Lecture Notes in Computer Science 15396

The series Lecture Notes in Computer Science (LNCS), including its subseries Lecture Notes in Artificial Intelligence (LNAI) and Lecture Notes in Bioinformatics (LNBI), has established itself as a medium for the publication of new developments in computer science and information technology research, teaching, and education.

LNCS enjoys close cooperation with the computer science R & D community, the series counts many renowned academics among its volume editors and paper authors, and collaborates with prestigious societies. Its mission is to serve this international community by providing an invaluable service, mainly focused on the publication of conference and workshop proceedings and postproceedings. LNCS commenced publication in 1973.

Leonardo Horn Iwaya · Liina Kamm ·
Leonardo Martucci · Tobias Pulls
Editors

Secure IT Systems

29th Nordic Conference, NordSec 2024
Karlstad, Sweden, November 6–7, 2024
Proceedings

Editors
Leonardo Horn Iwaya
Karlstad University
Karlstad, Sweden

Liina Kamm
Cybernetica
Tallinn, Estonia

Leonardo Martucci
Karlstad University
Karlstad, Sweden

Tobias Pulls
Karlstad University
Karlstad, Sweden

ISSN 0302-9743 ISSN 1611-3349 (electronic)
Lecture Notes in Computer Science
ISBN 978-3-031-79006-5 ISBN 978-3-031-79007-2 (eBook)
https://doi.org/10.1007/978-3-031-79007-2

This Springer imprint is published by the registered company Springer Nature Switzerland AG
The registered company address is: Gewerbestrasse 11, 6330 Cham, Switzerland

Preface

This volume contains the papers presented at the 29th Nordic Conference on Secure IT Systems (NordSec 2024). The conference was held from November 6 to 7, 2024, in Karlstad, Sweden.

The NordSec conference series started in 1996 with the aim of bringing together researchers and practitioners in computer security in the Nordic countries, thereby establishing a forum for discussion and cooperation between universities, industry, and computer societies. The NordSec conference series addresses a broad range of IT security and privacy topics. Over the years, it has developed into an international conference that takes place in the Nordic countries. NordSec is currently a key meeting venue for Nordic university teachers and students with research interests in information security and privacy.

NordSec 2024 received a total of 63 submissions, of which 59 were considered valid submissions and were double-anonymized and reviewed by at least three members of the Program Committee (PC). Submissions by members of the PC were handled using the EasyChair conflict declaration system. After the reviewing phase, 25 papers were accepted for publication and included in the proceedings (an acceptance rate of 42%).

We were honored to have the brilliant invited keynote speaker, Marit Hansen, State Data Protection Commissioner of Land Schleswig-Holstein and Chief of Unabhängiges Landeszentrum für Datenschutz (ULD).

We sincerely thank everyone involved in making this year's conference a success, including, but not limited to, the authors who submitted their papers, the presenters who contributed to the NordSec 2024 program, the PC members and additional reviewers for their thorough and constructive reviews, and EasyChair for their platform.

November 2024

Leonardo Horn Iwaya
Liina Kamm
Leonardo Martucci
Tobias Pulls

Organization

General Chairs

Leonardo Martucci	Karlstad University, Sweden
Liina Kamm	Cybernetica, Estonia

Program Committee Chairs

Leonardo Horn Iwaya	Karlstad University, Sweden
Tobias Pulls	Karlstad University, Sweden

Steering Committee

Audun Jøsang	University of Oslo, Norway
Aslan Askarov	Aarhus University, Denmark
Tuomas Aura	Aalto University, Finland
Mikael Asplund	Linköping University, Sweden
Karin Bernsmed	SINTEF ICT/NTNU, Norway
Sonja Buchegger	KTH, Sweden
Mads Dam	KTH, Sweden
Nils Gruschka	University of Oslo, Norway
Simone Fischer-Hübner	Karlstad University, Sweden
Lothar Fritsch	OsloMet, Norway
Dieter Gollmann	Hamburg University of Technology, Germany
René Rydhof Hansen	Aalborg University, Denmark
Ismail Hassan	OsloMet, Norway
Marcel Kyas	Reykjavik University, Iceland
Helger Lipmaa	University of Tartu, Estonia
Leonardo Martucci	Karlstad University, Sweden
Raimundas Matulevicius	University of Tartu, Estonia
Antonios Michalas	Tampere University, Finland
Simin Nadjm-Tehrani	Linköping University, Sweden
Tobias Pulls	Karlstad University, Sweden
Hans Peter Reiser	Reykjavik University, Iceland
Juha Röning	University of Oulu, Finland
Nicola Tuveri	Tampere University, Finland

Program Committee

Sedat Akleylek	University of Tartu, Estonia
Ala Sarah Alaqra	Karlstad University, Sweden
Anders Andersen	Arctic University of Norway, Norway
Mikael Asplund	Linköping University, Sweden
Matthias Beckerle	Karlstad University, Sweden
Karin Bernsmed	SINTEF ICT/NTNU, Norway
Svetlana Boudko	Norwegian Computing Center, Norway
Sigurd Eskeland	Norwegian Computing Center, Norway
Diego F. Aranha	Aarhus University, Denmark
Simone Fischer-Hübner	Karlstad University, Sweden
Ulrik Franke	RISE, Sweden
Lothar Fritsch	OsloMet, Norway
Christian Gehrmann	Lund University, Sweden
Dieter Gollmann	Hamburg University of Technology, Germany
Nils Gruschka	University of Oslo, Norway
Rene Rydhof Hansen	Aalborg University, Denmark
Ismail Hassan	OsloMet, Norway
Kirsi Helkala	Norwegian Defence College/NTNU, Norway
Erik Hjelmås	Gjøvik University College, Norway
Jaap-Henk Hoepman	Karlstad University, Sweden
Lejla Islami	Karlstad University, Sweden
Meiko Jensen	Karlstad University, Sweden
Hongyu Jin	KTH, Sweden
Farzaneh Karegar	Karlstad University, Sweden
Sokratis Katsikas	NTNU, Norway
Agnieszka Kitkowska	Jönköping University, Sweden
Kristjan Krips	University of Tartu, Estonia
Michael Kubach	Fraunhofer IAO, Germany
Marcel Kyas	Reykjavík University, Iceland
Joakim Kävrestad	Jönköping University, Sweden
Peeter Laud	Cybernetica, Estonia
Nuno Marques	OsloMet, Norway
Raimundas Matulevicius	University of Tartu, Estonia
Antonis Michalas	Tampere University, Finland
Nurul Momen	Blekinge Institute of Technology, Sweden
Simin Nadjm-Tehrani	Linköping University, Sweden
Boel Nelson	Uppsala University, Sweden
Hamed Nemati	KTH, Sweden
Mats Näslund	KTH and FRA, Sweden
Samuel Pagliarini	Tallinn University of Technology, Estonia

Paolo Palmieri	University College Cork, Ireland
Alisa Pankova	Cybernetica, Estonia
Panos Papadimitratos	KTH, Sweden
Danny Bøgsted Poulsen	Kiel University, Germany
Pille Pullonen-Raudvere	Cybernetica, Estonia
Siddharth Prakash Rao	Nokia Bell Labs, Finland
Jenni Reuben	Saab Aeronautics, Sweden
Juha Röning	University of Oulu, Finland
Einar Snekkenes	NTNU, Norway
Emre Süren	KTH, Sweden
Nicola Tuveri	Tampere University, Finland
Jan Willemson	Cybernetica, Estonia
Karel Wouters	Bancontact Payconiq Company, Belgium
Rose-Mharie Åhlfeldt	Skövde University, Sweden

Additional Reviewers

Mahdi Akil	Karlstad University, Sweden
Vjatšeslav Antipenko	University of Tartu, Estonia
Mariia Bakhtina	University of Tartu, Estonia
Fredrik Heiding	KTH, Sweden
Daniel Luoma	Tampere University, Finland
Alex Shaindlin	Tampere University, Finland
Charilaos Skandylas	Linköping University, Sweden

Contents

Cybersecurity and Policy

LLMs for Security

Formal Verification

Mobile and IoT

Network Security

Privacy

Authentication

Are Swedish Passwords Tougher Than the Rest?

Casper Jensen[1,2(✉)], Martin Karresand[2], Gurjot Singh Gaba[1], Andrei Gurtov[1], and Erik Öhrn[3]

[1] Department of Computer and Information Sciences (IDA), Linköping University, Linköping, Sweden
{gurjot.singh,andrei.gurtov}@liu.se

[2] Swedish Defence Research Agency (FOI), Linköping, Sweden
{casper.jensen,martin.karresand}@foi.se

[3] Swedish National Forensic Centre, Polisen, Linköping, Sweden

Abstract. In today's digital world, passwords are the keys that unlock our online lives, keeping our social media, financial accounts, and streaming services secure. However, creating strong passwords that are easy to remember is hard. Often an individual's language and cultural background influence password creation, which an attacker can exploit. This paper examines the importance of the User Context Bias (UCB) on Swedish passwords, versus international passwords stemming from multiple languages and cultures. This is done by employing four different password-cracking tools; Probabilistic Context Free Grammar (PCFG), Ordered Markov Enumerator (OMEN), Odinn, and Hashcat. The findings reveal that all the tools are able to crack a higher percentage of passwords when attacking those created by Swedish natives compared to their international counterparts. PCFG, in particular, is nearly twice as effective as the other tools against Swedish passwords after just 10,000 guesses, while OMEN is the best against Swedish passwords after 5 million guesses.

Keywords: cyber security · User Context Bias · password-crackers · password security · Swedish passwords

1 Introduction

An increasing part of our society is rapidly moving online, but has still not been able to move away from the use of password based authentication [8]. Strong passwords are hard to remember and therefore (involuntarily) affected by for example a user's personal preferences, native tongue and culture [1,2,13,25,26,31,40]. The user's effect on the strength of his or her passwords will be called the User Context Bias (UCB)[1] in the rest of the paper.

[1] We define *User Context Bias* as the factors in the local context of a user affecting the creation of a password, for example the user's native tongue, social values, education, age, gender, hobbies, occupation and place of living.

L. Horn Iwaya et al. (Eds.): NordSec 2024, LNCS 15396, pp. 3–21, 2025.
https://doi.org/10.1007/978-3-031-79007-2_1

Users also tend to circumvent any policies meant to strengthen the password security [32,34]. Furthermore a majority of users admit they reuse passwords [28,35]. The enormous amounts of passwords stored by every online service have also become the target of criminals, sometimes being able to steal millions of passwords at the same time. In 2022 alone over 24 billion passwords were stolen [35].

The stolen passwords are often found in hashed format, meaning that they have to be converted back to clear text by simple guessing, which is done by a password-cracking tool. Such tools are currently able to test millions of passwords per second [22]. Furthermore, the UCB will help by greatly reducing the amount of passwords to test. However, most leaks tend to be from websites primarily used by English-speaking people [6,7,24,39], a culturally diverse group from all around the world. Consequently the tools' performance on specific cultures and languages are less explored.

In 2023 the strength of Finnish passwords was found to be better than the average [21]. However, the work was done using only one password-cracking tool. This paper therefore explores the effect of the UCB on passwords using four different tools, testing the strength of Swedish passwords compared to an international collection of passwords.

Creating strong and easily recollectable passwords is hard, especially since they all should be unique. The recommendations also vary over time, depending on the latest research within the area. Consequently, this paper does not advise on how to create a strong password. Such advice would also soon be outdated. For the currently valid recommendations, please see for example [5,9,30,37].

The work in this paper is based upon the research made by C. Jensen [20].

1.1 Aim and Contribution

There is limited research on how the language and culture of training sets used in password-guessing attacks affect the outcome of these attacks. The aim of the research is therefore to test the importance of the UCB in passwords by evaluating the ability to crack passwords from a specific language and culture, compared to passwords collected from a diverse cultural and language background. This is tested by cracking Swedish and a broad set of international passwords and comparing the success rates. The work is done using several password-cracking tools to eliminate any effects of a specific tool.

The contribution of the work is to show to what extent the password cracking tools can utilize any UCB information found in password datasets. The chosen tools use different techniques to improve the success rate by extracting patterns from training datasets. This will be manifested by a faster password cracking process, or a higher number of cracked passwords. The work also shows the strengths and weaknesses of the tools and consequently will help improve future password-cracking sessions by allowing the optimal tool for a specific setting to be chosen.

1.2 Outline of Paper

The rest of the paper is organized as follows. Section 2 presents the used password-cracking tools and Sect. 3 elaborates on related work. Section 4 describes the method and details the datasets used for the research. Section 5 presents the results, which are then further discussed in Sect. 6. Lastly, the conclusion and future work can be found in Sect. 7.

2 Background

An attacker can use the predictability of the password structures (the UCB) by modifying a wordlist by applying different rules, such as adding numbers or replacing letters with numbers or other characters. These are called mangling rules, and a password-cracking tool that utilizes a wordlist and generates a larger set of potential passwords is called a password mangler.

A password-cracker/mangler can either be rule-based, utilizing predefined mangling rules, or generative, utilizing lists of passwords or memorable phrases and words to enhance the existing mangling rules. This is done by extracting patterns found in the given lists. The final result is password candidates of higher quality.

2.1 Rule-Based Password-Cracking Tools

Rule-based means that the tool expands a set of words by applying predefined rules to each word, for example replacing some or all "a":s with "@". The set of passwords can for example consist of older cracked passwords or any other kind of password candidates.

These tools and their corresponding rule sets, also called mangling rules, build upon the fact that humans tend to use common patterns in their password creation and that these can be used to make more probable guesses [24].

The rule-based password-cracking tool used in this research is Hashcat. Hashcat is a free tool that can perform several kinds of attacks, such as dictionary attacks, use rule sets for better guessing, and attack over 200 different hashing algorithms [17].

2.2 Generative Password-Cracking Tools

Generative password-cracking tools use a wordlist containing earlier cracked passwords or other words as a guessing basis, and from this wordlist, they extract the probability of specific character usage and word structures. Using the probabilities, it is possible to make more accurate password guesses. Probability as the basis for password guesses was first proposed by Narayanan et al. [29].

Wier et al. [39] created PCFG based on the work by Narayanan et al. PCFG uses the probability of specific word structures when creating password guesses, with the most probable guesses first. The probabilities are first collected from a training list. In the next step, PCFG generates the password guesses.

Another tool that builds on the work of Narayanan et al. is OMEN. It uses Markov models to apply probability distributions over sequences of symbols [29]. The password guesses are then made based on the most probable word structures in falling order of probability [7].

The third generative password-cracking tool used in this research is called Odinn [6]. Similarly to the other tools, Odinn uses a wordlist for training to generate better password guesses. Odinn can split passwords into their word stems and extract their semantic meaning. It then makes semantic password guesses, for example, extracting popular dates or sports terms and combining them.

3 Related Work

Kurasaki et al. [21] study the difference between passwords from a wide range of countries and how a rule-based password-cracker, Hashcat, succeed when attacking using a rule set. The authors observe that passwords of Finnish origin are much harder to crack compared to passwords from the United States. The authors use training sets corresponding to the different languages they attack. The training and target sets are collected from a large dataset of 1.4 billion passwords, which Kurasaki et al. divide into nationalities by the corresponding email address domains.

Li et al. [23] do a large study on the security of Chinese passwords when attacked with a generative password-cracker, PCFG. They observe that a change in password-guessing strategy can improve the amount of cracked passwords.

Maoneke et al. [27] attack passwords from South African university students using the generative password cracker PCFG. In their research, Manoeke et al. prove that the security of passwords increases when using passwords in a language other than English or if they consist of a mix of different languages. They also find that it is easier to guess a user's password if there is information available on the user's language background and cultural domicile because more specific word lists can be used. According to the authors, multilingual users more often include personal data (for example name and date of birth) in their passwords, than purely English-speaking users. The included names are both in local and English form.

Abbott and Garcia [1] study English and Spanish passwords. Almost 50% of the English passwords are based on a real word, which is only true for approximately 30% of the Spanish passwords. Another difference is that Spanish passwords ending in numbers always have at least two digits at the end, according to the authors. Abbott and Garcia also find that the English passwords contain a larger set of special characters than the Spanish passwords and overall contain 75% more characters.

AlSabah et al. [2] find that different nationalities from the Middle East tend to form their passwords differently, incorporating personal information such as phone numbers in different ways. The authors conclude that patterns can be found in how people form their passwords depending on their nationalities and cultural belonging.

Bonneau and Shutova [4] show that users have difficulties choosing random pass phrases. The phrases are more or less affected by the user's natural language. Most of the pass phrases in the study are grammatically correct, or at least formatted into an understandable expression. The connection frequency of pairs of words is close to that of natural language.

Malone et al. [26] note that there are differences in how users structure passwords in different language groups. They also see that the distribution of popular (well-known) passwords more or less follows Zipf's law.

Petrie et al. [31] get similar results to AlSabah et al. [2] when they study password creation in the UK, Turkey, and China. However, Petrie et al. find that gender is sometimes a larger factor than cultural belonging, for example regarding the longest passwords, which belong to women. Likewise men are having harder to remember their passwords, even though they generally have fewer passwords than women, according to the authors.

Wei et al. [38] study leaked and broken passwords from five different web services and conclude that when filtering out traditionally popular passwords most of the remaining passwords are related to the service in question. They also find that the password structure has connections to the native language of the users.

Yang et al. [40] find that numbers are very important in Chinese culture. For example is "4" similar in pronunciation to the Chinese word for death, "8" sounds as "create wealth" and "6" is regarded as a lucky number. There are also Chinese number sequences that are similar in pronunciation to different sentences, for example, "5201314", "1314520" and "7758520", which correspond to the phrases "I love you forever", "forever I love you" and "please kiss me since I love you", according to Yang et al.

Tihany et al. [36] compare different statistical properties of passwords in international and western databases. The authors find that the databases have similar properties, which contradicts the existence of cultural differences between passwords. However, the overall results still show some differences between the passwords in the databases at certain levels, but that the differences diminish at higher levels.

Yang. et al. [41] study the use of character patterns in passwords and find that half of the pattern-based passwords are based on keyboard patterns. The keyboard based passwords all follow four different patterns, described as

> (1) multiple consecutive keys starting from a certain key in the horizontal direction; (2) multiple consecutive keys starting from a certain key in the vertical direction; (3) Repetition of a certain key; (4) Combination of two or more of the above. [41, p. 160]

Merdenyan and Petrie [28] compare the password management behavior of young (18–22 years) computer science students and old computer users (at least 60 years old). They find that password reuse is highly likely in both groups (93% for students and 100% for old computer users), even though the student group grade themselves as knowledgeable in password security. Less than 5% of the participants in both groups follow recommendations on password length. The authors also find that old people tend to share passwords related to ebanking to a much higher degree than young students, while young students are more likely to share passwords related to entertainment. Young students also follow advice on password content to a higher degree than old people (18% versus 4%).

Renaud, Otondo and Warkentin [32] have studied the endowment effect connected to passwords. Users have a tendency to see their passwords and security routines as dear artifacts that they cannot just throw away, even against better knowledge, according to the authors. The study is based on the assumption that users are aware of relevant computer security requirements on passwords. Renaud, Otondo and Warkentin argue that the problem is complex and cannot be explained or solved by a single factor.

4 Method

The description of our work method is divided into three parts. First, several password datasets of good quality and language origin have to be collected. Then the selection of the used password-cracking tools is explained. Lastly, the password-guessing attacks have to be conducted using different password crackers, which in turn have to be trained on training sets of the corresponding language.

4.1 Password Datasets

The datasets used can be divided into two groups: training- and target sets. These groups are divided into Swedish training/target sets and international training/target sets. All datasets used consist of passwords acquired from earlier password leaks, and they have all been collected from online sources and torrent sites [12].

The training set is used by the password-cracking tool as a basis for making guesses. For example, PCFG will train on the probabilities of word structures for all the passwords in the training set. Then, the tools' guesses will be compared against the target set, and the number of matches between the guesses and the target passwords will be logged together with the total number of guesses.

The passwords in the target sets will be plain text and not hashed, this is because the focus of the experiments is to test the guesses made by the tools. Consequently, it is not necessary to hash the target passwords and the guessed passwords. It is also important to note that all the training- and target sets contain duplicates of passwords; this is because PCFG and OMEN need to get a correct probability of popular password patterns when training to make better and, therefore, more realistic guesses.

The division of the used passwords into training and target sets means that passwords from a certain leak only appear in one of the two. This is done to minimize the risk of password-cracking programs training on the same data they are attacking.

The Swedish training set consists of passwords coming from two primary sources. The first is a gathering of passwords from several different Swedish password leaks [11]. These leaks are from a wide range of websites, such as picture forums, government-related sites, porn sites etcetera.

The second part is a gathering of all passwords connected to a Swedish email domain in the Collection#1 [18] password leak. The domains are filtered on their country code top-level domains, where .se or .nu are classified as Swedish since they are administered by the Swedish Internet Foundation [19]. In total, the Swedish training set consists of 1,655,676 entries.

The Swedish target set consists of three separate datasets from different password leaks. The first two are all the passwords connected to email addresses with Swedish domains in the LinkedIn and Shein leaks. The LinkedIn leak is a massive data breach from 2012 [10], and the Shein leak is from 2018 [3]. The third part is a password leak from the Website Netdoktor.se [15], a Swedish medical counseling website hacked sometime before 2016.

Table 1 presents the number of passwords in the target set. The Swedish and international training sets are much larger than their corresponding target sets, because the tools need a large dataset on which to base their guesses. This also guarantees a broad coverage of passwords.

Table 1. Number of passwords in each dataset in the Swedish target set.

Dataset	Passwords
LinkedIn Swedish domains	71,382
Shein Swedish domains	17,550
Netdoktor.se	57,174

The international training set consists of 3 million password entries taken from a part of Collection#1 called *semi-private dumps*. The passwords are randomly selected from 200 separate leaks from several websites. It is a mix of travel sites, employment forums, travel websites, and more. There is also a mix of nationalities. However, a majority of the websites are of western, Japanese, and Russian origin. Because of the large diversity of leaked websites in this training set, there is also a diversity in password authors, meaning there is a mix of age- and socio-economic groups and nationalities.

The international target set consists of 100,000 randomly selected passwords from the LinkedIn leak and 100,000 from the Shein leak. Some tests used a Swedish and English dictionary as a training set, targeting all the target sets.

4.2 Selection of Password-Cracking Tools

As mentioned before there are two types of password-cracking tools used in this research, rule-based and generative. Rule-based tools build on the use of a predefined set of rules used to filter, modify, and extend the set of password guesses to be tested against a set of password hashes. The main difference between the rule-based password-cracking tools are their rule sets. Hashcat, which is said to be the"[w]orld's fastest password cracker" [14], was chosen because of its better rule set and higher cracking speed [24] compared to John the Ripper, another well-known rule-based password-cracking tool.

The generative password-cracker tools used are PCFG, OMEN, and Odinn. PCFG and OMEN are chosen because they have previously been compared to each other [7,33,39]. Odinn is used due to its focus on semantic meaning in passwords, an alternative approach that is interesting to compare to the other two in the context of this study. To avoid any bias from a specific tool or technique four well-established tools were used, enabling a better understanding of the reason(s) behind the results.

The new generation of generative password crackers that use deep learning, for example, PassGAN [16], has been excluded for several reasons. First of all the deep learning technique is still in its infancy and is therefore better suited for a dedicated study. Also, the rapid development within the deep learning research area makes it difficult to know if the same tool that is tested now will still be available in the future.

4.3 Password-Cracking Test Layout

The focus of the experiments lies in comparing the generated guesses to the target sets. The tools' performance will be measured by how many passwords they can crack in the different target sets. The layout of the tests will be different between the tools. Figure 1 presents a simplified flowchart explaining the steps in the tests.

The overall test layout is made so that all the tools would be measured on the same parameters. All four tools are trained on the Swedish and international training sets, except for Odinn, which uses subsets from both training sets. Then, each tool attacks the target sets corresponding to the language they trained on (Swedish or international). Then, this process is repeated, but instead of the tools using the training sets as a guessing basis, they use a Swedish and English dictionary. In total, there are 35 tests. For each test, Hashcat sends out status updates at regular intervals so that progress can be recorded over time. All the different password crackers are run on ordinary desktop computers.

Hashcat first uses the training sets and Swedish and English dictionaries as a guessing basis for a dictionary attack on the target sets. Then, the process is repeated but with the rule set RockYou-30,000 enabled. This rule set is chosen to create a large enough guessing space so the total number of guesses would reach more than one billion. The rule set is also broad and extensive, which should result in a higher number of cracked passwords.

When testing PCFG and OMEN, they are either trained on a training set of passwords taken from a data leak or trained on a Swedish or English dictionary. Then, they generate almost one billion guesses that are saved in a text file. This file of guesses is then used against each target set of their respective language.

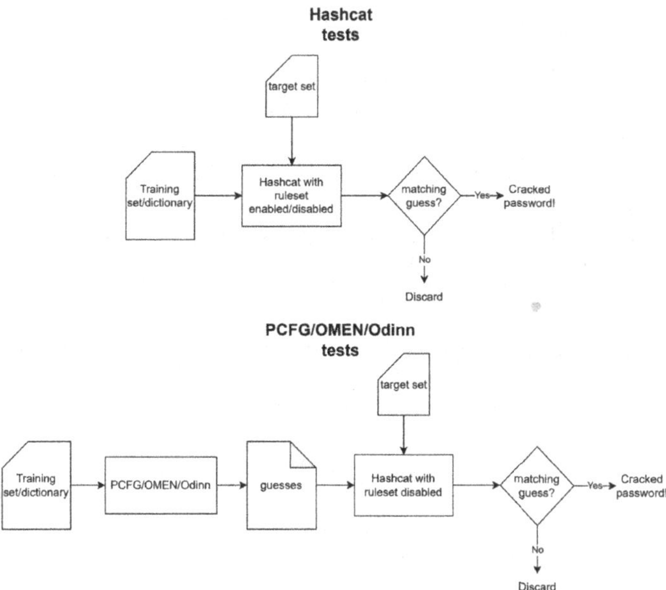

Fig. 1. Flowchart of the test layout. Hashcat tests use the training set/dictionary directly in the attacks. PCFG, OMEN, and Odinn train on the training set, and produce guesses that are used with Hashcat to attack the target sets.

Hashcat is then used to attack the target set with the file containing the guesses, with no rule set enabled. Odinn is not used in the same way as PCFG or OMEN because it crashed when training on a large training set. That is why randomly selected subsets of the Swedish and international training set are used, each containing 200,000 passwords. With this amount of passwords to train on, the tool produces five million guesses. They are written to a text file, which is then used to attack the target sets using Hashcat without any rule set enabled.

The reason for using Hashcat in the tests with PCFG, OMEN, and Odinn is that Hashcat can easily be used with an input list of guesses against a target list of passwords. None of the generative tools can attack a list of given passwords with their guesses directly and provide sufficient data during the cracking process. The guesses from the tools have to be either piped into another tool, such as Hashcat, or saved in a file that is used as a guessing base, as it is done in this research.

5 Result

The results of the experiments are presented as sub-sections that span different number of password guesses. This is done because it is interesting to see how the ratio of cracked passwords changes over the guessing space. Additionally, Odinn could only produce five million guesses and therefore the comparison between Odinn and the other tools is limited to that guessing space.

5.1 Attacks Without Any Rule Sets Enabled

Tables 2 and 3 show the percentage of cracked passwords when attacking the target sets using only the training sets or dictionaries without any rule set enabled. When using only a language dictionary the result is a poor coverage of the target sets. As can be seen in Table 2 usage of the English dictionary results in only 6% of the international LinkedIn target set passwords being cracked. Using the Swedish dictionary (Table 3) on the Swedish target sets result in approximately 3% of all passwords being cracked.

Table 2. Percentage of international passwords cracked using only the training sets and dictionaries without any rule set used.

Training set	Target set	Cracked [%]
International	LinkedIn int.	24.1
...	Shein Int.	9.1
English dict.	LinkedIn int.	6.0
...	Shein Int.	1.6

Table 3. Percentage of Swedish passwords cracked using only the training sets and dictionaries without any rule set used.

Training set	Target set	Cracked [%]
Swedish	LinkedIn Swe.	32.1
...	Shein Swe.	32.1
...	Netdoktor.se	30.5
Swedish dict.	LinkedIn Swe.	2.9
...	Shein Swe.	2.5
...	Netdoktor.se	3.6

There is a large difference between the amount of cracked passwords in the international Shein- and LinkedIn target sets. Only 9% of the passwords in the training set appear in the Shein target set, while 24% appear in the LinkedIn target set. The differences are clearly seen in the graphs in Figs. 2 and 3.

Almost 32% of the Swedish target sets were cracked when using only the Swedish training set. This shows that the Swedish training set has much better coverage than the international training set, i.e. it has a more coherent UCB.

5.2 Cracked Passwords Over 1 Billion Guesses

Figure 2 shows the numbers and percentage of passwords cracked after 1 billion guesses for the different target sets. It shows this for Hashcat using the RockYou-30,000 rule set, PCFG, and OMEN. The tools used have either been trained on the training sets or an English- or Swedish dictionary. Odinn is excluded from Fig. 2 due to a much lower amount of guesses.

An important note is that the left y-axes of the graphs show the number of cracked passwords in the target set. This is after duplicate passwords have been removed from the target sets, thus the international target sets have 100,000 passwords each in total but in practice, it is fewer because of duplicate passwords.

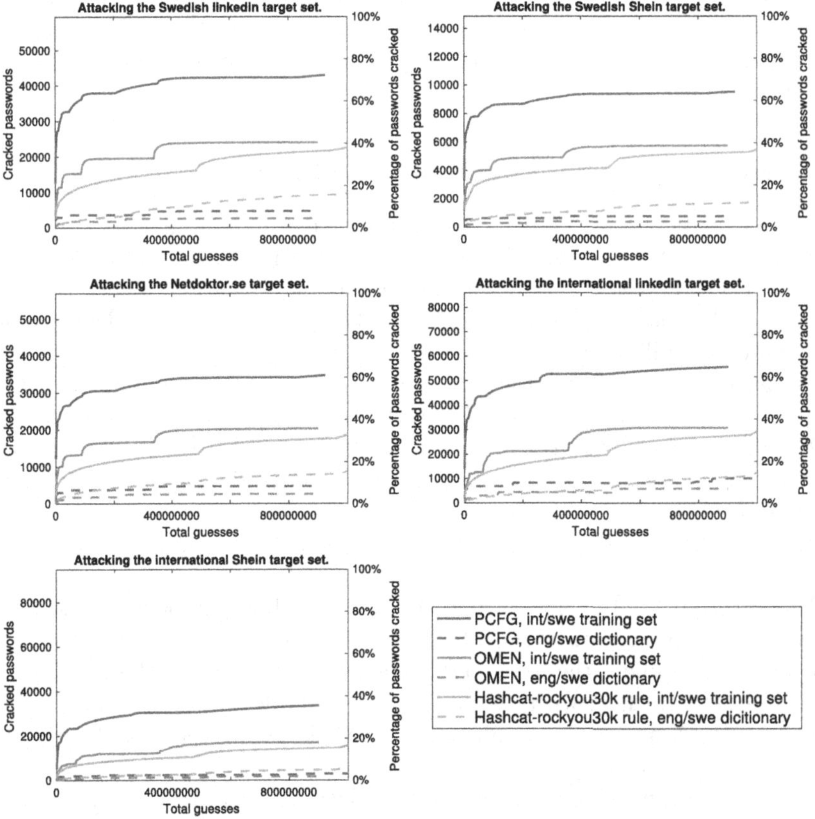

Fig. 2. Cracked passwords over 1 billion guesses for PCFG, OMEN, and Hashcat. Duplicate passwords are removed in the target sets.

The performance against the international Shein target set is much worse than the LinkedIn target set. Also, using a Swedish or English dictionary as a training set results in worse performance than using a list of real-world passwords. However, Hashcat, using the RockYou-30,000 rule set, outperforms PCFG and OMEN when they are trained on dictionaries only, but only after a significant number of guesses.

When studying the different tools used in the Swedish and international training sets, it is clear that PCFG is the best of the three. It reaches somewhere between 65–75% cracked passwords in the Swedish target sets after 900 million guesses, and 65% and 35%, respectively, for the international LinkedIn and Shein target sets. After 900 million guesses, OMEN reaches around 40% against all target sets except the international Shein one, where it reaches 20%. Hashcat, using the RockYou-30,000 rule set, can not reach the same levels of cracked passwords as the other two tools.

As can be seen in Fig. 2 the steepness of the graphs for OMEN and PCFG is high at the beginning of the cracking process. This indicates that both tools sort their guesses in order of descending probability, making them more efficient than Hashcat.

5.3 Cracked Passwords Over 5 Million Guesses

Figure 3 presents a zoomed-in view of the first five million guesses against the different target sets. The tools shown are Hashcat using the RockYou-30,000 rule set, PCFG, OMEN, and Odinn. Due to the higher resolution of the graphs the behavior of the tools at the start of the cracking process is more clearly shown, than in the one billion guesses graphs.

As can be seen in Fig. 3 there is a difference between the languages to be cracked, since both PCFG and OMEN perform better against the Swedish target set than against the international target set. PCFG is able to crack 35% and 15%, respectively, in the international target set and 40–45% in the Swedish target set. OMEN cracks double the percentage of passwords in the Swedish target set compared to the international target set, although at lower levels than the other tools.

When studying Odinn's performance, it is seen that it performs almost identically between the Swedish and international target sets. It can crack 5–7% in both target sets, where the lower performance corresponds to the international Shein target set. Hashcat with the Rockyou-30,000 rule set performs almost identically to OMEN and Odinn against the Swedish and international target sets for five million guesses.

From the graphs in Figs. 2 and 3, it is clear that PCFG performs better against the Swedish target set than the international target set. It is also possible to see that OMEN performs much better against the Swedish target set than the international when using the training sets consisting of passwords from the password leaks.

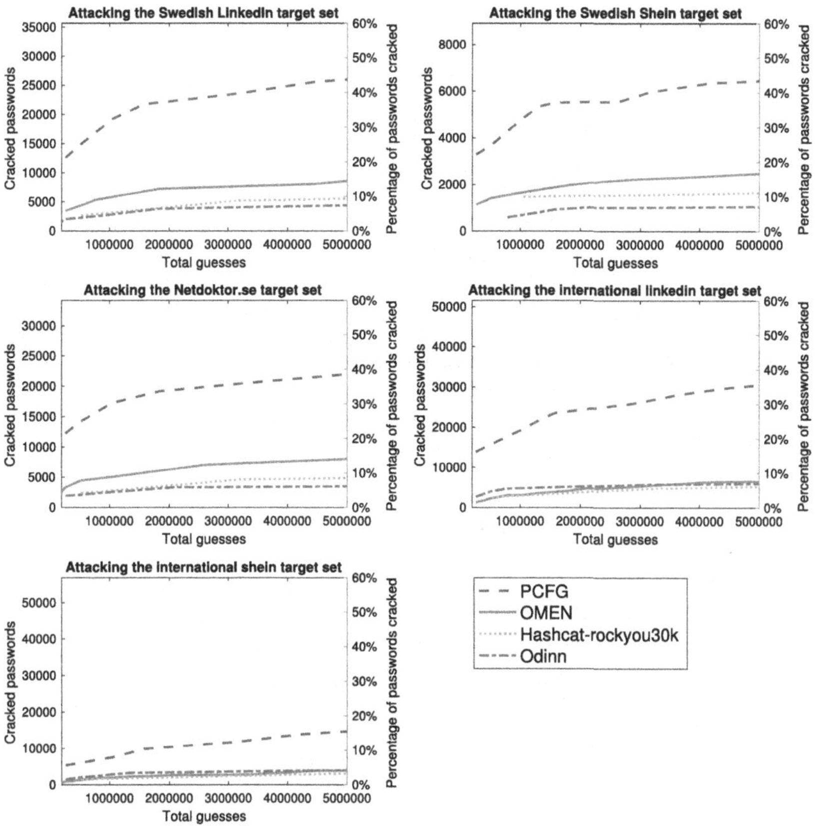

Fig. 3. Cracked passwords over the first 5 million guesses for PCFG, OMEN, Hashcat, and Odinn.

5.4 Cracked Passwords After 10,000 Guesses

Tables 4 and 5 presents the percentage of cracked passwords after 10,000 guesses for PCFG, OMEN, and Odinn. From the tables it is clear that PCFG outperforms the other generative tools with relatively few guesses. This behavior is shown for both the international (Table 4) and Swedish (Table 5) target sets.

There is a large difference in the performance between the different combinations of training and target sets. PCFG cracks almost double the amount of passwords against the Swedish target sets than the international, and OMEN cracks almost four times as many passwords in the Swedish target set than the international. Odinn cracks roughly the same percentage of passwords between the languages. However, it performs slightly better against the Swedish target sets.

Table 4. Percentage of international passwords cracked after 10,000 guesses.

Tool	Target set	Cracked [%]
PCFG	LinkedIn int.	4.8
PCFG	Shein int.	2.0
OMEN	LinkedIn int.	0.4
OMEN	Shein int.	0.3
Odinn	LinkedIn int.	1.3
Odinn	Shein int.	0.6

Table 5. Percentage of Swedish passwords cracked after 10,000 guesses.

Tool	Target set	Cracked [%]
PCFG	LinkedIn Swe.	6.6
PCFG	Shein Swe.	8.2
PCFG	Netdoktor.se	7.5
OMEN	LinkedIn Swe.	1.4
OMEN	Shein Swe.	2.1
OMEN	Netdoktor.se	1.4
Odinn	LinkedIn Swe.	1.4
Odinn	Shein Swe.	1.3
Odinn	Netdoktor.se	1.8

6 Discussion

There are many ways the strength of a password can be affected by the user who creates it [1,2,13,25,26,31,32,40]. Obvious factors are for example which language the user speaks, the user's obedience to (if any) password policies or recommendations, the user's favorite films, books or other cultural aspects and of course the names of family members and pets. The conclusion is that the amount of factors affecting the password creation process of a user is large and yet not fully covered. This paper has therefore introduced the term UCB as a meta-term covering all factors, known or yet unknown, affecting the password strength when a user creates a password.

Looking at the results the large difference in amount of cracked passwords between the international target sets probably originates from the fact that Shein is a Chinese online clothes store. Consequently, there is a possibility of a higher number of Chinese and non-Western users of the website. Since the international training set includes a mix of Western, Russian, and Japanese passwords, there is a difference in password culture between the training and target sets, hence the bad results compared to the pure Swedish datasets.

Almost $\frac{1}{4}$ of the LinkedIn passwords were cracked using only the training sets without any rule sets when attacking the international target set (Table 2). For the Swedish target set, it was even higher, almost $\frac{1}{3}$ of the Swedish LinkedIn passwords were cracked (Table 3). This is an indication that LinkedIn passwords are less varied than the other datasets. In other words, all LinkedIn users seem to have chosen similar, or weaker, passwords. We are not familiar with the password policy used by LinkedIn at that time, but it might have forced users to create weaker passwords.

The large fraction of passwords cracked using only the training sets without any rule sets affected the Swedish Shein and Netdoktor target sets too (Table 3). When using training sets from Swedish domains, more than 30% of the passwords were cracked. Using the same reasoning as for the international LinkedIn target set mentioned earlier, Swedish passwords seem to be weaker than the international passwords. However, this might also be an effect of the UCB in passwords. When a single language or culture is targeted, much noise (irrelevant passwords) is filtered out and consequently the cracking ability is improved.

Another reason for the high ratio of cracked passwords in the Swedish target set might be due to the small size of the Swedish-speaking population, which makes it much easier to gather a training set that covers a larger part of the user population, and consequently the password population, relative to larger language groups.

To further elaborate on the effect of the size of language groups, consider the following example: Suppose every person in Sweden has on average 100 passwords each, with a population of approximately 10 million, giving a total of 1 billion Swedish passwords. We have a training set consisting of 1.6 million passwords, covering 0.16% of all Swedish passwords. The same coverage of for example Chinese passwords would require 240 million passwords, assuming a population of 1.5 billion. If we add the fact that people tend to reuse passwords between accounts and use common words and phrases, the high percentage of cracked Swedish passwords is easier to understand.

The hypothesis on small languages being easier to crack seems to be contradicted by the findings of Kurasaki and Kanaoka, who found the Finnish language passwords to be hard to crack (Finland has a population of less than 6 million). However, Kurasaki and Kanaoka did not use as advanced password-cracking tools as we did. There is also a Swedish-speaking minority (approximately 290,000) in Finland, which might have introduced noise into their experiments. On the other hand, the Swedish population is more culturally and linguistically diverse than the Finnish population. Thus the problem is more complex than simply being related to the size of the population speaking the language.

The steepness of the graphs for OMEN and PCFG in Fig. 2 are high at the beginning of the cracking process. This means that the tools' guesses are much more accurate in the beginning, probably because they generate high-quality guesses early in the process. Since Hashcat is going through its training set sequentially without internal ordering, the order of the words in the set is the order of the guesses. Consequently the best guesses might be given at the end of the process.

The steps in graphs for PCFG and OMEN in Fig. 2 that appear for both training sets and against all target sets are interesting. A probable cause is that the tools switch guessing tactics, for example, trying a new password structure, thus increasing correct guesses. However, after a couple of million guesses, the guessing space is exhausted, and lower probability guesses are made until the structure changes.

The performance boost against the Swedish target set seen in the result of the five million guesses experiment has no obvious explanation. However, when observing the performance of the tools using an ordinary dictionary to train on, Hashcat, with the RockYou-30,000 rule set enabled, performs better than the other tools. A possible explanation is that there are no duplicate words in a dictionary, i.e. information on the frequency of specific words is missing. Thus, PCFG and OMEN can not calculate a realistic probability of common words. Additionally, there are no digits or special characters mixed into the words in a dictionary, hence PCFG and OMEN cannot extract that feature of passwords either.

7 Conclusions and Future Work

This work shows the importance of a good training set that reflects the language and culture of the passwords targeted in a guessing attack. The importance of the UCB of passwords is shown by using a Swedish-only password dataset and an international password dataset. We compared the number of cracked passwords in the Swedish target set with the international target set that had been attacked by the same password-cracking tools using a training set consisting of a collection of international passwords. A higher percentage of passwords in the Swedish target set were cracked.

The tool PCFG demonstrated significantly better performance against the Swedish target set after 10,000 guesses and reasonably better after 5 million and 1 billion guesses. The tool OMEN also performed significantly better against the Swedish target sets in all the different guessing ranges. Odinn performed almost identically between the languages, with a slightly higher percentage of passwords cracked in the Swedish targets. Hashcat with the Rockyou-30,000 rule set also performed similarly between the languages, but with a slightly better ratio of cracked passwords against the Swedish targets, than the international targets.

The work also highlights the importance of the UCB on password strength and invites to further research within the area. Better knowledge will help improve the performance of both types of password-cracking tools, but especially the rule-based tools, which cannot automatically extract the UCB features. The generative password-cracking tools implicitly extract the UCB features from the probabilities of patterns found in a training dataset and therefore make the most out of each dataset. However, utilizing knowledge on the UCB the extraction models of the rule-based tools can be further improved.

An interesting area of further research is whether the same conclusions made in this paper can be made when attacking another small language, such as Norwegian, Finnish, Dutch, or even German, using generative password crackers. The small language group study can then be expanded by comparing the results of attacks on languages with larger populations, for example, Russian, Chinese, or Spanish. Such a comparison would further test the theory that it is easier to gather a training set that has a high coverage when targeting a language with a small population, than a large one.

References

1. Abbott, J., Garcia, V.M.: Password differences based on language and testing of memory recall. Int. J. Inf. Secur. **2** (2015)
2. AlSabah, M., Oligeri, G., Riley, R.: Your culture is in your password: an analysis of a demographically-diverse password dataset. Comput. Secur. **77**, 427–441 (2018). https://doi.org/10.1016/j.cose.2018.03.014. https://www.sciencedirect.com/science/article/pii/S0167404818302979
3. BBC News: Shein owner Zoetop fined $1.9m over data breach response (2022). https://www.bbc.com/news/technology-63255661. Accessed 12 Aug 2024
4. Bonneau, J., Shutova, E.: Linguistic properties of multi-word passphrases. In: Blyth, J., Dietrich, S., Camp, L. (eds.) Financial Cryptography and Data Security, pp. 1–12. Springer, Heidelberg (2012)
5. Canadian Center for Cyber Security: Best practices for passphrases and passwords (2024). https://www.cyber.gc.ca/en/guidance/best-practices-passphrases-and-passwords-itsap30032. Accessed 29 Sept 2024
6. Coray, S.: Óðinn: a framework for large-scale wordlist analysis and structure-based password guessing. Master's thesis, University of Basel (2015)
7. Dürmuth, M., Angelstorf, F., Castelluccia, C., Perito, D., Chaabane, A.: OMEN: faster password guessing using an ordered Markov enumerator. In: Piessens, F., Caballero, J., Bielova, N. (eds.) Engineering Secure Software and Systems, pp. 119–132. Springer, Cham (2015)
8. Everett, C.: Are passwords finally dying? Network Security, pp. 10–14 (2016)
9. German Federal Office for Information Security: Creating secure passwords. https://www.bsi.bund.de/EN/Themen/Verbraucherinnen-und-Verbraucher/Informationen-und-Empfehlungen/Cyber-Sicherheitsempfehlungen/Accountschutz/Sichere-Passwoerter-erstellen/sichere-passwoerter-erstellen_node.html. Accessed 29 Sept 2024
10. Gunaratna, S.: Linkedin: 2012 data breach much worse than we thought (2016). https://www.cbsnews.com/news/linkedin-2012-data-breach-hack-much-worse-than-we-thought-passwords-emails/. Accessed 12 Aug 2024
11. Gustafsson, D.: Swedish passwords - analysis of Swedish password usage (2022). https://github.com/halvtomat/swedish-passwords. Accessed 20 Aug 2024
12. Hacxx-underground: Files (2023). https://github.com/hacxx-underground/Files/tree/main. Accessed 20 Aug 2024
13. Han, W., Li, Z., Yuan, L., Xu, W.: Regional patterns and vulnerability analysis of Chinese web passwords. IEEE Trans. Inf. Forensics Secur. **11**(2), 258–272 (2016)
14. Hashcat: Features. https://hashcat.net/hashcat/. Accessed 27 Sept 2024
15. Hashmob: Hashlist information: Netdoktor.se (2022). https://hashmob.net/hashlists/info/5366-netdoktor.se. Accessed 20 Aug 2024

16. Hitaj, B., Gasti, P., Ateniese, G., Pérez-Cruz, F.: PassGAN: a deep learning approach for password guessing. CoRR abs/1709.00440 (2017). http://arxiv.org/abs/1709.00440. Accessed 8 Sept 2023
17. Hranický, R., Zobal, L., Ryšavý, O., Kolář, D.: Distributed password cracking with BOINC and hashcat. Digit. Invest. **30**, 161–172 (2019). https://doi.org/10.1016/j.diin.2019.08.001
18. Hunt, T.: The 773 million record "Collection 1" data breach (2019). https://www.troyhunt.com/the-773-million-record-collection-1-data-reach/. Accessed 20 Aug 2024
19. Internetstiftelsen: Terms and conditions for .se and .nu domains (2023). https://internetstiftelsen.se/en/domains/how-to-register-a-domain-name/terms-and-conditions-for-se-and-nu-domains/. Accessed 20 Aug 2024
20. Jensen, C.: Asserting password crackers ability to target Swedish passwords: an analysis. Master's thesis, Department of Computer and Information Science, Linköping University (2023)
21. Kurasaki, S., Kanaoka, A.: Analysis of country and regional user password characteristics in dictionary attacks. In: Moallem, A. (ed.) HCI for Cybersecurity, Privacy and Trust, pp. 656–671. Springer, Cham (2023)
22. Lcubo Corp.: Hashcat GPU benchmarking table for Nvidia en AMD (2017). https://tutorials.technology/blog/08-Hashcat-GPU-benchmarking-table-Nvidia-and-amd.html. Accessed 20 Aug 2024
23. Li, Z., Han, W., Xu, W.: A large-scale empirical analysis of Chinese web passwords. In: 23rd USENIX Security Symposium (USENIX Security 2014), pp. 559–574. USENIX Association, San Diego, CA (2014)
24. Liu, E., Nakanishi, A., Golla, M., Cash, D., Ur, B.: Reasoning analytically about password-cracking software. In: 2019 IEEE Symposium on Security and Privacy (SP), pp. 380–397 (2019). https://doi.org/10.1109/SP.2019.00070
25. Lundberg, T.: Comparison of automated password guessing strategies. Master's thesis, Department of Electrical Engineering, Linköping University (2019)
26. Malone, D., Maher, K.: Investigating the distribution of password choices. In: Proceedings of the 21st International Conference on World Wide Web, WWW 2012, pp. 301–310. Association for Computing Machinery, New York, NY, USA (2012). https://doi.org/10.1145/2187836.2187878
27. Maoneke, P.B., Flowerday, S., Isabirye, N.: Evaluating the strength of a multilingual passphrase policy. Comput. Secur. **92**, 101746 (2020). https://doi.org/10.1016/j.cose.2020.101746
28. Merdenyan, B., Petrie, H.: Generational differences in password management behaviour. In: Proceedings of the 32nd International BCS Human Computer Interaction Conference (HCI), pp. 1–10 (2018). https://doi.org/10.14236/ewic/HCI2018.60
29. Narayanan, A., Shmatikov, V.: Fast dictionary attacks on passwords using time-space tradeoff. In: Proceedings of the 12th ACM Conference on Computer and Communications Security, CCS 2005, pp. 364–372. Association for Computing Machinery, New York (2005). https://doi.org/10.1145/1102120.1102168
30. National Institute of Standards and Technology (NIST): NIST special publication 800-63B—digital identity guidelines (2020). https://doi.org/10.6028/NIST.SP.800-63b. https://pages.nist.gov/800-63-3/sp800-63b.html. Accessed 29 Sept 2024
31. Petrie, H., Merdenyan, B.: Cultural and gender differences in password behaviors: evidence from China, Turkey and the UK. In: Proceedings of the 9th Nordic Conference on Human-Computer Interaction, NordiCHI 2016. Association for Computing Machinery, New York (2016). https://doi.org/10.1145/2971485.2971563

32. Renaud, K., Otondo, R., Warkentin, M.: "This is the way 'I' create my passwords"...does the endowment effect deter people from changing the way they create their passwords? Comput. Secur. **82**, 241–260 (2019). https://doi.org/10.1016/j.cose.2018.12.018
33. Shi, R., Zhou, Y., Li, Y., Han, W.: Understanding offline password-cracking methods: a large-scale empirical study. Secur. Commun. Netw. **2021**, 1–16 (2021)
34. Siponen, M., Puhakainen, P., Vance, A.: Can individuals' neutralization techniques be overcome? A field experiment on password policy. Comput. Secur. **88**, 1–12 (2020). https://doi.org/10.1016/j.cose.2019.101617. http://www.sciencedirect.com/science/article/pii/S0167404819301646
35. Stouffer, C.: 139 password statistics to help you stay safe in 2023 - Norton (2023). https://us.norton.com/blog/privacy/password-statistics. Accessed 18 Aug 2024
36. Tihanyi, N., Kovács, A., Vargha, G., Lénárt, Á.: Unrevealed patterns in password databases part one: analyses of cleartext passwords. In: Mjølsnes, S. (ed.) Technology and Practice of Passwords, pp. 89–101. Springer, Cham (2015)
37. US Cybersecurity & Infrastructure Security Agency (CISA): Use strong passwords—create long, random, unique passwords with a password manager for safer accounts. https://www.cisa.gov/secure-our-world/use-strong-passwords. Accessed 29 Sept 2024
38. Wei, M., Golla, M., Ur, B.: The password doesn't fall far: how service influences password choice. In: Proceedings of the Who Are You?! Adventures in Authentication 2018 Workshop (WAY) (2018)
39. Weir, M., Aggarwal, S., Medeiros, B., Glodek, B.: Password cracking using probabilistic context-free grammars. In: 2009 30th IEEE Symposium on Security and Privacy, pp. 391–405 (2009). https://doi.org/10.1109/SP.2009.8
40. Yang, C., Hung, J.L., Lin, Z.: An analysis view on password patterns of Chinese internet users. Nankai Bus. Rev. Int. **4**(1), 66–77 (2013)
41. Yang, K., Hu, X., Zhang, Q., Wei, J., Liu, W.: Studies of keyboard patterns in passwords: recognition, characteristics and strength evolution. In: Gao, D., Li, Q., Guan, X., Liao, X. (eds.) Information and Communications Security, pp. 153–168. Springer, Cham (2021)

Towards Exploring Cross-Regional and Cross-Platform Differences in Login Throttling

Minjie Cai[1], Xavier de Carné de Carnavalet[2(✉)], Siqi Zhang[3], Lianying Zhao[1], and Mengyuan Zhang[3]

[1] Carleton University, Ottawa, Canada
minjiecai@cmail.carleton.ca, lianying.zhao@carleton.ca

[2] The Hong Kong Polytechnic University, Hung Hom, Hong Kong SAR, China
xdecarne@polyu.edu.hk

[3] Vrije Universiteit Amsterdam, Amsterdam, The Netherlands
{s.zhang4,m.zhang}@vu.nl

Abstract. This study conducts an analysis of login throttling mechanisms on both websites and smartphone apps, focusing particularly on 20 large Chinese and non-Chinese services. Our research uniquely addresses discrepancies in authentication strategies between these services, which have not been extensively covered in existing literature. We manually simulate the behavior of persistent attackers who can circumvent common anti-bot measures, such as solving CAPTCHAs and employing non-suspicious IP addresses. Our findings reveal significant variations in CAPTCHA implementation, password guessing restrictions, and the integration of multiple login throttling mechanisms between app and web interfaces. Notably, Chinese services tend to deploy more complex CAPTCHA systems and additional verification, whereas non-Chinese services are more susceptible to continuous guessing attacks. This paper also proposes a procedure for analyzing and comparing the efficacy of authentication measures in mitigating password-based attacks, contributing to future enhancements to security practices for online services.

Keywords: Authentication · Login Throttling · CAPTCHA · Password Guessing · Online Services · China

1 Introduction

Passwords are among the most popular and widely used form of identity authentication by online services. Given the critical nature of password-related sensitive information, extensive research has been conducted to address the issue of password guessing [36]. In online guessing attacks, an attacker tries to log into an online service by attempting a list of candidate passwords. Passwords

L. Horn Iwaya et al. (Eds.): NordSec 2024, LNCS 15396, pp. 22–41, 2025.
https://doi.org/10.1007/978-3-031-79007-2_2

could be simply popular (e.g., *password*, *123456*) or derived from a user's personal information, in which case the success rate increases dramatically. Wang et al. [38] reported that they could reach an alarming 70% success rate with a mere 100 attempts in targeted online guessing attacks. As widely recognized, second-factor authentication (2FA) is a prevalent and recommended measure aimed at fortifying the security of password-based authentication, e.g., security tokens [28,30,35], emails and text messages (SMS), prompted after *successful* password-based authentication. Given the operational complexity and inconvenience, 2FA is not always active by default.

To prioritize usability, online services also tend to adopt mechanisms to strengthen the login process itself, e.g., login throttling against password guessing, usually presented after *failed* login attempts. Examples include CAPTCHAs [17], temporary blocking, and account lockout. CAPTCHAs help differentiate between human users and bots, while temporary restrictions and account lockout further rate-limit unsuccessful login attempts. Additionally, risk-based authentication (RBA) [41] is widely used to assess the risk level of a login attempt based on user behavior and environmental contexts, such as IP addresses, login modes, and device characteristics [25,41].

Prior work has attempted to characterize how login throttling mechanisms are deployed in the wild. Lu et al. [23] surveyed 182 websites to enumerate the maximum number of login attempts an attacker can perform. They bypassed blocking mechanisms when possible by switching IP addresses. However, their work did not consider more persistent attackers, e.g., solving CAPTCHAs when they encounter any. They also relied on public cloud IP addresses for their login attempts, which online services could consider as inorganic requests. Finally, they used a Selenium-instrumented browser, which could be fingerprinted and flagged as malicious automated logging attempts. Golla et al. [11] manually examined the rate-limiting mechanisms of 12 prominent websites, specifically focusing on CAPTCHAs and account lockout, and conducted separate analyses on each mechanism. However, their testing environment may not resemble that of an attacker who tries to remain stealthy as they attempted logins through the Tor browser, from which traffic is likely treated differently or even as malicious [16]. Overall, prior work misses an important factor: attackers may be stealthy and resourceful to bypass anti-bot detection and use non-suspicious devices/addresses. Last but not least, online services can exist in the form of either a website, or a smartphone app, or oftentimes both.

In our work, we conduct a measurement of the implementations of login throttling mechanisms using a procedure we propose with a special consideration of both website implementations and smartphone apps. We intend to mimic stealthy and persistent attackers by designing a manual procedure as is done by human (organic) users in the day-to-day use of a computing device. By choosing purely manual operations, we ensure our login attempts are ideal from the point of view of large-scale attackers; however, we also accept that the scale of our experiments is inherently limited by our manual testing ability and labor available. Furthermore, our selection of services also reflects significant influences of the services on individual users, e.g., user base, with at least 186 million active users each, covering diverse categories in our analysis. We also place a focus on Chinese services, as those services (and its users) have long been underrepresented in the literature, yet they have proved to possess unique security characteristics compared to non-Chinese ones [42]. Discussions on Chinese passwords [37] have also highlighted significant differences compared to passwords chosen by English-speaking users. Finally, such services potentially affect more than a fifth of the world population. Therefore, we selected a top 10 Chinese and top 10 non-Chinese services.[1]

Through our analysis, we have identified discrepancies between the web version and the app version of the same service, such as variations in CAPTCHA implementations, weaker restrictions on password guessing on certain platforms, and differences in combining various login throttling mechanisms. These behavior discrepancies between websites and apps can have a substantial impact on the overall security posture of the entire service. Furthermore, notable differences exist between Chinese and non-Chinese services, such as more complex CAPTCHA implementations and verification based on phone numbers (SMS) in Chinese services and a higher likelihood of successful login after continual guessing attacks in non-Chinese services.

Contributions. This paper contributes to the security research of password-based authentication in the following aspects:

1. We propose a procedure to analyze the authentication mechanisms adopted by major online services that support both web and mobile app accesses, with regard to their behavior in response to password guessing attempts.
2. We have uncovered, based on our observations, significant discrepancies between websites and their corresponding apps, leading to one platform being less secure (i.e., the weakest link) than the other. When an app is more permissive, testing the corresponding website's login security alone would mislead security analysts. Worse, when platforms are not in sync, attackers could combine the number of permitted login attempts across platforms.
3. We have also identified significant differences in the way Chinese services operate compared to their non-Chinese counterparts in terms of login security, including reliance on phone numbers, CAPTCHAs at the expense of usability, and more stringent lockouts.

2 Terminology and Threat Model

There have been multiple similar and sometimes overloaded terms used in authentication. We first clarify their definitions involved in this paper to facilitate subsequent discussions. *Rate-limiting* is a generic term to refer to mechanisms to limit the number of allowed failed attempts within a specific period of

[1] Data collected on data.ai, formerly known as APP Annie [24,33,39], on Dec 2023, https://www.data.ai/en/.

time, which is sometimes used interchangeably with *login throttling*. Such mechanisms include CAPTCHAs and temporarily blocking accesses, e.g., based on IP addresses or cookies. Certain previous research separated account lockout from rate-limiting as was done in the work of Lu et al. [23] and Florêncio et al. [7] because it disables login even by legitimate users with the correct password. In this paper, we consider both account lockouts and regular rate-limiting mechanisms for simplicity, referred to as login throttling, in line with other research works such as Golla et al. [11] and Bonneau et al. [5] as they both raise the bar for password guessing and slow down the attacker in one way or another.

In addition, there also exists another form of restriction we call *SMS/Email verification*, which could be triggered at different stages of the authentication process (usually after a correct password), and asks the user to enter a verification code received by either a text message or email. Its key distinction from the aforementioned rate-limiting is that SMS/Email verification per se is an authentication factor, often used in 2FA mechanisms. However, we do not set up any 2FA mechanisms in our experiments as none of the tested services required us to do so.

Although SMS/Email verification is not ideally secure (e.g. [20,31], it normally requires possession of or access to a device/account. Therefore, the appearance of SMS/Email verification will mark the end of the current password guessing attempt for the attacker.

Threat Assumptions. In our analysis, we assume the attacker, whose primary goal is to gain unauthorized access to the service (e.g., for information theft, financial fraud, or other malicious purposes), would try to remain as stealthy as possible (not flagged) and is capable of bypassing bot detection mechanisms like solving CAPTCHAs. We do not consider targeted attacks where the attacker has user-specific information. Additionally, this attacker is proficient in cleaning cookies and changing IP address to avoid RBA effectively. They avoid IP addresses that are associated with cloud providers and thus possibly with bad reputations. In our case, we achieve that by utilizing a range of university IP addresses as well as cellular networks that are known to require ID registration. To enhance the likelihood of successful guessing, the attacker exploits differences in security policies and authentication mechanisms across platforms. If blocked on one platform, they shift efforts to alternative platforms.

3 Selection of Services and Passwords

We describe below our selection of 20 services (10 Chinese and 10 non-Chinese) that offer both a website and an app version (hereafter referred to as platforms), and the lists of incorrect passwords we enter on those services based on our testing procedure presented in Sect. 4.

3.1 Websites and Apps

Chinese Services. To choose the Top 10 Chinese apps, we start with the top 50 apps from the Tencent App Store [34]. We discard apps without corresponding websites, those requiring real-name verification, and banking apps. Additionally, we filter out apps lacking password-based login support or relying solely on Single Sign-On (SSO). For companies with multiple services/apps, we only select their most popular service, e.g., we pick *Baidu* but exclude *BaiduWangpan*. We categorize apps based on the labels sourced from `data.ai` and Google Play (if an app is listed there), and keep only the apps with the highest ranking in each category if there are multiple apps in that category. Our list of top 10 Chinese apps is *QQ*, *Baidu*, *JD*, *Meituan*, *iQIYI*, *Weibo*, *58*, *Ctrip*, *MeituPic*, and *Bilibili*.

Non-Chinese Services. Similarly, we download the list of the top 500 non-Chinese apps from Androidrank [2] on Dec. 30, 2023. Then, we sort apps by the estimated number of app installations worldwide and apply the same filtering criteria used for the Chinese apps, excluding those without a website (e.g., *Chrome*, *WhatsApp Messenger*, those without password-based login.[2] We further remove apps subject to regional restrictions that impact us (*TikTok*), as well as online games without user accounts. We also noticed that many apps rely on SSO, such as *Youtube* (*Google* accounts), and *Messenger* (*Facebook* accounts). For apps from the same company, we keep only the most popular ones (*Facebook* over *Instagram*). Our list of top 10 non-Chinese apps is *Google*, *Facebook*, *Microsoft OneDrive*, *Snapchat*, *X* (formerly Twitter), *Spotify*, *LinkedIn*, *Zoom*, *Picsart*, and *Amazon Shopping*.

Account Creation. To ensure that the experimental accounts closely resemble real accounts, we register new accounts on the app and set passwords using our personal devices at IP addresses unrelated to the experimental environment.

3.2 Password Lists

To simulate an attacker carrying out a password guessing attack, we created a list of popular passwords that would likely be tested in an untargeted online guessing attack. Considering the different preferences of Chinese and non-Chinese users in password selection [12,21,37], we use separate password lists for Chinese and non-Chinese services.

For non-Chinese services, we pick the top passwords from the HaveIBeen-Pwned v6 [13] list,[3] and extract passwords of length 6 and above into a first list English-1class6. Top passwords include "123456" and "qwerty". We further extract passwords of length 7 and above, and mangle them using John the Ripper's [27] top 5th mangling rule (capitalize pure alphabetic words and append '1') to create passwords composed of 3 classes and length 8 and above into a second list English-3class8. Top passwords include "Password1" and "Iloveyou1".

---

[2] We also need to exclude websites bound to their app version by scanning a QR code (without password login), which is the case of WhatsApp.

[3] The list is available as cracked hashes at: https://gist.github.com/roycewilliams/226886fd01572964e1431ac8afc999ce. We first un-hexed Hahcat's `$HEX[]` entries and trimmed those with a trailing newline.

For Chinese services, we rely on a password leak from the Chinese service GFAN.com dating from 2013 [22], which is among the most recent Chinese passwords leaks publicly available. We obtained a list of 10.5M cracked account passwords, and extracted two lists Chinese-1class6 and Chinese-3class8 following the process described above. Top passwords include "123456" and "111111" in the former list, and "Zxcvbnm1", "Qwertyuiop1" in the latter one.

We select passwords from the 1class6 lists if the registration policy of a service lets users register with a 6-character password; otherwise, we select passwords from the 3class8 lists. Note that attackers may leverage their own curated list of top passwords, perhaps even with passwords targeted at specific users [29,38]. By testing more generic popular passwords, the tested services may detect our login attempts as a possible attack more easily, and therefore, our results might show more aggressive defense mechanisms.

4 Methodology

We detail below our procedure for testing the services, including our strategy to deal with various throttling mechanisms. Since these mechanisms may depend on the IP address or device used, we leverage different IP addresses and multiple devices as necessary. We leverage the Chrome browser in incognito mode to browse websites, and several Android smartphones for the counterpart apps. The procedure is illustrated in Fig. 1a and Fig. 1b. Experiment results are discussed in Sect. 5.

4.1 Testing Strategy

We give an overview of our testing strategy below then discuss specific aspects related to bypassing a) CAPTCHAs, b) blocking and account lockout, and c) SMS/Email verification. As part of our strategy, we also try to login with the correct account password to distinguish between various states and describe this step in more detail.

Overview. Our testing procedure starts by attempting to enter up to *25* incorrect passwords on a service's website, by following the password list compiled in Sect. 3.2. Before we reach this number though, we may encounter a number of mechanisms to limit/block our attempts. After each incorrect password, we expect three scenarios: CAPTCHAs, blocking/account lockout, or SMS/Email verification to throttle login attempts, as is commonly suggested in relevant guidelines (see NIST SP 800-63B [26]). In such cases, we try to solve CAPTCHAs or bypass other mechanisms by cleaning up the environment, and changing IP addresses. When we either exhaust our quota of incorrect passwords or we cannot bypass restrictions, we attempt to log in with the correct password. Similarly, we try to bypass any restriction by cleaning up the environment and changing IP address, and also switching platform. We then end the test on the website platform. If necessary, we wait for a day until the expiry of lockout periods or complete SMS/Email verification, so that we can then test the app from scratch by following the same testing strategy. We illustrate the complete procedure in Fig. 1, and further explain it below.

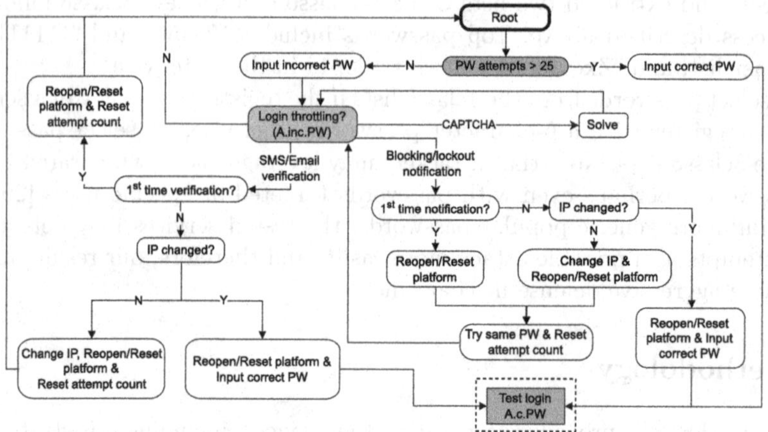

(a) General testing strategy starting from the top "Root" node. The module *Test login A.c.PW* (after correct password) depicted with a green box is expanded in the figure below.

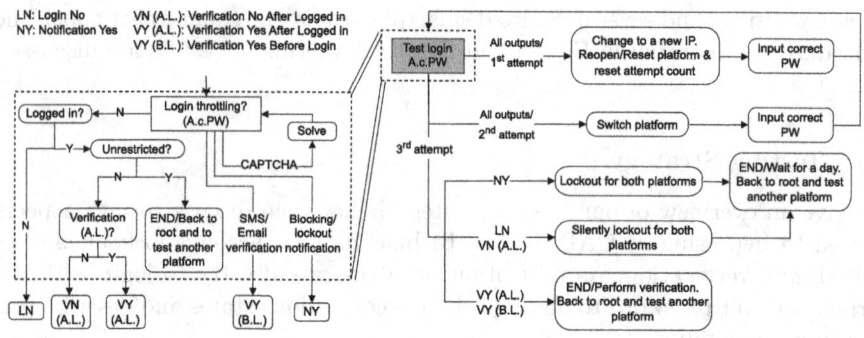

(b) Details of the *Test login A.c.PW* module. The left side depicts the inside of this module while the right side describes possible exits, re-entries, and ending conditions.

Fig. 1. High-level flow chart of our login throttling testing strategy (Color figure online)

CAPTCHAs. Such mechanisms temporarily block the login process until a user solves the challenge. While solving CAPTCHAs is intended to distinguish humans from bots, various CAPTCHA-breaking tools have been proposed [32] and could be employed to automate login attempts. Their accuracy could be even higher than solving by humans [32]. Therefore, differentiating bots and humans based on the successful solving of CAPTCHAs is less reliable now. Instead, the role of CAPTCHAs could be primarily considered as a login throttling mechanism. Given the scale of our experiments and the diversity of CAPTCHAs we may encounter, we simply solve them manually. In our experiments, we solved over 300 CAPTCHAs. Attackers could also leverage paid services employing humans to solve them [4]. We can then discover whether additional throttling mechanisms are in place.

If a website/app shows an outright login failure, we simply enter the next incorrect password. Otherwise, we handle other scenarios as described below.

Blocking and Account Lockout. While incorrect passwords are being attempted, a service may decide to stop serving login requests based on a number of factors. The service could block us thanks to cookie tracking or IP address. Such measures are usually temporary and could last for any duration. When the entire account is locked out, irrespective of which device state and IP address is used for login, even the legitimate user may face challenges to access the account. We learn that blocking or lockout has occurred when the service shows a notification. Our strategy is to try to bypass this verification process by clearing/resetting the browser state/app, and also changing IP address. We resume at the last incorrect password whose attempt was not finalized (we are not explicitly told whether it was a correct or incorrect password). Each time we attempt either of the two techniques, we also reset our attempt counter to zero (*Reset attempt count* in Fig. 1a) to accurately assess password guessing limits when they are not bypassed.

Afterwards, if we are still blocked, we enter the *correct* password through the last IP address that is being throttled, if possible, which helps simulate the case when an attacker stumbles upon the correct password. Services are not expected to treat this login attempt differently and should continue blocking the account. Finally, we change to a fresh IP address once again to enter the correct password on the last platform tested, but after reset, mimicking a legitimate user login. This last step helps distinguish the exact scenario, blocking or lockout. If unsuccessful, the account is locked out.

Sometimes, blocking/lockout occurs silently and the service keeps returning the same "incorrect password" error message, even against the correct password. This situation becomes apparent after we finish our series of 25 passwords and attempt to login with the correct password, as described further below.

SMS/Email Verification. Users could be required to enter a code or use a link received via SMS or email after submitting either a correct or incorrect password. We also try to bypass this verification process by clearing/resetting the browser state/app, changing IP address, and we also reset the attempt counter. Afterwards, if we are still required to verify the account, we enter the *correct* password through the last IP address that is being throttled, which helps simulate the case when an attacker stumbles upon the correct password, similar to our strategy when the account is blocked. Finally, we change to a fresh IP address once again to enter the correct password on the last platform tested, similar to how we assess the type of restriction in the case of blocking or account lockout. This last step assesses whether the service imposes the additional verification account-wise or simply based on the history of failed logins by IP address.

No Apparent Login Throttling. If none of the above login throttling mechanisms are observed, we simply try the next incorrect password within our defined limit of 25 passwords since the last throttling bypass. Depending on the exact testing path and service behavior, a total of 75 incorrect passwords may be attempted at a given service; however, in practice this number remains lower than 33. It is in line with a related work [11] in which the authors tested 25 incorrect passwords at non-Chinese website services, and is usually high enough for throttling to occur while remaining tractable by manual effort.

Testing the Correct Password. Once we exhaust all password attempts or cannot bypass throttling mechanisms, we enter the correct password using the last IP address used. This attempt may fail due to further SMS/Email verification, blocking or account lockout, which could be explicit or not, and that correspond respectively to the three outputs in Fig. 1b: VY (B.L.) (Verification Yes Before Login), NY (Notification Yes), and LN (Login No). We also distinguish whether we can effectively log in, i.e., we enter the account, and whether the service is restricted in some ways or may require further verification, corresponding to the outpus VN (A.L.) (Verification No After Logged in) or VY (A.L.) depending on the need for verification.

In all these cases, we change to a fresh IP address to observe whether a seemingly legitimate login attempt is granted. At this stage, new throttling could occur again. If this second attempt is also unsuccessful, we again change to a fresh IP address and try to log in on the alternative platform. The test conducted on this new platform assesses the consistency between the two platforms. Any inconsistent behavior between the two platforms could potentially present a larger attack surface for that service. Our tests end afterward.

4.2 Technical and Ethical Considerations

We provide below further rationale, technical and ethical elements to support our testing strategy.

Human Behavior. In our testing strategy, we ensure the behavior of an organic human user by manually entering passwords into each services. Our typing behavior and other movements on the websites naturally bypass behavioral-based anti-bot measures [1,15]. This effort significantly reduces the effect of anti-bot techniques on the login process therefore mimicking an adversary with significant resources to perform login attempts at scale.

IP Addresses. If the throttling mechanisms persist, we attempt to bypass them by switching to a new IP address. In our tests, we utilized Wi-Fi networks provided by our university and hotspots generated with cellular data to obtain IP addresses that differ by at least a /21 subnet from those used in the previous attempts. This step helps us determine whether the implemented mechanisms are based on IP addresses. Note that the IP addresses used in this study are not associated with a bad reputation such as being placed on notable blacklists, nor are they cloud IP addresses.

Considering the significant role of IP addresses in evaluating login risks [41], our testing method utilized the IP addresses from the same country as the registered account. In such cases, the risk score associated with our incorrect password login attempts in Risk-Based Authentication (RBA) system should be medium or even lower, especially as the IP addresses originate from reputable sources. We also factor in other indicators, such as monitoring login times against typical patterns and ensuring language consistency with registration. Therefore, our testing methodology is designed to avoid triggering negative reputations.

Ethical Considerations. This paper simulates online password guessing attacks to understand authentication mechanisms in popular services, identify potential weaknesses and vulnerabilities, and evaluate the security of the throttling mechanisms. We have only conducted a limited number of password guesses (32 unique passwords with few repetitions at most), strictly controlling the number and the frequency. Note that since our list is necessarily composed of very large services, thus our experiment cannot sensibly disrupt the operations of those services nor impact the accessibility of legitimate users.

4.3 Testing Environment

Website-Testing Platform. We select the Chrome browser as the platform for conducting website experiments considering its world-wide popularity. Since we manually interact with the website services, we do not leverage automated programs that may get fingerprinted, e.g., based on TLS ciphersuites or alert messages [6]. Consequently, our login attempts *feel* organic, which is the best-case scenario for real large-scale attacks. We start each experiment with a fresh incognito session, guaranteeing that Chrome refrains from storing any browsing history, cookies, or website data. By doing so, we ensure that each experiment commences in a pristine and untraceable state (however, see our limitations in Sect. 7), thereby eliminating any potential influence from prior browsing history on the experimental outcomes.

App-Testing Platform. We leverage physical Android phones to conduct our experiments. We selected three Google Pixel 3 XL mobile phones with the latest stock Android 12. When testing a service, we ensure that the phone used during the website platform testing (when the app is needed to try the correct password) is different than the phone used to perform all the tests for the app itself. We parallelize the experiments across two students. Note that Google phones are good choices since they are not enforcing geographical restrictions that would prevent the download of Chinese apps. The phones are only used for research experiments and have not been significantly associated with any user activity and no real identity.

Platform Reset. When any throttling mechanisms are encountered, we first try to reopen or reset the platform. Specifically, for website testing, we close the browser (incognito) window and reopen it, discarding all traces of browsing history. For app testing, we clear the Android app storage and cache to effectively reset it to its initial state. This step helps us evaluate whether the throttling mechanism relies solely on simple tracking methods, such as session cookies or stored identifiers.

5 Experiment Results and Takeaways

We illustrate the results of our tests on the 20 services in Table 1, highlight significant results and list takeaways below.

5.1 Chinese Services

Account Lockout Mechanisms. Six of the ten Chinese services implement account lockout mechanisms after a limited number of incorrect password attempts. For example, services like *iQIYI*, *JD*, *Meitu*, and *QQ* lock accounts after 10 incorrect attempts or fewer, often resulting in a temporary lockout period (e.g., 24 h in the case of *iQIYI* and 3 h for *Meitu*). These lockout mechanisms remain in place across IP changes and prevent both further incorrect attempts and legitimate logins until the lockout period expires.

SMS Verification as a Second Factor. Eight of the ten services leverage SMS verification, often required after the correct password is entered following multiple incorrect attempts. SMS verification serves as an additional layer of protection even when lockout mechanisms are bypassed, as with *QQ*, *iQIYI* web and *Bilibili* web. Notably, SMS verification is always persistent across IP address changes and platform switching, preventing attackers from gaining access even after successfully entering the correct password.

CAPTCHA Enforcement. CAPTCHAs are widely used across Chinese services to mitigate brute-force attacks, with all services leveraging CAPTCHAs on at least one platform. Most services deliver CAPTCHAs after every incorrect attempt, or after only a few attempts. Some services deploy more complex and multi-stage CAPTCHAs, such as those seen on platforms like *Bilibili* and *Ctrip*. In some cases, CAPTCHAs differ between the website and app versions, with the website requiring more frequent or different types of CAPTCHA tasks.

Disparities Between App and Website Platforms. Six of the ten Chinese services exhibit discrepancies in serving CAPTCHAs across platforms. CAPTCHAs could either be delivered more often or sooner on the website than the app platform, or vice versa.

Pre-login Notifications and Warnings. Several Chinese platforms provide users with pre-login notifications when nearing the incorrect password limit. For example, *iQIYI* displays a countdown notifying users of the remaining allowed attempts before the lockout, helping legitimate users avoid triggering account restrictions. This behavior is not universally seen across non-Chinese services and represents an additional user-friendly feature within Chinese platforms.

Table 1. Summary of our login throttling analysis results

Services		Guesses	CAPTCHA	Lockout		Login A.c.PW	Verification		General Flow
				Notified?	Bypass		By	Bypass	
Chinese services									
QQ	Web	8	Everytime	Y	**S.P.**	→	SMS	✗	→→
	App	6	Everytime	Y	**S.P.**	→	SMS	✗	→→
Baidu	Web	**25**	None	-	-		SMS	✗	→
	App	**25**	Randomly	-	-	()→	SMS	✗	()→
JD	Web	10	Everytime	Y	✗	→	-	-	→
	App	10	Everytime	Y	✗	→	-	-	→
Meituan	Web	25?	Everytime	N	✗	→	SMS	✗	→
	App	1	None	Y	-		-	-	
iQIYI	Web	10	New IP + c.PW	Y	**S.P.**	()→→	SMS	✗	→()→→
	App	10	New IP + c.PW	Y	✗	→	-	-	→→
Weibo	Web	**25**	Everytime	-	-		SMS	✗	→
	App	**25**	None	-	-		SMS	✗	→
58	Web	**25**	Everytime from 4	-	-		SMS	✗	→→
	App	**25**	Everytime	-	-		SMS	✗	→
Bilibili	Web	10+10	Everytime	Y	**C.U., S.P.**	→	SMS	✗	→→
	App	**25**	Everytime from 11	-	-		SMS	**S.P.**	→→→→
Ctrip	Web	**25**	None	-	-		SMS	✗	→
	App	**25**	Everytime from 5	-	-	→	SMS	✗	→→
Meitu	Web	7	Everytime until 8	Y	✗	→	-	-	→
	App	7	Randomly	Y	✗	()→	-	-	()→
Non-Chinese services									
Google	Web	**25**	Randomly	-	-		-	-	()→→
	App	**25**	None	-	-		-	-	→
Facebook	Web	25?	None	N	✗		-	-	→
	App	12	None	Y	✗		-	-	→
Microsoft	Web	9	None	Y	**c.PW**		-	-	→→→
OneDrive	App	9	None	Y	**c.PW**		-	-	→→→
Snapchat	Web	13+19	None	Y	**C.U., c.PW**		App	✗	→→
	App	**25**	None	-	-		-	-	→
X	Web	5+5	None	Y	**New IP**		-	-	→→→
	App	5+5	None	Y	**New IP**		-	-	→→→
Spotify	Web	25?	None	N	**New IP**		-	-	→→→
	App	**25**	None	-	-		-	-	→
LinkedIn	Web	20	Everytime from 6	Y	✗	→	-	-	→→
	App	15	Everytime from 6	Y	✗	→	-	-	→→
Zoom	Web	5	None	Y	✗		-	-	→
	App	5	None	Y	✗		-	-	→
Picsart	Web	**25**	None	-	-		-	-	→
	App	**25**	None	-	-		-	-	→
Amazon	Web	6+6+6	None	-	-		Email	**C.U.**	→→
	App	6+6+6	None	-	-		Email	**C.U.**	→→

Legend: "Guesses" represents the number of password guesses we could attempt; a sum represents the series of attempts after each bypass of a blocking or SMS/Email verification mechanism. "Lockout – Notified?" means we are blocked or the account is locked out and the service notifies this (Y), the service does it silently (N), or there is no blocking (–). Under "Login A.c.PW" (login after correct password): The correct password is accepted, no throttling occurs, and it leads to full control of the account (only), or any throttling mechanism occurs in the order given. Under sub-columns "Bypass": Mechanism bypassed by switching platform (S.P.), inputting the correct password (c.PW), and/or cleaning up the environment (C.U.), could not be bypassed (✗), or there is no mechanism to bypass (–). Under "Verification – By": Method of verification (SMS, Email, or service app) and always occured before login is completed, or there is no verification (–). "General Flow" represents the sequence of throttling mechanisms (or lack thereof) we encoutered until a successful login or an non-bypassable mechanism. Colored cells represent a discrepancy between the website and app's results for the same service. **Bold** results are noteworthy and discussed in Section 5.3. Icons: →CAPTCHA, →SMS/Email verification, →Account blocked/lockout notification, →No throttling, →Warning notification, →Login successful.

Permissive Guesses. Five services allow at least 25 incorrect login attempts on at least one platform (the maximum we tested), with either CAPTCHAs as the only throttling method or no throttling. This permissive threshold could allow an attacker to effectively find the correct password with enough attempts. However, in all cases, the attacker would be presented with an SMS verification request before successfully logging in, preventing the attack.

5.2 Non-Chinese Services

Account Blocking and Lockout. Seven of the 10 non-Chinese services implement blocking or account lockout. *Facebook*, *LinkedIn*, and *Zoom* implement a lockout that we could not bypass. *Facebook*'s website silently locks the account while the app only allows 12 incorrect attempts before announcing the lockout. Compared to Chinese services, two services (*Spotify* web, *X*) only block by IP address, and can therefore get bypassed by changing IP address.

CAPTCHAs. Only two services serve CAPTCHAs (*Google* and *LinkedIn*), sometimes randomly and not on both platforms. This result comes in direct opposition to how CAPTCHAs are used on Chinese services.

No Email/SMS Verification. None of the non-Chinese services rely on SMS as a channel for verification. These services do not always require a phone number to register either. *Snapchat* web requires the user to confirm from the *Snapchat* app. Amazon only suggests a "password assistance" after 6 login failures, which is easily bypassed by cleaning up the environment. There did not seem to be a limit after we tested already 18 incorrect passwords from the same IP address.

Failed and Silent Blocking. *Microsoft OneDrive* allows a user with the correct password to log in after the account is locked out. In other words, the blocking notification replaces the incorrect password message, but does not block an attacker. The same issue appears with *Snapchat* web. Cleaning up the browser state also helps bypass *Snapchat* web (similar to *Bilibili*). However, it will require verification through the *Snapchat* app after the user enters the correct password. Interestingly, for *Spotify* web, a notification appears that reads "Oops! Something went wrong, please try again or take a look at our help area" after continuously trying incorrect passwords. However, it keeps appearing after entering the correct password, indicating that the account is blocked silently. However, this can be bypassed by changing to a different IP address.

Disparities Between App and Website Platforms. Similar to Chinese services, half of the non-Chinese services exhibit some form of discrepancy across platforms. *Google* does not present CAPTCHAs on the app, *Facebook* web and *Spotify* web silently block login attempts but not on the app. *Snapchat* and *LinkedIn* allow different number of guesses.

Permissive Services. Four services allow at least 25 attempts from one platform, with only *Google* web randomly serving CAPTCHAs along the way. Amazon also appears to allow more than 18 incorrect attempts without further throttling mechanisms. Compared to Chinese services, non-Chinese services do not offer a default safety net to catch successful onliny guessing attacks.

5.3 Takeaways

From the results of our study and additional tests, we are able to draw the following takeaways.

Takeaway 1: Higher Reliance on SMS Verification in Chinese Services. Eight out of 10 Chinese services ultimately require authentication by a verification code sent via SMS or email; only a single non-Chinese service does the same. This measure prevents an attacker with the right password from successfully logging in, and cannot be bypassed easily.

To observe the platforms' default login mechanism and then define the function of SMS/email verification as a baseline, we conduct additional tests using our own regular accounts and enter the correct passwords in private browsing mode on the websites where SMS/Email verification was found.

We discovered that all those tested services need SMS/email verification. Its implementation can vary based on the service's security requirements and the perceived level of risk associated with a login attempt. On the one hand, it can serve as a secondary authentication factor (selectable) or as part of multiple mandatory authentication factors, enhancing the security of user accounts (*Weibo*, *Snapchat*). Take *Weibo* as an example, it indicates that "You have enabled login protection, please verify via SMS.". In this case, SMS verification acts as a secondary authentication factor to prevent an attacker from successfully logging in even with a correct password. On the other hand, it can be implemented as a risk-based authentication measure against an unusual or suspicious login attempt by detecting unfamiliar IP addresses, login devices, or browser metadata (*QQ*, *iQIYI*, *Meituan*, *58*, *Ctrip*). In this case, services tend to indicate that "There are risks in the current login. Please verify your mobile phone number before logging in." or "You are logging in on a new device and need to authenticate". Therefore, SMS/email verification functions as a throttling mechanism because it could appear selectively to reduce risks in certain situations.

Takeaway 2: Throttling Mechanisms not in Sync Between Platforms. In our study, each service offers two distinct platforms: a website and a mobile app. User accounts are the same on both platforms. Therefore, an account-wise security evaluation should be implemented to mitigate online password-guessing attacks. However, three services (*QQ*, *iQIYI*, and *Bilibli*) still implement security measures in isolation, focusing on a single platform rather than the account as a whole. On these services, blocking or SMS/Email verification on five of the six corresponding platforms is bypassed by switching to the alternative platform (see Table 1 columns "Lockout–Bypass" and "Verification–Bypass"). Consequently, this can elevate the risk and success rate of targeted attacks.

Takeaway 3: One Platform Allowing More Login Attempts. Websites (or apps) may enable attackers to carry out more login attempts before the attacker is blocked or additional authentication measures are triggered. Websites of *QQ* and *LinkedIn* (highlighted with red in Table 1 in the Guesses column) grant more login attempts, making the security of their websites weaker than their apps. Contrarily, the apps of *Bilibili*, *Snapchat*, and *Spotify* are less secure than their websites for the same reason, even allowing up to 25 login attempts before a successful login. Notably, *Meituan* exhibits a unique case where anomalies about mobile phone numbers trigger login blocks after a single incorrect password entry within the app, but the website still allows login attempts. This suggests that the app's security system may be more sensitive to changes in device and network environments, triggering warnings more easily than the website's system.

Takeaway 4: More Complex Throttling Mechanisms in Chinese Services. Interestingly, we have observed that all Chinese online services implement login throttling mechanisms, with a preference for CAPTCHA, often in conjunction with other throttling mechanisms. In contrast, for the 10 non-Chinese services, 2 out of them do not employ login throttling mechanisms, and 6 out of them solely set locking mechanisms. However, attackers can more easily bypass those locking mechanisms (see below). In this case, non-Chinese services are more susceptible than Chinese services to online password attacks.

Takeaway 5: Weaker Blocking Mechanisms in Non-Chinese Services. Non-Chinese services offer the least effective blocking mechanisms. By simply changing the IP address, a blocked attacker can resume five additional login attempts on *X*. Worse, while Microsoft or Snapchat (website version) appear to block further attempts, an attacker can still try to log in with the correct password from a fresh browser state. This suggests that no blocking measures are effective other than cookie-based, otherwise, even the correct password would be rejected. However, Chinese services do not suffer from these issues.

Takeaway 6: Potential DoS Attacks. In our analysis of four Chinese services, *QQ*, *iQIYI*, *JD*, and *Meitu*, and three non-Chinese services, *Facebook*, *LinkedIn*, and *Zoom*, we observed that these platforms (7/20) implement a security measure where accounts are locked out after several consecutive incorrect password attempts. This strategy is designed to enhance the security of user accounts by preventing unauthorized access through brute-force attacks. However, while this approach effectively safeguards user accounts, it also introduces a vulnerability to intentional Denial of Service (DoS) attacks. Specifically, this security measure can be exploited by attackers aiming to disrupt service for legitimate users. By intentionally entering incorrect passwords, attackers can trigger the account lockout mechanism, thereby blocking real users from accessing their own accounts. This is particularly crucial for services like *JD*, a shopping website. Attackers could strategically target legitimate users during peak promotional events, deliberately triggering account lockouts and thus preventing these users from taking advantage of time-sensitive deals. This not only frustrates customers but also poses a tangible threat to the service's revenue, as blocked users are unable to complete their purchases. Similarly, a DoS attack on legitimate users on *Zoom* could create critical consequences during this remote-work era, as it relies heavily on the availability and reliability of digital communication tools.

Takeaway 7: Difference During Registration. During account registration, we noticed that almost all Chinese services require a real (e.g., non-virtual, Chinese) phone number and verification code for registration without setting a password, while most of the non-Chinese services prefer to take an email address and allow for setting the password during the registration. Additionally, in most Chinese apps, the login and registration processes are integrated, i.e., upon successful verification of an unregistered mobile phone number, the user is automatically registered and logged in without providing a password or username. Subsequently, users have the option to update their account information at any time after logging in. We conjecture the main reason for the popularity of SMS verification in China is real-name authentication for each phone number [9,19].

Takeaway 8: More CAPTCHAs in Chinese Services. Chinese online services often utilize a wide variety of CAPTCHA mechanisms. Notably, some of these CAPTCHAs are specifically tailored to Chinese users, as they necessitate the understanding of Chinese characters or context to be solved. This language-specific approach adds an extra layer of security but also limits accessibility to users who can understand Chinese. In contrast, we only encountered two types of CAPTCHA in the experiments with non-Chinese services (e.g., orientation selection from *LinkedIn* and distorted text CAPTCHA from *Google*). While stronger CAPTCHA-based mechanisms appear more effective than none, complex and challenging CAPTCHAs can frustrate users, especially those with disabilities, leading to disengagement [10,40]. Implementing CAPTCHAs may result in indirect costs for the website, as it may lose users and potential revenue due to diminished user satisfaction and retention.

Takeaway 9: Different CAPTCHA Implementations Between Website and App. In Chinese services, distorted text CAPTCHAs are often implemented on websites, and slider-based CAPTCHAs are implemented on apps. The frequency and the time at which CAPTCHA appears also differ between the website and app. For example, *Bilibili* CAPTCHAs start to appear after 11 attempts on the app but every time on the website. Among the 20 services we examined, 12 of them deploy CAPTCHAs, with 8 utilizing different CAPTCHA implementations between their website and app, and 4 having CAPTCHAs on only one platform. An attacker may exploit this difference to bypass a platform with weaker CAPTCHA settings, allowing them to gain unauthorized access and conduct malicious activities.

6 Related Work

In an online guessing attack, attackers often gather lists of popular passwords from previous breaches and attempt to log in impersonating the legitimate user. Implementing login throttling mechanisms to mitigate such attacks has emerged as an important strategy for online services. However, research indicates that many online services lack this protective mechanism. Lu et al. [23] proposed a black-box approach to model and validate the implementation of authentication throttling mechanisms for 182 popular websites in the U.S. Their research revealed that 131 out of the 182 websites did not properly implement throttling mechanisms. Among the remaining 51 websites, 28 could block legitimate users with correct passwords. This means overly restrictive throttling strategies may also degrade user experience. Golla et al. [11] investigated differences in throttling mechanisms across 12 non-Chinese website services leveraging the Tor network, often successfully attempting 25 incorrect passwords and logging into half. By contrast, we compare Chinese and non-Chinese services as well as the corresponding Android apps (which is sometimes the main platform for a service, especially in China). We report notable new differences and takeaways.

Furthermore, Risk-based Authentication (RBA) [8] base on risk factors like IP address, device, cookies, login time, and failed attempts [14], assigning different risk levels (i.e., VPN connections are low-risk, unfamiliar devices medium-risk, and different locations high-risk, requiring additional verification) [3], protecting accounts from strong attackers guessing the correct password within a low number of attempts [41]. Wiefling et al. [41] found the IP address most critical in assessing login risk. In our work, in addition to IP addresses, we have also considered different devices to assess whether such changes in the website and app accesses affect login attempts.

7 Limitations

For practical reasons, we excluded services requiring real-name authentication, which might involve more stringent identity verification mechanisms that are worth exploring. Our experiments do not test hundreds or thousands of passwords. Such extensive activities could be blocked differently. We only performed one set of experiments per service. Results might vary due to factors beyond our control and could change with time or external conditions. Our tests were conducted from one country; multi-country failed login attempts (as could be achieved via a botnet) may trigger throttling in different ways. Despite resetting the incognito window and changing IP addresses, services might use browser fingerprinting to detect the same user [18]. Note that we leveraged a different device when entering a correct password on the alternative platform than the device used to perform all the tests.

8 Conclusion

In this paper, we analyze throttling authentication mechanisms employed to mitigate online guessing attacks, focusing on CAPTCHA, blocking/account lockout, and SMS/Email verification. We propose a procedure for exploring such mechanisms in the entire login process and analyze the discrepancy across platforms (i.e., between websites and apps) and across regions (i.e., between Chinese and non-Chinese services). Our results indicate that the same service may set different login throttling mechanisms (especially CAPTCHAs) on different platforms. Additionally, Chinese services tend to set complex CAPTCHAs and SMS verification, while there is a higher chance of bypassing throttling and successfully logging in on non-Chinese services. In summary, our research provides valuable takeaways regarding cross-platform and cross-region implementations of login throttling, highlighting both unexpected and flawed discrepancies as well as interesting variations in the user experience in and out of China. Different strategies should be further evaluated to advance user safety on online services.

References

1. Acien, A., Morales, A., Monaco, J.V., Vera-Rodriguez, R., Fierrez, J.: Typenet: deep learning keystroke biometrics. IEEE Trans. Biometrics Behav. Identity Sci. **4**(1), 57–70 (2022)
2. AndroidRank.com: List of Android most popular Google Play apps. https://www.androidrank.org/android-most-popular-google-play-apps?start=1&sort=4&price=all&category=all. Accessed 05 Jan 2024
3. Awati, R.: TechTarget: risk-based authentication (RBA). https://www.techtarget.com/searchsecurity/definition/risk-based-authentication-RBA
4. AZcaptchas: Auto Captcha Solver Service and Cheap Captcha Bypass Service Provider - AZcaptchas. https://azcaptcha.com/. Accessed 08 Jan 2024
5. Bonneau, J., Preibusch, S.: The password thicket: technical and market failures in human authentication on the web. In: Workshop on the Economics of Information Security (2010)
6. Cloudflare: What is rate limiting? https://www.cloudflare.com/en-gb/learning/bots/what-is-rate-limiting/. Accessed 05 Jan 2024
7. Florêncio, D., Herley, C., van Oorschot, P.C.: An administrator's guide to internet password research. In: Large Installation System Administration Conference (LISA) (2014)
8. Freeman, D., Jain, S., Dürmuth, M., Biggio, B., Giacinto, G.: Who are you? A statistical approach to measuring user authenticity. In: Network and Distributed System Security Symposium. The Internet Society, San Diego, California (2016)
9. Fu, K., Chan, C., Chau, M.: Assessing censorship on microblogs in China: discriminatory keyword analysis and the real-name registration policy. IEEE Internet Comput. **17**(3), 42–50 (2013)
10. Gafni, R., Nagar, I.: Captcha: impact on user experience of users with learning disabilities. Interdisc. J. e-Skills Lifelong Learn. **12**, 207–223 (2016)
11. Golla, M.; Schnitzler, T., Dürmuth, M., Görtz, H.: "Will any password do?" Exploring rate-limiting on the web. In: Who Are You?! Adventures in Authentication (WAY) (2016)
12. Han, W., Li, Z., Yuan, L., Xu, W.: Regional patterns and vulnerability analysis of Chinese web passwords. IEEE Trans. Inf. Forensics Secur. **11**(2), 258–272 (2016)
13. Hunt, T.: Pwned passwords, version 6. https://www.troyhunt.com/pwned-passwords-version-6/. Accessed 06 Jan 2024
14. Hurkała, A., Hurkała, J.: Architecture of context-risk-aware authentication system for web environments. In: The Third International Conference on Informatics Engineering and Information Science (2014)

15. Iliou, C., Kostoulas, T., Tsikrika, T., Katos, V., Vrochidis, S., Kompatsiaris, I.: Detection of advanced web bots by combining web logs with mouse behavioural biometrics. Digit. Threats **2**(3) (2021)
16. Khattak, S., et al.: Do you see what I see? Differential treatment of anonymous users. In: Annual Network and Distributed System Security Symposium (2016)
17. Kheshaifaty, N., Gutub, A.A.A.: Preventing multiple accessing attacks via efficient integration of CAPTCHA crypto hash functions. Int. J. Comput. Sci. Netw. Secur. **20**(9), 16–28 (2020)
18. Laperdrix, P., Bielova, N., Baudry, B., Avoine, G.: Browser fingerprinting: a survey. ACM Trans. Web **14**(2), 8:1–8:33 (2020)
19. Lee, J.A., Liu, C.Y.: Real-name registration rules and the fading digital anonymity in China. Washington Int. Law J. **25**, 1 (2016)
20. Lee, K., Kaiser, B., Mayer, J.R., Narayanan, A.: An empirical study of wireless carrier authentication for SIM swaps. In: Symposium on Usable Privacy and Security (SOUPS), pp. 61–79 (2020)
21. Li, Z., Han, W., Xu, W.: A large-scale empirical analysis of Chinese web passwords. In: USENIX Security (2014)
22. Liu, X.: Jifeng Forum was exposed to have leaked the information of 23 million users (translated), Beijing News article (2015). https://www.bjnews.com.cn/detail/155148659914920.html. Accessed 01 June 2024
23. Lu, B., Zhang, X., Ling, Z., Zhang, Y., Lin, Z.: A measurement study of authentication rate-limiting mechanisms of modern websites. In: Annual Computer Security Applications Conference (ACSAC) (2018)
24. Mao, S., Dewan, S., Ho, Y.I.: Personalized ranking at a mobile app distribution platform. Inf. Syst. Res. **34**(3), 811–827 (2023)
25. Markert, P., Schnitzler, T., Golla, M., Dürmuth, M.: "As soon as it's a risk, I want to require MFA": how administrators configure risk-based authentication. In: Symposium on Usable Privacy and Security (SOUPS) (2022)
26. National Institute of Standards and Technology: Digital identity guidelines: Authentication and lifecycle management, NIST Special Publication 800-63B
27. OpenWall.com: John the Ripper password cracker. https://www.openwall.com/john/. Accessed 05 Jan 2024
28. Oracle: Oracle: Java card technology. https://www.oracle.com/java/java-card/
29. Pal, B., Daniel, T., Chatterjee, R., Ristenpart, T.: Beyond credential stuffing: password similarity models using neural networks. In: IEEE Symposium on Security and Privacy (S&P) (2019)
30. Rescorla, E.: The transport layer security (TLS) protocol version 1.3. RFC **8446**, 1–160 (2018)
31. Sami Laine: SMS two-factor authentication - worse than just a good password?. https://sec.okta.com/articles/2020/05/sms-two-factor-authentication-worse-just-good-password
32. Searles, A., Nakatsuka, Y., Ozturk, E., Paverd, A., Tsudik, G., Enkoji, A.: An empirical study & evaluation of modern captchas. In: USENIX Security (2023)
33. Shahin, M., Zahedi, M., Khalajzadeh, H., Nasab, A.R.: A study of gender discussions in mobile apps. In: International Conference on Mining Software Repositories (2023)
34. Tencent: Tencent official website. https://sj.qq.com/. Accessed 06 Jan 2024
35. Thanh, D.V., Jørstad, I., Jønvik, T.E., van Thuan, D.: Strong authentication with mobile phone as security token. In: International Conference on Mobile Adhoc and Sensor Systems (MASS) (2009)

36. Thomas, K., et al.: Data breaches, phishing, or malware? Understanding the risks of stolen credentials. In: ACM Conference on Computer and Communications Security (2017)
37. Wang, D., Wang, P., He, D., Tian, Y.: Birthday, name and bifacial-security: understanding passwords of Chinese web users. In: USENIX Security (2019)
38. Wang, D., Zhang, Z., Wang, P., Yan, J., Huang, X.: Targeted online password guessing: an underestimated threat. In: ACM Conference on Computer and Communications Security (2016)
39. Wang, X., Markert, C., Sasangohar, F.: Investigating popular mental health mobile application downloads and activity during the COVID-19 pandemic. Hum. Factors **65**(1), 50–61 (2023)
40. Wentz, B., Pham, D.J., Tressler, K.: Exploring the accessibility of banking and finance systems for blind users. First Monday **22**(3) (2017)
41. Wiefling, S., Iacono, L.L., Dürmuth, M.: Is this really you? An empirical study on risk-based authentication applied in the wild. CoRR abs/2003.07622 (2020)
42. Chen, X., Zhou, Y.: Mobile login methods help Chinese users avoid password roadblocks. https://www.nngroup.com/articles/mobile-login-china/

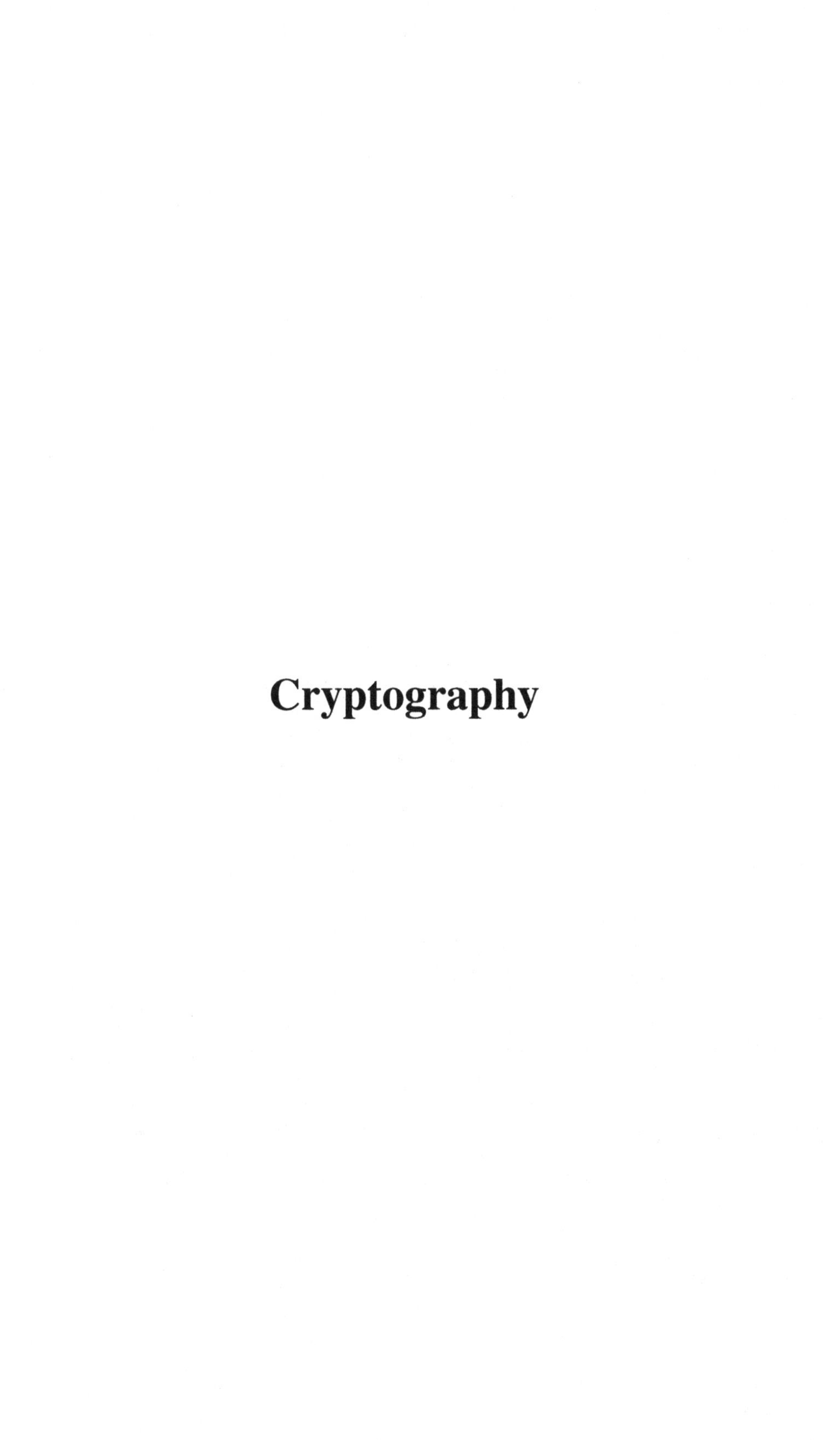

Cryptography

Determining the A5 Encryption Algorithms Used in 2G (GSM) Networks

Danielle Morgan(✉)

University of Tartu, Tartu, Estonia
danielle.morgan@ut.ee

Abstract. The algorithms used in GSM networks are known to be weak, and attackers can exploit them to perform various attacks, such as eavesdropping. However, 2G (GSM) networks are still widely used worldwide, especially by IoT devices, and as a fallback when networks utilising 4G and 5G technology are unavailable. Therefore, the security of GSM networks is still relevant today, and efforts should be made to ensure that these networks adhere to modern security standards. In this paper, we propose low-cost methods that can be used to determine the encryption algorithms employed by mobile operators in their GSM networks. We applied these methods to perform a case study, analysing the algorithms used by Estonian mobile operators. The results show that even in 2024, there are mobile operators who only support the `A5/1` encryption algorithm to secure communication privacy for devices operating in their network, leaving these devices vulnerable to eavesdropping attacks.

Keywords: GSM · 2G · A5/1 · SDR

1 Introduction

Globally, 90% of the population is covered by networks using 4G technology and 32% by 5G technology, with mobile operators expected to expand these networks in the coming years. However, networks using the older 2G (GSM) technology are and will still be in use, especially by mobile users in low and middle-income countries (LMICs) as well as older Internet of Things (IoT) applications [18]. These 2G networks also serve as fallback systems when the newer networks (4G and 5G) are unavailable. Additionally, an attacker can apply jamming attacks or bidding-down attacks [14] to force a mobile device to use 2G technology. Therefore, understanding the security of 2G communications is still relevant as mobile devices will use 2G technology in cases where 4G and 5G coverage is not present.

Radio communication in 2G networks between a mobile device and the mobile network is secured using A5 encryption algorithms. The four main encryption algorithms available are `A5/0`, `A5/1`, `A5/2` and `A5/3`. The `A5/3` encryption algorithm provides the best option for communication secrecy from these algorithms, as the other algorithms have practically exploitable flaws that allow an attacker

L. Horn Iwaya et al. (Eds.): NordSec 2024, LNCS 15396, pp. 45–61, 2025.
https://doi.org/10.1007/978-3-031-79007-2_3

to eavesdrop on communication. Therefore, by identifying which algorithms are in use in a mobile operator's network, it is possible to assess the security risks associated with the network. Furthermore, understanding the mobile operator's encryption practices can help formulate better security policies and regulations.

In this paper, we investigate tools that can be used to assess the A5 algorithms supported and used in 2G networks and propose two low-cost methods that can obtain this data:

1. a passive method that can be used to monitor A5 algorithm usage by eavesdropping on the signals transmitted by a mobile operator's cell tower;
2. an active method that can be used to quickly enumerate the A5 algorithms supported by a cell tower and determine which A5 algorithm is the preferred choice.

We applied these methods in a case study to analyse the A5 algorithms supported by Estonian mobile operators. The results show that:

1. there are mobile operators that do not support the `A5/3` algorithm, effectively leaving their 2G networks open to passive eavesdropping attacks;
2. in the 2G networks with `A5/3` support, a portion of the mobile traffic is still encrypted using the insecure `A5/1` algorithm.

The remainder of this paper is organised as follows: Sect. 2 contains the background necessary to understand encryption in 2G networks. Section 3 highlights related works focusing on assessing the security in 2G networks. Section 4 introduces the suggested methodology to assess networks, and Sect. 5 presents the results and discusses a case study using this methodology. Finally, Sect. 6 concludes the paper.

2 Background

Global System for Mobile Communications (GSM) is a standard developed by the European Telecommunications Standards Institute (ETSI) to describe the protocols used by 2G mobile networks. As such, GSM is often used to refer to 2G networks. This section provides an overview of this GSM standard in regard to the encryption algorithms available to secure radio communication.

2.1 A5 Encryption Algorithms Used in GSM Networks

The encryption algorithms implemented in 2G networks are fundamental to safeguarding the confidentiality of the data transmitted over these networks. This communication is usually secured using a 64-bit session key known as `Kc`. This key is used in conjunction with one of three encryption algorithms available: `A5/1`, `A5/2` or `A5/3`. The fourth encryption algorithm, `A5/0`, does not ensure confidentiality as communication is not encrypted. The GSM Association [13] provides guidance on the algorithm choice that should be implemented in 2G networks.

If `A5/0` is used, an attacker can read all messages exchanged in plaintext once the attacker has the correct tools to capture the communication. Therefore, the current recommendation from the GSM standard is to prohibit `A5/0` in networks to prevent impersonation attacks.

The first encryption algorithm, the stream cipher `A5/1`, has been shown to leak `Kc` with ciphertext-only attacks [3] and known plaintext attacks [4]. Today, `A5/1`-encrypted messages can be deciphered in real-time with tools such as rainbow tables [15,29], Kraken [12] or the Shoghi A5.1 Decryptor[1]. Therefore, the current recommendation for `A5/1` is only to have it activated to support legacy devices that do not support `A5/3`.

The second encryption algorithm `A5/2`, also a stream cipher, was proven to be weak, allowing `Kc` to be quickly recovered [3,11] and as per the GSM standard [2] the use of `A5/2` was banned. The `A5/2` algorithm was prohibited from devices, and the current recommendation is to not have it activated in networks. The algorithm is no longer included in manufactured mobile devices, and reputable mobile operators have eliminated the support for `A5/2` in their networks [22]. This left `A5/1` and `A5/3` as the only encryption algorithms available to secure the confidentiality of communications in GSM networks.

The third encryption algorithm, `A5/3`, is based on the block cipher KASUMI [1]. An attack to recover the encryption key from the `A5/3` algorithm was shown in 2010, but it was not applicable to the operation of 2G networks [9]. In 2024, a known-plaintext attack against the `A5/3` encryption algorithm as used in GSM networks was released [6]. This attack was described as being capable of decrypting a two-hour phone call with a probability of 0.43 in 14 minutes. At the time of writing, no publicly available tools or applications that implement this attack are available. As such, `A5/3` is currently still recommended as the GSM encryption algorithm of choice and should be activated in both devices and networks with a higher preference than `A5/1`.

A variant of the `A5/3` algorithm is the `A5/4` algorithm, which, like `A5/3`, is also based on the block cipher KASUMI. However, `A5/4` uses a 128-bit session key instead of the 64-bit key used by `A5/1`, `A5/2` and `A5/3`. Currently, implementing `A5/4` in devices and GSM networks is not mandatory, but when implemented should have a higher preference than `A5/3`.

Despite its security vulnerabilities, `A5/1` remains in the GSM standard as the bare minimum algorithm that needs to be supported by a device wishing to communicate with a 2G network [2]. As a result, all mobile operators must support this algorithm in their 2G networks. This opens the opportunity for an attacker to eavesdrop on the communication between the mobile network and a device and potentially gain access to sensitive information if `A5/1` is used to secure the communication. Therefore, it is important to understand how the A5 algorithm is negotiated in GSM networks.

[1] https://www.shoghicom.com/a5-decryptor.php.

2.2 Radio Communication in GSM Networks

The Base Transceiver Station (BTS) is the first connection a mobile device has to a GSM network, with these components exchanging information using wireless signals [10]. These wireless signals are sent on frequencies unique to each BTS in a specific location area identified by a location area code (LAC). In Europe, these frequencies fall in the 900 MHz (GSM-900) and 1800 MHz (GSM-1800) frequency bands[2]. Every mobile device is designed with specific GSM frequency bands that it can support. When a device attempts to connect to a network, it searches for Base Transceiver Stations (BTS) in the supported frequency ranges. The BTS, in turn, also emit `System Information` messages containing details about itself, such as its cell identifier (CID) and location area code (LAC).

Each of these BTS operates on a specified *downlink* frequency (the frequency the BTS uses to send information to the mobile device) and *uplink* frequency (the frequency the mobile device uses to send information to the BTS). The combination of the *uplink* and *downlink* frequency is encoded in the absolute radio-frequency channel number (ARFCN). For GSM-900 the ARFCN value ranges from 0 to 124 and 975 to 1023 and ranges from 512 to 885 for GSM-1800 [17]. The BTS that the device eventually attempts to connect to depends on the settings configured on the SIM card installed in the mobile device. If multiple BTS that operate with the specified SIM parameters are detected, the BTS with the strongest signal is usually selected.

Figure 1 gives an overview of the process used to connect a mobile device to the mobile network. During this process, the mobile device indicates the A5 algorithms it supports, the session key `Kc` is created, and the network chooses an encryption algorithm to secure communication.

The device first initiates contact with the mobile operator's BTS using the location update procedure. In this procedure, the first step involves the mobile device sending a message called the `Location Update Request` on the *uplink* frequency. This frame contains a unique identifier for the device, either an International Mobile Subscriber Identity (IMSI), a Temporary Mobile Subscriber Identity (TMSI) and/or an International Mobile Equipment Identity (IMEI). The IMSI is internationally unique to a SIM card, identifying the user to the network and used to keep track of the services linked to the SIM card [17]. The TMSI is a temporary identifier used to prevent the IMSI from being constantly sent across the network to prevent tracking. The IMEI is a unique identifier for mobile devices.

The network uses the identifier to determine if the device should have access to the network. If the device is allowed, the BTS sends `RAND` (a 128-bit random number) to the mobile device. The SIM card then uses a key stored in its memory known as `Ki` (a 128-bit key), and `RAND` to generate `Kc` [17]. At the same time, `Ki`, and `RAND` are used to produce `SRES`. `SRES` and `Kc` are then returned to the phone. The phone sends `SRES` back to the BTS, on the *uplink* frequency using the `Authentication Response` message. If the network accepts `SRES`, at this

[2] https://docdb.cept.org/document/480.

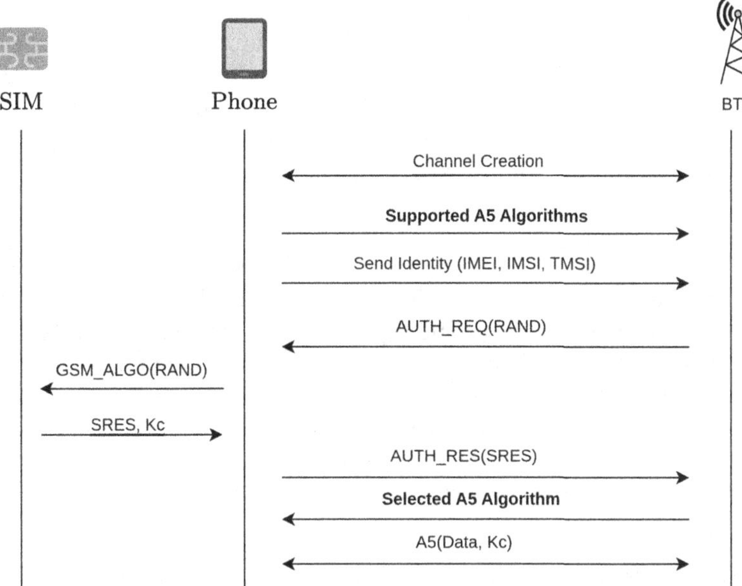

Fig. 1. Radio Communication in a GSM network

point, messages can be exchanged using `Kc` and one of the supported encryption algorithms. The status of the procedure is usually indicated by a `Location Update Accept` message if the device is accepted or `Location Update Reject` message if the device is not accepted.

Listing 1.1. Extract of a Classmark Information message showing the A5 algorithms supported by a device

```
DTAP Radio Resources Management Message Type: Classmark Change (0x16)
Mobile Station Classmark 2
Length: 3
...
.... 0... = A5/1 algorithm supported: encryption algorithm A5/1 available
...
.... ..0. = A5/3 algorithm supported: encryption algorithm A5/3 not available
.... ...1 = A5/2 algorithm supported: encryption algorithm A5/2 available
Mobile Station Classmark 3
Length: 5
...
.... 0000 = A5 bits: 0x00
.... 0... = A5/7 algorithm supported: encryption algorithm A5/7 not available
.... .0.. = A5/6 algorithm supported: encryption algorithm A5/6 not available
.... ..0. = A5/5 algorithm supported: encryption algorithm A5/5 not available
.... ...0 = A5/4 algorithm supported: encryption algorithm A5/4 not available
```

During the location update procedure, the network may assign a new TMSI to the device before issuing the `Location Update Accept` message. As this identifier is meant to prevent the user from being tracked, it is encrypted before it is sent to the device. To determine which A5 algorithm should be used for encryption, the network must first know the algorithms that the device supports. The device sends this information to the BTS using `Classmark information` (Supported A5 algorithms in Fig. 1) messages on the *uplink* frequency as seen in Listing 1.1.

To start encryption, the BTS sends a `Ciphering Mode Command` (Selected A5 Algorithm in Fig. 1) message to the device, and the device responds with the `Cipher Mode Complete` message [10,17]. The `Cipher Mode Command` as seen in Listing 1.2 contains the A5 algorithm, selected by the mobile network, that should be used to encrypt communication. The `Cipher Mode Complete` message sent by the device is encrypted using this algorithm and `Kc`. If the BTS is able to decipher this message, then the network accepts the device, and further communication between the device and BTS is encrypted, including the newly assigned TMSI.

Listing 1.2. Extract of a Cipher Mode Command message showing A5/1 selected as the encryption algorithm

```
DTAP Radio Resources Management Message Type: Ciphering Mode Command (0x35)
Cipher Mode Setting
        .... ...1 = SC: Start ciphering (1)
        .... 000. = Algorithm identifier: Cipher with algorithm A5/1 (0)
Cipher Mode Response
        ...1 .... = CR: IMEISV shall be included (1)
```

If the network chooses to use `A5/0` (no encryption), then the `Cipher Mode Command` is not sent to the device, and all messages exchanged between the BTS and the device would be sent in plaintext. Additionally, if the network does not support any of the algorithms the device has indicated, then the device may be denied access to the network even if the `SRES` value was accepted.

3 Related Work

Several tools and software applications have been developed over the years to assess the security of GSM networks. Mobile phones and Software Defined Radio (SDR) devices have been the main hardware equipment used in the implementations.

3.1 Mobile Applications

In 2014, Dabrowski et al. [7] introduced multiple methods of detecting artifacts in mobile networks with the express purpose of detecting IMSI catchers, resulting in the mobile application, mobile IMSI Catcher Catcher (mICC), that could be used with standard consumer-grade mobile phones, without the need to *root* or *jailbreak* them.

Android IMSI-Catcher Detector (AIMSICD) [5], an Android application first introduced in 2012, is another application that aims to detect IMSI-catchers but also provides warnings when ciphering is not available in the network (`A5/0` is used). AIMSICD also works on *non-rooted* Android devices.

Darshak [30] is an application for the Samsung Galaxy S3 phone using the stock Android 4.1.2 firmware with *root* access. The main purpose of Darshak is to detect any suspicious activity of tracking by the network and assess the capabilities of cellular providers, such as displaying whether authentication has been performed, the `RAND` used, and the ciphering algorithms utilised.

SnoopSnitch, introduced in 2014, is another popular Android application that assesses the security of GSM networks, which will be discussed in detail below.

SnoopSnitch. SnoopSnitch [26] is an Android application that offers several tests to assess the security of mobile devices and the mobile networks they use. The application must be used with a *rooted* Android device with a Qualcomm-based chipset. The application aims to determine whether a device is exposed to attacks or surveillance from the mobile network. SnoopSnitch's mobile network security test has an active and passive mode. In the active mode, three rounds of incoming and outgoing calls and SMS are sent to and from the testing device. In the passive mode, continuous analysis of the device's radio traffic is conducted. From these tests, SnoopSnitch can identify several security-related events, including which A5 algorithms are being used by the device in the network.

Users of the application can choose to upload detailed event logs to the SnoopSnitch servers. This data is then used to rate the security of several mobile operators worldwide, and the results are presented in reports. The data and the results are available at GSMmap [25]. The reports analyse both the 3G and 2G user protection features implemented in the networks. The values used in GSMmap are averaged over many samples for a network contributed by different users in different locations. As a result, the location, the type of SIM card used or the current load of the network are factors that influence the score a mobile operator may receive [27].

Currently, GSMmap offers the best overall analysis of a mobile operator's GSM network. Unfortunately, as mobile users switch to 4G and 5G networks, data collected by mobile phones for 2G networks is no longer readily available, leading to applications using SDR devices becoming more popular in GSM network analysis. Therefore, the methods outlined in this paper help to solve the limitations of SnoopSnitch specified below:

- *Rooted* devices with Qualcomm-based chipsets are required, which may be difficult to obtain or configure.
- The application can only detect the A5 algorithms used by the test device and cannot detect the algorithms used by other mobile devices connected to the same network.

- SnoopSnitch cannot enumerate the algorithms supported by a BTS or mobile network and is unable to determine a BTS's preferred A5 algorithm.

The passive method proposed in this work solves the issue of radio equipment by using readily available, low-cost SDR equipment. It can also detect the A5 algorithms used by the mobile devices connected to a BTS. Finally, the active method proposed can quickly enumerate the algorithms supported by a BTS and specify which A5 algorithm is preferred.

3.2 SDR and Other Projects

One popular choice for network analysis that relies on SDR is the gr-gsm project [24]. The open-source project, gr-gsm, is a collection of tools that uses low-cost SDR devices to receive information transmitted by GSM equipment and devices. We used the tools in this project to develop the passive method explained in this work.

Another low-cost option to actively interact with a mobile network is the Open source mobile communications BaseBand (OsmocomBB) project [19]. OsmocomBB is an open-source software that implements the GSM phone-side protocol stack. We used this software to develop the active method explained in this work.

4 Methods

This section describes two low-cost methods to determine the encryption algorithms supported and used in a GSM mobile network. One method focuses on passively collecting data, while the second focuses on actively interacting with the network. These methods were designed because the data obtained from a mobile network using a *rooted* and *non-rooted* device is limited. Additionally, these methods can give an overview of a mobile network and are not limited to the specifications of a mobile device. The source code and instructions for applying these methods are available at [8].

4.1 Passive Method

As mentioned in Sect. 2.2, the `Cipher Mode Command` sent from the BTS to the mobile device indicates the encryption algorithm that should be used to encrypt further communication in the GSM network. Therefore, the encryption algorithms used by a BTS can be determined by monitoring the A5 algorithms specified in the `Cipher Mode Command` message. To apply this method, a device capable of capturing GSM signals and software to decode these signals is required.

This method targets the encryption algorithms used by a specific BTS, allowing each BTS in a network to be assessed independently. Therefore, the following research question can be answered:

- **RQ1**: What encryption algorithms are used by the BTS in a mobile operator's network?

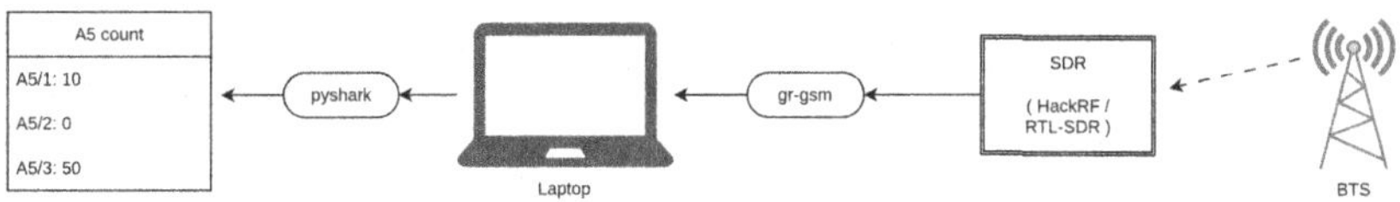

Fig. 2. Experiment setup for Passive method

Implementation. Figure 2 depicts the experiment setup for applying the passive method. To minimise the cost of the setup, we chose the RTL-SDR[3] (approximately €40), and HackRF (approximately €300) to capture signals and used gr-gsm to decode the GSM signals. Specifically, the tool `grgsm_livemon` from the gr-gsm project was used to monitor the activity of a BTS in real-time. The tool forwards GSM messages to the laptop's loopback interface, which can be viewed in Wireshark. The SDR, HackRF, can monitor all the GSM frequency ranges supported in the EU, but the RTL-SDR is sufficient in situations where the BTS under observation uses frequencies below 1800 MHz.

We created a Python program using Pyshark [16] to extract information from the GSM messages on the loopback interface. The program inspects each `Cipher Mode Command` and obtains the A5 algorithm used in the communication. A count of each algorithm encountered is maintained, and this information, along with the identifier for the BTS, is stored in JSON format once the monitoring is complete. Listing 1.3 shows a snippet of the information from one of the monitored BTS. During the two hours, the BTS was monitored, 79 `Cipher Mode Command` messages were discovered, and 4 of the messages specified communication should be encrypted using `A5/1` and 75 specified `A5/3` encryption.

Listing 1.3. Snippet of the output from the passive monitor

```
{
    "Start Time": "2024/08/16 18:17:08",
    "A5 count": 79,
    "A5/1 count": 4,
    "A5/2 count": 0,
    "A5/3 count": 75,
    "End Time": "2024/08/16 20:17:12",
    "Total Time": "2:00:03.900575"
}
```

Improvements. This method could be improved by monitoring the `Classmark information` messages transmitted by the mobile device to indicate the A5 algorithms it supports. By comparing the algorithms a device supports and the algorithm selected by the BTS, the preferred algorithm choice of the BTS can be

---

[3] The RTL-SDR is only capable of capturing signals from BTS that use the GSM-900 frequency range in the EU as the operating frequency range of the RTL-SDR is 24 MHz to 1750 MHz.

determined. However, this improvement is restricted by the capabilities of the SDR used. The mobile device sends the `Classmark information` messages, and therefore, `Classmark information` messages have a lower power level than messages sent by the BTS. This lower power level makes `Classmark information` messages difficult to detect using cheaper SDRs, such as the RTL-SDR and HackRF.

Another improvement would be determining how many devices the `Cipher Mode Command` messages are sent to during the monitoring period. Knowing the number of devices communicating with the BTS would indicate if one device is responsible for the `Cipher Mode Command` messages observed or if multiple devices were using the GSM mobile network. Messages containing a device's TMSI or IMSI can be monitored to identify the device receiving the `Cipher Mode Command` messages. However, if the TMSI of a device is updated often, it would be difficult to identify it *uniquely*. The device's IMEI would better serve as a unique identifier for the device in this case. However, the IMEI is usually sent in messages which are encrypted, and these messages would not be detected using `grgsm_livemon`.

Limitations. This method requires the data to be collected for a specific time period and would only provide information about the algorithms selected in the monitored time frame. This would also be heavily influenced by the capabilities of the devices using the GSM network during that time. For example, if devices that only support `A5/1` use the network during the monitoring period, the resultant data would indicate that the BTS only uses the `A5/1` algorithm. Additionally, as the `Cipher Mode Command` message is not sent when `A5/0` is used, this method would be unable to detect if the BTS uses the `A5/0` algorithm. Therefore, a method that can be executed independently of the users of a network and is less time-consuming is preferable.

4.2 Active Method

To determine the algorithms supported by a BTS, we can use a device that only supports one of the A5 algorithms to connect to the BTS. Furthermore, a device that supports all A5 algorithms will provide information about the preferred A5 algorithm of the BTS. This method requires a device that can be configured to use specific A5 algorithms and a SIM card with access to the network under observation.

This method is, therefore, useful in answering the following research questions:

- **RQ2**: What encryption algorithms are supported by the BTS in a mobile operator's network?
- **RQ3**: What is the preferred A5 algorithm for the BTS in a mobile operator's network?

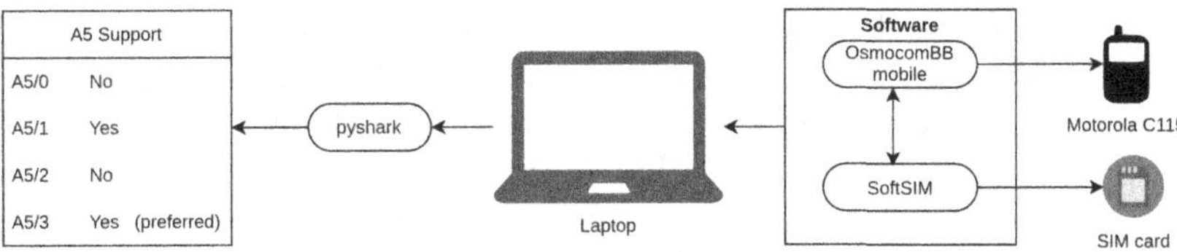

Fig. 3. Experiment setup for Active method

Implementation. Figure 3 depicts the experiment setup used to perform the active method. We used the OsmocomBB compatible phone [20], Motorola C115 (can be purchased second-hand for approximately €50), and the OsmocomBB `mobile` program [21] to produce a device with configurable A5 algorithms. We then used softSIM [23] to allow the OsmocomBB `mobile` program to communicate with the SIM card (usually less than €5 per card), creating a configurable mobile device.

To determine the supported algorithms, the OsmocomBB phone was configured to support only one of the A5 algorithms at a time. First, to simulate `A5/0`, the OsmocomBB `mobile` configuration file was set to support none of the A5 algorithms. The `mobile` program was then started, which initiated the location update procedure. The BTS was verified to support the `A5/0` algorithm tested if the location update procedure was successful, as indicated by the `Location Update Accept` message sent to the mobile device. These steps were repeated until each A5 algorithm was tested individually by setting the OsmocomBB `mobile` configuration file to support only `A5/1`, `A5/2`, and finally, `A5/3` before triggering the location update procedure with the `Location Update Accept` message used to indicate a successful connection.

Listing 1.4. Snippet of the messages exchanged between a BTS and the Osmocom phone during the location Update procedure

```
(UL) Location Updating Request
(DL) Location Updating Request
(UL) Classmark Change
(DL) Identity Request
(UL) Identity Response
(DL) Authentication Request
(UL) Authentication Response
(DL) Ciphering Mode Command
       Algorithm: A5/1
(UL) Ciphering Mode Complete
(DL) Identity Request
(UL) Identity Response
(DL) Location Updating Accept
(UL) TMSI Reallocation Complete
```

Next, to conclude the algorithm preferred by the network, the OsmocomBB `mobile` configuration file was set to support `A5/1`, `A5/2` and `A5/3` before the location update procedure was initiated. The preferred A5 algorithm was then determined by extracting the A5 algorithm specified in the `Cipher Mode Command` message sent during the location update procedure. A Python program was written using Pyshark to extract the messages exchanged between the OsmocomBB phone and the BTS. A sample of the communication can be seen in Listing 1.4, where (UL) indicates messages sent from the phone to the BTS and (DL) indicates messages sent to the phone from the BTS. During this exchange, the BTS requested the `A5/1` algorithm even though the OsmocomBB phone indicated that it supported `A5/3`.

Improvements. The A5 algorithm used in the location update procedure is not guaranteed to be used during calls and SMS communication, as the mobile operator may use a different algorithm to secure calls and SMS. The test could be improved by monitoring the A5 usage while sending text messages and calls from the OsmocomBB phone. This method, however, may incur costs. Theoretically, the preferred A5 algorithm the BTS uses should remain the same for all types of communication. An SMS or call may immediately follow the location update procedure, and the data will be encrypted using the previously specified algorithm.

Limitations. The main limitation of this method is that the BTS tested for algorithm support and preference is chosen when the OsmocomBB phone decides on the BTS it will connect to. The BTS selected during testing would depend on the strongest signal the OsmocomBB phone receives. There is no guarantee that each A5/x test will be executed on the same BTS. Hence, the test would have to be repeated multiple times in some cases to obtain the results from one BTS, even when the same SIM card is used. The SIM card used can also impact the results, as the mobile operator may have different configurations and/or settings specified for different types of cards.

Additionally, this method only indicates the A5 algorithms supported by a specific BTS. It does not give an overview of the algorithms other devices use in the mobile network, while such an overview is provided by the passive method. Therefore, combining the active and passive methods would provide a more comprehensive insight into the algorithms used in a GSM network.

5 Case Study

The methods outlined in Sect. 4 were used to collect data on select BTS located in Tartu, Estonia. The experiments were performed from February to August 2024. During that time, three mobile operators were active in Estonia - Elisa Eesti AS (Elisa), Tele2 Eesti AS (Tele2) and Telia Eesti AS (Telia). Data was collected from at least one BTS from each mobile operator. We present the results of the tests in two sections. Section 5.1 contains the results of the A5 usage in the networks, and Sect. 5.2 shows the A5 algorithms supported by the networks.

5.1 A5 Usage

This experiment was executed by first determining the frequencies used by the BTS. The `grgsm_scanner` tool, available in the gr-gsm project, was used to collect this information. The Python program was then used to monitor the *downlink* frequency of a BTS in set intervals. Overall, each BTS was monitored for at least 8 hours; the results collected in August 2024 can be seen in Table 1.

Table 1. A5 usage for observed BTS in Tartu, Estonia

Telecom	LAC	CID	Run-time	A5 encountered			
				Total A5	A5/1	A5/2	A5/3
Telia	5	5087	8 h	215	5	0	210
		5099	17 h 20 min	2571	28	0	2543
		6682	16 h 50 min	1936	200	0	1736
Elisa	41	50141	8 h	46	46	0	0
		50967	8 h	180	180	0	0
		52181	17 h 10 min	290	290	0	0
		52183	16 h 30 min	395	395	0	0
Tele2	1171	36748	16 h	241	241	0	0
		4154	20 h	450	450	0	0
		4156	8 h	38	38	0	0

The results indicate that in the Tele2 and Elisa networks, the `A5/3` algorithm was not used by any BTS during the monitoring period. From the observed `Cipher Mode Command` messages, 100% of the communication was encrypted using `A5/1`. As the readings were taken at different times and sometimes on different days, it was highly unlikely that a single device was responsible for all the `A5/1` encrypted communication. Telia networks showed better results, with the majority of communication encrypted using `A5/3`. Presumably, `A5/1` was used only when the device did not support `A5/3`. Overall, 95% of the communication was encrypted using `A5/3` and 5% by `A5/1`.

These results also indicate that `A5/3` is the preferred algorithm in Telia networks and is supported by most of the devices using the GSM network. The preferred option for Elisa and Tele2 appears to be `A5/1`. An alternative explanation for the preference in these two networks could be that only devices supporting `A5/1` connected to the BTS during the monitoring period, but this is unlikely. No `A5/2` encrypted traffic was detected in any of the networks, suggesting this algorithm was eliminated from these networks. Next, we attempted the active method on the networks to confirm the algorithm preference and whether the `A5/2` and `A5/0` algorithms were supported.

5.2 A5 Support

We obtained a prepaid SIM card from each mobile operator to perform this test. Each network was tested for `A5/0`, `A5/1`, `A5/2` and `A5/3` support and the preferred A5 algorithm using the acquired SIM cards. These tests were conducted in May, June and August 2024 on the same BTS identified in Table 1. Table 2 shows each mobile operator's results obtained by combining the data from the tested BTS of that operator.

Table 2. A5 preference for observed BTS in Tartu, Estonia.

	Telia Eesti	Elisa Eesti	Tele2 Eesti
A5/0 support	✖	✖	✖
A5/1 support	✔	✔	✔
A5/2 support	✖	✖	✖
A5/3 support	✔	✖	✖
Preferred A5	A5/3	A5/1	A5/1

The results of the active method show that Telia supports both `A5/1` and `A5/3`, with a preference for `A5/3`, as indicated by the results in Sect. 5.1. The results also verified that the Tele2 and Elisa networks do not support the `A5/3` algorithm, relying only on the `A5/1` algorithm. Finally, it was confirmed that the tested mobile networks do not support the `A5/0` and `A5/2` algorithms.

As stated in the limitations of this method, the SIM cards used in the experiment can significantly impact the results. For example, mobile operators may only use `A5/1` for prepaid cards or cards from other countries. The best results for the active method will be obtained if testing is performed using prepaid and postpaid SIM cards as well as SIM cards from foreign mobile operators. However, as the results in Sect. 5.1 reflect the findings in Table 2, it is unlikely that the configuration for the tested BTS varies per SIM card type. The prepaid SIM cards used for testing were sufficient to obtain information about the algorithms supported by the BTS.

5.3 Discussion

In 2014, Security Research Labs released a mobile network security report for Estonia [28]. The analysis was performed on information submitted by users of the SnoopSnitch application collected from the networks between October 2012 and December 2014. At the time, in all three mobile operator networks, 100%

of the communication was encrypted using `A5/1`. The results from the previous section show that only Telia has improved its network after the findings were published. Our experiments outlined in Sect. 4 obtained this data with a higher degree of certainty and in a fraction of the time specified in the report.

The passive method, while slightly time-consuming, provided data that was reflected by the results of the active method. Research question **RQ1** was successfully answered as the encryption algorithms used by the BTS were discovered. The results indicate that, in practice, the passive method might be sufficient to obtain the A5 preferences of a BTS.

The main advantage of the active method appears to be the ability to confirm A5 support and the speed at which the test can be executed, as the location update procedure can be completed in under 5 seconds. Research questions **RQ2** and **RQ3** were successfully answered, indicating the usefulness of this method. The A5 algorithms supported by the mobile operators' networks were obtained, and the preferred algorithm was determined in less than one minute.

The case study could be improved by conducting a wider survey. An analysis of all the BTS in Tartu or Estonia would be beneficial as the A5 settings may change in different areas of the country. When both methods are applied on such a large scale, it may even be possible to answer other research questions. For example, the data obtained could be used to identify a misconfigured BTS, such as if the BTS is using `A5/2`.

6 Conclusion

We have proposed two methods that can be used to determine the A5 algorithms used in a GSM network. The equipment required to execute these experiments is affordable and, therefore, can be used to perform similar studies on the networks in other countries.

The study performed on the BTS in Tartu, Estonia, shows that `A5/1` is still the preferred choice for encryption for some mobile networks, making these networks vulnerable to eavesdropping attacks. The study also highlighted that in the Telia mobile network where `A5/3` is supported and preferred, there are devices which only support `A5/1`.

We hope that this paper will contribute to making the security configuration of GSM networks available to a wider audience, thereby ensuring that users can make an informed choice when choosing their mobile network operator.

Acknowledgement. We would like to thank Arnis Parsovs for the feedback he provided on this paper. We would also like to thank the anonymous reviewers for taking the time to review the paper. We appreciate the comments and suggestions, many of which helped us to improve the quality of the paper.

Disclosure of Interests. The author has no competing interests to declare that are relevant to the content of this article.

References

1. 3rd Generation Partnership Project: 3G Security; Specification of the 3GPP confidentiality and integrity algorithms; Document 2: Kasumi specification (3GPP TS 35.202 version 17.0.0 Release 17). https://www.etsi.org/deliver/etsi_ts/135200_135299/135202/17.00.00_60/ts_135202v170000p.pdf. Accessed 04 Dec 2023
2. 3rd Generation Partnership Project: Digital cellular telecommunications system (Phase 2+); Security-related network functions (3GPP TS 03.20 version 8.6.0 Release 1999). https://www.etsi.org/deliver/etsi_ts/100900_100999/100929/08.06.00_60/ts_100929v080600p.pdf. Accessed 20 May 2024
3. Barkan, E., Biham, E., Keller, N.: Instant Ciphertext-Only Cryptanalysis of GSM Encrypted Communication. In: Boneh, D. (ed.) CRYPTO 2003. LNCS, vol. 2729, pp. 600–616. Springer, Heidelberg (2003). https://doi.org/10.1007/978-3-540-45146-4_35
4. Biham, E., Dunkelman, O.: Cryptanalysis of the A5/1 GSM Stream Cipher. In: Roy, B., Okamoto, E. (eds.) INDOCRYPT 2000. LNCS, vol. 1977, pp. 43–51. Springer, Heidelberg (2000). https://doi.org/10.1007/3-540-44495-5_5
5. CellularPrivacy: Android-IMSI-Catcher-Detector. https://github.com/CellularPrivacy/Android-IMSI-Catcher-Detector. Accessed 22 Dec 2023
6. Claverie, T., Avoine, G., Leblanc-Albarel, D., Carpent, X., Devine, C.: Time-Memory Trade-Offs Sound the Death Knell for GPRS and GSM. Springer (2024). https://doi.org/10.1007/978-3-031-68385-5_7
7. Dabrowski, A., Pianta, N., Klepp, T., Mulazzani, M., Weippl, E.: IMSI-catch me if you can: IMSI-catcher-catchers. In: Proceedings of the 30th Annual Computer Security Applications Conference, ACSAC 2014, pp. 246–255. Association for Computing Machinery, New York (2014). https://doi.org/10.1145/2664243.2664272
8. Morgan, D.: A5 identifier. https://github.com/morganedge/a5_identifier
9. Dunkelman, O., Keller, N., Shamir, A.: A Practical-Time Attack on the A5/3 Cryptosystem Used in Third Generation GSM Telephony. Cryptology ePrint Archive, Paper 2010/013 (2010). https://eprint.iacr.org/2010/013. Accessed 14 May 2023
10. Eberspächer, J., Vögel, H.J., Bettstetter, C., Hartmann, C.: GSM - Architecture, Protocols and Services, 3rd edn. Wiley (2009)
11. European Telecommunications Standards Institute: Security Algorithms Group of Experts (SAGE); Report on the specification and evaluation of the GSM cipher algorithm A5/2 (1996). https://web.archive.org/web/20131204061251/. http://www.etsi.org/deliver/etsi_etr/200_299/278/01_60/etr_278e01p.pdf. Accessed 24 Dec 2023
12. Stevenson, F.A.: kraken. https://github.com/0xh4di/kraken. Accessed 22 May 2023
13. GSM Association: Security Algorithm Deployment Guidance Version 3.0. Techncial report, GSMA (2022). https://www.gsma.com/solutions-and-impact/technologies/security/wp-content/uploads/2022/09/FS.35-v3.0.pdf
14. Karakoc, B., Fürste, N., Rupprecht, D., Kohls, K.: Never Let Me Down Again: Bidding-Down Attacks and Mitigations in 5G and 4G. In: Proceedings of the 16th ACM Conference on Security and Privacy in Wireless and Mobile Networks, WiSec 2023 (2023). https://doi.org/10.1145/3558482.3581774
15. Nohl, K.: Attacking phone privacy (2010). https://web.archive.org/web/20190301111108/https://www.srlabs.de/wp-content/uploads/2010/07/Attacking.Phone_.Privacy_Karsten.Nohl_1-1.pdf
16. KimiNewt: PyShark. https://kiminewt.github.io/pyshark/. Accessed 20 Aug 2024

17. Sauter, M.: From GSM to LTE-Advanced: An Introduction to Mobile Networks and Mobile Broadband, Revised Second Edition. Wiley (2014). https://learning.oreilly.com/library/view/from-gsm-to/9781118861929/. Accessed 21 Aug 2024
18. Shanahan, M., Bahia, K.: The State of Mobile Internet Connectivity 2023. Technical report, GSMA (2023). https://www.gsma.com/r/wp-content/uploads/2023/10/The-State-of-Mobile-Internet-Connectivity-Report-2023.pdf
19. Osmocom: OsmocomBB. https://osmocom.org/projects/baseband/wiki. Accessed 20 May 2024
20. Osmocom: OsmocomBB Compatible Phones. https://osmocom.org/projects/baseband/wiki/Phones. Accessed 20 May 2024
21. Osmocom: OsmocomBB mobile program. https://osmocom.org/projects/baseband/wiki/Mobile. Accessed 20 May 2024
22. Osmocom: Withdrawal of A5/2 algorithm support (2016). https://projects.osmocom.org/projects/security/wiki/A52_Withdrawal. Accessed 20 May 2024
23. Osmocom: softSIM (2022). https://osmocom.org/projects/baseband/wiki/SoftSIM. Accessed 07 June 2024
24. Krysik, P., Khassraf, R., Yanitskiy, V., Velichkov, V., Robyns, P.: The gr-gsm project. https://osmocom.org/projects/gr-gsm/wiki/Gr-gsm's_wiki. Accessed 10 May 2024
25. Security Research Labs: GSM Map. https://gsmmap.org/. Accessed 27 Aug 2024
26. Security Research Labs: SnoopSnitch. https://github.com/srlabs/snoopsnitch. Accessed 15 July 2023
27. Security Research Labs: SnoopSnitch FAQ. https://opensource.srlabs.de/projects/snoopsnitch/wiki/FAQ. Accessed 26 July 2023
28. Security Research Labs: Mobile network security report: Estonia (2014). https://gsmmap.org/assets/pdfs/gsmmap.org-country_report-Estonia-2014-12.pdf. Accessed 20 May 2024
29. Meyer, S.: Breaking GSM with rainbow Tables (2010). https://arxiv.org/pdf/1107.1086. Accessed 21 Aug 2024
30. Udar, S., Borgaonkar, R.: Darshak. https://github.com/darshakframework/darshak. Accessed 22 Dec 2023

Misbinding Raw Public Keys to Identities in TLS

Mariam Moustafa(✉), Mohit Sethi, and Tuomas Aura

Aalto University, Espoo, Finland
{mariam.moustafa,mohit.sethi,tuomas.aura}@aalto.fi

Abstract. The adoption of security protocols such as Transport Layer Security (TLS) has significantly improved the state of traffic encryption and integrity protection on the Internet. Despite rigorous analysis, vulnerabilities continue to emerge, sometimes due to fundamental flaws in the protocol specification. This paper examines the security of TLS when using Raw Public Key (RPK) authentication. This mode has not been as extensively studied as X.509 certificates and Pre-Shared Keys (PSK). We develop a formal model of TLS RPK using applied pi calculus and the ProVerif verification tool, revealing that the RPK mode is susceptible to identity misbinding attacks. Our contributions include formal models of TLS RPK with several mechanisms for binding the endpoint identity to its public key, verification results, practical scenarios demonstrating the misbinding attack, and recommendations for mitigating such vulnerabilities. These findings highlight the need for improved security measures in TLS RPK.

Keywords: TLS · raw public key · identity misbinding · formal modeling

1 Introduction

Development of standard security protocols, among which Transport Layer Security (TLS) [30] is the most prominent one, has significantly increased the usage of traffic encryption and integrity protection on the Internet [34]. The protocols have undergone rigorous security analysis [3], ensuring their robustness and reliability. Furthermore, numerous open-source implementations of TLS and other protocols are readily available, facilitating their widespread adoption. Consequently, many products [36,37], services [24,29], and standards [1,16] now readily incorporate TLS and other security protocols as fundamental building blocks.

Despite the rigorous analysis these protocols undergo during their specification and the extensive scrutiny of their open-source implementations, new attacks are continuously discovered. Many of these attacks originate from weaknesses in the implementation of the protocols, rather than flaws in the protocols themselves [23]. Nonetheless, attacks are also discovered from fundamental flaws in the protocol specification itself. For example, version 1.3 of TLS was specified

L. Horn Iwaya et al. (Eds.): NordSec 2024, LNCS 15396, pp. 62–79, 2025.
https://doi.org/10.1007/978-3-031-79007-2_4

at the Internet Engineering Task Force (IETF) after several years of deliberation and analysis. Yet, shortly after publication of the standard, an identity misbinding attack was discovered [12].

TLS supports three independent modes of authentication: (i) X.509 certificates (ii) Pre-Shared Keys (PSK), and (iii) Raw Public Keys (RPK). While the security properties of TLS authentication with X.509 certificates and PSKs have been extensively analyzed in literature [3,10,12], a similar thorough analysis of the RPK authentication mode in TLS is missing. Therefore, in this paper, we study the security properties of TLS when authentication is based on raw asymmetric key pairs. We develop a formal protocol model of TLS RPK using applied pi calculus and the ProVerif verification tool [6]. Our formal verification of TLS RPK security properties shows that it is susceptible to identity misbinding attacks. Based on our findings, we provide practical recommendations on how the attacks can be avoided in practice. Thus, the contributions of this paper are three-fold:

- Formal model of TLS RPK with different methods of binding the server and client identities to their public keys.
- Verification results that reveal server and client identity misbinding attacks, and example scenarios where the attacks can occur in practice.
- Discussion of the potential solutions available to the TLS RPK standards process and implementors.

The rest of the paper is organized as follows. Section 2 provides background information on the TLS RPK mode. Section 3 introduces our formal model of TLS RPK. Sections 4 and 5 detail the formal verification results, including an analysis of the identified misbinding attacks. Section 6 illustrates the ease of implementing these misbinding attacks in practice. Section 7 discusses potential solutions to prevent the identified attacks. Finally, Sect. 8 concludes the paper.

2 TLS with Raw Public Keys

This section provides background information on TLS and its raw public key mode, the security of which will be analyzed in the following sections.

2.1 The TLS Protocol

Transport Layer Security (TLS) is one of the most long-standing security technologies on the Internet, providing a critical foundation for secure communications. TLS version 1.0 [2] was standardized in 1999. For authentication, TLS adopted the web public key infrastructure (PKI) [7], which is based on the X.509 standard [21]. The certificates or certificate chains bind the endpoint public keys to their identities, such as host names. In typical web browsing, only the server has a certificate, but in other applications, the client can also have a certificate for mutual public-key authentication.

Over time, the protocol has evolved to improve its security and broaden its applications. As part of this evolution, new authentication methods have been defined. For instance, the Pre-Shared Key (PSK) authentication mode was introduced to avoid the computational expense of asymmetric operations and simplify key management in closed environments [35].

As vulnerabilities were discovered in earlier versions, TLS underwent significant revisions. TLS version 1.2 [31] focused on updating the cryptographic functions. Later, a *raw public key* (RPK) mode was incorporated into TLS 1.2 [38], offering a lightweight alternative to certificate-based authentication. TLS 1.3 [30] was a major update towards a more robust and formally verified protocol. It also incorporated three authentication methods: certificates, PSK, and RPK. Additionally, EAP authentication [26] was defined as an extension.

2.2 Raw Public Keys in TLS

The motivation for introducing the TLS raw public key (TLS RPK) was to reduce message size and processing cost. The *Certificate* message in the RPK mode contains only the *SubjectPublicKeyInfo* object [38], which comprises an algorithm identifier and the raw public key. Compared to the full X.509 [21] certificates and certificate chains, this significantly reduces the amount of data transmitted and simplifies the processing at the endpoint that receives the key, which usually is the TLS client. Only a minimalist ASN.1 parser is needed instead of the complex and error-prone code for certificate validation [9,15,25]. The reduced code footprint can be particularly beneficial in resource-constrained IoT devices. The trade-off is that the endpoints must establish the authenticity of the raw public key in some alternative way without being able to rely on X.509 certificates. Thus, the RPK mode forgoes both the complexity and the benefits of the public-key infrastructure (PKI).

Figure 1a illustrates TLS server authentication with RPK when the client is anonymous or authenticated separately inside TLS. The client sends the `server_certificate_type` extension in the *ClientHello* message. The extension informs the server which certificate types the client is willing to process [38]. In this case, the client asks for the *RawPublicKey* type. The server sends back the `server_certificate_type` extension in the *ServerHello* message, indicating that it agrees to use the RPK mode. The server then sends its raw public key in the *Certificate* message. While the raw keys are not certificates in the usual sense, the TLS specification treats them as one certificate type to unify the message structures in the different authentication modes.

TLS RPK also supports mutual authentication and has a corresponding `client_certificate_type` extension. Figure 1b shows a mutual RPK authentication where the client and server authenticate each other with raw public keys. The client first sends the `client_certificate_type` extension in the *ClientHello* message. This extension informs the server which certificate types the client can send. In the figure, the client only supports the *RawPublicKey* type. The server agrees to the RPK mode for client authentication by responding with a *Certifi-*

cateRequest for the same type. The client then sends a *Certificate* message that contains its RPK.

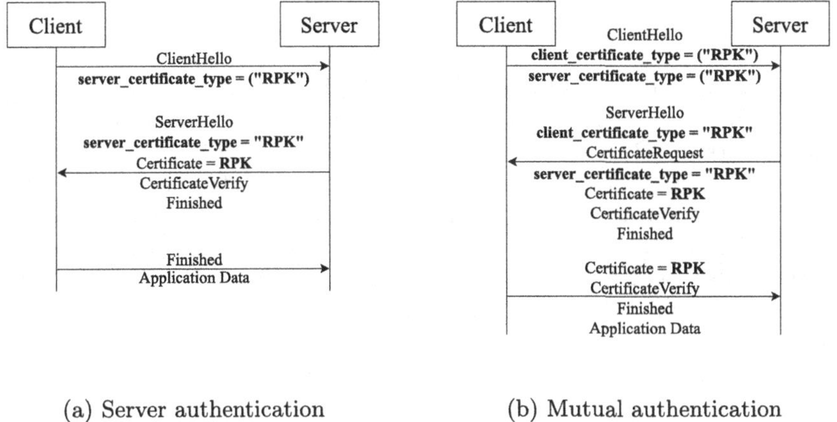

(a) Server authentication (b) Mutual authentication

Fig. 1. TLS 1.3 authentication with RPK

2.3 Authentication of the Raw Public Key

In public-key authentication, there must be some way of binding the public key to the identity of its owner. Since the RPK mode does not use a PKI, there must be another solution for this binding. The TLS RPK specification [38] suggests several methods for a client or a server to authenticate the other endpoint's raw public key.

Authentication with Pre-configured Keys. One possible solution is that the client and server have pre-configured lists of trusted public keys, which are configured by an out-of-band mechanism. While the standard does not provide further guidance, it is reasonable to assume that when there are multiple clients and servers, each of them has a local file or database indexed with the other endpoint's hostname or IP address, which will be looked up to verify the authenticity of its public key. The TLS client usually knows the server hostname, and when connecting to the server, it looks up the correct public key by the server hostname. In some constrained applications, such as sensor networks, the client may be configured with the server's IP address, in which case it looks up the correct public key by the server's IP address. Either way, this is quite natural because the TLS client looks up the correct public key by the same identifier that it uses for connecting to the server.

On the other hand, it is less clear how the server in mutual RPK authentication can verify the client's public key. The server does not know the hostname of the connecting client, and the client's IP address is rarely a reliable identifier because most clients have dynamic IP addresses or are behind a NAT. Unlike X.509 client certificates, which contain the client hostname, the RPK is just a key and does not give any indication of the client identifier. In some situations, such as closed sensor networks, the client's IP address may be a sufficient identifier for the lookup. We will assume this method in our analysis.

Server Authentication with DANE. The TLS RPK specification includes another method for TLS clients to verify the server's RPK: DNS-Based Authentication of Named Entities (DANE) [13,17]. DANE specifies a new DNS resource record (RR) type, TLSA, which binds a domain name to a public key or certificate. DANE can function as a replacement for the web PKI if, instead of trusting certificates issued by a CA, the client trusts the signed TLSA records in DNS Security Extensions (DNSSEC). When used to validate an RPK in TLS, a TLSA resource record will hold a public key or its hash.

It is worth noting that DNSSEC does not require proof of possession of the corresponding private key when the public key is registered in a TLSA RR. Authorization of the domain owner is sufficient for the updates. DANE also allows many-to-many relations between the domains and public keys. A single hostname can have multiple TLSA RR entries with different public keys, and different domains can have TLSA RR entries with the same public key.

Client Authentication with DANE. DANE currently does not support client authentication. However, there is an ongoing effort to standardize a mechanism for TLS servers to verify the client RPK or certificate with DANE [18]. The clients are identified by domain names, and the proposal defines a new extension to the TLS protocol to convey the TLS client identity to the server [19].

The proposed extension serves multiple purposes: (i) TLS client includes an empty DANE client identity extension in the *ClientHello* to indicate that it has an identity that can be authenticated with DANE. (ii) TLS server includes an empty DANE client identity extension in the *CertificateRequest* message to indicate that it is willing to authenticate the client's identity with DANE. (iii) TLS client includes a non-empty DANE client identity extension in its *Certificate* message. The non-empty extension contains the encrypted client domain name, which the server should then use to verify the authenticity of the client's RPK with DANE. While the above description is focused on TLS 1.3, which introduced the *EncryptedExtensions*, the proposal also considers TLS 1.2, where the client identity would be communicated unencrypted in the *ClientHello* and *ServerHello* messages.

2.4 Analysis of TLS RPK Implementations

Many open-source TLS libraries (for example, OpenSSL, wolfSSL, and GnuTLS) support TLS RPK. Their approaches to handling the raw public keys differ somewhat from each other. OpenSSL [33] allows an application to invoke the `SSL_get0_peer_rpk` function to learn and validate the received raw public key. WolfSSL [20] allows applications to register a callback function that validates the received raw public key. GnuTLS [14], on the other hand, maintains a database of trusted RPKs, which can be added with the `gnutls_store_pubkey` function. It also supports trust on first use (TOFU), where the endpoints store the received RPKs and verify them on subsequent connections with the same endpoint. (The verification can be explicitly invoked by calling the `gnutls_verify_stored_pubkey` function.)

Libcoap [28], a library for the Constrained Application Protocol (CoAP), supports RPK authentication of client Internet-of-Things (IoT) devices. However, the library documentation does not explain how a server can distinguish between client identities. When a client IoT device presents an RPK instead of an X.509 certificate, libcoap passes the RPK and the fixed CN string "RPK" to a callback function (registered with `coap_dtls_cn_callback_t`). It is up to the application to determine the client's identity from the received public key.

Some of these libraries also support DANE for authentication. OpenSSL [33] allows clients to input server TLSA RRs with the `SSL_add_expected_rpk` function. GnuTLS [14] allows the clients to invoke the `dane_verify_crt` function to verify the received server RPK via DANE. Apart from this DANE support, the libraries do not provide guidance to application developers on how to confirm that the received RPK belongs to the correct entity. The developers are left to implement their custom validation methods in the callback functions.

3 Formal Model of TLS RPK

This section explains the formal modeling methods used in the paper, describes the model of TLS RPK, including the TLS handshake and the methods for binding the endpoint identities to their public keys, and specifies the main security goals for the verification.

3.1 Symbolic Modeling Methods

ProVerif [6] is a symbolic modeling tool used to verify security protocols. It takes a protocol model written in applied pi calculus and considers all possible execution paths in a protocol to find potential attacks. ProVerif uses the Dolev-Yao attacker model [11], where the attacker controls the network and can read, modify, and inject messages. Security properties of a protocol are formalized as queries that are evaluated against the protocol model. Queries in ProVerif are written in terms of events. In particular, authentication is formalized as a correspondence between local events in the different concurrent processes. Proverif models are symbolic, and they treat cryptographic primitives, such as signatures and encryption, as abstract functions that are assumed secure. Unlike computational models [5], the symbolic approach does not consider the probability of breaking cryptographic primitives. The symbolic approach can find logical flaws in the protocol design.

TLS has previously been analyzed with symbolic modeling tools. Bhargavan et al. [3] used ProVerif to model TLS 1.3 draft 18, as well as the composition of TLS versions 1.3 and 1.2, to study the security properties in scenarios where clients and servers support both versions for backward compatibility. Cremers et al. [10] modeled TLS 1.3 draft 21 with the Tamarin [27] symbolic modeling tool. They analyzed, among other things, the key exchange mechanisms and session resumption with pre-shared keys. While earlier attempts at symbolic formal analysis of TLS have analyzed many protocol variants and found attacks, none explicitly study TLS with RPKs. The current paper aims to study the security properties of TLS when raw public keys are used for authentication.

3.2 Model Overview

We modeled server authentication and mutual authentication in TLS RPK with several key validation mechanisms. Since TLS RPK *Certificate* messages do not contain full certificates issued by a CA, an out-of-band mechanism is needed for binding an endpoint's identity to its public key. The TLS RPK standard discusses two out-of-band mechanisms to achieve this binding: pre-configured keys and DANE. We modeled the following TLS RPK scenarios:

1. Server authentication with DANE in TLS RPK
2. Mutual authentication with DANE in TLS RPK
3. Mutual authentication with pre-configured keys in TLS RPK

The ProVerif models are available for review online[1].

3.3 TLS Handshake Model

We wrote our own model of the TLS handshake with a focus on the features relevant to TLS RPK. In other respects, the handshake model is similar to previously published formal models of TLS. It closely follows the message flows, contents, and key derivation in the TLS 1.3 standard. There are two main processes: the server and client process. After the *ClientHello* and *ServerHello* messages are sent, both endpoints derive the master secret. All the following messages are encrypted and authenticated with keys created from the master secret. The server sends the client its raw public key in the *Certificate* message, a signed transcript hash in the *CertificateVerify* message, and a MAC of the transcript hash in the *Finished* message. The signature in the *CertificateVerify* message proves to the client that the server possesses the private key corresponding to the RPK.

Figure 2a shows the client and server events that we will use to formulate the security goals. The server and client emit the `ServerFinished` and `ClientFinished` events when sending their respective *Finished* messages. `ClientFinished` signals that the client has received the final handshake message and accepted the server authentication.

In the models with mutual authentication, the client sends its own *Certificate* and *CertificateVerify* messages before its *Finished* message. In this case, the

[1] https://github.com/Mariam-Dessouki/tls-rpk.

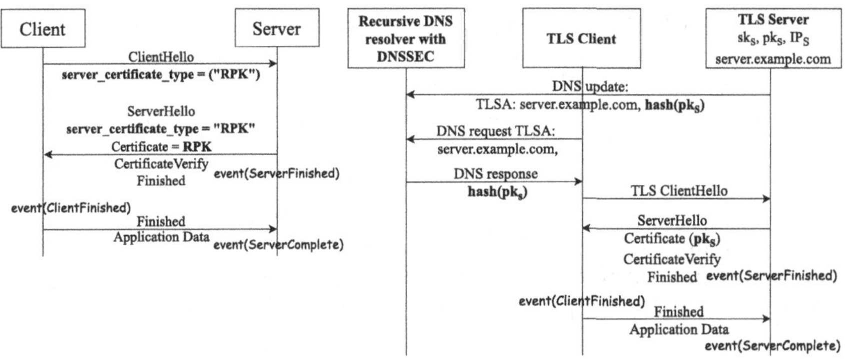

(a) Events in the TLS RPK models

(b) DANE registration

Fig. 2. Model details for TLS 1.3 authentication with RPK

additional `ServerComplete` event indicates that the server has accepted the client authentication.

3.4 RPK Binding Model

In addition to the TLS handshake, the TLS RPK authentication requires an out-of-band mechanism for binding the server's raw public key to its identity, such as its domain name. This part of our model is novel compared to the previously published TLS models.

DNS Registration in DANE. The DNS process receives queries and sends back signed resource records in the response. Additionally, the DNS process receives updates to the names. Each TLS endpoint can create TLSA resource records that bind its domain name to its public keys. The DNS update requires authorization, which can take many forms. For example, the domain owner could log in on the domain registrar's web portal to edit its domain's DNS records. We model the authorization in a relatively abstract way as a table of domain names and corresponding credentials. When an endpoint wants to update the TLSA resource records for its domain name, it sends an update message to the DNS protected by the credential.

A domain in the model can have multiple TLSA resource records with different public keys, and multiple domains can have the same public key in their resource records. DNS allows such many-to-many relationships between domains and public keys.

When a client wants to connect to a server, it initially knows the server name. The client queries the DNS for the TLSA records associated with the server name. Upon receiving the server RPK in the TLS handshake, the client checks that it matches one of the values in the TLSA records. The DNS update and request are shown in Fig. 2b.

We also model mutual authentication with the proposed client name extension (see Sect. 2.3). The server receives the client name, in addition to the RPK, in the Certificate message. The server queries the DNS for the TLSA records associated with the received name and checks that the received RPK matches one of them.

Compromised or attacker-owned domains are modeled by leaking the credentials of some endpoints to the attacker. The event `CompromiseDomain(d)` indicates that the domain's update credential has been given to the attacker. While the compromised domain itself cannot expect much security from DNS or DANE, the existence of some compromised domains should not endanger the security of other domains.

Pre-configured Keys. In the pre-configured keys scenario, we model mutual authentication where each endpoint has a table of bindings between endpoint identifiers and their public keys. For a concrete example, consider IoT hubs and devices identified by IP addresses. The device IP address and public key are registered to the hub, and the device is pre-configured with the hub IP address and public key.

An IoT device typically connects to one hub while the hub receives connections from multiple clients. In the pull communication pattern, however, the IoT hub could initiate connections to the devices. To cover all communication patterns, we model the relation between the TLS servers and clients as many-to-many. Thus, each TLS RPK server endpoint may be pre-configured with the public keys of many clients, and each client may be pre-configured with the public keys of many servers.

We also model the pre-registration step and allow the attacker to register its own devices to the hub. This extension to the model was inspired by the DANE model discussed above and turned out to be essential for the security analysis.

3.5 Security Goals

The main security goal of the TLS handshake is authentication, which is expressed as a correspondence between the events in the client and server processes.

The client should only accept the TLS connection if it is established with the server to which the client intended to connect. The following security query represents server authentication in ProVerif.

Listing 1. Server authentication goal

```
query s_domain:Id_t, rpk:PK_t, ms:K_t;
event(ClientFinished(s_domain, rpk, ms))
==> inj-event(ServerFinished(s_domain, rpk, ms))
    || event(CompromiseDomain(s_domain)).
```

The query states that if the (possibly anonymous) client accepts a TLS connection to a server with the server name `s_domain`, server public key `rpk` and master secret `ms` for protecting the TLS connection, then the server with the name s_domain and public key rpk must have derived the same master secret. An exception is allowed for the case where the domain is compromised, i.e., the attacker has compromised the DNS update credentials, or it is an attacker-owned domain to begin with.

A second query represents client authentication in the mutual authentication scenario.

Listing 2. Client authentication goal

```
query s_domain,c_domain:Id_t, spk,cpk:PK_t, ms:K_t;
event(ServerComplete(s_domain,c_domain,spk,cpk,ms))
==> event(ClientFinished(s_domain,c_domain,spk,cpk,ms))
     || event(CompromiseDomain(s_domain))
     || event(CompromiseDomain(c_domain)).
```

The query states that if a server with a name s_domain and public key spk accepts a TLS connection from a client with the client name c_domain, client public key cpk and master secret ms, then the client should have already accepted the corresponding connection to the server. An exception is allowed for the cases where the server's or the client's DNS domain is compromised.

Aditionally, there are secrecy goals related to the master secret. We omit them here for brevity and because the interesting results come from the queries above.

4 Misbinding Attack in RPK Registration

This section presents the main results of our formal modeling and analysis. They are misbinding attacks that exploit weaknesses in how the standard binds endpoint identity to its public key.

Server Misbinding Against TLS RPK with DANE. The query for server authentication in Listing 1 fails when DANE is used for authentication. The attack is illustrated in Fig. 3. A malicious domain owner, other.example.org in the figure, has full control over its own DNS zone and TLSA resource records. It can thus write the hash of the public key of the honest server server.example.com into a TLSA resource record of its own domain name. A client that wants to communicate with the malicious domain receives the public key belonging to the honest server. The attacker then redirects inbound connections from the malicious domain to the honest server. The client connects to the wrong server but successfully verifies the signature in the *CertificateVerify* message because the received RPK matches the one in the TLSA resource records of other.example.org. The client accepts the connection with the unintended server, and hence the server authentication goal fails. This attack is known as a misbinding [22, 32] or unknown key share attack [4].

The attack is easier to implement than one might think. First, the DNS registrar and server are not compromised. Instead, the malicious domain owner controls the DNS records for a domain which it has legitimately registered. Second, no advanced network attacks, such as forwarding connections or manipulating the network routing, are necessary. Instead, the malicious domain owner can redirect the connections to the honest server by copying the IP address of the honest server to an A resource record of `other.example.org`. This will cause the client to connect to the honest server instead of the intended one. Thus, no special skills or access to a specific network segment are needed for the attack implementation.

The attack clearly violates the security goals. The practical consequences of the misbinding attack can be difficult to understand because the client is willingly connecting to the malicious domain. This kind of behavior is, however, quite common on the Internet. For example, web browsers and email relays connect to untrusted servers, which could behave maliciously. We will present a more detailed scenario related to mail servers when discussing the attack implementation in Sect. 6.

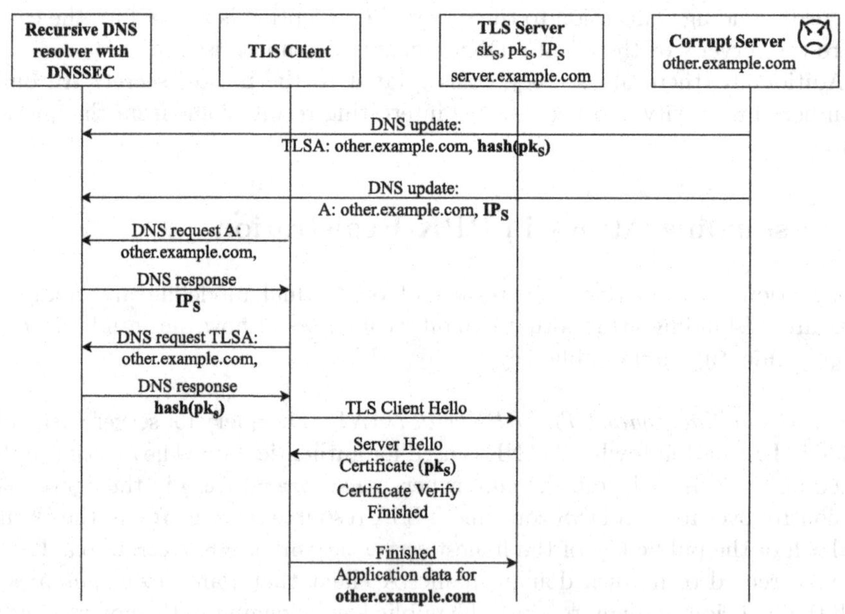

Fig. 3. Misbinding attack against TLS RPK with DANE, exploiting DNS registration

Server Misbinding with Pre-configuration. The query in Listing 1 also reveals an attack in the case of pre-configured public keys. We explain the attack in the context of an example IoT application. Consider a network of IoT devices, identified by their IP addresses or domain names, and a hub to which the devices are registered. Following the pull communication pattern, the IoT hub connects to the devices to collect data from them. Let `device1` be an honest IoT device.

A malicious user can copy the public key of `device1` and register a new (real or imaginary) device `device2` to the same hub with the same public key. When the hub polls `device2` for data over TLS RPK, the network attacker rewrites the device IP address in the network layer and redirects the connection to `device1`. The RPK received from `device1` in the TLS handshake matches the key registered for `device2`. Thus, the IoT hub falsely accepts the connection as coming from `device2`. The IoT hub then records the received data as coming from the wrong device.

Server Misbinding for Multi-named Server. As a matter of fact, there is a simpler attack on server authentication where no malicious registration is needed. DNS allows for a many-to-many relation between domains and public keys. Suppose there are two services: `coaps://service1.example.com` and `coaps://service2.example.com` that share the same public key as shown in Fig. 4. When the honest device connects to the server, a network attacker can redirect the connection from service1 to service2, or vice versa. Since the public keys are identical, the client accepts the RPK received in the TLS handshake even when connected to the wrong server.

There are practical scenarios where two servers could have the same public key. Hosting multiple online services on the same physical server is common, and cloud application gateways can hide any number of services behind the same application gateway and public IP address. The two different services could even have the same backend authentication server and the same client accounts for authenticating the user inside the TLS tunnel. The attack results in the client sending the application-layer data to the wrong service.

This attack is similar to one of the attacks presented in ALPACA [8]. If a certificate with multiple hostnames or a wildcard pattern in the common name field is used in communication, an attacker can reroute the connection to an unintended server with an SNI that matches one of the common name values in the certificate. The certificate would still be valid, but the client would be communicating with the wrong server.

Weakness in the TLS RPK Specification. The misbinding attacks presented in this section can be prevented by optional features in the TLS handshake. In TLS, the client can optionally send the *server name indication* (SNI) in the *server_name* extension of the *ClientHello* message. The server may optionally use the received SNI to select the public key, which implicitly means that the server checks the SNI value and rejects unrecognized names. If the client sends the extension and the server checks it, the misbinding attacks are prevented. The security queries succeed when both actions are added in the models. However, since these actions are optional in the standard, there is a lot of room for insecure implementations and usage.

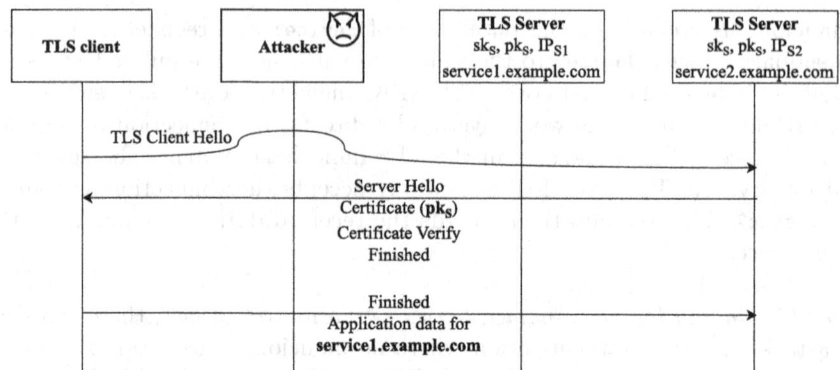

Fig. 4. Misbinding attack against TLS RPK, exploiting multi-name server

5 Analysis of Client Authentication

So far, we have discussed misbinding of the server identity, causing the client to connect to the wrong server. What about misbinding of the client identity in mutual authentication? The misbinding attacks in the literature typically have two possible directions, and the same could happen in TLS RPK. This section analyzes whether there are similar weaknesses in client authentication.

No Client Misbinding Against TLS RPK with DANE. Client authentication using DANE was modeled based on the Client Authentication proposal [18], which we discussed in Sect. 2.3. When RPK is used for client authentication, the client must send the *ClientName* extension [19] in the *Certificate* message. Knowing the client domain name allows the server to look up the client's public key from TLSA resource records in the DNS, and this provides a secure binding between the client domain name and its public key. Thus, the client authentication with DANE is not susceptible to a misbinding attack. The critical difference between client and server authentication with DANE is that *ClientName* is mandatory while *SNI* is optional and, even when the client sends the *SNI*, the server may ignore it.

Client Misbinding with Pre-configuration. An attack was found on client authentication with pre-configured public keys. Consider again the IoT hub and devices. In this case, the devices send push messages to the IoT hub, reversing the direction of the TLS connections compared to our earlier scenario. The hub identifies the devices by their IP address, which is visible in the IP header but not protected by the TLS handshake. A malicious user can register a new (real or imaginary) IoT device with the public key of another, honest device. When the honest device connects to the server, the network attacker performs address translation on the client's IP address, replacing the honest device's IP address with the malicious user's one. The IoT hub checks that the RPK received in the TLS handshake matches the one registered for the malicious user's device, and since it does, the hub accepts the connection. Consequently, the hub mistakenly believes that the data received over the TLS connection comes from the malicious user's device.

6 Attack Implementation

We successfully verified the practicality of the server misbinding attacks discovered by the formal analysis across three popular TLS libraries: OpenSSL, GnuTLS, and wolfSSL. Since TLS RPK with DANE and server authentication has the most complete and well-specified key registration solution, we focused on implementations that support DANE.

Initially, we deployed both an honest server and an attacker-controlled server, where the IP address and TLSA record of the attacker-controlled server were modified to match those of the honest server. The attack proved to be relatively straightforward. In practice, the attacker-controlled server was not even used. It was sufficient to modify the DNS entries of the compromised server. The unsuspecting client was redirected to the honest server and could not detect the misbinding.

Subsequently, we discovered a rare public mail server that supports TLS RPK for server authentication and has its TLSA record published in DNS. We set up a test SMTP client and server that use StartTLS with RPK and DANE. We then copied the public mail server's IP address and TLSA resource record to the DNS records of our test server. This caused the unsuspecting test client to connect to the public mail server instead of the intended test server.

The practicality of such attacks against TLS RPK in real-world applications depends on the underlying TLS libraries and on how the applications interact with them. For example, in OpenSSL, the client application can call the *SSL_set_tlsext_host_name* function to include an SNI into the *ClientHello* message. It is then up to the server implementation to verify or ignore the SNI value. The public mail server in our experiment accepted any SNI value without raising an alert. Even servers that adhere strictly to the standard specification [30] might only issue a warning-level TLS alert upon encountering an unrecognized SNI but nevertheless continue with the connection.

The outcome of the attack also depends on the application layer. For example, HTTPS clients (HTTP version 1.1 and above) send a Host header to the server, and the server may reject requests for an unrecognized server name in the header. Some reverse proxies and TLS gateways, however, are configured with a default forwarding rule that ignores the Host header.

7 Solutions for Preventing Misbinding

To prevent the misbinding attack, the endpoints of the session must agree on the authenticated identifiers associated with the session. In other words, the endpoint identities should be bound to the TLS session [4,22]. Several solutions can be employed for this purpose.

7.1 Sending the Identities in the TLS Handshake

As already mentioned, one way to bind the server or client identity to the session is to send them in the handshake messages. The SNI in the *ClientHello* message exists for this purpose. The SNI will automatically become part of the transcript hash, which is authenticated in the handshake. To prevent misbinding, all that is needed is to make the *server_name* extension mandatory in TLS RPK and require the server to check the received value.

A disadvantage of this solution is that it is not easy to transition to a stricter standard in an open system such as the Internet. The client cannot ensure that the server checks the received SNI, and if the server follows the new stricter rules, compatibility with legacy clients might break.

The equivalent extension for the client identity is currently a proposal and not yet a part of any standard. The DANE Client Identity draft [19] would make it mandatory for the client to send the `dane_clientid` extension when using an RPK. Since DANE for client authentication is still in the early draft stage, it would be possible to establish stricter rules for it. A disadvantage of the proposal is that it is specific to DANE and does not solve the problem in key pre-configuration and other out-of-band mechanisms.

Another possibility is to add new server and client identity extensions to the TLS specification for TLS RPK. They could be similar to the extensions `server_certificate_type` and `client_certificate_type` that were added to support TLS RPK. Sending the extension should probably be mandatory. Most importantly, checking the value should be mandatory at the receiving endpoint, raising a fatal alert if the value is not recognized.

The privacy of the client and server needs to be considered. The server identity would be sent as plaintext in the *ClientHello* message. The privacy of the client identity would depend on the TLS version. In TLS 1.3, the client could send its identity as an encrypted extension of the *Certificate* while, in TLS 1.2, it would have to be sent in plaintext.

7.2 Self-signed Certificates

One reason why the SNI is optional in TLS [30] is that, in certificate-based authentication, the server certificate identifies the server. The endpoints agree on the server name in the certificate, which is sufficient to prevent server misbinding.

TLS RPK could get the same benefit from self-signed certificates. DANE already supports storing a certificate hash in the TLSA RR. If an endpoint sends a self-signed certificate with the correct domain name (or another correct identifier) in the *Certificate* messages and the other endpoint validates the certificate following the PKIX validation rules [7], including checking the subject name, then misbinding of the subject is prevented. DANE already supports this solution with the Certificate Usage PKIX-EE(1). Self-signed certificates would also work well together with pre-configured public keys.

While self-signed certificates prevent the misbinding attack, they still have the same problems that TLS RPK was set out to fix. The entire certificate needs to be transmitted, and the endpoints must have full ASN.1 parsers for the X.509 standard.

7.3 Verify the Identities Inside the TLS Tunnel

Yet another solution is to verify the endpoint identities in the application layer inside the established TLS tunnel. As mentioned earlier, the Host header in the HTTP request can prevent misbinding if the server carefully checks the value. While such application-layer mechanisms can intentionally or accidentally fix the security issue, the solution does not work universally for all applications of TLS RPK. It also seems that the architecturally more correct approach is to fix TLS RPK security flaws in the TLS RPK protocol.

8 Conclusion

We have modeled and analyzed the TLS Raw Public Key (RPK) mode, focusing on scenarios where identity of the server and client are linked to their public keys through various out-of-band mechanisms, including secure DNS. We performed verification of the protocol, which led to the discovery of identity misbinding attacks. In addition to presenting the verification results and misbinding vulnerabilities, we show their significance by presenting concrete attack scenarios and providing guidance for enhancing the robustness of TLS RPK standard and implementations.

References

1. 3rd Generation Partnership Project (3GPP): Technical Specification Group Services and System Aspects; Security architecture and procedures for 5G system (Release 15). 3GPP (2020). https://www.3gpp.org/ftp/Specs/archive/33_series/33.501/, version 15.4.0. Accessed 24 July 2024
2. Allen, C., Dierks, T.: The TLS Protocol Version 1.0. RFC 2246 (1999). https://doi.org/10.17487/RFC2246. https://www.rfc-editor.org/info/rfc2246
3. Bhargavan, K., Blanchet, B., Kobeissi, N.: Verified models and reference implementations for the TLS 1.3 standard candidate. In: 2017 IEEE Symposium on Security and Privacy (SP), pp. 483–502 (2017). https://doi.org/10.1109/SP.2017.26
4. Blake-Wilson, S., Menezes, A.: Unknown key-share attacks on the station-to-station (STS) protocol. In: Imai, H., Zheng, Y. (eds.) PKC 1999. LNCS, vol. 1560, pp. 154–170. Springer, Heidelberg (1999). https://doi.org/10.1007/3-540-49162-7_12
5. Blanchet, B.: Computationally sound mechanized proofs of correspondence assertions. In: 20th IEEE Computer Security Foundations Symposium (CSF 2007), pp. 97–111. IEEE (2007). https://doi.org/10.1109/CSF.2007.16
6. Blanchet, B., Smyth, B., Cheval, V., Sylvestre, M.: Proverif 2.00: automatic cryptographic protocol verifier, user manual and tutorial. Version from, pp. 05–16 (2018)
7. Boeyen, S., Santesson, S., Polk, T., Housley, R., Farrell, S., Cooper, D.: Internet X.509 Public Key Infrastructure Certificate and Certificate Revocation List (CRL) Profile. RFC 5280 (2008). https://doi.org/10.17487/RFC5280. https://www.rfc-editor.org/info/rfc5280

8. Brinkmann, M., et al.: ALPACA: application layer protocol confusion - analyzing and mitigating cracks in TLS authentication. In: 30th USENIX Security Symposium (USENIX Security 2021), pp. 4293–4310. USENIX Association (2021). https://www.usenix.org/conference/usenixsecurity21/presentation/brinkmann
9. Brubaker, C., Jana, S., Ray, B., Khurshid, S., Shmatikov, V.: Using frankencerts for automated adversarial testing of certificate validation in SSL/TLS implementations. In: 2014 IEEE Symposium on Security and Privacy, pp. 114–129 (2014). https://doi.org/10.1109/SP.2014.15
10. Cremers, C., Horvat, M., Hoyland, J., Scott, S., van der Merwe, T.: A comprehensive symbolic analysis of TLS 1.3. In: Proceedings of the 2017 ACM SIGSAC Conference on Computer and Communications Security, CCS 2017, pp. 1773-1788. Association for Computing Machinery, New York, NY, USA (2017). https://doi.org/10.1145/3133956.3134063
11. Dolev, D., Yao, A.: On the security of public key protocols. IEEE Trans. Inf. Theory **29**(2), 198–208 (1983)
12. Drucker, N., Gueron, S.: Selfie: reflections on TLS 1.3 with PSK. J. Cryptol. **34**(3), 27 (2021)
13. Dukhovni, V., Hardaker, W.: The DNS-Based Authentication of Named Entities (DANE) Protocol: Updates and Operational Guidance. RFC 7671 (2015). https://doi.org/10.17487/RFC7671. https://www.rfc-editor.org/info/rfc7671
14. Foundation, F.S.: GnuTLS: The GNU Transport Layer Security Library (2024). https://www.gnutls.org, version 3.7.8
15. Georgiev, M., Iyengar, S., Jana, S., Anubhai, R., Boneh, D., Shmatikov, V.: The most dangerous code in the world: validating SSL certificates in non-browser software. In: Proceedings of the 2012 ACM Conference on Computer and Communications Security, pp. 38–49 (2012)
16. GSMA: SGP.01 embedded SIM remote povisioning architecture, version 4.1 (2020). https://www.gsma.com/esim/wp-content/uploads/2020/06/SGP.01-v4.1.pdf
17. Hoffman, P.E., Schlyter, J.: The DNS-Based Authentication of Named Entities (DANE) Transport Layer Security (TLS) Protocol: TLSA. RFC 6698 (2012). https://doi.org/10.17487/RFC6698. https://www.rfc-editor.org/info/rfc6698
18. Huque, S., Dukhovni, V.: TLS Client Authentication via DANE TLSA records. Internet-Draft draft-ietf-dance-client-auth-05, Internet Engineering Task Force (2024). https://datatracker.ietf.org/doc/draft-ietf-dance-client-auth/05/, work in Progress
19. Huque, S., Dukhovni, V.: TLS Extension for DANE Client Identity. Internet-Draft draft-ietf-dance-tls-clientid-03, Internet Engineering Task Force (2024). https://datatracker.ietf.org/doc/draft-ietf-dance-tls-clientid/03/, work in Progress
20. wolfSSL Inc.: wolfSSL: Embedded SSL/TLS Library (2024). https://www.wolfssl.com, version 5.5.0
21. International Telecommunication Union: ITU-T Recommendation X.509: Information technology - Open Systems Interconnection - The Directory: Public-key and attribute certificate frameworks. Technical report, International Telecommunication Union (2019). https://www.itu.int/rec/T-REC-X.509, series X: Data Networks, Open System Communications and Security; OSI Networking and System Aspects
22. Krawczyk, H.: SIGMA: the 'SIGn-and-MAc' approach to authenticated Diffie-Hellman and its use in the IKE protocols. In: Boneh, D. (ed.) CRYPTO 2003. LNCS, vol. 2729, pp. 400–425. Springer, Heidelberg (2003). https://doi.org/10.1007/978-3-540-45146-4_24

23. Levillain, O.: Implementation flaws in TLS stacks: lessons learned and study of TLS 1.3 benefits. In: Garcia-Alfaro, J., Leneutre, J., Cuppens, N., Yaich, R. (eds.) CRiSIS 2020. LNCS, vol. 12528, pp. 87–104. Springer, Cham (2021). https://doi.org/10.1007/978-3-030-68887-5_5
24. Ltd., S.: Surfshark VPN protocols (2024). https://surfshark.com/features/surfshark-vpn-protocols. Accessed 24 July 2024
25. Luo, M., Feng, B., Lu, L., Kirda, E., Ren, K.: On the complexity of the web's PKI: evaluating certificate validation of mobile browsers. IEEE Trans. Dependable Secure Comput. **21**(1), 419–433 (2023)
26. Mattsson, J.P., Sethi, M.: EAP-TLS 1.3: Using the Extensible Authentication Protocol with TLS 1.3. RFC 9190 (2022). https://doi.org/10.17487/RFC9190. https://www.rfc-editor.org/info/rfc9190
27. Meier, S., Schmidt, B., Cremers, C., Basin, D.: The TAMARIN prover for the symbolic analysis of security protocols. In: Sharygina, N., Veith, H. (eds.) CAV 2013. LNCS, vol. 8044, pp. 696–701. Springer, Heidelberg (2013). https://doi.org/10.1007/978-3-642-39799-8_48
28. libcoap Project: libcoap: C-Implementation of CoAP (2024). https://libcoap.net/, version 4.3.0
29. Project, F.: Filezilla SFTP using SSH-2 (2024). https://wiki.filezilla-project.org/Howto. Accessed 24 July 2024
30. Rescorla, E.: The Transport Layer Security (TLS) Protocol Version 1.3. RFC 8446 (2018). https://doi.org/10.17487/RFC8446. https://www.rfc-editor.org/info/rfc8446
31. Rescorla, E., Dierks, T.: The Transport Layer Security (TLS) Protocol Version 1.2. RFC 5246 (2008). https://doi.org/10.17487/RFC5246. https://www.rfc-editor.org/info/rfc5246
32. Sethi, M., Peltonen, A., Aura, T.: Misbinding attacks on secure device pairing and bootstrapping. In: Proceedings of the 2019 ACM Asia Conference on Computer and Communications Security, Asia CCS 2019, pp. 453–464. Association for Computing Machinery, New York, NY, USA (2019). https://doi.org/10.1145/3321705.3329813
33. The OpenSSL Project: OpenSSL: a toolkit for the transport layer security (TLS) and secure sockets layer (SSL) protocols (2024). https://www.openssl.org/. Accessed 24 July 2024
34. ThreatLabz, Z.: 2023 state of encrypted attacks report (2023). https://info.zscaler.com/resources-industry-reports-threatlabz-2023-state-of-encrypted-attacks-report. Accessed 24 July 2024
35. Tschofenig, H., Eronen, P.: Pre-Shared Key Ciphersuites for Transport Layer Security (TLS). RFC 4279 (2005). https://doi.org/10.17487/RFC4279. https://www.rfc-editor.org/info/rfc4279
36. WolfSSL Inc.: WolfSSL enables sensity systems to secure light sensory networks (LSNS). Case Study (2014). https://www.wolfssl.com/files/casestudy/casestudy_wolfssl_sensity.pdf
37. WolfSSL Inc.: Ewolfssl secures eimsig®smart home alarm system. Case Study (2015). https://www.wolfssl.com/files/casestudy/casestudy_wolfssl_eimsig.pdf
38. Wouters, P., Tschofenig, H., Gilmore, J.I., Weiler, S., Kivinen, T.: Using Raw Public Keys in Transport Layer Security (TLS) and Datagram Transport Layer Security (DTLS). RFC 7250 (2014). https://doi.org/10.17487/RFC7250. https://www.rfc-editor.org/info/rfc7250

Small Private Exponent Attacks on Takagi Family Schemes

George Teşeleanu[1,2(✉)]

[1] Advanced Technologies Institute, 10 Dinu Vintilă, Bucharest, Romania
tgeorge@dcti.ro

[2] Simion Stoilow Institute of Mathematics of the Romanian Academy, 21 Calea Grivitei, Bucharest, Romania

Abstract. Takagi's cryptosystem is a fast variant of RSA that offers improved decryption times. This scheme was further extended by Lim *et al.* to moduli of type $N = p^r q^s$, where p and q are balanced prime numbers (*i.e.* $q < p < 2q$). This family of cryptosystems uses the key equation $ed - k(p-1)(q-1) = 1$. In this paper, we study if small private key attacks based on continued fractions can be applied to the Takagi family of cryptosystems. More precisely, we argue that when $r > s$, such attacks do not appear to be applicable to this family.

1 Introduction

In 1978, Rivest, Shamir and Adleman [28] introduced RSA, one of the most popular and widely used encryption scheme. The standard RSA cryptosystem works modulo an integer $N = pq$, where p and q are two large prime numbers. Let $\varphi(N) = (p-1)(q-1)$ denote the Euler's totient function. To encrypt a message $m < N$, one computes $c \equiv m^e \bmod N$, where e is chosen such that $\gcd(e, \varphi(N)) = 1$. Decryption is done by computing $m \equiv c^d \bmod N$, where $d \equiv e^{-1} \bmod \varphi(N)$. (N, e) is a user's public key, while (p, q, d) is the corresponding private key. Traditionally, p and q are of similar bit-size (*i.e.* $q < p < 2q$). In this paper, we only consider this particular choice of primes.

In 1998, Takagi [34] introduced a method to improve the efficiency of the RSA decryption algorithm. This proposal was further extended by Lim *et al.* in [19]. This family of schemes uses the modulus $N = p^r q^s$, where $r \neq s \geq 1$. In this case, the Euler totient is $\varphi(N) = p^{r-1}q^{s-1}(p-1)(q-1)$. To set up the public exponent, we must have $\gcd(e, (p-1)(q-1)) = 1$. The corresponding private exponent is $d \equiv e^{-1} \bmod (p-1)(q-1)$ and not $d' \equiv e^{-1} \bmod \varphi(N)$.

According to [35,36], to ensure security against factoring algorithms such as the Number Field Sieve [18] and the Elliptic Curve Method [16], $r + s$ must be selected as in Table 1. Note that the maximum number of prime factors that N can have is provided in parenthesis. A simple analysis shows that these choices also prevent the application of Lattice Factoring Methods [5,10,11][1].

[1] The best lattice factoring attack works if $r \geq \log_2 p$ or $s \geq \log_2 q$.

L. Horn Iwaya et al. (Eds.): NordSec 2024, LNCS 15396, pp. 80–98, 2025.
https://doi.org/10.1007/978-3-031-79007-2_5

Table 1. Equivalent key sizes (bits)

Modulus key size	3072	7680	15360
Lenstra model	800(3)	1617(4)	2761(5)
Regression model	749(4)	1457(5)	2385(6)

To decrease decryption time, one may prefer to use a smaller d. Unfortunately, if d is too small the corresponding scheme becomes vulnerable to an important class of attacks known as small private key attacks. For RSA, Wiener showed in [37] that if $d < N^{0.25}/3$, then d can be retrieved from the continued fraction expansion of e/N, and thus factor N. Using a result developed by Coppersmith [9], Boneh and Durfee [4] improved Wiener's bound to $N^{0.292}$. Later, Herrmann and May [14] achieved the same bound with simpler techniques. A different approach was taken by Blömer and May [3], whom generalized Wiener's attack. Specifically, they showed that if there exist three integers x, y, z such that $ex - y\varphi(N) = z$, $x < N^{0.25}/3$ and $|z| < |exN^{-0.75}|$, then the factorisation of N can be recovered. When an approximation p_0 of p is known such that $|p - p_0| < N^{\delta}/8$ and $\delta < 0.5$, Nassr, Anwar and Bahig [23] present a method based on continued fractions for recovering d when $d < N^{(1-\delta)/2}$.

In the case of the Takagi family, there are two variants of decryption: the first one leads to the key equation

$$ed' - k\varphi(N) = 1, \tag{1}$$

while the second to

$$ed - k(p-1)(q-1) = 1. \tag{2}$$

Therefore, there are two classes of small private key attacks against the Takagi family. The first continued fraction attacks are found in [8,34]. In [34], the author studies the case $s = 1$ and provides the attack bound $d' \leq N^{1/2(r+1)}$. Takagi concluded the Wiener-type attacks do not seem possible for Eq. 2. Lim *et al.*'s proposal was studied in [8], and the following attack bound is proved $d' \leq N^{1/2(r+s)}$. Additionally, the authors provide the first lattice attack that can recover d'. As Takagi, the authors of [8] conclude that continued fraction and lattice attacks are probably not applicable to the key Eq. 2.

For $s = 1$, further lattice attacks against Eq. 1 can be found in [21,22,26,29,30]. The best attack bound for Lim et al.'s scheme is $d' < N^{1-(3r+s)/(r+s)^2}$ and uses lattices to recover d' [20]. This result was generalized in [1,25,27] to obtain more flexibility.

For the case $N = p^2q$, another continued fraction attack for recovering d' is provided in [2] and further generalized to $N = p^rq$ in [33], under the restriction

$$2p^{(3r+2)/(r+1)}|p^{(r-1)/(r+1)} - q^{(r-1)/(r+1)}| < 1/6 \cdot N^{\gamma},$$

for $\gamma \in (0.75, 0.8)$. When the condition $q^s < p^r < 2q^s$ holds, the authors of [32] devise a continued fraction attack and their result is further generalized to unbalanced primes in [31].

The only successful small private key attacks against Eq. 2 can be found in [15,20], and both are based on lattices. For $s = 1$, the authors of [15] provide the attack bound $d < N^{(2-\sqrt{2})/(r+1)}$, while for the general case, in [20] we can find an attack for $d < N^{(7-2\sqrt{7})/3(r+s)}$. The equivalence between factoring N and computing d when $s = 1$ is given in [17].

In this paper, we extend the attack bounds for d' provided in [8,34], which allow continued fraction attacks when $e < \varphi(N)$. We then argue that this attack cannot be applied when $e < (p-1)(q-1)$. Additionally, we show that our technique cannot be adapted to the key equation $ed - k(p-1)(q-1) = 1$. Therefore, we extend the interval in which continued fraction attacks are inapplicable for both key equations.

Structure of the Paper. In Sect. 2, we provide definitions and notions used throughout the paper. After proving several useful propositions in Sect. 3, we present a Wiener-type small private key attack in Sect. 4 for $e < \varphi(N)$ and argue why it does not apply to Takagi-type schemes (*i.e.* $e < (p-1)(q-1)$). Two concrete instantiations of our attack (for $e < \varphi(N)$) are provided in Sect. 5. We conclude our paper in Sect. 6.

2 Preliminaries

2.1 Continued Fraction

For any real number ζ there exists a unique sequence $(a_n)_n$ of integers such that

$$\zeta = a_0 + \cfrac{1}{a_1 + \cfrac{1}{a_2 + \cfrac{1}{a_3 + \cfrac{1}{a_4 + \cdots}}}},$$

where $a_k > 0$ for any $k \geq 1$. This sequence represents the continued fraction expansion of ζ and is denoted by $\zeta = [a_0, a_1, a_2, \ldots]$. Remark that ζ is a rational number if and only if its corresponding representation as a continued fraction is finite.

For any real number $\zeta = [a_0, a_1, a_2, \ldots]$, the sequence of rational numbers $(A_n)_n$, obtained by truncating this continued fraction, $A_k = [a_0, a_1, a_2, \ldots, a_k]$, is called the convergents sequence of ζ. Note that the coefficients a_i can be computed in polynomial time using the Euclidean algorithm. For more details, we refer the reader to [37].

According to [13], the following bound allows us to check if a rational number u/v is a convergent of ζ.

Theorem 1. *Let $\zeta = [a_0, a_1, a_2, \ldots]$ be a positive real number. If u, v are positive integers such that $\gcd(u, v) = 1$ and*

$$\left|\zeta - \frac{u}{v}\right| < \frac{1}{2v^2},$$

then u/v is a convergent of $[a_0, a_1, a_2, \ldots]$.

2.2 Takagi Family Schemes

In [19], Lim *et al.* propose a generalization of Takagi's cryptosystem [34], which is itself a generalization of RSA [28]. Instead of using a classical RSA modulus, they propose the use of $N = p^r q^s$, where $r, s \geq 1$. Note that in this case, Euler's totient is $\varphi(N) = p^{r-1}q^{s-1}(p-1)(q-1)$. Remark that when $r = s$, the scheme only makes sense for $r = s = 1$.[2] However, for completeness, we further present the scheme in a generic way. Note that λ denotes a security parameter.

Setup(λ): Let $r, s \geq 1$ be two integers. Randomly generate two distinct large prime numbers p, q such that $p, q \geq 2^\lambda$ and compute the product $N = p^r q^s$. Compute $L = (p-1)(q-1)$. Choose an integer e such that $\gcd(e, L) = 1$ and compute d such that $ed \equiv 1 \bmod L$. Output the public key $pk = (N, e)$. The corresponding secret key is $sk = (p, q, d)$.
Encrypt(pk, m): To encrypt a message $m \in \mathbb{Z}_N$ we compute $c \equiv m^e \bmod N$. Output the ciphertext c.
Decrypt(sk, c): Using the method described in [19], we first compute $m_p \equiv m \bmod p^r$ and $m_q \equiv m \bmod q^s$. The original message m can be recovered using the Chinese Remainder Theorem.

Remark 1. An alternative decryption method is to compute $d' \equiv e^{-1} \bmod \varphi(N)$ and $c \equiv m^{d'} \bmod N$. Note that, this method is slower than the ones presented in [19,34], that use $d \equiv e^{-1} \bmod L$.

Remark 2. Depending on the choice of parameters, faster decryption can be achieved compared to RSA [28] ($r = s = 1$). Takagi proposed $r > 1$ and $s = 1$, but Lim *et al.* showed that better running times can be obtained for $N = p^{r+1}q^r$ or $N = p^{r+1}q^{r-1}$ if $r \equiv 0 \bmod 4$ or $N = p^{r+2}q^{r-2}$ if $r \equiv 2 \bmod 4$.

3 Useful Properties of $\varphi(N)$

In this section we provide a few useful properties of $\varphi(N)$. Using the following result, we will compute a lower and upper bound for Euler's totient.

Lemma 1. *Let $N = p^r q^s$ be the product of unknown primes with $q < p < 2q$. Then the following property holds*

$$\frac{2^{s/(r+s)}}{2} N^{1/(r+s)} < q < N^{1/(r+s)} < p < 2^{s/(r+s)} N^{1/(r+s)}.$$

Proof. From $q < p < 2q$ we obtain $q^s < p^s < 2^s q^s$. Multiplying by p^r we obtain $N < p^{r+s} < 2^s N$ or equivalently

$$N^{1/(r+s)} < p < 2^{s/(r+s)} N^{1/(r+s)}.$$

[2] If $N = p^r q^r$, then we can try to factor $\sqrt[r]{N} = pq$ instead of N, and this lowers the scheme's security.

Since $q^s = N/p^r$, we have

$$\frac{1}{2^{rs/(r+s)}N^{r/(r+s)}} < \frac{1}{p^r} < \frac{1}{N^{r/(r+s)}} \Leftrightarrow \frac{N}{2^{rs/(r+s)}N^{r/(r+s)}} < q^s < \frac{N}{N^{r/(r+s)}}$$
$$\Leftrightarrow \frac{N^{s/(r+s)}}{2^{rs/(r+s)}} < q^s < N^{s/(r+s)}$$
$$\Leftrightarrow \frac{N^{1/(r+s)}}{2^{r/(r+s)}} < q < N^{1/(r+s)},$$

just as desired. □

Remark 3. When $(r, s) = (1, 1)$ and $(r, s) = (2, 1)$, [24, Lemma 1] and [2, Lemma 1] become a special case of Lemma 1. Another special case of our lemma is [33, Lemma 2.1] that considers $s = 1$.

Before continuing our analysis, we first express $\varphi(N)$ as a function in p, when N, r and s are fixed. More precisely, we observe that plugging $q = (N/p^r)^{1/s}$ in $\varphi(N)$ leads to the following function

$$\begin{aligned} f(p) &= p^{r-1}\left(\frac{N}{p^r}\right)^{(s-1)/s}(p-1)\left(\left(\frac{N}{p^r}\right)^{1/s}-1\right) \\ &= p^{(r-s)/s}N^{(s-1)/s}(p-1)\cdot p^{-r/s}(N^{1/s}-p^{r/s}) \\ &= p^{-1}N^{(s-1)/s}(p-1)(N^{1/s}-p^{r/s}) \\ &= p^{-1}N^{(s-1)/s}(pN^{1/s}-p\cdot p^{r/s}-N^{1/s}+p^{r/s}) \\ &= N^{(s-1)/s}\left(N^{1/s}-p^{r/s}-\frac{N^{1/s}}{p}+\frac{p^{r/s}}{p}\right) \\ &= N - N^{(s-1)/s}p^{r/s} - \frac{N}{p} + N^{(s-1)/s}p^{(r-s)/s}, \end{aligned}$$

with p as a variable. The next lemma tells us when, under certain conditions, f is a strictly decreasing function.

Proposition 1. *Let $N > 2^{r-2s}$ be a positive integer. Then for any integer $N^{1/(r+s)} < x < 2^{s/(r+s)}N^{1/(r+s)}$, we have that the function*

$$f(x) = N - N^{(s-1)/s}x^{r/s} - \frac{N}{x} + N^{(s-1)/s}x^{(r-s)/s},$$

is strictly decreasing with x when $r \geq s$.

Proof. To determine whether the function f increases or decreases, we need to compute the derivative

$$f'(x) = -\frac{r}{s}\cdot N^{(s-1)/s}x^{(r-s)/s} + \frac{N}{x^2} + \frac{r-s}{s}\cdot N^{(s-1)/s}x^{(r-2s)/s}.$$

We first consider the case $r > s$. We distinguish three subcases: $r > 2s$, $r = 2s$ and $2s > r > s$.

Case $r > 2s$: We obtain that

$$\begin{aligned} f'(x) &< -\frac{r}{s}\cdot N^{\frac{s-1}{s}} N^{\frac{r-s}{s(r+s)}} + \frac{N}{N^{\frac{2}{r+s}}} + \frac{r-s}{s}\cdot N^{\frac{s-1}{s}} 2^{\frac{r-2s}{r+s}} N^{\frac{r-2s}{s(r+s)}} \\ &= -\frac{r}{s}\cdot N^{\frac{r+s-2}{r+s}} + N^{\frac{r+s-2}{r+s}} + \frac{r-s}{s}\cdot 2^{\frac{r-2s}{r+s}} N^{\frac{r+s-3}{r+s}} \\ &= N^{\frac{r+s-3}{r+s}}\left(\left(1-\frac{r}{s}\right)\cdot N^{\frac{1}{r+s}} + \frac{r-s}{s}\cdot 2^{\frac{r-2s}{r+s}}\right) \\ &= \frac{r-s}{s}\cdot N^{\frac{r+s-3}{r+s}}(-N^{\frac{1}{r+s}} + 2^{\frac{r-2s}{r+s}}) < 0, \end{aligned}$$

since $N > 2^{r-2s}$.
Case $r = 2s$: We have

$$\begin{aligned} f'(x) &< -2\cdot N^{\frac{s-1}{s}} N^{\frac{1}{3s}} + \frac{N}{N^{\frac{2}{3s}}} + N^{\frac{s-1}{s}} \\ &= -2\cdot N^{\frac{3s-2}{3s}} + N^{\frac{3s-2}{3s}} + N^{\frac{s-1}{s}} \\ &= N^{\frac{s-1}{s}}\left(-N^{\frac{1}{3s}} + 1\right) < 0. \end{aligned}$$

Case $2s > r > s$: We obtain

$$\begin{aligned} f'(x) &< -\frac{r}{s}\cdot N^{\frac{s-1}{s}} N^{\frac{r-s}{s(r+s)}} + \frac{N}{N^{\frac{2}{r+s}}} + \frac{r-s}{s}\cdot N^{\frac{s-1}{s}}\cdot \frac{1}{N^{\frac{2s-r}{s(r+s)}}} \\ &= -\frac{r}{s}\cdot N^{\frac{r+s-2}{r+s}} + N^{\frac{r+s-2}{r+s}} + \frac{r-s}{s}\cdot N^{\frac{r+s-3}{r+s}} \\ &= N^{\frac{r+s-3}{r+s}}\left(\left(1-\frac{r}{s}\right)\cdot N^{\frac{1}{r+s}} + \frac{r-s}{s}\right) \\ &= \frac{r-s}{s}\cdot N^{\frac{r+s-3}{r+s}}(-N^{\frac{1}{r+s}} + 1) < 0. \end{aligned}$$

Therefore, we can conclude that f is a strictly decreasing function when $r > s$.
When $r = s$ we have that

$$f'(x) = -N^{(s-1)/s} + \frac{N}{x^2} < -N^{(s-1)/s} + \frac{N}{N^{1/s}} = 0,$$

since $N^{1/2s} < x$. Therefore, we have that f is a strictly decreasing function. □

By applying the function f to the inequality given in Lemma 1, we can derive the following bounds for $\varphi(N)$.

Corollary 1. *Let $N = p^r q^s$ be the product of unknown primes with $q < p < 2q$. Then the following property holds*

$$N^{\frac{r+s-2}{r+s}}\left(N^{\frac{2}{r+s}} - \frac{3}{2}\cdot 2^{\frac{r}{r+s}}\cdot N^{\frac{1}{r+s}} + 2^{\frac{r-s}{r+s}}\right) < \varphi(N) < N^{\frac{r+s-2}{r+s}}\left(N^{\frac{1}{r+s}} - 1\right)^2,$$

when $r \geq s$.

Proof. By Lemma 1 we have that

$$N^{1/(r+s)} < p < 2^{s/(r+s)} N^{1/(r+s)},$$

which, according to Proposition 1, leads to

$$f(N^{1/(r+s)}) > f(p) > f(2^{s/(r+s)} N^{1/(r+s)}).$$

Thus, we need to evaluate the endpoints

$$\begin{aligned} f(N^{\frac{1}{r+s}}) &= N - N^{\frac{s-1}{s}} N^{\frac{r}{s(r+s)}} - \frac{N}{N^{\frac{1}{r+s}}} + N^{\frac{s-1}{s}} N^{\frac{r-s}{s(r+s)}} \\ &= N - 2N^{\frac{r+s-1}{r+s}} + N^{\frac{r+s-2}{r+s}} \\ &= N^{\frac{r+s-2}{r+s}} \left(N^{\frac{1}{r+s}} - 1\right)^2, \end{aligned}$$

and

$$\begin{aligned} f(2^{\frac{s}{r+s}} N^{\frac{1}{r+s}}) &= N - N^{\frac{s-1}{s}} \cdot 2^{\frac{r}{r+s}} N^{\frac{r}{s(r+s)}} - \frac{N}{2^{\frac{s}{r+s}} N^{\frac{1}{r+s}}} + N^{\frac{s-1}{s}} \cdot 2^{\frac{r-s}{r+s}} N^{\frac{r-s}{s(r+s)}} \\ &= N - 2^{\frac{r}{r+s}} N^{\frac{r+s-1}{r+s}} - \frac{N^{\frac{r+s-1}{r+s}}}{2^{\frac{s}{r+s}}} + 2^{\frac{r-s}{r+s}} N^{\frac{r+s-2}{r+s}} \\ &= N^{\frac{r+s-2}{r+s}} \left(N^{\frac{2}{r+s}} - \frac{3}{2} \cdot 2^{\frac{r}{r+s}} \cdot N^{\frac{1}{r+s}} + 2^{\frac{r-s}{r+s}}\right), \end{aligned}$$

and we obtain our desired bounds. □

When $r = s = 1$, the following result proven in [7] becomes a special case of Lemma 1.

Corollary 2. *Let $N = pq$ be the product of two unknown primes with $q < p < 2q$. Then the following property holds*

$$N - \frac{3}{\sqrt{2}}\sqrt{N} + 1 < \varphi(N) < (\sqrt{N} - 1)^2.$$

We can use Corollary 1 to find a useful approximation of φ. This result will be useful when devising our attack against the Takagi family.

Proposition 2. *Let $N = p^r q^s$ be the product of unknown primes with $q < p < 2q$. We define*

$$\varphi_0(N) = \frac{1}{2} \cdot N^{\frac{r+s-2}{r+s}} \left[\left(N^{\frac{1}{r+s}} - 1\right)^2 + \left(N^{\frac{2}{r+s}} - \frac{3}{2} \cdot 2^{\frac{r}{r+s}} \cdot N^{\frac{1}{r+s}} + 2^{\frac{r-s}{r+s}}\right)\right].$$

Then the following holds

$$|\varphi(N) - \varphi_0(N)| \le \frac{1}{2} \cdot N^{\frac{r+s-1}{r+s}} \left(\frac{3}{2} \cdot 2^{\frac{r}{r+s}} - 2\right),$$

when $r \ge s$.

Proof. According to Corollary 1, $\varphi_0(N)$ is the mean value of the lower and upper bound. Let $\delta = |\varphi(N) - \varphi_0(N)|$. Then we have

$$\begin{aligned}\delta &\leq \frac{1}{2} \cdot N^{\frac{r+s-2}{r+s}} \left[\left(N^{\frac{1}{r+s}} - 1\right)^2 - \left(N^{\frac{2}{r+s}} - \frac{3}{2} \cdot 2^{\frac{r}{r+s}} \cdot N^{\frac{1}{r+s}} + 2^{\frac{r-s}{r+s}}\right)\right] \\ &= \frac{1}{2} \cdot N^{\frac{r+s-2}{r+s}} \left(-2N^{\frac{1}{r+s}} + \frac{3}{2} \cdot 2^{\frac{r}{r+s}} \cdot N^{\frac{1}{r+s}} + 1 - 2^{\frac{r-s}{r+s}}\right) \\ &\leq \frac{1}{2} \cdot N^{\frac{r+s-1}{r+s}} \left(-2 + \frac{3}{2} \cdot 2^{\frac{r}{r+s}}\right),\end{aligned}$$

as desired. □

When $r = s = 1$, the following property presented in [7] becomes a special case of Proposition 2.

Corollary 3. *Let $N = pq$ be the product of two unknown primes with $q < p < 2q$. Then the following holds*

$$|\varphi(N) - \varphi_0(N)| < \frac{3 - 2\sqrt{2}}{2\sqrt{2}}\sqrt{N}.$$

4 Application of Continued Fractions

In this section, we provide two impossibility results. More precisely, we argue that Wiener-type attacks appear to be impossible for the Takagi family.

4.1 The Key Equation $ed' - k\varphi(N) = 1$

We start the section by studying what happens when $e < \varphi(N)$. We provide a Wiener-type attack for the key equation

$$ed' - k\varphi(N) = 1.$$

More precisely, we provide an upper bound for d' such that we can use the continued fraction algorithm to recover d' without knowing the factorisation of the modulus N. Note that our bound is an improvement on the bound presented in [8], namely

$$d' < \sqrt{N^{\frac{1}{r+s}}}.$$

Theorem 2. *Let $N = p^r q^s$ be the product of unknown primes with $q < p < 2q$ such that $r \geq s$. If $e < \varphi(N)$ satisfies $ed' - k\varphi(N) = 1$ with*

$$d' < \sqrt{\frac{2^{\frac{s}{r+s}} N \left(N^{\frac{1}{r+s}} - 3 \cdot 2^{\frac{r}{r+s}}\right)}{3e}}, \tag{3}$$

then we can recover d' in polynomial time.

Proof. Since $ed' - k\varphi(N) = 1$, we have that

$$\left|\frac{k}{d'} - \frac{e}{\varphi_0(N)}\right| \le e\left|\frac{1}{\varphi_0(N)} - \frac{1}{\varphi(N)}\right| + \left|\frac{e}{\varphi(N)} - \frac{k}{d'}\right|$$
$$= e\frac{|\varphi(N) - \varphi_0(N)|}{\varphi_0(N)\varphi(N)} + \frac{1}{\varphi(N)d'}.$$

Let $\varepsilon = N^{\frac{r+s-2}{r+s}}\left(N^{\frac{2}{r+s}} - \frac{3}{2}\cdot 2^{\frac{r}{r+s}}\cdot N^{\frac{1}{r+s}} + 2^{\frac{r-s}{r+s}}\right)$. Using $d' = (k\varphi(N)+1)/e$ and Proposition 2 we obtain

$$\left|\frac{k}{d'} - \frac{e}{\varphi_0(N)}\right| \le \frac{eN^{\frac{r+s-1}{r+s}}(3\cdot 2^{\frac{r}{r+s}} - 4)}{4\varphi_0(N)\varphi(N)} + \frac{e}{\varphi(N)(k\varphi(N)+1)}$$
$$\le \frac{eN^{\frac{r+s-1}{r+s}}(3\cdot 2^{\frac{r}{r+s}} - 4)}{4\varepsilon^2} + \frac{e}{\varepsilon(k\varepsilon+1)}$$
$$\le \frac{eN^{\frac{r+s-1}{r+s}}(3\cdot 2^{\frac{r}{r+s}} - 4)}{4\varepsilon^2} + \frac{e}{\varepsilon^2}$$
$$\le \frac{e(N^{\frac{r+s-1}{r+s}}(3\cdot 2^{\frac{r}{r+s}} - 4) + 4)}{4N^{\frac{2(r+s-2)}{r+s}}\left(N^{\frac{2}{r+s}} - \frac{3}{2}\cdot 2^{\frac{r}{r+s}}\cdot N^{\frac{1}{r+s}}\right)^2}.$$

Note that

$$\frac{N^{\frac{r+s-1}{r+s}}(3\cdot 2^{\frac{r}{r+s}} - 4) + 4}{4N^{\frac{2(r+s-2)}{r+s}}\left(N^{\frac{2}{r+s}} - \frac{3}{2}\cdot 2^{\frac{r}{r+s}}\cdot N^{\frac{1}{r+s}}\right)^2} = \frac{3\cdot 2^{\frac{r}{r+s}}\cdot N^{\frac{r+s-1}{r+s}} - 4\left(N^{\frac{r+s-1}{r+s}} - 1\right)}{4N^{\frac{2(r+s-1)}{r+s}}\left(N^{\frac{1}{r+s}} - \frac{3}{2}\cdot 2^{\frac{r}{r+s}}\right)^2}$$
$$< \frac{3\cdot 2^{\frac{r}{r+s}}\cdot N^{\frac{r+s-1}{r+s}}}{4N^{\frac{2(r+s-1)}{r+s}}\left(N^{\frac{1}{r+s}} - \frac{3}{2}\cdot 2^{\frac{r}{r+s}}\right)^2}$$
$$= \frac{3\cdot 2^{\frac{r}{r+s}}}{4N^{\frac{r+s-1}{r+s}}\left(N^{\frac{1}{r+s}} - \frac{3}{2}\cdot 2^{\frac{r}{r+s}}\right)^2}$$
$$< \frac{3\cdot 2^{\frac{r}{r+s}}}{4N\left(N^{\frac{1}{r+s}} - 3\cdot 2^{\frac{r}{r+s}}\right)}.$$

and thus

$$\left|\frac{k}{d'} - \frac{e}{\varphi_0(N)}\right| < \frac{3\cdot 2^{\frac{r}{r+s}}e}{4N\left(N^{\frac{1}{r+s}} - 3\cdot 2^{\frac{r}{r+s}}\right)}. \tag{4}$$

To apply Theorem 1, we need

$$\left|\frac{k}{d'} - \frac{e}{\varphi_0(N)}\right| \le \frac{1}{2d'^2}.$$

Therefore, using Eq. 4 we obtain

$$d'^2 < \frac{2N\left(N^{\frac{1}{r+s}} - 3 \cdot 2^{\frac{r}{r+s}}\right)}{3 \cdot 2^{\frac{r}{r+s}} e},$$

just as in our hypothesis. Therefore, we obtain that k/d' is a convergent of the continued fraction expansion of $e/\varphi_0(N)$. Hence, d can be recovered in polynomial time. □

When $r = s = 1$ the bounds presented in [6]

$$d < \sqrt{\frac{8N\sqrt{N}}{e}}$$

and in [12]

$$d < \sqrt{\frac{\sqrt{2}N\left(\sqrt{N} - \frac{2(\sqrt{2}+1)^2}{(\sqrt{2}-1)^2}\right)}{e(\sqrt{2}-1)^2}} \simeq \sqrt{\frac{8.24N(\sqrt{N} - 67.94)}{e}},$$

are better than ours.

Corollary 4. *Let $N = pq$ be the product of two unknown primes with $q < p < 2q$. If $e < \varphi(N)$ satisfies $ed' - k\varphi(N) = 1$ with*

$$d' < \sqrt{\frac{\sqrt{2}N\left(\sqrt{N} - 3\sqrt{2}\right)}{3e}} \simeq \sqrt{\frac{0.47N\left(\sqrt{N} - 4.24\right)}{e}}$$

then we can recover d' in polynomial time.

When $s = 1$, the bound presented in Corollary 5 improves on the bound provided by Takagi [34], namely

$$d' < \sqrt{N^{\frac{1}{r+1}}}.$$

Corollary 5. *Let $N = p^r q$ be the product of unknown primes with $q < p < 2q$. If $e < \varphi(N)$ satisfies $ed' - k\varphi(N) = 1$ with*

$$d' < \sqrt{\frac{2^{\frac{1}{r+1}}N\left(N^{\frac{1}{r+1}} - 3 \cdot 2^{\frac{r}{r+1}}\right)}{3e}},$$

then we can recover d' in polynomial time.

We further check if Theorem 2 can be applied under the restriction $e < (p-1)(q-1)$ instead of $e < \varphi(N)$. We start with some useful bounds for d'.

Lemma 2. *If* $1 < e < (p-1)(q-1)$, *then* $d' > p^{r-1}q^{s-1}$.

Proof. We assume that $1 < d' < p^{r-1}q^{s-1}$. Then $1 < ed' < \varphi(N)$, and thus the product never wraps around. Therefore, we obtain a contradiction with $ed' \equiv 1 \bmod \varphi(N)$. □

Applying Lemmas 1 and 2 we obtain the following corollary.

Corollary 6. *If* $1 < e < (p-1)(q-1)$, *then*

$$d' > \frac{1}{2^{\frac{r(s-1)}{r+s}}} N^{\frac{r+s-2}{r+s}}.$$

Now we are able to verify if the bound provided in Theorem 2 is compatible with the restriction $e < (p-1)(q-1)$.

Theorem 3. *Let* $N = p^r q^s > 2^{\frac{2rs}{r+s-5}}$ *be the product of unknown primes with* $q < p < 2q$ *such that* $r > s$ *and* $r + s \geq 5$. *If* $e < (p-1)(q-1)$ *then we cannot recover* d' *using Theorem 2.*

Proof. Using Theorem 2 and Corollary 6 we obtain

$$\frac{1}{2^{\frac{r(s-1)}{r+s}}} N^{\frac{r+s-2}{r+s}} < \sqrt{\frac{2^{\frac{s}{r+s}} N \left(N^{\frac{1}{r+s}} - 3 \cdot 2^{\frac{r}{r+s}} \right)}{3e}} < N^{\frac{r+s+1}{2(r+s)}} \sqrt{\frac{2^{\frac{s}{r+s}}}{3e}}. \tag{5}$$

When $s = 1$, Eq. 5 becomes

$$N^{\frac{r-1}{r+1}} < N^{\frac{r+2}{2(r+1)}} \sqrt{\frac{2^{\frac{1}{r+1}}}{3e}} < N^{\frac{r+2}{2(r+1)}} \Leftrightarrow N^{\frac{r-4}{2(r+1)}} < 1,$$

which leads to a contradiction when $r > 4$.

When $s \geq 2$, Eq. 5 is equivalent to

$$N^{\frac{r+s-5}{2(r+s)}} < \sqrt{\frac{2 \cdot 2^{\frac{r(2s-3)}{r+s}}}{3e}} < 2^{\frac{r(2s-3)}{2(r+s)}} < 2^{\frac{2rs}{2(r+s)}} \Leftrightarrow N < 2^{\frac{2rs}{r+s-5}}.$$

Therefore, we obtain a contradiction when $r + s > 5$.

When $r + s = 5$, we have that $r = 4$ and $s = 1$, and this leads to the following contradiction

$$N^{\frac{3}{5}} < N^{\frac{3}{5}} \sqrt{\frac{2^{\frac{1}{5}}}{3e}} \Leftrightarrow 3e < 2^{\frac{1}{5}} < 1.15,$$

or $r = 3$ and $s = 2$, and which leads to

$$\frac{1}{2^{\frac{3}{5}}} N^{\frac{3}{5}} < N^{\frac{3}{5}} \sqrt{\frac{2^{\frac{2}{5}}}{3e}} \Leftrightarrow 3e < 2 \cdot 2^{\frac{3}{5}} < 3.04,$$

and thus we obtain our desired result. □

Lemma 3. *Let $N = p^3q$ be the product of unknown primes with $q < p < 2q$. If $e < (p-1)(q-1)$ then we cannot recover d' using Theorem 2.*

Proof. When $r = 3$ and $s = 1$, Eq. 5 becomes

$$N^{\frac{2}{4}} < N^{\frac{5}{8}}\sqrt{\frac{2^{\frac{1}{4}}}{3e}} \Leftrightarrow e < \frac{2^{\frac{1}{4}} \cdot N^{\frac{1}{4}}}{3} < N^{\frac{1}{4}} = p^{\frac{3}{4}}q^{\frac{1}{4}} < p.$$

Since $\gcd(e, \varphi(N)) = 1$, we can refine the bound to $e < p-1$. In this case, using the same arguments as in Lemma 2, we obtain that $d' > p^2(q-1)$. But this is in contradiction with the bound provided in Theorem 2

$$p^2(q-1) < d' < N^{\frac{5}{8}} < p^{\frac{15}{8}}q^{\frac{5}{8}} < p^2q^{\frac{5}{8}} \Leftrightarrow q \leq q^{\frac{5}{8}},$$

hence we cannot recover d'. □

Lemma 4. *Let $N = p^2q$ be the product of unknown primes with $q < p < 2q$. If $e < (p-1)(q-1)$ then we cannot recover d' using Theorem 2.*

Proof. When $r = 2$ and $s = 1$, Eq. 3 becomes

$$d' < \sqrt{\frac{2^{\frac{1}{3}}N^{\frac{4}{3}}}{3e}} < N^{\frac{2}{3}} = p^{\frac{4}{3}}q^{\frac{2}{3}} < p^2.$$

Therefore, $e > (q-1)$. The updated Eq. 3 is

$$d' < \sqrt{\frac{2^{\frac{1}{3}}N^{\frac{4}{3}}}{3e}} < \sqrt{\frac{2^3q^4}{2e}} = \frac{2q^2}{\sqrt{e}} < \frac{2q^2}{(q-1)^{\frac{1}{2}}}.$$

Hence,

$$e > \frac{p(p-1)(q-1)(q-1)^{\frac{1}{2}}}{2q^2} > \frac{(q-1)^{\frac{3}{2}}}{2} > \frac{(q-1)^{\frac{3}{2}}}{4}.$$

In this case, Eq. 3 becomes

$$d' < \frac{4q^2}{(q-1)^{\frac{3}{4}}},$$

and the new bound is

$$e > \frac{p(p-1)(q-1)(q-1)^{\frac{3}{4}}}{4q^2} > \frac{(q-1)^{\frac{7}{4}}}{4}.$$

Again, this updates our bounds

$$d' < \frac{4q^2}{(q-1)^{\frac{7}{8}}},$$

and

$$e > \frac{p(p-1)(q-1)(q-1)^{\frac{7}{8}}}{4q^2} > \frac{(q-1)^{\frac{15}{8}}}{4}.$$

We further employ induction to prove that the interval for d continuously decreases in size. Hence, we assume that $e \geq (q-1)^{(2^{i+1}-1)/2^i}/4$ for an i. Equation 3 leads to a smaller interval for d

$$d \leq \frac{4q^2}{(q-1)^{(2^{i+1}-1)/2^{i+1}}},$$

and the corresponding interval for e

$$e > \frac{p(p-1)(q-1)(q-1)^{(2^{i+1}-1)/2^{i+1}}}{4q^2} > \frac{(q-1)^{(2^{i+2}-1)/2^{i+1}}}{4}.$$

Since our rationale works for any i, we cannot devise a Wiener-type attack. □

To conclude we provide the following corollary. Note that we ignore the case $r = s = 2$ (see Sect. 2.2 for justification). Also, the case $r = s = 1$ coincides with RSA and continued fraction attacks are feasible (see [6,12] and Corollary 4).

Corollary 7. *Let* $N = p^r q^s > 2^{\frac{2rs}{r+s-5}}$ *be the product of unknown primes with* $q < p < 2q$ *such that* $r > s$ *and* $r + s > 2$. *If* $e < (p-1)(q-1)$ *then we cannot recover* d' *using Theorem 2.*

Remark 4. Note that for Lim *et al.*'s cryptosystem, a different argument is provided in [8] explaining why Wiener-type attacks seem impossible for the relation $ed' - k\varphi(N) = 1$ when $e < (p-1)(q-1)$. Since our bound is larger (see Theorem 2), our argument extends this impossibility result.

4.2 The Key Equation $ed - k(p-1)(q-1) = 1$

We can also try to devise a Wiener-type attack for the relation $ed - k(p-1)(q-1) = 1$, when $r, s \neq 1$. In this case, we get the relation

$$\left|\frac{k}{dp^{r-1}q^{s-1}} - \frac{e}{\varphi_0(N)}\right| \leq e\left|\frac{1}{\varphi_0(N)} - \frac{1}{\varphi(N)}\right| + \left|\frac{e}{\varphi(N)} - \frac{k}{dp^{r-1}q^{s-1}}\right|$$
$$= e\frac{|\varphi(N) - \varphi_0(N)|}{\varphi_0(N)\varphi(N)} + \frac{1}{\varphi(N)d},$$

since $edp^{r-1}q^{s-1} - k\varphi(N) = p^{r-1}q^{s-1}$. Therefore, the bound

$$\left|\frac{k}{dp^{r-1}q^{s-1}} - \frac{e}{\varphi_0(N)}\right| < \frac{3 \cdot 2^{\frac{r}{r+s}} e}{4N\left(N^{\frac{1}{r+s}} - 3 \cdot 2^{\frac{r}{r+s}}\right)}, \tag{6}$$

holds. Using Lemma 1 we have that

$$\frac{1}{2^{\frac{(r-1)s}{r+s}} N^{\frac{r-1}{r+s}}} \cdot \frac{1}{N^{\frac{s-1}{r+s}}} = \frac{1}{2^{\frac{(r-1)s}{r+s}} N^{\frac{r+s-2}{r+s}}} \leq \frac{1}{p^{r-1}q^{s-1}},$$

and thus we can apply Theorem 1 if

$$\left| \frac{k}{dp^{r-1}q^{s-1}} - \frac{e}{\varphi_0(N)} \right| \leq \frac{1}{2\left(d \cdot 2^{\frac{(r-1)s}{r+s}} N^{\frac{r+s-2}{r+s}}\right)^2} \leq \frac{1}{2(dp^{r-1}q^{s-1})^2}.$$

Therefore, using Eq. 6, we obtain the necessary bound for a Wiener-type attack to be successful

$$d^2 2^{\frac{2(r-1)s}{r+s}} N^2 N^{\frac{-4}{r+s}} < \frac{2N\left(N^{\frac{1}{r+s}} - 3 \cdot 2^{\frac{r}{r+s}}\right)}{3 \cdot 2^{\frac{r}{r+s}} e}$$
$$\Leftrightarrow d < \sqrt{\frac{2N^{\frac{4}{r+s}}\left(N^{\frac{1}{r+s}} - 3 \cdot 2^{\frac{r}{r+s}}\right)}{3 \cdot 2^{\frac{2(r-1)s+r}{r+s}} Ne}}.$$

We observe that

$$\frac{2N^{\frac{4}{r+s}}\left(N^{\frac{1}{r+s}} - 3 \cdot 2^{\frac{r}{r+s}}\right)}{3 \cdot 2^{\frac{2(r-1)s+r}{r+s}} Ne} < \frac{2N^{\frac{5}{r+s}}}{3 \cdot 2^{\frac{2(r-1)s+r}{r+s}} Ne} < \frac{N^{\frac{5}{r+s}}}{2^{\frac{2(r-1)s+r}{r+s}} N} < \frac{1}{N^{\frac{r+s-5}{r+s}}} \leq 1.$$

Unfortunately, this leads to $d < 1$ when $r + s \geq 5$. Therefore, a Wiener-type attack seems infeasible for the equation $ed - k(p-1)(q-1) = 1$.

Lets see what happens in the cases $2 < r + s < 5$. When $r + s = 4$, we have that $r = 3$ and $s = 1$,[3] which leads to

$$d < \sqrt{\frac{2N\left(N^{\frac{1}{4}} - 3 \cdot 2^{\frac{3}{4}}\right)}{3 \cdot 2^{\frac{7}{4}} Ne}} = \sqrt{\frac{N^{\frac{1}{4}} - 3 \cdot 2^{\frac{3}{4}}}{3 \cdot 2^{\frac{3}{4}} e}} < \sqrt{N^{\frac{1}{4}}} = p^{\frac{3}{8}} q^{\frac{1}{8}} < p^{\frac{1}{2}}. \quad (7)$$

Using the same arguments as in Lemma 2, we obtain that $e > (p-1)^{\frac{1}{4}}(q-1)$. Therefore, we obtain the updated Eq. 7

$$d < \sqrt{\frac{N^{\frac{1}{4}}}{e}} < \frac{p^{\frac{3}{8}} q^{\frac{1}{8}}}{(p-1)^{\frac{1}{4}}(q-1)^{\frac{1}{2}}} < \frac{2^{\frac{3}{8}} \cdot q^{\frac{1}{2}}}{(q-1)^{\frac{3}{4}}} < 2^{\frac{3}{8}} < 1.30,$$

which is a contradiction. Therefore, we cannot devise a Wiener-type attack in this case.

When $r + s = 3$, we have that $r = 2$ and $s = 1$, and this leads to

$$d < \sqrt{\frac{2N^{\frac{4}{3}}\left(N^{\frac{1}{3}} - 3 \cdot 2^{\frac{2}{3}}\right)}{3 \cdot 2^{\frac{4}{3}} Ne}} = \sqrt{\frac{N^{\frac{1}{3}}\left(N^{\frac{1}{3}} - 3 \cdot 2^{\frac{2}{3}}\right)}{3 \cdot 2^{\frac{1}{3}} e}} < N^{\frac{1}{3}} = p^{\frac{2}{3}} q^{\frac{1}{3}} < p. \quad (8)$$

[3] The case $r = s = 2$ is ignored (see Sect. 2.2 for justification).

Hence, we obtain that $e > q$ since $ed \equiv 1 \bmod (p-1)(q-1)$. The updated Eq. 8 is

$$d < \sqrt{\frac{N^{\frac{2}{3}}}{2 \cdot 2^{\frac{1}{3}} e}} < \sqrt{\frac{q^2}{e}} = \frac{q}{\sqrt{e}} < \sqrt{q}.$$

Again, this updates our bound on $e \geq (p-1)(q-1)^{\frac{1}{2}}$. Updating Eq. 8 again we have that

$$d \leq \frac{q}{(p-1)^{\frac{1}{2}}(q-1)^{\frac{1}{4}}} < \frac{q}{(q-1)^{\frac{3}{4}}} = (q-1)^{\frac{1}{4}} + \frac{1}{(q-1)^{\frac{3}{4}}} \Leftrightarrow d \leq (q-1)^{\frac{1}{4}}.$$

Therefore, $e \geq (p-1)(q-1)^{3/4}$. Equation 8 becomes

$$d \leq \frac{q}{(p-1)^{\frac{1}{2}}(q-1)^{\frac{3}{8}}} < \frac{q}{(q-1)^{\frac{7}{8}}} = (q-1)^{\frac{1}{8}} + \frac{1}{(q-1)^{\frac{7}{8}}} \Leftrightarrow d \leq (q-1)^{\frac{1}{8}}.$$

Therefore, $e \geq (p-1)(q-1)^{7/8}$. We further employ induction to prove that the interval for e continuously decreases in size. Hence, we assume that $e \geq (p-1)(q-1)^{(2^i-1)/2^i}$ for an i. Equation 8 becomes

$$d \leq \frac{q}{(p-1)^{\frac{1}{2}}(q-1)^{\frac{(2^i-1)}{2^{i+1}}}} < \frac{q}{(q-1)^{\frac{2^{i+1}-1}{2^{i+1}}}} \Leftrightarrow d \leq (q-1)^{\frac{1}{2^{i+1}}},$$

and thus we obtain a new smaller interval $e \geq (p-1)(q-1)^{(2^{i+1}-1)/2^{i+1}}$. Since our rationale works for any i, we cannot devise a Wiener-type attack.

Remark 5. Note that for Takagi's cryptosystem ($s = 1$), a different argument is provided in [34] explaining why Wiener-type attacks seem impossible for the relation $ed - k(p-1)(q-1) = 1$. Since our bound is larger (see Corollary 5) and more generic, our argument extends this impossibility result.

5 Experimental Results

For completeness we provide an example for $(r, s) = (4, 1)$ (Takagi's scheme example) and $(r, s) = (3, 2)$ (Lim *et al.* 's scheme example) for Theorem 2. Note that for both examples we used the following prime numbers

$$p = 211977819903685906870781 9,$$
$$q = 142230570862221395680680 7.$$

5.1 Case $(r, s) = (4, 1)$

For our attack we use the following public key

$$N = 287180295746212179967635961859891926834489875444 0$$
$$727753428875494233165107431169089552645439477024 6$$
$$822306372008982647820647,$$
$$e = 247920826007715486919646278686053036654317195572 1$$
$$770343837966865885139334096080693938872337686987 5$$
$$7951808933201286653956 7.$$

Remark that $e \approx N^{0.9912}$ and Theorem 2's bound is $d' \leq 2946311427171$. We use the Euclidean algorithm to compute the continued fraction expansion of $e/\varphi_0(N)$ and obtain the first 25 partial quotients

$$[0, 11, 1, 1, 2, 2, 31, 1, 4, 1, 9, 1, 2, 1, 6, 1, 1, 3, 1, 15, 1, 2, 2, 2, 7, \ldots].$$

According to Theorem 2, the set of convergents of $e/\varphi_0(N)$ contains all the possible candidates for k/d'. We note that the $27th$ convergent leads to our desired decryption exponent

$$\frac{k}{d'} = \frac{59082139876}{684380843519}.$$

5.2 Case $(r, s) = (3, 2)$

In this case, we use the following public key

$$\begin{aligned} N = {} & 19268910975178443654929867054408975206933337522 51\\ & 14440277859080482915042481528835799755326535729 55\\ & 3433325220074840056954 91, \\ e = {} & 16918698227018759606395262827350765058501324868 81\\ & 34626298590944422128068784903820313100330746657 02\\ & 8854904104082670956116 07. \end{aligned}$$

Note that $e \approx N^{0.9995}$ and Theorem 2's bound is $d' \leq 951428599246$. Applying the continued fraction expansion of $e/\varphi_0(N)$, we get the first 25 partial quotients

$$[0, 1, 7, 5, 32, 1, 42, 6, 1, 4, 1, 9, 10, 4, 6, 1, 7, 1, 10, 318, 3, 1, 5, 1, 1, \ldots].$$

We see that the $19th$ convergent leads to the correct d'

$$\frac{k}{d'} = \frac{600907491802}{684380843519}.$$

6 Conclusions

In this paper, we provided two impossibility results for the Takagi family schemes when $r > s$. Firstly, in Sect. 4.1, we presented a continued fraction attack for the key equation $ed' - k\varphi(N) = 1$ when $e < \varphi(N)$, and then we showed that it cannot be applied when $e < (p-1)(q-1)$. Note that this result extends the impossibility result presented in [8]. Our second result, given in Sect. 4.2, concerned the key equation $ed - k(p-1)(q-1) = 1$. We showed that the continued fraction strategy presented in Sect. 4.1 cannot be applied. This extends another impossibility result, namely the one presented in [34].

Future Work. We have not been able to extend our results for the case $r < s$ (namely, Proposition 1). Therefore, we leave this case as an open problem. Another interesting problem is to adapt our results to balanced halves (*i.e.* $q^s < p^r < 2q^s$).

References

1. Alquié, D., Chassé, G., Nitaj, A.: Cryptanalysis of the multi-power RSA cryptosystem variant. In: Beresford, A.R., Patra, A., Bellini, E. (eds.) Cryptology and Network Security, CANS 2022. LNCS, vol. 13641, pp. 245–257. Springer, Cham (2022). https://doi.org/10.1007/978-3-031-20974-1_12
2. Asbullah, M., Ariffin, M.: New attacks on RSA with modulus $N = p^2q$ using continued fractions. J. Phys: Conf. Ser. **622**(1), 012019 (2015)
3. Blömer, J., May, A.: A generalized Wiener attack on RSA. In: Bao, F., Deng, R., Zhou, J. (eds.) PKC 2004. LNCS, vol. 2947, pp. 1–13. Springer, Heidelberg (2004). https://doi.org/10.1007/978-3-540-24632-9_1
4. Boneh, D., Durfee, G.: Cryptanalysis of RSA with private key d less than $N^{0.292}$. In: Stern, J. (ed.) EUROCRYPT 1999. LNCS, vol. 1592, pp. 1–11. Springer, Heidelberg (1999). https://doi.org/10.1007/3-540-48910-X_1
5. Boneh, D., Durfee, G., Howgrave-Graham, N.: Factoring $N = p^rq$ for large r. In: Wiener, M. (ed.) CRYPTO 1999. LNCS, vol. 1666, pp. 326–337. Springer, Heidelberg (1999). https://doi.org/10.1007/3-540-48405-1_21
6. Bunder, M., Nitaj, A., Susilo, W., Tonien, J.: A new attack on three variants of the RSA cryptosystem. In: Liu, J.K., Steinfeld, R. (eds.) ACISP 2016. LNCS, vol. 9723, pp. 258–268. Springer, Cham (2016). https://doi.org/10.1007/978-3-319-40367-0_16
7. Bunder, M., Tonien, J.: A new attack on the RSA cryptosystem based on continued fractions. Malays. J. Math. Sci. **11**, 45–57 (2017)
8. Ciet, M., Koeune, F., Laguillaumie, F., Quisquater, J.J.: Short private exponent attacks on fast variants of RSA. Technical report, Ser. CG-2003/4, University Catholique de Louvain Crypto Group (2003)
9. Coppersmith, D.: Small solutions to polynomial equations, and low exponent RSA vulnerabilities. J. Cryptol. **10**(4), 233–260 (1997). https://doi.org/10.1007/s001459900030
10. Coron, J.-S., Faugère, J.-C., Renault, G., Zeitoun, R.: Factoring $N = p^rq^s$ for large r and s. In: Sako, K. (ed.) CT-RSA 2016. LNCS, vol. 9610, pp. 448–464. Springer, Cham (2016). https://doi.org/10.1007/978-3-319-29485-8_26
11. Coron, J.-S., Zeitoun, R.: Improved factorization of $N = p^rq^s$. In: Smart, N.P. (ed.) CT-RSA 2018. LNCS, vol. 10808, pp. 65–79. Springer, Cham (2018). https://doi.org/10.1007/978-3-319-76953-0_4
12. Cotan, P., Teşeleanu, G.: Small private key attack against a family of RSA-like cryptosystems. In: Fritsch, L., Hassan, I., Paintsil, E. (eds.) Secure IT Systems, NordSec 2023. LNCS, vol. 14324, pp. 57–72. Springer, Cham (2023). https://doi.org/10.1007/978-3-031-47748-5_4
13. Hardy, G.H., Wright, E.M., et al.: An Introduction to the Theory of Numbers. Oxford University Press, Oxford (1979)
14. Herrmann, M., May, A.: Maximizing small root bounds by linearization and applications to small secret exponent RSA. In: Nguyen, P.Q., Pointcheval, D. (eds.) PKC 2010. LNCS, vol. 6056, pp. 53–69. Springer, Heidelberg (2010). https://doi.org/10.1007/978-3-642-13013-7_4
15. Itoh, K., Kunihiro, N., Kurosawa, K.: Small secret key attack on a variant of RSA (due to Takagi). In: Malkin, T. (ed.) CT-RSA 2008. LNCS, vol. 4964, pp. 387–406. Springer, Heidelberg (2008). https://doi.org/10.1007/978-3-540-79263-5_25
16. Lenstra, H.W., Jr.: Factoring integers with elliptic curves. Ann. Math. 649–673 (1987)

17. Kunihiro, N., Kurosawa, K.: Deterministic polynomial time equivalence between factoring and key-recovery attack on Takagi's RSA. In: Okamoto, T., Wang, X. (eds.) PKC 2007. LNCS, vol. 4450, pp. 412–425. Springer, Heidelberg (2007). https://doi.org/10.1007/978-3-540-71677-8_27
18. Lenstra, A.K., Verheul, E.R.: Selecting cryptographic key sizes. J. Cryptol. **14**(4), 255–293 (2001). https://doi.org/10.1007/s00145-001-0009-4
19. Lim, S., Kim, S., Yie, I., Lee, H.: A generalized Takagi-cryptosystem with a modulus of the form $\mathrm{p^r q^s}$. In: Roy, B., Okamoto, E. (eds.) INDOCRYPT 2000. LNCS, vol. 1977, pp. 283–294. Springer, Heidelberg (2000). https://doi.org/10.1007/3-540-44495-5_25
20. Lu, Y., Peng, L., Sarkar, S.: Cryptanalysis of an RSA variant with moduli $N = p^r q^l$. J. Math. Cryptol. **11**(2), 117–130 (2017)
21. Lu, Y., Zhang, R., Peng, L., Lin, D.: Solving linear equations modulo unknown divisors: revisited. In: Iwata, T., Cheon, J.H. (eds.) ASIACRYPT 2015. LNCS, vol. 9452, pp. 189–213. Springer, Heidelberg (2015). https://doi.org/10.1007/978-3-662-48797-6_9
22. May, A.: Secret exponent attacks on RSA-type schemes with moduli $N = p^r q$. In: Bao, F., Deng, R., Zhou, J. (eds.) PKC 2004. LNCS, vol. 2947, pp. 218–230. Springer, Heidelberg (2004). https://doi.org/10.1007/978-3-540-24632-9_16
23. Nassr, D.I., Bahig, H.M., Bhery, A., Daoud, S.S.: A new RSA vulnerability using continued fractions. In: AICCSA 2008, pp. 694–701. IEEE Computer Society (2008)
24. Nitaj, A.: Another generalization of Wiener's attack on RSA. In: Vaudenay, S. (ed.) AFRICACRYPT 2008. LNCS, vol. 5023, pp. 174–190. Springer, Heidelberg (2008). https://doi.org/10.1007/978-3-540-68164-9_12
25. Nitaj, A., Boudabra, M.: Improved cryptanalysis of the multi-power RSA cryptosystem variant. In: El Mrabet, N., De Feo, L., Duquesne, S. (eds.) Progress in Cryptology – AFRICACRYPT 2023. LNCS, vol. 14064, pp. 252–269. Springer, Cham (2023). https://doi.org/10.1007/978-3-031-37679-5_11
26. Nitaj, A., Rachidi, T.: New attacks on RSA with moduli $N = p^r q$. In: El Hajji, S., Nitaj, A., Carlet, C., Souidi, E.M. (eds.) C2SI 2015. LNCS, vol. 9084, pp. 352–360. Springer, Cham (2015). https://doi.org/10.1007/978-3-319-18681-8_28
27. Nitaj, A., Susilo, W., Tonien, J.: A generalized attack on the multi-prime power RSA. In: Batina, L., Daemen, J. (eds.) Progress in Cryptology – AFRICACRYPT 2022. LNCS, vol. 13503, pp. 537–549. Springer, Cham (2022). https://doi.org/10.1007/978-3-031-17433-9_23
28. Rivest, R.L., Shamir, A., Adleman, L.: A method for obtaining digital signatures and public-key cryptosystems. Commun. ACM **21**(2), 120–126 (1978)
29. Sarkar, S.: Small secret exponent attack on RSA variant with modulus $N = p^r q$. Des. Codes Crypt. **73**, 383–392 (2014)
30. Sarkar, S.: Revisiting prime power RSA. Discret. Appl. Math. **203**, 127–133 (2016)
31. Shehu, S., Abdullahi, H., Ibrahim, A.A., Ahmad, R.: Breaking modulus of the form $N = p^r q^s$ with improved polynomial attacks. J. Adv. Math. Comput. Sci. **38**(8), 33–46 (2023)
32. Shehu, S., Abubakar, S.I.: Cryptanalysis attacks for factoring generalized Takagi's scheme $N = p^r q^s$. New Trends Math. Sci. **10**(1) (2022)
33. Shehu, S., Ariffin, M.R.K.: New attacks on prime power $N = p^r q$ using good approximation of $\varphi(N)$. Malays. J. Math. Sci. **11**, 121–138 (2017)
34. Takagi, T.: Fast RSA-type cryptosystem modulo $p^k q$. In: Krawczyk, H. (ed.) CRYPTO 1998. LNCS, vol. 1462, pp. 318–326. Springer, Heidelberg (1998). https://doi.org/10.1007/BFb0055738

35. Teşeleanu, G.: The case of small prime numbers versus the Joye-Libert cryptosystem. Mathematics **10**(9), 1577 (2022)
36. Teşeleanu, G.: The case of small prime numbers versus the Okamoto-Uchiyama cryptosystem. In: NuTMiC 2024, LNCS. Springer (2024)
37. Wiener, M.J.: Cryptanalysis of short RSA secret exponents. IEEE Trans. Inf. Theory **36**(3), 553–558 (1990)

Cyber-Physical Systems

A Comparison of Deep Learning Approaches for Power-Based Side-Channel Attacks

Roberto Capoferri[1](✉), Alessandro Barenghi[1], Luca Breveglieri[1], Niccolò Izzo[2], and Gerardo Pelosi[1]

[1] Politecnico di Milano, 20133 Milan, Italy
{roberto.capoferri,alessandro.barenghi,luca.breveglieri, gerardo.pelosi}@polimi.it

[2] Micron Semiconductor Italia Srl, 20871 Vimercate, MB, Italy
niccoloizzo@micron.com

Abstract. Side-channel attacks aim to recover cryptographic secrets by exploiting involuntary information channels coming from the computational platform of the targeted cipher implementation, e.g., power consumption or electromagnetic emissions. Among them deep learning based attacks have recently obtained great attention from both industry and academia, due to their greater efficiency and accuracy with respect to other methodologies. We provide a systematic comparison of the effectiveness of deep learning based attacks by considering different data acquisition and training methods. We also tackle the problem of the portability of the derived information leakage model, by analysing multiple instances of the same device, an ARM Cortex-M4 32-bit processor, running a software implementation of the AES-128 cipher. We complement the exploration of the attack space by considering datasets corresponding to cipher executions employing, for each run, either the same fixed secret key or a randomly chosen one. Furthermore, we generalize the set of inputs considered to build the model, by adding also the plaintexts fed to each cipher run. Finally, from the perspective of efficiency, we point out several unexpected and counterintuitive benchmark points.

Keywords: Side-channel Analysis · Deep Learning · Applied Cryptography

1 Introduction

Side-channel Attacks (SCAs) are a very relevant threat to the security of computing devices that offer cryptographic functions. There are various examples of attacks that target real-world devices, such as smartphones [21] or secure elements [36]. These kinds of attack require a physical access to the device, for measuring information leakage, which is a realistic scenario with the diffusion of mobile and IoT devices. Deep learning (DL) based SCAs against cryptographic implementations have become an active subject of research in recent years, resulting in similar if not better performance with respect to other types of profiled attacks, such as the template attacks [22].

L. Horn Iwaya et al. (Eds.): NordSec 2024, LNCS 15396, pp. 101–120, 2025.
https://doi.org/10.1007/978-3-031-79007-2_6

Attacks based on the analysis of the profile of both the dynamic power consumption or the electromagnetic radiation observed during the execution of a cryptographic algorithm (either in hardware or in software) define an important category of side-channel attacks. For each input provided to the cryptographic implementation at hand, assumed to be known in any possible detail (except for the value of the secret key), the numerical time series, a.k.a. *trace*, resulting from the measurement of one of the aforementioned parameters is recorded. The *divide-et-impera* observation at the core of the attack assumes that the secret key is composed as a long binary string that is processed, by the underlying computational platform, one (small) fragment at a time. Since the operation computed by employing the key fragment is known, it is easy to derive the switching activity (toggle count) resulting from its computation, by guessing the value of the key fragment and knowing the input fed into the algorithm. Repeating such a guessing for each possible value of the key fragment allows the attacker to derive a "model", which in turn can be correlated with the actual switching activity measured out from the execution of the target cryptographic implementation, for different inputs to the algorithm.

Over the years, numerous techniques have been designed to successfully execute a (secret-)key recovery attack. Many of these techniques, e.g., [9,13,20], make use of statistical tools to infer the value of the secret key, starting from both the model of a proper operation executed by the cryptographic algorithm and a set of traces. Other techniques, e.g., [11], assume the availability of multiple instances of the same computational platforms, therefore many analyses can be performed on just one of them to the end of quickly derive the secret-key employed in a device deployed on field. In recent years, the replacement of the statistical tools applied to execute a power-based SCA with deep-learning techniques has become more and more common, with interesting improvements in terms of effectiveness, robustness and performance [28].

Contributions. In this work, we provide a systematic comparison of the effectiveness of DL SCAs by considering different data acquisition and training methods. In particular, we explore the use of different datasets composed by traces collected from three distinct instances of the device under test, which is based on an ARM Cortex-M4 32-bit processor, running a software implementation of the AES-128 cipher. Traces are also distinguished (especially when training DL models) by whether they were measured from runs of the target cryptographic implementation in which the secret key was kept either fixed, or chosen randomly each time. The use of different devices is important to determine the degree of *portability* of the conclusions that can be drawn about the SCA vulnerability of a particular device instance, to the whole family of devices. In fact, common DL operations such as *tuning* and *training* are performed on device instances other than those that are being attacked. At the best of our knowledge, this is the first assessment of the application of DL SCAs techniques and their portability that addresses a (quite complex) 32-bit microcontroller as target computational platform. From the perspective of efficiency, we also point out several interesting (not expected and not intuitive) benchmark points during the exploration of the attack space generated by DL analyses. Finally, the source code [35] developed to perform our analysis, as well as the employed datasets [33,34], are made available for reproducibility.

Paper Organization. The rest of the paper is organized as follows. In Sect. 2 we present some background notions regarding deep learning techniques and side-channel analysis. In Sect. 3 and its subsections we describe the methodology defined for the exploration of the attack space, i.e., data collection, model selection and training. The results are described in Sect. 4, followed by a discussion of related work in Sect. 5. Finally, Sect. 6 reports our conclusions.

2 Background

In the following, we briefly recall the relevant notions about neural networks (NNs), which underlie every DL technique, and the main concepts regarding power-based SCAs, detailing how NNs are used in profiled side-channel attacks.

Deep Learning. It is a subset of machine learning that uses multi-layered NNs, to simulate a complex decision-making power. While there are several ways of building a neural network, in this work we consider the Multi-Layer Perceptron (MLP) [15,23] for its ability to learn nonlinear relationships among data and well modeled tasks such as classification, regression, and pattern recognition. An MLP is the extension of a single perceptron, i.e., the unit able to linearly combine its inputs and fed an evaluation function, by introducing multiple layers of fully connected neurons (each with a nonlinear kind of activation function [37]), and is organized in a feed-forward manner. As shown in Fig. 1, the structure of an MLP includes:

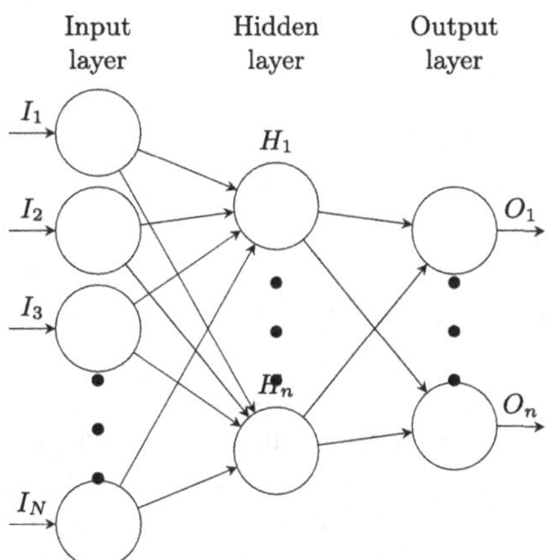

Fig. 1. Structure of an MLP

- An *input layer* $\mathbf{x} = [I_1, I_2, \dots, I_N]$, where each perceptron takes as input an input data feature I_j.
- $\ell \geq 1$ *hidden layers*. In each of these layers, each perceptron out of ℓ_k, $1 < k \leq \ell$, takes an input from each perceptron in layer $k-1$ and forwards its output to each perceptron in layer k. Any value moved from the i-th perceptron at layer $k-1$ to the j-th perceptron at layer $k-1$, is multiplied by a weight coefficient $w_{j,i}$, prior to be part of a summation computed by perception k, which is in turn fed into its activation function [37] to provide its output.

$$\mathbf{W}_1 = \begin{pmatrix} w_{1,1} & w_{1,2} & \cdots & w_{1,\ell_1} \\ w_{2,1} & w_{2,2} & \cdots & w_{2,\ell_1} \\ \cdots & \cdots & \cdots & \cdots \\ w_{N,1} & w_{N,2} & \cdots & w_{N,\ell_1} \end{pmatrix}, \quad \mathbf{W}_2, \quad \dots, \quad \mathbf{W}_\ell$$

- An *output layer* $\mathbf{y} = [y_1, y_2, \dots, y_n]$, where each perceptron yields a component of the final output. The number of nodes in the output layer depends on the nature of the task.

The weights in an MLP are updated during the training process, by using an optimization algorithm called *backpropagation algorithm*, often combined with the *Gradient Descent* (GD) procedure [2]: after feeding an input to the network, the output is compared against the desired result $\overline{y_i}$ and an error is computed by means of a *loss function*. For multi-class classification tasks, a typical loss function is the categorical cross-entropy L, which is defined as follows:

$$L = -\sum_{i=1}^{n} (\overline{y_i} - y_i) \cdot \log(y_i)$$

This process is repeated for each piece of data in the dataset used as training set, concluding an *epoch* of the training process. Multiple epochs are performed to minimize the loss function, thus finding the set of weight values that best models (fits) the training data, with the given structure of the MLP.

Side-Channel Attacks. They are a class of non-invasive security threats that exploit the observation of time series (a.k.a. *traces*) related to environmental parameters, e.g., execution time, dynamic power consumption [19] and electromagnetic radiation [30] (a.k.a. side-channel information), during the execution of a cryptographic primitive on a target computational platform, to derive the value of the secret parameters employed by the algorithm. The main idea consists of targeting an operation of the executed algorithm that involves the use of a portion of the secret key, guesses the value of such a key portion out of all possible values, and assesses the value of a *leakage function* fed with the said key hypothesis and the other possible inputs to the considered operation. The evaluation of such a leakage function is meant to mimic (or, better, to be directly proportional) to the actual side-channel measured from the executing device. In case of a power-based side-channel, the CMOS technology employed for most electronic devices suggests to use as leakage function related to the dynamic power consumption triggered by the switching activity induced by the data processing of the targeted operation [25], either the Hamming weight of the computed value or the computed value itself. The values of the leakage function for each possible guess of the considered key can be used in statistical and computational tools that are employed to correlate them with the values derived from the actual side-channel measurement taken from the device.

In *Non-profiled Side-channel Attacks*, the attacker targets directly the device she/he wants to break and collects traces from it. Examples of such techniques are Differential Power Analysis (DPA) [20] and Correlation Power Analysis (CPA) [8]. Our interest is towards another class of attacks called *Profiled Side-channel Attacks*, where the attacker is assumed to have access to another instance of the same device. In such a scenario, she/he performs her/his analysis on such an additional instance and computes a leakage model by taking as many measurement as necessary from the additional device (*profiling phase*). In a subsequent step, the attacker measures the side-channel from the attacked device only a few times (ideally, one time) to combine such data with the pre-computed model and so derive the secret key of the targeted device (*attack phase*). This is the base upon which Template Attacks (TA) [11] and Deep Learning SCAs are performed. The main difference between the two approaches is in the construction of the leakage model, which is performed applying a statistical approach for TAs, while a data-driven approach is followed when a DL technique is applied.

Deep Learning Side-Channel Attacks. These are a particular class of Profiled SCAs that leverage DL to retrieve the secret key, which has been shown to outperform traditional machine learning techniques [22]. Their advantage over other profiled methods is that there is no need to use data preprocessing, although sometimes it can improve performance [26], or to make assumptions about the noise distribution. The ability of NN to perform automatic feature extraction allows the profiling phase, also called training phase (we will use the two terms interchangeably), to be completely automated. In many cases only a few traces from the target device are required during the attack phase to fully retrieve the secret key [28]. While many approaches are possible, the two main types of model used are the Convolutional Neural Network (CNN), which has also shown resilience against temporal misalignment in the trace measurements [10], and the Multilayer Perceptron. In general one cannot *a priori* prefer one type of network architecture over another, as seen in other works [26].

To have a realistic attack scenario, the profiling and attack devices must be different, thus making sure that the resulting model is more general and that it does not overfit on the specific peculiarities of the device. This topic has been explored in detail in [6], concluding that the performance of an attack can be vastly overestimated if only a single device is considered during the training and testing phases. This is due to the *portability problem*. The authors propose the Multiple Device Model (MDM) as a solution to the problem, where the NN is trained using traces from different devices.

3 Methodology

The objective of this work is to evaluate different approaches to the dataset collection and training method in the context of DL-SCA.

For this purpose, we have collected datasets that use a fixed or random key from multiple devices of the same type, as detailed in Sect. 3.1, by covering the first round *SBox* operation of the AES cipher. To select the best model, multiple models are trained and evaluated by using a genetic algorithm to select the best set of hyperparameters from the best performing ones; this procedure is described in Sect. 3.2. After this selection, the best performing model is trained on the whole dataset available. Different options are explored. Details on the training process are in Sect. 3.3:

- **target**: observe the effect of using different target intermediates on the network performance. In particular we use the identity leakage model, by taking directly the output of the *SBox* as label for the network (`SBOX_OUT` scenario) or its Hamming weight (`HW_SO` scenario)
- **multi-device**: validate the work in [6], by checking whether our device is also affected by the portability problem, and see if the performance improves when using traces from multiple devices in the training set and attacking the same or different devices.
- **plaintext**: find out what happens when giving more information to the NN besides the raw trace data. Giving the plaintext used during the encryption as additional input to the NN is possible, since during the profiling phase the attacker has a full control on the device, and also during testing it is necessary to have this information when retrieving the key. This is also easy to implement and does not require additional preprocessing of data. To our knowledge, such an approach has not been tested yet in the literature. We indicate the two scenarios with "ptx" when the plaintext is used, and "no ptx" when it is not used.

All the evaluation work was carried out on a virtual machine running Debian 12, with 20 CPU cores, 128 GB of RAM and two Nvidia A100 40 GB GPUs. The computational times reported below refer to this system. The GPUs are used to train two models in parallel to speed up the results.

3.1 Dataset Collection

Figure 2 shows the Riscure Pinata [32] board employed in our experiments, which is based on an STM32F4 microcontroller with an ARM Cortex-M4, a widely used low-power processor that features a 32-bit architecture and is clocked at 168 MHz. The power consumption is measured with a current probe connected in series with the board, which asserts a trigger signal on one of its GPIO pins at the beginning of the *SBox* computation of the first AES round, and desserts it when the operation concludes, just before the *MixColumns* operation. The cipher is implemented in software without the use of countermeasures or optimizations,

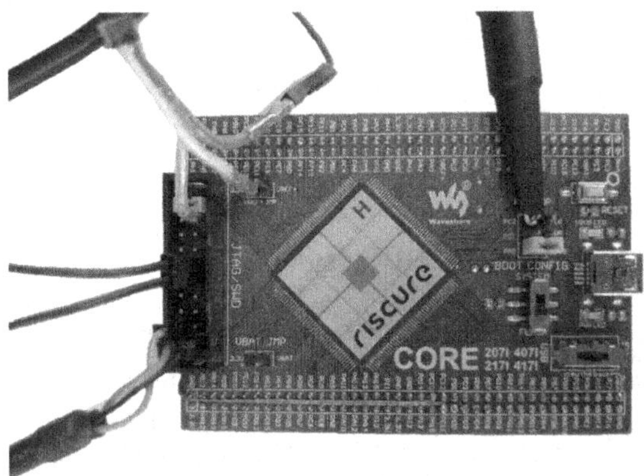

Fig. 2. Capturing setup. Blue, white and grey wires in the upper left are connected to the current probe to measure power consumption. In the bottom left there is the serial connection to the capturing machine. The probe to the right on the PC2 pin is the trigger connected to the scope (Color figure online)

and the *SBox* operation specifically is realized as a lookup in a precomputed table stored in memory. This signal is used by an oscilloscope, a Tektronik MSO58, to start the capture of the power trace from the current probe, and ensures that all the traces are temporally well aligned. The sampling rate is set to 625 MHz, with a vertical resolution of 8 bits. A single capture consists of 4,402 samples. The traces are then resampled at 168 MHz in order to reduce the number of input neurons to the NN, thus obtaining traces with 1,183 samples.

To be able to test the portability scenario, the traces were captured from three different boards, denoted as D1, D2 and D3. For each board the data collected consists of:

- 200,000 traces collected with a fixed 128-bit key, `key 0`, see Table 1. This is used in the fixed key scenario. Collection time is about 4 h.
- 200,000 traces collected using a randomly generated key for each capture, so that each trace uses a different key. This is used in the random key scenario. This is similar to the ASCAD [5] variable key dataset, however in ASCAD one third of the measured traces uses a single fixed key, while in our dataset all traces use random keys. Collection time is about 5 hours, longer than the fixed key scenario because an additional command is needed to set the key at every capture.
- 30,000 traces collected with a fixed 128-bit key, namely `key 1`, see Table 1, different from `key 0`. This is used during the testing phase to evaluate the performance of the network. Collection time is about 40 min.

The plaintext is selected randomly at each capture, and is stored in the trace metadata together with the key used and the resulting ciphertext. The software used to perform the capture is `Riscure Inspector` [31], so the traces are saved in the `.trs` format. The fixed key dataset is available at [33] and the random key one at [34].

Table 1. Fixed keys used

key	purpose	value (bytes)
key 0	training	98 84 37 ED BA 40 4D DF 83 27 59 57 43 DF D4 FF
key 1	testing	36 A0 0A BD F4 01 B9 4E 15 78 E1 B7 02 5E 58 F7

Table 2. Hyperparameter space

parameter	possible values
hidden layers	[1, 2, 3, 4, 5]
hidden neurons	[100, 200, 300, 400, 500]
dropout rate	[0.0, 0.1, 0.2, 0.3]
l2	$[0.0, 5 \cdot 10^{-2}, 1 \cdot 10^{-2}, 5 \cdot 10^{-3}, 1 \cdot 10^{-3}, 5 \cdot 10^{-4}, 1 \cdot 10^{-4}]$
optimizer	['adam', 'rmsprop', 'sgd']
learning rate	$[5 \cdot 10^{-3}, 1 \cdot 10^{-3}, 5 \cdot 10^{-4}, 1 \cdot 10^{-4}, 5 \cdot 10^{-5}, 1 \cdot 10^{-5}]$
batch size	[128, 256, 512, 1024]

Table 3. Parameters for the genetic algorithm

nGen	popSize	selPerc	scProb	mProb
20	15	30%	20%	20%

3.2 Hyperparameter Tuning

The MLP input layer has as many neurons as the samples in the trace, plus one extra neuron for the models trained with plaintext information, while the output layer can have either 256 neurons in the SBOX_OUT scenario or 9 neurons when targeting HW_SO. The SOFTMAX activation function gives a probability distribution over all the possible values of the selected target intermediate.

To build the network a hyperparameter tuning is performed, by searching for the optimal parameters in the space defined in Table 2. To perform the tuning a genetic algorithm [24] is employed. The specific genetic algorithm chosen here is the one used by Matt Harvey et al. [17]. Settings for the algorithm are reported in Table 3. The algorithm starts by generating *popSize* different networks by selecting a random combination of hyperparameters from the *hpSpace*, reported in Table 2. Then, each element of the initial population is used to build an MLP, which is successively trained on the training set and evaluated on the validation set. The validation loss of each network is stored and used to compare the performances of all the networks in order to select the top *selProb* best performing ones, and also some bad performing ones with *scProb* probability, to add diversity to the population. The selected combinations are used to generate *offsprings* that will compose the new population. Offspring combinations are composed by randomly choosing from the selected parents, but sometimes a random *muta-*

Table 4. Selected hyperparameters for all the possible cases

dataset	target	variant	n. devices	layers	neurons	dropout	l2
fixed key	SBOX OUT	no ptx	1	4	200	0.1	$1 \cdot 10^{-2}$
			2	4	300	0.2	$1 \cdot 10^{-2}$
		ptx	1	4	500	0.0	0.0
			2	5	200	0.0	0.0
	HW SO	no ptx	1	4	100	0.1	$1 \cdot 10^{-3}$
			2	5	500	0.3	$5 \cdot 10^{-4}$
		ptx	1	3	200	0.1	0.0
			2	5	300	0.0	$1 \cdot 10^{-4}$
random key	SBOX OUT	no ptx	1	4	200	0.1	$1 \cdot 10^{-4}$
			2	4	300	0.2	0.0
		ptx	1	5	400	0.2	0.0
			2	5	400	0.3	0.0
	HW SO	no ptx	1	5	400	0.2	0.0
			2	5	500	0.3	0.0
		ptx	1	4	400	0.3	$5 \cdot 10^{-3}$
			2	4	100	0.0	$5 \cdot 10^{-3}$

tion can happen to some hyperparameters with probability *mProb*. In this case a random value from Table 2 is selected. This process is repeated *nGen* times, and at the end the best performing configuration is selected, according to the validation loss. The results of the selection are reported in Table 4. Optimizer, learning rate and batch size are not included due to lack of space. The optimizer selected was always `adam`. The time required to complete the tuning varies considerably, depending on the complexity of the models that are selected during the process, ranging from a few hours to almost a full day per case. Considering all the different cases that have been tested, this is the most time consuming part of the process.

3.3 Training

After choosing the optimal model, a neural network with the selected hyperparameters is built and trained on the dataset. The dataset composed of 200, 000 traces (fixed key or random key, depending on the specific model) is loaded and labeled according to the selected target (`SBOX_OUT` or `HW_SO`), then the traces are randomly shuffled. If multiple devices are used in training, the total number of traces is always 200, 000, coming in equal amount from every device, and selecting a random subset of all the available traces from each one.

The loaded data is then divided into a training set and a validation set, using a 90/10 training/validation split, and scaled to fit in the $[0-1]$ range as follows.

$$X_{\texttt{scaled}} = \big(X - \mathbf{min}(X)\big) \; / \; \big(\mathbf{max}(X) - \mathbf{min}(X)\big)$$

If the plaintext is used, the corresponding byte is appended at the end of the trace. We tried both scaling it to the same range and not doing that. The networks trained without scaling the plaintext consistently perform slightly better than the ones with the scaled plaintext. Therefore, we avoided scaling the appended byte in all the experiments. At this point the neural network is built according to the selected hyperparameters, which specify the number of layers, the number of neurons and all the other network parameters. All the code related to the NN was implemented by using TENSORFLOW 2.14.0 [1] and KERAS 2.14.0 [12], and it is available at [35]. Some regularization options are also enabled, which help in preventing overfitting and render the network more robust:

- **Dropout:** which percentage of neurons to turn off in a layer during training. This value is tuned during the hyperparameter search.
- **L2 regularization**: limits the value of the weights by adding a penalty to larger values. This value is also tuned.
- **Batch normalization** [18]: normalizes the input to each layer, thus helping in stabilizing the training process.
- **Early stopping** [29]: monitors training and validation accuracy, and stops the training process if overfitting is detected, i.e., when the training accuracy keeps increasing but the validation accuracy starts decreasing.

The resulting network is trained on the training set for 200 epochs or until the early stopping monitor blocks the process, targeting the fifth byte of the AES key. Learning rate scheduling is used to reduce the learning rate when the validation loss becomes stable.

3.4 Evaluation Metric

The Guessing Entropy (GE) is often used during the evaluation of the attack [38]. It is defined as the average rank of the correct key byte when sorting the key predictions by their probability value in ascending order. The probabilities from different predictions are multiplied together [39]. Ideally, the more traces are added, the more the compound probability of the correct key among all predictions should increase, thus leading to a GE of 0 (first place in the ranking is at index 0). The graphs reported in Sect. 4 report the evolution of the correct key position from 1 to 300 traces used in the prediction, thus highlighting when it reaches 0. Since we have $30,000$ test traces, it is possible to divide them in 100 disjoint sets of 300 traces and average the results. The number of traces required for the GE to converge is an indicator of the performance of the network. A better model will need fewer traces to correctly guess the key byte.

4 Performance Results

In this section, the attack performance results are presented, classified by the dataset and training method used. Both attack targets `SBOX_OUT` and `HW_SO` are considered, in each section, highlighting similarities and differences. Finally, the results are summarized in Tables 5 and 6. All the graphs are structured in the same way so that they can be compared easily, by reporting the average GE value w.r.t. the number of traces used to perform the attack. All the figures are also available in svg format on the code repository [35], so that one can easily download and inspect them at a higher resolution.

In each graph there are three color-coded lines, which represent three different scenarios, with a slightly different interpretation depending on whether the model was trained with a fixed or random key. In the fixed key case we consider the same scenario as in [6], excluding the "same device and same key" one since it is trivially unrealistic:

- The green line, labeled `same_devs_diff_key`, represents the scenario that does not consider portability, as the targeted device is the same as the profiling one, while the test traces are collected using a different fixed key.
- The blue line, labeled `diff_devs_same_key`, identifies the case in which the device under attack is different from the one used in training, but the attack traces used are collected using the same key. This is only used to compare against the full portability scenario, detailed below.
- The red line, labeled `diff_devs_diff_key`, represents the full portability scenario, where during the attack both the device and the key used are different from the ones in the training set. This is the realistic attack scenario and the one that should be used to evaluate the attack performance.

In the random key case we also have the three graphs, but the concept of same/different key no longer applies. Instead, the three scenarios become:

- The green line, labeled `same_devs_key_1`, targets the same device used during training, by means of traces captured with `key 1`.
- The blue line, labeled `diff_devs_key_0`, targets different devices from the ones used during training, by means of traces captured with `key 0`.
- The red line, labeled `diff_devs_key_1`, targets different devices from the ones used during training, by means of traces captured with `key 1`. These last two scenarios are useful to check whether performance changes significantly depending on the specific target key.

In every case the vertical dashed line represents the number of traces needed to achieve $GE < 0.5$, and that is the value reported in the legend.

4.1 Training with Fixed-Key Dataset

In Fig. 3 we can see the evolution of the GE with an increasing number of traces. This is the most common case that matches the expectations and results in the related literature, employing also similar or different computational platforms, e.g., 8-bit microcontrollers. Indeed, we can see that both methods can successfully recover the correct key byte, with the `SBOX_OUT` performing slightly better than the `HW_SO`. The portability concern is also evident here, as the performance

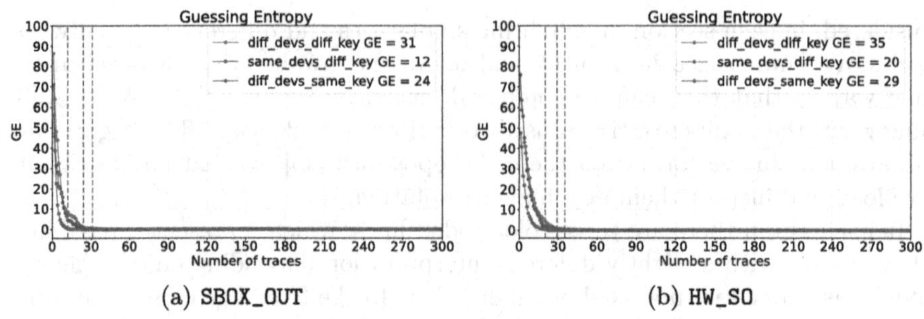

(a) `SBOX_OUT` (b) `HW_SO`

Fig. 3. Fixed key, training with 1 device

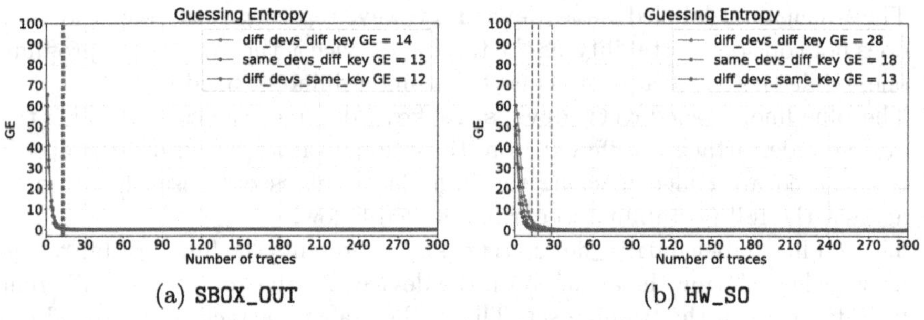

(a) `SBOX_OUT` (b) `HW_SO`

Fig. 4. Fixed key, training with 2 devices

decreases when attacking a different device from the one used during the profiling phase.

When using the multi-device model, taking traces from two different devices to train the network, we can see in Fig. 4 that the performance increases, requiring fewer traces to recover the key. This shows that, at least for a fixed training key dataset, using multiple devices for profiling is to be preferred, thus confirming the results found in [6]. Also when considering the `SBOX_OUT`, we can see that the portability becomes much less prominent, with all three graphs becoming almost identical, showing that the obtained model is more general and can be applied to different devices without a significant performance hit.

When adding the plaintext information during the training, the performance of the network gets worse, as reported in Fig. 5. This was not expected, as in principle more information should be beneficial to the network. In particular we see a confirmation of this in two different cases. On one hand, training on the `SBOX_OUT` target appears to be overfitting on the specific key value, since when guessing against traces taken from another device but using the same key, the line in blue, the network only needs one trace to correctly recover it. Further investigating the motivation underlying this behaviour, we found that the weights of the network are heavily biased in correspondence of the plaintext information. This may lead to an underestimation of the leakage due to the key. On the other hand, the cases against a different key show a decrease in

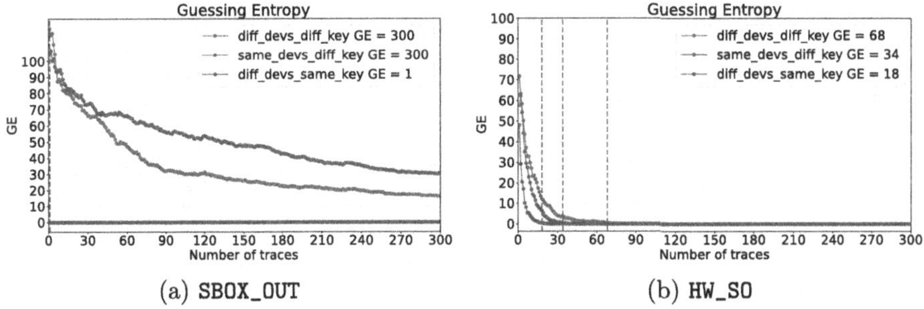

(a) SBOX_OUT (b) HW_SO

Fig. 5. Fixed key, training with 1 device and plaintext

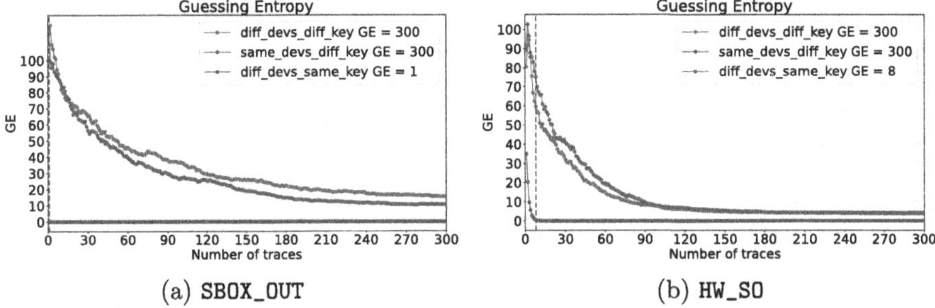

(a) SBOX_OUT (b) HW_SO

Fig. 6. Fixed key, training with 2 devices and plaintext

performance of more than one order of magnitude. For the HW_SO we also see a decrease in performance, but not so severe, and the network is still able to learn how to extract the key in all three cases, and the portability scenario in red still proves to be more difficult than the other two.

When considering multiple devices, SBOX_OUT behaves the same, while HW_SO gets worse, as it can be seen in Fig. 6, with two out of three scenarios not converging to $GE = 0$ but flattening out at $GE = 5$. Counterintuitively, we repeatedly confirmed that when using a dataset with a fixed key and providing the plaintext information to the network, this yields to worse performance overall.

4.2 Training with Random-Key Dataset

In the case of random key, it is evident that the performance is worse both for SBOX_OUT and HW_SO. The trend of the former performing better than the latter is still present here. The interesting behaviour that appears from the graphs, is that in this case the performance of the model also depends on the key used during testing. For instance, in Fig. 7 using `key 0` performs better than using `key 1` (Fig. 8).

However, we also maintain the problem of the portability when training with a single device. In fact, the GE converges to 0 faster when attacking traces captured with `key 1` on the same device used during training, while it needs

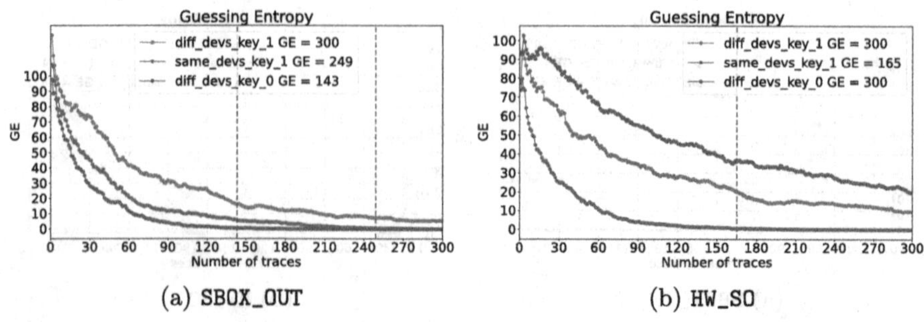

(a) SBOX_OUT (b) HW_SO

Fig. 7. Random key, training with 1 device

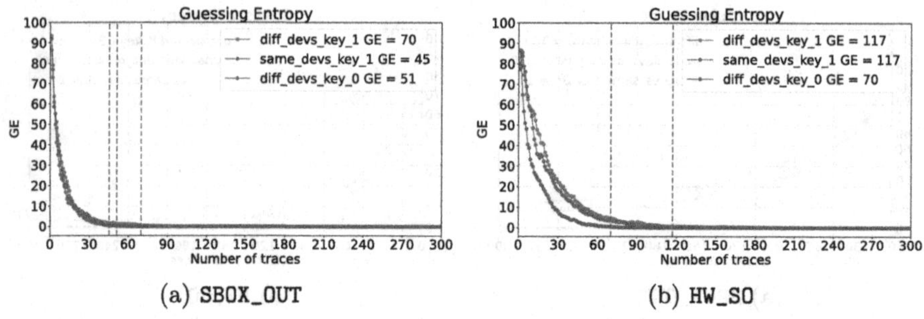

(a) SBOX_OUT (b) HW_SO

Fig. 8. Random key, training with 2 devices

more traces when attacking the same `key 1` but with traces from a different device. Similarly to the fixed key scenario, also when using a random key the performance increases when using the Multi-Device Model, but in this case the increase is more significant, although w.r.t. fixed key the overall performance is still lower. We see a difference from the fixed key scenario when considering what happens with the plaintext. When considering only one training device, the performance increases in both SBOX_OUT and HW_SO w.r.t. not using the plaintext. This contrasts what was seen with the fixed key, where performance became significantly worse. When considering two training devices (see Fig. 10), in the HW_SO the network seems to learn with greater difficulty, requiring a great number of traces to lower the guessing entropy. Instead, when considering the SBOX_OUT case the performance is better than without plaintext, and approaches the performance of the fixed key case, also closing the gap in the portability scenario, as the network requires just five more traces to correctly guess the key when considering a different target device (Fig. 9).

4.3 Comparisons

Here we summarize all the guessing entropy behaviours discussed in Sect. 4 in Tables 5 and 6. We note that having a dataset of traces collected using a single fixed key is the best option, both for a single or multiple training devices.

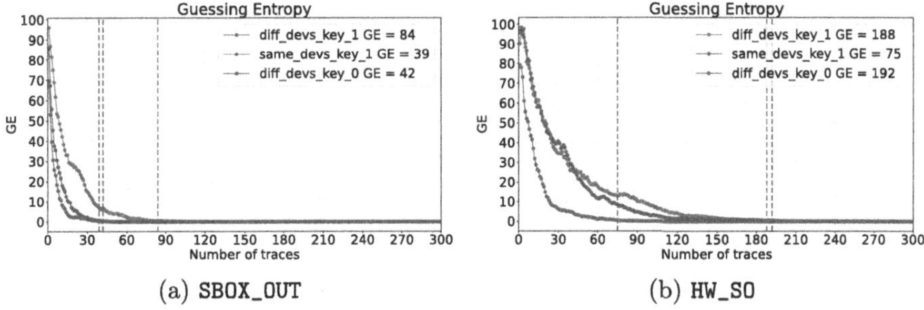

(a) `SBOX_OUT` (b) `HW_SO`

Fig. 9. Random key, training with 1 device and plaintext

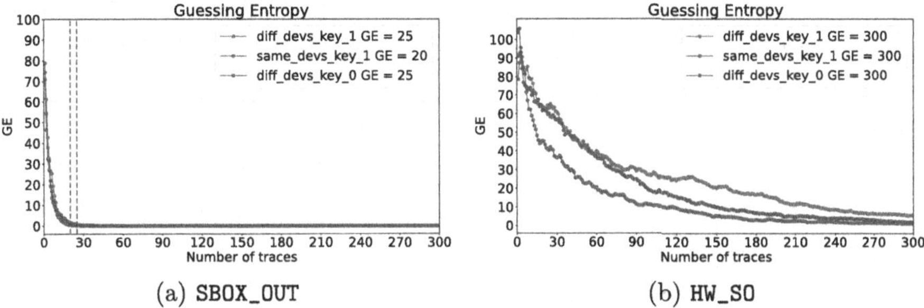

(a) `SBOX_OUT` (b) `HW_SO`

Fig. 10. Random key, training with 2 devices and plaintext

Unexpectedly, the use of the plaintext information should be avoided in this case. It can instead be a great advantage when using a dataset collected using random keys, depending on the target leakage function that is selected to train the network and on the number of devices used.

5 Related Work

There is a number of publicly available datasets that target AES-128, both with and without countermeasures in place [4,5,7,14,16], but all of them only capture traces from a single device for both the training and testing phases, making them unfit for testing the portability scenario. The dataset that we sampled and used in our analyses, which we also made publicly available in [33,34], provides the advantage of including measurements from a set of distinct instances of the same device. This feature makes our dataset more suitable for testing realistic attack scenarios.

Concerning the definition of the leakage function as the Hamming weight of the result of the considered operation, i.e., SBOX output, our conclusions align with those in [27], that is, the performance of DL-based attacks decreases because of the imbalance induced by the set of Hamming weight values, as they allow to gather the dataset samples in nine classes with quite different cardinalities.

Table 5. Results for the 'fixed key' dataset. No. of traces to get $GE < 0.5$

target	variant	n. devices	same_devs_diff_key	diff_devs_same_key	diff_devs_diff_key
SBOX OUT	no ptx	1	12	24	31
		2	13	12	14
	ptx	1	>300	1	>300
		2	>300	1	>300
HW SO	no ptx	1	20	29	35
		2	18	13	28
	ptx	1	34	18	68
		2	>300	8	>300

Table 6. Results for the 'random key' dataset. No. of traces to get $GE < 0.5$

target	variant	n. devices	same_devs_key_1	diff_devs_key_0	diff_devs_key_1
SBOX OUT	no ptx	1	249	143	>300
		2	45	51	70
	ptx	1	39	42	84
		2	20	25	25
HW SO	no ptx	1	165	>300	>300
		2	117	70	117
	ptx	1	75	192	188
		2	>300	>300	>300

Concerning the portability of the DL-SCA vulnerability proved when considering a single device instance or multiple device instances during the training phase, we mostly confirm the results provided in [6], where the attackers considered an AES-128 software implementation for an 8-bit microprocessor clocked at only 16 MHz (in contrast to our 32-bit CPU clocked at 168 MHz). Indeed we show that, when only one device is used for profiling, attacking a device different from the profiled one leads to a decrease in the performance of the model. We also show that using traces from multiple device instances for training, in general, helps the model to better generalize and to become more portable.

In our study, see Fig. 10b, a notable discrepancy is highlighted by the use, during the training phase, of the plaintext values fed to each cipher run and of traces obtained with a random key, when a worsening of the attack performance is observed only in the case of a dataset composed by traces coming from multiple device instances (two).

6 Concluding Remarks

We have provided a systematic comparison of different approaches to train an MLP for power-based SCA against a software implementation of AES. We have tested the effect of changing different parameters, such as the type of traces used, i.e., with fixed or random key, the target leakage function used, and the usage of plaintext information. We have validated results on a 32-bit CPU platform, namely the Riscure Pinata. In addition, we have provided a new study on the use of the plaintext information during the training, thus showing that its influence depends on other factors, like the choice of target or the available data. In the end, using the plaintext provides a benefit when dealing with datasets collected using a random key. We have found that when collecting a dataset, using a single fixed key is the better choice in terms of attack performance, but that it is also possible to get a similar, albeit lower, performance by using random keys and providing plaintext information. We have performed our tests also considering the portability of the model, and we have confirmed that using traces from multiple training devices helps in building a better model. Finally, we provide a new dataset to perform further studies concerning the portability on a complex target, thus filling the gap present in the currently available public datasets.

Future work will consider protected AES implementations, e.g., by masking, and the effect of selecting other points of interest (other than the *SBox* output) from the traces. It would also be interesting to study the behaviour of optimized AES implementations. In all these cases, different intermediate values need to be chosen, thus leading to the use of different and potentially more complex leakage models. Further experimentation is needed to evaluate the attack effort required. This also applies if we consider ciphers other than AES. Since the leakage behaviour is tightly related to the microarchitectural details of the processor [3], our results are representative for targets based around the same processor, i.e., Cortex M4, which is widely diffused. Processors with a significantly different microarchitecture may exhibit other behaviours.

Acknowledgments. This work was supported in part by project SERICS (PE00000014) under the NRRP MUR program funded by the EU - NGEU. We also thank Luca Castellazzi for his initial realization of our NN models.

References

1. Abadi, M., et al.: TensorFlow: Large-Scale Machine Learning on Heterogeneous Systems (2015). https://www.tensorflow.org/. Software available from tensorflow.org
2. Aggarwal, C.C.: Neural Networks and Deep Learning - A Textbook. Springer (2018). https://doi.org/10.1007/978-3-319-94463-0
3. Barenghi, A., Pelosi, G.: Side-channel security of superscalar CPUs: evaluating the impact of micro-architectural features. In: Proceedings of the 55th Annual Design Automation Conference, DAC 2018, San Francisco, CA, USA, 24–29 June 2018, pp. 120:1–120:6. ACM (2018). https://doi.org/10.1145/3195970.3196112
4. Bellizia, D., Bronchain, O., Cassiers, G., Momin, C., Standaert, F.X., Udvarhelyi, B.: Spook SCA CTF (2021). https://doi.org/10.14428/DVN/W2SV5G

5. Benadjila, R., Prouff, E., Strullu, R., Cagli, E., Dumas, C.: Deep learning for side-channel analysis and introduction to ASCAD database. J. Cryptogr. Eng. **10**(2), 163–188 (2020). https://doi.org/10.1007/S13389-019-00220-8
6. Bhasin, S., Chattopadhyay, A., Heuser, A., Jap, D., Picek, S., Shrivastwa, R.R.: Mind the portability: a warriors guide through realistic profiled side-channel analysis. In: 27th Annual Network and Distributed System Security Symposium, NDSS 2020, San Diego, California, USA, 23–26 February 2020. The Internet Society (2020). https://www.ndss-symposium.org/ndss-paper/mind-the-portability-a-warriors-guide-through-realistic-profiled-side-channel-analysis/
7. Bhasin, S., Jap, D., Picek, S.: Repository for AES_HD (2018). https://github.com/AESHD/AES_HD_Dataset
8. Brier, E., Clavier, C., Olivier, F.: Optimal statistical power analysis. IACR Cryptol. ePrint Arch. 152 (2003). http://eprint.iacr.org/2003/152
9. Brier, E., Clavier, C., Olivier, F.: Correlation power analysis with a leakage model. In: Joye, M., Quisquater, J.-J. (eds.) CHES 2004. LNCS, vol. 3156, pp. 16–29. Springer, Heidelberg (2004). https://doi.org/10.1007/978-3-540-28632-5_2
10. Cagli, E., Dumas, C., Prouff, E.: Convolutional neural networks with data augmentation against jitter-based countermeasures. In: Fischer, W., Homma, N. (eds.) CHES 2017. LNCS, vol. 10529, pp. 45–68. Springer, Cham (2017). https://doi.org/10.1007/978-3-319-66787-4_3
11. Chari, S., Rao, J.R., Rohatgi, P.: Template attacks. In: Kaliski, B.S., Koç, K., Paar, C. (eds.) CHES 2002. LNCS, vol. 2523, pp. 13–28. Springer, Heidelberg (2003). https://doi.org/10.1007/3-540-36400-5_3
12. Chollet, F., et al.: Keras (2015). https://keras.io
13. Clavier, C., Feix, B., Gagnerot, G., Roussellet, M., Verneuil, V.: Horizontal correlation analysis on exponentiation. In: Soriano, M., Qing, S., López, J. (eds.) ICICS 2010. LNCS, vol. 6476, pp. 46–61. Springer, Heidelberg (2010). https://doi.org/10.1007/978-3-642-17650-0_5
14. Coron, J.S., Kizhvatov, I.: Trace Sets with Random Delays - AES_RD (2009). https://github.com/ikizhvatov/randomdelays-traces
15. Cybenko, G.: Approximation by superpositions of a sigmoidal function. Math. Control Signals Syst. **2**(4), 303–314 (1989). https://doi.org/10.1007/BF02551274
16. Fei, Y.: Northeastern University TeSCASE Dataset - AES_HD_MM (2014). https://chest.coe.neu.edu/?current_page=POWER_TRACE_LINK&software=ptmasked
17. Harvey, M., Heckscher, N.: Evolve a neural network with a genetic algorithm (2017). https://github.com/harvitronix/neural-network-genetic-algorithm
18. Ioffe, S., Szegedy, C.: Batch normalization: accelerating deep network training by reducing internal covariate shift. In: Bach, F.R., Blei, D.M. (eds.) Proceedings of the 32nd International Conference on Machine Learning, ICML 2015, Lille, France, 6–11 July 2015. JMLR Workshop and Conference Proceedings, vol. 37, pp. 448–456. JMLR.org (2015). http://proceedings.mlr.press/v37/ioffe15.html
19. Kocher, P., Jaffe, J., Jun, B.: Differential power analysis. In: Wiener, M. (ed.) CRYPTO 1999. LNCS, vol. 1666, pp. 388–397. Springer, Heidelberg (1999). https://doi.org/10.1007/3-540-48405-1_25
20. Kocher, P.C., Jaffe, J., Jun, B., Rohatgi, P.: Introduction to differential power analysis. J. Cryptogr. Eng. **1**(1), 5–27 (2011). https://doi.org/10.1007/S13389-011-0006-Y
21. Lisovets, O., Knichel, D., Moos, T., Moradi, A.: Let's take it offline: boosting brute-force attacks on iPhone's user authentication through SCA. IACR Trans. Cryptogr.

Hardw. Embed. Syst. **2021**(3), 496–519 (2021). https://doi.org/10.46586/TCHES.V2021.I3.496-519

22. Maghrebi, H., Portigliatti, T., Prouff, E.: Breaking cryptographic implementations using deep learning techniques. In: Carlet, C., Hasan, M.A., Saraswat, V. (eds.) SPACE 2016. LNCS, vol. 10076, pp. 3–26. Springer, Cham (2016). https://doi.org/10.1007/978-3-319-49445-6_1
23. McCulloch, W.S., Pitts, W.H.: A logical calculus of the ideas immanent in nervous activity. In: Boden, M.A. (ed.) The Philosophy of Artificial Intelligence. Oxford Readings in Philosophy, pp. 22–39. Oxford University Press, Oxford (1990)
24. Mitchell, M.: An Introduction to Genetic Algorithms. MIT Press, Cambridge (1998)
25. Ng, L.L., Yeap, K.H., Goh, M.W.C., Dakulagi, V.: Power consumption in CMOS circuits. In: Song, H.Z., Yeap, K.H., Goh, M.W.C. (eds.) Electromagnetic Field in Advancing Science and Technology, chap. 5. IntechOpen, Rijeka (2022). https://doi.org/10.5772/intechopen.105717
26. Perin, G., Wu, L., Picek, S.: Exploring feature selection scenarios for deep learning-based side-channel analysis. IACR Trans. Cryptogr. Hardw. Embed. Syst. **2022**(4), 828–861 (2022). https://doi.org/10.46586/TCHES.V2022.I4.828-861
27. Picek, S., Heuser, A., Jovic, A., Bhasin, S., Regazzoni, F.: The curse of class imbalance and conflicting metrics with machine learning for side-channel evaluations. IACR Trans. Cryptogr. Hardw. Embed. Syst. **2019**(1), 209–237 (2019). https://doi.org/10.13154/TCHES.V2019.I1.209-237
28. Picek, S., Perin, G., Mariot, L., Wu, L., Batina, L.: SoK: deep learning-based physical side-channel analysis. ACM Comput. Surv. **55**(11), 227:1–227:35 (2023). https://doi.org/10.1145/3569577
29. Prechelt, L.: Early stopping - but when? In: Montavon, G., Orr, G.B., Müller, K. (eds.) Neural Networks: Tricks of the Trade. LNCS, 2nd edn, vol. 7700, pp. 53–67. Springer, Heidelberg (2012). https://doi.org/10.1007/978-3-642-35289-8_5
30. Quisquater, J.-J., Samyde, D.: ElectroMagnetic analysis (EMA): measures and counter-measures for smart cards. In: Attali, I., Jensen, T. (eds.) E-smart 2001. LNCS, vol. 2140, pp. 200–210. Springer, Heidelberg (2001). https://doi.org/10.1007/3-540-45418-7_17
31. Riscure: Inspector (2024). https://www.riscure.com/security-tools/inspector-sca/
32. Riscure: Pinata (2024). https://www.riscure.com/products/pinata-training-target/
33. Capoferri, R.: Fixed-key dataset for three Riscure Pinata devices (2024). https://zenodo.org/records/11443025
34. Capoferri, R.: Random-key dataset for three Riscure Pinata devices (2024). https://zenodo.org/records/11199202
35. Capoferri, R.: Source code and models (2024). https://github.com/RobertoCapoferri/DLSCA-article
36. Roche, T.: EUCLEAK. Cryptology ePrint Archive, Paper 2024/1380 (2024). https://eprint.iacr.org/2024/1380
37. Silva, T.C., Zhao, L.: Machine Learning in Complex Networks. Springer, Heidelberg (2016). https://doi.org/10.1007/978-3-319-17290-3
38. Standaert, F.-X., Malkin, T.G., Yung, M.: A unified framework for the analysis of side-channel key recovery attacks. In: Joux, A. (ed.) EUROCRYPT 2009. LNCS, vol. 5479, pp. 443–461. Springer, Heidelberg (2009). https://doi.org/10.1007/978-3-642-01001-9_26

39. Wu, L., et al.: On the attack evaluation and the generalization ability in profiling side-channel analysis. Cryptology ePrint Archive, Paper 2020/899 (2020). https://eprint.iacr.org/2020/899

Binary-Level Code Injection for Automated Tool Support on the ESP32 Platform

Benjamin Plach, Matthias Börsig(✉), Maximilian Müller, Roland Gröll, Martin Dukek, and Ingmar Baumgart

FZI Research Center for Information Technology, Karlsruhe, Germany
publications@benjamin-plach.de,
{boersig,m.mueller,groell,dukek,baumgart}@fzi.de

Abstract. The analysis and testing of proprietary ESP32 firmware by independent security experts is often hampered by the lack of specialized tools that provide the necessary capabilities and ease of use to effectively support these tasks.

This paper presents a novel binary rewriting framework that addresses this challenge by allowing additional instructions to be inserted into ESP32 firmware without altering its original functionality. The framework leverages two already existing tools, Esptool and ESP32-Image-Parser, to extract firmware from ESP32 devices and convert it to ELF format, simplifying both the implementation of the framework and the development of subsequent tools.

In addition, an assembler has been developed to encode Xtensa assembly instructions without the need for linking the code afterward, facilitating the development of patch code. The framework includes a new patching methodology adapted from x86 patching tactics to the Xtensa architecture. These tactics have been implemented in a binary rewriting framework capable of inserting code at almost arbitrary locations without affecting the original firmware functionality.

A proof of concept tool that inserts fuzzing instrumentation was implemented to demonstrate the utility of the framework. This tool successfully integrates functional coverage information into ESP32 binaries. This framework represents a significant advancement in the tools available for firmware analysis and security testing of ESP32 devices.

Keywords: Static Binary Rewriting · Internet of Things · Embedded Systems · ESP32 · Xtensa · Microcontroller Security · Fuzzing

1 Introduction

The ESP32 platform has become increasingly prominent in the growing market for Internet of Things (IoT) devices due to its capabilities and cost-effectiveness. The proliferation of these devices has also led to an increased focus on their security. IoT devices are particularly vulnerable to security issues due to several

L. Horn Iwaya et al. (Eds.): NordSec 2024, LNCS 15396, pp. 121–138, 2025.
https://doi.org/10.1007/978-3-031-79007-2_7

factors: The rush to bring products to market often results in inadequate security testing, there is a general lack of regular patching and the mechanisms for applying patches are often ineffective.

Independent security testing is important as it offers an unbiased evaluation of the security posture of devices. Manufacturers may overlook or underestimate vulnerabilities. Independent testing can circumvent these issues, providing a more thorough and objective assessment. Moreover, external testers, utilizing techniques like automated fuzzing, can probe systems in ways that internal teams might not consider, uncovering hidden vulnerabilities.

We propose to adopt a solution that involves the insertion of instrumentation into existing binaries via binary rewriting. This introduced approach automates the process of security testing by modifying the binary code of the firmware to include additional code that facilitates fuzzing and vulnerability detection. A crucial element of our method is utilizing binary rewriting while maintaining the original control flow. By preserving the original program flow, our technique ensures that the functionality and behavior of the firmware remain unchanged while still allowing the insertion of necessary instrumentation for effective fuzzing.

In this paper, we detail the method for binary-level code injection on the ESP32 platform. Our goal is to fill a gap in current security testing tools and provide a robust framework for improving the security of IoT devices built on the ESP32 platform.

Our contribution includes the development of a binary rewriting framework designed to modify and extend existing firmware binaries without disrupting their overall functionality. This includes the ability to insert patches into specific sections of the binary, primarily the `.flash.text` section. Additionally, we adapted patching tactics originally developed for the Complex Instruction Set Computer (CISC)-based x86-64 architecture to suit the Reduced Instruction Set Computer (RISC)-based Xtensa Instruction Set Architecture (ISA). We implemented a proof of concept to show the viability of these tactics. Lastly, our work includes assembler integration. We support a limited set of Xtensa ISA instructions and directives in the current assembler framework, with plans to expand this capability or integrate an external assembler to support a broader range of instructions.

2 Related Work

Duck et al. developed E9Patch, a static binary rewriter that capitalizes on the trampoline rewriting technique, which relies on the x86 long relative jump opcode [5]. E9Patch makes only minimal assumptions about the binary it alters, specifically avoiding dependencies on the binary's source language, compiler, debug information, or explicit control flow analysis. It does assume that patched instructions are neither accessed as data nor modified by the program itself, ruling out self-modifying code or overlapping instructions.

This approach has shaped our research direction, inspiring the method we adopted. Unlike E9Patch, which is tailored for x86-64 Linux binaries, our work focuses on adapting similar techniques to the Xtensa architecture of ESP32 devices, addressing specific challenges and leveraging unique opportunities in this context.

For the task of binary rewriting, various tools have been developed for different architectures and purposes. Performance optimization is the primary focus for tools like Lancet [12], Vulcan [1], and OM [15], while security hardening is targeted by others such as Zipr [8], RevARM [9], and CFI CaRE [11].

Binary rewriters are classified into dynamic and static types. Dynamic rewriters, like Dynamo [2], STRATA [14], and Pin [10], modify code at runtime, right before execution, which makes them unsuitable for embedding instrumentation into the firmware of ESP32 devices due to the need for pre-runtime modification.

Static binary rewriters, in turn, can be subdivided into categories based on their approach and functionality. Intermediate Representation (IR) rewriters such as mctoll [18] and revng [6] utilize LLVM as an intermediate language, enabling certain types of code manipulation that are beneficial for analysis and optimization. Meanwhile, reassemblable disassemblers like ddisasm [7], Retrowrite [4], and Uroboros [16] focus on the ability to disassemble and then reassemble binary code, offering a different set of capabilities. However, a common limitation across both categories is their inability to preserve the original structure of the binary. Maintaining the original structure is crucial for gaining useful insights from security testing.

Despite the rich ecosystem of binary rewriters detailed in comprehensive surveys by Wenzel et al. [17] and Schulte et al. [13], none of these existing approaches support the Xtensa architecture used in ESP32 devices. This highlights a gap that our work aims to address by adapting and extending binary rewriting techniques specifically for the Xtensa architecture.

3 Background

This section gives an overview about ESP23 firmware images and the code location problem that arises when trying to rewrite binaries as well as different categories of binary rewriting, i.e., static and dynamic rewriting.

3.1 ESP32

The ESP32 is a versatile, low-power and cost-effective microcontroller family from Espressif Systems, aimed at IoT applications. As an advancement over the ESP8266, it offers enhanced functionality with various options such as single or dual Xtensa LX6 cores, Xtensa LX7 cores, or a RISC-V core, along with various memory configurations. The ESP32 also features integrated Wi-Fi and Bluetooth, alongside a set of peripherals such as touch sensors, SD card interfaces, and Ethernet.

Firmware Images. An overview of the ESP32 firmware image can be found in Fig. 1. It contains three main components: the bootloader, the partition table, and at least one app partition containing the application code. The bootloader

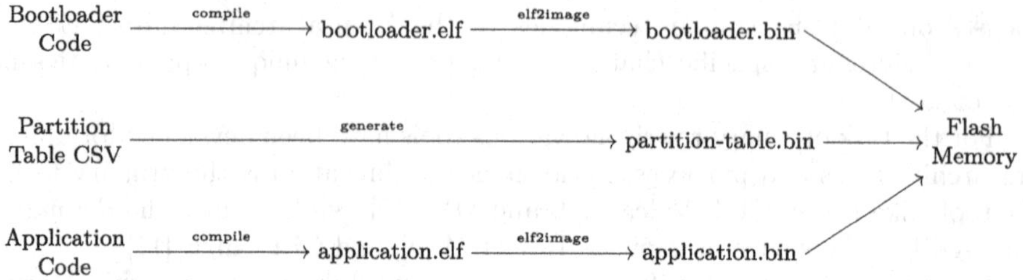

Fig. 1. The build and flash process

and application code are compiled into Executable and Linkable Format (ELF) binaries and are then converted into a binary format suitable for the ESP32.

These binaries are flashed together to the microcontroller. Although they are not combined into a single image, the bootloader, partition table, and application image are collectively referred to as the firmware image in this paper. Modifying or swapping any of these components typically results in a failure of the firmware to function correctly.

Bootloader. The bootloader runs first when the ESP32 is powered up or reset. It initializes the hardware, sets the clock, configures the memory, and verifies the integrity of the application code before passing control to the application.

Partition Table. The partition table defines the layout of the ESP32's flash memory, including the location and size of the bootloader, the application, and other partitions.

Application Image. The application image is the main firmware that contains the code for the functionality of the ESP32. After the bootloader initializes the system, it transfers control to the application image, which then carries out the device's intended operations.

Xtensa ISA. The Xtensa ISA is a customizable and extensible RISC-based ISA designed to be configurable via different options. These allow designers to tailor the instruction set to specific performance, power, and area requirements by extending it with custom instructions and registers.

While the Xtensa ISA follows most of the typical RISC conventions, such as load/store architecture or single-cycle instructions, it deviates from on in particular. When the "Code Density Option" is activated, which is almost always the case, additional 16-bit versions of the regular 24-bit instructions are introduced. This option enables more efficient memory usage, an important advantage in embedded systems where memory resources are often limited. In an average ESP32 binary around half of the instructions are 16-bit instructions.

The "Windowed Register Option" introduces additional general purpose registers, bringing the total number from 16 to 64. To avoid having to introduce

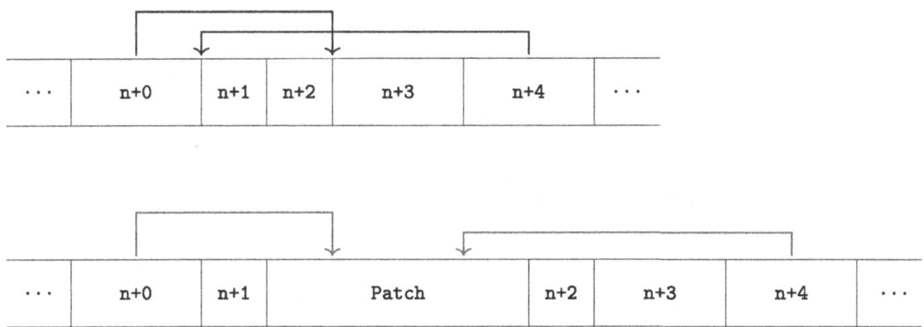

Fig. 2. The code location problem

new instructions with larger register encodings (from 4 to 6 bit per register used in the instruction), the number of visible registers stays at 16. During function calls this window of visible registers can be shifted by a multiple of 8. This option reduces the amount of registers that have to be saved on the stack before a function call.

3.2 The Code Location Problem

The code location problem arises when modifying the binary code of a program. This issue is prevalent in any system where instructions use relative addressing, such as jump and branch instructions that calculate their targets based on their position in memory. When new instructions are inserted or existing ones are altered, these changes can shift the positions of subsequent instructions (as seen in Fig. 2), potentially causing incorrect jumps, crashes, or unpredictable behavior.

3.3 Binary Rewriting

Binary rewriting can be broadly categorized into static and dynamic methods, each with distinct approaches and trade-offs.

Static rewriting involves modifying the binary code without executing it, resulting in a new, modified binary file. This method allows for comprehensive analysis and optimization prior to execution. However, it has the disadvantage that jump targets within the code must be recalculated without runtime information or kept at their current positions, making it difficult to make changes to the code. It also struggles with self-modifying code.

Dynamic rewriting modifies the binary code during execution, enabling adjustments based on real-time behavior and conditions. While it is better suited to handle dynamic and self-modifying code, it introduces runtime overhead, which can negatively impact performance.

For IoT devices, static rewriting is generally preferred because dynamic rewriting often relies on virtualization. Although there is a QEMU implementa-

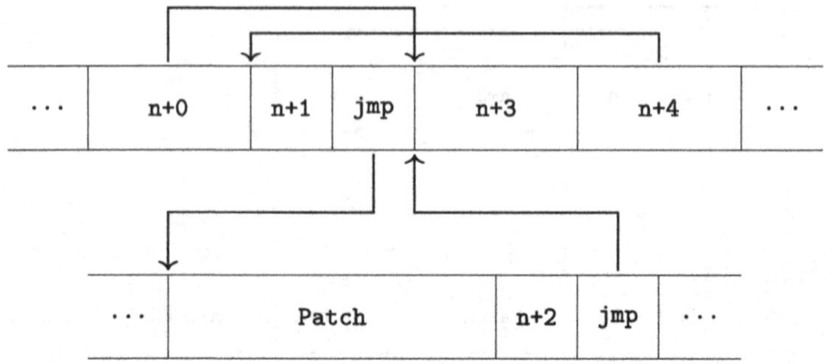

Fig. 3. Trampoline rewriters offer a solution to the code location problem.

tion for the Xtensa architecture, it does not support network interfaces, which is an important feature for most IoT applications.

Static rewriters can either convert the binary to an IR, like assembly, make changes at that level of abstraction, and then reassemble the binary. While this is a small overhead, the original control flow is lost, and new bugs may be introduced.

Static trampoline rewriters place patches in unused areas of the binary and redirect control flow to those patches using jump instructions, as shown in Fig. 3, this allows the original order of control flow to be preserved.

4 Design

Our design consists of several steps: extracting of the binary, rewriting the binary by applying different patching tactics, and reflashing the modified binary.

4.1 Binary Recovery

The binary recovery starts with extracting a complete flash dump of the ESP32 device. Following this, we recover the partition table and use its information to identify the application binary. A crucial transformation in this process is converting the recovered binary image into an ELF file format, which simplifies subsequent analysis and modification tasks. The general idea of this extraction and reflashing process is shown in Fig. 4.

4.2 Rewriter

The rewriter consists of several patching tactics, solving individual patch cases, and a broader binary-wide strategy. The tactics are presented in the order of their attempted application, e.g., if the jump tactic fails to apply the patch, the punned jump tactic is tried next.

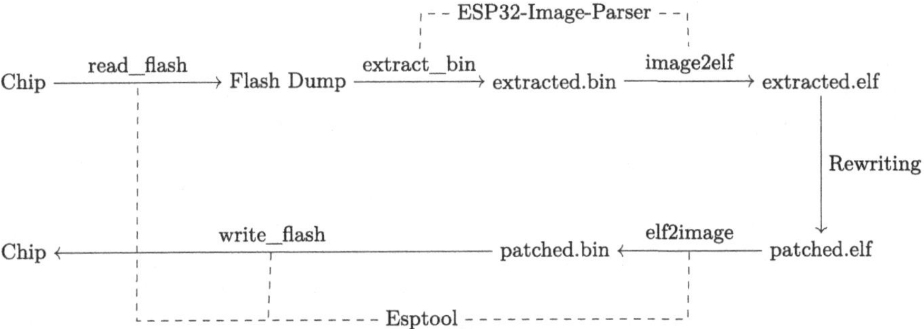

Fig. 4. Binary recovery, rewriting, and re-flashing process

Patching Tactics. The rewriter component is responsible for modifying the recovered ELF binary to insert the necessary instrumentation. We use various patching tactics to accomplish this without disrupting the original program flow.

Jump Tactic. The jump tactic involves redirecting the control flow from the original code to the newly inserted instrumentation and then back to the original code. This is accomplished by inserting jump instructions instead of the original instruction that is moved to the trampoline code. Figure 5 illustrates the application of the jump tactic to the Xtensa architecture, using the following syntax: The original instruction (red) is removed and replaced by the jump instruction (green), while the `X` represents an arbitrary selectable value. However, the opcode of the jump instruction is six bits, leaving 18 bits for the relative offset to address the target location. These 18 bits are displayed as five `X`s, each representing a half-byte in hexadecimal encoding, but is followed by a `/4` (right shift by 2 bits) to indicate that the two Most Significant Bits (MSBs) are cut off because they are part of the opcode. This jump instruction now points to the beginning of the trampoline (right side) where the patch is inserted, including the original instruction at the end. The last instruction in the trampoline points to the first instruction after the jump.

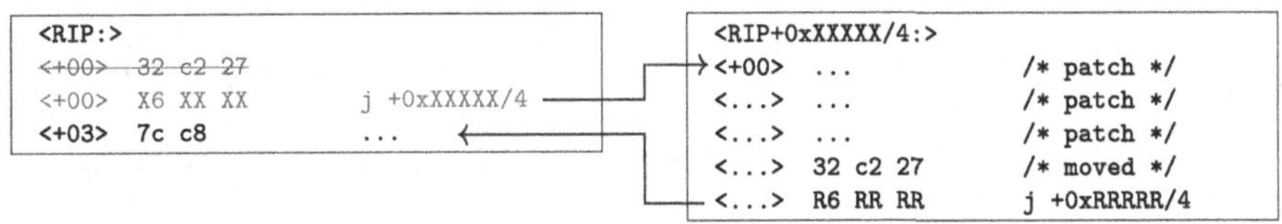

Fig. 5. Applying the jump tactic on Xtensa (Color figure online)

Punned Jump Tactic. The punned jump tactic is a variation of the jump tactic used when the target instruction that would be replaced with the jump instruction is a short 16 bit instruction and not a 24 bit instruction. In such cases, the initial byte of the subsequent instruction can be incorporated into the current instruction, a technique known as instruction punning [3]. Figure 6 demonstrates the punned jump tactic. In addition to the explanation above, we now have punned bytes of the following instruction (orange), which cannot be changed and limit the range of our jump command. Depending on the program, it may be harder to find free space for the trampoline. This limitation is deliberately accepted in order to open up new possibilities, allowing us to insert the jump in tight spaces and use the patch in situations that would otherwise be impossible.

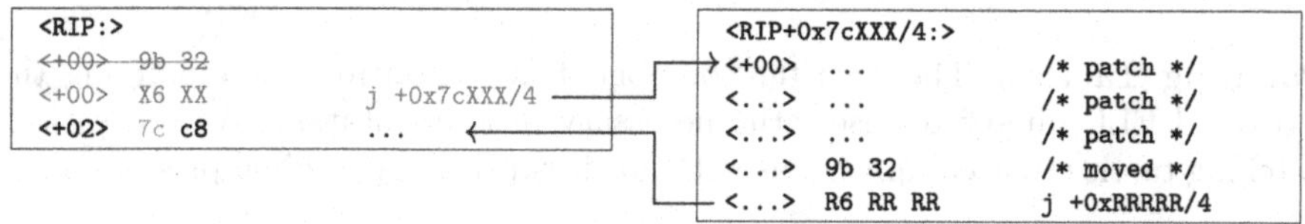

Fig. 6. Applying the punned jump tactic on Xtensa (Color figure online)

Successor Eviction Tactic. If the previous tactic is unsuccessful, the subsequent eviction tactic, which also moves the next instruction to a different code area (using any of the above tactics), can be used. Moving both the original instruction and its successor gives us additional options for finding unused code locations. The displaced instructions are relocated to a new address within the binary, and the control flow is adjusted to ensure the program continues to execute correctly. Figure 7 demonstrates this tactic. The main difference from the last patch tactic is that we now have two replacements, giving us options in cases where the instruction punning tactic fails to find a suitable area for the trampoline code.

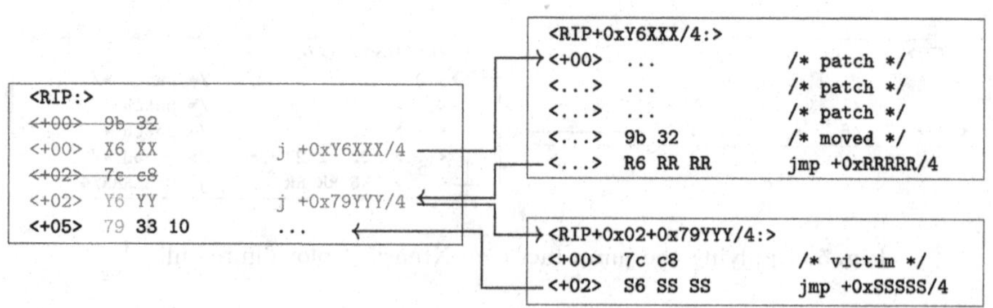

Fig. 7. Applying the successor tactic on Xtensa

Neighbor Eviction Tactic. The neighbor eviction tactic is another possible option if the successor eviction tactic fails and is similar to it, but it evicts an instruction after the patch point. This approach, shown in Fig. 8, provides even more flexibility in finding unused code locations. As the Xtensa ISA does not provide a short relative jump, this tactic exploits the `bnez.n` branch instruction, a 16-bit instruction that performs a relative jump when a register is not zero. The `a0` register holds the return address, and thus should never be zero, resulting in a guaranteed branch.

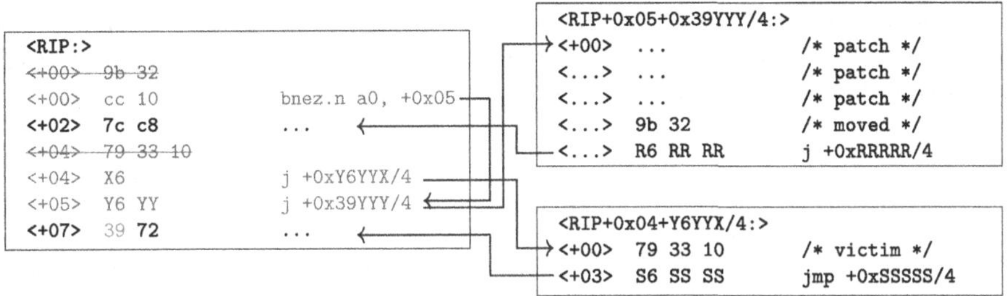

Fig. 8. Applying the neighbor eviction tactic on Xtensa

Patching Strategy. For every patch, the tactics are tried sequentially, until one can successfully apply the patch. If the last one fails, the patch can not be applied.

All patches are applied in reverse order, meaning that patching starts from high addresses and moves to lower ones. This behavior avoids "locking in" the following bytes that might need to be changed too. To better understand this, imagine the second instruction in the punned jump tactic example in Fig. 6 needed to be moved for a patch too. If the first instruction was patched first (normal order), the first byte of the second instruction would be "locked in" and a patch could not be applied. If this second instruction is patched first (reverse order), the instruction punning of the first instruction might still succeed with the new byte `Y6` as punned byte.

5 Implementation

The following shows the implementation of design discussed in the previous section. Our implementation is specifically designed to work on the ESP32-WROOM-32 model, which is a widely used version of the ESP32.

5.1 Binary Recovery

First, a complete flash dump of the target ESP32 device is extracted using Esptool[1]. Afterward, the ESP32-Image-Parser[2] is used to locate and extract the application image from the flash dump, and to transform it into the ELF format. However, this tool is outdated and requires several bug fixes. A fixed version with extended functionality can be found on GitHub[3].

5.2 Rewriter

The rewriter tool is our main contribution and is used for modifying the recovered binary to insert the necessary instrumentation for tasks such as fuzzing. Figure 9 shows the relationship to the other components.

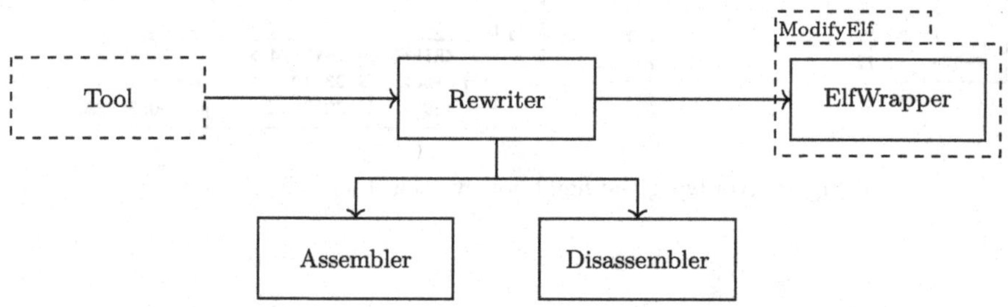

Fig. 9. The structure of our approach

The rewriter is structured to support future tool development. We implemented an adapter for the Radare2 disassembler and a new assembler. The ModifyElf library allows manipulating ELF binaries. It encapsulates the complexities of the ELF format and provides both, a low-level and a high-level interface. The low-level interface is provided by the `ElfRaw` class, which allows detailed and precise modifications, while the `ElfWrapper` class provides a more abstract interface for ease of use.

Patching Tactics. Each patching tactic takes the patch location and patch code as input and returns whether the patching attempt was successful or not. An optional parameter allows the moved statement to be executed before or after the patch code, with the default being execution before the patch code.

---

1 https://github.com/espressif/esptool/.
2 https://github.com/tenable/esp32_image_parser.
3 https://github.com/benjamin-plach/esp32-binary-rewriting-paper.

Patching Strategy. The patching strategy function takes a list of patches and attempts to apply them in reverse order to their target location. For each patch, the function sequentially applies the available patching tactics. Currently, it first attempts the jump tactic, followed by the punned jump tactic.

The method provides feedback on the success of each patch attempt, and summarizes the coverage information at the end.

Assembler. The assembler produces code that requires no further linking. It takes a start address along with the instruction stream as input, allowing the assembler to correctly encode instructions with relative offsets such as jumps or relative load instructions.

The assembler supports the basic features of assembly language coding: the encoding of several Xtensa assembler instructions from the Xtensa ISA Summary[4], assembler directives such as `.align 4` for 4-byte alignment, labels for code locations, and comments.

5.3 Flashing the Rewritten Binary Back Onto the Device

Once the rewriting is complete, the binary can be converted from the ELF format back into the ESP application image format and flashed back on the device.

The address specified in the rewrite command must be the same address from which the binary was recovered. Otherwise, the bootloader will not find it. This address can be looked up in the recovered partition table.

6 Proof of Concept

The binary rewriter has several applications, such as inserting arbitrary code or applying third-party security patches without changing the original program's control flow. To demonstrate its potential, we have developed a proof-of-concept tool that focuses on fuzzing instrumentation. This tool is designed to showcase the potential of the binary rewriter. Consequently, it focuses on collecting coverage information for function calls only, without tracking branches or loops.

6.1 Designing an Example Tool

Three options were considered for implementing the counters needed to collect fuzzing coverage information:

- **Flash Memory:** Using an unused area of flash memory to store counter variables can offer performance benefits. However, this approach introduces risks like losing the information stored in the memory to a power loss or device crash.

[4] https://www.cadence.com/content/dam/cadence-www/global/en_US/documents/tools/silicon-solutions/compute-ip/isa-summary.pdf.

- **Non-Volatile Storage (NVS) Partition:** Adding an NVS partition to the firmware to store counter information can be an efficient solution. However, it requires modifying the partition table and implementing NVS access in assembly language.
- **Monitoring Messages:** Sending unique function identifiers to a connected device through monitoring messages allows for function call counting. On the ESP32, data sent to `stdout` and `stderr`, e.g., via `printf`, is forwarded to a monitoring device. This option is the easiest to implement but can not be used to get coverage information for all functions, as inserting a counter at the start of the chosen function, e.g., `printf`, and any function it calls would result in an infinite loop.

For this proof of concept, we have chosen to implement monitoring messages using the `printf` function, which is a natural choice given the task. While fuzzing standard library functions like `printf` is important for comprehensive software security, the inability to do so here is a negligible disadvantage since our primary focus is on custom application code.

6.2 Implementing the Example Tool

Strings on ESP32. On the ESP32, strings are stored in the `.flash.rodata` section. The Xtensa ISA's 24-bit instruction size does not allow to directly encode 32-bit absolute addresses and the `l32r` instruction used for loading 32-bit values has a limited range. Therefore, pointers to strings are placed at the beginning of the `.flash.text` section and loaded into registers using the `l32r` instruction before calling `printf`.

Listing 1.1. Strings on ESP32

```
<.flash.rodata:>
0x3f4041a8:     48 65 6c 6c 6f    ; Hello
                20 77 6f 72 6c    ;  Worl
                64 21 00          ; d!\0

<.flash.text:>
0x400d0618:     a8 41 40 3f       ; pointer to 0x3f4041a8

0x400d500f:     a1 82 ed          ; l32r a10, -0x049f7
0x400d5012:     e5 77 05          ; call8 <printf>
```

Patch Code. Initial attempts to use custom strings in the patch code failed, likely due to memory access restrictions or alignment issues that prevent the hardware from reading bytes directly from the `.flash.text` section. However, leveraging existing strings within the binary – such as those used by system functions – proved to be an effective alternative for instrumentation purposes.

It is important to note that while the ability to insert custom strings into the binary might be desirable in certain scenarios, it is not a critical requirement for many forms of security testing, such as fuzzing or coverage-based instrumentation. The primary objective of our rewriter is to inject observational instructions without disturbing the control flow of the firmware, and this goal is achieved regardless of the source of the strings. Therefore, the use of pre-existing strings offers a practical solution without affecting the utility or effectiveness of the framework.

Consequently, existing strings in the binary were used, with several criteria:

- **Availability:** The string must be present in all ESP32 binaries. Strings in FreeRTOS, a small operating system commonly used in ESP32 applications, that are compiled into ESP32 code fulfill this criterion.
- **Position:** The pointer to the string must be close enough for the `l32r` command to load it.
- **Structure:** The string must accept a 32-bit integer as its last parameter. This ensures that data, containing the current address of the function call, can be output directly without requiring additional conversions.

The string "`W (%lu) %s: Flash clock frequency round down to %d`" has been selected and cut. Its pointer and the address of the `printf` function must be present when the tool is initialized.

The core function `add_fuzzing_counter` assembles the patch code, loads the string pointer and truncates the string, loads the counter address and calls `printf`.

Listing 1.2. Defining the patch

```
def add_fuzzing_counter(self, addr:int):
    fuzzing_counter_patch = [
        "               l32r a10, " + hex(self.
            __addr_string_pointer),
        "               addi a10, a10, 52", # trim start
            of string
        "               j jmplabel", # jump over data
        "               .align 4",
        "addrlabel:     .uint32 " + hex(addr),
        "jmplabel:      l32r a11, addrlabel", # always -4
        "               call8 " + hex(self.
            __addr_printf_function)
    ]

    self.rewriter.add_patch(addr, fuzzing_counter_patch
        , moved_after_patch=True)
```

The registers `a10` and `a11` can be utilized without the risk of overriding meaningful data, because the register window was just shifted by 8 during the function call.

Patches are applied to the `entry` instruction, which marks the starting point of each function. This ensures that every counter is only triggered once per function call, as the control flow will never be redirected to the `entry` instruction within one function call.

Monitoring. A monitoring script is implemented to collect `printf` output on the monitoring device, filtering data from the `stdout` stream and counting addresses sent by the patch code. After a specified time, the counting is stopped and the results are displayed.

6.3 Utilizing the Example Tool

The example tool can now be utilized to insert fuzzing instrumentation into an existing binary. After reflashing it back onto the device, the monitoring script is used to collect the results.

First, the tool must be initialized by providing the path to the extracted binary. Once initialized, the fuzzing counters can be added. After loading the binary, fuzzing counters can be added. Currently, the user must identify the addresses where the counters should be placed himself, e.g., by using a disassembler. These addresses can then be added using the `add_fuzzing_counter` method. In addition, the user must inform the framework where additional code can be safely inserted without overwriting existing functionality using the `add_free_space` method. This step is critical to maintaining the integrity and proper execution of the original program.

Once these steps have been completed, the patches can be applied. This step handles the actual insertion of the patches into the binary, ensuring that the new instructions are correctly placed and aligned with the existing code structure, and that any jumps are correctly targeted. Finally, the rewritten ELF binary needs to be saved to a file, that can be flashed back onto the device.

Listing 1.3. Using the example tool

```
inserter = Fuzzing_Instrumentation_Inserter('extracted.
   elf')

inserter.add_fuzzing_counter(0x400e248c)
inserter.add_fuzzing_counter(0x400d4fc0)
inserter.add_fuzzing_counter(0x400d4fdc)

inserter.add_free_space(0x400e23a8, 0x400e2489)

inserter.apply_patches()
util.save_file("patched.elf", inserter.get_elf_bytes())
```

Once the binary is rewritten and flashed back to the device, the monitoring script can be run to collect the coverage information. The script tracks the `printf` calls made by the patch code. After the run is completed the results are displayed.

Listing 1.4. Running the monitoring script

```
 > python3 monitoring.py
[COUNTER] 0x400d4fdc
[COUNTER] 0x400d4fc0
  [...]
[COUNTER] 0x400e248c
[COUNTER] 0x400e248c

[CONTROL] Terminating Run!

[RESULTS] 0x400d4fdc: 1
[RESULTS] 0x400d4fc0: 5
[RESULTS] 0x400e248c: 15
```

7 Limitations

Several limitations were encountered during this research. A primary constraint is the limited space available on the ESP32 device for patches. While small patches can be accommodated in padding areas, larger modifications may require extending existing code sections within the binary or modifying the bootloader to load additional code at boot time.

One set of instructions that can currently not be moved are instruction with relative offsets encoded into them, but the relocation of these instructions would require a recalculation of their offsets. Avoiding this is a core design philosophy of trampoline rewriters.

The current implementation only supports a limited set of assembler instructions, restricting the complexity of patches that can be applied. Additionally, the current patching strategies are limited to the Jump and Punned Jump tactics. Implementing the Successor Eviction and Neighbor Eviction tactics, which both require a more in-depth disassembler integration, will increase the rate of successfully applied patches.

8 Future Work

Future work could focus on addressing the identified limitations and enhancing the capabilities of the binary rewriter. One potential area of improvement is the automatic extension of binary sections, particularly the `.flash.text section`, to create additional space for patching without affecting other parts of the binary. Additionally, expanding assembler support to include the full range of Xtensa ISA instructions, or integrating an external assembler, would provide greater flexibility in applying more complex patches.

The patching tactics Successor Eviction and Neighbor Eviction were not necessary for our proof of concept tool, and therefore not implemented. More sophisticated tools would greatly benefit from implementing them. Besides these two tactics, exploring new patching tactics that leverage specific features of the Xtensa architecture could also increase the efficiency of the rewriter.

The reverse-order patching strategy, while effective, may not be optimal in all scenarios. Improving patching strategies, by experimenting with heuristic-based or randomized approaches, could further enhance the success rate of patch applications.

The fuzzing instrumentation inserter was chosen as a proof of concept because it is a promising use case to utilize the binary rewriting framework. As showcased, the tool shows great potential for third-party security testing, but needs to be developed further before it can be applied in real-world scenarios. This could include automated detection of the fuzzing instrumentation locations, and the addition of counters for loops and branches.

9 Conclusion

This paper addresses the gap in tool support for independent security experts to analyze and test proprietary ESP32 firmware. We propose a binary rewriting framework that enables the insertion of additional instructions into existing ESP32 firmware without altering its original functionality and control flow.

The framework simplifies the process of firmware analysis and modification by converting the extracted firmware into a more manageable format, allowing for precise changes while maintaining the integrity of the original code. It introduces novel patching methodologies tailored to the Xtensa architecture, adapting established techniques to meet the specific needs of ESP32 devices. The effectiveness of the framework was demonstrated by a proof of concept fuzzer that successfully added coverage information to ESP32 binaries. This approach involves inserting a counter that records the number of times a particular section of code is executed. By using this feedback, the fuzzer can explore different execution paths more efficiently, increasing the likelihood of finding bugs and vulnerabilities. This demonstrates the potential for further development of the framework to improve the security of ESP32 firmware.

Future work should focus on enhancing the versatility of the framework by implementing additional patching tactics and developing new ones, especially to address more complex patching scenarios. Continued refinement of this framework will expand its capabilities and further support the security analysis of ESP32 devices.

References

1. Srivastava, A., Edwards, A., Vo, H.: Vulcan: binary transformation in a distributed environment (2001). https://www.microsoft.com/en-us/research/wp-content/uploads/2016/02/tr-2001-50.pdf

2. Bala, V., Duesterwald, E., Banerjia, S.: Transparent dynamic optimization: the design and implementation of dynamo (1999). https://homes.cs.washington.edu/~bodik/ucb/cs703-2002/papers/dynamo-full.pdf
3. Chamith, B., Svensson, B.J., Dalessandro, L., Newton, R.R.: Instruction punning: lightweight instrumentation for x86–64. SIGPLAN Not. **52**(6), 320–332 (2017). https://doi.org/10.1145/3140587.3062344
4. Dinesh, S., Burow, N., Xu, D., Payer, M.: RetroWrite: statically instrumenting COTS binaries for fuzzing and sanitization. In: 2020 IEEE Symposium on Security and Privacy, SP 2020, San Francisco, CA, USA, 18–21 May 2020, pp. 1497–1511. IEEE (2020). https://doi.org/10.1109/SP40000.2020.00009
5. Duck, G.J., Gao, X., Roychoudhury, A.: Binary rewriting without control flow recovery. In: Donaldson, A.F., Torlak, E. (eds.) Proceedings of the 41st ACM SIGPLAN International Conference on Programming Language Design and Implementation, PLDI 2020, London, UK, 15–20 June 2020, pp. 151–163. ACM (2020). https://doi.org/10.1145/3385412.3385972
6. Federico, A.D., Payer, M., Agosta, G.: rev.ng: a unified binary analysis framework to recover CFGs and function boundaries. In: Wu, P., Hack, S. (eds.) Proceedings of the 26th International Conference on Compiler Construction, Austin, TX, USA, 5–6 February 2017, pp. 131–141. ACM (2017). http://dl.acm.org/citation.cfm?id=3033028
7. Flores-Montoya, A., Schulte, E.M.: Datalog disassembly. In: Capkun, S., Roesner, F. (eds.) 29th USENIX Security Symposium, USENIX Security 2020, 12–14 August 2020, pp. 1075–1092. USENIX Association (2020). https://www.usenix.org/conference/usenixsecurity20/presentation/flores-montoya
8. Hawkins, W.H., Hiser, J.D., Co, M., Nguyen-Tuong, A., Davidson, J.W.: Zipr: efficient static binary rewriting for security. In: 47th Annual IEEE/IFIP International Conference on Dependable Systems and Networks, DSN 2017, Denver, CO, USA, 26–29 June 2017, pp. 559–566. IEEE Computer Society (2017). https://doi.org/10.1109/DSN.2017.27
9. Kim, T., et al.: RevARM: a platform-agnostic ARM binary rewriter for security applications. In: Proceedings of the 33rd Annual Computer Security Applications Conference, Orlando, FL, USA, 4–8 December 2017, pp. 412–424. ACM (2017). https://doi.org/10.1145/3134600.3134627
10. Luk, C., et al.: Pin: building customized program analysis tools with dynamic instrumentation. In: Sarkar, V., Hall, M.W. (eds.) Proceedings of the ACM SIGPLAN 2005 Conference on Programming Language Design and Implementation, Chicago, IL, USA, 12–15 June 2005, pp. 190–200. ACM (2005). https://doi.org/10.1145/1065010.1065034
11. Nyman, T., Ekberg, J., Davi, L., Asokan, N.: CFI care: hardware-supported call and return enforcement for commercial microcontrollers. CoRR abs/1706.05715 (2017). http://arxiv.org/abs/1706.05715
12. Put, L.V., et al.: LANCET: a nifty code editing tool. In: Ernst, M.D., Jensen, T.P. (eds.) Proceedings of the 2005 ACM SIGPLAN-SIGSOFT Workshop on Program Analysis For Software Tools and Engineering, PASTE 2005, Lisbon, Portugal, 5–6 September 2005, pp. 75–81. ACM (2005). https://doi.org/10.1145/1108792.1108812
13. Schulte, E., Brown, M.D., Folts, V.: A broad comparative evaluation of x86-64 binary rewriters. In: CSET 2022: Cyber Security Experimentation and Test Workshop, Virtual Event, 8 August 2022, pp. 129–144. ACM (2022). https://doi.org/10.1145/3546096.3546112

14. Scott, K., Kumar, N., Velusamy, S., Childers, B.R., Davidson, J.W., Soffa, M.L.: Retargetable and reconfigurable software dynamic translation. In: Johnson, R., Conte, T., Hwu, W.W. (eds.) 1st IEEE/ACM International Symposium on Code Generation and Optimization (CGO 2003), 23–26 March 2003, San Francisco, CA, USA, pp. 36–47. IEEE Computer Society (2003). https://doi.org/10.1109/CGO.2003.1191531
15. Wall, D.W., Srivastava., A.: A practical system for intermodule code optimization at link-time (1992). https://web.stanford.edu/class/cs343/resources/om.pdf
16. Wang, S., Wang, P., Wu, D.: Reassembleable disassembling. In: Jung, J., Holz, T. (eds.) 24th USENIX Security Symposium, USENIX Security 15, Washington, D.C., USA, 12–14 August 2015, pp. 627–642. USENIX Association (2015). https://www.usenix.org/conference/usenixsecurity15/technical-sessions/presentation/wang-shuai
17. Wenzl, M., Merzdovnik, G., Ullrich, J., Weippl, E.R.: From hack to elaborate technique - a survey on binary rewriting. ACM Comput. Surv. **52**(3), 49:1–49:37 (2019). https://doi.org/10.1145/3316415
18. Yadavalli, S.B., Smith, A.: Raising binaries to LLVM IR with MCTOLL (WIP paper). In: Chen, J., Shrivastava, A. (eds.) Proceedings of the 20th ACM SIGPLAN/SIGBED International Conference on Languages, Compilers, and Tools for Embedded Systems, LCTES 2019, Phoenix, AZ, USA, 23 June 2019, pp. 213–218. ACM (2019). https://doi.org/10.1145/3316482.3326354

Detecting Cyber and Physical Attacks Against Mobile Robots Using Machine Learning: An Empirical Study

Levente Nyusti[1(✉)], Sabarathinam Chockalingam[1], Patrick Bours[2], and Terje Bodal[3]

[1] Department of Risk and Security, Institute for Energy Technology, 1777 Halden, Norway
{Levente.Nyusti,Sabarathinam.Chockalingam}@ife.no

[2] Department of Information Security and Communication Technology, Norwegian University of Science and Technology, 2815 Gjøvik, Norway
Patrick.Bours@ntnu.no

[3] Department of Applied Data Science, Institute for Energy Technology, 1777 Halden, Norway
Terje.Bodal@ife.no

Abstract. As more industries employ robots to perform critical tasks, the need to secure such robots are increasing. Mobile robots are more vulnerable to being attacked, as these are not always deployed in well-controlled environments. Therefore, security of mobile robots is essential, where cyber- and physical-attacks can lead to catastrophic events like physical injury, even loss of life. In some cases, such mobile robots include limited to no security controls. Preventing such cyber-attacks is not always possible. However, timely detection of such attacks or attempted attacks might lead to the deployment of appropriate response actions, which limit the negative consequences of the attack and potentially block corresponding attack-vector. When considering intrusion detection in mobile robots, it is necessary to monitor both the cyber and physical domain, as by their nature, attacks conducted in the cyber realm can lead to severe damage in the physical realm. However, there is limited research done on how such cyber and physical attacks against mobile robots can be detected.

Therefore, in this paper, we developed a system for intrusion detection in mobile robots, using a Machine Learning-based approach. This developed system can detect cyber- and physical-attacks, even when the robot is deployed in a previously unknown environment. Our proposed system shows promising results when evaluated utilizing datasets that we collected from *Spot* robot. To assess the performance of this system, we performed two physical- and two cyber-attacks against the robot, which were identified as a part of the review on threat landscape for mobile robots. This system can be applicable to all mobile robots, to detect attacks in both the cyber- and physical-domain, as the data used for intrusion detection in the context of this study should be available in other mobile robots.

Keywords: Anomaly detection · Cyber-physical systems · Cyber security · Intrusion detection · Machine learning · Mobile robots · Robotics

L. Horn Iwaya et al. (Eds.): NordSec 2024, LNCS 15396, pp. 139–157, 2025.
https://doi.org/10.1007/978-3-031-79007-2_8

1 Introduction

Over the recent years, industries use robots to perform a predetermined task, like site-monitoring, patrolling, serving as a guide for humans [1]. For these robots to be safe, trustworthy, and usable for such use-cases, security is of high importance. This is to ensure the Confidentiality, Integrity, and Availability (CIA) of the data collected, such as sensor readings and mission-critical details, while also ensuring that the robot successfully completes the mission. Currently, robotic systems have weak security, or no security implemented at all [2]. For instance, it has been demonstrated how trivial it is to hijack a drone by broadcasting false Global Positioning System (GPS) data [3–5].

An attack in the cyber realm, such as Man-in-the-Middle (MitM), has the potential to intercept, modify, and cut-off communication between the operator and the mobile robot. Therefore, it is of high importance to detect any attempts of gaining unauthorized access to these mobile robots or detecting any unexpected behavior [6, 7]. This is especially problematic when considering mobile robots, as they often operate in environments where humans are also present. This makes these robots potentially dangerous, e.g., controlling such robots to crash into objects or humans [8, 9].

As security mechanisms, like authentication before allowing control over such robots, which aim to keep such systems secure, might get circumvented, detection of such attacks is crucial. Early detection of an attack allows the operator to quickly deploy appropriate countermeasures, to block the attackers, and limit the negative consequences of such attacks. However, existing research on intrusion detection in mobile robots is limited, as our literature review reveals a significant gap in this area. Therefore, this paper develops a system for intrusion detection on mobile robots, which can detect both cyber- and physical-attacks using Machine Learning (ML). An ML-based anomaly detection approach is well-suited for this task, as these models can effectively learn patterns of normal behavior and subsequently identify and alert when deviations from this norm occurs.

In order to develop such a detection system, we formulated the following Research Question (RQ) in this study:

RQ. Can we use machine learning for intrusion detection in mobile robots to detect both cyber- and physical-attacks?

We have further formulated two Research Objectives (ROs) to tackle the RQ:

RO1. To gather relevant data from mobile robots for intrusion detection.

RO2. To identify which ML models perform well.

Learning-based ML approaches are highly effective in many fields [10]. While acknowledging the effectiveness of learning-based ML approaches for some tasks, the authors also state: "*Even with large datasets, learning-based approaches cannot enumerate and cover exhaustive scenarios in robots, and thus their statistical norm models are less accurate and rigorous*" [10]. The authors describe how robots obey physical laws, which learning-based approaches ignore. However, in this study, we intend to conduct experiments to test the above-mentioned hypothesis in the context of our RQ.

The remainder of this paper is structured as follows: Sect. 2 presents the threat landscape for mobile robots in addition to existing research on ML-based Intrusion Detection System (IDS) and non-ML based IDS for mobile robots. Section 3 describes the research methodology that we used, in addition to the research environments and datasets used. Section 4 describes the ML models with the best performance on Spot datasets. Section 5 describes the scenarios chosen for our experiments. Section 6 presents the results achieved on the collected datasets. In Sect. 7, we discuss our findings. Finally, Sect. 8 presents our conclusions and further research directions.

2 Related Work

2.1 Threat Landscape for Mobile Robots

Mobile robots rely on a wide range of sensors, such as GPS for localization, to gather critical information. Consequently, an attacker could potentially steer these robots off course by injecting false data, such as incorrect GPS coordinates. This could not only result in the mission being ruined, but also result in the robot causing damage or harming humans, as it may fail to detect and avoid obstacles. In addition, it is also possible for malicious actors to steal the robot, inject malicious software or data, damage the robot, access files stored locally on the robot, gain control over its operations, or even replace legitimate hardware with malicious components. Previous studies have explored potential attacks on mobile robots. For instance, the study in [11] reviews the threat landscape and attack surface of social robots operating in public spaces. Since Spot is used as a mobile robot in public spaces in our scenario, this paper serves as a foundation for investigating the threat landscape relevant to our robot. Therefore, it is important to map out the threat landscape for our system evaluation. The importance of identifying threats during the design of a security system is also stated in [12]. Given that [11] provides a comprehensive and up-to-date literature review, we mainly relied on this study for the threat landscape. Table 1 presents a selection of cyber- and physical-attacks discussed in [11].

Table 1. Threat Landscape for Mobile Robots – An Excerpt

Type of Attack	Physical Attack	Cyber Attack
Malware		X
GPS spoofing		X
Code injection		X
Denial of Service		X
Information theft		X
Buffer overflow		X
Illegal authorization		X
Man-in-the-Middle attack		X
Physical (Harm to robot)	X	
Physical (Obstructing robot path)	X	
Theft	X	

2.2 Intrusion Detection Systems

Professionals often differentiate between two categories when discussing IDS: signature-based IDS and anomaly-based IDS [13]. First, we discuss the difference between these two categories, before introducing ML-based anomaly detection and corresponding challenge.

Signature-Based Detection
In signature-based detection, cyber security personnel create a signature for an attack which can be used to uniquely identify that specific attack. After creating a signature for all the expected and known attacks, these signatures are collected into a database. The IDS then checks for these signatures in the network traffic to search for these attacks. An advantage of this approach is that it can reliably detect attacks for which a signature has been created, assuming the attack is not changed in a way that it will not be detected using the signature created against it. A disadvantage of this approach, however, is that it is only able to detect attacks for which a signature has already been created. This means that new and unseen attacks will not be detected [14].

Anomaly-Based Detection
In anomaly-based detection, cyber security personnel create a baseline which describes the system in the normal state. The IDS then uses this baseline to monitor the system, looking for behavior which deviates from the defined baseline. An advantage of this IDS is that the detection is not limited to already known attacks, meaning it can detect new and unseen attacks. However, a disadvantage of this system is that it has a higher False Positive Rates (FPRs), as it will generate an alarm for everything that deviates from the baseline. Deviations could include non-malicious actions, simply because these are not present in the baseline. Another weakness of this approach is that it may not be as reliable in detecting already known attacks as a signature-based IDS [15].

In the case of mobile robots, an anomaly-based IDS is desirable. This is mainly because creating labeled training data is both time-consuming and challenging. In addition, generating datasets for all possible cyber-attacks is impractical due to constantly evolving threat landscape. Similarly, the authors of [16] also suggest that especially in the case of robot security, attacks are highly challenging to predict and recreate.

ML-based anomaly detection systems can be sorted into four categories: fuzzy logic, genetic algorithm, Bayesian network, and neural network [17, 18]. The authors of [19] highlight that conventional anomaly detection methods can no longer address the challenges presented by Cyber-Physical Systems (CPS). To address this, several Deep Learning-based Anomaly Detection (DLAD) methods have been proposed. As such models adopt semi-supervised and unsupervised learning, these are capable of anomaly detection, even when trained in a one-class classification manner. Such models include: ConvLSTM, RNN, and Autoencoders [19]. However, neural networks have their limitation. One such limitation is that these models ultimately work as a black-box, where users do not have insight into the decision process, meaning these lack interpretability [20]. This is especially limiting in an anomaly detection system, as the neural network itself is not capable of pinpointing the cause of the alarm. This results in the need of involving a user to deep dive into the logs and decide whether there is a cause for the alarm or if it was a False Positive (FP).

3 Methodology

3.1 Experimental Setup

The Mobile Robot – Spot
We used Boston Dynamic's Spot robot as the subject for our work. This is a highly advanced mobile robot with state-of-the-art capabilities like opening doors, climbing stairs, and navigating challenging terrains [21]. As these robots are under constant development, there are different generations of Spot. The Spot robot used in this work is the first generation, updated to the latest software, v3.3.1 at the time of this study.

Spot comes with a controller, which is meant as a platform to control the robot manually or program it to execute a mission. This controller also has a screen, through which the operator can inspect Spot's environment always using the cameras. Spot uses a regular wireless or wired Local Area Network (LAN) to communicate with the controller, or other computers.

Spotcore
Spotcore is a payload, which is essentially an edge computing device [22]. This payload can be mounted on *Spot* and be utilized for different tasks like data processing, while the robot is completing a mission. In our work, we used this payload to gather data from *Spot*.

3.2 Datasets

During our work, we collected several physical sensor datasets and network datasets from Spot. In this Section, we introduce these datasets, describe the data collection methodology for these and introduce some of the features collected. These datasets were collected to evaluate the effectiveness of our system in detecting both physical- and cyber-attacks.

Physical Datasets
As a part of this study, we collected multiple physical sensor datasets from *Spot*. This process was conducted in several iterations, beginning with data collection from *Spot's* physical sensors such as perception and positional sensors. In the first iteration, we gathered eight datasets containing only physical sensor data. Each dataset includes approximately 35000 datapoints from *Spot*, while it is performing different movements to establish a general patrolling baseline. Each datapoint consists of 80 features.

In addition to the eight datasets, we also collected data from the same sensors during *Spot's* auto-mission, resulting in five additional datasets. This auto-mission followed a different path than the one used during the training data collection. This variation is crucial for ensuring the validity of our proposed system, as one of our key requirements is generalizability across different missions. Figure 1 shows the auto-mission path.

Features Collected
As previously mentioned, each datapoint collected from the physical sensors consists

of 80 features. However, not all these features are suitable for anomaly detection. Features such as "charge_%", "current", "time_sec" and "time_nano" were excluded before training the model. The features "charge_%", "time_sec" and "time_nano" were deemed irrelevant for anomaly detection given our scenarios. Although the feature "current" could be useful for detecting attacks that result in high power consumption or tampering with the battery monitoring sensor, it was not included as it is not pertinent to our system's focus. While some attacks might alter this feature, addressing such modifications is beyond the scope of this study.

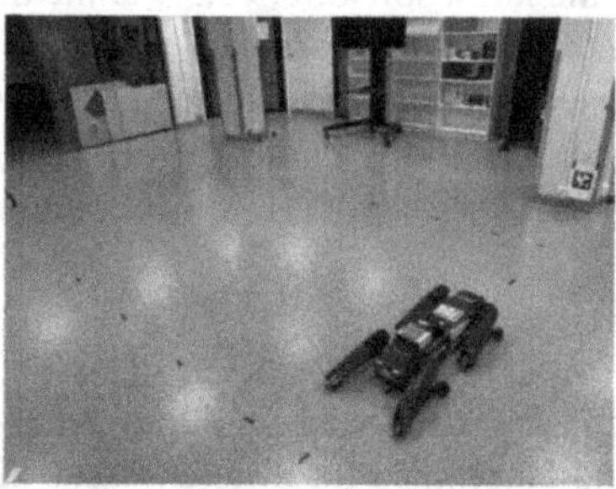

Fig. 1. Our Auto-Mission Path

Physical Dataset Collection Methodology

To ensure that all the desired movements were captured in the recorded data, we initiated the recording script, while *Spot* was already turned on and in a sitting position. Once the recording started, we instructed *Spot* to stand up, and begin moving like shown in Fig. 2. Half of the recordings were made while *Spot* was moving in the direction as shown in Fig. 2, and the other half were recorded with *Spot* moving in the opposite direction. This approach was used to ensure that a balanced dataset with an equal number of left and right turns. Recording lasted while *Spot's* battery ranged from 100% to 20%. Once the battery dropped below 20%, the recording stopped, and the file was closed. The battery typically took about an hour to discharge from full charge to 20%. This measure was implemented to prevent any performance degradation due to a low battery. Our data

Fig. 2. Our Training Environment and Path

collection script for the physical sensors operated at an average of 10Hz, resulting in 10 datapoints per second.

Network Datasets
To evaluate our system's capability to detect cyber-attacks against the robot, we collected all network traffic to and from *Spot*. We employed a similar strategy as with the physical sensor data, gathering several datasets, each lasting one hour.

Network Dataset Collection Methodology
To capture all network traffic between the robot, *Spotcore*, and the controller, we configured the network so that all network traffic going to and from *Spot* was routed through *Spotcore*. This network configuration is shown in Fig. 3. This setup allowed us to easily capture all communication by running a program on *Spotcore*. We used the program tshark [23] to collect all network traffic across all interfaces on *Spotcore*. This approach ensured that we could also analyze network traffic directed at *Spotcore*, addressing potential attacks on this device rather than just *Spot*. For this study, we chose to collect all available information, as we could then later apply feature selection to achieve best results. The collected features in the network data include source IP, source port, destination IP, destination port, frame, and protocol.

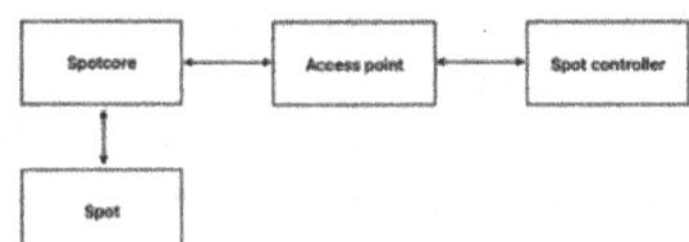

Fig. 3. Network Configuration for Experiments

Attack Datasets
The attack datasets consist of the same features as the training datasets, for both physical and network data. However, the collection method differs significantly for all the attacks. The most significant difference in capture methodology for all tested attacks is the duration of the recordings. The detailed description of capturing methodology is described in Sect. 4, where we also describe the specific attacks performed against *Spot* in more detail.

3.3 Data Labelling

Since the data from Spot was not pre-labeled, we developed an algorithm to assign labels to the recorded data. We experimented with two physical-attack scenarios: Spot encountering an unexpected obstacle and Spot being subjected to physical harm.

Each scenario was recorded separately, resulting in distinct recordings for each attack angle (i.e., front, right, left, and back), with each angle repeated 10 times. These attack datasets are described in more detail in Sect. 4. The labelling methodology was as follows: the features "charge_%", "wifi_state", "hard_estop", "payload_estop", "soft_estop" were removed from each dataset. The remaining features were scaled using the MinMaxScaler [24]. We then calculated the difference between consecutive datapoints and summed the absolute values of these differences for each row, providing an indication of Spot's movement between datapoints. Since Spot starts from a stationary position, this approach helps to determine when an attack occurred and how long it took for Spot to regain control.

To label an instance as an attack, we used the average movement value within the dataset. Given the relatively short and varied lengths of the datasets, despite consistent attack durations, we adjusted the average movement threshold using the following formula: average * (0.85 + (dataset length/500)), where the dataset length ranged from 20 to 70 rows. The adjustment was applied to prevent the average value from falling with the range where Spot had been attacked.

For labelling datasets where Spot encountered obstacles, we employed a similar approach, but focused on identifying periods of no movement instead of detecting movement. When Spot encountered an obstacle, it paused momentarily before returning to its home position. We labeled these periods as true when no movement was detected.

3.4 Data Preprocessing

Data normalization and other data preprocessing measures are used to transform the raw data to a format that is more desirable for ML applications [25]. Data normalization is required when features in a dataset vary significantly in range [26]. Since our datasets have considerable range differences, data normalization is necessary. For this purpose, we used the MinMaxScaler algorithm to normalize the data in our datasets [24].

In contrast, for the network datasets, a considerable amount of data preprocessing was required, as we collected everything the program tshark could collect. We chose this extensive collection methodology, as it does not introduce a challenge to collect everything, making it possible to later extract the features of interest. Additionally, not all the features collected could be used for anomaly detection, as nearly all data communication to and from Spot is encrypted. As we do not have access to the decryption key to perform anomaly detection on the unencrypted data, we are required to use the features that are not encrypted.

The authors of [27] presented methods for representing encrypted network traffic. From this work, we adopted the Flow-Level representation method, which utilizes source and destination IP, source, and destination port in addition to protocol. Furthermore, we included source and destination MAC addresses, as this would enable detection of cyber-attacks like ARP spoofing on LAN.

Encoding refers to the process of translating data to a format that is preferable for ML applications, which is necessary for certain data types like IP addresses [28]. To make these features interpretable by ML models, we used encoding techniques. We reviewed various approaches in the literature to determine the most effective method for encoding IP addresses. Based on the findings in [28], we applied the best-performing encoding method for IP addresses in our datasets. This method split the IP address into separate features, treating each octet treated as an individual feature, a method referred to as the split IP method by the authors. Additionally, we also applied this encoding method for the MAC addresses, converting them from their hex representation to decimal. Finally, the "protocol" feature was encoded using LabelEncoder [29].

3.5 Alarm Generation

Since robots are CPS that operate in different terrains and sometimes under sub-optimal conditions, it is challenging to develop an IDS that balances sensitivity and specificity. An IDS that is too strict may result in high False Positive Rate (FPR), while one that is too lenient may lead to a high False Negative Rate (FNR). To address this, as a part of our system, we developed a methodology for generating alarms based on anomalous datapoints. During our analysis, we observed that while some datapoints were labeled as anomalous by the model, these datapoints were often isolated with large intervals of normal datapoints before and after. Given our sampling rate of 10 Hz, we conclude that these anomalous datapoints were likely due to minor disturbances (i.e., noise) rather than significant issues. To filter out such noise, we implemented a threshold where an alarm is only generated if at least three consecutive datapoints are classified as anomalous. We chose three consecutive datapoints as the threshold, because this represents a duration of 0.3 s (3/10 of a second), meaning that Spot spent enough time, at least 0.3 s, recovering from a disturbance. Only under these conditions will an alarm be generated and sent to the operator.

4 Models Implemented

To address RO2, we implemented and evaluated several ML models using datasets collected from Spot. We experimented with several ML models, including One-Class Support Vector Machines (OC-SVM), isolation forest, Local Outlier Factor (LOF), Generative Adversarial Network (GAN), and autoencoders. To evaluate the performance of these models, we used commonly applied metrics for evaluating ML models: Recall, Precision and F1-score [30–32]. The models with the best performance were LOF, GAN, and autoencoder.

LOF is a model which relies on calculating and comparing distances [33]. More specifically, the algorithm measures the local deviation of a given datapoint with respect to its k-nearest neighbors, compared to the local deviations of the other points in the dataset. For every new datapoint which needs to be classified, the algorithm calculates the LOF score. If the LOF score is low, the data point is considered similar to those in the training data. A high LOF score indicates that the datapoint has lower density than those in the training set. As such, the data point will be marked as an anomaly.

GAN is a deep learning-based model that is capable of one-class classification. A GAN consists of two networks working against each other, training one another [34]. These two networks are called generator and discriminator. The generator takes a noise vector and generates fake data, which the discriminator takes as input in addition to a real data point. The discriminator then attempts to correctly label the inputs as either real or fake. During learning, these two networks are trained in an adversarial manner, where the generator learns to create more realistic fakes, while the discriminator tries to correctly label these data points.

Autoencoders are a type of neural network, which contains two main parts: encoding and decoding [35]. One of the most used autoencoder model is the so called undercomplete autoencoders. During the encoding phase of an undercomplete autoencoder, the model extract features to represent the datapoints using a decreasing number of neurons. When the observation is represented by the least number of neurons, the observation is in a so-called latent representation. The next step is then to decode the observation from its latent representation to the original state. Once the decoding is finished and the observation is reconstructed, the model compares the input to the reconstructed form, resulting in a reconstruction error. High reconstruction error means the autoencoder failed to reconstruct the datapoint correctly, meaning that the datapoint is anomalous.

Since the autoencoder showed the superior performance based on the evaluation metrics described in Sect. 3, we provide a detailed presentation of the results for this model.

5 Model Experiments

In this section, we describe the scenario we chose for Spot's normal operation. In addition, we also describe the attack scenarios which will be performed against Spot to evaluate the models' detection capabilities.

5.1 Normal Operation of *Spot*

In our scenario, we aim to detect anomalies while Spot is patrolling on a flat terrain. We chose this scenario because it represents a common real-world use case for mobile robots, which are frequently employed for environment patrolling [36]. Such patrolling could serve various purposes, including site inspection, environment survey, and routine inspection of environment. While the robot is patrolling, it will perform the most basic movements, such as walk forward, turn left, and turn right, with a constant speed throughout the mission. This approach reflects typical actions a robot makes while patrolling an environment. Furthermore, in our scenario, the patrolled environment is accessible by both authorized and unauthorized personnel. The robot is not expected to interact with humans during its patrol. As unauthorized personnel have access to the environment, the robot might be exposed to both cyber- and physical-attacks. To that end, we aim to evaluate our proposed system against both cyber- and physical-attacks.

In addition, to test the FPR during mission completion, we used the five datasets collected while Spot was completing the auto-mission.

5.2 Attack Scenarios

Based on the list of attacks identified in the literature review presented in Table 1, we chose two cyber-attacks and two physical-attacks to evaluate our system's detection capabilities. The attacks tested were Denial of Service (DoS), ARP spoofing, physical harm to the robot, and obstructing the robot's path. We chose these attacks because they are feasible to carry out given the resources and access available, and they are unlikely to render the robot non-operational or cause irreparable damage. However, these attacks could still lead to significant harm or increased security risks. Specifically, DoS and ARP Spoofing are categorized as cyber-attacks, while physical harm to the robot and obstructing the robot's path are classified as physical-attacks. There are possibilities of hybrid cyber-physical attacks, which are out-of-the-scope of this study.

DoS Attack

To conduct a DoS attack against *Spot*, we performed a de-authentication attack against *Spotcore*, while *Spot* is in a standstill position, waiting for commands from the controller. This attack does not require attacker to be authenticated on the network beforehand. It exploits the authentication process of clients to an access point and the ability of adversaries to read the MAC addresses of devices on unauthenticated networks. Consequently, the attacker can send spoofed de-authentication packets to either the access point or the target device, using the respective MAC address. This results in the victim being de-authenticated from the LAN for a duration specified by the attacker [37]. We chose this attack because it is relatively easy to execute and causes the robot to enter a faulty state due to sudden loss of network connection.

As a result, *Spot* would be stuck in a position, requiring an operator to physically intervene and relocate the robot. This could lead to severe damage, especially if the attack occurs while *Spot* is in a sensitive position, such as climbing stairs. In such a case, *Spot* might fall, leading to damage to components, the robot itself or even harm nearby humans. Furthermore, if *Spot* is operating in a hazardous environment, retrieving it could pose additional risks.

To gather data for this attack scenario, we first connected a screen and keyboard directly to *Spotcore*. This setup was necessary because the SSH connection would be interrupted once the attack began, stopping data collection. We maintained the same connection configuration as used for the normal network dataset collection, as shown in Fig. 3. *Spotcore* was chosen as the attack target because compromising it would result in complete loss of control over both *Spot* and *Spotcore*.

For data collection, we used the 'tshark' tool on *Spotcore*. In the same manner as we did for the physical attack data collection, we gathered 10 datasets for this attack to ensure result validity. Each dataset was recorded while *Spot* was stationary with the controller connected. The recordings lasted 15 s, with first 5 s capturing normal network traffic and the remaining 10 s recording attack data.

Address Resolution Protocol (ARP) Spoofing

ARP is used in LANs to map an IP address to a MAC address. However, since ARP lacks authentication, it is vulnerable to spoofing attacks [38]. An attacker can exploit this vulnerability by sending a spoofed packet to the router or switch, falsely claiming that the victim's IP address now corresponds to the attacker's MAC address. Simultaneously, the attacker sends ARP packets to the victim's machine, stating that the router's IP address is associated with the attacker's MAC address. This allows the attacker to intercept and forward packets between the victim and the router or switch, effectively placing them in the middle of the communication, thereby executing a MitM attack. Figure 4 illustrates this attack.

This attack is particularly severe because it grants the attacker control over the communication flow, potentially allowing the attacker to perform further attacks such as

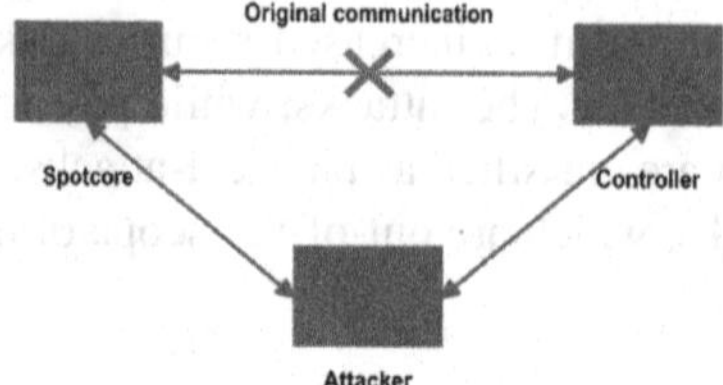

Fig. 4. ARP Spoofing

packet sniffing, DNS cache poisoning, and malware delivery [39]. In the case of packet sniffing, once ARP spoofing is successful, the attacker can inspect the intercepted packets to extract sensitive information like usernames and passwords. To collect datasets for this attack, we used SSH to connect to Spotcore, maintaining the same network configuration as in the normal network and DoS attack dataset recordings. The 'tshark' tool was also used for data collection.

We gathered 20 datasets in total for this attack scenario. In 10 of the datasets, the ARP spoofing attack was initiated only after the recording began, while in the other 10, the attack was already in progress when the recording started. Each recording lasted 15 s. In the 10 relevant datasets, the robot was controlled normally for the first 5 s before the attack was launched, and then Spot was controlled for the remaining duration under the influence of the attack.

Physical Harm to the Robot

In this scenario, we pushed Spot in various directions, ensuring that the force applied was minimal enough for the robot to regain its balance and remain upright. The purpose of this test is to evaluate whether the system can detect slight pushes, as this might be a form of stealthy attack aimed at disrupting the mission. If the system successfully identifies these minor pushes, from which the robot quickly recovers, we can reasonably expect it to detect more severe physical attacks that might cause Spot to fall or sustain damage, leading to mission disruption. This issue is particularly relevant, as identified in [40], where several instances of mobile robots being subjected to violence, sometimes resulting in the robots being completely destroyed.

To collect data for this attack scenario, we started by placing Spot in a starting position, which was a standstill position. After this, the data collection script was started. Once the script was running, we pushed Spot, waited until it returned to the starting position after which we stopped the data collection script. As these datasets are captured in seconds, these are much shorter, containing about 20 samples per dataset. As both before and after we push Spot is in an accepted state, we expect to see several normal datapoints in these datasets, in addition to the anomalous ones.

Obstructing Robot Path

This physical attack scenario is less destructive but can still result in damage and mission failure. In this attack, the attacker obstructs robot's path by either standing in its way or placing an object in its planned route. While Spot is equipped with an excellent object avoidance algorithm, it might still fail depending on the size and nature of the obstruction. Although the severity of the damage is expected to be low, the primary concern is the robot's failure to complete its mission. This issue is particularly relevant in the context of mobile robots operating in the physical realm, as stated in [41], where the authors discuss instances of children obstructing or abusing mobile robots.

To collect data for this scenario, we programmed a mission for Spot in which it was supposed to walk in a rectangular pattern. The recording began when Spot was in a stationary position, ready to start the mission. During the mission, we placed objects of varying sizes in the robot's path to observe how the robot responded to different obstacles. The recording was stopped once Spot either successfully completed the mission or failed and returned to the starting position. The resulting datasets contains approximately 140 datapoints each.

6 Results

In this section, we present the results obtained from our system. We evaluated the performance of the ML models including autoencoders using Precision, Recall, and F1-score on the physical datasets. Since the network datasets were not labelled, we only present the detection rate for them.

6.1 Physical Datasets

Table 2 presents the performance of our system based on the evaluation metrics mentioned earlier.

Table 2. Evaluation Results for Physical Attack Detection

	Total Datapoints	Precision	Recall	F1-score
Attack from back	187	0.82	0.63	0.71
Attack from left	238	0.89	0.67	0.77
Attack from front	158	0.76	0.74	0.75
Attack from right	177	0.91	0.84	0.87
Mission obstruction	1500	0.06	0.01	0.02

Alarm Generation

In addition, we explored methods for classifying attacks based on the anomalous datapoints in a meaningful way as detailed in Sect. 3.5. This is significant because we do not intend to generate an alarm for each anomalous datapoint, as this would result in a high number of false alarms being sent to the operator. Table 3 shows the total number of alarms generated for each attack category. In every category where alarms were raised, the system generated a single alarm per dataset.

Table 3. Total Number of Alarms Generated per Attack Category

	Number of Datasets	Alarms Generated
Attack from back	10	9
Attack from left	10	10
Attack from front	10	10
Attack from right	10	10
Normal (unseen dataset)	1	0
Normal (auto-mission)	5	0
Attack during auto-mission	10	4

6.2 Network Datasets

Similar to the physical datasets, the network datasets were also unlabeled during collection. Consequently, we cannot precisely evaluate the model's performance. Instead, we relied on analyzing the number of anomalies detected across different datasets and comparing this to the total number of datapoints, referred to as the detection rate. Table 4 provides an overview of the network datasets collected and analyzed.

Table 4. Evaluation Results for Cyber-attack Detection

	Total Datapoints	Anomalies Detected	Detection Rate
Normal unseen datasets	1843401	11	5.97*10–6
ARP Attack	148422	272	0.0018
DoS Attack	39486	142	0.004

7 Discussion

In this section, we discuss the results related to the physical and network datasets, evaluate our hypothesis, and conclude by addressing the limitations of this work.

Physical Datasets: The labeling of physical attack datasets was performed after data collection, introducing some uncertainty regarding the accuracy of the labels used for performance evaluation. Using timestamps to improve labeling of the physical attack datasets might not result in greater accuracy, as the time *Spot* takes to regain balance can vary.

- **Physical harm to the robot:** As shown in Table 2, the model performs better at detecting attacks from the sides compared to those from the front or back. This may be due to the recording process, as we did not perform sideways movement with *Spot* during data collection. Nevertheless, the model effectively detects physical attacks on the robot, when using the described filtering mechanism.

- **Obstructing Robot Path:** Table 2 indicates a decrease in model performance for obstruction-related attacks compared to physical-harm attacks. This is because the robot makes multiple corrections to stay on its predefined path while executing the mission. These adjustments are not introduced by the operator, as it is easier for the operator to identify and follow the correct path. The system's performance during auto-mission is expected to improve if the operator records data while the robot executes such missions.

Network Datasets: Similar to the physical datasets, the network datasets were not labeled during or after collection. Also, due to the complexity of network communications, estimating the number of anomalous datasets is challenging. Therefore, we relied on the detection rate to determine if it is higher for datasets where attacks occurred.

- **ARP Spoofing:** Since the features we can extract from the network data are limited due to encryption, estimating the number of anomalous datapoints in the attack datasets is challenging. One crucial feature excluded due to encryption is "info", which in ARP packets indicates the MAC address associated with each IP address. We expect that this feature would allow the model to accurately identify malicious ARP packets. However, even without this feature, the model should still be able to detect anomalies because *Spot* is interacting with a new device. As described in Sect. 5, our attack was launched systematically, so the number of anomalous datapoints per dataset might differ marginally. In addition, we expect the detection rate for these anomalous datasets to be significantly higher compared to that of normal unseen dataset.
- **DoS Attack:** Estimating the number of anomalous datapoints in the DoS attack datasets is also challenging. In this case, the attack results in a severed connection between *Spotcore* and the network, causing all the anomalous datapoints will appear towards the end of the dataset. However, this approach is not suitable for real-time monitoring of *Spot*. Therefore, we rely on the detection rate to determine whether the model effectively detects this attack.

Performance of Learning-Based Approach: As mentioned in Sect. 1, the authors of [10] state that a learning-based approaches generally yield less accurate performance. Although the results in terms of traditional metrics may not be entirely promising, our experiments demonstrate the appropriate features are extracted and the model's hyperparameters are carefully tuned. Utilizing our filtering approach further enhances these results, as shown in Table 3. Furthermore, by focusing on generalizability and selecting data features that are applicable to other mobile robots, our approach shows significant promise. Specifically, our results show that a sampling rate of 10 Hz for collecting physical sensor data is sufficient for the model to establish a proper baseline of the robot's normal behavior. A lower sampling rate would extend duration of data collection and may fail to capture minor manipulations from which the robot can quickly recover. This is because a lower rate would require much more time to capture the whole normal baseline for the mobile robot. Conversely, a higher sampling rate could improve the speed at which normal behavior is captured, but we recommend utilizing a lower sampling rate such as 10 Hz once the system is deployed. A higher sampling rate demands more computational resources from the robot, which would have a negative impact on the overall performance of the robot. Therefore, a sampling rate of 10 Hz effectively balances the need to detect slight manipulations while minimizing computational overhead.

Filtering to Detect Attacks: Filtering reduces false positives in alarm generation and shifts the focus to assessing the model's ability to detect attacks within the datasets, rather than pinpointing the exact anomalous datapoints. This not only limits the number of false positives, but also provides a more reliable methodology for attack detection. As shown in Table 3, the system successfully generated 39 alarms for the 40 physical harm datasets. The single dataset without an alarm was found to involve a minor attack, which led the model to classify only two consecutive datapoints as anomalous.

8 Conclusions and Future Work Directions

This paper presents a ML-based system for intrusion detection in mobile robots, capable of detecting both cyber- and physical-attacks, even in unfamiliar environments. To evaluate the ML-based system, we collected data from Spot robot during two separate physical- and cyber-attacks. This was done by experimenting with the Spot API, identifying a relevant script for data collection, and then developing our own data collection script using the Spot API, followed by feature extraction, addressing RO1. Our choice of ML approach involved experimenting with several models to identify the most effective for anomaly detection, using Precision, Recall and F1-Score for evaluation, addressing RO2. Among the models tested, such as LOF, OC-SVM, and autoencoder, the autoencoder demonstrated the best performance.

Additionally, we implemented a filtering mechanism to reduce false alarms sent to operators during the detection process. The autoencoder produced promising results, confirming that ML can be effectively used for intrusion detection in mobile robots, even when trained only on normal operation data from the robot. While the metrics scored relatively low, after filtering the model correctly generated alarm for 39 out of 40 physical attacks. Future work directions include: (i) enhancing data collection by implementing real-time labeling of anomalous datapoints to improve the accuracy of performance assessment, (ii) experimenting with transformer models to compare their performance and time complexity with the autoencoder, particularly given their potential with time-series data, (iii) evaluating the system's generalizability by implementing it on different mobile robots, adjusting sampling rates, optimizing model hyperparameters, and testing with both normal and attack datasets.

Disclosure of Interests. The authors have no competing interests to declare that are relevant to the content of this article.

References

1. Cebollada, S., Payá, L., Flores, M., Peidró, A., Reinoso, O.: A state-of-the-art review on mobile robotics tasks using artificial intelligence and visual data. Expert Syst. Appl. **167**, 114195 (2021). https://doi.org/10.1016/j.eswa.2020.114195

2. Kirschgens, L.A., Ugarte, I.Z., Uriarte, E.G., Rosas, A.M., Vilches, V.M.: Robot hazards: from safety to security (2021). http://arxiv.org/abs/1806.06681, https://doi.org/10.48550/arXiv.1806.06681
3. Zheng, X.-C., Sun, H.-M.: Hijacking unmanned aerial vehicle by exploiting civil GPS vulnerabilities using software-defined radio. Sens. Mater. **32**, 2729 (2020). https://doi.org/10.18494/SAM.2020.2783
4. Feng, Z., et al.: Efficient drone hijacking detection using onboard motion sensors. In: Design, Automation & Test in Europe Conference & Exhibition (DATE), pp. 1414–1419 (2017). https://doi.org/10.23919/DATE.2017.7927214
5. Noh, J., et al.: Tractor beam: safe-hijacking of consumer drones with adaptive GPS spoofing. ACM Trans. Priv. Secur. **22**(12), 1–12:26 (2019). https://doi.org/10.1145/3309735
6. Vuong, T.P., Loukas, G., Gan, D.: Performance evaluation of cyber-physical intrusion detection on a robotic vehicle. In: 2015 IEEE International Conference on Computer and Information Technology; Ubiquitous Computing and Communications; Dependable, Autonomic and Secure Computing; Pervasive Intelligence and Computing, pp. 2106–2113 (2015). https://doi.org/10.1109/CIT/IUCC/DASC/PICOM.2015.313
7. Mitchell, R., Chen, I.-R.: A survey of intrusion detection techniques for cyber-physical systems. ACM Comput. Surv. **46**, 55:1–55:29 (2014). https://doi.org/10.1145/2542049
8. Liu, S.B., Roehm, H., Heinzemann, C., Lütkebohle, I., Oehlerking, J., Althoff, M.: Provably safe motion of mobile robots in human environments. In: 2017 IEEE/RSJ International Conference on Intelligent Robots and Systems (IROS), pp. 1351–1357 (2017). https://doi.org/10.1109/IROS.2017.8202313
9. Markis, A., Papa, M., Kaselautzke, D., Rathmair, M., Sattinger, V., Brandstötter, M.: Safety of mobile robot systems in industrial applications. Presented at the May 9 (2019). https://doi.org/10.3217/978-3-85125-663-5-00
10. Guo, P., Kim, H., Virani, N., Xu, J., Zhu, M., Liu, P.: RoboADS: anomaly detection against sensor and actuator misbehaviors in mobile robots. In: 2018 48th Annual IEEE/IFIP International Conference on Dependable Systems and Networks (DSN), pp. 574–585 (2018). https://doi.org/10.1109/DSN.2018.00065
11. Oruma, S.O., Sánchez-Gordón, M., Colomo-Palacios, R., Gkioulos, V., Hansen, J.K.: A systematic review on social robots in public spaces: threat landscape and attack surface. Computers. **11**, 181 (2022). https://doi.org/10.3390/computers11120181
12. Dudek, W., Szynkiewicz, W.: Cyber-security for mobile service robots – challenges for cyber-physical system safety. J. Telecommun. Inf. Technol. 29–36 (2019)
13. Yaacoub, J.-P.A., Noura, H.N., Salman, O., Chehab, A.: Robotics cyber security: vulnerabilities, attacks, countermeasures, and recommendations. Int. J. Inf. Secur. **21**, 115–158 (2022). https://doi.org/10.1007/s10207-021-00545-8
14. Alrajeh, N.A., Khan, S., Shams, B.: Intrusion detection systems in wireless sensor networks: a review. Int. J. Distrib. Sens. Netw. **9**, 167575 (2013). https://doi.org/10.1155/2013/167575
15. Bezemskij, A., Loukas, G., Anthony, R.J., Gan, D.: Behaviour-based anomaly detection of cyber-physical attacks on a robotic vehicle. In: 2016 15th International Conference on Ubiquitous Computing and Communications and 2016 International Symposium on Cyberspace and Security (IUCC-CSS), pp. 61–68 (2016). https://doi.org/10.1109/IUCC-CSS.2016.017
16. Olivato, M., Cotugno, O., Brigato, L., Bloisi, D., Farinelli, A., Iocchi, L.: A comparative analysis on the use of autoencoders for robot security anomaly detection. In: 2019 IEEE/RSJ International Conference on Intelligent Robots and Systems (IROS), pp. 984–989 (2019). https://doi.org/10.1109/IROS40897.2019.8968105
17. Kaur, H., Singh, G., Minhas, J.: A review of machine learning based anomaly detection techniques (2013). http://arxiv.org/abs/1307.7286, https://doi.org/10.48550/arXiv.1307.7286
18. Jyothsna, V., Prasad, R., Prasad, K.M.: A review of anomaly based intrusion detection systems. Int. J. Comput. Appl. **28**, 26–35 (2011)

19. Luo, Y., Xiao, Y., Cheng, L., Peng, G., Yao, D. (Daphne): deep learning-based anomaly detection in cyber-physical systems: progress and opportunities. ACM Comput. Surv. **54**, 106:1–106:36 (2021). https://doi.org/10.1145/3453155
20. Zhang, Y., Tiňo, P., Leonardis, A., Tang, K.: A survey on neural network interpretability. IEEE Trans. Emerg. Top. Comput. Intell. **5**, 726–742 (2021). https://doi.org/10.1109/TETCI.2021.3100641
21. Spot. https://bostondynamics.com/products/spot/. Accessed 31 Oct 2023
22. Spot CORE Payload (Legacy). https://support.bostondynamics.com/s/article/Spot-CORE-payload-reference. Accessed 04 June 2024
23. tshark(1). https://www.wireshark.org/docs/man-pages/tshark.html. Accessed 03 Oct 2023
24. sklearn.preprocessing.MinMaxScaler. https://scikit-learn/stable/modules/generated/sklearn.preprocessing.MinMaxScaler.html. Accessed 12 Nov 2023
25. Iliou, T., Anagnostopoulos, C.-N., Nerantzaki, M., Anastassopoulos, G.: A novel machine learning data preprocessing method for enhancing classification algorithms performance. In: Proceedings of the 16th International Conference on Engineering Applications of Neural Networks (INNS), pp. 1–5. Association for Computing Machinery, New York (2015). https://doi.org/10.1145/2797143.2797155
26. Muhammad Ali, P., Faraj, R.: Data normalization and standardization: a technical report (2014). https://doi.org/10.13140/RG.2.2.28948.04489
27. Shen, M., et al.: Machine learning-powered encrypted network traffic analysis: a comprehensive survey. IEEE Commun. Surv. Tutor. **25**, 791–824 (2023). https://doi.org/10.1109/COMST.2022.3208196
28. Shao, E.: Encoding IP address as a feature for network intrusion detection (2019). https://hammer.purdue.edu/articles/thesis/Encoding_IP_Address_as_a_Feature_for_Network_Intrusion_Detection/11307287/1, https://doi.org/10.25394/PGS.11307287.v1
29. sklearn.preprocessing.LabelEncoder. https://scikit-learn/stable/modules/generated/sklearn.preprocessing.LabelEncoder.html. Accessed 13 Nov 2023
30. Xu, J., Wu, H., Wang, J., Long, M.: Anomaly transformer: time series anomaly detection with association discrepancy (2022). http://arxiv.org/abs/2110.02642, https://doi.org/10.48550/arXiv.2110.02642
31. Zhou, C., Paffenroth, R.C.: Anomaly detection with robust deep autoencoders. In: Proceedings of the 23rd ACM SIGKDD International Conference on Knowledge Discovery and Data Mining, pp. 665–674. Association for Computing Machinery, New York (2017). https://doi.org/10.1145/3097983.3098052
32. Li, D., Chen, D., Goh, J., Ng, S.: Anomaly detection with generative adversarial networks for multivariate time series (2019). http://arxiv.org/abs/1809.04758, https://doi.org/10.48550/arXiv.1809.04758
33. Cheng, Z., Zou, C., Dong, J.: Outlier detection using isolation forest and local outlier factor. In: Proceedings of the Conference on Research in Adaptive and Convergent Systems, pp. 161–168. Association for Computing Machinery, New York (2019). https://doi.org/10.1145/3338840.3355641
34. Creswell, A., White, T., Dumoulin, V., Arulkumaran, K., Sengupta, B., Bharath, A.A.: Generative adversarial networks: an overview. IEEE Signal Process. Mag. **35**, 53–65 (2018). https://doi.org/10.1109/MSP.2017.2765202
35. Bank, D., Koenigstein, N., Giryes, R.: Autoencoders. In: Rokach, L., Maimon, O., Shmueli, E. (eds.) Machine Learning for Data Science Handbook: Data Mining and Knowledge Discovery Handbook, pp. 353–374. Springer, Cham (2023). https://doi.org/10.1007/978-3-031-24628-9_16
36. Case Studies – Spot. https://bostondynamics.com/case-studies/. Accessed 11 Nov 2023

37. Nguyen, T.D., Nguyen, D.H.M., Tran, B.N., Vu, H., Mittal, N.: A Lightweight solution for defending against deauthentication/disassociation attacks on 802.11 networks. In: 2008 Proceedings of 17th International Conference on Computer Communications and Networks, pp. 1–6 (2008). https://doi.org/10.1109/ICCCN.2008.ECP.51
38. Hijazi, S., Obaidat, M.S.: Address resolution protocol spoofing attacks and security approaches: a survey. Secur. Priv. **2**, e49 (2019). https://doi.org/10.1002/spy2.49
39. Son, S., Shmatikov, V.: The Hitchhiker's guide to DNS cache poisoning. In: Jajodia, S., Zhou, J. (eds.) SecureComm 2010. LNICST, vol. 50, pp. 466–483. Springer, Heidelberg (2010). https://doi.org/10.1007/978-3-642-16161-2_27
40. Tan, X.Z., Vázquez, M., Carter, E.J., Morales, C.G., Steinfeld, A.: Inducing bystander interventions during robot abuse with social mechanisms. In: 2018 13th ACM/IEEE International Conference on Human-Robot Interaction (HRI), pp. 169–177 (2018)
41. Brščić, D., Kidokoro, H., Suehiro, Y., Kanda, T.: Escaping from children's abuse of social robots. In: 2015 10th ACM/IEEE International Conference on Human-Robot Interaction (HRI), pp. 59–66 (2015)

Cybersecurity and Policy

A Gamified Learning Approach for IoT Security Education Using Capture-the-Flag Competitions: Architecture and Insights

Mohammad Hamad[1(✉)], Andreas Finkenzeller[1], Monowar Hasan[2], Marc-Oliver Pahl[3], and Sebastian Steinhorst[1]

[1] Technical University of Munich, Munich, Germany
{mohammad.hamad,andreas.finkenzeller,sebastian.steinhorst}@tum.de

[2] Washington State University, Washington, USA
monowar.hasan@wsu.edu

[3] IMT Atlantique, Rennes, France
marc-oliver.pahl@imt-atlantique.fr

Abstract. Cybersecurity is one of the most critical issues for Internet of Things (IoT) systems today and in the future. Therefore, it is essential to educate students about cybersecurity and provide them with the skills needed to design and protect secure IoT systems. We share the experience we gained using a gamified learning approach to IoT security by integrating Capture the Flag (CTF) competitions into our university course. During the semester, students form teams and compete against each other in hacking various educational systems designed in a practically relevant way on our CTF platform. In our paper, we introduce the architecture of the CTF platform and provide student feedback on its effectiveness in teaching IoT security. The evaluation reflects student feedback over three semesters. We also share our lessons learned from creating and maintaining the CTF platform and discuss ideas on how to improve it further. Overall, the students engaged extensively in the CTF, had positive experiences with the provided platform and challenges, and were highly satisfied with our teaching approach. Based on the positive feedback, we believe our approach is an effective way to educate students in IoT security, and we encourage others to adopt this method.

Keywords: Active Learning · Security · Capture the Flag · Internet-of-Things

1 Introduction

There is an increasing prevalence of Internet of Things (IoT) devices in many critical sectors, such as healthcare, smart homes, transportation, and industrial systems. Due to the high value of these systems to adversaries, cyber-attacks on IoT systems are also on the rise. Hence, the future workforce must be trained with IoT

L. Horn Iwaya et al. (Eds.): NordSec 2024, LNCS 15396, pp. 161–175, 2025.
https://doi.org/10.1007/978-3-031-79007-2_9

security in mind. IoT systems have unique features and security requirements, demanding tailored security education [6]. Especially for core topics of student education, such as cybersecurity, advanced learning methods, including practical hands-on experiences, are needed [16]. Teaching a critical topic like cybersecurity requires providing students with hands-on experiences using various established tools and addressing multiple aspects of the field. Traditional homework and exam-based study for IoT security training are insufficient, as they lack the realism that can be reached with realistic environments, emulated attacks, and using practical defense strategy implementations and evaluation. Also, interaction among students that prepares them for teamwork is often ignored—leaving students inadequately prepared for real-world operations and challenges. Without new teaching techniques focused on active and student-centered learning, the gaps in cybersecurity education within high-level institutions and the industrial sector will persist and increase [5].

Game-based learning has been proven to enhance student motivation and educational outcomes [17]. Applying this approach to cybersecurity education can effectively engage students and improve their understanding of complex security concepts [14]. There exist gamification approaches, including card games [11], serious games [19], and capture-the-flag (CTF) competitions [7,10,21]. CTF challenges emerged outside the classical university curriculum. They are considered an excellent method for teaching cybersecurity, as they enhance students' cybersecurity skills and actively engage them in practical learning experiences [4,9].

Contributions. This paper presents our experiences adapting the CTF methodology for IoT security training to a university curriculum, including tools, setup, and the challenges we faced. We summarize our observations from the successful deployment of IoT security CTF modules in a leading European university over the last three semesters.

In this work, we made the following contributions:

- We introduce our CTF system architecture for hands-on Industrial Internet of Things (IIoT) security learning, targeting reproducibility and usability for other instructors (Sect. 2).
- Using the data from three semesters, we present student evaluations of using the CTF as part of our course, including performance analysis of our pedagogical modules (Sect. 3).
- We share our observations and lessons that can assist instructors who are interested in adopting the CTF methodology to their curriculum using our system, and we discuss possible improvements to enhance the system further (Sect. 4).

Other educators, upon request, will have access to our CTF tools, including blueprints for the implementations, challenges, and related course materials.

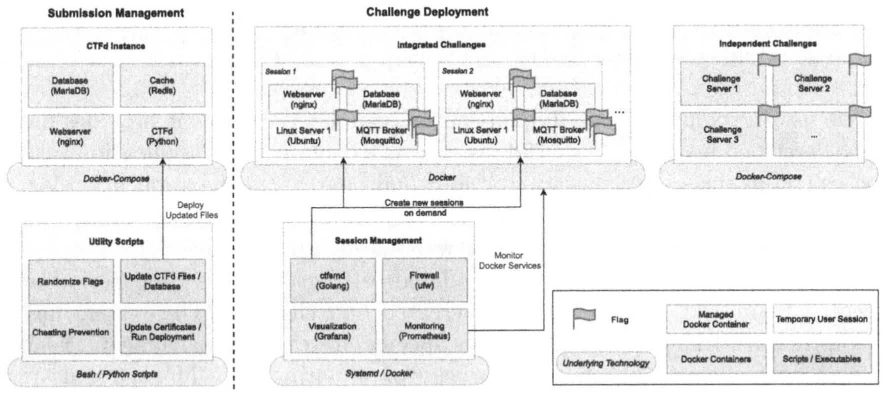

Fig. 1. High-level schematic of our CTF-based IoT cybersecurity training framework.

2 CTF-Based Active Learning

A CTF is primarily a competition where individual students or teams solve challenges to earn points within a limited time period. The team with the highest score, or the first to get the total score, wins the competition. Our CTF-based training approach provides a gamified learning environment for students to explore practical IoT security challenges in a safe environment. We do so by designing a hands-on IoT security course. The course was taught at the Technical University of Munich in the summer semester of 2021 (SS 21) and continued in the winter semesters of 2021–2022 (WS 21–22) and 2022–2023 (WS 22–23). We are currently adapting the materials for the Future-IoT PhD Summer School (a part of the German-French Academy for the Industry of the Future event) [2] and Washington State University's critical infrastructure security course (a required course in the BS in cybersecurity curriculum).

Figure 1 depicts the high-level illustration of our system design. The CTF ecosystem is primarily divided into two components. One unit is **submission management**, which deals with management-related (i.e., back-end) tasks, such as user and team management, flag submissions, hints, and scoreboard display. The second part manages the **challenge deployment**, i.e., provides the technical infrastructure for the students to deliberately attack to obtain the flags.

2.1 Submission Management

To keep track of all scores, every CTF needs a management system that properly documents the progress of each user and team. Hence, we need a system that handles user and team registration and tracks the collected points. Besides, the students need to know *(a)* what challenges are available, *(b)* how many points each challenge gives, and *(c)* which challenges the team has already solved. In addition, we need the possibility for the students to submit flags and a system that checks for correct submissions and ideally prevents cheating. An important additional feature in an educational CTF is challenge hints to help students overcome thinking barriers. Further, a public scoreboard keeps up the motivation in the competition [16].

We use the commonly used open-source system `CTFd` [1] as it provides most of the described features. The `CTFd` instance is a containerized application (using Docker [15] in this case) consisting of four main parts: *(a)* the application logic, *(b)* a database, *(c)* a web server, and *(d)* a cache for fast access. Once the system runs, the CTF can be configured via a web-based Admin panel.

New challenges and general CTF-related settings, such as time period and accepted team size, can be manually created and changed. The system has a backup feature that saves and restores specific states of an ongoing CTF. We use this mechanism to automate the process of preparing the CTF each semester. The set of provided challenges changes slowly over time due to the required effort to create new challenges. However, we change the flag strings each semester to prevent copy-pasting old flags from a previous semester. For this, a script randomizes the flags and builds a "backup" from a template that can be uploaded to the `CTFd` system to start a clean run. In addition, we also run other *scripts* like detecting suspicious submissions to prevent cheating attempts. These steps are automated to deploy a fresh CTF each semester with new flags by executing only one command.

2.2 Challenge Deployment

The challenges/flags can be deployed in static forms, such as complementary files, or more dynamically with some server interaction. For static files, `CTFd` provides a built-in mechanism for users to download the files from the challenge description. Server interaction, however, requires custom implementation. We use Docker containers to deploy these interactive challenges. We support two distinct approaches. In one approach, the tasks are **independent**, and one challenge/flag is hosted by one Docker container. This is convenient because adding or removing challenges is simpler as there are no dependencies on other tasks.

As this does not reflect the full complexity of actual IoT systems, we implement another approach offering a more involved experience. We name this as **integrated** challenges. For this, we deploy multiple containers that constitute a complete infrastructure. An example contains a web server, a database, or an entire virtual network with several hosts. The flags are then hidden within the application and not specifically in a single container. This makes the infrastructure significantly more complex, introducing another problem. Since now the task is not limited to stateless server connections, anyone accessing the system can experience a shared system state. This could include created files on a server or a command history that might unintentionally reveal parts of the solution to other teams. Hence, we use individual sessions per user (i.e., team) with a unique state that others cannot access.

The *session management* is a custom implementation and always keeps some sessions available for fast access. Once a user requests a session, another one is created to maintain the desired number of available sessions. A session expires after a certain time, which the course instructors can set. Once the student knows the issue, the required steps to get a flag are not time-consuming. We implement the challenges so the students can reasonably solve them within a few hours. Besides being more motivating, another benefit of short sessions is that once a system is unintentionally broken due to rash student actions (e.g., file deletion), a student can start from scratch with a new session. Since the session management is based on managing containers via the Docker APIs,[1] the current state can be monitored and visualized with existing tools (e.g., Prometheus[2] and Grafana[3]).

2.3 CTF Competitions

Our semesters are 15 weeks long. Each semester, we run two CTF competitions. The first one is held in Week 5, and the second one is in Week 10. The first CTF includes 18 independent challenges, the main topic of which is Cryptography for IoT. The second CTF includes 14 challenges. These challenges are divided into three groups, each with multiple "integrated" tasks. Students must solve one challenge to be able to solve the next one, and so forth.

The second CTF's challenges cover topics related to IoT communications, such as HTTP and Message Queuing Telemetry Transport (MQTT) protocols [12,18,20], different attacks such as Machine-In-The-Middle (MITM) attacks, and IoT web security attacks. Figure 2 shows the architecture of one MQTT challenge. The challenge is set up using four nodes: 3 act as publishers, and one acts as both a publisher and a subscriber. Additionally, there is a Mosquitto broker[4] that allows the nodes to exchange messages (publish and subscribe) on different topics. The flags in this challenge represent security issues in the MQTT implementation, such as the use of default credentials, weak usernames and passwords, spoofing the communication between the different nodes, and the broker. The team will try to connect to the broker (attacker node) and retrieve all the flags. The challenges in both CTFs vary in difficulty from easy to hard. Each CTF is open for ten days, followed by two days for students to submit their report detailing the steps to collect the flag for each challenge.

Students are allowed to form teams of a maximum of 2 students. Teams that solve all the challenges receive full marks, with the remaining teams graded on a sliding scale. To encourage students to finish faster and maintain the competitive spirit of the CTF, we offer a bonus to the first 3 teams, which could be used if they did not perform well in the final exam. The CTFs contributed 40% of the final grade.

---

1 https://docs.docker.com/engine/api/.
2 https://prometheus.io/.
3 https://grafana.com/.
4 https://mosquitto.org/.

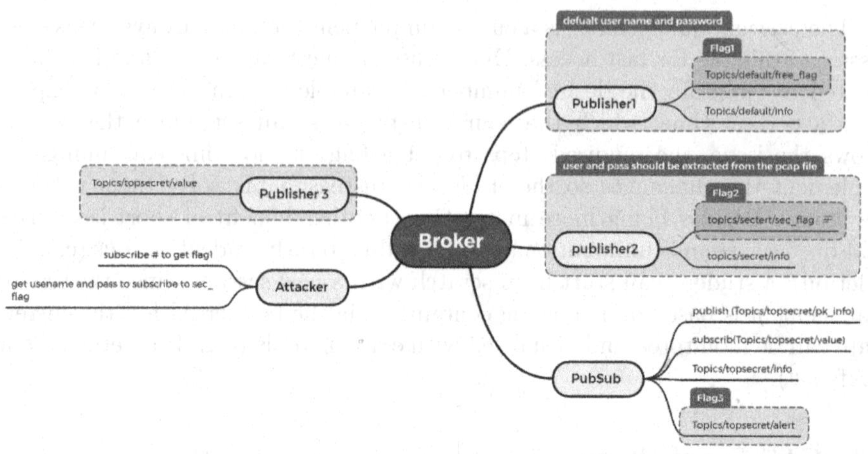

Fig. 2. Sample of challenges: MQTT challenges

The course was taught in the Summer semester of 2021 (SS 21) and continued in the Winter Semesters of 2021–2022 (WS 21–22) and 2022–2023 (WS 22–23). Additionally, it was recently being offered this semester, SS 2024.

3 Student Response and Feedback

We conducted *extensive surveys* to obtain students' reactions and feedback about our CTF-based learning components. Specifically, to collect student feedback about their experience with the CTF, we conducted **three surveys** each semester: *(a)* the *preliminary survey* at the beginning of the course, *(b)* the first CTF survey after the first CTF, and *(c)* the *second CTF* survey at the end of second CTF (the end of the course).

All surveys are designed to allow students to participate *anonymously* and are open for 10 days. Each survey includes multiple questions to collect student feedback about the CTF experience. Besides these three surveys we designed, there is also the *official course evaluation*, which is managed by the department and conducted before the end of the semester. As part of the first and the second CTF surveys, we also asked students to express their opinions about the overall experience of using the CTF as the main tool to learn and better understand IoT cybersecurity aspects. The feedback is very positive. The course was even *nominated for the Best Course Award.* The survey questions, student feedback, and the official course evaluation are available and accessible to other educators upon request.

Table 1. Student participation in the surveys.

Surveys		Semester			
		SS 21	WS 21–22	WS 22–23	SS 24
First CTF	Total	20	26	26	28
	Participated	13	24	20	17
	Response Rate	**65.0%**	**93.4%**	**76.9%**	**60.7%**
Second CTF	Total	20	26	26	28
	Participated	12	17	16	15
	Response Rate	**60.0%**	**65.4%**	**61.5%**	**53.6%**

Participation. Table 1 presents the total enrollment, students who participated in the first CTF and second CTF surveys across three semesters, and the corresponding percentage of participation. As the table shows, at least 65% of the students provided their feedback for the first CTF survey and 60% for the second CTF survey each semester. We ensured that student feedback was completely voluntary and did not pose an additional burden on the students to participate. Despite anonymity, we also set the survey deadline after announcing the official CTF results to reassure students that negative feedback would not impact their grading.

3.1 Key Survey Questions

Although our survey comprised several questions, we focus on the following three aspects for the brevity of our discussion.

Q1. *How many hours did each student spend on solving all challenges?*

The goal of this question is to assess the *(a) engagement level* of the students, *(b)* willingness to spend *extended* time on challenges, and *(c)* other aspects such as the difficulty of the challenges and student motivation. The answer to this question is based on the results of the *first and second CTF surveys.*

Q2. *How was the system running during the whole duration of the CTF?*

This question aims to provide insights into the overall student experience with our platform. We answer this question based on the results obtained from the *second CTF surveys.*

Q3. *Would a current student recommend the course to other students?*

This question relates to student satisfaction and benchmarks the course's success. We rely on the *official course evaluation* results to obtain the findings.

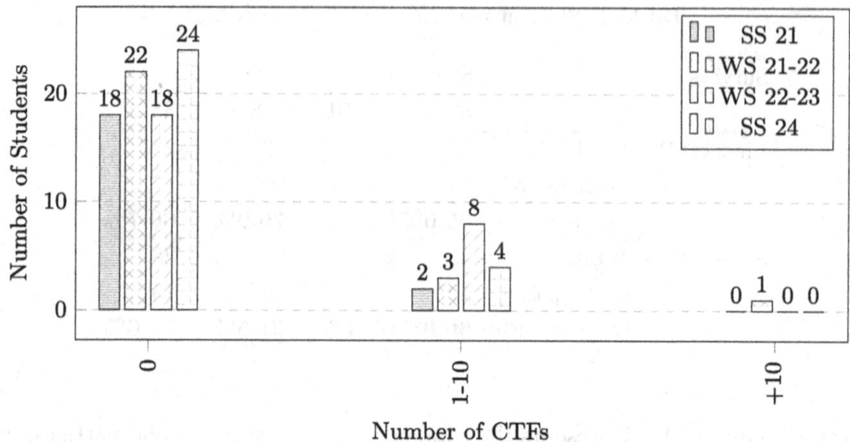

Fig. 3. The number of CTFs students participated in before joining the course across different semesters. Most of the students were participating for the first time.

3.2 Observations

Our observations and findings from the student participation for the past three offerings are summarized below.

Pre-knowledge of CTFs. As mentioned earlier, we conducted a *preliminary survey* at the start of each semester to assess students' initial programming and cybersecurity skills. The goal is to identify areas that need emphasis during the semester. Additionally, we asked students if they were familiar with CTF principles and if they had previously participated in any CTFs. Figure 3 depicts the results of this question across three semesters. As the figure shows, most students had never played any CTFs and were unfamiliar with them before attending the course (90% in SS 21, 85% in WS 21–22, 70% in WS 22–23, and 87% in SS 24). One noticeable trend is the increase in the number of students who have played CTFs before and are willing to attend the course.

Student Engagement. To better understand how using CTF challenges to teach IoT cybersecurity is engaging for students, we asked them how many hours they spend on solving the problems (**Q1**, see Sect. 3.1). The result of this question is presented in Fig. 4. The figures show that students were willing to spend a long time playing the CTF and trying to get the flags (i.e., solutions) of the challenges. We note that more than 95% of the teams obtained all the challenges, which implies students kept playing until they obtained all the flags.

We find that having previous experience with CTFs may have some impact. In one case, the student managed to finish in less than 10 h, as seen in Figs. 4c and 4d. This is the same year where we had a student with more than 10 CTF experiences (see Fig. 3). However, this is our speculation, as the results are anonymous. Another observation is that the independent challenges may take longer

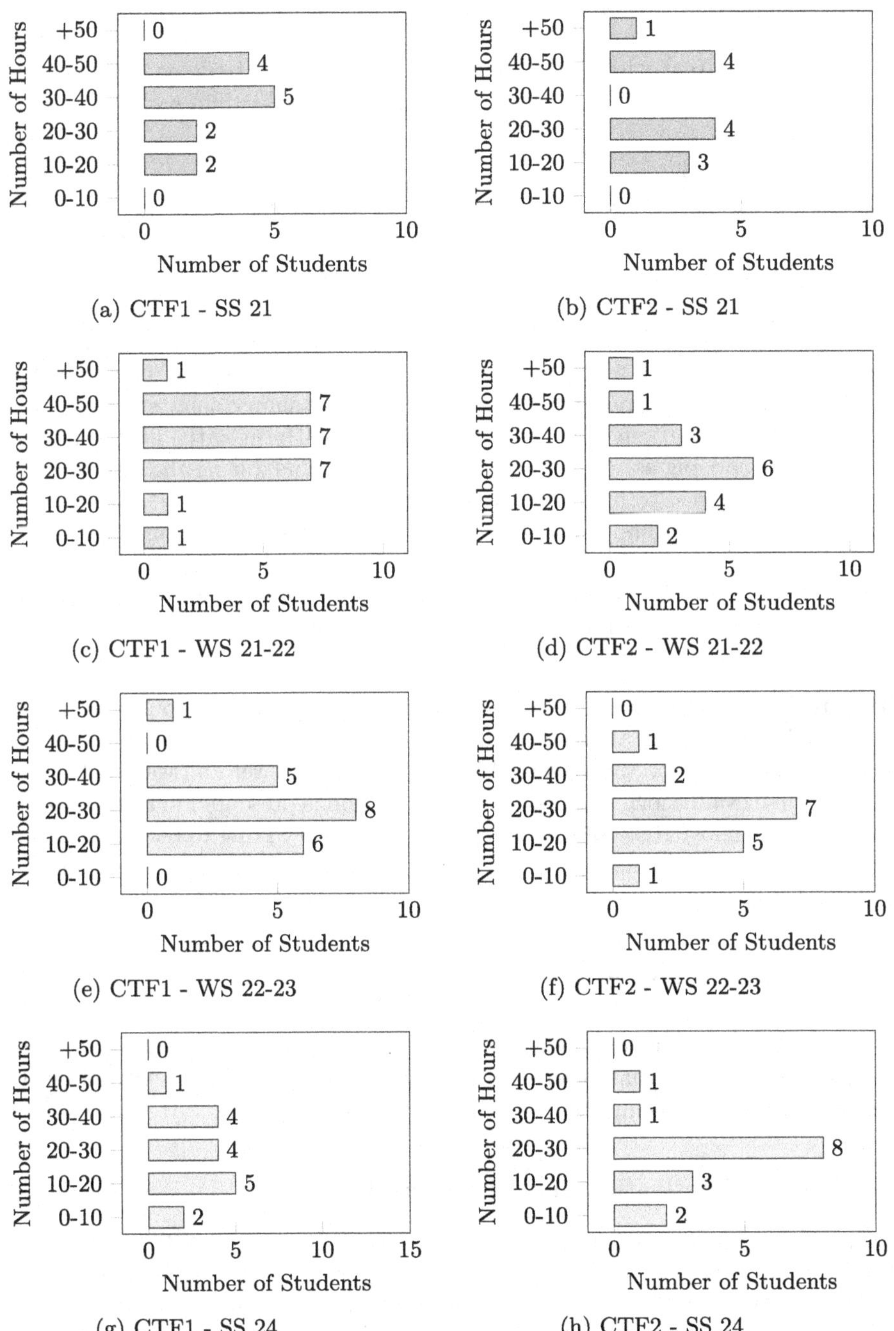

(a) CTF1 - SS 21

(b) CTF2 - SS 21

(c) CTF1 - WS 21-22

(d) CTF2 - WS 21-22

(e) CTF1 - WS 22-23

(f) CTF2 - WS 22-23

(g) CTF1 - SS 24

(h) CTF2 - SS 24

Fig. 4. The hours spent by students to solve all the challenges for the first and second CTFs across the three semesters.

to solve compared to the integrated ones (see Fig. 4). This can be explained by the gained experience (e.g., with the platform and the mindset) from the first CTF and the context where the integrated challenges are built on one another, leading the students on a more gradual path toward individual solutions.

Platform Usability. As part of the second CTF survey, we asked the students how the system was performing during the competitions (see **Q2**, Sect. 3.1). Specifically, we asked them to reflect on their experience in both CTFs. The possible choices they were given were: *(a)* the system was running flawlessly, *(b)* mostly smoothly, *(c)* with some errors, *(d)* with many major errors, and *(e)* with unacceptable errors. We also asked the students to provide detailed descriptions of the errors they faced and to offer suggestions for improving the platform. We present the students' responses in Fig. 5. As the figure shows, some students were not fully satisfied and reported some errors in the platform in the first semester. This is not surprising as the system was not fully stable during the first offering of the CTF. We tried to fix all the errors and adopt the students' suggestions to improve the usability and responsiveness of the platform. This improvement is reflected in the answers from the recent times we offered the course (WS 22–23 and SS 24), where all the students were satisfied with the performance of the platform (see Fig. 5c and Fig. 5d).

Student Satisfaction. To assess student satisfaction with our course, students were asked whether they would recommend the course to other students (**Q3**, see Sect. 3.1). The question was designed for a Yes or No answer and was part of the official course evaluation. The result of this question is presented in Fig. 6. As the figure shows, almost 100% of the students were always willing to recommend our course. Hence, our gamification strategy has a positive influence on the students' learning experience.

4 Lessons Learned

We now summarize our experience with the past three offerings. We share the challenges we faced so that other educators are cognizant of them while adopting similar gamification techniques.

4.1 Student Motivation and Enthusiasm

By implementing the "learning by doing" approach through CTF challenges, students gain practical experience in IIoT cybersecurity. The game-like hands-on activities engage students and create an entertaining and gamified learning environment—this is also apparent from student survey responses. Our observations in the last three semesters where we integrated CTF into our course are also akin to the others who use CTF-based pedagogical modules [9].

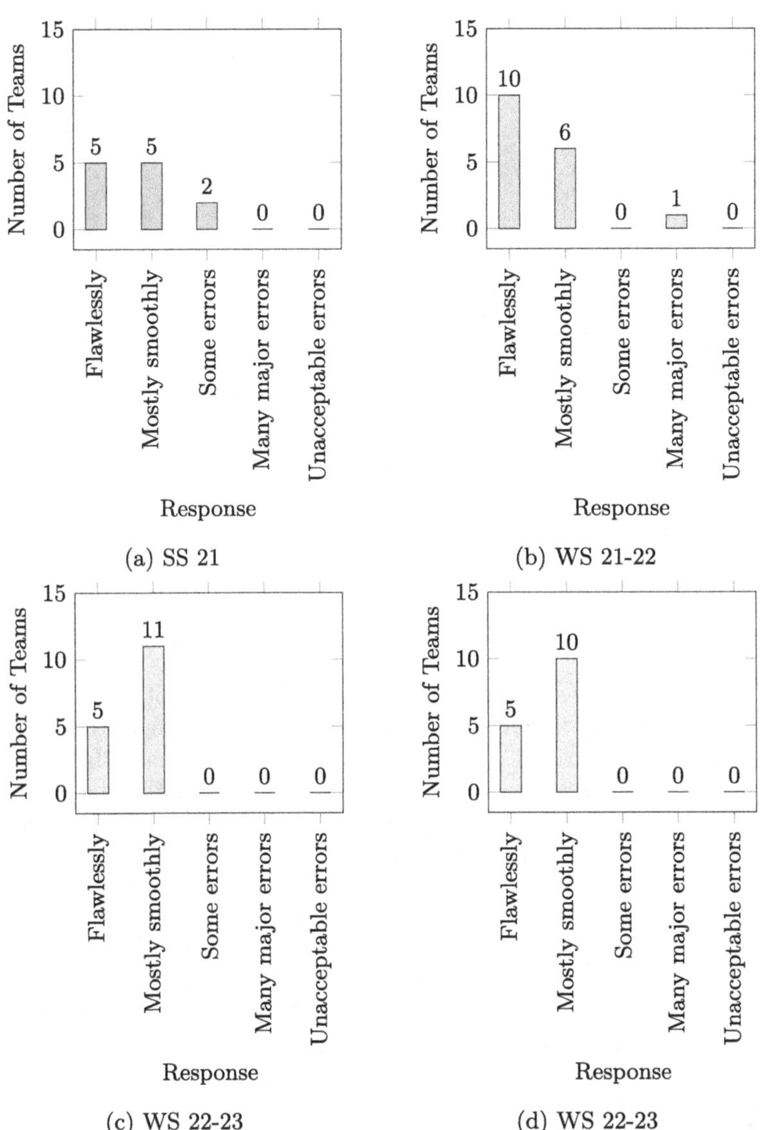

Fig. 5. Students' responses about the platform usability across three semesters.

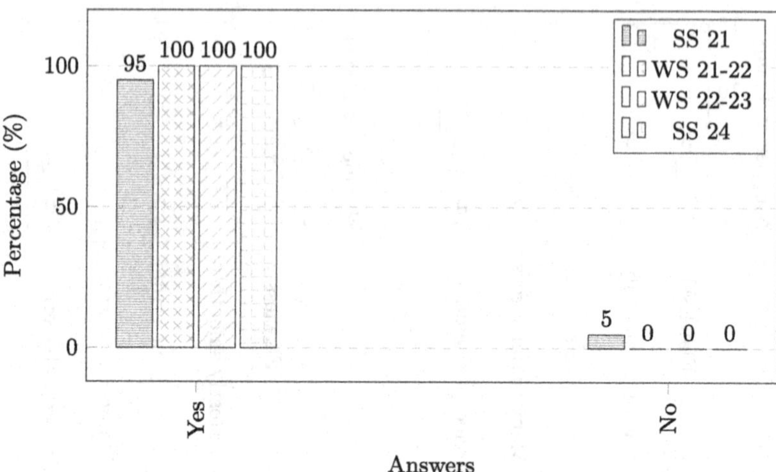

Fig. 6. The students' answers about their willingness to recommend the course to other students.

4.2 Cheating Prevention

Cheating in the form of sharing flags between teams is one of the pitfalls of our existing system. This is, however, also an issue in any CTF-like learning modules. Although we try to mitigate this by asking students to share their write-ups and randomly selecting teams to present how they solved the challenges, it is still imperfect. Implementing cheating prevention mechanisms, for instance, that analyze logs and traces left by students in the system [8,13] can be used to detect if they followed certain patterns to reach each flag. Integrating such mechanisms is one of our ongoing activities. We strongly recommend that instructors consider using similar cheating prevention mechanisms. One could argue that students can still share the instructions on how to get the flags. However, we believe learning concepts is still useful if students attempt to understand instructions and adapt their results rather than simply copying solutions directly.

4.3 Collaborative Challenge Creation

Another way to prevent cheating is the deployment of new challenges for each semester. While this would be theoretically an ideal setup, in practice, we have two major hurdles: *(a)* the significant effort required to create the challenges in each semester and *(b)* the challenges associated with adapting the lecture contents and theoretical materials to reflect the new CTFs. However, a community-driven approach could ease this process. For instance, several instructors can contribute to creating and sharing challenges and corresponding theoretical concepts/algorithms, which will reduce the effort required by each individual to develop a completely new set of challenges each semester or year. We initiate this process by collaborating with two other institutions in different countries (one in Europe and the other in North America, see Sect. 2).

4.4 Team Isolation

Since we built the platform mostly from scratch, we faced development challenges in reaching the current stable stage. One major difficulty was the lack of a session management system. We had only one set of containers for all students. This shared state could be modified and seen by all teams. While this approach theoretically worked, in practice, it impacted our intended challenges in two ways. First, teams could unintentionally get hints by looking at the "bash history" in Linux to see what commands others used to solve challenges. This limits students' learning. Second, teams could change the running system by creating or deleting files and scattering misleading hints. The instructors need to consider such technical challenges while building their CTF environment.

4.5 Student-Driven Flag Exploration

We find that asking students to submit and present a write-up about their methodology and journey to capture each flag has been extremely helpful. This approach allows us to see how creative some students are and helps us identify and close unintended vulnerabilities in the system. Additionally, it gives students the opportunity to perform live attack demonstrations and supports a *flipped classroom model* [3].

4.6 Competition Duration

We learned that extending the duration of CTFs to 10 days, unlike the typical one or two-day non-educational CTFs, is beneficial for students who have other obligations such as classes and work. This longer timeframe allows all participants to fully engage without time pressure. Some teams finished within the first two days, while many others completed the tasks on the last day, demonstrating the need for a flexible schedule. We awarded bonus points to the top teams who finished first to maintain their competitive spirit and motivation. This balance of extended duration and competitive incentives was well-received by students.

4.7 The Role of a Final Exam

By observing the flag submissions on the CTF platform, we noticed that some team members were actively participating while others were less engaged. Although this variation could be considered normal, ensuring that all team members are engaged in the learning activities is essential. Therefore, we conducted an oral or written exam at the end of the course. The final exam ensured that all students actively participated in the CTF challenges and acquired the necessary knowledge to achieve the intended learning outcomes.

5 Conclusion

As IoT systems become inseparable from modern everyday life, security threats to those critical systems are also rising. A well-trained workforce is needed to improve security posture and protect those systems from cyber breaches. Teaching and training students for this critical domain require techniques beyond traditional methods. CTF competitions are one such way to provide hands-on IoT security training experience through a gamified learning approach. Our CTF-based training methodology, which has been successfully executed for the last three semesters, will inspire other institutions to build similar frameworks for IoT security learning.

Acknowledgments. This work is supported by *(a)* the Federal Ministry of Education and Research (BMBF) and the Free State of Bavaria under the Excellence Strategy of the Federal Government and the Länder in the context of the German-French Academy for the Industry of the Future of Institut Mines-Télécom (IMT) and Technical University of Munich (TUM), *(b)* FEDER development fund of the Brittany region of France and *(c)* the US National Science Foundation Award 2312006. Any findings, opinions, recommendations, or conclusions expressed in this paper are solely those of the authors and do not necessarily reflect the sponsors' views.

References

1. CTFd: Capture the flag platform. https://ctfd.io/
2. Future-IoT PhD School. https://school.future-iot.org. Accessed 25 sept 2024
3. Al-Samarraie, H., Shamsuddin, A., Alzahrani, A.I.: A flipped classroom model in higher education: a review of the evidence across disciplines. Educ. Tech. Res. Dev. **68**(3), 1017–1051 (2020)
4. Balon, T., Baggili, I.: CyberCompetitions: a survey of competitions, tools, and systems to support cybersecurity education. Educ. Inf. Technol. **28**(9), 11759–11791 (2023)
5. Blažič, B.J.: Changing the landscape of cybersecurity education in the EU: will the new approach produce the required cybersecurity skills? Educ. Inf. Technol. **27**(3), 3011–3036 (2022)
6. Canbaz, M.A., OHearon, K., McKee, M., Hossain, M.N.: IoT privacy and security in teaching institutions: inside the classroom and beyond. In: 2021 ASEE Virtual Annual Conference Content Access (2021)
7. Carlisle, M., Chiaramonte, M., Caswell, D.: Using CTFs for an undergraduate cyber education. In: 2015 USENIX Summit on Gaming, Games, and Gamification in Security Education (3GSE 2015) (2015)
8. Chetwyn, R.A., Erdődi, L.: Cheat detection in cyber security capture the flag games-an automated cyber threat hunting approach. In: Proceedings of the 28th C&ESAR, p. 175 (2021)
9. Cole, S.V.: Impact of capture the flag (CTF)-style vs. traditional exercises in an introductory computer security class. In: Proceedings of the 27th ACM Conference on on Innovation and Technology in Computer Science Education, vol. 1. pp. 470–476 (2022)

10. Collins, J., Ford, V.: Teaching by practice: shaping secure coding mentalities through cybersecurity CTFs. J. Cybersecur. Educ. Res. Pract. **2022**(2), 9 (2023)
11. Denning, T., Shostack, A., Kohno, T.: Practical lessons from creating the {Control-Alt-Hack} card game and research challenges for games in education and research. In: 2014 USENIX Summit on Gaming, Games, and Gamification in Security Education (3GSE 2014) (2014)
12. Hamad, M., Finkenzeller, A., Liu, H., Lauinger, J., Prevelakis, V., Steinhorst, S.: SEEMQTT: secure end-to-end MQTT-based communication for mobile IoT systems using secret sharing and trust delegation. IEEE Internet Things J. **10**(4), 3384–3406 (2022)
13. Kakouros, N., Johnson, P., Lagerström, R.: Detecting plagiarism in penetration testing education. In: Nordsec 2020, The 25th Nordic Conference on Secure IT Systems, 23–24 November 2020, Online (2020)
14. Karagiannis, S., Papaioannou, T., Magkos, E., Tsohou, A.: Game-based information security/privacy education and awareness: theory and practice. In: Themistocleous, M., Papadaki, M., Kamal, M.M. (eds.) Information Systems, pp. 509–525. Springer, Cham (2020)
15. Miell, I., Sayers, A.: Docker in Practice. Simon and Schuster (2019)
16. Pahl, M.O.: The iLab concept: making teaching better, at scale. IEEE Commun. Mag. **55**(11), 178–185 (2017). https://doi.org/10.1109/MCOM.2017.1700394
17. Papastergiou, M.: Digital game-based learning in high school computer science education: impact on educational effectiveness and student motivation. Comput. Educ. **52**(1), 1–12 (2009). https://doi.org/10.1016/j.compedu.2008.06.004
18. Soni, D., Makwana, A.: A survey on MQTT: a protocol of internet of things (IoT). In: International Conference on Telecommunication, Power Analysis and Computing Techniques (ICTPACT-2017), vol. 20, pp. 173–177 (2017)
19. Švábenský, V., Vykopal, J., Cermak, M., Laštovička, M.: Enhancing cybersecurity skills by creating serious games. In: Proceedings of the 23rd Annual ACM Conference on Innovation and Technology in Computer Science Education, pp. 194–199 (2018)
20. Wukkadada, B., Wankhede, K., Nambiar, R., Nair, A.: Comparison with HTTP and MQTT in internet of things (IoT). In: 2018 International Conference on Inventive Research in Computing Applications (ICIRCA), pp. 249–253. IEEE (2018)
21. Zouahi, H.: Gamifying cybersecurity education: a CTF-based approach to engaging students in software security laboratories (2024). https://ojs.library.queensu.ca/index.php/PCEEA/article/view/17071

NIS2 Directive in Sweden: A Report on the Readiness of Swedish Critical Infrastructure

Ebba Rehnstam, Wera Winquist, and Simon Hacks(✉)

Stockholm University, Stockholm, Sweden
wera.w@live.se, simon.hacks@dsv.su.se

Abstract. This study evaluates the preparedness of Swedish critical infrastructure for the NIS2 directive, which sets enhanced EU standards for information- and cybersecurity. The research reveals a generally low competence level, highlighting a lack of readiness for the directive's requirements. Variations in competence are influenced by organizational size, resource availability, and existing strategic processes. Larger organizations with roles like CISOs tend to have higher competence levels, yet significant gaps remain in meeting the directive's demands. The study emphasizes the need for comprehensive business and gap analyses to identify critical areas for improvement. Organizations should adopt strategic, systematic approaches to cybersecurity that integrate with existing processes. Enhancing competencies requires increased investment in education and training, supported by leadership committed to fostering a robust security culture. The NIS2 directive should be seen not as a regulatory burden but as an opportunity to enhance resilience against cyber threats. Methodologically, the study uses a consistent semi-structured interview approach with experts and authorities to ensure validity and reliability. Although the qualitative nature of the research limits generalizability, it offers critical insights into Sweden's cybersecurity readiness and the need for strategic improvements.

Keywords: NIS2 Directive · Cybersecurity Readiness · Information Security Competence · Swedish Critical Infrastructure

1 Introduction

Digital information and systems security is crucial in today's increasingly interconnected world. Cyber threats are becoming more sophisticated and frequent, posing significant risks to individuals and organizations [10]. Recognizing these challenges, the European Union (EU) has proactively strengthened its cybersecurity framework to protect the digital infrastructure across its member states. In 2020, the EU introduced a comprehensive cybersecurity strategy to enhance its resilience against such threats, aiming to safeguard essential services and promote a secure digital environment [7].

L. Horn Iwaya et al. (Eds.): NordSec 2024, LNCS 15396, pp. 176–195, 2025.
https://doi.org/10.1007/978-3-031-79007-2_10

The EU launched the Network and Information Security Directive 2 (NIS2) [9] in 2022 as part of this initiative. This directive is an evolution of the original NIS directive [8] and sets out more rigorous cybersecurity requirements for a broader range of sectors. NIS2 aims to establish a high common level of cybersecurity across the EU by enforcing stricter regulations on key sectors, including energy, healthcare, finance, and digital infrastructure. The directive mandates these critical sectors to adopt robust cybersecurity practices to prevent, detect, and respond to cyber incidents effectively.

Despite these advancements, Sweden's critical infrastructure must comply with the NIS2 directive [9]. These critical services, including energy supply, healthcare, and electronic communications, are essential for maintaining the country's societal and economic stability. However, the increased cybersecurity requirements pose significant challenges for these sectors, which may lack the necessary resources and expertise to meet the new standards.

Accordingly, we formulate our research question: *How prepared is Sweden's critical infrastructure for the NIS2 directive?* To explore this, we also investigate two sub-questions: *What is the current level of information security competence among the critical infrastructure?* and *What competencies are required to comply with future EU regulatory requirements on information security?*

To answer these questions, we conducted semi-structured interviews with information security consultants and relevant authorities familiar with Sweden's critical infrastructure. This qualitative approach allows an in-depth understanding of existing skills and preparedness levels. The data collected from the interviews were analyzed using thematic analysis, enabling us to identify key themes and patterns related to the competencies and challenges faced by these entities.

The structure of this paper is as follows: First, we provide an extended background and review relevant literature to explain key concepts in information and cybersecurity. We then describe the research method used to collect and analyze data. The results section presents our findings, highlighting the current preparedness and identified skill gaps. Finally, the discussion section interprets the findings in the context of existing literature, offering conclusions and recommendations for future research and policy implementation.

2 Background

2.1 NIS2 Directive

The Network and Information Security Directive 2 (NIS2) [9] is a regulatory initiative by the European Union (EU) to enhance cybersecurity across its member states. As part of the EU's broader strategy introduced in 2020, NIS2 builds on the foundations of the original NIS directive, extending its scope and establishing stricter cybersecurity requirements to protect essential services and infrastructures from growing cyber threats.

The introduction of the NIS2 directive in 2022 responds to the escalating risks associated with cyber threats in an increasingly digital and interconnected world [9]. This directive aims to create a high common level of cybersecurity across the EU by requiring member states to implement more comprehensive and uniform cybersecurity measures [17]. NIS2 broadens the range of sectors covered, encompassing both essential and important entities, which include sectors such as energy, transportation, banking, health, and digital infrastructure [16].

The directive shall strengthen the resilience of network and information systems critical to the internal market and the well-being of European citizens. It mandates that these entities adopt robust risk management practices to effectively address cybersecurity challenges and enhance the EU's collective cyber defense [11]. NIS2 states several key obligations on entities covered by the directive to improve their cybersecurity:

- **Risk Management** Entities must establish comprehensive risk management frameworks, including regular risk assessments and appropriate security measures to manage and mitigate cybersecurity risks effectively [5].
- **Incident Reporting** Covered entities must report significant cybersecurity incidents to their national Computer Security Incident Response Teams, facilitating timely responses and information sharing across the EU [2].
- **Supply Chain Security** The directive emphasizes the need to secure the entire supply chain of network and information systems, ensuring that third-party suppliers adhere to cybersecurity standards [19].
- **Training and Awareness** NIS2 highlights the importance of cybersecurity hygiene and awareness among personnel. Entities must implement training programs to ensure employees can recognize and respond to cyber threats [3].
- **Governance and Accountability** The directive holds management bodies of essential entities accountable for ensuring compliance with cybersecurity obligations, fostering a culture of cybersecurity within organizations [4].

Member states must transpose NIS2 into national law by October 2024 [16]. This transition poses challenges, including increased investment in cybersecurity infrastructure and skills development to meet the directive's requirements [17].

2.2 Information Security in Sweden

The Swedish Civil Contingencies Agency (MSB) plays a crucial role in enhancing the cybersecurity posture of Sweden's public sector. As cyber threats evolve and increase in sophistication, robust information security measures and competencies become important. To address these challenges, MSB has developed initiatives such as "Cybersäkerhetskoll and Kompetensförsörjning"[1] to assess and improve Swedish organizations' cybersecurity readiness and capabilities.

Cybersäkerhetskollen, including Infosäkkollen[2] and IT-säkkollen[3], is an initiative to evaluate the systematic work on information and cybersecurity within Swedish municipalities, regions, and government agencies. TMSB conducted

[1] English: Cybersecurity Check and Skills Supply.
[2] English: Information Security Check.
[3] English: IT-Security Check.

Infosäkkollen between May 17 and September 29, 2023, and involved 211 participating organizations [13]. The initiative aims to provide a comprehensive overview of how these entities manage information security, highlighting areas of strength and identifying gaps that must be addressed to meet upcoming regulatory requirements like the NIS2 directive.

The assessment uses a four-level scale to indicate the maturity of an organization's information and cybersecurity efforts [13]: (1) Basic information and cybersecurity practices; (2) Systematic work with improved fundamentals; (3) Qualified content in information and cybersecurity work; (4) Continuous improvements in security practices. The results from Cybersäkerhetskollen showed that 69% of the participating organizations did not meet the basic requirements of level 1, indicating a significant need for improvement in their information security practices. Only about 3% achieved level 3 or 4, highlighting a critical need for enhanced engagement and prioritization of cybersecurity efforts [13].

In 2021, MSB conducted a preliminary study on the state of information- and cybersecurity competencies in Sweden. They identified a global and national shortage of skilled professionals, with a growing demand for expertise [12]. The study emphasized that organizations must focus on developing existing staff and attracting new talent to fill the competency gaps. MSB's Kompetensförsörjning initiative addresses these challenges by focusing on two main groups: current professionals and those not yet in the workforce. The initiative seeks to improve professionals' skills through training and development programs. At the same time, for those not yet in the workforce, it aims to create pathways into the field through education, certifications, and partnerships with companies [12].

2.3 Related Work

A study by da Veiga [18] explored how data protection regulations influence the information security culture within organizations across various jurisdictions, including Mauritius, Switzerland, Guernsey, South Africa, the UK, and Australia. The findings indicated that countries with established data protection laws, such as Mauritius and Switzerland, generally exhibited higher levels of information security culture than those without such regulations, like South Africa. However, the results also showed variability, with some countries like the UK and Australia performing lower than expected, suggesting that the mere existence of regulations does not guarantee a strong security culture.

Chowdhury et al. [3] examined how critical infrastructure companies approach cybersecurity awareness and training in Norway. The research found that most of these organizations had invested in technical infrastructure and cybersecurity expertise to enhance security. Many also cited regulatory requirements as key drivers for implementing cybersecurity training initiatives. The study emphasized the importance of involving all staff in security training to foster a culture of awareness and resilience against cyber threats.

Dedeke and Masterson [6] conducted a comparative analysis of cybersecurity implementation frameworks in Australia, the UK, and the USA. The study highlighted that while all frameworks emphasized risk management, they differed significantly in their coverage of security domains. The Australian framework was noted for its broad risk management coverage but lacked detailed incident response and recovery guidance. The UK framework aligned strongly with NIST standards yet missed some specific measures.

South Korea presents a unique case where cybersecurity regulations are dispersed across various sector-specific laws rather than an overarching cybersecurity law [14]. This fragmented approach emphasizes sector-specific needs but poses challenges for ensuring uniform compliance and coordination across industries. The South Korean model highlights the complexity of balancing sector-specific regulations with overarching cybersecurity goals.

The international studies underscore the importance of tailored cybersecurity approaches, considering each country's unique regulatory, cultural, and operational contexts. Effective cybersecurity strategies often involve a combination of strong regulatory frameworks, comprehensive training programs, and active engagement with all organizational stakeholders. For Sweden, these international insights can inform the implementation of the NIS2 directive by emphasizing the need for a balanced approach that incorporates both regulatory compliance and the cultivation of a strong security culture. Lessons from countries like Norway, where regulatory requirements drive training and awareness initiatives, can help Swedish entities prioritize these aspects in their cybersecurity strategies.

3 Research Method

This study employed a qualitative research approach, utilizing semi-structured interviews to gather in-depth insights into the preparedness of Sweden's critical infrastructure for the NIS2 directive. The qualitative method was chosen to capture the complexities of information security practices and competencies within these entities. The research was conducted through a series of semi-structured interviews[4] with key stakeholders in information security. We applied two guidelines for the interviews (cf. Appendix). On the one hand, we had a guideline for the authorities. On the other hand, we had a guideline for the consultancy. This approach allowed for a flexible yet focused exploration of the participants' perspectives and experiences, enabling the researchers to delve deeply into specific topics while allowing respondents to express their insights in detail.

The study involved a purposive sample of 11 participants (cf. Table 1) selected for their expertise and relevance to the research questions. The interviews were conducted face-to-face or via digital platforms, depending on participant preferences and logistical considerations. Each interview was recorded with the participant's consent and subsequently transcribed for analysis.

These participants included:

- **Five Information Security Consultants** Professionals with extensive experience advising organizations on cybersecurity practices and compliance

[4] See appendices for the translated interview guidelines. All interviews were held in Swedish.

with regulatory frameworks. These consultants provided valuable insights into the current state of information security within Swedish critical infrastructure and the challenges posed by the NIS2 directive.
- **Five Representatives from Relevant Authorities** Officials from Swedish government agencies responsible for overseeing and supporting critical societal functions. These authorities included MSB and other regulatory bodies identified as key players in implementing the NIS2 directive [16].
- **Two Representatives from Post- och Telestyrelsen (PTS)** Participants from Sweden's national regulatory authority for electronic communications and postal services participated in a joint interview to provide insights into the telecommunications sector's preparedness for the directive.

Table 1. Demographic Information of Respondents

ID	Organisation	Role	Experience	Formal Education
R1	Consultancy	Managing Director	>10 years	No
R2	Transport-styrelsen[a]	NIS and Cyber Inspector	0–5 years	Training via job
R3	Consultancy	Director	>10 years	No
R4	Consultancy	Information Security Consultant	>10 years	Training via job
R5	Consultancy	Manager	5–10 years	Master's in Information Systems
R6	MSB[b]	Officer & NIS Coordinator	5–10 years	Computer Science
R7.1	PTS[c]	Officer	0–5 years	Training via job
R7.2	PTS	Lawyer	0–5 years	No
R8	Stockholms Länsstyrelse[d]	Regulatory Officer	5–10 years	Computer and Systems Science, Certification, Training via job
R9	Consultancy	Director	>10 years	Training via job, Certification
R10	Energi-myndigheten[e]	Unit Manager	0–5 years	Systems Science, Training via job

[a] English: Swedish Transport Agency
[b] English: Swedish Civil Contingencies Agency
[c] English: Swedish Post and Telecom Authority
[d] English: Stockholm's County Administrative Board
[e] English: Swedish Energy Agency

Data analysis was done using thematic analysis, which involves identifying and interpreting patterns and themes within qualitative data [1]. This approach enabled the researchers to systematically categorize and analyze the data, highlighting key competencies and challenges in implementing the NIS2 directive.

4 Results

The study's results shed light on Sweden's critical infrastructure preparedness for the upcoming NIS2 directive. Through thematic analysis of interviews with information security experts and authorities, key themes and categories were identified, summarizing the current competence levels and future needs. Notable gaps in skills, organizational challenges like resource allocation, and the importance of training and awareness programs were highlighted. The readiness for NIS2 compliance, particularly in developing risk management strategies, is also assessed. Table 2 summarizes the identified themes and categories.

Table 2. Identified Themes and Categoires

Theme	Category
NIS2 at Authorities	Actual Knowledge
	Planning
NIS2 in Critical Infrastructure	Actual Knowledge
	Challenges
	Needed Competencies
	Readiness
General Information- and Cybersecurity Activities	Critical Competencies
	Actions to Improve Competencies
	Common Mistakes
Awareness	Security Culture
	Education

4.1 NIS2 at Authorities

Actual Knowledge. The results show that some authorities acknowledge their limited understanding of the directive, while others believe they are well-informed. Authorities with previous experience with NIS tend to express a higher knowledge level about the directive than those without NIS experience. R10 states that they have quite a good understanding of information security and the relevant legislation. In contrast, R8 responds that their level of knowledge is low.

R2 sees NIS2 as a natural continuation of NIS: *"We see it as quite a natural continuation of NIS, so NIS2 is just a more structured version of what NIS was. I mean, more sectors. There will be higher fines. There will be even clearer requirements for management. Like more specific, clearer requirements around certain risk management and security measures"*.

R7.1, who previously worked with NIS, believes their knowledge of NIS2 is good in the central parts and the parts concerning their authority. R6 explains that they see NIS2 in a coordinated way, that it is important to create a secure society, and that all parts of the organization must be addressed.

Planning. This category highlights the responses from authorities regarding their planning for NIS2. Several respondents mentioned that planning has not progressed far due to delays in investigating how NIS2 will be implemented in Swedish law. R6 mentioned that before the investigation was completed, they knew little more than what was stated in the directive text on the EU's website. There are still many uncertainties: *"What risk management measures should organizations take to achieve a higher level of cybersecurity? We still don't know. It just says, 'Use these cryptographic strategies.' But it's still quite vague"*. Some frustration was expressed over not receiving clear instructions on what is expected, which has hindered planning. There is also pressure concerning the time available to organizations, as the directive is set to take effect on January 1, 2025: *"It's very clear that it has become a bit rushed. I think this law should have been introduced in October. But it will probably be from January instead. And for it to work from January, we must work very hard to have all the regulations in place so that everyone knows what applies. There is some pressure".* (R2)

The data shows, however, that some have worked and planned for NIS2 more than others. R2 said they have been involved in the investigation. Another respondent was involved in the investigation, and they could read drafts before publication: *"This past year, at least since I came in, you could say I have been working. Most of our work time is spent analyzing and looking at NIS2, what will happen, and planning how this will look in national regulation. It has become a huge part of our work".* (R7.2)

A single authority will also have several new sectors to supervise, and it is believed that it would be helpful to have a tool that organizations can use to determine if they are affected by NIS2 (R7.1). This will make it easier for authorities to identify affected organizations since they have to register with the supervisory authority if they are covered.

4.2 NIS2 in Critical Infrastructure

Actual Knowledge. According to R6, organizations today struggle to meet the minimum level of cybersecurity, but it is not necessarily the competence within the organizations that is the problem; instead, it is the lack of management engagement. Management must take responsibility for educating themselves and their staff. R9 responded that they assumed that competence is low and alarmingly low in authorities regarding understanding the significance of information security. According to R9, many understand technical IT security and are good at protection mechanisms and security measures, but organizations are not as good at understanding the breadth that NIS2 aims for.

R2 replied that most organizations have potential for improvement. Still, it depends on the organization's size and whether there is, for example, a Chief Information Security Officer (CISO). R2 further states that organizations with strategic work and management systems are better positioned. R2 also points out that some organizations do not even know if they are affected by NIS2. Both R1 and R5 believe that larger companies generally have greater maturity. R8 responded that the level of knowledge is *"very low"* and that there is a lack of competence. According to R8, recruiting people with information security skills is difficult, especially regarding technical aspects.

R5 suggests there are differences between domains, such as having a higher level of maturity. R3 also states it is difficult to say generally because the market is not homogeneous, and some industries have good knowledge and work methodically. At the same time, R3 agrees with other respondents that there is relatively low and poor competence concerning NIS2. R3 believes this is because the previous NIS did not have clear requirements. Furthermore, R3 suggests it may have negative consequences if the EU names NIS2 after the previous NIS directive. This could lead operators following the previous directive to be lulled into a false sense of security, thinking they are already compliant when they might not fully understand what NIS2 entails. R3 believes that if the organization is already working systematically and is certified, for example, ISO 27000, understands risks and risk management, and works with incident handling, they are well positioned in terms of competence for the directive.

R7 explains that the organizations affected by NIS today, for which they conduct risk analysis oversight, especially the larger organizations, have a good level of knowledge in information security, with some also being ISO 27000 certified. These organizations work systematically and take the necessary measures. This includes monitoring changes and logging. According to R7, however, there is a noticeable difference with smaller organizations with fewer employees and resources.

Challenges. According to R9, it will be a challenge not to create separate silos for NIS2 but instead to integrate the directive into the existing business and its information security. Furthermore, R9 points out that security awareness within organizations easily becomes more of a *"tick in the box"*. The respondent indicates that it is not taken seriously enough and that continuous work is not being done. R6 suggests that the overlapping regulations, for example, in municipalities that will be affected by several different sector-specific regulations and will have oversight for multiple sectors, will be a challenge. R6 argues that MSB ensures that this oversight coordination is conducted effectively.

R3, R4, and R9 mention that meeting the high requirements on incident handling and incident reporting may be challenging. R3 elaborates on this by saying that it is not just about capturing and reporting incidents that have occurred but also incidents that almost occurred or could have happened.

R2, R3, and R5 mention risk management as a challenge, and R3 elaborates on this by stating that it is no longer enough to have a *"risk assessment"* on two risks but that one must do a thorough job with a comprehensive and all-encompassing risk assessment within the business. R3 and R5 mention the term *"all hazards approach"* in terms of risk management, and R5 links this to the need for the organization to find out all risks and potential threats, which is a major difference in NIS2 compared to NIS.

Regarding challenges with the NIS2 directive, R3 mentioned the management of third-party suppliers, which the directive will impose requirements. R7 also believes it will be challenging for businesses to manage security in the supply chain. R9 also suggests that handling supply chains can be challenging, as the respondent indicates that businesses are generally poor at this.

Furthermore, R2 suggests that a challenge will be making their interpretation of what the regulations will mean for their own business and getting management's engagement. R7.2 also highlights that it may be difficult for organizations with the legal interpretation of the new laws that come with the NIS2 directive.

Needed Competencies. Regarding essential competencies, R2 responded: *"One should not focus too much on cybersecurity; instead, one must understand that it is about an all-risk perspective on information security"*. At the same time,

R2 stated that cybersecurity competence must increase. R2 and R5 mention the CISO's role as an important competence, whereas R2 believes that the CISO contributes strategically. R4 also mentions strategic information security work as an important competence. Furthermore, R2 suggests that various competence profiles are needed and mentions ENISA's European Cybersecurity Skills Framework (ECSF). ECSF is a framework created by ENISA that includes a document listing twelve important profiles for cybersecurity roles, including the CISO role. R1 mentions project management roles for implementing management systems and believes that it is important while being a major challenge to update and maintain the management system.

R3, R7, R9, and R10 state that more general competence in information security is needed, and R3 further suggests that competence needs to be enhanced at all levels within the organization, with management having the greatest responsibility for this. R8 and R6 also highlight management competence as important. R4 also discussed different layers of competence and said that specialized competence, such as incident management, would be required. R1, R4, R5, and R7 suggest that legal competence will be needed to interpret the directive. Thus, it is not just a question of information security competence but various forms of competence. R5 and R8 mention competence in IT security. R5 and R7 believe that competence in incorporating systematic work is important.

Readiness. R1 stated that an important step is to look at industry standards and mentioned ISO 27000 and the NIST framework as examples. R2, R7, R8, and R9 also believe working with a management system is beneficial, with ISO 27000 being mentioned. Furthermore, both R7 and R9 emphasize that it is important in combination with ensuring that the organization conducts systematic work.

R4 highlights the importance of systematic work and suggests that the organization should consider other industry-specific regulations. R4 further underscores the importance of incremental work, where the organization works with strategic goals broken down into internal governance for everything that affects them. R4 believes it is important to move away from compliance-driven security work. R4 also emphasizes that organizations should not handle NIS2 requirements separately, as this would undermine their own security culture.

R2 and R3 stress the importance of structured work, and R3 builds on this by saying that it is also important to involve the entire organization so that everyone is informed about what applies. Furthermore, R3 emphasizes that organizations should create clear roles and responsibilities. A concrete step R3 also mentions for organizations is to create a current state description and a gap analysis against the NIS2 directive to more easily identify their shortcomings and then follow up with an implementation or action plan, for example. This should be done with a risk-based approach with risk assessments to identify vulnerabilities, according to R3. R6 suggests that the organization conduct a business analysis to examine how they are affected and what needs to be done to follow up.

R5 suggests that the organization conduct an impact assessment and identify its five most critical issues and follow up with crisis exercises where they can immerse themselves in the scenario to gain that perspective.

Ahead of NIS2, R5 believes it is important to keep track of the Swedish law that will be adopted and monitor the requirements set at the EU level. In addition, R5 states that it is important for the organization to ensure active collaboration with its supervisory authority and keep an eye on the guides that will be released. R5 also mentions the importance of conducting risk assessments and a thorough risk analysis. Furthermore, R5 believes it is important to note that NIS2 applies to the entire company, and the organization should review its operations and include all parts. Besides this, R5 underscores the importance of resource allocation and management engagement.

R1 mentions supplier follow-up and provides examples of reviewing agreements with suppliers from which IT operations services are purchased. R1 also highlights that incident management is complex and expensive and that there is a need for standard packages for organizations to manage this. R6 and R7 recommend seeking support from MSB and their guidance.

4.3 General Information and Cybersecurity Activities

Critical Competencies. R2 believes that the needed competencies depend on the essential service and its systems, but it is vital to understand and identify risks. In addition, R2 mentions IT security competence and competence related to the organization's vulnerabilities. R2 highlights the necessity of having *"iron-clad"* knowledge of the organization and the systems it depends on.

R3 argues that the most critical competence involves a comprehensive view and not working in silos. Furthermore, R3 emphasizes the importance of achieving a holistic view regarding risks and the incident chain. R7 also mentions that various competencies, such as legal, security expertise, and technical understanding, are needed. R8 believes it is essential to have people with technical IT security competence and those who work with softer values, such as management systems. R6 argues that it is not necessarily a lot of technical, specialized competence that is needed but rather the overarching, systematic competence.

R4 responded that a mix of generalists and specialists is needed. This includes the technical aspect, strategy, and connection to the organization's goals and visions: *"I'm a bit cynical about my industry because there is no intrinsic value. Everything is about ensuring that businesses can continue as they should according to their goals and vision. So both parts are needed"*. R4 also mentions a case where an organization hired a senior psychologist and behavioral scientist to communicate security issues. R4 argues that communication regarding security can often become problematic if the recipient lacks the knowledge or experience. Still, it is very important to understand the target audience when disseminating security work throughout the organization.

R5 brings up the importance of having a coordinator, such as someone in a CISO position and having an information security person sitting with management. R1 underscores the importance of working with change and that there must be understanding within the board and management.

Actions to Improve Competencies. According to R9, "management buy-in" is required, meaning governing functions must understand the importance of information- and cybersecurity. R9 further emphasizes that it is essential to understand that many security aspects are important – not just technical or physical protections but also awareness training. R9 also argues that one must understand supplier risks and not relinquish responsibility just because of outsourcing: *"[...] you can outsource functions, but not the problem"*. R7.1 underscores that knowledge and information must reach all channels, from Parliament and the government to agencies and companies. In addition, R7.1 believes that it must receive more media attention. R7.1 says that it starts with management and comes from the top down. R8 thinks that MSB has an important role and needs to release more materials and support.

R5 brings up that organizations should hire more people with backgrounds in information and cybersecurity and that more people who work with information security are generally needed internationally, especially in Sweden. Both R5 and R10 emphasize that it is a problem that it is harder for public companies to attract people with the right skills because individuals are more easily drawn to the private sector since it can offer higher salaries.

Common Mistakes. R3 argues that a common mistake is the abdication of responsibility. That is, responsibility is distributed among several people who do not understand the overarching picture, leading to problems because the overall picture is lost. R3 also mentions that third-party suppliers are not monitored, and follow-up is missed. R5 also points out that management shifting responsibility is a common mistake. R5 believes it is the responsibility of all employees, but management must integrate information security and, therefore, has a significant responsibility. Furthermore, R5 also mentions that organizations allocate too small a budget and that more resources are often required than are provided.

According to R9, a common mistake is working in silos. That is, working in silos with different regulations when they all deal with the same fundamental risk, which leads to a wrong focus: *"I think that is a huge risk in the work today. It's so easy to have your little bubble and your thinking. Which is why it's so incredibly important to get this holistic view and comprehensive process, both for risks and, yes, the incident chain, and so on"*.

R3 and R5 continue to explain that a common mistake is thinking it is only IT's responsibility to keep track of information- and cybersecurity. This doesn't seem right because information security should, among other things, set requirements for IT in connection with other parts and processes in the organization. R5 compared this to GDPR, where a data protection officer was lifted out so that they could be separated from and impose requirements on the organization, and said that this was a good solution.

R4 responded that a mistake was making technical shifts too quickly. They mention the NIST framework as an example, based on the parts *"identify, protect, detect, and respond"*. In projects that use this framework, R4 argues that organizations spend too little time in the identification phase, quickly leading to the project becoming expensive and failing.

4.4 Awareness

Security Culture. R4 responded that it is important to work with the security culture and not just focus on technology or processes, which is common in cybersecurity work: *"I would almost call it strategic security culture work. Seeing it as a crucial part of building your information and cybersecurity capabilities. People talk a lot about technology, especially in the cybersecurity track, and sometimes about processes. But we rarely focus on people"*. R4 further said: *"I think most organizations would benefit from starting to work a little more focused on the security culture within the organization. Because it is, for me anyway, a slightly bigger issue than just doing some onboarding and weekly awareness, which can be a bit off the mark"*. R4 also mentions that risk-based awareness is essential and that it should be targeted and adapted to one's role and the information one handles within the organization. In addition, R4 emphasizes that the organization should measure how well the awareness training is going and ensure that every employee understands why security work is important.

R4 also believes it is important for all employees to understand that it is a joint effort and not something that only affects certain departments or individuals. R3 and R5 responded that increasing general awareness is important. R3 believes it is essential to do this for all employees, regardless of their level, and management engagement is essential. R8 and R2 also emphasize the importance of management's involvement. They say that starting with management can increase control over the organization and examine several parts of it, such as continuity planning, risks, and more. In line with this, R4 underscores that management plays a vital role in ensuring that work is not pushed down into the organization. They also believe it is important to focus on the people in the organization regarding information and cybersecurity capabilities. Furthermore, R3 mentions that the awareness required by the directive must be ensured and increased, especially awareness of risks.

R2 brings up the requirement for cyber hygiene and believes it is connected to security culture: *"I can add that the term cyber hygiene pops up sometimes, and that's what I would like to convey, somehow. [...] It is related to security culture somehow, and it is very important to meet high standards with systematic information security work. Still, it's crucial-excuse my language-that you clean up the foundation, so to speak, raise the baseline. That you have this basic cyber hygiene. And there are requirements for that, too. You must ensure that everyone is involved – you can't have the weakest link in the chain because there will be a vulnerability that a potential antagonist could exploit to sabotage"*. R6 also mentions NIS2's requirement for cyber hygiene and the most basic measures as an important aspect linked to awareness, security culture, and education.

Education. R8 believes that there are not many cybersecurity courses at universities and that more are needed: *"Since the lack of competence is so significant, we must educate people"*. R1 thinks it is important to have more specialized education in information security, and R2 and R5 also mention education as important and that more people need to be trained in information and cybersecurity. Regarding critical areas of competence to maintain good information security, R1 states that it is important to work with education actively: *"There might be a course related to pure security, and then you do your master's in NIS2. I now feel that there are quite a few general courses related to cybersecurity, and that's fine. However, I think there should be something a bit more specialized".* R10 mentions education in terms of competence that will be important to meet the NIS2 directive: *"We need to invest even more in education, all the way down to primary school. And what is it called? High school. And also within universities and colleges".*

Regarding essential measures, several respondents mention education and awareness creation. R10 expresses that organizations should give their employees basic training as an important step to increase awareness. R7.1 and R6 mention the NIS2 requirement that management must educate themselves and their employees. R7.1 also stresses the need to find a way to get employees to understand why it is important and beneficial for the organization: *"Few people have formal, like cyber or information security training. At least we do. I can't say we have a handle on the market, but it isn't easy to find people who know this if we hire people, for example. It might be a problem because they don't work at agencies or want to work at an agency".*

5 Discussion

The results indicate that the overall level of competence regarding NIS2 in critical societal functions is generally perceived as low, although it varies depending on the organization. Several respondents suggested that the competence level is somewhere between one and two on MSB's model, with some organizations struggling to meet even the lowest level. This aligns with the findings of Waizel [19], which identified a knowledge gap related to NIS2 among EU organizations. Despite the overall low competence level, respondents perceived it as somewhat higher than the findings of MSB's "infosäkkollen", although both studies highlight significant deficiencies.

The variation in maturity levels towards NIS2 is attributed to several factors, with organizational size being a key determinant affecting resources, role availability, and budget. Respondents noted that organizations with a CISO or those working systematically with management systems tend to have higher competence levels. Larger, more established organizations are perceived to have higher competence than smaller ones. Some respondents expressed concern that naming NIS2 after its predecessor, NIS, might lead to a false sense of competence among critical entities. Organizations previously working actively with NIS tend to have higher competence levels, yet many authorities acknowledged their limited knowledge, partly due to delays in legislative preparations. This aligns with findings by Da Veiga [18], which suggest that countries with implemented laws typically have higher levels of information security culture.

The primary challenges identified concerning the NIS2 directive include incident handling and risk management. With its reporting requirements, the incident management process is considered complex and challenging. Respondents noted the necessity of identifying potential incidents before they occur, requiring significant resources and expertise.

Risk management is highlighted as challenging due to the directive's higher demands, requiring organizations to identify all risks, not just a few, and necessitating more extensive resource allocation. This aligns with Vandezande's [17] assertion that risk management will be a significant challenge for entities affected by NIS2. Additionally, managing supply chains and third-party vendors was cited as challenging due to the current low levels of engagement with these issues, highlighting a gap in compliance.

Given these challenges, the consensus among respondents is that Sweden's critical infrastructure is not sufficiently prepared to meet the requirements of NIS2, with the directive's minimum standards perceived as significantly higher than the current maturity levels.

Respondents identified a need for a mix of competencies to meet the requirements of the upcoming EU directive. While many highlighted the need to enhance information and cybersecurity skills, other factors were deemed necessary to complement these skills. Roles such as CISO and project managers are crucial for meeting the directive's requirements. There is a recognized need to elevate management competence to ensure high collective competence within organizations.

The results indicate a need for both technical and soft skills, including legal knowledge and a broader understanding of information security. Emphasis is placed on developing strategic, systematic, and cyclical information and cybersecurity processes to ensure seamless integration into business operations and continuity. Organizations need to develop clear roles with specific competencies related to information and cybersecurity, with leadership responsible for coordinating efforts and fostering a strong security culture.

To bridge the gap between current maturity levels and the requirements of the NIS2 directive, respondents suggest that organizations should not approach compliance as isolated requirements but as a strategic effort integrated with existing processes. Key aspects include systematic, structured, and cyclical work with information and cybersecurity, focusing on continuous improvement and resilience against threats and incidents.

Proposed preparatory measures include conducting business analyses, gap analyses, impact assessments, and thorough supplier follow-up and incident management planning. MSB's role as a support function for critical societal functions is emphasized, with calls for more materials and support from MSB to facilitate compliance efforts.

Respondents emphasize the need for diverse competencies to achieve good information- and cybersecurity levels, and a mix of generalists and specialists is needed. There is a consensus on the importance of a comprehensive approach, avoiding working in silos with regulations and cybersecurity. Instead, information security should be central to organizations, integrated with processes and continuous efforts.

Engaging management and enhancing their competence is critical to maintaining high information security standards, with management responsible for setting a high standard reflected throughout the organization. This aligns with MSB's findings that greater management engagement is needed to strengthen information security efforts. Respondents also highlighted the need for societal efforts to raise competence levels, including government and media outreach.

Awareness is crucial for raising competence levels, and organizations must strategically and systematically strengthen security culture through ongoing internal training. This aligns with Siponen's [15] assertion that increased awareness can enhance organizational security effectiveness.

NIS2's cyber hygiene requirements are closely tied to security culture, aiming to raise the minimum standard across organizations to minimize vulnerabilities. Respondents stress the importance of offering more specialized education, from primary school to university level, to address the need for skilled information and cybersecurity professionals. This demand for competence aligns with MSB's preliminary study findings. The essential role of management and the need for increased awareness across all employees echo findings from Chowdhury et al. [3] emphasizing the need for deep understanding among management roles.

6 Conclusion

The overall competence level of Swedish critical infrastructure is insufficient concerning the NIS2 directive's requirements, posing significant challenges for these organizations. The findings suggest they are unprepared to meet the new EU information and cybersecurity demands. To enhance readiness and achieve compliance, organizations must take several key actions. Conducting business and gap analyses to identify critical areas is essential. Organizations should establish a framework for information and cybersecurity efforts that align with existing strategic processes, ensuring a dynamic, systematic approach capable of continuous improvement. Adopting an all-hazards perspective will enable a comprehensive understanding of potential risks to the organization.

Improving competence requires both societal and internal investments in education. Allocating more resources is crucial for real change, which can only be achieved if leaders understand the critical role of information- and cybersecurity in sustaining societal and organizational operations. Awareness of information- and cybersecurity is essential to raising standards, as the weakest link poses the most significant vulnerability. This awareness must flow from the top down, with leadership fostering a robust security culture throughout society and the organization.

The study's validity is supported by a consistent interview approach, with semi-structured formats and equal treatment of respondents, ensuring comparable data collection. Ten interviews provided nuanced insights, contributing to the study's credibility. The involvement of information security experts and experienced authorities offers a well-founded perspective on the research topic.

However, the need for occasional interpretation of responses may impact validity, though not significantly. Variability in interview settings, such as face-to-face versus video calls, could affect external validity.

Reliability is a challenge in qualitative research due to the dynamic nature of social environments. The study documents its methodology transparently, enabling potential replication with similar results if respondents with comparable backgrounds are selected. While different entities may yield varied outcomes, a consistent semi-structured interview enhances internal reliability. All interviews were transcribed for accurate representation, and a thematic analysis method was consistently applied, further supporting reliability.

External reliability is weaker due to the qualitative approach's context dependency, limiting generalizability. There is some transferability to other EU nations' critical societal functions, considering similarities in security culture and capabilities. However, the application of the directive varies by country, and the study's focus on Sweden may hinder broader applicability.

Disclosure of Interests. The authors have no competing interests to declare relevant to this article's content.

A Appendix

A.1 Interview Guideline – Authorities

- **Introduction**
  - What is your title?
  - Could you please tell us more about your work and the organization?
  - Do you have any formal information and/or cybersecurity education?
  - How long have you been working in the industry?
- **NIS2**
  - What knowledge do you have about NIS2?
  - How are you approaching your role as a supervisory authority for the NIS2 directive?
    - ⋆ Have you developed any plans?
    - ⋆ How long do you expect it will take?
  - Concerning NIS2, what competencies do you see in the critical societal functions in Sweden today?
    - ⋆ How deep is this knowledge? Based on the following levels from MSB's infosäkkollen:
      - · Level 1: Corresponds to the basics of information and cybersecurity work
      - · Level 2: Information and cybersecurity work is conducted with some systematics and a better understanding of the basics
      - · Level 3: Achieved qualified content in information and cybersecurity work
      - · Level 4: Continuous improvements are made.

- What areas of NIS2 are potential challenges requiring more organizational focus?
- How do you think organizations should structure their information and cybersecurity work to meet these new requirements?
- What competencies are important to address the NIS2 directive?

– **General Questions**
- To ensure a strong security culture, how do you engage employees to increase the organization's awareness of information and cybersecurity?
- What do you consider an important step to take to improve information and cybersecurity competence?
- What are the most critical competency areas or skills within an organization to maintain good information and cybersecurity?
- Do you use any other frameworks or regulations?

– **Outro**
- Related to the topic, is there any question we haven't asked that you think we should have?
- Is there anything you would like to add beyond what has already been said and beyond what we have asked for?

A.2 Interview Guideline – Consultancy

– **Introduction**
- What is your title?
- Could you please tell us more about what you do and the company in general?
- Do you have any formal information and/or cybersecurity education?
- How long have you been working in the industry?

– **NIS2**
- Concerning NIS2, what competencies do you see in the market today?
    - ⋆ How deep is this knowledge? Based on the following levels from MSB's infosäkkollen:
        - · Level 1: Corresponds to the basics of information and cybersecurity work
        - · Level 2: Information and cybersecurity work is conducted with some systematics and a better understanding of the basics
        - · Level 3: Achieved qualified content in information and cybersecurity work
        - · Level 4: Continuous improvements are made.
- What areas of NIS2 are potential challenges requiring more organizational focus?
- How do you think organizations should structure their information and cybersecurity work to meet these new requirements?
- What competencies are important to address the NIS2 directive?

– **General Questions**
- What do you consider an important step to take to improve information and cybersecurity competence?

  - What are the most critical competency areas or skills within an organization to maintain good information and cybersecurity?
  - What are common mistakes organizations make in improving information and cybersecurity? How do you think these can best be avoided?
- **Outro**
  - Related to the topic, is there any question we haven't asked that you think we should have?
  - Is there anything you would like to add beyond what has already been said and beyond what we have asked for?

References

1. Braun, V., Clarke, V.: Using thematic analysis in psychology. Qual. Res. Psychol. **3**(2), 77–101 (2006). https://doi.org/10.1191/1478088706qp063oa
2. CERT-SE: Samverkan. CERT-SE (2024). https://www.cert.se/samverkan/. Accessed 09 Aug 2024
3. Chowdhury, N., Nystad, E., Reegård, K., Gkioulos, V.: Cybersecurity training in Norwegian critical infrastructure companies. Int. J. Saf. Secur. Eng. **12**(3), 299–310 (2022). https://doi.org/10.18280/ijsse.120304 https://doi.org/10.18280/ijsse.120304
4. Christen, M., Gordijn, B., Loi, M. (eds.): The Ethics of Cybersecurity. International Library of Ethics, Law and Technology. Springer, Cham (2020). https://doi.org/10.1007/978-3-030-29053-5
5. Darko Galinec, D.M., Guberina, B.: Cybersecurity and cyber defence: national level strategic approach. Automatika **58**(3), 273–286 (2017). https://doi.org/10.1080/00051144.2017.1407022
6. Dedeke, A., Masterson, K.: Contrasting cybersecurity implementation frameworks (CIF) from three countries. Inf. Comput. Secur. **27**(3), 373–392 (2019). https://doi.org/10.1108/ICS-10-2018-0122
7. European Commission: The EU's cybersecurity strategy for the digital decade. European Union Publications Office (2020). https://digital-strategy.ec.europa.eu/en/library/eus-cybersecurity-strategy-digital-decade. Accessed 09 Aug 2024
8. European Union: Directive (EU) 2016/1148 of the European parliament and of the council of 6 July 2016 concerning measures for a high common level of security of network and information systems across the union (NIS directive). Official Journal of the European Union (2016). https://eur-lex.europa.eu/legal-content/EN/TXT/?uri=CELEX:32016L1148. Accessed 09 Aug 2024
9. European Union: Directive (EU) 2022/2555 of the European parliament and of the council of 14 December 2022 on measures for a high common level of cybersecurity across the union, amending regulation (EU) no 910/2014 and directive (EU) 2018/1972 (NIS2 directive). Official Journal of the European Union (2022). https://eur-lex.europa.eu/legal-content/EN/TXT/?uri=CELEX:32022L2555. Accessed 09 Aug 2024
10. European Union Agency for Cybersecurity (ENISA): ENISA threat landscape 2023 (2023). https://www.enisa.europa.eu/publications/enisa-threat-landscape-2023. Accessed 09 Aug 2024
11. Europeiska Kommissionen: Direktiv om åtgärder för en hög gemensam cybersäkerhetsnivå i hela unionen (nis2-direktivet). European Commission (2023). https://digital-strategy.ec.europa.eu/sv/policies/nis2-directive. Accessed 09 Aug 2024

12. Myndigheten för samhällsskydd och beredskap (MSB): Kompetens inom informations- och cybersäkerhet: En förstudie om kompetensförsörjning för samhället. MSB Report (2021). https://www.informationssakerhet.se/siteassets/kompetensutveckling/kompetens-inom-informations--och-cybersakerhet---en-forstudie-om-kompetensforsorjning-for-samhallet.pdf. Accessed 09 Aug 2024
13. Myndigheten för samhällsskydd och beredskap (MSB): Det systematiska informations- och cybersäkerhetsarbetet i den offentliga förvaltningen resultatredovisning av infosäkkollen och it-säkkollen 2023. MSB Report (2024). https://rib.msb.se/filer/pdf/30598.pdf. Accessed 09 Aug 2024
14. Park, K.B., Chae, S., Lee, H.: Korea's cybersecurity regulations and enforcement related to security incidents. Int. Cybersecur. Law Rev. 47–59 (2021). https://doi.org/10.1365/s43439-021-00028-5
15. Siponen, M.T.: A conceptual foundation for organizational information security awareness. Inf. Manag. Comput. Secur. **8**(1), 31–41 (2000). https://doi.org/10.1108/09685220010371394
16. Statens Offentliga Utredningar (SOU): SOU 2024:18. Utredningen om genomförande av NIS2- och CER-direktiven. Nya regler om cybersäkerhet: delbetänkande. Swedish Government Official Reports (2024). https://www.regeringen.se/rattsliga-dokument/statens-offentliga-utredningar/2024/08/sou-202418/. Accessed 09 Aug 2024
17. Vandezande, N.: Cybersecurity in the EU: how the NIS2-directive stacks up against its predecessor. Comput. Law Secur. Rev. **52**, 105890 (2024)
18. da Veiga, A.: The influence of data protection regulation on the information security culture of an organisation–a case study comparing legislation and offices across jurisdictions. In: Proceedings of the Human Aspects of Information Security and Assurance (HAISA), pp. 65–79 (2017)
19. Waizel, G.: The potential effects of recent EU cybersecurity and resilience regulations on cloud adoption and EU cyber resilience. In: Centre for European Studies (CES) Working Papers, vol. 15, no. 3 (2023)

The Cyber Alliance Game: How Alliances Influence Cyber-Warfare

Gergely Benkő[1] and Gergely Biczók[1,2,3](✉)

[1] CrySyS Lab, Department of Networked Systems and Services, Budapest University of Technology and Economics, Budapest, Hungary
benkogergely@edu.bme.hu, biczok@crysys.hu
[2] BME-HUN-REN Information Systems Research Group, Budapest, Hungary
[3] University of Michigan, Ann Arbor, MI 48109, USA

Abstract. Cyber-warfare has become the norm in current ongoing military conflicts. Over the past decade, numerous examples have shown the extent to which nation-states become vulnerable if they do not focus on building their cyber capacities. Adding to the inherent complexity of cyberwar scenarios, a state is usually a member of one or more alliances. Alliance policies and internal struggles could shape the individual actions of member states; intuitively, this also holds for the cyber domain.

In this paper, we define and study a simple Cyber Alliance Game with the objective of understanding the fundamental influence of alliances on cyber conflicts between nation-states. Specifically, we focus on the decision of whether to exploit a newly found vulnerability individually or share it with the alliance. First, we characterize the impact of vulnerability-sharing rewards on the resulting equilibrium. Second, we study the implications of the internal power structure of alliances on cyberwar outcomes and infer the expected behavior of Dictator, Veto, and Dummy players. Finally, we investigate how alliances can nudge their members via rewards and punishments to adhere to their defensive or offensive cyber policy. We believe that our results contribute to the fundamental understanding of real-world cyber-conflicts by characterizing the impact of alliances.

Keywords: Cyber-Warfare · Weighted Voting · Game Theory · Alliances

1 Introduction

The ongoing Russo-Ukrainian war highlights the importance of military cyber operations and the significant difference between cyber- and traditional warfare in its dynamics, points of conflict, and applied weaponry [21]. Cyberattacks can be broadly categorized into two types: they could target either military or civilian objects, e.g., weapon guidance systems[1] or telecommunication companies such as Kyivstar [22] (see Appendix A for examples from both sides).

[1] https://www.wired.com/story/dire-possibility-cyberattacks-weapons-systems/.

L. Horn Iwaya et al. (Eds.): NordSec 2024, LNCS 15396, pp. 196–216, 2025.
https://doi.org/10.1007/978-3-031-79007-2_11

While the decision situations in an ongoing cyber conflict can be complex in themselves, most countries are also part of military and/or economic alliances, which have strict admission criteria, internal rules, and a common purpose. Once a nation-state becomes a member of an alliance, it represents both its own interests and those of the alliance through its actions and behavior. During the collaboration, members align their military and economic objectives; nowadays, a common cyber defense strategy has also been implemented in most alliances, blurring the lines between military and other alliances. The European Union has been advocating for harsh sanctions against cybercrime and supporting joint research and knowledge sharing [9]. BRICS+ countries research three main topics within the framework of the CyberBRICS project [5]: protection of personal data, secure digital transition, and regulation of artificial intelligence [10]. While NATO has prioritized the defense of information systems [13] and employs a policy of deterrence through cyber exercises and capability enhancement, the operations, regulations, and guidelines of the Collective Security Treaty Organization (CSTO), which includes post-Soviet successor states, receives less public attention regarding cyberspace [11]. (See Appendix B for more details.)

Military operations have been a fertile application domain for studying strategic decision-making via game theory since its inception [4]. Recently, cyber-warfare has also been studied with a similar toolset, but existing studies have not considered alliance systems and their impact on the actors. For instance, in their seminal work [17], the authors modeled and studied the discovery process, stockpiling, and weaponization of (software) vulnerabilities in the cyber-conflict of two nation-states. Their main finding was that at least one state has the incentive to act as an aggressor as opposed to focusing on defensive efforts in a wide range of scenarios.

In this paper, we ask the question: *how do the presence of alliances influence the outcomes of cyber-warfare?*. Inspired by the Cyber Hawk game [17], we construct and analyze the equilibria of the *Cyber Alliance Game (CAG)*. Specifically, through games of increasing complexity and with the help of weighted voting theory [18], we show how i) alliances can encourage peaceful, defensive outcomes via rewards for sharing newly discovered vulnerabilities, ii) the internal power structure within an alliance affects the equilibria, and iii) how the fundamental posture of alliances (defensive or offensive) perturb the resulting strategy profiles. Although our model is quite generic and high-level, we believe that our results can help better understand and perhaps predict real-world cyber-warfare-related decisions of various member states of different alliances.

The rest of the paper is structured as follows. Section 2 lays out the terminology, the basics of weighted voting, and related modeling efforts. Section 3 defines our baseline game CAG and analyzes its possible outcomes. Section 4 extends CAG with intra-alliance power structures. Section 5 further extends the model with the fundamental defensive/offensive posture of alliances. Finally, Sect. 6 provides a discussion on the implications of our results and concludes the paper.

2 Background

2.1 Terminology

Here, we define the basic cybersecurity concepts used throughout the paper. A *vulnerability* constitutes an opportunity for attack. If previously undiscovered or undisclosed, it can be referred to as a *zero-day*. Software vulnerabilities are the most common, but there also exist hardware, organizational, and human vulnerabilities. An *exploit* is a weaponized vulnerability; the attacker develops a piece of code with which he can corrupt the system through the identified vulnerability. A discoverer of a specific vulnerability can never be certain whether they are the sole possessor of that piece of knowledge (unless it was made public or they were attacked through that exact vulnerability), it is possible that they just made a *rediscovery* [19].

Nevertheless, a strategic discoverer can choose between several actions [17]. First, they can *stockpile*, storing a discovered vulnerability for later offensive usage. Note that alleged zero-days can also be acquired from the black market, resulting in a similar situation [2]. Second, they can *patch* their own system via fixing the vulnerability, but at the cost of eliminating the possibility of an attack (patching makes the vulnerability public, hence other actors can also patch their system, resulting in an overall increased level of cybersecurity). The actual patch development is usually done by software vendors [20], but a nation-state might also be able to fix critical vulnerabilities. A glimpse into the economics of a real-world vulnerability disclosure process and related actions of the United States was given in [7] based on a redacted version of the document and a blog post by the former White House Cybersecurity Coordinator. Finally, in relation to alliances, an actor can choose to *share* the vulnerability results with its alliance. With this step, the discoverer forfeits the opportunity for individual exploitation and places the decision in the hands of the alliance and its internal processes.

2.2 Game Theoretical Models of Cyber-Warfare

Although there has been much research in modeling different aspects of attacker-defender dynamics in the cyber domain [14,16], the cyber struggle specific to nation-states has received considerably less attention in the game theory literature. In the seminal paper already mentioned above [17], Moore et al. study two simple cyberwar games (one on stockpiling and one on weaponizing/exploiting the discovered vulnerability) between two nation-states. The factors they take into account are the technical sophistication of the states and their willingness to attack. Although the equilibrium outcomes are influenced by these factors, the key takeaway is that there is no all-defensive equilibrium: at least one of the players (whether based on perceived technical superiority or a more aggressive posture) will choose stockpile/attack.

Next, Bao et al. present a comprehensive game-theoretical framework to be used as an automated tool in cyber-strategy development [3]. This paper relaxes the many simplifying assumptions of previous works and develops a computationally feasible algorithm for deriving equilibria in the complex model. Focusing on algorithmic details, this paper does not offer high-level insights on cyber-warfare.

Chen et al. [8] introduced a practical framework for governments that, utilizing various parameters, rapidly determines whether the attacker's exploitation of a vulnerability or patching it would yield greater benefits. If a country's systems are affected or if the manufacturer is located within the territory of that country, patching becomes significantly more cost-effective. Another important finding (in line with [17]) is that technically inferior countries are more likely to opt for publicly disclosing the vulnerability. Finally, Wang et al. focused on a two-player two-stage conflict [27], where one player can both invest into attacking and stockpiling in the first stage, while it can also use the stockpile created in the second stage; the other player defends in both stages. The paper studied how players managed the trade-off in exerting their efforts across the two periods depending on asset valuations, asset growth, time discounting, and contest intensities.

As opposed to the related literature, we analyze simple two-player cyber-warfare games inspired by [17] and focus exclusively on the impact of alliances. This approach enables us to i) compare to a baseline without alliances and ii) isolate the effect of alliances, adding a new dimension to the strategic understanding of cyber-warfare situations.

2.3 Weighted Voting

Weighted voting is a crucial mechanism for making collective decisions [18], especially in environments where various stakeholders have differing levels of expertise, resources, and risk exposure. Weighted voting assigns different weights to the votes of different participants, reflecting their relative importance, expertise, or investment in the outcome [25]. In the context of (cyber) alliances, such mechanisms are widely used to establish the joint decisions of the member states.

Terminology. Each entity casting a vote is called a *Player* in the election. They're often denoted as P_1,P_2,P_3,...,P_N where N is the total number of voters. A player is given a *Weight*, which represents how many votes they get. The *Quota* is the minimum aggregated weight needed for the votes to be approved; the quota must be larger than 50% and not larger than 100% of the total number of votes. The *Coalition* is a group of players who voted in the same way. A coalition is a *Winning coalition* if it has enough weight to reach the quota. A Player is *Critical* if the coalition loses the vote without them. A weighted voting system is often represented in a shorthand form: $[q{:}w_1,w_2,w_3,...,w_N]$. In this form, q is the quota, while w_i is the weight of Player i.

Power Relations. Players of different powers may fall into distinct categories of importance. A player is a *Dictator* if their weight is equal to or greater than the quota. A player has *Veto* power if their support is essential to reach the quota. Finally, a player is a *Dummy* if they are never essential to reach the quota. In general, the power of a player can be characterized by the Banzhaf Power Index that determines the proportion of all winning coalitions where the given player is critical, analogously to the Shapley-Shubik index in cooperative games [24].

3 The Cyber Alliance Game

Cyber conflicts entail the risk of escalation, but they also present a completely new opportunity for the aggressor. If there is reason to believe that escalation is unlikely, cyber conflicts offer an opportunity to increase the influence of nation-states. During the strategic decision-making process, the cyber commander must leverage their belief in the likelihood of the adversary exploiting a specific vulnerability. The statutes of most alliances condemn private actions and may even introduce sanctions against members, tarnishing the reputation of the alliance. Nevertheless, the members of these alliances are diverse, autonomous entities driven by entirely different objectives and motivations.

Below, we define the Cyber Alliance Game (CAG); our investigation revolves around how the alliance environment influences the decisions of two opposing nation-states belonging to different alliances. The model deals with the costs and benefits of exploiting or sharing vulnerabilities without considering the outcomes of an actual conflict; as such, CAG is inspired by the Cyber Hawk game and adopts its base parameters (p and q, see later) and mechanics regarding how the game is played [17]. The game is played by two players who are members of two different alliances.

3.1 Strategies and Game Mechanics

Each player can choose from two strategies.

Attack. The player discovers a vulnerability and develops an exploit from it but keeps it secret from the alliance (and the world). An attack is considered successful when a player discovers a vulnerability and uses it before any other player does. The reward for being the first to launch a successful attack is 1, while being subjected to an attack results in a cost of -1, making this a zero-sum strategy.

Share. The player discovers a vulnerability and shares it with their allies. The alliance then decides whether to develop an exploit and collectively utilize it or to forward it to the vendor [8]. To preserve clarity, decision-making after sharing the vulnerability is omitted from CAG. The first player who shares a specific vulnerability with their alliance receives a payout; the alliance's reward to the Player. In this situation, the other player receives a payout of 0, making sharing a non-zero-sum strategy.

Using Fig. 1, we illustrate the mechanics of the game. Decision nodes are represented by circles, and leaf nodes by rectangles. Nodes can be labeled with either the letter "C" for chance or the number of the player. A numbered node and its children have two edges labeled "A" for Attack and "S" for Share, denoting the two possible moves. The edges between chance nodes and their children are labeled with probabilities. At the leaves of the tree, the first number in the rectangle represents the payoff for Player 1, while the second number represents the payoff for Player 2. The game starts at the root of the tree, indicated by a double circle.

3.2 Game Parameters

Three parameters influence the payoffs and, thus, the equilibrium of CAG. These are the following:

p. The parameter p takes a value between 0 and 1 and measures the player's technical savvy in discovering vulnerabilities. The value of $1 - p$ represents the technical sophistication of the other player. Smaller values of p indicate that Player 1 is less sophisticated than Player 2, while larger values indicate the opposite. If the two players are evenly matched, then $p = 0.5$. CAG interprets p as the probability of discovering a new vulnerability.

q. The parameter q measures the willingness of each player to launch an attack after discovering a vulnerability. Its value ranges from 0 to 1 and indicates how aggressive a player is. The value of $1 - q$ represents the attack willingness of the other player. Smaller values of q indicate that Player 1 is more restrained in launching attacks, while larger values indicate that Player 1 is "trigger-happy". If the two players are evenly matched, then $q = 0.5$.

$\mathbf{R}_i$**.** The R_i value represents the alliance's reward to a member who shared a valuable vulnerability. The value of R_i also falls between 0 and 1. In real-world scenarios, various factors can affect the magnitude of alliance rewards, such as the exploitability of the vulnerability or the number of affected systems. By introducing this reward, CAG becomes a non-zero-sum game (unlike the Cyber Hawk game) and enables modeling the influence of the alliance environment on the player's decision regarding the discovered vulnerability.

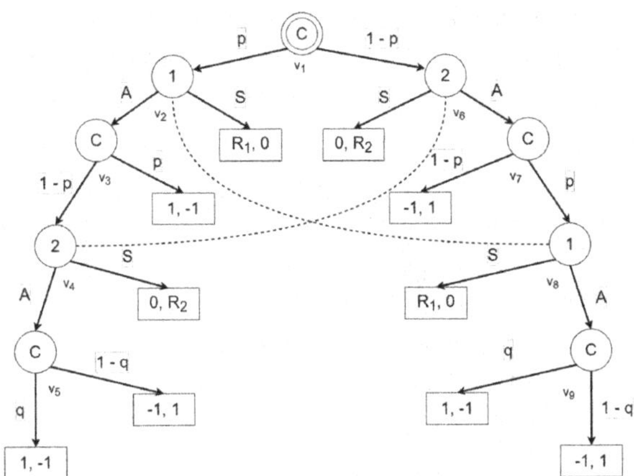

Fig. 1. Cyber Alliance Game in extensive form

3.3 Payoffs

To find a Nash equilibrium, we need to determine the payoff for each player for every possible strategy profile. A strategy profile is referred to as the pair (S_1, S_2), where S_1 represents the first player's strategy, and S_2 represents the second player's strategy. The corresponding expected payoffs are denoted as $u_i(S_1, S_2)$.

The expected payoffs are determined following the game mechanics. At nodes labeled with "C", the probability of reaching a specific child is associated with the value on the corresponding edge. At numbered nodes, the respective player must choose between the actions Attack (A) and Share (S). After making the choice, the game proceeds along the edge labeled with the chosen action. Leaf nodes signify the end of the game: the players receive the payoff specified in the leaf.

Let's determine the payoff for Player 1 when it chooses Attack (A), and their opponent chooses Share (S): u_1(A, S). The game starts at the root, which is the node v_1. Initially, the game proceeds along the left branch with a probability of p. Upon reaching the node v_2, Player 1 is faced with a decision and chooses to Attack (A). After this choice, we arrive at the chance node v_3, where the game ends with a probability of p. In this case, the first Player receives a payoff of 1. Otherwise, With a probability of $1 - p$, Player 2 rediscovers the vulnerability, leading to node v_4. At node v_4, the Player 2 chooses the Share (S) action, resulting in a payoff 0 for the first Player. Thus we get:

$$u_1(A, S) = p \cdot (p * 1 + (1 - p) \cdot 0) + (1 - p) \cdot 0 = p \cdot (p \cdot 1) = p^2$$

Note that at the root node, Player 2 discovers the vulnerability first with probability $1-p$; in this case, the game progresses along the right branch instead.

It is important to emphasize that player nodes belong to two distinct information sets (v_2 and v_8 versus v_4 and v_6, see the dashed lines in Fig. 1). Owing to imperfect information, a player does not know which exact node they are at inside their own information set; they do not know whether they are the first to discover a specific vulnerability.

Following the method above, we determine the expected payoff for each strategy profile:

$$\begin{aligned}
u_1(A, S) &= p^2 \\
u_1(S, A) &= -p2 + 2 \cdot p \cdot R_1 + 2p - p^2 R_1 - 1 \\
u_1(S, S) &= p \cdot R_1 \\
u_1(A, A) &= 2p^2 + 4pq - 4p^2 q - 1 \\
u_2(A, S) &= -p2 - p2R_2 + R_2 \\
u_2(S, A) &= (1 - p)^2 \\
u_2(S, S) &= (1 - p) * R_2 \\
u_2(A, A) &= -2p^2 - 4pq + 4p^2 q + 1.
\end{aligned}$$

Table 1. CAG payoffs, $p = 0.6$, $q = 0.3$, $R1 = 0.7$, $R2 = 0.45$.

P_1/P_2	S	A
S	0.42, 0.18	0.428, 0.16
A	0.36, −0.072	0.008, −0.008

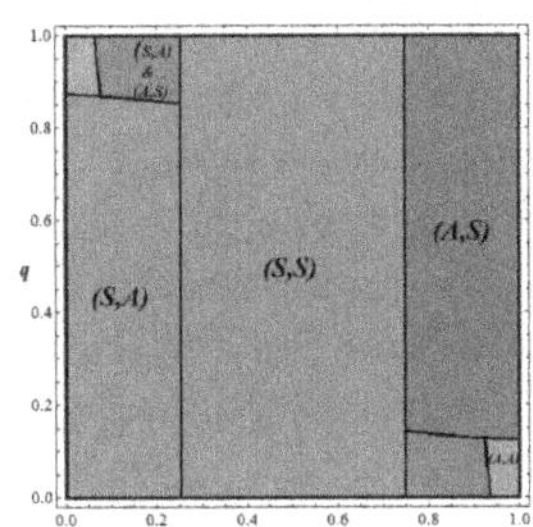

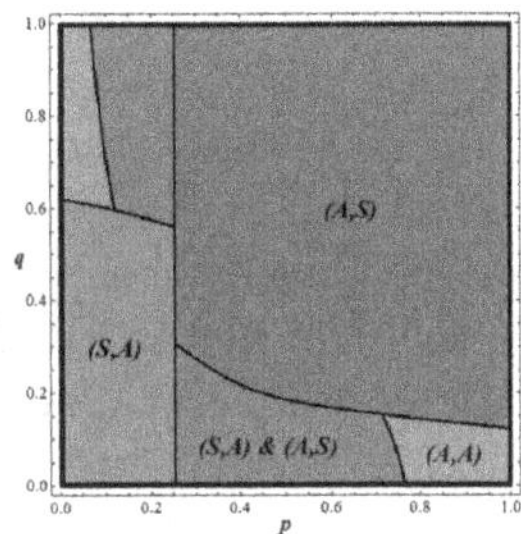

Fig. 2. Left: $R_1 = 0.1$, $R_2 = 0.1$; Mid: $R_1 = 0.75$, $R_2 = 0.75$; Right: $R_1 = 0.25$, $R_2 = 0.75$ (Color figure online)

Note that in the case of the (A, A) strategy profile, the expected payoff depends on who attacks first (Player 1 with a probability of q and Player 2 with a probability of $1 - q$).

Afterward, we can represent the game in a 2-by-2 matrix format (see Table 1). In the example, we use the following parameter values: $p = 0.6$, $q = 0.3$, $R1 = 0.7$, $R2 = 0.45$.

3.4 Equilibrium Analysis

Similarly to [17], we utilize simple (pure strategy) Nash Equilibrium (NE) as our solution concept (as opposed to more involved sequential equilibrium concepts [15]). We can do this because a strategy in an extensive-form game with imperfect information is a function that maps information sets to actions; in fact, all the nodes in an information set have identical available actions. In CAG, this means that a player's strategy is either A or S, and the same action is played in either node of a given player.

In CAG, there are three parameters, each of which can take a value between 0 and 1. For solving and visualizing CAG instances, we wrote a Python script[2]. Specifically, we generate NE diagrams where the x-axis represents p, the y-axis represents q, and the R_i values are fixed according to various criteria.

If both players receive equally low rewards from their alliance for sharing the discovered vulnerability, they tend to choose attack for a wide range of (p, q) values (left plot in Fig. 2). As rewards go towards zero, CAG essentially transforms into the Cyber Hawk game [17]. Moreover, if the players' technical proficiency

[2] Available at https://anonymous.4open.science/r/cyberwar-8F21/.

(p) and aggressiveness (q) are similar, they both opt for attack (orange), resulting in a risk of conflict escalation. Since most real-world alliances are defensive, it is in their best interest to offer high(er) rewards for vulnerability sharing to maintain peace.

As we begin to concurrently increase the rewards above a value of 0.5, the (S, S) equilibrium emerges (blue), promoting sharing in case of similar technical proficiency p (middle plot in Fig. 2). As we approach maximum symmetric rewards, states will share vulnerabilities for any (p,q), trusting the alliance with the ultimate decision concerning a cyberattack.

If alliance rewards are highly asymmetric, the player with the higher reward is more likely to play S, while the under-rewarded player will attack (red (A,S) NE, the right plot in Fig. 2). Note that the behavior of an alliance member can be predicted from the alliance's rewards. This enables the other player (if familiar with this information) to optimize its own payoff; treating rewards as top-secret is advised.

4 The Cyber Alliance Game with Power Structure

Our base game did not include the power distribution among the members of a given alliance. To illustrate the influence of allies, we will use the previously presented weighted voting system and the Banzhaf Power Index. Alliances are considered static, i.e., players in our model cannot change their weight value. In the present model, we differentiate between two types of alliances for visualization purposes: Dictatorial and Democratic. This allows us to examine the behavior of players with similar and significantly different alliance backgrounds. The dictatorial alliance is composed of a single Dictator and multiple Dummies such as $[10 : 11, 2, 2, 2]$. The number and weight of Dummy members in the dictatorial alliance do not significantly change the voting mechanism, as the Dummy players always make decisions in line with the Dictator's interests. In the Democratic alliance, chosen to be $[20 : 5, 5, 5, 5]$, each player has Veto power. Naturally, an alliance might have many members and unequal weights; nevertheless, even with such changes, the behavioral characteristics typical of Veto players remain consistent with the presented findings of this study.

4.1 Parameters

The meaning of parameters p, q, and R_i remain consistent with their definitions in the base game. We introduce a new parameter B_i to measure Player i's influence within the alliance. The value of B_i ranges from 0.1 to 1.5, and it appears as a multiplier alongside the R_i parameter in the payoff function. This captures the impact of how much the Player is capable of influencing the decision regarding the use of the vulnerability after sharing it with the alliance. B_i is calculated using the following formula: $B_i = 1.4 \cdot P_i + 0.1$, where P_i is the Banzhaf Power Index. The addition of the 0.1 value is necessary due to the Dummy Players, as a Dummy Player has a 0 power index, thus it would lose any sharing reward which

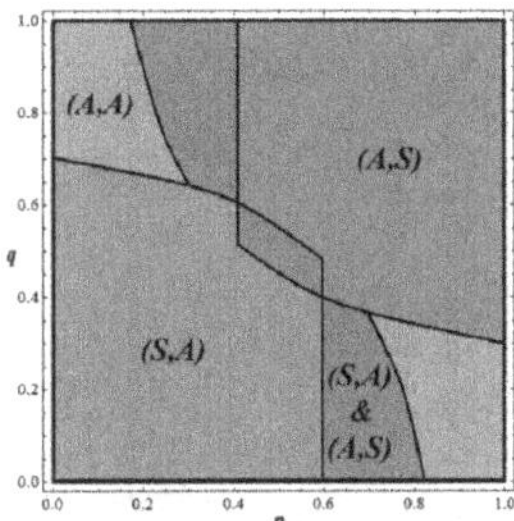

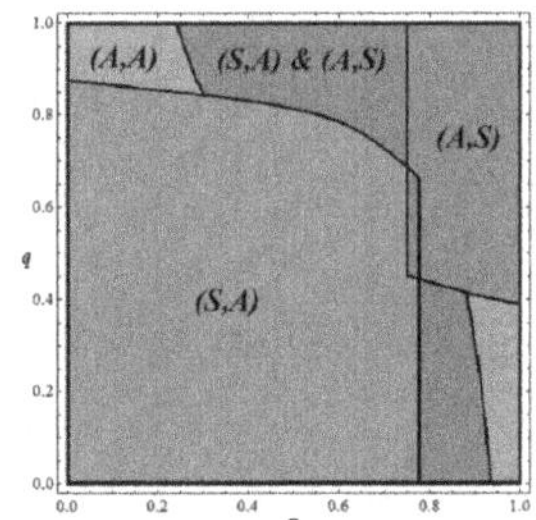

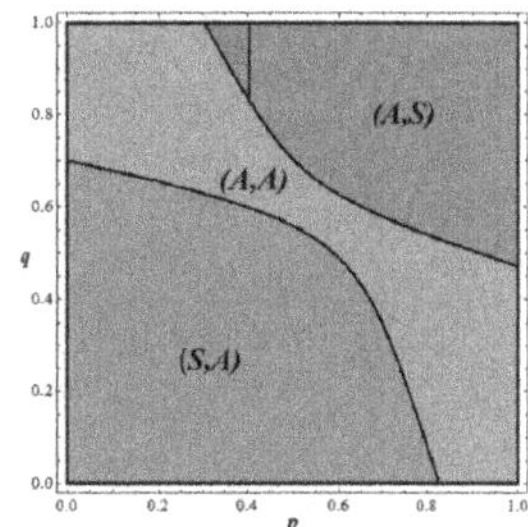

Fig. 3. Left: Veto vs. Veto, $R_1 = R_2 = 0.9$; Mid: Dict. vs. Veto, $R_1 = R_2 = 0.5$; Right: Veto vs. Dummy, $R_1 = 0.9$, $R_2 = 0.5$. (Color figure online)

is not realistic. In the case of a Dictator, it results in a maximum reward increase of +50% when sharing with the alliance. For Veto players, it implies a moderate decrease because, in a Democratic alliance, all players must decide the fate of the vulnerability in the same way; accounting for the possibility that the alliance may make a decision unfavorable to the Veto player. If a Dummy player shares the vulnerability, they have very little influence over their subsequent fate and must execute the Dictator's decision, which results in losing 90% of the reward.

4.2 Equilibrium Analysis

Veto vs. Veto (Democratic vs. Democratic). If two Veto players from different democratic alliances face each other, one player will almost always find sharing with the alliance to be profitable (left plot in Fig. 3). Therefore, the (S,A) (green) and (A, S) (red) strategy profiles dominate when alliances reward their members appropriately. In our setting, each member's power index is $P_i = 0.25$; however, real-world alliances can have various compositions. In general, the higher a player's power index, the lower the reward needs to be provided by the alliance for sharing.

Dictator vs. Veto (Dictatorial vs. Democratic). In a standoff between a Dictator and a Veto player, the Veto player frequently opts for Attack, while the Dictator almost always chooses to share with the alliance (green area, middle plot in Fig. 3)). By increasing the reward for the Veto Player, the democratic alliance can make it less likely that the player will attack.

Veto vs. Dummy (Democratic vs. Dictatorial). In the case of a Veto and Dummy player, it is not surprising that the Dummy prioritizes the Attack strategy. By increasing the reward for the Veto player, we can avoid the occurrence of the (A,A) strategy profile in cases of nearly identical technological development and aggressiveness. Naturally, increasing the reward for the Dummy player does not have an impact: it only chooses Sharing if both its technical sophistication and aggression are much lower compared to the Veto player (red area, right plot in Fig. 3).

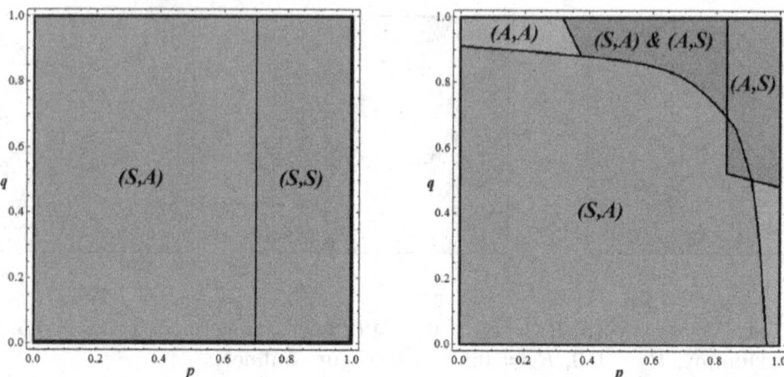

Fig. 4. Left: Dict. vs. Dict., R_1=0.9, R_2=0.2; Right: Dict. vs. Dummy, R_1=0.55, R_2=0.4 (Color figure online)

Dummy vs. Dummy (Dictatorial vs. Dictatorial). If two Dummy players from different dictatorial alliances face each other, the alliance's reward practically does not matter, regardless of how large it may be. In a dictatorial alliance, once a Dummy has shared its vulnerability, it can no longer have a say in how it will be handled going forward. Therefore, Dummies with balanced technological development and aggressiveness will find the all-attack (A,A) strategy profile optimal.

Dictator vs. Dictator (Dictatorial vs. Dictatorial). When two leaders of dictatorial alliances face each other, even with moderate but symmetric rewards, they almost always choose to share their discovered vulnerability with their alliance. This is because they alone decide the fate of vulnerability, and the members of the alliance are obliged to accept the directive. The (S,A) profile is optimal if R_2 is low, and player 2 is not lagging much behind regarding technological development (green area, left plot in Fig. 4). Dictators only choose the (A, A) strategy profile against each other in the case of insufficient sharing incentives from their alliance.

Dictator vs. Dummy (Dictatorial vs. Dictatorial). In situations where a Dictator and a Dummy from a different alliance are clashing, it is not surprising that the Dummy will typically choose to initiate the attack, while the Dictator, even in the presence of a moderate reward, will share the vulnerability with its alliance (green area, right plot in Fig. 4). Only in extreme cases, when the Dictator possesses overwhelming technological superiority and high aggressiveness, will the Dummy choose to share the vulnerability with its alliance.

Summary. Their influence within their alliance greatly influences a player's behavior in specific decision-making situations. Knowing a player's power position allows for more accurate prediction of their behavior in a cyber-conflict.

Dictators wield total power within their own alliance. Discovered vulnerabilities are shared with the alliance at a very high rate, and attacks are chosen only in rare instances, as the alliance is leveraged to achieve the Dictator's objectives. Consequently, most other players find aggression to be the most appropriate response when facing a Dictator. An exception to this is when the Dictator possesses overwhelming technical and/or aggressiveness superiority. Therefore, if a Dictator wishes to avoid continuous attacks, they must demonstrate their superiority and/or aggressiveness at significant real-world financial expenditures. This is in line with the behavior of dominant leaders in both human society and the animal world.

Veto Players are driven by sharing rewards from their Democratic alliance. In case of low rewards, Veto Players are more likely to attack. Between Veto players, the (S, A) or (A, S) strategy profiles often represent an NE, reducing the likelihood of conflict escalation. Veto players with lower power might have to be compensated excessively by their alliance in order to choose not to attack.

Dummy players have no influence on alliance decisions; they essentially execute the decisions of the Dictator within the alliance. Consequently, in the vast majority of cases, Dummy players choose to attack. In fact, a Dummy may be better off outside the alliance (regarding cyber-conflicts) if they are technologically advanced (an unlikely situation).

5 Incorporating Alliance Policy

Alliances, in addition to the rules and guidelines outlined in their founding documents, are typically governed by numerous internal regulations and agreements. When an alliance admits a new member, the new member must adopt the alliance's guidelines and values. If this does not occur, the behavior of the alliance member reflects on the entire alliance, meaning that, e.g., launching an individual cyberattack could potentially affect all members negatively. In order to avoid such inefficiency, alliances strive to nudge members towards closer cooperation or deter them from violating the rules. In the second extension of our model, we introduce the alliance's policy, which is another tool at the alliance's disposal to influence the decisions of its members.

5.1 Alliance Posture

In modern times, most alliances have had a defensive orientation. Their objective is not to initiate joint offensives but rather to deter enemies by demonstrating strength [12]. Nevertheless, we must not disregard alliances with an offensive orientation, which may arise along the lines of common interests in the event of a potentially escalated conflict or an already ongoing cyberwar.

The *defensive alliance* aims to deter its members from deviating from the alliance's guidelines, in this case, deterring from exploiting a vulnerability for individual gain rather than sharing it with the alliance. Therefore, the alliance applies a penalty in the event of an attempted attack, thus reducing the payoff of the deviating member state. On the other hand, the *offensive alliance* evaluates the actions of its members, as this type of alliance typically forms during an ongoing or emerging conflict. Therefore, the offensive-oriented alliance also rewards successful attacks.

5.2 Parameters

The meaning of parameters p, q, R_i, and B_i remain consistent with their definitions established in the Cyber Alliance Game with Power Structure. We introduce a new parameter E_i that conveys the alliance's punishment/reward on the payout generated by an individual cyberattack. For an offensive alliance, the values of E_i can range from 1.1 to 1.6 (reward), while for a defensive alliance, this value ranges from 0.9 to 0.4 (penalty), i.e., a reward or penalty of ±10% to ±60%. Note that these value sets were determined only for demonstration purposes. The resulting extended game tree is shown in Fig. 5.

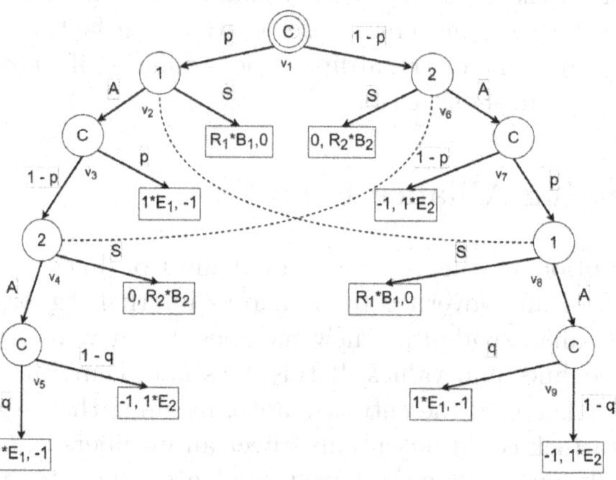

Fig. 5. Cyber Alliance Game with both power and policy structure in extensive form

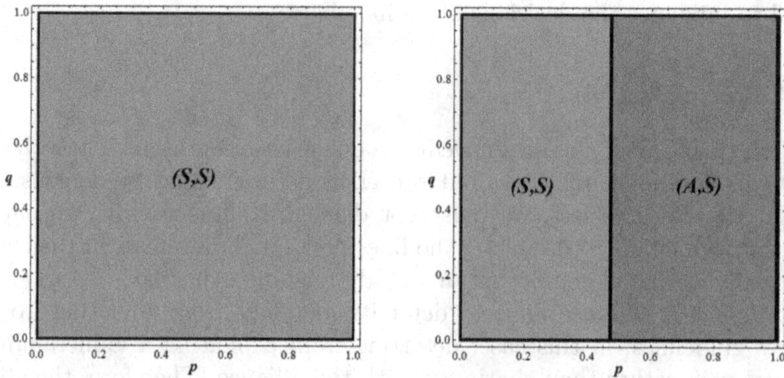

Fig. 6. Left: Defensive Dictator vs. Defensive Dictator ; Right: Defensive Dictator vs. Offensive Dictator (Color figure online)

5.3 Equilibrium Analysis

Dictator vs. Dictator. In the case of Dictators, we could see in the first extension that sharing with the alliance often represents the most profitable decision for the players; they alone can decide as Dictators about the further fate of the vulnerability while also pocketing some sharing rewards. Therefore, the punishment for an attack in the case of a Dictator only encourages more sharing with the alliance (see the left plot in Fig. 6). In contrast, influencing the Dictator's decision is possible with the reward for the attack. If the attack is sufficiently rewarded and the sharing reward of the alliance is low, then the Dictator Player is more likely to attack, especially when being technologically more advanced than its enemy (red area, right plot in Fig. 6).

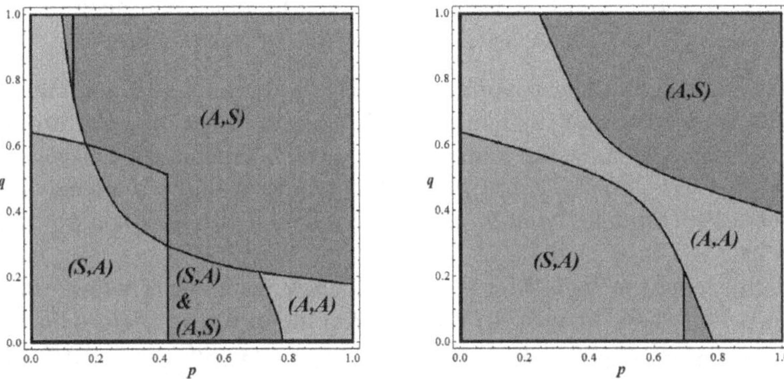

Fig. 7. Left: Defensive Dummy vs. Defensive Veto; Right: Defensive Dummy vs. Offensive Veto

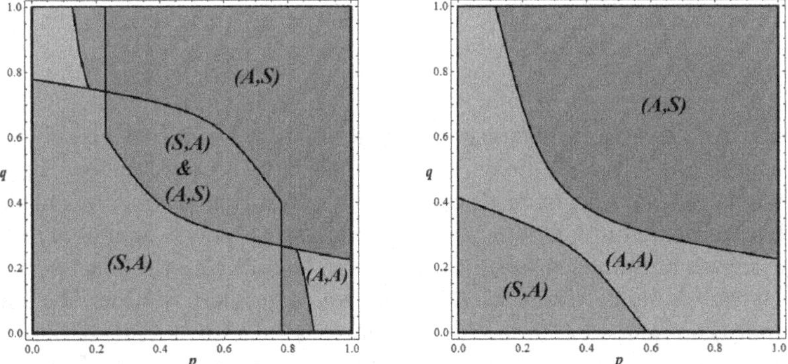

Fig. 8. Left: Defensive Dummy vs. Defensive Dummy; Right: Offensive Dummy vs. Defensive Dummy

Veto vs. Dummy. The actions of Veto players can be influenced to the greatest extent by the reward or punishment for an attack. Through the reward for sharing and the reward/punishment for an attack, the alliance is almost fully capable of controlling the decisions of Veto members in certain situations. With a low reward for sharing and a high reward for attacking, Veto Players can be encouraged to attack, while punishing the attack and rewarding high sharing can persuade them to cooperate with the alliance (see Fig. 7). Note that we chose to show Dummy vs. Veto to isolate the effects of alliance policy on the Veto player.

Dummy vs. Dummy. As we have seen earlier, Dummy Players most often choose to attack because sharing their discovered vulnerability with the alliance brings them very little benefit. They have no influence over how the vulnerability is utilized, and as members of the alliance, they must accept the decision. Therefore, Dummies can be best persuaded to cooperate with the alliance via a stringent penalty for attacking. However, an all-sharing equilibrium emerges very rarely (see Fig. 8), as at least one of the Dummies will achieve a higher payoff attacking (with the exception of very high attack penalties).

Summary. Changing the payout for attacks is a useful tool for alliances to influence the decisions of their members in certain situations. Dictators in an offensive-oriented alliance are more likely to attack than in a defensive alliance. Veto players can be greatly controlled by the alliance's ability to change the payout for attacks. Dummies can be encouraged to cooperate based on punishments for attacks.

By influencing the payout for attacks, alliance members are more exposed to the influence of their alliance. In a dictatorial alliance, the Dictator can shape the decisions of Dummy players according to their preferences. If the alliance provides a low reward for sharing but supports attacking, Dummy players will invariably choose the attack. On the contrary, with high attack penalties and high alliance rewards, they will choose to share. Thus, Dummy players are even more dependent on the will of the Dictator in such situations.

6 Conclusion

The Cyber Alliance Game demonstrates that alliances can incentivize their members to cooperate with the alliance through rewards, as cooperation without such incentives would only occur in extreme cases, given that advantages achievable through attacks are only possible through payouts. However, members may have varying degrees of influence within the alliance. Introducing the concept of power to The Cyber Alliance Game with Power Structure, derived from the Banzhaf Power Index, allows us to model the differences among members. Dictator, Veto, and Dummy players have unique roles and fates within the life of an alliance, which can be exploited by either the opposing parties or the allies themselves. Ultimately, by considering the possibility of changing the payouts resulting from attacks, alliances can exert even greater control over their members. Defensive and offensive alliances could change the default behavior of their member states to the alliance's own benefit by punishing or rewarding individual attacks. In real life, knowing the opponent well, understanding how their alliance operates, and their position within the alliance can help predict the decisions of a given nation-state.

6.1 Democratic Defensive Alliances

In a Democratic alliance, the majority of members respond well to alliance rewards and punishments, making defensive behavior sustainable for almost every member in practice. The alliance democratically decides on the exploitation of vulnerabilities, making vulnerability sharing favorable for members. Such an alliance is most useful during peacetime, as the balance can be maintained by adjusting reward parameters. If members engage in too many individual actions, the trend can be reversed by increasing penalties for attacks and/or increasing rewards for sharing. On the other hand, if members share vulnerabilities excessively, meaning they do not carry out individual actions and overly direct their local problems toward the alliance globally, there is an opportunity to reduce the punishment for attacks.

During peacetime, maintaining and joining the Democratic Defensive alliance is the optimal decision for a Veto player. The power values of Veto players may vary a little but not much; consequently, the alliance's response to changes in rewards and punishments is almost uniform, rendering the alliance predictable. The behavior of alliance members formed by Veto players can be shifted towards a higher proportion of sharing and a higher proportion of attacks, although this incurs relatively high costs for the alliance. Therefore, Veto players in Democratic alliances respond well to changes in parameters, but the alliance may only divert them from their individually preferred behavior with very high rewards or punishments; this strengthens the sovereignty of member states.

6.2 Dictatorial Offensive Alliances

The formation of a Dictatorial Offensive alliance is usually advisable in cases of pre-existing conflicts. The alliance founder is typically the Dictator, who gathers weaker members into the alliance. Since members do not receive high rewards through sharing, they will constantly choose to attack, engaging in individual conflicts. In contrast, the Dictator almost always shares vulnerabilities with the alliance, forcing members to act based on the Dictator's decision. If a Dictator discovers a very large number of vulnerabilities or a critical weakness, it is worth sharing them with the alliance, as this can prompt all members to engage in a large-scale coordinated cyberattack.

During peacetime, it is recommended to incentivize Dummy players to better align with the alliance's interests. However, this incurs significant costs. To address this, the Dictator must either increase the penalty stakes or, during peace, implement some form of democratization within the alliance, a subject not explored in this paper. Additionally, the Dictator must be vigilant regarding technological advancements or high levels of aggressiveness, as most adversaries would likely target the Dictator, given the knowledge that they almost always refrain from an individual attack. Therefore, the role of the Dictator is highly effective in an established conflict from the Dictator's perspective but can be prohibitively costly during peacetime.

6.3 Limitations and Future Work

We made several simplifications in order to i) provide tractable models and ii) be able to compare to the baseline Cyber Hawk game [17]. Attacks are always assumed successful, and there is no potential for retaliation against the attacker. The game is myopic, and we restrict the number of players to two. We did not delve into how the alliance generates player rewards, and we did not model the alliance's decision after a vulnerability was shared. We restricted the alliances to two fixed types, Democratic and Dictatorial, although a mixed form may occur with an infinite number of combinations for member count and power index. Furthermore, when it comes to penalties in defensive alliances, we did not consider potential negative payouts or the exclusion of a player from the alliance. In future work, we plan to relax our assumptions and characterize long-sighted equilibria with repeated interactions, the potential for retaliation, heterogeneous alliances, and dynamic alliance posture.

Acknowledgements. This work has been funded by Project no. 138903, implemented with the support provided by the Ministry of Innovation and Technology from the National Research, Development, and Innovation Fund, financed under the FK_21 funding scheme.

Appendix

A Real-World Cyber-Warfare

Cyberattacks can be broadly categorized into two types: they could target military or civilian objects. Military targets entail the leadership and command of armed forces, as well as weapon guidance systems. Civilian targets encompass critical infrastructure, administrative systems, banking systems, the private sector, and high-ranking political or economic leaders. In the current Ukrainian conflict, we are witnessing an unprecedented, prolonged, intensive cyberwar between two nation-states; even involving civilian volunteers in the operations. In the following, we will examine the largest cyberattacks against civilian targets during the Russo-Ukrainian war.

Ukraine Power Grid. In December 2015 and again in December 2016, Ukraine's electrical grid experienced severe cyberattacks [6]. In both instances, the Supervisory Control and Data Acquisition (SCADA) system of the electricity transmission company was targeted. While the infrastructure of the electrical network was not physically harmed during the attack, approximately 200,000 people were left without service for several hours. Due to their long lifespan, SCADA systems often carry unpatched vulnerabilities and become targets of attacks [1].

Kyivstar. The largest cyberattack in the telecommunications sector was suffered by Kyivstar [22]. The company, which had 24 million users, saw its phone and internet services and website become completely inaccessible due to the attacks. In some areas, even air raid alert systems became inoperative. Additionally, the attackers caused significant damage to the company's systems, particularly concerning cloud-based virtual environments.

VTB. Russia's second-largest bank, VTB, was subjected to the largest DDoS attack in history[3], during which most of its services, including the mobile app and website, became inaccessible. The company issued a brief statement informing its customers about the attack originating from "abroad".

IPL Consulting. Russia's largest and most advanced company specializing in the implementation of industrial IT systems was hit by a cyberattack[4]. The attackers infiltrated the company's IT systems, destroyed vast amounts of data, and rendered numerous servers and services inoperative. The company's clients include major companies in the automotive, aerospace, and defense industries.

B (Cyber-)Alliances

To complicate matters, most countries are part of some form of military or economic alliance. These alliances usually have strict admission criteria, internal rules, and a common purpose. The primary objectives of these alliances used to be defensive. Once a nation-state becomes a member of an alliance, it represents both its own interests and those of the alliance through its actions and behavior. If a member is under attack, the other members typically come to their aid according to internal regulations. Earlier, during collaborations, members aligned their military and economic objectives, and nowadays, a common cyber defense strategy has also been implemented in most alliances, blurring the lines between military and other alliances. The alliances presented below effectively demonstrate the diverse objectives, power structures, and internal regulations they can operate with.

European Union. The European Parliament, the Council of the European Union, and the European Commission form the legislative branch of the alliance. The EU has been advocating for harsh sanctions against cybercrime, the detection of abuse of non-paper-based payment instruments, the introduction of quantum encryption, as well as joint research and knowledge sharing [9]. A recent barrage of new cybersecurity-related regulations, including the Network and Information Security (NIS2), the Digital Operational Resilience Act (DORA), the Cyber Resilience Act (CRA), and others [26], compulsory to adopt in member states, ensure that cybersecurity (including building defensive capacity against

---

[3] https://www.reuters.com/business/finance/russian-state-owned-bank-vtb-hit-by-largest-ddos-attack-its-history-2022-12-06/.

[4] https://kyivindependent.com/military-intelligence-claims-cyberattack-on-russian-defense-ministry-gave-access-to-classified-documents/.

cyberattacks, swiftly patching vulnerabilities, and reporting cyber-incidents to the national and EU authorities with a short deadline) is a first-order priority.

BRICS+. In 2006, Brazil, Russia, India, and China created the "BRIC" alliance. The group was designed to bring together the world's most important developing countries and challenge the political and economic power of the wealthier nations of North America and Western Europe. Since its founding, 5 additional countries have joined the alliance, now referred to as BRICS+, with several other prospective members and interested countries. The economic alliance encompasses more than 44% of the world's population and over 28% of the world's economic power. The member countries, within the framework of the CyberBRICS project [5], aim to create a uniformly structured and secure cyberspace. CyberBRICS is an international research project with three main areas: protection of personal data, secure digital transition, and regulation of artificial intelligence [10].

North Atlantic Treaty Organization (NATO). As the military alliance with the most member countries, NATO has prioritized the importance of information systems defense [13]. In 2012, NATO decided to centralize the protection of all communication networks within the alliance. Following a decision in 2016, NATO began to intensify its cooperation with the private sector, leading to the inclusion of "NATO-compatible" products among the top-tier offerings of most major manufacturers. The highest political decision-making body is the North Atlantic Council, where each member country is represented. Decisions affecting the operation of the alliance, such as admitting a new member, require the consent of every member country. However, the level of technological advancement, the number of experts, the amount of resources allocated, etc., vary significantly across nations, resulting in widely differing power positions within the alliance. The alliance employs a policy of deterrence through cyber exercises and enhancing their capabilities [11].

Collective Security Treaty Organization (CSTO). The CSTO is a military alliance consisting of five former Soviet successor states alongside Russia. The organization's operations, regulations, and guidelines have received less publicity compared to NATO [11]. Article 4 of the CSTO charter adopted in 2002 states that if one of the Member States undergoes aggression (armed attack menacing to safety, stability, territorial integrity, and sovereignty), it will be considered by the Member States as aggression to all the Member States of this Treaty. Neither the Article nor other agreements address how the alliance handles cyberattacks. Generally speaking, the organization pays significant attention to the development of cyber capabilities and the use of "hybrid technologies". Additionally, there is a significant willingness for cooperation among the countries to combat domestic cybercrime and impose stricter cyber hygiene.

Five Eyes. The alliance consisting of 5 Anglo-Saxon countries is one of the most successful intelligence cooperations since World War II [28]. The main area of cooperation among the countries is Signals Intelligence (SIGINT), within which they share information collected from adversarial countries. The key to successful collaboration is global reach, high technological readiness, similar legal systems, and, last but not least, a common language and culture. In most cases, the members follow and adhere to decisions made by their allies in a predictably disciplined manner. However, certain steps can cause tension and even public debate among the member countries. Recently, a divisive issue was the restriction of products from Chinese companies Huawei and ZTE [23].

References

1. Alanazi, M., Mahmood, A., Chowdhury, M.J.M.: Scada vulnerabilities and attacks: a review of the state-of-the-art and open issues. Comput. Secur. **125**, 103028 (2023)
2. Allodi, L.: Economic factors of vulnerability trade and exploitation. In: Proceedings of the 2017 ACM SIGSAC Conference on Computer and Communications Security, pp. 1483–1499 (2017)
3. Bao, T., Shoshitaishvili, Y., Wang, R., Kruegel, C., Vigna, G., Brumley, D.: How shall we play a game?: a game-theoretical model for cyber-warfare games. In: 2017 IEEE 30th Computer Security Foundations Symposium (CSF), pp. 7–21 (2017). https://doi.org/10.1109/CSF.2017.34
4. Beckmann, K.B., Reimer, L.: Dynamics of military conflict: an economics perspective. Rev. Econ. **65**(2), 193–215 (2014). https://doi.org/10.1515/roe-2014-0205
5. Belli, L.: CyberBRICS: Cybersecurity Regulations in the BRICS Countries. Springer, Cham (2021)
6. Case, D.U.: Analysis of the cyber attack on the Ukrainian power grid. Electr. Inf. Sharing Anal. Cent. (E-ISAC) **388**(1-29), 3 (2016)
7. Caulfield, T., Ioannidis, C., Pym, D.: The us vulnerabilities equities process: an economic perspective. In: Decision and Game Theory for Security: 8th International Conference, GameSec 2017, Vienna, Austria, 23–25 October 2017, pp. 131–150. Springer (2017)
8. Chen, H., Han, Q., Jajodia, S., Lindelauf, R., Subrahmanian, V., Xiong, Y.: Disclose or exploit? A game-theoretic approach to strategic decision making in cyber-warfare. IEEE Syst. J. **14**(3), 3779–3790 (2020)
9. Christou, G.: The challenges of cybercrime governance in the European union. Eur. Polit. Soc. **19**(3), 355–375 (2018)
10. CyberBRICS: Cyberbrics: Policies and practices for cybersecurity and digital governance. https://cyberbrics.info/. Accessed 24 June 2024
11. Elamiryan, R., Bolgov, R.: Comparing cybersecurity in NATO and CSTO: legal and political aspects. In: GigaNet: Global Internet Governance Academic Network, Annual Symposium (2018)
12. Hoag, M.W.: NATO: deterrent or shield? Foreign Affairs **36**(2), 278–292 (1958). http://www.jstor.org/stable/20029283
13. Hunker, J.: Cyber war and cyber power. Issues for NATO doctrine (2010)
14. Hunt, K., Zhuang, J.: A review of attacker-defender games: current state and paths forward. Eur. J. Oper. Res. **313**(2), 401–417 (2024). https://doi.org/10.1016/j.ejor.2023.04.009, https://www.sciencedirect.com/science/article/pii/S0377221723002916
15. Kreps, D.M., Wilson, R.: Sequential equilibria. Econometrica **50**(4), 863–894 (1982). http://www.jstor.org/stable/1912767

16. Merrick, K., Hardhienata, M., Shafi, K., Hu, J.: A survey of game theoretic approaches to modelling decision-making in information warfare scenarios. Future Internet **8**(3) (2016). https://doi.org/10.3390/fi8030034, https://www.mdpi.com/1999-5903/8/3/34
17. Moore, T., Friedman, A., Procaccia, A.D.: Would a 'cyber warrior' protect us: exploring trade-offs between attack and defense of information systems. In: Proceedings of the 2010 New Security Paradigms Workshop, pp. 85–94 (2010)
18. Nordmann, L., Pham, H.: Weighted voting systems. IEEE Trans. Reliab. **48**(1), 42–49 (1999)
19. Ozment, A., Schechter, S.E.: Milk or wine: does software security improve with age? In: USENIX Security Symposium, vol. 6, pp. 10–5555 (2006)
20. Rescorla, E.: Is finding security holes a good idea? IEEE Secur. Priv. **3**(1), 14–19 (2005)
21. Robinson, M., Jones, K., Janicke, H.: Cyber warfare: issues and challenges. Comput. Secur. **49**, 70–94 (2015)
22. Santora, M.: Huge cyberattack knocks Ukraine's largest mobile operator offline. The New York Times (Digital Edition) (2023)
23. Shoebridge, M.: Chinese cyber espionage and the national security risks Huawei poses to 5G networks. Macdonald-Laurier Institute for Public Policy (2018)
24. Strafiin Jr, P.D.: The Shapley-Shubik and Banzhaf power indices as probabilities. In: The Shapley Value: Essays in Honor of Lloyd S. Shapley, p. 71 (1988)
25. Tran, C.D.: Math C100: Liberal Arts Mathematics. Coastline College (2024)
26. Vandezande, N.: Cybersecurity in the EU: how the nis2-directive stacks up against its predecessor. Comput. Law Secur. Rev. **52**, 105890 (2024)
27. Wang, G., Welburn, J.W., Hausken, K.: A two-period game theoretic model of zero-day attacks with stockpiling. Games **11**(4) (2020). https://doi.org/10.3390/g11040064, https://www.mdpi.com/2073-4336/11/4/64
28. Wells, A.R.: Between Five Eyes: 50 Years of Intelligence Sharing. Casemate Publishers (2020)

LLMs for Security

Evaluating Large Language Models in Cybersecurity Knowledge with Cisco Certificates

Gustav Keppler(✉), Jeremy Kunz, Veit Hagenmeyer, and Ghada Elbez

Institute for Automation and Applied Informatics, KASTEL Security Research Labs, Karlsruhe Institute of Technology (KIT), Karlsruhe, Germany
{gustav.keppler,jeremy.kunz,veit.hagenmeyer,ghada.elbez}@kit.edu

Abstract. As generative artificial intelligence evolves, understanding the capabilities in the cybersecurity domain becomes crucial. This paper examines the capability of Large Language Models (LLMs) models in solving cybersecurity certification Multiple Choice Question Answering (MCQA) exams, comparing proprietary and open-weights models. Challenges related to test-set leakage, notably on the widely used MMLU benchmark, emphasize the need for continuous validation of benchmarking results. Open-weights models, namely Mistral Large 2, Qwen 2, and Phi 3, seem to overfit the MMLU Computer Security and indicate less usability for cybersecurity knowledge tasks. The study also introduces the first visual cybersecurity MCQA benchmark, assessing the capability of Large Multimodal Models (LMMs) in interpreting and responding to visual questions. Among the tested models, the proprietary Anthropic Claude 3.5 Sonnet and OpenAI GPT-4o outperformed others in the language and vision-language setting. However, Llama 3.1 model series demonstrated significant advancement in the open-weights domain, signaling potential parity in cybersecurity knowledge with proprietary models in the near future. Code and datasets are available at: https://github.com/GKeppler/GenAICyberSecMCQA.

Keywords: Large Language Models (LLMs) · MCQA · Benchmarking · Cybersecurity · Large Multimodal Models (LMMs) · Visual Question Answering

1 Introduction

Generative Artificial Intelligence (AI), particularly LLMs, represents an advancement in how machines process and generate human language. These models are trained on extensive datasets comprising diverse human language inputs with trillions of words [5]. At the center of modern LLMs is the transformer architecture [24], which has evolved natural language processing (NLP) due to its effectiveness in handling large-scale language data.

L. Horn Iwaya et al. (Eds.): NordSec 2024, LNCS 15396, pp. 219–238, 2025.
https://doi.org/10.1007/978-3-031-79007-2_12

One of the leading applications of this technology is OpenAI's GPT-4 [20], a model based on the Generative Pre-trained Transformer. It demonstrates profound capabilities in generating textual content, programming code, and even poetry in various stylistic imitations. GPT-4 and competitors have also showcased their utility in the cybersecurity domain [19,28,30], outperforming traditional commercial tools in some areas, for example, automated program repair methods [27].

LMMs, which interpret and generate information across various forms of data like text, audio, and images, further expands the applicability of generative AI [10,13]. These advancements underscore the importance of understanding the characteristics and capabilities of LMMs in critical fields such as cybersecurity, where these models have not yet been explored.

MCQA is crucial for assessing LLMs capabilities, used widely for its deterministic measurement and compatibility with human testing protocols. In MCQA, models are tested for comprehension, application of pre-training knowledge, and reasoning abilities by providing answers from a set of options. Such assessments are essential for ranking LLMs in recognized benchmarks, including the Holistic Evaluation of Language Models benchmark [17].

One of the most widely used MCQA benchmarks is the Massive Multitask Language Understanding (MMLU) [12] which also features a computer security subtask of 100 questions. As LLMs advance, their performance on the MMLU has plateaued, making it difficult to discern differences in model capabilities. The MMLU-Pro [25] aims to address the plateauing performance by incorporating more complex, reasoning-intensive questions to better differentiate model capabilities in language comprehension and reasoning across various domains. However, it no longer features the computer security subtask of the MMLU.

Also, given the importance of MCQA in evaluating LLMs, it is vital to ensure that the accuracy obtained through MCQA reflects the abilities being measured. However, static benchmarks can face issues with test set leakage, which leads to accidental contamination of the training data of the LLMs or overfitting on the test set [21]. Developers who access these test sets might incorporate them into the training datasets, either unknowingly or intentionally inflating performance metrics. Widely used benchmarks, like the MMLU, pose this risk especially as the data is widespread on the internet.

This limits their reliability and suggests more benchmarks to mitigate contamination risks [9], which is addressed in this study. The key findings are summarized as follows:

- Performance in Cybersecurity Certifications: Proprietary models such as Anthropic's Claude 3.5 Sonnet and OpenAI's GPT-4o consistently achieved at least an 80% passing grade on Cisco certifications. In contrast, open-source models like Llama3.1 showed variability, excelling in CCNA exams more consistently than in CCNP.
- Model Overfitting: The overfitting in several models, including Qwen2 and Phi-3 as demonstrated by their inconsistent performance on CCNA, CCNP, and MMLU benchmarks is observed. In contrast, models like Llama3.1,

Claude 3.5 Sonnet, and GPT-4o exhibited more consistent results across these benchmarks, suggesting more adapted training methodologies.
- Vision-based Question Answering: Both GPT-4o and Claude 3.5 Sonnet achieve high accuracy on vision-based cybersecurity exams, maintaining accuracy comparable to text-based questions and indicating their prowess across modalities.

The rest of the paper is organized as follows. Section 2 presents related work, while Sect. 3 presents a detailed overview of the methodology adopted for evaluating the performance on cybersecurity certification questions, including the creation and utilization of the first visual cybersecurity MCQA dataset. Section 4 analyzes the data, discussing the accuracy of both open-weights and proprietary models in various testing scenarios and exploring potential biases caused by training on the test set. Sections 5 and 6 evaluate and discuss the implications of the results for the field, emphasizing the challenges and opportunities identified through the study. Finally, Sect. 7 concludes the paper.

2 Related Work

There is a variety of specialized benchmarks used for evaluating the cybersecurity knowledge of LLMs. From assessing the generation of insecure code to measuring the understanding and application of security principles, these benchmarks provide critical insights into the capabilities of LLMs within the cybersecurity domain.

As mentioned above, MCQA benchmarks are widely utilized. Besides the MMLU Computer Security, WMDP [16] features 3668 multiple-choice questions that evaluate LLMs' expertise in biosecurity, cybersecurity, and chemical security. All questions were generated and controlled by experts in the field. The dataset is intended to be a proxy-benchmark that can be used to untrain highly sensitive knowledge in LLMs. SecEval [14] offers a set of multiple-choice questions covering various security domains. It utilizes OpenAI's GPT-4 to generate questions by sourcing content from authoritative materials including open-licensed textbooks, official documentation, and industry guidelines and standards. SecQA [18] also leverages GPT-4 to generate questions based on a security textbook. However, GPT-3.5-Turbo and GPT4 reach almost 100% accuracy, indicating a lack of difficulty. The quality assessment of the generated questions is done by researchers review, but not specified further. The CyberMetric [23] benchmark series, with datasets ranging from 80 to 10,000 questions, evaluates LLMs cybersecurity knowledge using questions generated from textbooks via GPT-3.5 and Retrieval-Augmented Generation. Developed questions underwent expert validation. However, this setting reaches 96.25% GPT-4, indicating a benchmark saturation.

Overall, GPT plus Retrieval Augmented Generation (RAG) created benchmarks offer customizable, scalable, and cost-effective assessment tools that can provide extensive coverage of topics. However, they lack quality assurance of the generated questions and answers. Therefore, using industry-recognized professional certification exams provides an authentic and standardized benchmark that is highly respected in the field. Tann et al. [22] test LLMs question-answering capabilities across Cicso certification exams. The aim is to determine if LLMs can pass these industry-recognized professional certification exams. To the best of the author's knowledge, this only works by benchmarking the knowledge of LLMs with Cisco certification exams. However, their datasets are not publicly available and they use outdated Cisco exams.

3 Experimental Setup

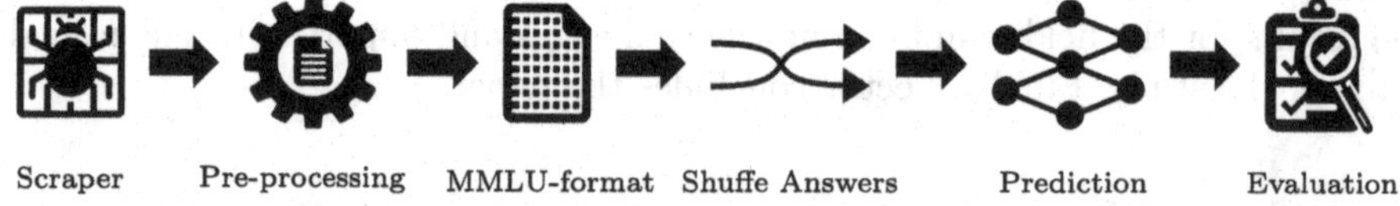

Fig. 1. Overview of the data collection, processing, and evaluation of the multiple choice questions answering benchmarks using LLMs.

In this section, the methodologies employed to evaluate the capability of LLMs in answering multiple-choice cybersecurity certification questions are outlined. This includes the shuffling of the answer possibilities [7], evaluation of an LLM overfitting on the test set. Additionally, as not only one answer per question can be correct, the score per question depends on the proportion of correct and incorrect options chosen by the LLMs. The process is shown in Fig. 1

3.1 MCQA Task Definition

The MCQA task [7] for LLMs is defined as: 1) a question q; and 2) a set of choices of varying length $\mathcal{C} = \{c_a, c_b, c_c, c_d, c_e\}$, were one or multiple are correct. Utilizing these as inputs, the LLM must give one or multiple letters of the correct option $a \in$ { (A), (B), (C), (D), (E) }.

In this study, a 5-shot approach is employed, where models are provided with five examples before answering each question. The standard MCQA prompt is a full prompt, including the 5 few-shot examples, the question q, and choices $\mathcal{C}$:

> Question: q
> Choices:
> (A) c_a
> (B) c_b
> (C) c_c
> (D) c_d
> (E) c_d
> Your response should end with "The best answer is [the_answer_letter(s)]" where the [the_answer_letter(s)] is/are of A, B, C, D, E, ...
> The best answer is a

As visual question answering is also examined in this study, a separate benchmark has been included to assess LMMs capabilities. The same 5-shot templates as for the language-only multiple-choice questions benchmarks are utilized, adding the picture to the question. The few-shot examples were not adapted to the visual setting.

To assess the accuracy of the benchmark, the following considerations are made: If all correct options and no incorrect ones are selected, the answer is considered completely correct. Partial accuracy and exact accuracy are computed by averaging these scores and the number of wholly correct answers over the entire question set, respectively. This is further described in Algorithm 1.

```
Input: QSet: multiple-choice questions, LLMSet: large language models
Output: PartialAccuracy, ExactAccuracy: accuracy of LLMs in
        answering questions correctly
Function EvaluateMCQ(QSet, LLMSet):
    foreach LLM in LLMSet do
        CorrectAnswers ← 0
        PartialCorrectAnswers ← 0
        foreach Q in QSet do
            Answer ← LLM(Q)
            T ← len(CorrectOptions)
            C ← number of correct options
            W ← number of incorrect options
            Score ← max(0, C/T − W/T)
            PartialCorrectAnswers ← PartialCorrectAnswers + Score
            if C == T and W == 0 then
                CorrectAnswers ← CorrectAnswers + 1
            end
        end
        PartialAccuracy[LLM] ← PartialCorrectAnswers / len(QSet)
        ExactAccuracy[LLM] ← CorrectAnswers / len(QSet)
    end
    return PartialAccuracy, ExactAccuracy
```

Algorithm 1: Multiple-Choice Question Answering Accuracy

3.2 Model Selection: Open-Weights and Closed-Weights Models

The selection of models for the project was guided by comprehensive performance evaluation and specialization across various platforms. The HELM MMLU Leaderboard [17] offers a third-party evaluation of the accuracy for each of the 57 topics in the MMLU - including Computer Security - for a variety of open-weights and proprietary LLMs. The Chatbot Arena [11] is additionally used for model selection as it offers human-evaluated instruction following capability scoring, as all models selected for this study are instruction-following tuned. This results in the following models:

The Llama3.1 [5] 405B Instruct stood out by achieving the highest scores overall on the HELM MMLU and the Chatbot Arena Leaderboard from an open-weights model. Additionally, the Llama3.1 70B Instruct and the Qwen2 72B Instruct were chosen as the medium-size models due to their performance on the MMLU HELM. The Qwen2 series are the best open-weights models available from a Chinese company. Mistral Large 2-2407 was selected as it was the top-performing open-weights LLM in the Chatbot Arena-Hard category [15] and is the most prominent model from a European provider.

In the realm of proprietary models, Anthropic Claude 3.5 Sonnet [4] with its latest update from June 20th, 2024, achieved the highest score in the HELM MMLU overall and also specifically in MMLU Computer Security. OpenAI GPT-4o [3] version from May 13, 2024, is also included in our selection. Although it ranked fourth on the HELM MMLU overall - lower than the open-weights Llama 3.1 405b Instruct - it achieved the highest scores in the Chatbot Arena [11] overall. Both models offer multi-modal capabilities, making them suitable for the vision datasets.

Furthermore the Phi-3 series models [6], Phi-3-mini-128k-instruct and Phi-3-medium-4k-instruct were selected, due to their MMLU score of 70.9% and 78% (self-reported, as not mentioned on the HELM leaderboard). Despite their relatively smaller size of only 3.8B/14B parameters, they outperform larger models such as the Llama 2 70B, which scored 69.5% in HELM results. The vision-language version of the Phi-3-mini model, the Phi3-vision-128k-instruct LMMs is used to compare to the proprietary vision-language models.

The recent release of open-weights LLMs include pre-trained, and a further instruction-tuned version of the model. In this work, only the instruction-tuned versions are compared, as the State-of-the-Art closed-weight Models are only available as instruction-tuned or chat variations. These models use a chat template with special tokens indicating the roles in a multi-turn conversation. The raw model of the proprietary models cannot be accessed. There are three distinct methods to prompt open-weights models. Firstly, the raw mode where the conversation tokens

```
<|eot_id|><|start_header_id|>assistant<|end_header_id|>
```

need to be inserted manually. Contrarily, the chat completion mode relies on a chat template, which is compatible with the OpenAI API and is therefore used for this work as closed-weights and open-weights models can be compared. The templates used in this work can be examined in Appendix A.

3.3 Shuffeling and Parameters

Shuffling the answer options can be employed as a strategy to determine the consistency and variance in the accuracy of LLMs when operating at a temperature of zero. By rearranging the order of these choices, it can assess whether the model's performance is stable across different presentations of the same question, thereby providing a clearer understanding of its reliability.

For open-weight models, testing is conducted in an unquantized fp16 state, as this configuration delivers superior performance compared to quantized models, although with increased computational requirements. The temperature is set to zero with a sampling rate of 1, aligning with the testing procedure used for MMLU. If the output cannot be serialized into the answer format with the used regex-pattern, there will be no resampling with for example higher temperature performed. In the scenario of 5-shot tasks, the number of shuffles is set to 5, and the maximum output tokens one can generate is set to 10. For 0-shot Chain of Thought (CoT) [26] prompting, there is no shuffling applied, and the maximum output tokens are significantly higher, set at 1000, allowing for the more expansive generation of answer explanation. This allows the model to explain its reasoning step-by-step.

When processing answers from model-generated content, the primary method involves a regex pattern ‘answer is \[?([A-J]+)\]?’. The regex ‘.*[aA]nswer:\s*([A-J]+)’ is used in addition. For CoT prompting, first the regex ‘answer is ([^.]*?)\.’ is used to match an answer sequence, and then all uppercase letters ‘[A-Z]’ are extracted from the segment.

4 Dataset

The tested MCQA benchmarks in this study include the MMLU Computer Security [12], as a subtask of the wildly used MMLU benchmark, as well as the CISCO Career certification exams [1] 200-301 CCNA and 350-701 SCOR are also used. The exam questions were scraped from the internet [2], as the scraping policy allows it. They were chosen as promising candidates that meet the following requirements for LLM knowledge benchmarks for the cybersecurity domain:

- Possess sufficient difficulty to prevent benchmark plateau and effectively distinguish between models with high confidence.
- Reduced test-set leakage that exists for wildly used benchmarks.
- Address quality assurance issues prevalent in the GPT self-generation of datasets.

Regarding the first point, the scraped exams represent two levels of certification difficulty: The Cisco Certified Network Associate (CCNA) certification, though not strictly focused on cybersecurity, provides fundamentals - which include routing, switching, and security concepts - that are crucial for a cybersecurity career. There are no prerequisites for this certification, and the difficulty level ranges from entry-level to intermediate. The required exam for this certification is the 200-301 CCNA.

The advanced Cisco Certified Network Professional Security (CCNP Security) certification provides an in-depth knowledge of securing Cisco networks. This knowledge encompasses firewall technologies, VPNs, intrusion prevention, and endpoint security. To pursue this certification, a valid CCNA certification or equivalent experience is required. The core exam for this certification is the 350-701 SCOR, and a choice of an additional topic needs to be completed for certification.

Table 1. Two examples from the 201-301-CCNA (orange) and 350-701-CCNP (blue) vision datasets. The correct answer is bolt and the exhibit is shown at the bottom.

201-301-CCNA Vision	**350-701-CCNP Vision**
Question: Refer to the exhibit. Which type of route does R1 use to reach host 10.10.13.10/32?	**Question:** Refer to the exhibit. What does the API do when connected to a Cisco security appliance?
Options: (A) default route **(B) network route** (C) host route (D) floating static route	**Options:** (A) create an SNMP pull mechanism for managing AMP (B) gather network telemetry information from AMP for endpoints (C) get the process and PID information from the computers in the network **(D) gather the network interface information about the computers AMP sees**

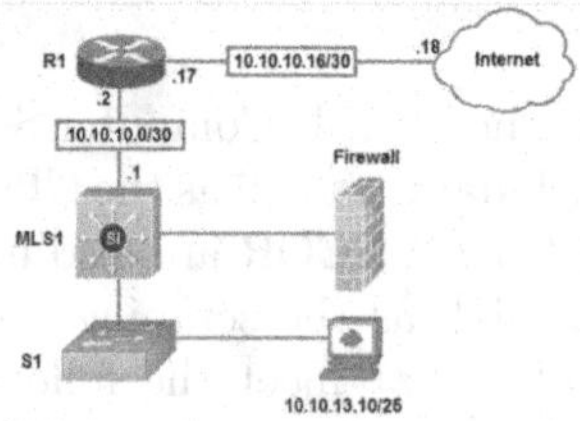 R1 .17 10.10.10.16/30 .18 Internet
.2 10.10.10.0/30 .1 Firewall
MLS1
S1 10.10.13.10/25
R1#sh ip ro
Gateway of last resort is 10.10.10.18 to network 0.0.0.0
10.0.0.0/8 is variably subnetted, 4 subnets, 3 masks
C 10.10.10.0/30 is directly connected, FastEthernet0/1
O 10.10.13.0/25 [110/6576] via 10.10.10.1, 06:58:21, FastEthernet0/1
C 10.10.10.16/30 is directly connected, FastEthernet0/24
O 10.10.13.144/28 [110/110] via 10.10.10.1, 06:58:21, FastEthernet0/1
B* 0.0.0.0/0 [20/0] via 10.10.10.18, 01:17:58
	import requests
	client_id = 'a1b2c3d4e5'
	api_key = 'a1b2c3d4-e5f6-g7h8'
	url = 'https://api.amp.cisco.com/v1/computers'
	response = requests.get(url, auth=(client_id, api_key))
	response_json = response.json()
	for computer in response_json['data']:
	    network_addresses = computer['network_addresses']
	    for network_interface in network_addresses:
	        mac = network_interface.get('mac')
	        ip = network_interface.get('ip')
	        ipv6 = network_interface.get('ipv6')
	        print(mac, ip, ipv6)

In terms of test-set leakage, the lack of disclosure regarding the training data of the compared models makes it difficult to determine whether CCNA and CCNP questions were included. However, this new benchmark likely gains an advantage from its relatively limited representation in internet text. Unlike widely established benchmarks such as MMLU, the lesser-known status of this benchmark potentially reduces the risk of test-set leakage, as its questions may be less exposed during the models' training phases.

Compared to the MMLU Computer Security exams, Cisco multiple-choice question exams present a few key differences. Cisco exams can have varying lengths of answer possibilities, allow for multiple answer choices within a single question, as indicated by prompts such as "choose two.", and include vision-based questions.

The MMMU [29] benchmark includes vision-based multi-choice questions, however, it does not include computer security questions, only computer science questions. Therefore, there is no related vision-language benchmark available for the cybersecurity domain, and the "201-301-CCNA Vision" and "350-701-CCNP Vision" are the first of their kind - example questions are shown in Table 1.

The pre-processing of the scraped questions and answers involves the following steps:

- **De-duplication:** Perform de-duplication regarding the questions.
- **Low-quality images:** Drop questions that feature low-quality images with less than 100×100 pixels.
- **Drag-and-drop questions:** Remove questions where not at least one answer possibility is given, as they are not multiple choice questions, but query-answer matching tasks.
- **Sampling:** Sample from the remaining questions for 100 questions, if available. The image-based questions are less.
- **MMLU-Format conversion:** Convert questions, answers, and choices to the MMLU format, for easy integration of the benchmark into other packages.

Regarding the data quality of new benchmarks, Multiple choice questions generated by models like GPT from textbook data are susceptible to issues of hallucination and general quality assurance problems, because these models

Table 2. An overview multiple-choice question answering benchmarks for the cybersecurity domain. The amount of questions, the source of the questions, and the reported GPT-4 accuracy are shown.

Name	Count	Development	GPT4 Acc.
MMLU Computer Security [12]	100	Domain experts	86
SecEval [14]	2126	GPT-4	79.07
SecQA [18]	210	GPT-4 + RAG	98.0
CyberMetric [23]	10000	GPT-3.5 + RAG, human verified	88.50
WMDP-Cyber [16]	1,987	Domain experts	–
201-301-CCNA	100	Domain experts	–
350-701-CCNP	100	Domain experts	–
201-301-CCNA Vision	70	Domain experts	–
350-701-CCNP Vision	15	Domain experts	–

sometimes generate content that blends learned knowledge with confabulated details. While the model attempts to understand and replicate the information style and content from textbooks, its inability to perfectly discern facts from plausibility can lead to hallucinations [8]. Therefore, without rigorous vetting and quality control, the use of such AI-generated quiz content could compromise the benchmark quality. An overview of the scarped datasets, as well as other publicly available MCQA datasets in the cybersecurity domain, is shown in Table 2.

5 Evaluation of Results

In this chapter, the accuracy of LLMs on the cybersecurity certification exams, comparing open-weights and proprietary models across different prompting strategies and modalities, while also examining potential training data leakage and dataset quality is analyzed.

5.1 Solving Cybersecurity Certification Questions

In the following section, the performance of various language models on the CCNA and CCNP certification exams is evaluated by comparing 5-shot with 0-shot CoT prompting. The CCNA and CCNP have a passing grade assumed at 80% as shown in Fig. 2. Among the models, Anthropic Claude 3.5 Sonnet and OpenAI GPT-4o stood out, consistently exceeding the 80% threshold across, with Anthropic Claude 3.5 Sonnet scoring as high as 88% in CCNP. However, it is unclear why the CCNP score is higher than the CCNA for this model, as the difficulty of the CCNP exam is higher.

Llama3.1 405B is the only open-weights model passing CCNA every time, and the CCNP one out of five times. Qwen2.72B Instruct, Llama3.1 70B Instruct,

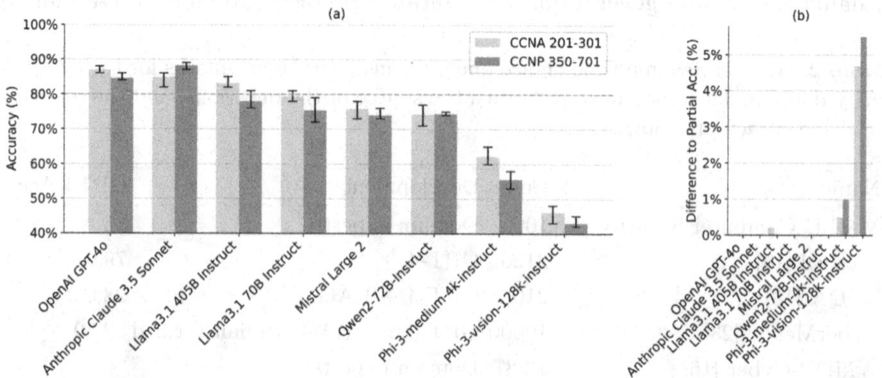

Fig. 2. (a) Overview of the accuracy of LLMs on the CCNA 201-301 and CCNP 350-701 5-shot. The error bar indicates the min. and max. accuracy of 5 shuffled runs. The red horizontal line is the assumed passing accuracy for the exams. (b) Accuracy gains if partial points are given, e.g. 0.5 point if [A] is answered, but [A, B] is correct.

and Mistral Large 2 did not meet the passing grade in the certification metrics. The Phi 3 models, Phi-3-medium and Phi-3-vision consistently fell short across all metrics, although they are more conservative when multiple answer options per question are correct, achieving partial points as shown in Fig. 2(b). The benchmark mostly states if multiple options should be selected, indicated with "choose two." Phi-3-vision often ignores this and answers with only one option, achieving partial points. This is also the case for one question in the CCNA exam and the Llama 3.1 405b model.

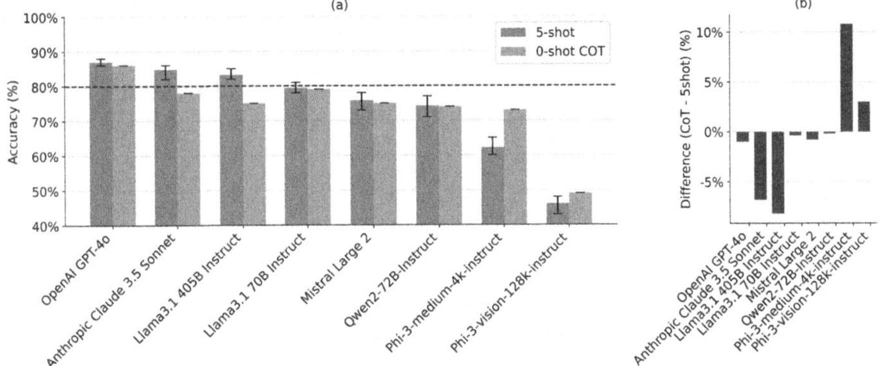

Fig. 3. (a) Overview of the accuracy comparing 5-shot vs 0-shot Chain of Thought prompting on the 200-301 CCNA benchmark. (b) Difference in the accuracy of the 5-shot vs 0-shot Chain of Thought prompting techniques.

The results presented in Fig. 3 showcase the comparison of model accuracy between 5-shot and 0-shot CoT prompting. The range of accuracy over 5 shuffled runs is shown, while for the CoT prompting one unshuffled run was done. Across the models, the 5-shot setting outperforms the 0-shot CoT approach, besides the Phi-3 models. While the accuracy for the GPT-4o, Llama3.1 70b, Mistral and Qwen2 models are similar for both promoting techniques, the Claude 3.5 Sonnet and Llama3.1 405b show a notable decrease in accuracy with over 5%. The Phi-3 models benefit from the CoT prompting with the Phi-3-medium model showing over 10% accuracy increase, while the Phi-3-vision-128k-instruct model slightly surpasses the 5-shot method. Overall, the findings are highly variable.

Overall, the comparative analysis shows that only the proprietary models, namely Anthropic Claude 3.5 Sonnet and OpenAI GPT-4o, consistently achieved 80% passing grade across both datasets. Llama3.1 405B is the only open-weights model passing CCNA every time, and the CCNP one out of five times.

5.2 Trained on the Test-Set

The leakage of benchmark test sets on the internet poses a significant risk of contaminating training datasets in machine learning practices. As a result, models may appear to perform exceptionally well on tests not because they genuinely learned the underlying patterns and generalized well, but because they were indirectly trained on the test data. This compromises the integrity of performance evaluations and could lead to misleading conclusions about a model's effectiveness when deployed in real-world scenarios. Figure 4 shows that the better-performing models exhibit similar accuracy on the MMLU Computer Security benchmark compared to the CCNA 201-301 and CCNP 350-701 benchmarks. Starting with the Mistral Large 2, notable declines in the certification question accuracy compared to their performance on the MMLU benchmark. These models may overfit on commonly used benchmarks or even specifically trained on the MMLU test-set. This discrepancy is larger for Qwen2, Mistral Large 2, and especially Phi-3, while it is less pronounced for Llama3.1, Claude, and GPT-4o, potentially reflecting better data handling and training practices.

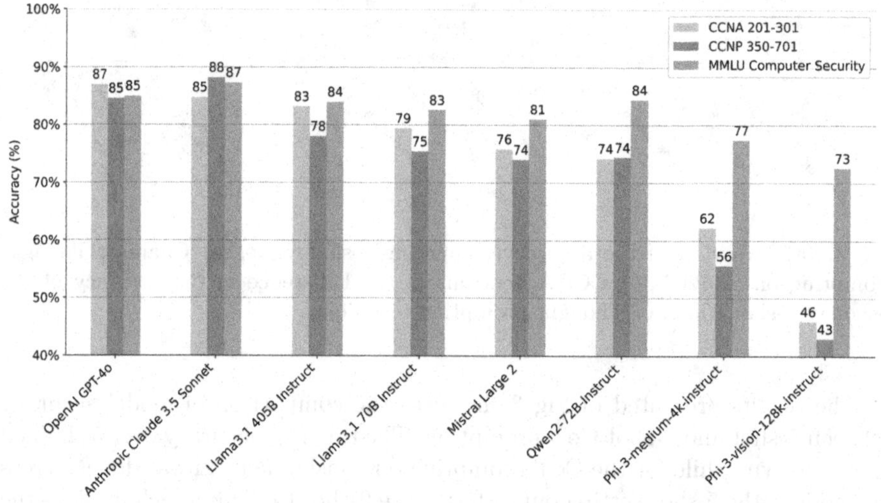

Fig. 4. Overview of the LLMs mean accuracy in the CCNA 200-301, CCNP 350-701, and the MMLU Computer Security benchmarks of 5 shuffled runs. The difference may indicate test-data leakage to the training data of the model.

5.3 Solving Visual Questions

Figure 5 highlights the vision capabilities of LMMs when tasked with solving image-based questions from the CCNA 201-301 vision and CCNP 350-701 vision datasets. The results indicate a notable variance in performance across the models. OpenAI GPT-4o and Anthropic Claude 3.5 Sonnet demonstrate relatively high accuracy. In contrast, Phi-3-vision-128k-instruct shows significantly lower performance, particularly on the CCNA dataset. These results suggest that while advanced models like GPT-4o and Claude 3.5 Sonnet exhibit strong vision capabilities, also smaller multimodal models such as Phi-3-vision-128k-instruct achieve notable accuracy. However, the accuracy for CCNP 350-701 vision is higher for all tested models, indicating that the questions are easier to solve. This may be caused by a low number of samples in the CCNP 350-701 vision dataset of only 15 questions, where relatively easy questions may be present. In general are GPT-4o and Claude 3.5 Sonnet capable of solving vision-based questions with high accuracy, comparable to language questions. However, the overall separability for the CCNA vision benchmark is higher. Phi-3-vision shows lower accuracy.

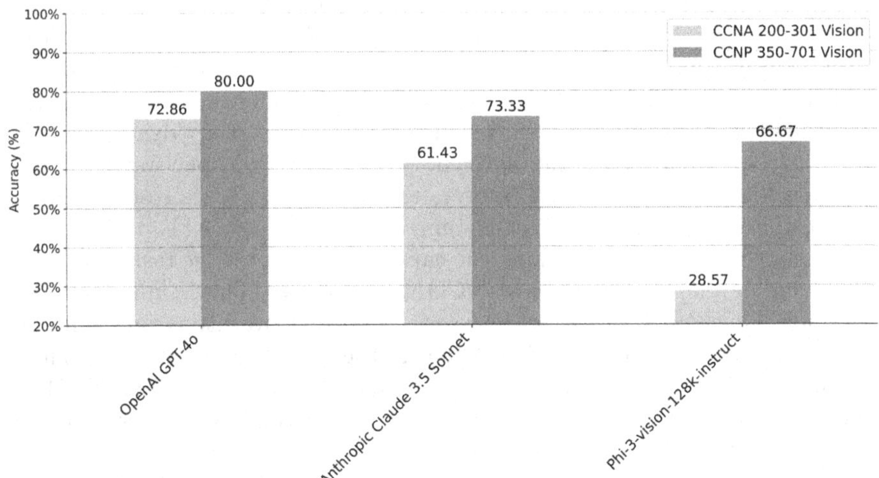

Fig. 5. Overview of the CCNA 201-301 Vision and CCNP 350-701 Vision accuracy.

6 Discussion

The dataset utilized was scraped from an online learning portal, as obtaining it through official channels was not feasible for publication. Despite the lack of formal validation, it benefits from being a community dataset, where the quality and relevance have been informally verified through widespread use and feedback within the community. This "community validation" offers assurance about the dataset's utility and applicability, although it may still contain inconsistencies.

Regarding the variance in prompting techniques, the results are consistent with the MMLU evaluations in the literature, where no prompting technique is advancing for all compared models [5]. Llama 3 70B and Llama 3 405B, benefit in the MMLU benchmark from the 0-shot CoT prompting, showing improved performance over the 5-shot method, while GPT-4o and Claude 3.5 Sonnet achieve better results in the 5-shot setting. However, the high drop in accuracy for the Anthropic and LLama3.1 405b models, as well as the large increase for the Phi-3-medium model is unclear but might be due to sensitivity to the provided prompts. This is left for future work.

The leakage of benchmark test sets on the internet poses a significant risk of contaminating training datasets in machine learning practices. As a result, models may appear to perform exceptionally well on tests not because they genuinely learned the underlying patterns and generalized well, but because they were indirectly trained on the test data. This compromises the integrity of performance evaluations and could lead to misleading conclusions about a model's effectiveness when deployed in real-world scenarios. This study demonstrated a varying gap in accuracy for the different proprietary and open-weights LLMs on the evaluated benchmarks. However, the aim is not to call one company out with the accusation of test-set training. Instead, the focus is on increasing transparency in both benchmarking the capability in knowledge tasks for cybersecurity and developing more robust MCQA benchmarks. The training data that is used for the LLMs is disclosed, however, to prevent overfitting on commonly used benchmarks for Llama 3, they state that the pre-training data was sourced and processed by an independent team incentivized to avoid benchmarks [5]. As other teams do not highlight, this may be unique for the Llama 3 series models compared to the open-weights competitors.

The visual question-solving capabilities of different LMMs indicate that although GPT-4o and Claude 3.5 Sonnet showcased similar vision capabilities, the smaller Phi-3-vision-128k-instruct managed to achieve higher accuracy compared to the language-only CCNP exam. Also, a generally higher performance across all models on the CCNP 350-701 vision dataset is shown, likely influenced by its smaller size and possibly less complex content, contrary to CCNP language-only questions. The higher seperability of the CCNA 200-301 vision benchmark, enables a better model capability judgement.

In general, the introduced CCNA and CCNP benchmarks show higher separability compared to the MMLU computer security dataset, which ensures sufficient complexity to prevent benchmark plateauing and effectively distinguish between models. These characteristics show that the CCNA and CCNP exams provide a challenging testing environment that measures the capabilities of LLMs and LMMs. The findings from this study underscore the significant role that benchmarks play in assessing the domain-specific capabilities of LLMs. By examining the performances across different models and prompting techniques, this research offers an additional data point. Practically, these insights can guide the selection and application of LLMs in cybersecurity settings.

Future plans include expanding the visual datasets to cover a broader array of topics within the field of cybersecurity and evaluating them with more open-weights models. The influence of prompting techniques and their impact on accuracy, as well as improving the interpretability of the models' decision-making processes is also left for future work. Moreover, it can be investigated to differentiate between knowledge-based questions and those that require analytical reasoning. While certain questions draw predominantly on the retrieval of factual data, others necessitate a more intricate, stepwise reasoning approach to derive solutions. As the domain advances, there is a shift towards prioritizing reasoning-based tasks. This shift highlights the growing imperative of constructing models capable of not only the recall of information but also the emulation of human cognitive processes, including logical analysis and sophisticated problem-solving strategies.

7 Conclusion

This study evaluates the capabilities of LLMs and LMMs in solving cybersecurity certification questions, highlighting the stronger performance of proprietary models Anthropic Claude 3.5 Sonnet and OpenAI GPT-4o in exceeding accuracy thresholds necessary for certification. However, open-weights models - especially the Llama 3.1 models - are improving performance, demonstrating their potential to bridge the gap between open-sourced and proprietary models in the near future. The introduced CCNA and CCNP benchmarks show high separability compared to the MMLU computer security dataset, making them suitable for measuring cybersecurity knowledge in language-only and language-vision tasks.

The research also reveals potential overfitting to familiar datasets such as the MMLU, underscoring the need for ongoing attention to the validity of benchmark results. The training data for the models is disclosed, but to avoid benchmark overfitting the pre-training data of models should intentionally avoid benchmark data. Additionally, this study introduces the first visual cybersecurity multiple-choice question-answering dataset. Exploring vision integration in problem-solving shows varying success, with proprietary models demonstrating significant capabilities in multi-modal contexts.

Acknowledgments. This work was supported by funding from the topic Engineering Secure Systems of the Helmholtz Association (HGF) and by KASTEL Security Research Labs (structure 46.23.02).

Disclosure of Interests. The authors have no competing interests to declare that are relevant to the content of this article.

A Appendix

Cisco 5-SHOT

```
"""<|start_header_id|>user<|end_header_id|>

The following are multiple choice questions (with answers
    ) about network fundamentals, network access, security
      fundamentals, automation and programmability.
Question: Which two options are the best reasons to use
    an IPV4 private IP space? (Choose two.)
A. to enable intra-enterprise communication
B. to implement NAT
C. to connect applications
D. to conserve global address space
E. to manage routing overhead
Your response should end with \"The best answer is [
    the_answer_letter(s)]\" where the [the_answer_letter(s
    )] is/are of A, B, C, D, E, F,...
<|eot_id|><|start_header_id|>assistant<|end_header_id|>

The best answer is AD.<|eot_id|><|start_header_id|>user<|
    end_header_id|>

The following are multiple choice questions (with answers
    ) about network fundamentals, network access, security
      fundamentals, automation and programmability.
Question: Security Group Access requires which three
    syslog messages to be sent to Cisco ISE? (Choose three
    .)
A. IOS-7-PROXY_DROP
B. AP-1-AUTH_PROXY_DOS_ATTACK
C. MKA-2-MACDROP
D. AUTHMGR-5-MACMOVE
E. ASA-6-CONNECT_BUILT
F. AP-1-AUTH_PROXY_FALLBACK_REQ
Your response should end with \"The best answer is [
    the_answer_letter(s)]\" where the [the_answer_letter(s
    )] is/are of A, B, C, D, E, F,...
<|eot_id|><|start_header_id|>assistant<|end_header_id|>

The best answer is BDF.<|eot_id|><|start_header_id|>user
    <|end_header_id|>
```

```
The following are multiple choice questions (with answers
    ) about network fundamentals, network access, security
      fundamentals, automation and programmability.
Question: Which two authentication stores are supported
    to design a wireless network using PEAP EAP-MSCHAPv2
    as the authentication method? (Choose two.)
A. Microsoft Active Directory
B. ACS
C. LDAP
D. RSA Secure-ID
E. Certificate Server
Your response should end with \"The best answer is [
    the_answer_letter(s)]\" where the [the_answer_letter(s
    )] is/are of A, B, C, D, E, F,...
<|eot_id|><|start_header_id|>assistant<|end_header_id|>

The best answer is AB.<|eot_id|><|start_header_id|>user<|
    end_header_id|>

The following are multiple choice questions (with answers
    ) about network fundamentals, network access, security
      fundamentals, automation and programmability.
Question: The corporate security policy requires multiple
      elements to be matched in an authorization policy.
    Which elements can be combined to meet the requirement
    ?
A. Device registration status and device activation
    status
B. Network access device and time condition
C. User credentials and server certificate
D. Built-in profile and custom profile
Your response should end with \"The best answer is [
    the_answer_letter(s)]\" where the [the_answer_letter(s
    )] is/are of A, B, C, D, E, F,...
<|eot_id|><|start_header_id|>assistant<|end_header_id|>

The best answer is B.<|eot_id|><|start_header_id|>user<|
    end_header_id|>

The following are multiple choice questions (with answers
    ) about network fundamentals, network access, security
      fundamentals, automation and programmability.
Question: Which three posture states can be used for
    authorization rules? (Choose three.)
A. unknown
```

```
B. known
C. noncompliant
D. quarantined
E. compliant
F. no access
G. limited
Your response should end with \"The best answer is [
    the_answer_letter(s)]\" where the [the_answer_letter(s
    )] is/are of A, B, C, D, E, F,...
<|eot_id|><|start_header_id|>assistant<|end_header_id|>

The best answer is ACE.<|eot_id|><|start_header_id|>user
    <|end_header_id|>

The following are multiple choice questions (with answers
    ) about network fundamentals, network access, security
     fundamentals, automation and programmability.
Question: {Exam_Question}
{Exam_Choices}
Your response should end with \"The best answer is [
    the_answer_letter(s)]\" where the [the_answer_letter(s
    )] is/are of A, B, C, D, E, F,....<|eot_id|>"""
```

Cisco 0-SHOT COT Template

```
"""The following are multiple choice questions (with
    answers), choose the best answer.
Question: {Exam_Question}
{Exam_Choices}

- For simple problems:
Directly provide the answer with minimal explanation.

- For complex problems:
Use this step-by-step format:
## Step 1: [Concise description]
[Brief explanation]
## Step 2: [Concise description]
[Brief explanation]

Regardless of the approach, always conclude with:
The best answer is [the_answer_letter(s)].
where the [the_answer_letter(s)] is one or multiple of A,
    B, C, D, E, F...
Let's think step by step."""
```

References

1. Current Exam List. https://www.cisco.com/c/en/us/training-events/training-certifications/exams/current-list.html
2. Free Exam Prep By IT Professionals | ExamTopics. https://www.examtopics.com/
3. Hello GPT-4o. https://openai.com/index/hello-gpt-4o/
4. Introducing Claude 3.5 Sonnet. https://www.anthropic.com/news/claude-3-5-sonnet
5. The Llama 3 Herd of Models | Research - AI at Meta. https://ai.meta.com/research/publications/the-llama-3-herd-of-models/
6. Abdin, M., et al.: Phi-3 technical report: a highly capable language model locally on your phone. https://doi.org/10.48550/arXiv.2404.14219
7. Balepur, N., Ravichander, A., Rudinger, R.: Artifacts or abduction: how do LLMs answer multiple-choice questions without the question? https://doi.org/10.48550/arXiv.2402.12483
8. Bang, Y., et al.: A multitask, multilingual, multimodal evaluation of ChatGPT on reasoning, hallucination, and interactivity. https://doi.org/10.48550/arXiv.2302.04023
9. Carlini, N., et al.: Extracting training data from large language models. https://doi.org/10.48550/arXiv.2012.07805
10. Chen, X., et al.: PaLI-X: on scaling up a multilingual vision and language model. https://doi.org/10.48550/arXiv.2305.18565
11. Chiang, W.L., et al.: Chatbot arena: an open platform for evaluating LLMs by human preference. https://doi.org/10.48550/arXiv.2403.04132
12. Hendrycks, D., et al.: Measuring massive multitask language understanding. https://doi.org/10.48550/arXiv.2009.03300
13. Li, F., Liang, K., Lin, Z., Katsikas, S.K. (eds.): Security and Privacy in Communication Networks: 18th EAI International Conference, SecureComm 2022, Virtual Event, October 2022, Proceedings, Lecture Notes of the Institute for Computer Sciences, Social Informatics and Telecommunications Engineering, 1st edn., vol. 462. Springer (2023). https://doi.org/10.1007/978-3-031-25538-0
14. Li, G., Li, Y., Guannan, W., Yang, H., Yu, Y.: SecEval: a comprehensive benchmark for evaluating cybersecurity knowledge of foundation models. https://github.com/XuanwuAI/SecEval
15. Li, T., et al.: From crowdsourced data to high-quality benchmarks: arena-hard and BenchBuilder pipeline. https://doi.org/10.48550/arXiv.2406.11939
16. Li, N., et al.: The WMDP benchmark: measuring and reducing malicious use with unlearning. https://doi.org/10.48550/arXiv.2403.03218
17. Liang, P., et al.: Holistic evaluation of language models. https://openreview.net/forum?id=iO4LZibEqW
18. Liu, Z.: SecQA: a concise question-answering dataset for evaluating large language models in computer security. https://doi.org/10.48550/arXiv.2312.15838
19. Motlagh, F.N., Hajizadeh, M., Majd, M., Najafi, P., Cheng, F., Meinel, C.: Large language models in cybersecurity: state-of-the-art. http://arxiv.org/abs/2402.00891
20. OpenAI: GPT-4 technical report. https://arxiv.org/pdf/2303.08774.pdf
21. Sainz, O., et al.: NLP evaluation in trouble: on the need to measure LLM data contamination for each benchmark. https://doi.org/10.48550/arXiv.2310.18018
22. Tann, W., Liu, Y., Sim, J.H., Seah, C.M., Chang, E.C.: Using large language models for cybersecurity capture-the-flag challenges and certification questions. https://arxiv.org/pdf/2308.10443.pdf

23. Tihanyi, N., Ferrag, M.A., Jain, R., Bisztray, T., Debbah, M.: CyberMetric: a benchmark dataset based on retrieval-augmented generation for evaluating LLMs in cybersecurity knowledge. https://doi.org/10.48550/arXiv.2402.07688
24. Vaswani, A., et al.: Attention is all you need. https://arxiv.org/pdf/1706.03762.pdf
25. Wang, Y., et al.: MMLU-Pro: a more robust and challenging multi-task language understanding benchmark. https://doi.org/10.48550/arXiv.2406.01574
26. Wei, J., et al.: Chain-of-thought prompting elicits reasoning in large language models. https://doi.org/10.48550/arXiv.2201.11903
27. Xia, C.S., Wei, Y., Zhang, L.: Practical program repair in the era of large pre-trained language models. https://doi.org/10.48550/arXiv.2210.14179
28. Xu, H., et al.: Large language models for cyber security: a systematic literature review. https://doi.org/10.48550/arXiv.2405.04760
29. Yue, X., et al.: MMMU: a massive multi-discipline multimodal understanding and reasoning benchmark for expert AGI. https://doi.org/10.48550/arXiv.2311.16502
30. Zhang, J., Bu, H., Wen, H., Chen, Y., Li, L., Zhu, H.: When LLMs meet cybersecurity: a systematic literature review. https://doi.org/10.48550/arXiv.2405.03644

How to Train Your Llama – Efficient Grammar-Based Application Fuzzing Using Large Language Models

Ibrahim Mhiri[1], Matthias Börsig[2](✉), Akim Stark[2], and Ingmar Baumgart[2]

[1] 1&1 Mail & Media, Karlsruhe, Germany
ibrahim.mhiri@1und1.de

[2] FZI Research Center for Information Technology, Karlsruhe, Germany
{boersig,stark,baumgart}@fzi.de

Abstract. Fuzzing is an automated testing technique that generates random input to identify software bugs and vulnerabilities by provoking unexpected behavior. Although effective, traditional fuzzing lacks input generation guidance, which often leads to inefficiency and wasted time, especially for complex programs, because many inputs are invalid and are rejected. Grammar-based fuzzers address this problem by generating inputs that match the syntactic structure of the program, although they require expert knowledge to define accurate grammars.

Large Language Models (LLMs) show remarkable capabilities in Natural Language Processing (NLP), improving efficiency in various domains. These models can be used to generate input for fuzzers, as they can quickly learn or already have familiarity with the required input formats. This paper explores the integration of LLMs with fuzzing methods to streamline directed input generation and thereby increase fuzzing efficiency. We specifically adapt Llama2 for use with American Fuzzy Lop (AFL), focusing on Extensible Markup Language (XML) due to its commonality as a structured file format. Our approach demonstrates the potential of LLMs to enhance traditional fuzzing by providing targeted, intelligent input generation. Experimental results show that our approach can achieve up to six times more code coverage after 24 h compared to using AFL alone. Furthermore, in our tests, our method provides up to 50% more coverage than a grammar-based fuzzer.

Keywords: Grammar-Based Fuzzing · XML · Fuzzing · Large Language Models · Llama2 · Fine-Tuning · Prompt-Tuning

1 Introduction

Fuzzing is an important technique in IT security for identifying vulnerabilities in software by automatically testing programs with both expected and malformed inputs. This automated testing approach deliberately inputs a wide range of data to the software, looking for instances where unexpected or faulty responses, such

L. Horn Iwaya et al. (Eds.): NordSec 2024, LNCS 15396, pp. 239–257, 2025.
https://doi.org/10.1007/978-3-031-79007-2_13

as crashes, unhandled exceptions, or security vulnerabilities, are triggered [4]. Grammar-based fuzzing, a specialized testing method, targets applications that handle structured input by using the expected input grammar of the application to generate syntactically correct test cases aimed at exploring the limits of its data handling capabilities.

The recent rise of Large Language Models (LLMs) has significantly impacted various fields by their ability to generate text and to predict sequences of text based on the context provided to them [18]. The application of LLMs to fuzzing, in particular grammar-based fuzzing, offers a new approach to improving software testing by generating complex and varied test inputs that can reveal hidden vulnerabilities beyond the reach of traditional fuzzing methods.

This paper explores the use of LLMs in grammar-based fuzzing to improve vulnerability detection by generating grammar-compliant input. We aim to optimize LLMs for specific tests and refine input generation through feedback, providing a more effective method of testing complex applications than traditional approaches.

We conduct a comparative evaluation against current fuzzing techniques to assess the efficacy of our LLM-enhanced fuzzing approach. The goal is to demonstrate not merely the applicability of LLMs to grammar-based fuzzing but also to highlight the broader implications for testing software that processes complex structured inputs. This investigation underscores the potential of leveraging LLMs to advance the field of software testing, emphasizing the scientific inquiry into their practical application rather than an uncritical endorsement of their capabilities. In summary, our paper makes the following contributions:

- Adaptation of a pre-trained Llama2 13B LLM: As a proof of concept, we adapt a pre-trained Llama2 model to represent the grammar of XML files. This adaptation allows the LLM to generate optimized XML patterns, which are particularly valuable for fuzzing applications that depend on XML data.
- Integration of an LLM into American Fuzzy Lop (AFL): We illustrate how the integration of an LLM for input generation improves the efficiency of the AFL fuzzing framework. This cooperation facilitates the generation of new input files, allowing the fuzzer to explore deeper states more effectively.
- Continuous and dynamic improvement strategy: We propose a feedback loop approach to consistently and dynamically improve the fuzzer's performance throughout the fuzzing process. This approach ensures that the effectiveness of the model is maintained over time.

2 Related Work

Hu et al. [6] introduce ChatFuzz, an extension of grey box fuzzers like AFL++ that integrates generative AI. The system uses large language models to generate XML inputs that conform to the format specifications of programs with structured input. The work uses an LLM (ChatGPT) without further Fine-Tuning or Prompt-Tuning, which performs worse in edge coverage compared to our approach.

The work of Zhang et al. [27] implements LLAMAFUZZ. It also recognizes the ability of LLMs to generate structured input as test cases for fuzzing. However, their approach focuses exclusively on Fine-Tuning LLMs to handle input seed mutations and evaluating performance improvements using AFL++ as the baseline fuzzer. In contrast, our work explores different strategies, such as Prompt-Tuning and Fine-Tuning, to determine which approach yields better results for input generation. Unlike Zhang et al., we do not delegate the mutation process to the LLM; instead, the LLM generates the initial inputs while the fuzzer retains control over the mutations.

Xia et al. [21] present Fuzz4All, a generic fuzzing tool that uses LLM to test different target programs. The tool has two phases: Autoprompting, which refines user input using LLMs, and the fuzzing loop, which generates input for testing. Fuzz4All prioritizes generality over efficiency and is tailored for compilers. This differs from our approach, where we try to learn one grammar at a time and focus on intensive fuzzing.

Meng et al. [10] introduce CHATAFL, an LLM-guided protocol fuzzer using pre-trained models for human-readable specifications. CHATAFL's systematic interaction with LLMs enhances state and code coverage by learning the protocol specification and guiding the fuzzer. Although the Fine-Tuning approach is used to enhance the capabilities of an LLM, it differs from our methodology as it is only a part of our approach. Additionally, it operates in a different domain. While we investigate XML parsers, it focuses on learning a network protocol.

In the field of fuzzing, various methods use LLM to improve specialized fuzzers. Yang et al. [24] introduce KernelGPT, which extends kernel fuzzing by using LLM to automatically infer specifications for Syzkaller, one of the most widely studied kernel fuzzers. Deng et al. [3] present TitanFuzz, a generative LLM that creates seed programs for fuzzing Deep Learning (DL) APIs. TitanFuzz uses a multi-armed bandit algorithm for mutation operations and demonstrates effectiveness in detecting bugs across CPU and GPU backends. In a follow-up paper, Deng et al. [2] introduce FuzzGPT, an extension of TitanFuzz, automating varied input program creation to fuzz DL libraries with LLMs. FuzzGPT improves error detection and has uncovered many bugs in PyTorch and TensorFlow. Liu et al. [9] demonstrated the use of LLMs for fuzz target generation, presenting a generalized approach for input generation.

Le Mieux et al. [7] present CodaMosa, a tool for Search-Based Software Testing (SBST). The paper shows that LLMs can be used to derive new test cases based on existing ones, leading into an increase in the overall test coverage.

Ackerman and Cybenko [1] propose an NLP-driven approach using a LLM to address software vulnerabilities from format specification ambiguity.

Prior to the advent of LLM, significant research and various other efforts, including experiments with Machine Learning (ML) and DL, aimed at improving the efficiency of (grammar-based) fuzzing [4,16,19,20,23].

3 Background

3.1 Large Language Models

LLMs are trained on large amounts of text data to understand and generate human language. They are based on the transformer model, which uses an encoder-decoder architecture. The encoder processes the input data by converting it into a continuous representation, while the decoder generates the output sequence from this representation. The model uses a self-attention mechanism to process input data in parallel, allowing it to assess the relationships between words, even over long distances in a sentence, and to effectively weigh the importance of words. As a result, LLMs can predict the next word or phrase based on learned patterns and produce coherent output. They excel at tasks such as answering questions, summarizing information and producing structured text.

3.2 Model Tuning

The machine learning community has created open access to a wealth of pre-trained LLMs. These models often encompass a diverse range of both natural (e.g., English, French, German) and programming (e.g., JavaScript, Python) languages, making them versatile tools for various applications. Platforms like Hugging Face[1] offer convenient access to these pre-trained LLMs, which, while operationally ready for immediate tasks, often require further refinement, like Fine-Tuning or Prompt-Tuning, to excel in specific applications.

3.3 Fine-Tuning

Fine-Tuning involves the precise adjustment of the parameters of a pre-trained LLM to tailor it for a particular task or dataset, such as enhancing its capability in sentiment analysis, question-answering, or the generation of structured data like Extensible Markup Language (XML) for fuzzing purposes. This adaptation process necessitates additional training on a target-specific dataset, enabling the model to Fine-Tune its parameters for optimized performance. Although this method is potent, it is also marked by its high demand for resources. The substantial number of parameters in current LLMs, potentially reaching into the billions, entails a significant computational burden. As a result, the process demands specialized computational resources, like advanced Graphical Processing Units (GPUs) or Tensor Processing Units (TPUs), and can extend over prolonged periods, posing potential constraints on its applicability [22].

3.4 Prompt-Tuning

LLMs undergo extensive pre-training across vast datasets, equipping them with a broad exposure to various languages. This pre-training instills in them a foundational capability to process diverse linguistic structures and grammars. In many

[1] https://huggingface.co/.

cases, this extensive pre-training makes it inefficient to adjust the entire model for specific applications through Fine-Tuning. Instead, a more targeted approach, known as Prompt-Tuning (a specific Parameter-Efficient Prompt Tuning (PEFT) technique), proves to be more effective [11].

PEFT optimizes a pre-trained LLM for particular tasks by altering only a select subset of the parameters of a model. This process involves introducing specific input-output pairs that guide the model towards generating the desired outcomes for particular tasks. By freezing the original weights of the model and focusing adjustments on a smaller set of prompt parameters, PEFT facilitates the adaptation of the model with minimal modifications. This approach leverages the extensive pre-trained knowledge of the model while ensuring a resource-efficient adaptation process. As models grow in complexity, the advantages of Prompt-Tuning might become even more pronounced, providing a practical method for tailoring LLM to specialized tasks without extensive retraining [8,26].

3.5 Model Inference

During the inference phase, an LLM uses its trained pattern recognition to generate outputs from given inputs (prompts). This phase demonstrates the model's ability to adapt to new, unseen data. "Inference" here refers to the use of statistical algorithms to produce text based on learned patterns, not to make judgments or inferences [13,25].

In practical terms, inference is where the theoretical capabilities of an LLM lead to tangible results, such as answering questions, generating text, or creating code. The efficiency and accuracy of inference are critical because they directly affect the real-world utility and effectiveness of the model. Advances in model architectures, training methods, and computational technologies continue to improve LLMs, making them increasingly valuable in a variety of industries.

4 Design

Our prototype focuses on a specialized input generator for XML parsers. The core of our design involves crafting malformed XML packets using ML techniques, employing the AFL as our choice of fuzzing engine due to its advanced functionality and adaptability. AFL is widely regarded as one of the best multipurpose fuzzers available. It combines extensive capabilities with a compact code base, allowing for easy modification and extension. AFL++, an advanced version of AFL, incorporates numerous scientific advances that make it one of the most powerful fuzzers currently available. These enhancements, however, also increase the complexity of the codebase, making custom extensions to AFL++ more difficult to implement. Therefore, we choose AFL as the basis for the experimental setup. This allows us to focus on the interface between ML and the fuzzer with little modification on the AFL side. AFL orchestrates the fuzzing operation by methodically feeding inputs to the ML parser, monitoring its behavior, and recording any crashes, hangs and anomalies.

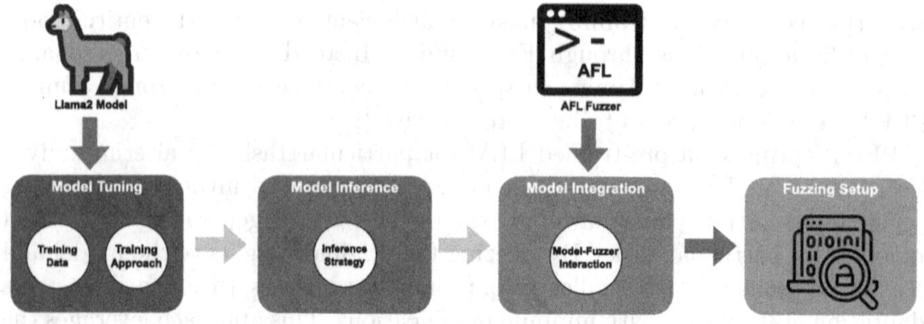

Fig. 1. Concept overview of our approach

On the machine learning side, we require an LLM that can effectively handle context-free grammars and generate complex input. With Llama2 13B, we choose a well-known and freely available LLM [17], as its ability to efficiently parse and generate complex structures perfectly matches our goal of systematically generating malformed XML packages.

We focus on XML, because its human-readable format allows immediate visual verification of results. This also fits well with our ML methods, allowing the systematic production of malformed packets to test the robustness of the parser. In addition, the ubiquity of XML provides a wealth of test cases, and its structured nature further aids the verification of results, making it easier to identify parser weaknesses. Since XML can be represented as a formal grammar, it furthermore allows us to compare our results with a grammar-based fuzzer, providing a benchmark for evaluating the effectiveness of our approach. Figure 1 illustrates the concept of our solution, necessitating two principal inputs: An LLM, specifically Llama2, and the AFL fuzzing tool. Our method consists of three phases:

- **Model Tuning:** Initially, we refine the ability of the model to process the input grammar of the target program by selecting an optimal dataset and training method. This phase results in an LLM tailored to process input structures relevant to the target program, enhancing its efficiency in generating meaningful input variations.
- **Model Inference:** Following the tuning, this phase involves deploying the model to produce test inputs for the fuzzing process. The focus here is on employing a strategic inference mechanism that enables the generation of diverse test cases.
- **Model Integration:** This final step ensures the model works smoothly with the fuzzing tool. We outline a straightforward method for the LLM to feed inputs directly into the fuzzing process, aiming for seamless collaboration between the two.

This structured approach results in a comprehensive fuzzing environment, encompassing an LLM proficient in generating targeted input samples and an AFL instance refined to leverage these samples effectively.

4.1 Dataset

We gather a dataset consisting of both malicious and benign XML files. For the malicious files, we obtain 56 XML files from the Exploit Database[2], primarily containing XML External Entity (XXE) injection payloads that exploit real-world application vulnerabilities. For the benign files, we choose the KIT Motion-Language Dataset [12] as the source and randomly select 100 XML files from there to keep benign and malicious samples roughly in balance.

While this seems to be a fairly small set of training data, it is a challenging task to obtain a larger variety of distinct malicious XML files. This, however, should not be a problem, as Llama2 is pre-trained on large amounts of publicly available XML files found on the Internet, providing a strong foundation for the model's understanding of the XML structure.

4.2 Training Approach

The training phase involves obtaining data aligned with the goals of the project, where the generative LLM is utilized to supply AFL with a balanced mix of benign and malicious samples, ensuring a thorough evaluation of the functionality of the target program. Following dataset preparation, we proceed to determine the optimal model tuning method.

Although Fine-Tuning requires significant computational resources, Prompt-Tuning offers a more cost-effective alternative, as only a portion of the model is modified. Given these considerations, we prioritize Prompt-Tuning for its efficacy, with Fine-Tuning serving to establish a robust comparative baseline.

4.3 Inference Strategy

Inference strategies for generating fuzzing samples broadly fall into two primary categories: sampling-based strategies, that explore the input space using randomness, and deterministic strategies, that use a predefined algorithm or heuristics. Deterministic strategies, which produce the same sequences for given tokens and probability tuples, lack the variability necessary for effective fuzzing. Such predictability, coupled with scalability issues related to memory and execution time, renders deterministic strategies impractical for our application.

Our chosen approach is the top-k sampling method, which belongs to the category of sampling-based strategies. The adaptability of top-k sampling makes it ideal for generating a wide range of fuzzing inputs, facilitating a more comprehensive evaluation of the vulnerabilities of the target program. This technique involves selecting the top-k most likely tokens at each step, introducing randomness into the process to ensure a varied set of generated XML samples. The key advantage of this method is its ability to maintain a balance between generating diverse inputs and keeping the selection process efficient and manageable. This balance is crucial for fuzzing applications where both the diversity of inputs and the practicality of generating them are important.

[2] https://www.exploit-db.com/.

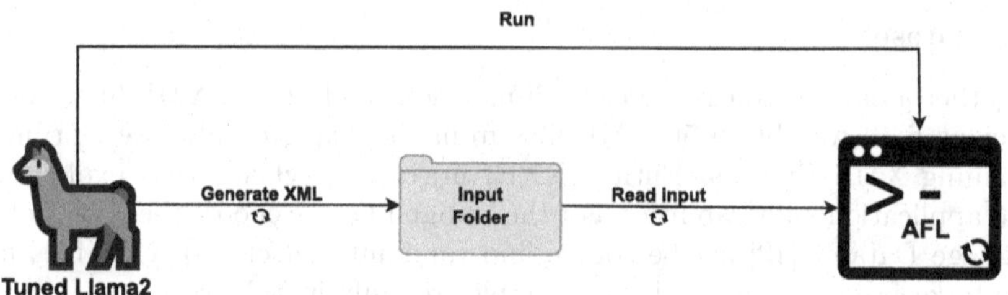

Fig. 2. LLM Integration into the Fuzzing Test

4.4 Model Integration

With the LLM prepared for inference, we outline an integration strategy enabling the application of the model within the fuzzing tests. Unlike conventional tools that depend on predefined grammars, our approach benefits from directly incorporating generated XML samples into the fuzzing workflow.

This integration necessitates modifying AFL to accommodate the seamless transfer of generated samples, detailed further in Sect. 5. As shown in Fig. 2, the Llama2 model is activated to produce a predetermined number of XML samples. These samples are directly sent to an input directory, making them readily available for AFL processing. The operation is cyclic, with new samples generated and assessed by AFL throughout the duration of the fuzzing test.

The cycle begins with the LLM initiating AFL to start a fuzzing session that is scheduled to run continuously for 24 h. The initial time required for the LLM calculations is not subtracted from the AFL fuzzing time, as this time can be calculated in advance. In real-world scenarios, testing time is often limited and typically begins as soon as the program is ready. After the 24-hour period, sample generation stops and AFL exits. This termination is managed either by a direct stop signal from the LLM or by a predetermined timeout mechanism set at the start of the test.

4.5 Feedback Loop

An integral component of our system, as depicted in Fig. 3, is the feedback loop that enhances the performance of the LLM over time. During the fuzzing test, the LLM adapts based on the feedback of the fuzzer. Specifically, the feedback loop (illustrated by red arrows in the figure) analyzes AFL outcomes to pinpoint XML samples instrumental in uncovering new vulnerabilities or pathways in the target program. These samples are then reintegrated into the training routine of the LLM during regular Prompt-Tuning sessions. This allows the model to improve its process of generating examples for future tests. This iterative cycle allows the model to continuously refine its output, aligning more closely with the evolving landscape of potential vulnerabilities in the target software.

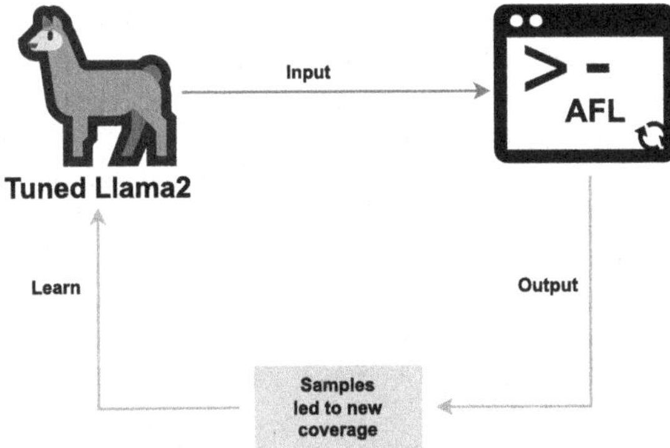

Fig. 3. Llama2 learns through a Feedback Loop

5 Implementation

We develop a Proof of Concept (PoC) leveraging the synergies between the 13B model of Llama2 and the AFL for an enhanced fuzzing framework. Our PoC, hosted on GitHub[3], demonstrates the practical application of integrating an LLM with a leading fuzzing tool to uncover software vulnerabilities through structured XML inputs.

5.1 Model Training and Integration with AFL

Fine-Tuning. To begin our implementation, we perform a full Fine-Tuning of the Llama2 model, which was specifically chosen for its balance between computational efficiency and model performance.

This Fine-Tuning process is performed over three epochs with a learning rate of 0.003. This learning rate value is determined through empirical testing to strike a balance between rapid model adaptation and the risk of overfitting. Fine-Tuning is performed using a curated dataset as described in Sect. 4.1.

Prompt-Tuning. We also use a Prompt-Tuning approach using the Transformers library, training the model on the same dataset mentioned in Sect. 4.1.

To compare the results, we use the 3072 and 4096 tokenization settings. With 3072 tokenization, the model processes queries up to 3072 tokens long, while with 4096 tokenization it processes queries up to 4096 tokens long. This difference affects the contextual information available for output generation.

5.2 Continuous Data Integration Mechanism

Our enhancements to the AFL framework includes the implementation of a continuous data integration mechanism, distinguishing our approach from traditional fuzzing methods. This mechanism allows AFL to dynamically apply new

[3] https://github.com/IbraMhiri/LLaMa-Fuzzer.

test cases throughout the fuzzing process, rather than relying on a static set of inputs. By modifying the `read_testcases()` function of AFL to periodically scan a predefined input folder, our system ensures a constant influx of fresh, model-generated XML samples for testing. To prevent redundancy, we incorporated a function to track and skip previously scanned samples, optimizing the efficiency of the fuzzing process. We have also configured AFL to store the test cases responsible for detecting new unique paths within the target binary, as well as any hangs or crashes. These test cases are not only stored in the internal AFL seed pool, but also in a predefined folder. This folder serves as a repository for cases that will later be used by the feedback loop mechanism to further improve our model.

5.3 Optimization Technologies

To further improve the scalability and efficiency of our implementation, we integrate optimization technologies such as Accelerate [5], DeepSpeed [15] and Zero [14,15]. These tools are instrumental in enabling the rapid training and execution of the LLM on hardware configurations that are accessible to a broad range of researchers. In addition, our implementation takes advantage of technologies such as Accelerate, which provides optimization techniques to improve the efficiency and scalability of training and using large neural network models.

5.4 Dynamic Feedback Loop

Our approach is to use a dynamic feedback loop mechanism to review the results of each fuzzing iteration.

First, AFL reads the XML files generated by the LLM and starts fuzzing. Then the analysis phase begins: we evaluate the effectiveness of different XML patterns to identify those that successfully reveal new execution paths or cause program crashes. Patterns (XML files) that contribute to new code coverage are then fed back to the LLM. Conversely, patterns that do not add code coverage are retained in the AFL seed pool, but are not fed back to the LLM. The LLM then runs Prompt-Tuning on these samples to improve its performance.

The LLM is then Prompt-Tuned using these samples to improve its performance. Following the Prompt-Tuning process, the LLM generates new XML files that AFL uses as input for further fuzzing. This feedback loop allows us to prioritize XML patterns that have proven effective in exploring new paths or triggering crashes. This iterative process facilitates continuous improvement in the effectiveness of the fuzzing approach over time.

In the meantime, AFL works as usual. However, as new XML files are received from the LLM, they are read and added to the seed pool for further fuzzing. AFL then resumes normal operation, actively looking for new code coverage.

6 Evaluation

We used the developed PoC as described in Sect. 5 to evaluate our approach.

The development environment and hardware played a crucial role in determining the results of this research, given the intensive computational requirements of training and using LLMs. We used a server equipped with a NVIDIA A100 GPU with 80 GB of VRAM. The server also had 720 GB of RAM, 2.03 TB of storage and was powered by an AMD EPYC 75F3 CPU.

To ensure comparability between runs, we ran each fuzzing session for 24 h, allowing full access to GPU resources while restricting the fuzzing process to a single CPU core (default setting of AFL). In real-world scenarios, resources are typically not the bottleneck for fuzzing. Running AFL in parallel on multiple cores does not scale linearly because of the need to share results and data, which introduces overhead.

For our evaluation, we tested the fuzzing setup we developed against several target programs, including libxml2 and TinyXML-2.

6.1 Evaluation Metrics

The following metrics provided by AFL have been used for the evaluation:

- Total Paths Found: This metric represents the total number of unique paths found within the target program during the fuzzing test.
- Crashes: These are unique test cases that cause fatal errors in the tested program, such as `SIGSEGV`, `SIGILL`, `SIGABRT`, and others.
- Hangs: These are unique test cases that cause the unit under test to time out. In AFL, the default time limit before a test-case is classified as a hang is 1 s.

For our evaluation we rely on two widely used XML parsers. A common method of evaluating the effectiveness of a fuzzer is to introduce deliberate bugs into the tested program and measure how many of them are detected by the fuzzer. However, we take an alternative approach by testing real-world programs, as intentionally introduced bugs are more obvious and lack the subtlety often found in accidentally introduced bugs. Consequently, if no bugs are found – often because the program has been thoroughly tested and simpler bugs have already been patched – code coverage (total paths found) becomes the most reliable metric. It serves as an indicator of how deeply the fuzzer has explored the program.

6.2 Experimental Approaches

To evaluate our prototype, we conducted experiments using different approaches, each of which yielded different results:

- AFL Fuzzing: This approach uses the native functionality of the AFL fuzzing tool, with the training data used for the LLM as input.
- Pre-Trained LLM Fuzzing: This method uses the original pre-trained Llama2 model (13B version) as input provider to AFL.
- Fine-Tuned LLM Fuzzing: This method uses a Fine-Tuned version of Llama2 to provide input to AFL.

- Prompt-Tuned LLM Fuzzing: This approach uses a Prompt-Tuned Llama2 model.
- Feedback Loop LLM Fuzzing: The final approach, our PoC, uses a Prompt-Tuned Llama2 model to provide input samples to AFL. In addition, this model undergoes real-time Prompt-Tuning during the fuzzing test using feedback from the fuzzer, specifically samples that lead to the discovery of new paths.
- Nautilus[4] and AFL Fuzzer combined: This approach uses Nautilus 2.0, a coverage-guided, grammar-based fuzzer, in combination with AFL as a baseline. AFL synchronizes with Nautilus, allowing AFL to import Nautilus input, but not vice versa. We used the example of a XML structure that comes with nautilus (`grammar_py_exmaple.py`).

These approaches allow us to compare the effectiveness and efficiency of different methods in the context of our fuzzing framework.

6.3 Experimentation Results

The plots in Fig. 4 illustrate the number of paths detected by the fuzzer within libxml2 and TinyXML-2, respectively, over 24 h. The LLM enhanced fuzzing methods outperform the traditional AFL approach, as shown in the figure. All AFL variants integrated with an LLM show superior performance compared to using AFL alone, with tests using Prompt-Tuned LLMs showing significant improvement. In the following, we discuss and interpret our results.

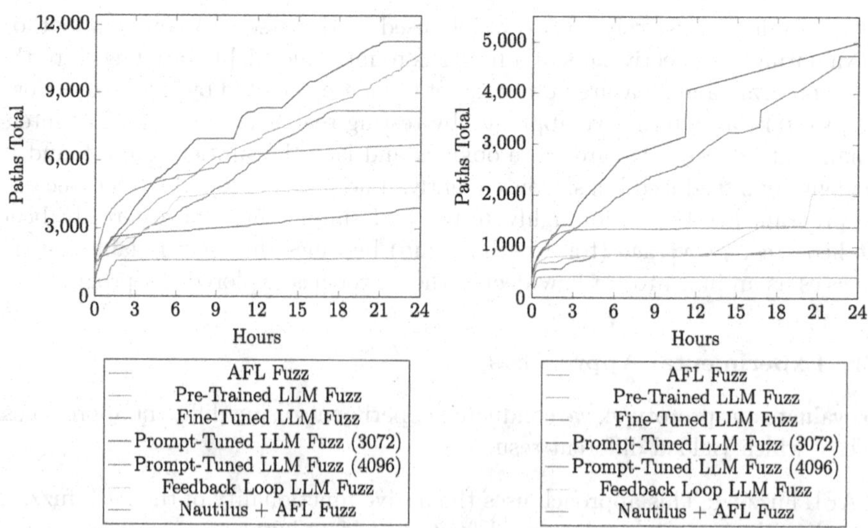

Fig. 4. Total path coverage of the different approaches in libxml2 (left) and TinyXML-2 (right) over 24 h

[4] https://github.com/nautilus-fuzz/nautilus.

For libxml2, the traditional AFL detected 1698 paths, while LLM-enhanced AFL detected 10705 paths. The Prompt-Tuned LLM 4096 model detected 8203 paths, and the Prompt-Tuned LLM 3072 model detected 11290 paths. The Fine-Tuned LLM model detected 6719 paths, while the grammar-based fuzzer Nautilus combined with AFL detected 4826 paths.

For TinyXML-2, AFL detected 411 paths, while LLM-enhanced AFL detected 894 paths. The Prompt-Tuned LLM 4096 model detected 4745 paths, and the Prompt-Tuned LLM 3072 model detected 5000 paths. The Fine-Tuned LLM model detected 924 paths, while the grammar-based fuzzer Nautilus combined with AFL detected 1396 paths.

The Fine-Tuned model, however, shows relatively poor results compared to other LLM-based tests. This prototype has undergone a minimal amount of training (only three epochs), which is not enough to learn the required grammar, but was directly determined by the limitations of our hardware resources.

Conversely, fuzzing approaches that use Prompt-Tuned Llama2 models, such as Prompt-Tuned and feedback loop models, outperform the pre-trained model. The increase in history provides Llama2 with more information to compute the most likely next tokens. Prompt-Tuned models are adept at learning new XML patterns, especially from malicious examples, thereby improving results and coverage. Adjusting the context length of Prompt-Tuned LLMs can further optimize performance, however considering a bigger context length can result in a worse performance as shown in Fig. 4. Even though we could not derive a definite reason behind the deviation between the performance of the Prompt-Tuned LLM 4096 model and the Prompt-Tuned LLM 3072 model, our assumption is that using a bigger context length, can result in an overhead, which can introduce a considerable impact on the performance of the model over the 24 h of the test period.

In our fuzzing tests, the combination of AFL with a Prompt-Tuned LLM using a context length of 3072 showed superior performance to all other methods when evaluated against both libxml2 and TinyXML-2.

Comparatively, the feedback loop model shows slightly fewer detected paths than the Prompt-Tuned model. This is due to the learning overhead of the feedback loop model, which periodically undergoes a tuning process using XML samples detected by the fuzzer.

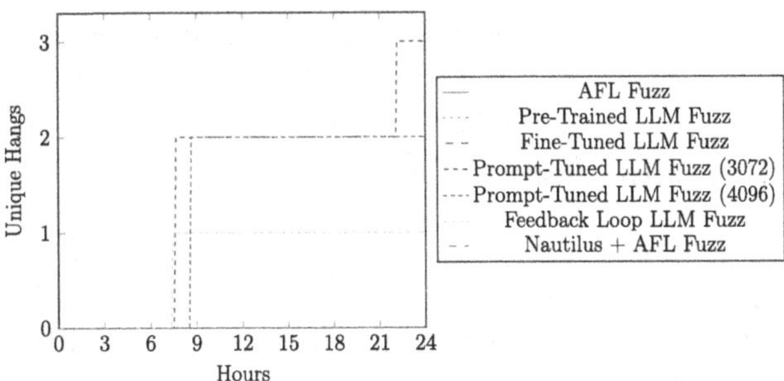

Fig. 5. Found hangs in libxml2 for the different approaches over 24 h.

Figure 5 shows the number of hangs that occurred during the 24 h of fuzzing libxml2. Again, the Prompt-Tuned fuzzing approaches outperformed the others, finding up to 3 unique hangs during the test period. However, it is worth mentioning that our approach, feedback loop fuzzing, follows right behind with one hang found. Standard AFL fuzzing, pre-trained LLM fuzzing, and Fine-Tuned LLM fuzzing did not find any hangs during the test. It is also worth noting that during a 24-hour fuzzing session targeting TinyXML-2, no hangs were detected regardless of the approach used. Also, no crashes were detected in either of the two programs tested.

Table 1. Number of Generated Samples per Fuzzing Test

Model	Pre-Trained	Fine-Tuned	Prompt-Tuned	Feedback Loop
Total number of Samples per Run	6060 Samples	980 Samples	13980 Samples	2390 Samples
Sample generation time	14.04 s	89.49 s	5.99 s	–

With the goal to better understand the potential direct factors that lead to the results presented in the previous paragraphs, we considered observing details related to samples generating. Table 1 represents the total number of generated samples per run as well as the required time to generate a single sample using the different LLM-based approaches that we introduced in our work. As we can notice here, the generation time of samples can significantly vary depending on the model type, which leads to a remarkable deviation within the total number of resulting samples. The original pre-trained Llama2 model generated 6060 samples within 24 h, during which our test was running. On the other hand, the Fine-Tuned version generated only 980 samples. This is due to the complexity and extra layer that traditional Fine-Tuning adds to the model, which has a significant impact on the time required to generate a sample. The Prompt-Tuned (3072) model was the best performing model with 13980 samples. This result demonstrates the effectiveness of the Prompt-Tuning approach in improving the suitability and performance of the model for a specific use case without adding complexity or extra layers. However, the feedback loop showed suboptimal performance in terms of samples generated. This is primarily due to our design, where the model periodically pauses sample generation to undergo a training phase.

7 Limitations and Future Work

The approach of combining a fuzzer with an LLM proves to be significantly more effective than using the fuzzer alone. In our study, we show that this hybrid approach can also yield superior results compared to traditional grammar-based fuzzers.

Traditional fuzzers rely heavily on mutation to explore new program paths, which often requires considerable luck to stumble upon meaningful variations.

Even when fuzzers randomly generate new input, their inspiration often comes from the existing data initially provided to the fuzzer. In contrast, LLMs can generate arbitrarily complex XML files based on learned patterns from existing data, allowing them to penetrate deeper into the program logic directly.

These tests initially focused on XML, which is well suited for representation using grammar-based methods. In practice, however, we can test programs of arbitrary complexity.

The Prompt-Tuned LLM fuzzing approach emerged as the most successful method in our evaluation. Its effectiveness underscores the potential of integrating language models into fuzzing techniques to improve testing results and vulnerability detection.

When considering the strengths and limitations of using XML as our target domain, several factors come into play. The structured format and well-defined syntax of XML make it an ideal candidate for fuzzing, allowing for the systematic generation of test cases to assess parser robustness. However, the complexity of XML can also present challenges, especially when dealing with nested or deeply nested elements. In addition, XML parsers can vary in their handling of edge cases and error conditions, requiring extensive testing to identify potential vulnerabilities.

One of the key advantages of the Prompt-Tuned LLM fuzzing approach is its independence from explicit knowledge of the input grammar. Unlike traditional fuzzing methods that require a predefined grammar for input generation, Prompt-Tuned LLM fuzzing leverages the ability of the language model to implicitly learn and understand the grammar. This eliminates the need for manual grammar specification, streamlining the fuzzing process and enabling effective testing even in cases where the grammar is not accessible.

Furthermore, the adaptability of the approach extends beyond XML parsing to other applications, such as PDF parsing, that isn't context free. By leveraging the ability of the language model to reproduce and adapt complex structures, Prompt-Tuned LLM fuzzing provides a versatile solution for automated testing across different software systems.

In conclusion, the success of the Prompt-Tuned LLM fuzzing approach highlights the potential of integrating language models into fuzzing methodologies. By harnessing the power of natural language understanding, this approach offers a novel and effective means of automated testing that can be applied to diverse domains beyond XML parsing.

While this research has yielded positive results, it is important to acknowledge several limitations that have affected the results and interpretations. These limitations and challenges are listed below:

- Meanwhile, Llama3.1 has been released, which may offer improved results, but this work focuses on demonstrating feasibility rather than achieving the best performance with the fastest LLM. In addition, there are now more code-specific models such as Code Llama. However, we believe that standard LLMs are more appropriate for our data generation purposes.

- The choice of language models was constrained by the hardware described in Sect. 5. Experimenting with larger language models for fuzzing tests holds the potential for better results, as they have more tunable parameters and a better understanding of context and languages.
- The proof of concept used 56 malicious and 100 benign XML examples. Exploring different data types and ratios of malicious to benign instances could improve the effectiveness of the proposed approach.
- The top-k sampling-based strategy, chosen to minimize sample generation time, warrants further investigation and optimization. Balancing generation time and sample quality through parameter tuning, taking into account other inference strategies, could further improve the results.
- The feedback learning loop, as discussed in Sect. 6, affects the number of samples generated during fuzzing tests. Optimization through asynchronous processes for learning and generation phases could improve this approach.

Looking forward, this research also opens up opportunities for further investigation and possible research directions. Some suggested topics arising from this work include:

- Exploring AI Alternatives: Investigating the viability of alternative AI models, such as Generative Adversarial Networks (GANs) and Sequence to Sequence (Seq2Seq) models, to improve the efficiency of fuzzing tests. In addition, the application of Low-Rank Adaptation (LoRA) could improve the results of Fine-Tuning LLMs with small datasets.
- LLM-Enhanced Mutation-Based Fuzzing: Examining the potential of LLM-based methods to augment and enhance the mutation operations performed by advanced fuzzing tools such as AFL. This examination could include developing techniques to use the contextual understanding provided by LLMs to more effectively guide mutation strategies, leading to improved test case generation and vulnerability discovery.
- Domain-Specific Adoption: Researching the applicability of the proposed solution in domains beyond XML-based applications, particularly in programs that deal with input governed by specific grammars that may challenge traditional fuzzing methods. It is important to consider how to extend our approach and in what format these adaptations can be made effectively, emphasizing the need to explore appropriate formats and methodologies for integration into different domains. This adoption requires the adaptation of the tuning phase of our approach by using appropriate samples of the target domain, for instance learning PDF files.

As outlined in Sect. 8, this research addresses various aspects of LLM-based fuzzing and represents a promising direction for future research. The evaluation presented in Sect. 6 demonstrates the potential of even a simple pre-trained Llama2 model to contribute to automated testing, thereby increasing the efficiency of fuzzing tests for security-critical applications such as XML parsers. Future work could also address the limitations outlined above: Opting for the latest version of Llama, optimizing the top-k sampling strategy, using more hardware resources and training on a larger dataset could further evaluate the applicability of our approach.

8 Conclusion

In this work we explored the potential of improving fuzzing tests using LLMs, with a focus on applications that parse XML. Our method, introduced in Sect. 4, revolves around Fine-Tuning and Prompt-Tuning a pre-trained LLM to capture the nuances of XML grammar and tailor it to the task of generating suitable XML samples for fuzzing tests. This involved training the model on a combination of normal and malicious data through Prompt-Tuning.

To demonstrate these concepts, we developed a PoC and made it available on GitHub to facilitate public access and collaborative improvement. Building upon the pre-trained Llama2 model, we applied our method and integrated the enhanced model into AFL, a state-of-the-art fuzzing tool.

Our experimental phase primarily examined the XML parsers libxml2 and TinyXML-2, revealing notable enhancements in the efficiency of AFL when incorporating LLMs. The evaluation demonstrated significant advancements in the discovery of new paths and increased bitmap coverage over set periods. The study not only highlights these key outcomes but also delves into several technical specifics encountered throughout the research.

Our fuzzing tests showed that the use of AFL in conjunction with a Prompt-Tuned LLM with a context length of 3072, outshone other tested methods in terms of code path coverage for both libxml2 and TinyXML-2. Noteworthy is the ability of our method to uncover three distinct unique hangs in libxml2 during fuzzing, underscoring the potential of integrating LLMs into fuzzing workflows for improved testing efficacy.

Acknowledgments. This publication is based on the research project SofDCar (19S21002), which is funded by the German Federal Ministry for Economic Affairs and Climate Action.

A Appendix

A central aspect of the inference evaluation is runtime. The required time for each model to generate an XML sample was recorded and represented in this part of the evaluation.

Table 2. Top-k variation impact on XML Generation Time

$Top - k$ Value	5	25	50	150	250
Pre-Trained LLM	13,12 s	14,04 s	14,34 s	14,56 s	14,68 s
Fine-Tuned LLM	89,82 s	89,49 s	90,67 s	89,52 s	91,35 s
Prompt-Tuned LLM	5,05 s	5,99 s	6,5 s	6,97 s	7,32 s

The Table 2 shows the required time by the model to generate an XML sample in seconds for several $top - k$ values. A high value can impact the generation time of XML samples (with slight variations). However, aside from this aspect, an interesting behavior shown in this table is that the generation time of XML samples can significantly vary depending on the model type (fine-tuned, prompt-tuned, or pre-trained). This table shows that the prompt-tuned LLM is the fastest model, whereas the fine-tuned one is very slow.

References

1. Ackerman, J., Cybenko, G.: Large language models for fuzzing parsers (registered report). In: Proceedings of the 2nd International Fuzzing Workshop, FUZZING 2023, pp. 31–38. Association for Computing Machinery, New York (2023). https://doi.org/10.1145/3605157.3605173
2. Deng, Y., Xia, C., Yang, C., Zhang, S., Yang, S., Zhang, L.: Large language models are edge-case generators: crafting unusual programs for fuzzing deep learning libraries. In: Proceedings of the IEEE/ACM 46th International Conference on Software Engineering, ICSE 2024, Los Alamitos, CA, USA, pp. 830–842. IEEE Computer Society (2024). https://doi.org/10.1145/3597503.3623343
3. Deng, Y., Xia, C.S., Peng, H., Yang, C., Zhang, L.: Large language models are zero-shot fuzzers: fuzzing deep-learning libraries via large language models (2023). https://doi.org/10.48550/arXiv.2212.14834
4. Godefroid, P., Peleg, H., Singh, R.: Learn&fuzz: machine learning for input fuzzing. In: 2017 32nd IEEE/ACM International Conference on Automated Software Engineering (ASE), Los Alamitos, CA, USA, pp. 50–59. IEEE Computer Society (2017). https://doi.org/10.1109/ASE.2017.8115618
5. Gugger, S., et al.: Accelerate: training and inference at scale made simple, efficient and adaptable (2022). https://github.com/huggingface/accelerate
6. Hu, J., Zhang, Q., Yin, H.: Augmenting greybox fuzzing with generative AI (2023). https://doi.org/10.48550/arXiv.2306.06782
7. Lemieux, C., Inala, J.P., Lahiri, S.K., Sen, S.: CodaMosa: escaping coverage plateaus in test generation with pre-trained large language models. In: Proceedings of the 45th International Conference on Software Engineering, ICSE 2023, Los Alamitos, CA, USA, pp. 919–931. IEEE Press (2023). https://doi.org/10.1109/ICSE48619.2023.00085
8. Lester, B., Al-Rfou, R., Constant, N.: The power of scale for parameter-efficient prompt tuning (2021). https://doi.org/10.48550/arXiv.2104.08691
9. Liu, D., Metzman, J., Chang, O.: AI-powered fuzzing: breaking the bug hunting barrier. Google Open Source Security Team (2023). https://security.googleblog.com/2023/08/ai-powered-fuzzing-breaking-bug-hunting.html
10. Meng, R., Mirchev, M., Böhme, M., Roychoudhury, A.: Large language model guided protocol fuzzing. In: Proceedings of the 31st Annual Network and Distributed System Security Symposium (NDSS). The Internet Society, Reston (2024). https://doi.org/10.14722/ndss.2024.24556
11. Pathak, H.: Parameter-efficient fine-tuning (PEFT) and how it's different from fine-tuning (2024). https://medium.com/@harshnpathak/parameter-efficient-fine-tuning-peft-and-how-its-different-from-fine-tuning-3f6b95c73bac
12. Plappert, M., Mandery, C., Asfour, T.: The KIT motion-language dataset. Big Data **4**(4), 236–252 (2016). https://doi.org/10.1089/big.2016.0028
13. von Platen, P.: How to generate text: using different decoding methods for language generation with transformers (2020). https://huggingface.co/blog/how-to-generate

14. Rajbhandari, S., Ruwase, O., Rasley, J., Smith, S., He, Y.: Zero-infinity: breaking the GPU memory wall for extreme scale deep learning. In: Proceedings of the International Conference for High Performance Computing, Networking, Storage and Analysis, SC 2021. Association for Computing Machinery, New York (2021). https://doi.org/10.1145/3458817.3476205
15. Rasley, J., Rajbhandari, S., Ruwase, O., He, Y.: DeepSpeed: system optimizations enable training deep learning models with over 100 billion parameters. In: Proceedings of the 26th ACM SIGKDD International Conference on Knowledge Discovery & Data Mining, KDD 2020, pp. 3505–3506. Association for Computing Machinery, New York (2020). https://doi.org/10.1145/3394486.3406703
16. Salem, H.A.A., Song, J.: A review on grammar-based fuzzing techniques. Int. J. Comput. Sci. Secur. (IJCSS) **13**(3), 114–123 (2019). http://www.cscjournals.org/library/manuscriptinfo.php?mc=IJCSS-1481
17. Touvron, H., et al.: Llama 2: open foundation and fine-tuned chat models (2023). https://arxiv.org/abs/2307.09288
18. Touvron, H., et al.: Llama 2: open foundation and fine-tuned chat models (2023). https://doi.org/10.48550/arXiv.2307.09288
19. Wang, Y., Jia, P., Liu, L., Huang, C., Liu, Z.: A systematic review of fuzzing based on machine learning techniques. PLoS ONE **15**(8), 1–37 (2020). https://doi.org/10.1371/journal.pone.0237749
20. Wu, Z.: A study of grammar-based fuzzing approaches. Master's thesis, California Polytechnic State University (2022). https://doi.org/10.15368/theses.2022.69
21. Xia, C.S., Paltenghi, M., Tian, J.L., Pradel, M., Zhang, L.: Fuzz4All: universal fuzzing with large language models (2024). https://doi.org/10.48550/arXiv.2109.05687
22. Xu, R., et al.: Raise a child in large language model: towards effective and generalizable fine-tuning (2021). https://doi.org/10.48550/arXiv.2109.05687
23. Yang, C., et al.: White-box compiler fuzzing empowered by large language models (2023). https://doi.org/10.48550/arXiv.2310.15991
24. Yang, C., Zhao, Z., Zhang, L.: KernelGPT: enhanced kernel fuzzing via large language models (2023). https://doi.org/10.48550/arXiv.2401.00563
25. Yemme, A., Garani, S.S.: A scalable GPT-2 inference hardware architecture on FPGA. In: 2023 International Joint Conference on Neural Networks (IJCNN), Los Alamitos, CA, USA, pp. 1–8. IEEE Computer Society (2023). https://doi.org/10.1109/IJCNN54540.2023.10191067
26. Yong, Z.X., et al.: BLOOM+1: adding language support to BLOOM for zero-shot prompting (2023). https://aclanthology.org/2023.acl-long.653
27. Zhang, H., Rong, Y., He, Y., Chen, H.: LLAMAFUZZ: large language model enhanced greybox fuzzing (2024). https://arxiv.org/abs/2406.07714

The Dual-Edged Sword of Large Language Models in Phishing

Alec Siemerink[1], Slinger Jansen[1,2], and Katsiaryna Labunets[1(✉)]

[1] Utrecht University, Heidelberglaan 8, 3584 CS Utrecht, The Netherlands
{slinger.jansen,k.labunets}@uu.nl

[2] LUT University, Yliopistonkatu, 34, 53850 Lappeenranta, Finland

Abstract. *Background:* With the rise of Large Language Model (LLM) technologies and LLM-based chatbots like ChatGPT, Copilot or Gemini, cyberattacks such as phishing are getting more sophisticated by using AI to craft personalized phishing messages. This poses a challenge for cybersecurity. *Aim:* This study explores the complexities of AI-enhanced phishing strategies, their success factors, and how LLMs can be used to improve cybersecurity defenses against phishing. *Method:* We delve into how LLMs, especially GPT 3.5 and 4, can detect and combat phishing. By experimenting with prompting techniques such as zero-shot, multi-shot, and chain-of-thought, we assess how these models fare in spotting phishing emails across various datasets. *Results:* The findings show that while GPT-4 demonstrates high precision and recall, the decision to deploy LLMs must consider cost-effectiveness, given their computational demand and operational costs.

Keywords: Large Language Models · Phishing Detection · Cybersecurity · Prompt Engineering · GPT

1 Introduction

Integrating generative AI into digital communication started a transformative era, offering high potential for innovation and efficiency for work automation. However, this progress also poses big cybersecurity challenges, especially in phishing. The National Institute of Standards and Technology defines phishing as *"a technique for attempting to acquire sensitive data, such as bank account numbers, through a fraudulent solicitation in email or on a website, in which the perpetrator masquerades as a legitimate business or reputable person"*[1]. Sophisticated phishing attacks leverage LLM to create highly personalized and convincing scams. According to Verizon's Data Breach Investigations Report 2023[2], incidents involving social engineering have seen a significant rise. Advanced cybersecurity defences need to be revised to mitigate these evolved threats.

[1] https://csrc.nist.gov/glossary/term/phishing.

[2] Verizon. Data Breach Investigations Report 2023. Link: https://www.verizon.com/business/en-nl/resources/reports/dbir/.

L. Horn Iwaya et al. (Eds.): NordSec 2024, LNCS 15396, pp. 258–279, 2025.
https://doi.org/10.1007/978-3-031-79007-2_14

This research explores the evolving threat of email-based phishing, focusing on both broad-scale phishing and spearphishing tactics, as well as Business Email Compromise content, which is included under the umbrella of phishing. This topic is crucial given the rise of LLMs, which have also become powerful tools for threat actors [18]. The ability of LLMs to mimic human communication increases the deceptiveness of phishing emails, making them more convincing and difficult to detect. By examining the psychological and linguistic strategies used in these emails, the research aims to uncover the sophisticated methods that contribute to their success, emphasizing the need for advanced cybersecurity solutions to defend against these AI-enhanced threats.

We considered two aspects:

a) the content within phishing and spearphishing emails, including linguistic and psychological tactics used to deceive recipients and
b) the characteristics that make phishing content persuasive and effective, focusing solely on the textual and communicative strategies employed.

To keep our research practical, we decided to focus only on the above aspects and excluded the operational tactics, financial implications, and the aftermath of phishing schemes. We have also excluded phishing attacks that are conducted through non-email channels such as SMS, voice calls, or social networks. Our study aims to answer the following research question: *"What is the efficacy of using LLMs such as GPT-3.5 and GPT-4 as a mechanism for phishing attack detection?"*

Our results revealed that GPT-4 offers enhanced performance in phishing detection with higher precision and recall rates, reducing false positives and improving overall security compared to GPT-3.5. However, the increased computational demands and costs of GPT-4 may not be justifiable for all organizations, particularly SMEs with smaller budgets. This makes GPT-3.5 a more cost-effective option despite its lower precision.

Summary of Contributions. Our main contributions are:

- We are filling the gap in the understanding of using LLMs for phishing detection, particularly by showing the capabilities of GPT-3.5 and GPT-4 models.
- We used several prompting techniques to enhance the models' detection accuracy without additional training to provide a resource-effective approach for detecting phishing messages.
- We conducted a comparative analysis across different datasets and offered insights into the effectiveness and operational considerations of deploying LLMs in real-world cybersecurity contexts.

Finally, this paper contributes to the topic of LLMs in cybersecurity by providing suggestions for future research, including the research of multi-modal LLMs in the context of phishing detection.

2 Background and Related Work

2.1 Phishing Campaign Success Factors

Phishing attacks have become a serious security concern due to their ability to bypass traditional defences and exploit human factors. Understanding the factors that contribute to the success of these attacks is crucial for developing more effective countermeasures.

Persuasive Content and Personalization: Karamagi et al. [12] highlights the role of realism and contextual appropriateness in creating phishing attacks. By creating emails that are not only convincing but also fit perfectly into the target's expectations, attackers significantly enhance the chance of success in their phishing attempts. The integration of details familiar to the potential victim creates a false sense of legitimacy, making the deceptive lure all the more irresistible.

The paper also describes how targeted attacks increase the perceived legitimacy of phishing emails. These personalized emails, especially when coupled with the right context for the target, transform the phishing attempt into a real threat. The accuracy of these attacks, based on details relevant to the individual's professional or personal life, blurs the line between authenticity and phishing [12]. Through this approach, phishing schemes bypass the initial scepticism of users and exploit the innate trust in familiar information [12].

Psychological Exploitation: A basic factor of susceptibility to phishing threats is authority bias, meaning how people adhere to the instructions or suggestions provided by a person who is recognized as an authority or an expert [9,21], such as their boss at work or an industry expert. Attackers exploit this bias by sending emails that appear to be formatted and signed by reputable officials or organizations, creating unwarranted trust and prompting victims to act against their own interests.

The recency effect, which prioritizes recently acquired information, represents another cognitive bias that phishing attackers exploit. By timing their campaigns to coincide with recent events or emergencies, attackers amplify the perceived urgency and relevance of their message, often bypassing the individual's critical assessment and sparking impulsive actions [21]. Hackers, spammers, and other attackers exploit this sense of urgency based on recent information [25].

Another cognitive bias used in phishing campaigns is the halo effect, where the overall opinion or perception of a person or brand influences thoughts about their qualities or intentions [21]. Attackers create a false sense of security by using familiar brands or names, such as influencers or well-known companies.

Hyperbolic discounting, which describes a person's preference for immediate rewards over delayed benefits, is also often exploited in phishing emails [9]. Offers of immediate gains or urgent warnings are designed to use this bias, leading victims to prioritize short-term rewards or avoid perceived immediate threats, often at the expense of their own security.

Curiosity, a fundamental human trait, is exploited through vague or intriguing messages designed to lure victims into seeking more information, leading them into traps set by attackers. This underscores the effectiveness of phishing campaigns that leverage natural human tendencies [9].

The strategy of invoking urgency aims to minimize the victim's critical thinking and prompt them to act swiftly, often by suggesting a limited-time offer or negative consequences if the victim does not act immediately [21]. Fear induction, another common tactic, exploits the victim's instinct for self-preservation, prompting actions aimed at avoiding perceived threats [9].

Lastly, the tactic of enticement plays on human desires, presenting seemingly beneficial opportunities that lure victims into a trap. A great example of this is the well-known'You have won a free iPhone' scam that exploits people's excitement [25]. The integration of AI allows for the customization and scaling of these tactics, presenting a sophisticated challenge to cybersecurity defenses.

2.2 Enhancing Phishing Campaign Effectiveness with LLM

Enhanced Content Authenticity

Content Creation: AI technologies such as GPT 3.5 and 4.0 have made the creation of phishing content easier and faster. Numerous studies demonstrate that these tools can successfully generate realistic and contextually appropriate material, enhancing the risk of phishing attempts [8,10]. This capability makes it more challenging to distinguish between genuine and fraudulent communication, highlighting the need for being more careful and implementing sophisticated cybersecurity strategies. Besides the initial contact, LLMs can also be leveraged to maintain continuous, authentic-looking conversations with the victim [3]. This capability enables threat actors to establish and maintain the trust of their victims.

Personalized and Contextually Relevant Attacks: The critical role of targeted, grammatically correct, and contextually relevant content in phishing emails, underscoring the premise that personalized content significantly boosts the success rate of phishing attacks, is highlighted by research [15]. Furthermore, the ability of artificial intelligence to absorb and analyze vast amounts of personal data enables the creation of highly customized and situation-specific deceptive messages, further amplifying the persuasiveness of these attacks.

Psychological Manipulation via Cognitive Biases

Exploitation of Innate Cognitive Biases: Phishing strategies are particularly insidious because they exploit inherent human cognitive biases. By embedding content that triggers authority bias, recency or halo effects, hyperbolic discounting, and the curiosity effect, attackers can manipulate the decision-making processes of the recipients. Such psychological manipulation is aimed at inducing compliance with the malicious directives of the phishing attempt. Research has successfully tasked ChatGPT based on GPT-3 model to create phishing content based on these biases [14]. According to Langford and Payne, instructing the model with prompts such as "Rewrite the email with a more authoritative tone" or "Rewrite the email to imply urgency" shows success in creating manipulative content that has even been shown to be effective on victims with high cybersecurity awareness [14].

Inducement of Emotional Responses: The integration of AI technologies significantly amplifies the potency of phishing attacks through the sophisticated manipulation of psychological cues. By leveraging AI, attackers can more effectively instil a sense of urgency and fear or offer enticements, crafting highly personalized and contextually relevant messages. This enhancement enables more precise targeting of victims' emotional triggers, making the phishing attempts more convincing and increasing the likelihood of eliciting immediate, often irrational, actions from the targets. AI's capability to analyze and exploit human psychology thus marks a significant evolution in the strategy and effectiveness of phishing campaigns [10].

Accessibility and Adaptability of Phishing Campaigns. The rise of LLM technologies is exemplified by services like ChatGPT, an LLM-based chatbot. It has significantly lowered the entry barriers for individuals aiming to engage in cyberattacks, even for those with minimal technical expertise. This development is critical in the cybersecurity landscape, as outlined in the work by Falade et al. [4], which discusses how LLMs facilitate the execution of sophisticated phishing campaigns and broaden the spectrum of potential threat actors. The ease with which these advanced attacks can now be carried out underscores an urgent need for enhanced cybersecurity defences to address the risks introduced by the democratization of hacking capabilities through AI [4].

2.3 Related Work

The closest work to ours is by Chataut et al. [2], who evaluated the effectiveness of LLMs in phishing detection using GPT-3.5, GPT-4, and a customized version of ChatGPT on a curated dataset of 324 phishing and 504 legitimate emails from the Kaggle Phishing Email Detection dataset [1]. Their findings showed that while all models were effective, GPT-4 and the customized ChatGPT demonstrated higher accuracy compared to GPT-3.5, highlighting their potential for enhancing cybersecurity. Similarly, we studied GPT-3.5 and GPT-4 models on a sample of 750 emails, including both real-world and synthetic phishing emails.

Sayyafzadeh et al. [24] studied the effectiveness of ChatGPT (GPT-4) combined with VADER sentiment analysis for phishing detection. They integrated NLP techniques such as VADER for sentiment detection and GPT-4 for email content analysis, employing a few-shot learning strategy on the PhishTank dataset[3]. Their system achieved 92% accuracy, demonstrating the

[3] PhishTank Dataset. Link: https://phishtank.org/developer_info.php.

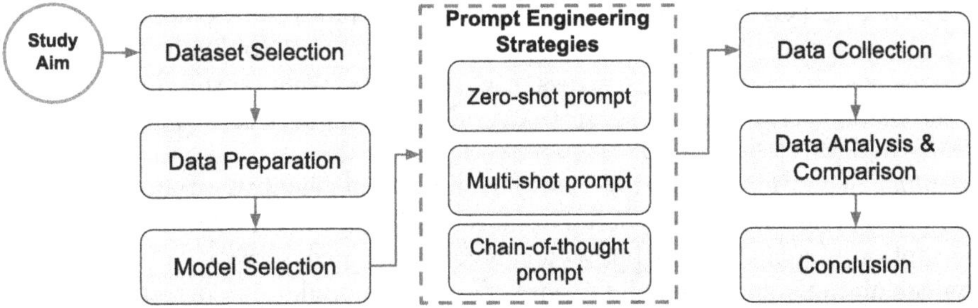

Fig. 1. Research Approach

potential of combining LLMs and sentiment analysis for phishing detection. Sayyafzadeh et al.used few-shot prompting and incorporated metadata (e.g., URLs and sender details), while our study focused solely on various prompting strategies without metadata analysis.

Recently, Trad and Chehab [27] explored LLMs for phishing URL detection using both prompt engineering and fine-tuning. They used models like GPT-3.5-turbo and Claude 2 for prompt engineering and fine-tuned models such as GPT-2, Bloom, and Baby LLaMA on a phishing dataset by Hannousse and Yahiouche [11], containing 11,430 URLs balanced between phishing and legitimate. Fine-tuning achieved superior performance, with a peak F1-score of 97.29% and an AUC of 99.56%, outperforming prompt engineering's best F1-score of 92.74%. In contrast, we focused on prompt engineering strategies like zero-shot, multi-shot, and CoT without fine-tuning.

3 Research Approach

This section outlines the research methodology, including data collection, model selection, and prompt engineering for detecting phishing content. Figure 1 demonstrate the main phases of our research approach. For data sampling and preparation, we used phishing email datasets to test the efficacy of standard LLMs in identifying phishing content. The initial phase involves selecting datasets providing phishing content. These datasets serve as the foundation for measuring the accuracy of AI in distinguishing phishing messages.

The main criterion for selecting suitable datasets was pre-labeled as deceptive or non-deceptive messages for testing the efficacy of the phishing detection capabilities of the selected models. Furthermore, we only want to include datasets that have phishing and non-phishing email content. We did not consider other factors, such as headers, sender addresses, etc. Using these requirements, we selected the following datasets:

- **Generalized Deception Dataset**: This dataset includes 15 336 emails, with 6 134 identified as deceptive (phishing) and 9 202 as truthful (non-phishing). It serves as the primary resource for assessing the models' ability to distinguish between phishing and legitimate emails [29].

- **Synthetic (GPT-generated) Dataset**: It includes 5 001 emails, artificially generated using advanced language models to simulate sophisticated phishing attempts and containing only deceptive messages. We used this dataset to test the models' effectiveness against AI-crafted phishing content [16].

Sampling: To ensure statistical relevance and manageability, sample sizes were calculated to achieve a 95% confidence level with a 5% margin of error, under the assumption of a 50/50 split between categories for a conservative estimation [7]. The calculations employed the formula for finite population correction, considering the datasets' total size and the distribution of phishing and non-phishing emails. The Generalized Deception dataset, containing 15 336 emails, required a sample size of 375 emails to be representative and manageable. For the Synthetic dataset, with a total of 5 001 emails, the calculated sample size was 357. However, for consistency, we used a sample size of 375 emails for both datasets.

Data Preparation: To ensure the analysis consistency, we prepared our dataset following these steps:

Step 1: Based on the calculated sample sizes, we created stratified samples for each dataset, ensuring the reliability and validity of the experimental results. This involved selecting samples from each category (e.g., phishing and non-phishing) to maintain the original distribution in the dataset.

Step 2: We (re)labeled the sample datasets with the label *is_deceptive* that has a boolean value, with 'True' indicating deceptive content and 'False' indicating non-deceptive content. We decided to use a boolean label across all datasets to streamline further statistical analysis.

3.1 Model Selection

For this experiment, we selected OpenAI's *gpt-4-turbo-preview* and the *gpt-3.5-turbo-1106* models. These models are selected due to their widespread use, and both are the most advanced models of their respective versions available through the OpenAI's API [20]. Using two models allowed us to compare their performance in detecting phishing content and the cost of using each model.

- **Advanced Natural Language Understanding**: GPT-4 exhibits state-of-the-art performance in understanding and generating human-like text. Its deep learning architecture enables it to grasp the nuances, context, and subtleties of language, making it compatible with tasks that require a sophisticated understanding of text content, such as distinguishing between deceptive and non-deceptive emails.
- **High Accuracy and Reliability**: GPT-4's performance on natural language processing tasks is benchmarked among the highest across various models, making it a reliable choice for achieving accurate and consistent labeling. Its ability to process and analyze large volumes of text data can significantly enhance the precision of the experiment's outcomes [19].

- **Rich Contextual Understanding**: GPT-4 can consider the broader context of each email beyond mere keyword spotting or surface-level analysis. This capability is crucial for accurately identifying deceptive emails, which may employ sophisticated tactics or subtleties to mislead recipients.

These quality criteria enhance the probability of the models being effective in analyzing messages and detecting whether they are phishing messages or not.

3.2 Prompt Engineering

The most crucial part of our research is creating a prompt tailored to our aim, detecting phishing content. Prompt engineering is developing as a proper field of study, with over 25 individual prompt engineering techniques and methods identified in recent literature [22]. In this research, we followed the Google guidelines [6], focusing on how to structure the input to elicit the most accurate output from an LLM. Our development process included three parts: context setting, prompt construction, and desired output. We applied it to develop and test the performance of the three prompt types that we explain below.

To ensure structured responses that are easy to parse and evaluate in all cases, we asked the model to provide the output in JSON format with clear parameters (IS_DECEPTIVE and explanation). This format supports both quantitative analysis (through the boolean value) and qualitative insights (through the textual explanation). The boolean IS_DECEPTIVE directly corresponds to the email's classification as phishing or not with a clear binary outcome. The requested explanation gives insight into the model's reasoning process and allows for a qualitative assessment of how well the model understands phishing content. It is important to evaluate the model's reasoning capabilities beyond its final decision, offering a window into potential areas of confusion or uncertainty that can be addressed in future iterations or with more complex prompting strategies.

Zero-Shot: The zero-shot prompting represents a straightforward approach in the context of detecting phishing content. It involves providing the model with a direct task without any prior examples or context. Our zero-shot prompt is designed to assess the model's innate ability to analyze email content and determine its nature, whether it is phishing or not, based solely on the provided instructions. This prompt is particularly challenging as it relies on the model's pre-existing knowledge and training to make accurate judgments [6]. Section A.1 in the Appendix shows the created zero-shot prompt. The prompt is straightforward, directing the model to analyze the email content presented to it. By asking for a classification, we prompted the model to use its understanding of phishing indicators to make a judgment.

Prompting with Examples (One-, Few-, and Multi-shot): The CoT prompting strategy enriches the LLM's context by providing one or more clear, descriptive examples of psychological traits and cognitive biases to evaluate phishing attempts [6]. We chose the psychological traits and cognitive biases to be provided to the model based on the findings of our literature analysis (cf. Sect. 2). This approach prompts the model to determine the nature of the email and understand the underlying tactics that might make it deceptive. It leverages the model's capability for deeper analysis, reflecting on specific psychological and linguistic cues to make a more informed decision. Section A.2 in the Appendix shows the multi-shot prompt that we used.

The prompt outlines key psychological traits and cognitive biases, encouraging the model to apply these concepts in its analysis. We expected that this approach would enhance the model's ability to scrutinize emails more deeply, considering both the content and the psychological manipulation techniques. By including examples for each psychological trait and cognitive bias, the prompt aids the model in understanding and identifying similar patterns in the email text. This component is critical for enabling the model to apply abstract concepts to concrete instances, improving its phishing detection accuracy. Specifying the output format ensures that the analysis results are organized and easily interpretable. The prompt also highlights the importance of evaluating the email's general presentation, including language subtlety, grammar, and unusual requests. This comprehensive view encourages a holistic analysis, considering the above-mentioned phishing indicators.

Chain-of-Thought (CoT) Prompting: This prompting type enables complex reasoning capabilities through intermediate reasoning steps [28]. In combination with few-shot prompting, we expected to obtain better results in more complex tasks that require some reasoning. Section A.3 in the Appendix shows the prompt that we created. This prompt represents an application of the CoT strategy, incorporating a framework of psychological traits and cognitive biases into the analysis process. It guides the LLM through a comprehensive examination of potential phishing emails, leveraging a structured approach to identify and reason through various deception indicators.

The prompt outlines a multi-step analysis process, focusing on the identification and application of psychological traits and cognitive biases commonly exploited in phishing attempts. We structured it as follows:

- *Introduction*: The prompt begins by introducing a list of psychological traits and cognitive biases, providing explanations and examples for each. This foundational knowledge equips the model with a clear understanding of the manipulation tactics to look for in the analysis.
- *Step-by-step analysis framework*: The prompt then outlines a detailed, step-by-step process for analyzing each email, from identifying relevant traits and biases to making a reasoned conclusion about the email's nature.
- *CoT reasoning*: By structuring the analysis into discrete steps that build upon one another, the prompt encourages the model to apply CoT reasoning. This approach fosters a deeper understanding of how different elements within an email can collectively indicate a phishing attempt.

- *Conclusion*: Finally, the model is instructed to conclude whether the email is likely a phishing attempt based on the identified traits, biases, and the overall context of the email.

This advanced prompting strategy elicits a nuanced understanding of phishing tactics from the model, guiding it through a logical process of deduction and reasoning. The detailed framework for analysis ensures that the model considers a wide range of indicators before reaching a conclusion. By requiring the model to apply critical thinking and use of knowledge of psychological manipulation with provided context, the prompt aims to enhance the accuracy and reliability of the phishing detection process.

3.3 Data Collection and Analysis

For the purpose of collecting data, we created a Python script that iterates over the sample datasets, selects the email content, sets the prompt, and queries the OpenAI API. This returned data is then saved to a CSV file, on which statistical analysis is done. This process is repeated for each sample, prompt, and model, resulting in 12 CSV files containing the email text, the label given by the model, and the explanation in keywords for the decision.

In our data analysis, we evaluated the performance of the GPT-3.5 and GPT-4 models across various datasets and prompting strategies. To measure the models' performance, we calculated accuracy, precision, F1 scores, and recall which are commonly adopted performance variables in the machine learning area [5,23]. The data is available through Github [26].

4 Results

We begin by examining the models' performance distinctions between the *Generalized Deception* and *Synthetic* datasets. After, we assess how each prompt strategy impacts the detection capabilities of GPT-3.5 and GPT-4, providing insights into the operational efficiencies and potential limitations of these AI tools in phishing detection. Table 1 provides accuracy, precision, F1 scores, and recall values for each model.

Table 1. Comparison of Phishing Detection Performance: GPT-3.5 vs GPT-4

Dataset & Prompt	GPT-3.5				GPT-4			
	Accuracy	Precision	Recall	F1	Accuracy	Precision	Recall	F1
Generalized - Zero-shot	88.77%	82.04%	91.95%	86.71%	92.51%	94.16%	86.58%	90.21%
Generalized - Multi-shot	87.43%	82.69%	86.58%	84.59%	93.58%	93.71%	89.93%	91.78%
Generalized - CoT	84.22%	72.50%	97.32%	83.09%	94.12%	95.04%	89.93%	92.41%
Synthetic - Zero-shot	94.96%	100.00%	94.96%	97.41%	98.32%	100.00%	98.32%	99.15%
Synthetic - Multi-shot	87.68%	100.00%	87.68%	93.43%	97.20%	100.00%	97.20%	98.58%
Synthetic - CoT	92.00%	89.80%	93.62%	91.67%	93.84%	100.00%	89.36%	96.82%

4.1 Datasets

The evaluation of the models across the *Generalized Deception* and *Synthetic* datasets revealed significant differences in detection capabilities. GPT-4 consistently outperforms GPT-3.5, particularly on the *Generalized Deception* dataset where real-world emails are present. GPT-4's higher performance, with a notable 94.12% accuracy and 92.41% in F1 score using the CoT prompting, demonstrates its advanced ability to parse and understand nuanced phishing attempts.

The *Synthetic* dataset, composed of AI-generated emails, also serves as a test for the models' responses to machine-generated phishing attacks. Both models perform well on this dataset, but GPT-4's high precision and recall underscore its robustness against modern, AI-driven phishing strategies. This dataset highlights the growing importance of using advanced AI to combat phishing, as cyber threats increasingly leverage similar technologies for attack execution.

4.2 Prompt Performance

The effectiveness of various prompt strategies demonstrates varied results between GPT-3.5 and GPT-4, highlighting each model's capabilities and limitations in handling phishing detection tasks.

Zero-Shot Prompting: This strategy tests the inherent capabilities of the models based on their training. For the *Generalized* dataset, GPT-4 shows better handling of context and subtleties, achieving an accuracy of 92.51% and outperforming GPT-3.5 in F1 scores. In the *Synthetic* dataset, GPT-4 also achieved high accuracy, and GPT-3.5 reached a precision of 100%. These results suggest that GPT-4 can better capture nuanced differences, while GPT-3.5 can operate well in environments where quick, general assessments are needed without additional contextual information.

Multi-shot Prompting: Introducing a few contextual examples improved detection capabilities for both models, but with different outcomes depending on the dataset. For the *Synthetic* dataset, both GPT-4 and GPT-3.5 demonstrated notable enhancements, with GPT-3.5 reaching a precision of 100%, which highlights its ability to adapt effectively and learn from additional context. However, for the *Generalized* dataset, GPT-3.5's performance actually worsened compared to zero-shot prompting, showing a decline in both accuracy and precision, indicating challenges in adapting to the increased complexity of real-world examples.

CoT Prompting: Employing a more complex reasoning process through the CoT approach significantly enhanced GPT-4's performance, achieving the highest accuracy and F1 scores, particularly for the *Generalized* dataset. This suggests that the CoT strategy allowed GPT-4 to better understand and reason through the nuances of real-world phishing attempts. For GPT-3.5, the CoT approach also improved performance, mainly in recall metrics, which suggests it can effectively identify a broad range of phishing attempts when guided through a detailed analysis process, although its precision still lagged behind that of GPT-4.

Comparative Analysis: This comparative analysis highlights that while GPT-4 generally outperforms GPT-3.5, the latter still demonstrates effectiveness, particularly in synthetic scenarios and when enhanced by sophisticated prompt strategies. The performance differences between the models are most evident in the Generalized dataset, where GPT-4 is superior in handling complex and nuanced phishing attempts, while GPT-3.5's limitations become apparent, particularly with multi-shot prompting. The choice between using GPT-3.5 or GPT-4 should therefore consider specific cybersecurity needs and available resources: GPT-4 offers superior performance in precision and nuanced threat detection, whereas GPT-3.5 is a more cost-effective solution for broader detection, particularly in simpler, synthetic contexts.

4.3 GPT3.5 vs GPT4

The enhanced performance of GPT-4 is reflective of its deeper and more nuanced understanding of context and semantics, a critical factor in distinguishing sophisticated phishing attempts. The multi-shot and CoT prompts highlight GPT-4's advanced efficiency in learning from examples and applying complex reasoning. This is particularly notable in scenarios involving synthetic phishing emails, where GPT-4 demonstrates high precision and recall. This indicates a robust capability to adapt to and recognize AI-generated content, a growing concern in cybersecurity.

As we evaluate the performance of GPT-3.5 and GPT-4, it is crucial to note the different costs associated with each model. While GPT-4 demonstrates higher accuracy and F1 scores, it also incurs significantly higher operational costs compared to GPT-3.5. This cost factor is crucial for organizations considering the balance between budget constraints and cybersecurity effectiveness. A deeper analysis of these financial implications will follow in Sect. 5.

To conclude, GPT-4's advancements, as outlined by OpenAI's continuous model upgrades, enhance its phishing detection capabilities and its applicability in safeguarding against increasingly sophisticated cyber threats. The decision between deploying GPT-3.5 or GPT-4 should consider both the organization's specific security needs and the trade-offs between cost and performance efficiency.

4.4 Qualitative Analysis of Indicators

A small pragmatic qualitative analysis of the explanations given for the labeling decision by the model reveals that "Authority Bias" and "Urgency" are the most frequently identified cognitive biases and psychological traits in the explanations. These results align with the understanding that phishing attempts often leverage perceived authority and create a sense of urgency to manipulate recipients. Lesser extent factors such as "Fear", "Curiosity Effect", and "Personal Information" also play roles in phishing strategies, according to the AI's analysis.

Notably, "Poor Grammar" and "Unusual Requests", while traditional indicators of phishing attempts, were not highlighted in the model's explanations, suggesting that the model's emphasis was more focused on psychological manipulation than on these aspects. This is a result of our prompting strategy, where the choice was made to focus on identifying psychological traits and cognitive biases. This insight could be valuable for refining phishing detection strategies or prompts and instructions to focus not only on the psychological and behavioral cues but also on other common factors in phishing emails.

5 Discussion

5.1 Models Comparison

Costs. The cost implications of choosing GPT-4 over GPT-3.5 for phishing detection tasks must be carefully considered. While GPT-4's enhanced performance could significantly improve detection rates and reduce false positives, leading to better overall security posture and user trust, the higher cost of almost 20 times more than GPT-3 might not be justifiable for all organizations. Smaller businesses or those with tighter budget constraints might find the cost-benefit ratio of using GPT-4 less favourable, especially if their volume of email traffic is manageable with slightly less advanced models.

- **GPT-4's higher cost** at $10.0 per 1M tokens for standard usage and $30.0 per 1M tokens for output is a significant investment compared to GPT-3.5's more affordable $0.5 per 1M tokens input and $1.5 for output[4].
- **Cost-Effectiveness**: The higher performance of GPT-4, as shown by the high precision and recall in detecting phishing emails, suggests that it could offer a more reliable defence against sophisticated phishing tactics. For organizations that prioritize cybersecurity and are particularly vulnerable to phishing attacks, the higher accuracy and efficiency of GPT-4 might justify its higher cost, especially if it leads to a reduction in the costs associated with phishing attacks, e.g., data breaches, loss of reputation and money.

Performance Comparison. The comparison of GPT-4 and GPT-3.5 in phishing detection demonstrates clear strengths and weaknesses in terms of precision, recall, computational demand, and overall efficiency. GPT-4 shows high precision performance, achieving 100% across all tested prompting strategies in the Synthetic Dataset. This accuracy minimizes false positives, a crucial feature for maintaining communication channel efficiency by ensuring legitimate emails are not mistakenly flagged as phishing. Achieving 100% precision can be explained by the fact that the synthetic datasets used might have been simpler for the models to classify, potentially lacking the variability and complexity found in real-world phishing campaigns. While these results are interesting, they do not guarantee that the models would perform similarly on more challenging and diverse datasets. The synthetic data may have contained distinct patterns or

[4] Open Ai Pricing. Link: https://openai.com/api/pricing/.

language cues that were easy for the models to learn and identify, which might not necessarily translate well to less structured, real-world data.

The optimal balance between precision and recall, as evidenced by an F1 score of 99.15% in the zero-shot prompting strategy, underscores GPT-4's ability to address phishing threats effectively without generating excessive false positives. However, this superior performance potentially leads to increased operational costs, which is especially significant for organizations with limited resources. The higher operational costs associated with GPT-4 must be carefully considered when assessing its feasibility for widespread deployment.

In contrast, GPT-3.5 shows a different set of performance characteristics. It shows high recall, particularly in the Generalized Deception Dataset, with a recall rate of 97.32% using CoT prompting. This high recall indicates GPT-3.5's capacity to detect a broad range of phishing attempts, which is crucial for minimizing the likelihood of overlooking potentially harmful communications. GPT-3.5 also presents a cost-effective solution for organizations that prioritize extensive detection over precision, as its lower computational demands and costs make it an attractive option. However, the trade-off is a lower precision rate, particularly in the Generalized Deception Dataset, which may lead to more false positives and inefficiencies in reviewing flagged communications. For organizations willing to accept a higher rate of false positives to achieve broader detection coverage, GPT-3.5 offers a viable and budget-friendly alternative.

General Comparison. The decision between using GPT-3.5 and GPT-4 for phishing detection requires a detailed understanding of the trade-offs between performance and operational costs. GPT-4's high precision significantly reduces false positives, which can decrease the workload of cybersecurity teams by reducing the number of legitimate emails falsely flagged for review. This makes GPT-4 particularly well-suited for environments where minimizing false positives is essential to maintaining efficient communication and where resources are available to support higher computational requirements.

On the other hand, GPT-3.5's high recall is advantageous in environments where the goal is to identify as many phishing attempts as possible, even at the cost of higher false positives. This characteristic makes GPT-3.5 a good candidate for organizations with limited budgets but still in need of a broad detection system. The lower precision rate implies a higher tendency for legitimate communications to be incorrectly flagged as phishing, which could lead to alert fatigue and inefficiencies in email review processes. Nevertheless, the lower operational costs and the potential for performance improvements through fine-tuning or targeted training make GPT-3.5 an appealing option for many use cases, particularly for small and medium-sized enterprises (SMEs).

Finally, the selection between GPT-3.5 and GPT-4 is not straightforward and should consider factors such as operational needs, risk management strategies, budget constraints, and the specific context of the phishing threats faced by the organization. Organizations must weigh their tolerance for false positives against the need for high detection rates and determine which model best aligns with their cybersecurity objectives. A combined approach, leveraging the strengths of each model or integrating them with other detection methods (such as metadata analysis), could provide a more comprehensive solution to the growing challenge of phishing attacks.

Prompt Engineering. Prompt engineering is developing into a proper field of study, with numerous techniques and methods recently identified in the literature [22]. We briefly discuss some of the categories identified by Sahoo and explain how they relate to our research. First, *New Tasks Without Extensive Training* are tasks that are given without context or examples, such as the zero-shot prompting method we used. Secondly, *Reasoning and Logic* include techniques such as our CoT technique, but also chain-of-symbol techniques, which allow LLMs to become more effective on, for instance, spatial tasks. Thirdly, in the *Reduce Hallucination* category, techniques such as retrieval augmented generation are classified, which reduce hallucinations and lead to higher quality responses by using current sources and ranking techniques for those sources. This technique could be a logical extension for our work, to take current examples of identified phishing emails and use them to better identify older and newer phishing attacks.

Fourthly, the category of *User Interface* techniques involves techniques that actively reason with the end-user to collaboratively come to a conclusion. This technique is less easy to use in our scenario but could involve an active operator scanning emails before they arrive at the desk of the attacked person. In the fifth category of prompt engineering techniques, there are *Knowledge-Based Reasoning and Generation* techniques, which include more tools for expert tasks. In the case of phishing detection, there are, of course, many more fraud recognition techniques, such as verified senders, scanning attachments, and scanning the URLs in an email to see whether they lead to verified sites. We believe that a combination of such techniques with our techniques will lead to even higher rates of recognition and more efficient phishing detection.

Finally, the sixth technique we wish to discuss here is *Understanding User Intent*, which has the goal of understanding what it is the user is trying to do. Generally, employees do not wish to expose their passwords to a bad actor, so we could block certain actions, such as logging in on a malicious site, based on this user intent. This technique can also be used to better identify what the sender of an email wants to do. In this way, email conversations could be guided better, for instance, by helping employees prioritize their most important emails. There are more techniques discussed by Sahoo that are relevant to this work, but for reasons of brevity, we have left them out.

5.2 Limitations and Future Research

A limitation of this research is the use of small sample sizes and only two relatively small datasets due to constrained resources. This restricts the generalizability of the results and highlights the need for further research with larger datasets and varied prompting strategies. The synthetic datasets used in this study, while useful for demonstrating model performance, may not fully capture the variability and complexity of real-world phishing campaigns. This restricts the generalizability of our results. Future research should involve testing the models with larger and more diverse datasets that better represent actual phishing attempts, such as datasets containing real emails gathered from various industries. This would allow us to evaluate the model's robustness and adaptability in more realistic settings.

Also, this study focused solely on the textual content of emails for phishing detection. Other elements, such as sender details, domain names, URLs, email timing, and contextual aspects, should be considered to enhance detection mechanisms. We are excited to see how this field is rapidly moving forward. One of the yet unpublished works related closely to ours is the work on ChatSpamDetector [13], which finds similar results but does not go as deeply into the details of social and cost factors as ours.

Future research could explore integrating multimodal AI models that analyze various inputs, such as text, images, and audio [17], to evaluate a broader range of phishing content. Expanding to include advanced and diverse AI models will provide deeper insights into their capabilities. Further, incorporating models from different vendors, such as Google's Bard or Meta's LLaMA, and comparing them with OpenAI's GPT-3.5 and GPT-4 would enable a broader understanding of LLM capabilities and improve the generalizability of our findings.

6 Conclusion

In this paper, we studied the application of LLMs, particularly GPT-3.5 and GPT-4, to detect phishing emails. Using zero-shot, multi-shot, and CoT prompting strategies combined with real and synthetic data, we found that GPT-4 shows increased precision and recall rates. The results indicate that using the latest models for phishing detection can yield good results without the need for earlier training.

The adoption of untrained models coupled with different prompting techniques offers an accessible and resource-efficient way for organizations to enhance their cybersecurity measures. The data collected and analyzed underscore the capabilities of these models to analyze and classify phishing content accurately, providing a foundation for deploying AI-driven defences against cyber threats.

However, the cost implications of using GPT-4, which is significantly more expensive than GPT-3.5, must be carefully considered. While GPT-4 enhanced performance can improve detection rates and reduce false positives, making it a strong candidate for organizations prioritizing cybersecurity, SMEs with limited budgets may opt for GPT-3.5. Additionally, the increased computational demand of GPT-4 could lead to higher operational costs. Also, as these costs generally fluctuate strongly with the advent of newer and more efficient models, we must update our data and keep track of these models consistently, for instance, using MLPerf, an "open source" industry benchmarking tool.

The limitations of this study, such as the use of small sample sizes and a focus on textual content only, highlight the necessity for future research. Investigations into a wider array of LLMs, integration of multi-modal models, and inclusion of additional phishing email characteristics are essential steps forward.

This paper contributes to the evolving discourse on the intersection of AI and cybersecurity, advocating for a balanced approach to harnessing LLMs' potential. As phishing schemes become increasingly sophisticated, leveraging advancements in AI technologies becomes a necessity. Through continuous research and innovation, we hope to stay ahead of cybercriminals in the digital age.

Data Availibility Statement. Code and datasets underlying this research study are made available via the GitHub platform [26].

A Appendix – Prompts

A.1 Prompt 1: Zero-Shot

Analyze this email, and classify it as phishing or not phishing **Instructions**: provide the analysis result in json format with the following parts:
is_deceptive: Boolean (True for phishing, False for not phishing)
explanation: Text explaining in keywords the reasoning behind the decision.

A.2 Prompt 2: Multi-shot

Analyze the provided email text to determine if it is a phishing attempt, using the detailed contextual framework of psychological traits and cognitive biases. For each email, decide whether it is a phishing email or not and explain your reasoning.

Apply the following psychological traits and cognitive biases in your analysis, with their explanations and examples:

1. *A Sense of Urgency*: Pressuring the recipient to make quick decisions, often leading to insufficient consideration of consequences. *Example*: An email claiming account suspension within 24 h unless a link is clicked.
2. *Inducing Fear by Threatening*: Invoking fear to coerce compliance, threatening negative outcomes. *Example*: Email from 'tax authority' threatening legal action for unpaid taxes.
3. *Enticement with Desire*: Playing on desires with too-good-to-be-true offers. *Example*: Email congratulating on a lottery win, requesting personal info.
4. *Authority Bias*: Trust in suggestions from authority figures. *Example*: Email from the CEO directing urgent fund transfer.
5. *Recency Effect*: Prioritizing the most recently presented information. *Example*: Urging donations to a fraudulent charity after a disaster.
6. *Halo Effect*: Influence of overall brand impression on character feelings. *Example*: Email mimicking a respected brand to steal credentials.

7. *Hyperbolic Discounting*: Preferring immediate rewards over larger, delayed benefits. *Example*: Offering an immediate discount for quick action.
8. *Curiosity Effect*: Leveraging curiosity to entice seeking more information. *Example*: Email with a vague subject line and a malicious attachment.

Additionally, consider other phishing indicators such as poor grammar and unusual requests for personal information.

Analyze the overall context, language subtlety, and presentation of the email. Instructions: provide the analysis result in json format with the following parts:
is_deceptive: Boolean (True for phishing, False for not phishing)
explanation: Text explaining in keywords the reasoning behind the decision.

A.3 Prompt 3: Chain-of-Thought

Given an email, your task is to analyze the email to determine if it is a phishing attempt. Apply a CoT process by following this detailed framework, which includes psychological traits and cognitive biases, complete with explanations and examples. For the email, proceed through the steps outlined below, utilizing your critical thinking and knowledge to guide your analysis and conclusions.

Step 1: Identify Psychological Traits and Cognitive Biases
Before analyzing the emails, understand these psychological traits and cognitive biases that phishers exploit, along with explanations and specific examples:

A Sense of Urgency
Explanation: Creating a sense of urgency pressures the recipient into making decisions quickly, often without sufficient time to consider the consequences. Examples: Email claiming account suspension within 24 h unless a link is clicked. Notification of an outstanding invoice requiring immediate payment.

Inducing Fear by Threatening
Explanation: This involves invoking fear to coerce individuals into complying with the attacker's demands, under the threat of negative outcomes. Examples: Message claiming to be from the tax authority threatens legal action and fines for supposedly unpaid taxes. Email falsely claiming that personal data has been compromised in a security breach.

Enticement with Desire
Explanation: This tactic plays on desires or greed, offering something too good to be true to lure individuals into performing specific actions. Examples: Email congratulating on winning a large sum of money, requesting personal information or a fee to process the winnings. Message offering an exclusive deal or a significant discount on high-value products.

Authority Bias
Explanation: This bias makes individuals more likely to trust and follow suggestions or orders from a figure of authority or someone perceived as an expert. Examples: Email purportedly from the company's CEO directs the employee to

transfer funds urgently or share sensitive information. Communication claiming to be from a government agency, demanding personal information for verification purposes.

Recency Effect
Explanation: This effect describes the tendency to remember and prioritize the most recently presented information over older data. Examples: Phishing campaign following a natural disaster, urging donations to a fraudulent charity. Emails advertising a recent technological breakthrough, offering early access in exchange for personal details or financial information.

Halo Effect
Explanation: The halo effect occurs when an overall impression of a person or brand influences feelings and thoughts about their character or properties. Examples: Email mimicking a well-respected brand, such as Apple or Microsoft, to trick individuals into disclosing login credentials. Messages claiming a celebrity endorses a product or investment scheme, urging immediate action to take advantage of the offer.

Hyperbolic Discounting
Explanation: This describes the preference for smaller, immediate rewards over larger, delayed benefits, exploiting the human tendency to want instant gratification. Examples: Email offering an immediate but limited-time discount, requiring quick action to provide payment information. Message promising a high return on investment in a short period, asking for an upfront payment or financial details.

Curiosity Effect
Explanation: This effect leverages human curiosity to entice individuals into seeking more information, often leading them into risky situations. Examples: Email with a vague but intriguing subject line, tempting the recipient to open an attached file that contains malware. Message that piques curiosity with a vague promise of a unique opportunity, directing users to a phishing site designed to harvest personal data.

This comprehensive understanding of psychological traits and cognitive biases will serve as a critical foundation for your email analysis. Keep these traits and examples in mind as you examine each email in the dataset, looking for signs that indicate the use of these tactics.

Step 2: Examine the Email
For every email, look for indications of these traits and biases. Consider:

- Does the email create an urgent need to act?
- Is there a threat that induces fear?
- Are there offers that entice with desire or seem too good to be true?
- Does the email falsely claim authority or expertise?
- Are recent events exploited to make the message seem more urgent or relevant?

- Is there an implication of a reputable brand or celebrity endorsement to gain trust?
- Are there offers for immediate rewards?
- Does the email pique curiosity with vague promises or intriguing attachments?

Step 3: Implementation Description
Describe how each identified trait or bias is implemented within the email. This involves considering:

The language and tone used: Is it pressing, threatening, overly enticing, or authoritative? The context: Are there references to current events, reputable brands, or authorities? The offer: Is there a promise of immediate gain or a solution to a provoked fear or problem?

Step 4: Apply Chain-of-Thought Reasoning
Reflect on your findings and apply reasoning:

If multiple traits and biases are present, how do they interact? Do the specific examples provided in the framework match the tactics used in the email? Considering the overall context and presentation, does the email align with common phishing strategies?

Step 5: Make a Conclusion
Based on the analysis, conclude whether the email is likely a phishing attempt or not. Consider:

The number and nature of phishing characteristics identified. How closely the email follows known phishing patterns and examples. Any external knowledge or phishing indicators, such as suspicious sender addresses or requests for personal information.

Reflecting on the Analysis Process[5]

This CoT approach encourages a comprehensive examination of each email, ensuring no detail is overlooked. By methodically considering each step and applying reasoned judgment, you'll be better equipped to identify and understand phishing attempts within your dataset.

Instructions: provide the analysis result in json format with the following parts: is_deceptive: Boolean (True for phishing, False for not phishing) Explanation: Text explaining in keywords the reasoning behind the decision.

References

1. Chakraborty, S.: Phishing Email Detection (2023). https://www.kaggle.com/dsv/6090437. Accessed 30 Sept 2024
2. Chataut, R., Gyawali, P.K., Usman, Y.: Can AI keep you safe? A study of large language models for phishing detection. In: Proceedings of CCWC'24, pp. 0548–0554. IEEE (2014)

[5] By adding this short 'summary' of the nature of the previously given instruction, the model is reminded of the approach to be taken after taking into account all the given context. This helps counter hallucinations or outright disregarding the initial instruction to use chain-of-thought.

3. Chowdhury, M., Rifat, N., Latif, S., Ahsan, M., Rahman, M.S., Gomes, R.: ChatGPT: the curious case of attack vectors' supply chain management improvement. In: Proceedings of eIT'23, pp. 499–504. IEEE (2023)
4. Falade, P.V.: Decoding the threat landscape: ChatGPT, FraudGPT, and WormGPT in social engineering attacks. Int. J. Sci. Res. Comput. Sci. Eng. Inf. Technol. (2023)
5. Flach, P.: Performance evaluation in machine learning: the good, the bad, the ugly, and the way forward. In: Proceedings of the AAAI'19, pp. 9808–9814 (2019)
6. Google Developers. Machine Learning Resources: Prompt Engineering (2024). https://developers.google.com/machine-learning/resources/prompt-eng
7. Gravetter, F.J., Wallnau, L.B., Forzano, L.-A.B., Witnauer, J.-D.E.: Essentials of Statistics for the Behavioral Sciences. Cengage Learning (2020)
8. Grbic, D.V., Dujlovic, I.: Social engineering with ChatGPT. In: Proceedings of INFOTEH'23, pp. 1–5. IEEE (2023)
9. Greitzer, F.L., Li, W., Laskey, K.B., Lee, J., Purl, J.: Experimental investigation of technical and human factors related to phishing susceptibility. ACM Trans. Soc. Comput. **4**(2) (2021)
10. Gupta, M., Akiri, C., Aryal, K., Parker, E., Praharaj, L.: From ChatGPT to ThreatGPT: impact of generative AI in cybersecurity and privacy. IEEE Access (2023)
11. Hannousse, A., Yahiouche, S.: Web page phishing detection, Amsterdam, The Netherlands (2021). https://doi.org/10.17632/c2gw7fy2j4.3
12. Karamagi, R.: A review of factors affecting the effectiveness of phishing. Comput. Inf. Sci. **15**(1) (2022). Available at SSRN: https://ssrn.com/abstract=4355455. https://ssrn.com/abstract=4355455
13. Koide, T., Fukushi, N., Nakano, H., Chiba, D.: ChatSpamDetector: leveraging large language models for effective phishing email detection. arXiv preprint arXiv:2402.18093 (2024)
14. Langford, T., Payne, B.: Phishing faster: implementing ChatGPT into phishing campaigns. In: Proceedings of FTC'23, pp. 174–187. Springer (2023)
15. Mäses, S., Maennel, O.M., Matulevičius, R.: How to conduct email phishing experiments. MA thesis, University of Tartu (2018). https://core.ac.uk/download/pdf/237084453.pdf. Accessed 20 Mar 2024
16. Mehdi Gholampour, P., Verma, R.M.: Adversarial robustness of phishing email detection models. In: Proceedings of IWSPA'23, pp. 67–76 (2023)
17. Meta. Multimodal Generative AI Systems (2023). https://ai.meta.com/tools/system-cards/multimodal-generative-ai-systems/. Accessed 12 Dec 2023
18. Microsoft. How AI is changing phishing scams (2023). https://www.microsoft.com/en-us/microsoft-365-life-hacks/privacyand-safety/how-ai-changing-phishing-scams. Accessed 22 Mar 2024
19. OpenAI. GPT-4 Technical report. OpenAI (2023). https://openai.com/research/gpt-4
20. OpenAI. OpenAI Models Documentation (2024). https://platform.openai.com/docs/models. Accessed 20 Mar 2024
21. Rashid, F.Y.: Phishing attacks exploit cognitive biases, research finds. VentureBeat (2021). https://venturebeat.com/ai/phishing-attacks-exploit-cognitive-biases-research-finds/. Accessed 24 Sept 2023
22. Sahoo, P., Singh, A.K., Saha, S., Jain, V., Mondal, S., Chadha, A.: A systematic survey of prompt engineering in large language models: techniques and applications. arXiv preprint arXiv:2402.07927 (2024)

23. Sarker, I.H., Abushark, Y.B., Alsolami, F., Khan, A.I.: IntruDTree: a machine learning based cyber security intrusion detection model. Symmetry **12**(5), 754 (2020)
24. Sayyafzadeh, S., Weatherspoon, M., Yan, J., Chi, H.: Securing against deception: exploring phishing emails through ChatGPT and sentiment analysis. In: Proceedings of SERA'24, pp. 159–165. IEEE (2024)
25. Shahriar, S., Mukherjee, A., Gnawali, O.: Improving phishing detection via psychological trait scoring. arXiv preprint arXiv:2208.06792 (2022)
26. Siemerink, A.: Code and datasets underlying research study "The Dual-Edged Sword of Generative AI in Phishing" (2024). https://github.com/alecsiemerink/thesis-ai-phishing-countermeasures
27. Trad, F., Chehab, A.: Prompt engineering or fine-tuning? A case study on phishing detection with large language models. Mach. Learn. Knowl. Extract. **6**(1), 367–384 (2024)
28. Wei, J., et al.: Chain of thought prompting elicits reasoning in large language models. CoRR abs/2201.11903 (2022). https://arxiv.org/abs/2201.11903
29. Zeng, V., Liu, X., Verma, R.M.: Generalized deception dataset (2022)

Formal Verification

Analysing TLS Implementations Using Full-Message Symbolic Execution

Johannes Wilson[1,2(✉)] and Mikael Asplund[1]

[1] Linköping University, Linköping, Sweden
{johannes.wilson,mikael.asplund}@liu.se
[2] Sectra Communications, Linköping, Sweden
johannes.wilson@sectra.com

Abstract. In this paper, we present a methodology for performing thorough analysis of TLS protocol implementations using dynamic symbolic execution. This method explores all possible inputs by treating entire messages as symbolic using KLEE. We are able to analyse the message parsing logic in detail, showing fulfilment of requirements from the protocol specification. This has previously not been performed for whole messages in complex protocols such as TLS. We tackle several problems that cause state space explosion by providing appropriate abstractions of implementation primitives. Additionally, we explore how protocol design choices impact the feasibility of analysis and argue for a strict TLS specification. We have applied our method to the ServerHello message parsing in several versions of the WolfSSL TLS 1.3 implementation. Our analysis revealed two vulnerabilities in the client implementation which were both assigned CVEs, one of them marked as high severity.

Keywords: Dynamic Symbolic Execution · Program Analysis · Protocol Analysis · Transport Layer Security

1 Introduction

Cryptographic protocols such as Transport Layer Security (TLS) are fundamental to internet security, as they provide the basic guarantees of authenticity and confidentiality. Implementation flaws can be fatal to security, as demonstrated by vulnerabilities such as Heartbleed [22] found in OpenSSL. Traditional test methods such as unit tests and fuzzing are necessarily incomplete, and cannot cover all cases. As a consequence, they cannot prove absence of bugs.

While modern protocol analysis tools such as Tamarin [24] and ProVerif [10] enable analysis of TLS 1.3 [8,18,19], analysis is limited to abstract models. Attempts to bridge the gap between symbolic verification and implementation analysis have either required the use of less common programming languages [7,9,21], or extract an implementation from the abstract model, requiring manual verification effort to prove memory safety [2,29]. We argue that new methods are needed in order to effectively analyse also *existing* protocol implementations, since such implementations account for the majority of everyday usage.

L. Horn Iwaya et al. (Eds.): NordSec 2024, LNCS 15396, pp. 283–302, 2025.
https://doi.org/10.1007/978-3-031-79007-2_15

We propose a method based on symbolic execution, where we systematically explore the state space of accepted messages during protocol execution. By treating messages symbolically, we exhaustively find all possible messages which advance the protocol state. This allows us to prove the absence of certain errors for individual messages. We adapt KLEE [12], a dynamic symbolic execution engine, to allow for dynamic symbolic execution of network protocols.[1] We analyse the found execution traces with respect to the requirements given by the protocol specification. The novelty of our method lies in combining symbolic sockets and abstracted symbolic functions for memcmp and cryptographic primitives, in order to support the analysis of fully symbolic messages. While there is previous work on these topics individually, we are first to demonstrate how they can be combined to analyse a real full-scale TLS implementation.

We apply the proposed method on the ServerHello message parsing in the WolfSSL implementation of TLS 1.3. WolfSSL TLS is a lightweight implementation targeting embedded systems with widespread usage. The ServerHello message establishes the negotiated parameters, notably the key group and version to be used for the rest of the session. Our analysis of this implementation revealed two flaws which both negatively affects the security of the protocol. The bugs are non-obvious and hard to uncover through manual inspection, since they rely on sending non-conformant messages. The vulnerabilities were both assigned CVEs and have been fixed in up-to-date versions. To the best of our knowledge, this is the first symbolic analysis of a real-world full-scale TLS implementation where the entire input message is treated symbolically. We do not only discover vulnerabilities, but we additionally demonstrate the absence of errors in corrected versions, as our method allows us to verify that an implementation only accepts conformant ServerHello messages.

A dynamic symbolic execution engine dynamically executes a System Under Test (SUT) while treating certain variables as symbolic. The engine tests for possible branches using a constraint solver, resulting in a disjunction of the program state if multiple paths are possible. We identify several implementation primitives and features in the TLS specification that gives rise to a large number of such disjunctions. We describe several abstractions which we have implemented in KLEE as part of making verification tractable in a wider range of cases. Moreover, we exemplify how design choices in protocols can impact the testability of protocol implementations. We showcase how a strict TLS specification that limits the number of choices and possible configurations can allow for more efficient symbolic execution, enabling thorough analysis while still allowing normal protocol operation.

With the help of Strict TLS and abstracted primitives, we were able to analyse ten different versions of WolfSSL. We show fulfilment of nine requirements extracted from the TLS specification for the corrected version. We measure running time of symbolic execution for each version. The contributions of this paper are as follows.

[1] Our code is made available at https://gitlab.liu.se/ida-rtslab/public-code/2024_full-message_symbolic_execution.

- We propose and evaluate a method for thorough analysis of TLS implementations using KLEE.
- We propose Strict TLS, a hardening of the TLS specification which provides increased testability and transparency.
- We show the applicability of our method by applying it on the widely used WolfSSL TLS implementation for ServerHello messages.
- We discover two previously unknown CVEs in WolfSSL, and describe their security implications in detail.

2 Method Overview

Our method consists of three parts. First, we perform some modifications to the KLEE symbolic execution engine to enable symbolic execution of protocol implementations. Next, we construct the test harness for the SUT, which in our case is WolfSSL. Finally, we run KLEE on the SUT to find messages which progress the protocol and analyse the successful traces. We highlight the steps in Fig. 1. The modifications we have made to KLEE in Step 1 are generic and are not specific to any particular implementation or protocol. In Step 2 we write a test-harness specific for WolfSSL. The analysis performed in Step 3 can be the same for any program which implements the same protocol. In addition to these steps, we propose and explain our motivation for considering a strict TLS specification during our experiments.

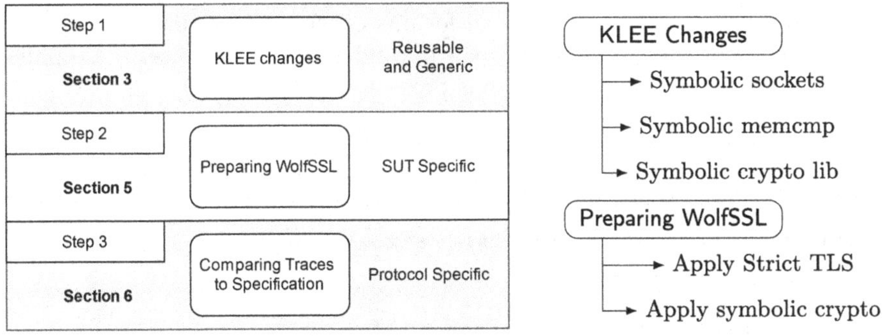

Fig. 1. Method Overview.

Our changes to KLEE include implementing the symbolic sockets, symbolic memcmp and cryptographic functions, as described in Subsects. 3.1, 3.2, and 3.3, respectively. Before presenting changes to the SUT, we introduce Strict TLS in Sect. 4. We believe that a strict TLS specification is worthwhile in its own right, but it also helps in making symbolic execution tractable. The changes made and the procedure for making changes to the SUT are presented in Sect. 5. We instantiate Strict TLS on the WolfSSL implementation, as described in Subsect. 5.1

and we additionally explain how to use the symbolic cryptographic library to create a test harness for WolfSSL in Subsect. 5.2. Finally, we explain our methods for analysing the generated test cases for improperly formatted messages in Sect. 6.

3 KLEE Changes

We will now proceed to present Step 1, detailing the additions and modifications we made to KLEE. Our changes are implemented as abstractions of library functions augmented to handle symbolic input.

3.1 Reading Symbolic Sockets

Symbolic sockets allow us to analyse how the TLS implementation handles all possible message contents. Our method relies on turning all reads from TCP sockets into symbolic bytes. These symbolic bytes serve as the only symbolic variables during execution.

When implementing symbolic sockets, we must specify what should happen in the case the length of the buffer is symbolic. Filling the buffer with the number of bytes specified would cause many branches, one for each possible buffer size. Instead, we find the maximum value which the symbolic size may take, and treat this as our effective size. The benefit is that the symbolic execution engine does not need to fork execution immediately due to the symbolic buffer length, maintaining only a single path, instead of a path for every possible buffer length. We assume that the buffer is not used for any other purpose than reading from the network, and that data is not read beyond the returned size. A simplified example of our symbolic socket code is presented in Listing 1.1.

Listing 1.1. Reading symbolic sockets using maximal buffer length. Code is simplified for ease of readability. Not shown in the simplified example is the addition of a message record type and handshake message type to signify ServerHello.

```
int symbolic_read(void *buf, size_t count){
    size_t max_read;
    // find size we may maximally read into buf
    if (klee_is_symbolic(count)){
        // we have symbolic input, find maximal size
        max_read = klee_get_max_value(count);
    }
    else{ max_read = count; }
    // fill buffer with max_read # symbolic bytes
    _array_symbolic(buf, max_read, "sym_read");
    return klee_range(0, count); // and symbolic return
}
```

A related, but different problem, also caused by the symbolic size of messages, occurs whenever message buffers need to be allocated to have appropriate sizes to fit the input message. This causes the implementation to allocate memory based on a symbolic value. KLEE handles calls to *malloc* by allocating a concrete region of memory, and is therefore forced to concretize the size of the allocated memory. The default behaviour is to only perform a few guesses for sizes when receiving a symbolic size in *malloc*. We modify KLEE in order to allocate memory that is guaranteed to be larger than the next handshake message when encountering a symbolic input to *malloc*. At the same time, we avoid allocating too much superfluous memory which might slow down execution. By only considering memory allocation of sufficient sizes, we may miss errors from reading beyond the buffer, since an error might only occur at a particular allocation size. This is because our modification may cause a buffer overflow to still land within allocated memory, which prevents KLEE from detecting this as an error. Our KLEE version treats the allocation size as a parameter which may be selected from the command line.

Note that this does not mean that we assume a concrete (fixed) value for the message size. Instead, we allow the message length to vary by maintaining it as symbolic, even after allocating a fix amount of memory for the buffer, and when reading the symbolic TCP socket. This ensures that we do not fixate on a particular message length. Rather, we allow any message which may fit the allocated buffer (including any shorter message length).

The benefit of our combined approach for memory allocation and symbolic sockets is that we effectively maintain a single execution path rather than one execution path for each possible concrete length. By delaying the concretisation of message length parameters, a major source of state space explosion is avoided, as the length is only concretised through the necessary restrictions imposed by the message parsing itself. An alternative approach, described in [15], instead performs length concretisation while also applying known message length restrictions early, immediately upon reading the message, in a process named meta-level search.

3.2 Handling Memcmp Symbolically

Even symbolic bytestrings of constant length can pose a challenge to symbolic execution engines by introducing significant state space explosion. We provide function abstractions in KLEE for some functions which cause a large state space explosion, in particular the standard C *memcmp* function, and several cryptographic functions.

The function *memcmp* is typically used as a comparison between two arrays, however symbolic analysis of the function will cause a large number of paths, one for each byte being different. Our abstracted *memcmp* function instead creates three branches: one branch where all bytes are equal, one where the first array is lexicographically before the second array, and one where the second array is lexicographically before the first array. The constraint for each branch can be given as a single expression. The first branch is given as a conjunction of equalities between each byte, while the second and third branches are given as a conjunction of equalities of previous bytes disjoint with a greater-than comparison.

This abstraction is not perfectly sound since the return value cannot be perfectly captured, as the semantics of *memcmp* require that the exact difference between the first differing byte is returned. With our abstraction we at the very least allow for branches that either test a lexicographic ordering, or test equality.

3.3 Dealing with Cryptographic Functions

We proceed to describe a simple mechanism to abstract away from the cryptographic functions. Cryptographic protocols such as TLS use a number of cryptographic primitives, including hashes, encryption, decryption, and signatures. Such primitives form the basis of the security guarantees for any cryptographic protocol. However, symbolic analysis of cryptographic functions is not feasible.

In this work, we are interested in the correct parsing of messages, rather than potential weaknesses in the implementation of the cryptographic primitives which is an orthogonal problem. Therefore, we follow the approach of Vanhoef and Piessens [32], which is to abstract the cryptographic primitives into entirely symbolic functions. Their work additionally describes how to record the relationship between the results of cryptographic functions. This is not necessary for our experiments since we only consider a single message at a time, however it would be necessary when considering sequences of messages.

In our symbolic cryptographic functions, the output of the cryptographic function is replaced by an array of symbolic bytes. This means that we allow any output to be the result of a cryptographic function. As an added optimisation, we additionally ensure that cryptographic functions which only take concrete input will use the original concrete implementation, resulting in a concrete output rather than a symbolic one. This avoids creating unnecessary symbolic values when the value would otherwise be known exactly.

4 Strict TLS Specification

Choices in protocols can give rise to significant state space explosion during symbolic execution. We started out with a supposition that many protocols are designed to perform a sequence of messages with very limited internal state. Highly adaptable and configurable protocols challenge this view. In TLS, the version, ciphers, key groups, and signature algorithms all need to be negotiated during the initial handshake, creating a vast number of possible handshake procedures, not to mention the possibility of using DTLS, pre-shared keys, or early data in TLS 1.3. Such diversity is important for purposes of adaptability to future needs, as well as compatibility with older versions or lightweight implementations. However, it is typically not beneficial for security, as the increase in complexity makes analysis difficult. We cannot analyse every possible combination of configurations in TLS, instead we must settle for a configuration at a time. Therefore, we propose Strict TLS, a specification with limited configuration, and some additional restrictions of the TLS implementation behaviour which otherwise hinder symbolic execution. These restrictions do not affect the ability of the protocol to establish a secure connection, but may affect interoperability with versions who do not conform to our strict TLS specification or configuration. In some sense, we trade compatibility and extensibility for increased security, testability, and readability. Strict TLS may be useful for security critical TLS implementations, since it may be desirable to use a standardised protocol, while enabling a more thorough analysis of the implementation. The configuration and restrictions of WolfSSL we have used are listed in Appendix A. In the following sections we motivate some of the restrictions by exemplifying how they affect symbolic execution.

4.1 Complexity from Extensions

The TLS specification states that extensions may appear in any order in the list. As a consequence, implementations need to parse extensions in the order they appear. Bugs may appear only when one extension is parsed after another. If we want to verify an implementation, we have to verify every order and combination of extensions. Even for a relatively small numbers of extensions, this can cause significant state space explosion.

We argue that there may be a benefit to limiting the number of combinations to test by imposing an order on the number of extensions. Requiring the extensions to follow a pre-defined ordering would not have any impact on the function of the protocol, yet it would reduce state space explosion significantly, simplifying testing. By only imposing an ordering, we reduce the state space from a factorial one to an exponential one, which for small values of n may be sufficient to make the problem tractable.

The lack of an order for extensions causes another problem. There is a particular extension which must be parsed first according to the specification, namely the *supported versions* extension. The version to use must be decided first, before any other extensions are handled. However, the *supported versions* extension is not guaranteed to be the first in the list, meaning any extensions before it must be skipped in the initial parsing of the *supported versions* extension. During symbolic execution this gives rise to a large number of forked executions before we know through parsing if a particular extension is allowed or has the correct format and length. To simplify testing and to enable efficient symbolic execution of the extension parsing, we force the *supported versions* extension to be the very first extension in the extension list in Strict TLS.

4.2 Disallowing Message Fragmentation

Another cause of state space explosion present in TLS, is that messages may be fragmented. In TLS, fragmented messages can introduce an arbitrary amount of extra record messages. To see this, consider that handshake messages can be fragmented at any length. A handshake message consisting of 300 bytes could be split into 300 records each containing a single byte, or into two records each with 150 bytes, or any combination of fragment lengths which add up to 300. Testing all combinations of message fragmentations is impractical, since each message of length n can be split in 2^{n-1} ways if we count unique ordered partitions ($1 + 2$ is distinct from $2 + 1$). The reason being that there are $n - 1$ places where we may split the message, where either we do or don't split at each byte, giving 2^{n-1} possibilities. To improve testability and transparency of Strict TLS, we restrict the fragmentation of messages to only occur when strictly necessary, meaning the message length exceeds the maximal allowed record length. Such a restriction does not significantly impact the function of the protocol to our knowledge.

5 Preparing WolfSSL

We now explain the necessary steps for creating a test harness for the SUT. We proceed to describe how we adapted WolfSSL to our strict TLS specification in Sect. 5.1. Additionally, we adapt the WolfSSL client implementation to use the abstracted cryptographic functions and describe the process in Sect. 5.2.

5.1 Conforming to Strict TLS

We instantiate Strict TLS by using a limited configuration of the WolfSSL TLS 1.3 implementation. Most of the instantiation can be handled through already existing compilation options for WolfSSL. We modify the implementation to disallow unknown extensions. We also note that while it is a requirement in the TLS specification that known but unsupported extensions are rejected, the WolfSSL implementation will instead ignore some extensions as they are implemented in 1.3 by default. We modify the implementation to disallow skipping known but unsupported extensions. Moreover, we modify two locations for the purpose of disabling message fragmentation. The first change ensures that we read complete messages from the sockets, as we could technically read messages one byte at a time. The other change disables fragmented messages by stopping analysis after receiving a complete record, regardless if the whole handshake message was read. Finally, we force the *supported versions* extension to be the very first extension in the extension list by rejecting paths which do not parse it during the first iteration.

5.2 Replacing Cryptographic Functions

To enable symbolic execution using our method, the original SUT must be modified so that concrete cryptographic implementations are replaced by the symbolic ones presented in Sect. 3.3. Replacing a concrete implementation of a function with a symbolic one requires that the original implementation is side-effect free, or else the behaviour of the program is altered. Some cryptographic functions are not entirely side-effect free, requiring some additional modification. In particular, hash functions in WolfSSL are built as running hashes. This means that the implementation maintains an internal state of the hash so far, while allowing an output to be extracted at any point. Because of this, changes to the hash data-structure and functions were required in order to allow both concrete hashes, and symbolic outputs whenever we had encountered a symbolic input value previously.

Some changes are also required outside of the implemented cryptographic functions themselves. We disable the sanity check on any server-provided keys since such checks were also cryptographic in nature, causing expensive queries which attempt to find all valid keys. In order to still match the expected key length, we add a check to compare the length of the submitted public key to the expected length (256 bytes for FFDHE2048) in the *key share* extension.

In total, we changed 114 lines of code in the SUT. A breakdown of the changes can be found in Appendix B. Most of our changes can be found in sha256.c, where we implemented a symbolic version of the hashing algorithm, and in tls.c, where we exclude some extensions from analysis and force the order of others.

6 Comparing Traces to Specification

We now describe how we compared the artefacts produced by KLEE to the requirements given by the TLS 1.3 specification. After a successful run, KLEE will have found a number of paths throughout the program which reach the target state, in our case an accepted ServerHello message. For each path, KLEE will output a path condition and a representative test case. Since our method covers all paths, the disjunction of all path conditions give the complete input-space of allowed ServerHello messages for our configuration, given the restrictions on message size and fragmentation.

In each test case, a concrete bytestring is given for the ServerHello which arrived at the completed message state. We parse the concrete bytestrings for all test cases and ensure that the ServerHello messages that were found to advance the client state conform to the extracted list of requirements. These tests are not specific to WolfSSL, and may be reused to test any ServerHello message generated for any implementation.

We ensure that all test cases produced by KLEE describe valid ServerHello messages. We do this by extracting requirements on ServerHello messages from the specification described by RFC 8446. Specifically, we look for keywords such as MUST or SHOULD describing a condition on the ServerHello messages. We adapt conditions to account for our specific configuration. We identified the following list of requirements for ServerHello messages.

- **Legacy Version 1.2.** The legacy version field should indicate TLS 1.2 during a TLS 1.3 handshake for backward compatibility with middleboxes.
- **Not Retry.** The field for the random variable should not contain the static string indicating a HelloRetryRequest.
- **Session ID Match.** The session ID should match the one sent in the ClientHello, and should therefore be empty.
- **Cipher Match.** The cipher field should match one of the ciphers sent in the ClientHello, and should therefore indicate AES-128-GCM-SHA256.
- **No Compression.** The legacy compression method field should be zero.

- **Requires Version.** The list of extensions must contain a SupportedVersion extension.
- **Version 1.3.** The SupportedVersion extension should indicate version 1.3.
- **Requires Key Share.** The list of extensions should contain the KeyShare extension, since the use of PSK is disabled.
- **Boundary Aligns.** The record boundary must align with the end of the ServerHello message.

While some of these requirements might seem mundane or trivial, violating them can in fact lead to security issues as we will see in Sect. 8. We were able to capture all requirements in the standard except one which is that the key entry contains a valid key for the group provided by the client. Our abstraction of the cryptographic functions does not allow us to test this case.

Note that, for simplicity, we compared the requirements to the test cases and not the path conditions. This may lose some precision, as the test cases only give a single concretisation of each path conditions, and there may be multiple choices for each concretisation. In the future, we would like to instead perform a query based on the path conditions, as this would ensure that we cover any possible concretisation. However, in this particular case, we deemed the test cases to be representative enough for the types of requirements we checked in order for a missed test to be very unlikely.

7 Method Evaluation

In this section, we demonstrate that our method can be used to analyse real-world protocol implementations by applying it to the WolfSSL TLS 1.3 implementation. We test the implementation of the ServerHello message parsing, and attempt to find violations of the message requirements described in Sect. 6. While analysis of the ServerHello message parsing is a limited analysis of the entire handshake protocol, we note that the ServerHello message is crucial for establishing the correct version and keys for the rest of the protocol. Furthermore, symbolic analysis of certificate parsing has already been treated in works by Chau et al. [14,15]. We measure the runtime of our experiments to show how long it takes to exhaustively search through the valid ServerHello messages. To investigate whether changes in the implementation affect the runtime of our experiment, we perform tests using multiple versions of the WolfSSL implementation.

We set up our experiments to initialise the client as normal using a provided example echoclient implementation, allowing it to send its first ClientHello as normal, and then inserting an abort statement in the code immediately after accepting a ServerHello message. We apply our SUT changes to 10 versions of WolfSSL, demonstrating the feasibility of automatically reapplying the necessary changes to the SUT. We perform our experiments using a virtual machine running Ubuntu 22.04, with 16 virtual cores and 32 GB RAM. We performed three runs for each version. Our initial experiments found two implementation flaws, described in Sect. 8, which were reported to, and fixed by, the developers of WolfSSL. We additionally run our experiment on a fixed up-to-date version to verify that no errors are present, namely version 5.6.6.

Figure 2 shows the time it took to run our experiments for each version. KLEE execution time varies considerably between versions, with versions between 5.5.2 and 5.5.4 taking over three times longer to run compared to versions 5.5.1 and prior. For all versions we used a size of 512 bytes for symbolic allocation sizes.

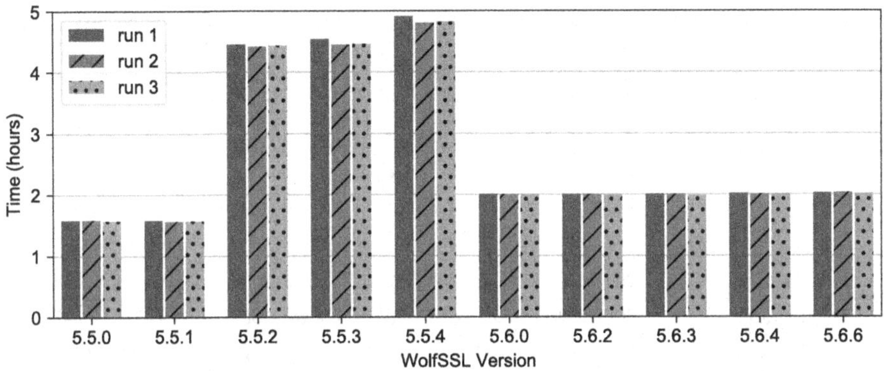

Fig. 2. Elapsed experiment duration across WolfSSL versions.

The overall results for each version is summarized in Table 1. Data across runs for the same version was consistent, unless otherwise indicated. The increased execution times for versions 5.5.2, 5.5.3, and 5.5.4 seem to correlate strongly with the increased number of queries. Surprisingly, the number of paths explored for versions 5.5.1 and 5.5.2 are the exact same, as well as versions 5.5.4 and 5.6.0, indicating that the change in the number of queries might have been caused by the heuristic of KLEE prioritising different queries for different versions, and not by any addition of branches in the code. Finding the specific change which caused the increase in execution time is non-trivial, especially as the difference between versions can be quite substantial. Between stable releases 5.5.2 and 5.5.1 there were 173 files changed and over 70k changed lines of code.

All generated test cases contained a correctly negotiated cipher and TLS version. Versions past 5.6.2 require the KeyShare extension to be present, while versions before that did not, shown as crosses in the table. Omitting the KeyShare extension has implications for the security of the protocol and results in a weak key being used by the client. We describe this vulnerability in detail in Sect. 8.1. Similarly, the lack of record boundary alignment of the ServerHello message, present across all tested versions except for version 5.6.6, results in another vulnerability, described in Sect. 8.2. We tested these bugs using an unmodified version of WolfSSL, confirming they were not false-positives.

Table 1. Number of messages and formatting errors for ServerHello messages for each version of WolfSSL. A checkmark indicates that all generated test cases for the tested version behave correctly, while a cross indicates that at least one trace allows for a message to be sent which breaks the requirement.

Version	5.5.0	5.5.1	5.5.2	5.5.3	5.5.4	5.6.0	5.6.2	5.6.3	5.6.4	5.6.6
Successful Paths	16	16	16	16	16	16	8	8	8	8
Legacy Version 1.2	✓	✓	✓	✓	✓	✓	✓	✓	✓	✓
Not Retry	✓	✓	✓	✓	✓	✓	✓	✓	✓	✓
Session ID Match	✓	✓	✓	✓	✓	✓	✓	✓	✓	✓
Cipher Match	✓	✓	✓	✓	✓	✓	✓	✓	✓	✓
Empty Compression	✓	✓	✓	✓	✓	✓	✓	✓	✓	✓
Requires Version	✓	✓	✓	✓	✓	✓	✓	✓	✓	✓
Version 1.3	✓	✓	✓	✓	✓	✓	✓	✓	✓	✓
Requires Key Share	✗	✗	✗	✗	✗	✗	✓	✓	✓	✓
Boundary Aligns	✗	✗	✗	✗	✗	✗	✗	✗	✗	✓
Total Paths	2614	2614	2614	2614	2638	2638	2638	2638	2654	2658
Total queries	6005	6005	85717	85717	86069	6661	6661	6669	6701*	6797
Total Instructions	1.5M	1.5M	2.4M	2.4M	2.4M	2.5M	2.5M	2.5M	2.5M	2.5M

*Third run performed 6700 queries
1M = One Million

8 New Vulnerabilities

We discovered two previously unknown vulnerabilities in the WolfSSL TLS 1.3 implementation using our proposed method. Both vulnerabilities were assigned CVEs (CVE-2023-3724 and CVE-2023-6937) by WolfSSL. The first vulnerability, presented in Sect. 8.1, allows ServerHello messages without KeyShare extensions to be accepted by the client, causing trivially computable keys to be used for the rest of the session. The second vulnerability, presented in Sect. 8.2, allows encryption of handshake messages to be partially bypassed using message coalescing.

8.1 Missing Key Exchange

We found that the latest WolfSSL client implementation at the time of our initial analysis did not ensure that either a KeyShare extension or a pre-shared key extension had been received from the server before accepting the ServerHello message and progressing the protocol (CVE-2023-3724). Based on our reporting, this has been fixed in WolfSSL versions starting from 5.6.2.

The bug was discovered by analysing the output from KLEE in relation to the correctness properties described in Sect. 6. The requirement that the KeyShare extension is present was violated by some of the test cases produced by KLEE. Further investigation revealed that when the client continued the protocol, it would still perform key derivation as normal, deriving keys using default empty vectors as input key material instead of both the PSK and the DH secret as shown in Fig. 3. Further keys are derived using the message transcripts, and so different sessions will still derive different keys, but the PSK and the DH secret are the only secrets used during the key derivation. The result is that *trivially insecure keys are being used for the rest of the protocol*, which any passive attacker may derive by listening to protocol messages.

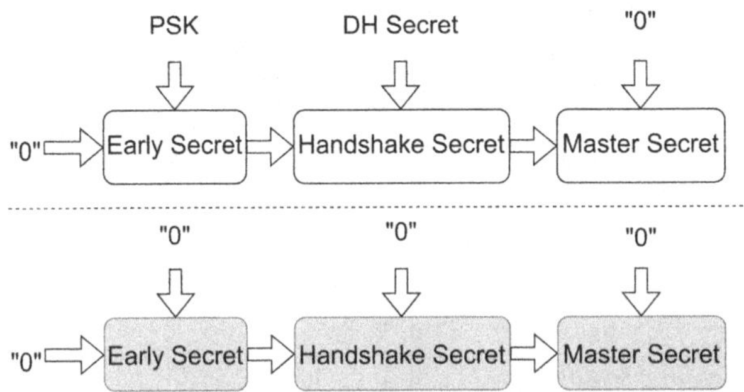

Fig. 3. Derivation of secrets using PSK and DH Secret (top) compared to trivially computable inputs due to missing KeyShare extension (bottom). Secrets are meant to be derived using either PSK, DH, or both, but not neither as in bottom example. Not shown are the keys which are derived from a combination of the secrets, a static unique string for each key, and a transcript of the handshake messages so far. Red colour indicates that a secret may be derived using only message transcript. (Color figure online)

The vulnerability on its own does not allow an adversary to bypass the authentication mechanisms present in TLS 1.3. For an adversary to inject the faulty ServerHello and then succeed during authentication, the adversary would need a valid CertificateVerify message, requiring a signature on the message transcript using the server long term key. This is because the client implementation assumes that certificate authentication is to be used when receiving the faulty ServerHello. Furthermore, an adversary cannot use the server as an oracle for such a message, since an honest server would always include key parameters, meaning the message transcripts will always differ on the ServerHello message between honest and dishonest sessions.

8.2 Coalesced Handshake Messages

TLS 1.3 requires encryption of all messages as soon as the first set encryption keys can be derived. As encryption is applied at the record layer, record boundaries need to be properly aligned with new encryption keys for encryption to be applied properly. If a new encryption key is derived, then all following messages must be encrypted using the new key, and so successive messages should be encapsulated in new records. Our analysis shows that no restriction was placed on the record boundary for the ServerHello message. Further manual testing revealed that a WolfSSL client accepts all handshake messages coalesced (CVE-2023-6937). This has been corrected in version WolfSSL version 5.6.6.

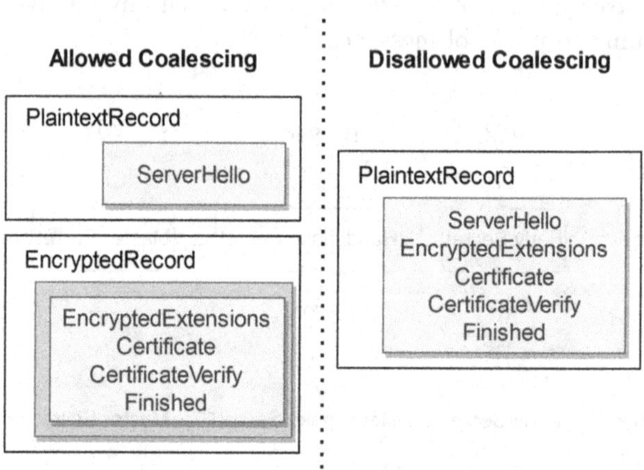

Fig. 4. Comparison between allowed and disallowed coalescing of handshake messages. Encryption is highlighted in red. On the left, the ServerHello and the following handshake messages are contained in separate records, with only the ServerHello being unencrypted. On the right, all handshake messages are combined in the same record without encryption. A client should reject the handshake on the right, since the record boundary does not align with the ServerHello. (Color figure online)

Since the ServerHello is the last handshake message which is sent in plaintext, coalescing together the ServerHello and successive messages bypasses the record layer encryption entirely. As a consequence, encryption of *all* handshake messages could be bypassed completely, on the condition that all messages could fit inside a single record header, as seen in Fig. 4.

There is no break of authentication, even during a PSK handshake, thanks to the inclusion of the derived key as part of the hash contained in the Finished message. Had it been possible to also send a valid Finished message, then an adversary would have been able to complete the full PSK handshake as the server without ever having derived the negotiated keys, tricking the client into believing the server is active.

Even if the handshake is not completed, the adversary can reach further into the protocol than would normally be possible without access to the handshake keys, as it allows sending handshake message unencrypted by coalescing them with the ServerHello. Note that it is possible to inject the EncryptedExtension by manipulating the length of the record containing the ServerHello. This could allow an adversary to guess the negotiated encrypted extensions and test if the guess was correct. They would perform this by sending the EncryptedExtensions handshake message in plaintext while dropping the real EncryptedExtensions, assuming the real EncryptedExtensions is contained in a single record. If the handshake completed, it would indicate a correct guess. This works because the record layer is not included in the message transcript, while the contents of the EncryptedExtensions message is. Therefore, the lack of encryption is not visible in the transcript hashes, but an incorrectly guessed EncryptedExtensions would not produce the same hash for both the server and the client and would cause the connection to be rejected.

9 Related Work

One of the earlier papers discussing cryptographic analysis of protocol implementations is from 2005 by Goubault-Larrecq and Parrennes [23] who translated C program code into verifiable Horn clauses, verifying the program against a Dolev-Yao adversary. The translation assumed an idealized semantic of C code without buffer overflows, and partially relied on manually inserted trust assertions to identify cryptographic functions and their behaviour. Udrea et al. [31] perform static analysis of C implementations of the SSH and RCP protocols. Abstract interpretation was used to compare code to protocol rules written in a specification language, using ghost variables to track protocol state. Another early approach, ASPIER [13], relies on predicate abstraction to extract an abstract model of the protocol. Because the abstraction gives an overapproximation, counterexamples do not always give concrete attacks. To refine the abstraction, counterexample guided abstraction refinement [16] was used. However, in ASPIER, pointers, bitwise operations, and floating-point operations were not handled soundly, and only bounded verification was performed.

Using symbolic execution for the purpose of extracting verifiable cryptographic models from C implementations was performed in 2011 for small code examples by Aizatulin et al. [1]. A symbolic model is extracted and can then be analysed in ProVerif. Their analysis is limited along a single execution path. The restriction to only analyse a single execution path was lifted in recent work by Nasrabadi et al. [25]. Their tool performs model extraction at the binary level. Case studies were performed for TinySSH and for the implementation of Wireguard for Linux. They handle bounded loops using a loop-summarization technique [30] which allows symbolic execution of loops to scale. This technique cannot precisely handle any possible loop and may result in overapproximations of the number of possible paths, but worked well for the programs which they analysed. They require some manual effort to specify the location of cryptographic functions and their abstract Proverif or CryptoVerif counterpart.

Several works have used KLEE for the purpose of protocol implementation analysis [3,4,14,15,17,32]. Corin and Manzano [17] present an in-depth formalism for replacing cryptographic functions with symbolic ones during dynamic symbolic execution using KLEE. They showcase their approach on a small code example. Vanhoef and Piessens [32] analyse the WPA2 4-way handshake, and also deal with problems arising during symbolic analysis of cryptographic functions. We take a similar approach to cryptographic functions in our work. Additionally, they restrict parts of the messages to concrete types and lengths, similar to how we applied some restrictions of our own to the protocol implementation.

Asadian et al. [4] used KLEE specifically to test TLS implementations, focusing on the implementation of DTLS whereas we consider non-datagram TLS. Their method relies on manually inserted assertions based on requirements from the specification. The main difference compared to our work is that symbolic execution is performed on selected fields at a time. Further development [3] allows specifying requirements through separate monitors which monitor protocol state, minimising modification of the SUT by allowing the monitor to identify faulty behaviour. Our approach instead tries to maximise coverage, at the cost of additional changes to the SUT and increased run time of experiments.

Other works [14,15] investigate the implementation of certificate validation and signature verification in common TLS libraries, finding deviations from the specification in the implementations. The use of symbolic execution in these works is focused on the portions of code which perform the certificate validation or signature verification.

Some approaches explore the state space of protocol implementations using pre-built messages, which already conform to the specifications [6,20]. Such analysis is limited to sending messages according to a known input corpus, and sending them out of order. However, not all vulnerabilities can be found using only client messages which conform to specification. Similarly, testing interoperability [26] is limited to sending messages of some implementation.

Cloud9 [11] is an extension to KLEE which allows more scalable analysis by leveraging parallel dynamic symbolic execution. The framework includes an extended environment model to handle multi-threaded applications as well as network applications. Their analysis of memcached was able to explore all possible paths after the implementation received two symbolic packets.

Many other frameworks and techniques for symbolic execution exist [5]. angr [27] is a dynamic symbolic execution which performs analysis at the binary level, rather than at source code level. angr provides extensive support of library functions through symbolic summaries. Symbolic summaries are abstractions of library functions which can significantly speed up execution when dealing with symbolic input. In addition to many other functions, symbolic summaries are provided to support sockets, memcmp and malloc, similar to the way we implement these in KLEE. However, as described in the angr documentation, there are a number of unsupported or incomplete symbolic summaries, including some required by WolfSSL. Because of this, we were not able to apply the angr engine to our SUT. Using function summaries in order to abstract from external function calls was also discussed in [28].

10 Conclusions

In this paper, we propose a method for applying dynamic symbolic execution using KLEE to analyse protocol message parsing in detail. We describe how to apply efficient abstractions of implementation primitives, circumventing state space explosion caused by message length variance, array operations like *memcmp*, cryptographic primitives, and protocol choices. We highlight how seemingly minor choices in protocol design can drastically affect analysability, such as the parsing behaviour for extensions. Had we not limited analysis to our Strict TLS specification, there would have been a practically infinite state space to symbolically analyse, since there is normally no restriction on unknown extensions. While Strict TLS does limit the interoperability of the protocol, it may still be useful for security-critical implementations.

We successfully apply our method on the WolfSSL TLS 1.3 client implementation and find two previously unknown vulnerabilities which effectively circumvent the encryption of handshake messages, and which may be used to establish insecure keys with affected clients. Importantly, we are able to show that up-to-date versions of the implementation only accepts ServerHello messages which are permitted by the specification. While our experiments take a significant amount of time, on the order of several hours, the gain is also substantial. As opposed to most automated testing methods, we are able to show absence of requirement violations for all possible inputs, not just subsets thereof.

Responsible Disclosure. All discovered vulnerabilities have been reported to the developers of WolfSSL, who have corrected the bugs and published fixes in current versions. The developers of WolfSSL have given permission for public disclosure of both vulnerabilities.

Code Availability. Our results can be replicated using the code provided by the repository at https://gitlab.liu.se/ida-rtslab/public-code/2024_full-message_symbolic_execution.

Acknowledgements. We would like to thank the anonymous reviewers for their valuable comments and feedback. Additionally, we would like to thank the developers of WolfSSL for their quick responses and helpful insights.

This work was partially supported by the Wallenberg AI, Autonomous Systems and Software Program (WASP) funded by the Knut and Alice Wallenberg Foundation.

A StrictTLS Requirements

- Only version 1.3 of TLS is used, with prior versions disabled. This ensures that we only ever use the latest and most secure version, and do not risk any downgrade attacks. Servers which only use prior versions will be incompatible.
- Only a single cipher is selected by the client. This gives the client the most control over which cipher we deem secure. Servers may support multiple versions but selection is done by the client.
- The client will only support and generate keys for a particular supported key group. The key group decides the strength of the DH key exchange, and is as such vital to the security of the handshake. Servers which do not support the preferred key group will be rejected.

- Extensions must follow a predefined order.
- The supported versions extensions must be the first extensions in both the ClientHello and the ServerHello messages.
- Records may not be fragmented unless they exceed the record size limit.
- Pre-shared keys are not be used. Testing PSK handshakes may be done separately, as a separate protocol.
- DTLS is not used. The DTLS protocol differs from TLS in many aspects, in particular regarding reordering and retransmission of messages. For this reason we treat DTLS as a separate protocol entirely.
- Early data (0-RTT) is not used. Security of early data is known to be weaker, since authentication is performed after some data has already been sent.
- Unknown extensions must result in a rejected connection.

B Summary of Changes to SUT

(See Table 2).

Table 2. Number of code lines changed in SUT, not counting comments or ifdef macros.

Filename	# of Lines	Reason
echoclient.c	2	exit silently on error
internal.c	4	public key, fragmented reads
tls.c	35	extensions, keyshare length
tls13.c	6	hello-retry, fragmented reads
dh.c	8	symbolic key derivation
random.c	6	symbolic random numbers
sha256.c	50	symbolic sha256
sha256.h	3	symbolic sha256

References

1. Aizatulin, M., Gordon, A.D., Jürjens, J.: Extracting and verifying cryptographic models from C protocol code by symbolic execution. In: Proceedings of the 18th ACM Conference on Computer and Communications Security, CCS '11, pp. 331–340. Association for Computing Machinery, New York (2011)
2. Arquint, L., et al.: Sound verification of security protocols: from design to interoperable implementations. In: 2023 IEEE Symposium on Security and Privacy (SP), pp. 1077–1093 (2023)
3. Asadian, H., Fiterau-Brostean, P., Jonsson, B., Sagonas, K.: Monitor-based testing of network protocol implementations using symbolic execution. In: Proceedings of the 19th International Conference on Availability, Reliability and Security, ARES '24. Association for Computing Machinery, New York (2024)

4. Asadian, H., Fiterău-Broştean, P., Jonsson, B., Sagonas, K.: Applying symbolic execution to test implementations of a network protocol against its specification. In: 2022 IEEE Conference on Software Testing, Verification and Validation (ICST), pp. 70–81 (2022)
5. Baldoni, R., Coppa, E., D'elia, D.C., Demetrescu, C., Finocchi, I.: A survey of symbolic execution techniques. ACM Comput. Surv. **51**(3) (2018)
6. Beurdouche, B., et al.: A messy state of the union: taming the composite state machines of TLS. Commun. ACM **60**(2), 99–107 (2017)
7. Bhargavan, K., et al.: Layered symbolic security analysis in DY*. In: Tsudik, G., Conti, M., Liang, K., Smaragdakis, G. (eds.) Computer Security – ESORICS 2023, pp. 3–21. Springer, Cham (2024)
8. Bhargavan, K., Blanchet, B., Kobeissi, N.: Verified models and reference implementations for the TLS 1.3 standard candidate. In: 2017 IEEE Symposium on Security and Privacy (SP), pp. 483–502 (2017)
9. Bhargavan, K., Fournet, C., Gordon, A.D., Tse, S.: Verified interoperable implementations of security protocols. ACM Trans. Program. Lang. Syst. **31**(1) (2008)
10. Blanchet, B.: Modeling and verifying security protocols with the applied PI calculus and ProVerif. Found. Trends® Priv. Secur. **1**(1–2), 1–135 (2016)
11. Bucur, S., Ureche, V., Zamfir, C., Candea, G.: Parallel symbolic execution for automated real-world software testing. In: Proceedings of the Sixth Conference on Computer Systems, EuroSys '11, pp. 183–198. Association for Computing Machinery, New York (2011)
12. Cadar, C., Dunbar, D., Engler, D.: KLEE: unassisted and automatic generation of high-coverage tests for complex systems programs. In: Proceedings of the 8th USENIX Conference on Operating Systems Design and Implementation, OSDI'08, USA, pp. 209–224. USENIX Association (2008)
13. Chaki, S., Datta, A.: ASPIER: an automated framework for verifying security protocol implementations. In: 2009 22nd IEEE Computer Security Foundations Symposium, pp. 172–185 (2009)
14. Chau, S.Y., et al.: SymCerts: practical symbolic execution for exposing noncompliance in X.509 certificate validation implementations. In: 2017 IEEE Symposium on Security and Privacy (SP), pp. 503–520 (2017)
15. Chau, S.Y., Yahyazadeh, M., Chowdhury, O., Kate, A., Li, N.: Analyzing semantic correctness with symbolic execution: a case study on PKCS#1 v1.5 signature verification. In: Network and Distributed Systems Security (NDSS) Symposium 2019 (2019)
16. Clarke, E., Grumberg, O., Jha, S., Lu, Y., Veith, H.: Counterexample-guided abstraction refinement. In: Emerson, E.A., Sistla, A.P. (eds.) Computer Aided Verification, pp. 154–169. Springer, Heidelberg (2000)
17. Corin, R., Manzano, F.A.: Efficient symbolic execution for analysing cryptographic protocol implementations. In: Erlingsson, Ú., Wieringa, R., Zannone, N. (eds.) Engineering Secure Software and Systems, pp. 58–72. Springer, Heidelberg (2011)
18. Cremers, C., Horvat, M., Hoyland, J., Scott, S., van der Merwe, T.: A comprehensive symbolic analysis of TLS 1.3. In: Proceedings of the 2017 ACM SIGSAC Conference on Computer and Communications Security, CCS '17, pp. 1773–1788. Association for Computing Machinery, New York (2017)
19. Cremers, C., Horvat, M., Scott, S., van der Merwe, T.: Automated analysis and verification of TLS 1.3: 0-RTT, resumption and delayed authentication. In: 2016 IEEE Symposium on Security and Privacy (SP), pp. 470–485 (2016)

20. de Ruiter, J., Poll, E.: Protocol state fuzzing of TLS implementations. In: 24th USENIX Security Symposium (USENIX Security 15), Washington, D.C., pp. 193–206. USENIX Association (2015)
21. Delignat-Lavaud, A., et al.: Implementing and proving the TLS 1.3 record layer. In: 2017 IEEE Symposium on Security and Privacy (SP), pp. 463–482 (2017)
22. Durumeric, Z., et al.: The matter of heartbleed. In: Proceedings of the 2014 Conference on Internet Measurement Conference, IMC '14, pp. 475–488. Association for Computing Machinery, New York (2014)
23. Goubault-Larrecq, J., Parrennes, F.: Cryptographic protocol analysis on real C code. In: Cousot, R. (ed.) Verification, Model Checking, and Abstract Interpretation, pp. 363–379. Springer, Heidelberg (2005)
24. Meier, S., Schmidt, B., Cremers, C., Basin, D.: The tamarin prover for the symbolic analysis of security protocols. In: Sharygina, N., Veith, H. (eds.) Computer Aided Verification, pp. 696–701. Springer, Heidelberg (2013)
25. Nasrabadi, F., Künnemann, R., Nemati, H.: CryptoBap: a binary analysis platform for cryptographic protocols. In: Proceedings of the 2023 ACM SIGSAC Conference on Computer and Communications Security, CCS '23, pp. 1362–1376. Association for Computing Machinery, New York (2023)
26. Pedrosa, L., Fogel, A., Kothari, N., Govindan, R., Mahajan, R., Millstein, T.: Analyzing protocol implementations for interoperability. In: 12th USENIX Symposium on Networked Systems Design and Implementation (NSDI 15), Oakland, CA, pp. 485–498. USENIX Association (2015)
27. Shoshitaishvili, Y., et al.: SoK: (state of) the art of war: offensive techniques in binary analysis. In: 2016 IEEE Symposium on Security and Privacy (SP), pp. 138–157 (2016)
28. Song, D., et al.: BitBlaze: a new approach to computer security via binary analysis. In: Sekar, R., Pujari, A.K. (eds.) Information Systems Security, pp. 1–25. Springer, Heidelberg (2008)
29. Sprenger, C., et al.: Igloo: soundly linking compositional refinement and separation logic for distributed system verification. Proc. ACM Program. Lang. **4**(OOPSLA) (2020)
30. Strejček, J., Trtík, M.: Abstracting path conditions. In: Proceedings of the 2012 International Symposium on Software Testing and Analysis, ISSTA 2012, pp. 155–165. Association for Computing Machinery, New York (2012)
31. Udrea, O., Lumezanu, C., Foster, J.S.: Rule-based static analysis of network protocol implementations. Inf. Comput. **206**(2), 130–157 (2008). Joint Workshop on Foundations of Computer Security and Automated Reasoning for Security Protocol Analysis (FCS-ARSPA '06)
32. Vanhoef, M., Piessens, F.: Symbolic execution of security protocol implementations: handling cryptographic primitives. In: 12th USENIX Workshop on Offensive Technologies (WOOT 18), Baltimore, MD. USENIX Association (2018)

Formal Verification of Browser Fingerprinting and Mitigation with Inlined Reference Monitors

Nathan Joslin(✉), Phu H. Phung, and Luan Viet Nguyen

Department of Computer Science, University of Dayton, Dayton, OH 45469, USA
{joslinn1,phu,lnguyen1}@udayton.edu

Abstract. Browser fingerprinting is a technique that identifies user devices by exploiting differences in software and hardware configurations. This technique is used in both benign applications, such as multi-factor authentication, and malicious ones, like web tracking and the disclosure of private information. Existing work has proposed various defense mechanisms against malicious browser fingerprinting and evaluated them using empirical experiments and analysis. While this approach demonstrates the effectiveness of mitigation methods, it does not provide proof of reliability. As browser fingerprinting research continues to advance and gain popularity across the web, there is an increasing need to verify the safety of user data and the reliability of protection mechanisms. In this paper, we develop formal models of both a browser fingerprinting tool and a controller capable of enforcing fingerprinting mitigation techniques. Specifically, we model an Inlined Reference Monitor for a canvas fingerprinter that intercepts JavaScript function calls and provides runtime policy enforcement. Our framework is highly extensible, allowing it to model a wide range of fingerprinting strategies and defenses. Using Computation Tree Logic, we formally define safety and liveness properties, demonstrating that our model successfully enforces key anti-fingerprinting techniques, such as randomization and API blocking.

Keywords: Formal Verification · Formalization · Browser Fingerprinting · Privacy · Security · Mitigation Techniques · UPPAAL

1 Introduction

In response to growing concerns over data privacy, many countries have begun updating legislation to meet the requirements of the digital age, with the European Union's General Data Protection Regulation (GDPR) and the ePrivacy directive being particularly influential [6,38]. These regulations require web pages to be more transparent on how and why they collect user data. The effect of these regulations is frequently seen in the form of consent pop-up windows for browser cookies [38]. The combination of increasing transparency and efforts put forth by regulatory bodies has led many users to decline the usage of browser

L. Horn Iwaya et al. (Eds.): NordSec 2024, LNCS 15396, pp. 303–321, 2025.
https://doi.org/10.1007/978-3-031-79007-2_16

cookies, which has driven cookie-based web trackers to explore alternatives, such as browser fingerprinting. Recent studies estimated that over 25% of the top 1,000 websites and nearly 10% of the top 100,000 use browser fingerprinting in some forms [17,35]. Browser fingerprinting presents significant challenges for web users seeking greater control over their digital footprint [40]. As a stateless mechanism, unlike cookies, browser fingerprints can be collected by web pages, allowing for the tracking of user activity without their knowledge or consent [20]. This method is particularly concerning because it even affects users who may not be uniquely identifiable, leaving them vulnerable to attacks that exploit software with known vulnerabilities [9]. Additionally, browser fingerprinting can lead to the exposure of sensitive information [19], the re-spawning of cookies after deletion [14], and even the identification of users through the linkage of fingerprints to social media accounts [20]. When used for involuntary tracking or unauthorized data collection, such practices clearly violate user privacy and can be deemed malicious.

However, it is important to recognize that browser fingerprinting also serves a protective role in certain contexts. For instance, it is increasingly used as an additional layer in multi-factor authentication schemes, particularly on login pages, where it helps safeguard users from fraud and phishing attacks [9,24, 35]. According to the United States Federal Trade Commission, this particular application has become increasingly important in recent years as online fraud and phishing attacks continue to grow, significantly contributing to the overall 14% increase in fraud between 2022 and 2023 [12]. Fingerprinting's utility in these scenarios is evident, as it is commonly employed on login and sign-up pages to enhance security and prevent unauthorized access [35]. Thus, while browser fingerprinting poses significant risks to user privacy, it also plays a crucial role in enhancing online security. The challenge lies in balancing these competing interests—ensuring fingerprinting is used responsibly to protect users without infringing on their privacy rights.

As a stateless tracking mechanism, it is challenging for average users not only to protect themselves from malicious actors but also to allow fingerprinting from trusted sources. Although some tools exist, e.g., fingerprint randomization in the Brave browser [36], there is still much work needed to increase the transparency, effectiveness, and, most importantly, reliability of anti-fingerprinting technologies. The first step to gaining control over browser fingerprinters is detection, as demonstrated in many studies with different proposed methods [1,11,17,18]. The second step is the design and empirical evaluation of mitigation methods, many of which have already been proven to be effective [2,7,20,25]. With extensive research conducted on these initial two steps, particularly in recent years, we are now well-positioned to shift our focus toward the next step: formalizing browser fingerprinting and its mitigation methods. This step allows researchers and developers alike to know the exact limitations and effectiveness of both fingerprinters and the defenses against them. A few works have proposed formal definitions of browser fingerprinting [4,21]. However, no prior work has built formal models or used formal methods to mathematically prove or verify the reliability of fingerprinters or the defenses against them.

In this paper, we develop formal models for a fingerprinting system and a corresponding defense mechanism using the formal modeling and verification framework UPPAAL [27]. Our approach involves defining three components: a fingerprinter, a server, and a controller, which together form a network of timed automata operating in parallel during the verification process [3]. The controller adopts the Inlined Reference Monitor (IRM) approach [10], which models the interception of functions executed by the fingerprinter at runtime. The IRM approach is particularly versatile, supporting the enforcement of several well-established fingerprinting mitigation strategies, including randomization, which introduces variability to fingerprinting data; normalization, which standardizes outputs to reduce uniqueness; and API blocking, which prevents unauthorized access to critical browser functions. We have designed our models to be extensible, providing a foundational framework that can be easily adapted to model more sophisticated fingerprinting techniques or advanced defense mechanisms. This extensibility is crucial, as it allows for the integration of future developments in both fingerprinting tactics and corresponding countermeasures.

We evaluate our model's effectiveness in enforcing these mitigation techniques by abstracting them into formally defined safety and liveness properties using Computation Tree Logic (CTL) [34]. Finally, through our formal evaluation using tools like UPPAAL, we aim to demonstrate the practical viability of our approach. Our results suggest that it is indeed possible to selectively allow or deny fingerprinting by domain as well as through more fine-grained policy enforcement depended on runtime factors; such as the methods used to fingerprint or how often the fingerprint is collected. This capability is particularly significant because it addresses an often overlooked aspect of existing anti-fingerprinting research: the need to balance security with usability. By enabling fine-grained control over which domains can perform fingerprinting, our model offers a more nuanced and practical solution to the challenges of browser fingerprinting in real-world applications. This work lays the groundwork for future research, which could explore more sophisticated fingerprinting techniques, further enhance the adaptability of the framework, and bridge the gap between theoretical models and practical implementation in web security. The models are available on Github[1].

2 Background and Related Work

2.1 Browser Fingerprinting

Modern web browsers provide significant information to the web pages they render, such as their configurations or the software running them. Individually, these pieces of information are often referred to as attributes and provide great value to the web pages that use them. Attributes as simple as a device's screen

[1] https://github.com/nathan-joslin/BrowserFingerprintingFormalization.

size allow web pages to properly format themselves to provide the best user experience for as many devices as possible. This aggregation of browser data is known as browser fingerprinting and has been proven to be able to uniquely identify browsers [9,20,24] and even track activity across the web [28,32,39,40].

Browser fingerprinters target attributes based on their potential entropy, or information gain, in an effort to yield a collision-resistant identifier. A fingerprint of one browser will differ from another as a result of variations in software and hardware configuration, such as installed fonts or the user agent [9,24]. More complex fingerprinters will introduce data-generating fingerprinting methods. Instead of simply collecting attributes, these methods generate unique data by running scripts[2] that exploit particular browser APIs. One of the most studied data-generating methods is canvas fingerprinting. Due to its prevalence in research, proven effectiveness [24,29], active use in both public and commercial libraries [37], and increased complexity compared to other methods, we choose to model a canvas fingerprinter to evaluate the effectiveness of mitigation methods. An example of a canvas fingerprint and the results of a simple mitigation method can be seen in Fig. 1.

Fig. 1. An example of a canvas fingerprint generated with amiunique.org [23]. The second image was subject to a simple implementation of a mitigation method known as canvas poisoning, which draws hashes of the current date and time randomly on the element.

2.2 Browser Fingerprinting Mitigation Approaches

Related work has demonstrated a variety of anti-fingerprinting mechanisms, which can be organized into three basic groups: normalization, randomization, and blocking [7]. First, the normalization technique takes a "hide in the crowd" approach. Also known as *attribute standardizing*, this method aims to reduce the entropy of fingerprints by setting attributes to a value shared among a sufficiently sized user base [7]. It is important to note that even minor deviations from the normalized user base can make users stand out more than they typically would without the technique. Not only has this method been shown to be effective [2,7], but it is also actively used by the Tor Browser [7,15]. The second well-known mitigation method is randomization. Also known as *attribute varying*, this method aims to create a "moving target" [7]. This technique will regularly change browser attributes or introduce noise to those that are generated in order

[2] Data generating fingerprinting scripts are often referred to as *challenges*.

to change the collected fingerprint. Random alterations to the data each time a fingerprint is collected make it increasingly difficult to track a user over time or across the web. Related works have shown that randomization is one of the most effective methods [24,26]. Finally, we have blocking techniques. Also known as *interaction blocking*, these methods block the execution of a particular API or interactions with particular third-party domains [7]. While some techniques block entire APIs, such as Tor blocking the canvas API [15], other techniques use partial or temporal API blocking [17]. This technique can be particularly aggressive, leading to frequent major and minor website breakage [17].

Many works have demonstrated the effectiveness of normalization, randomization, and blocking methods through empirical evaluation. While the contributions of these works are extremely valuable, they are limited in their ability to evaluate the reliability of these mitigation methods. As far as we know, few works have used formal methods in the domain of browser fingerprinting. In particular, two works have proposed formal definitions for browser fingerprinters with respect to their properties, such as uniqueness, robustness, or stability [4,21]. However, no work has used formal modeling and verification techniques to mathematically validate that defenses against fingerprinters behave as their empirical analyses show in all possible scenarios. The purpose of this work is to complement the aforementioned related works that perform empirical analyses by applying formal methods to the same mitigation techniques they propose.

2.3 Inlined Reference Monitors

Inlined Reference Monitors (IRMs) are a robust security mechanism that embeds runtime policy enforcement directly into applications, ensuring that execution adheres to predefined security policies [10]. By integrating policy checks within the code, IRMs can effectively regulate and modify behavior during runtime, making them particularly suitable for controlling JavaScript execution in web environments [31]. They operate by intercepting targeted JavaScript functions and enforcing actions as dictated by the specified security policies [16]. The versatility of IRMs extends beyond simple function interception. In more complex scenarios, it is necessary to monitor not only the initial function call but also the behavior of objects returned by these functions. This layered monitoring capability allows IRMs to adapt to dynamic and evolving threats by providing fine-grained control over both the inputs and outputs of function calls. The context-aware nature of IRMs—gained through runtime interception enables the enforcement of nuanced, fine-grained security policies that can account for the specific parameters and conditions of each function call [13].

These capabilities make IRMs highly effective in implementing well-known browser fingerprinting mitigation strategies such as normalization, randomization, or API blocking. In the cases of normalization or randomization, such a controller is able to modify the output of the function it intercepts, thereby standardizing or adding noise to the output value. In cases of API blocking, the controller is able to return an empty or nil value to prohibit the caller from further working with the output value, perhaps even throwing an error. Their ability to enforce all three mitigation methods highlights their suitability as a core component of our proposed controller model.

3 System Modeling

3.1 UPPAAL and Timed Automata

UPPAAL is a tool for automatically verifying system requirements specified as temporal logic, such as CTL. It provides a framework for modeling, simulating, and verifying real-time systems, where the correctness of the system is essential for ensuring reliability and safety [8,27]. The system in question is represented as a network of finite-state machines extended with real-valued clocks, a formalism known as timed automata, which allows for the modeling of systems where timing constraints are critical [5,27]. Each component of a timed automaton is characterized by a set of locations (representing states), an initial location, location invariants (conditions that must hold as long as the system remains in a particular location), a set of clocks (real-valued variables that progress uniformly), a set of actions (events that trigger transitions), and edges (transitions) between locations, each labeled with actions. These elements collectively define the dynamic behavior of the system, including how the system evolves over time and how it responds to various events.

In UPPAAL, the model is composed of one or more timed automata running in parallel, synchronized through channels or shared variables. This parallel composition enables the modeling of complex systems, where multiple components operate concurrently while adhering to strict timing constraints. The global state of the system is determined by the combined states of all automata and the values of global variables, with transitions occurring according to the rules defined by the automata and the constraints imposed by the clocks. In this work, we leverage UPPAAL as a framework for modeling and verifying a browser fingerprinting system along with its associated safety and liveness requirements, expressed as CTL formulas. In the following sections, we will provide a detailed presentation of the proposed formal model using UPPAAL.

3.2 System Overview

In this section, we provide a comprehensive overview of our system, which effectively models a fingerprinting attack and an Inlined Reference Monitor (IRM) enforcing defense mechanisms. The defined system has three main components: a **Fingerprinter**[3], a **Controller**, and a **Server**. Components communicate with one another using designated synchronization channels over state transitions. To model the **Controller** as an IRM, the **Fingerprinter** component is instrumented with a channel synchronization and corresponding state invariant for each monitored function while the **Controller** listens to those same channels in parallel. These channels are optionally instrumented with corresponding shared

[3] System components are emphasized in **bold**.

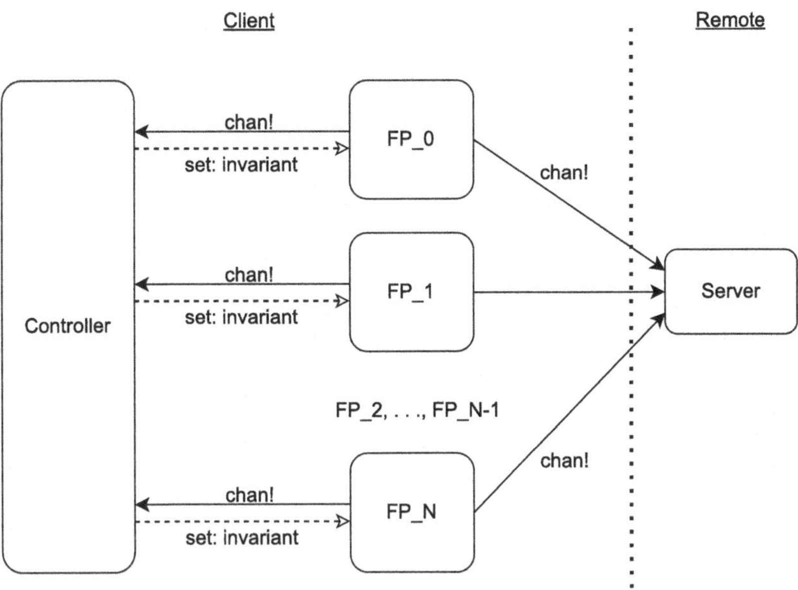

Fig. 2. Overview of communication between components. Unique synchronization channels, with corresponding state invariants, are defined for all functions monitored by the **Controller** for each **Fingerprinter**, with additional channels for submitting data to the **Server**. As such, for any system configuration, the total number of channels is defined by $f(x, y) = xy + y$; where x is the number of functions monitored by the **Controller** and y is the number of **Fingerprinter** components.

variables that represent the context around the function call, such as parameters. With this approach, the total number of active channels is determined by the abstracted functions the **Controller** monitors as well as how many **Fingerprinter** components are in the declared system. By defining a unique set of channels for each **Fingerprinter**, the system is able to model an IRM that's capable of enforcing policies on a per-component basis. Likewise, we define unique location invariants for the **Fingerprinter** to complement the unique set of channels. This completes the instrumentation of the **Fingerprinter** to support the IRM approach. As such, components may model a specific domain running a script or actions on a particular JavaScript object. This aspect of the design is crucial in giving the template the flexibility to support a wide variety of fingerprinting schemes as well as defense mechanisms. More information on how each component behaves during synchronizations on state transitions is described in detail in subsequent sections. The full implementation of our models is available on Github[4].

[4] https://github.com/nathan-joslin/BrowserFingerprintingFormalization.

3.3 Modeling the Fingerprinter

The **Fingerprinter** component is an abstraction of a fingerprinting technique created through static analysis of multiple scripts to identify similarities in API usage. Due to the vast scope of browser fingerprinting, we focus on one of the more complex techniques - dynamic data generation. In particular, we abstract a well-known method that exploits the widely available canvas API [20,22,29]. Although we only provide a model of a canvas fingerprinter, analogous approaches may be used for other data-generating methods, such as `AudioContext` fingerprinting [33], or even more trivial methods that simply aggregate data rather than generate it [9,20,40]. By modeling one of the more complex methods while considering extensibility, our goal is to design a system that can serve as a template for modeling entire fingerprinting schemes with the ability to evaluate a broad range of fingerprinting defenses. At a minimum, the system has a single **Fingerprinter** component; however, it easily scales to handle multiple ones.

We analyzed two implementations of canvas fingerprinters to base our model on, one from a real-world application and the other from related research. The first is from the widely used and open-sourced browser fingerprinting library `fingerprintjs2` [37], which provides a wide variety of fingerprinting functions allowing developers to easily integrate browser fingerprinting methods into the functionality of their websites. The second is from related work done by Laperdrix et al. [22,24], who push the limits of what canvas fingerprinting is capable of through rigorous analysis and experimentation.

The **Fingerprinter** component, depicted in Fig. 3b, models the main steps taken by canvas fingerprinting algorithms. The steps include creating a canvas element, getting the canvas context, drawing on the context, collecting the fingerprint value, and finally sending the value to a database. Within our model, these main steps are represented by the following locations respectively: *Create*[5], *Context*, *FillText*, *Collect*, and *Send*. As the automata is an abstraction of a running script, it follows the edges leading into each state model function execution, with the states themselves modeling the successful completion of the function call. Most of the modeled functions are only executed once, with the exception of drawing on the canvas context, which is the expected behavior of a well-written script. The remaining locations and transitions are added instrumentation to allow a wider variety of simulations that may require singular or repetitive fingerprinting. This particular mechanism is useful for evaluating the behavior of fingerprinting defenses over time; such as mitigation through randomization, which aims to ensure the fingerprint value is different each run. As mentioned previously, the channel synchronizations on state transitions are added instrumentation to model the **Controller** as an IRM; which is discussed further in the next section. Finally, the majority of locations of the **Fingerprinter** include timing constraints to support the verification of liveness properties.

[5] Locations of system components are emphasized in *italics*.

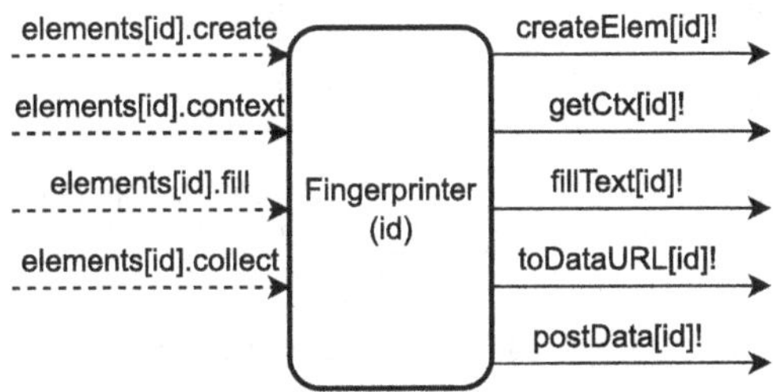

(a) **Fingerprinter Component**

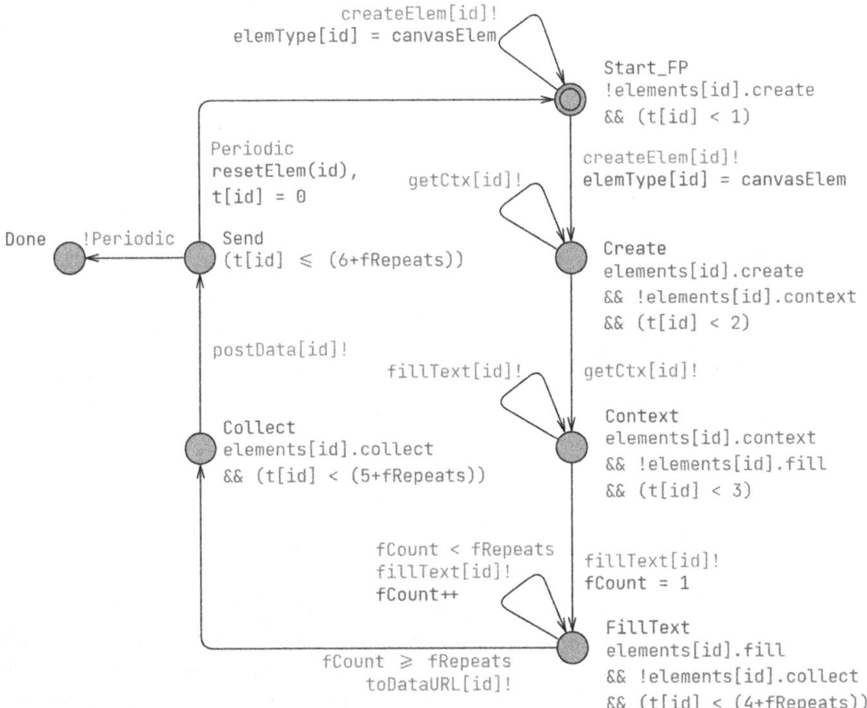

(b) **Fingerprinter Automata**

Fig. 3. The **Fingerprinter** models a running canvas fingerprinting script. The main transitions, see right and bottom, synchronize with the **Controller** via designated channels for each function. The invariants on transition destination states are managed by the **Controller**, which allows or denies particular actions based on the policy configuration. The remaining transitions, see left and top, post the data to the server and either terminate or reset the component.

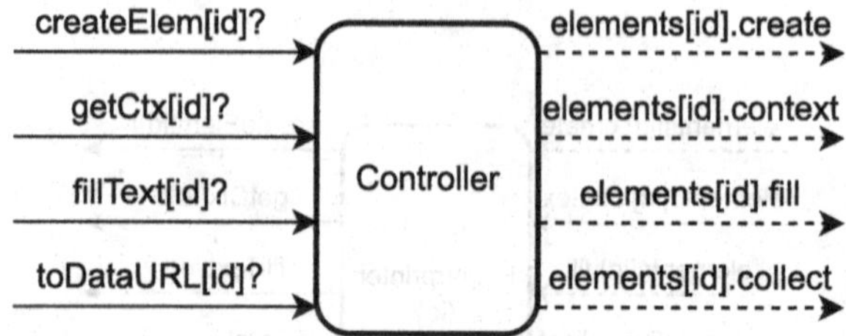

(a) **Controller Component**

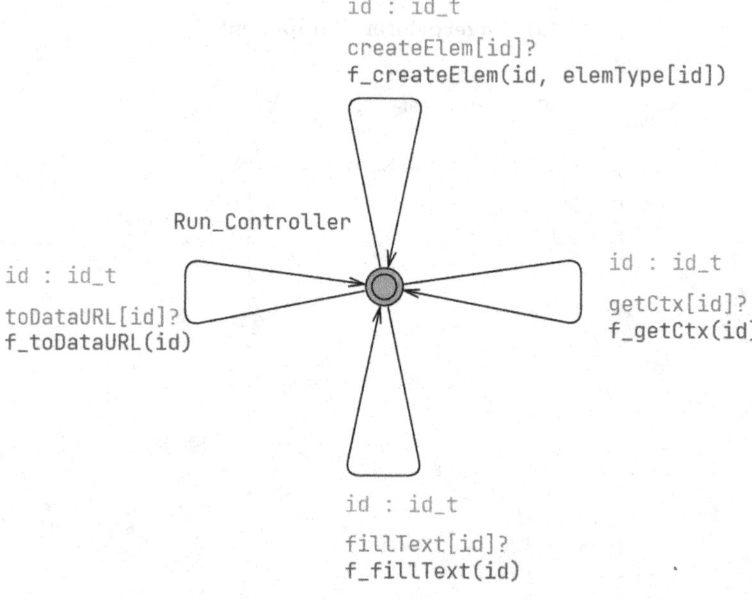

(b) **Controller Automata**

Fig. 4. The **Controller** models a running Inlined Reference Monitor actively intercepting the function calls it observes. Each transition is synchronized with a sending **Fingerprinter**, with the update functions performing the policy evaluation. Internally, the policy evaluation will set the appropriate sending **Fingerprinter** state invariant.

3.4 Modeling the Controller

The **Controller** abstracts an IRM running in a client's browser. The system always has a single **Controller** as we aim to model the fingerprinting of one client. We find this to be sufficient as the purpose of this work is to formally verify the defense mechanisms themselves, discussed in Sect. 2.2, not the effects they have on an entire fingerprinting scheme. Such an endeavor may require modeling hundreds of thousands, if not millions, of clients at the same time; which current formal verification tools are not equipped to handle. We refer readers to empirical analyses in related work for more information [7,25,26]. Furthermore, it follows that the behavior and capabilities of the same controller on different clients would be identical.

As previously mentioned, the **Fingerprinter** is instrumented with channel synchronizations and state invariants for each monitored function. This allows us to accurately model the behavior of an active IRM. The **Controller** listens to this set of channels, and upon receiving a channel synchronization, it evaluates some arbitrary set of policies that determine if the monitored function is allowed to be called. During this evaluation time, the **Controller** can take a variety of actions to support more fine-gained approaches other than simply allowing or blocking, such as calling the original function and then modifying the data returned by it before returning to the **Fingerprinter**. Ultimately, the **Controller** appropriately sets the **Fingerprinter's** corresponding state invariant, either allowing it to continue to the next state or preventing it. We note that based on the purpose of the **Controller** to immediately react to actions taken by the **Fingerprinters**, as reflected by the synchronization channels and invariant controls, it follows that we do not instrument it with timing constraints. Finally, Table 1 displays the Controller Transition Update Functions. These functions are invoked when channel synchronizations are initiated by the **Fingerprinter** and received by the **Controller**. The update functions evaluate the relevant policies and set the appropriate invariants for the sending **Fingerprinter**.

Table 1. Controller Transition Update Functions. Update functions are called when the channel synchronizations are sent by a **Fingerprinter** and received by the **Controller**. The related policies are evaluated by the update functions, which ultimately set the invariants for the sending **Fingerprinter** appropriately.

Function	Meaning	Policies	Invariant
f_createElem	Create a DOM element	p_createElement	create
f_getCtx	Get canvas' drawing context	p_getCtx	context
f_fillText	Generate data by drawing on canvas context	p_fillText	fill
f_toDataURL	Collect fingerprint value	p_poison p_toDataURL	collect

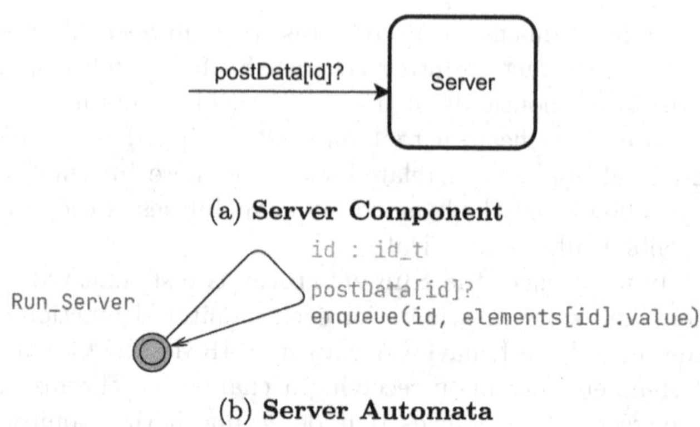

(a) **Server Component**

(b) **Server Automata**

Fig. 5. The **Server** models a remote server receiving fingerprint values. Upon receiving a channel synchronization from a **Fingerprinter**, the **Server** will read and store the fingerprint data from a shared variable.

3.5 Modeling the Server

The **Server** abstracts a remote server and database as a singular component. Although separate server and database components would be a more accurate representation of a real-world system, we choose to combine the two as an evaluation of the remote subsystems is not within the scope of this paper. Similarly, we do not include support for **Server** responses to the **Fingerprinter**. In doing so, we still fulfill the purpose of this component, instrumenting our model to enable the evaluation of fingerprint attributes' values over time while reducing the state space of our model.

The **Server** component, depicted in Fig. 5, models the storing of fingerprint data in a remote location. The **Server** blocks until it receives a channel synchronization from any **Fingerprinter**, subsequently storing the **Fingerprinter**'s attribute value in an underlying database. To further reduce state space, the underlying database is equipped with a configurable capacity. Upon submission of fingerprint data when at capacity the **Server** will remove the oldest value before storing the new one.

4 Verification Regarding Unsafe Regions

In this section, we discuss and evaluate several requirements that a client may have when looking to defend against browser fingerprinting attacks. We will first discuss these requirements informally, then translate them into formal safety properties, and finally utilize UPPAAL's simulation and verification tools to evaluate our model. It is important to note that we have chosen the following system setup and configuration to illustrate the capabilities of our model; however, it can easily be extended to handle more components or more complex requirements.

Table 2. Informal System Requirements. The evaluated system's policy configuration expressed as a set of informal requirements.

Component	Requirement	Mitigation Method
FP_0	Allow fingerprints to be freely collected, without intervention.	None
FP_1	Allow fingerprints to be collected, but poison its data.	Randomization
FP_2	Do not allow fingerprints to be collected whatsoever.	API Blocking

4.1 Informal Requirements and Policy Configuration

The following requirements, shown in Table 2, aim to evaluate the capability of our model to enforce well-known browser fingerprinting mitigation methods, in particular randomization and API blocking. Note that although we do not model the normalization technique, the enforcement mechanism itself remains the same as randomization; however, instead of adding noise to the attribute value, it would simply be set to a standard one. It follows that an evaluation of our model's capability to enforce the randomization method transfers over to normalization. Note that we do not evaluate the necessary amount of noise to add when randomizing values or the proper value to spoof when normalizing. Such an endeavor is not possible with current formal verification tools due to the state space expansion that results from modeling a sufficiently sized user base. We refer the reader to empirical analyses from related works for more information [9,24, 29,40]. Furthermore, we evaluate our models ability to simultaneously mitigate attacks from some components while allowing it from others.

In Table 2, the first requirement does not mitigate at all, instead allowing the fingerprinting to occur as if the **Controller** was not there. This serves to demonstrate the system's ability to permit fingerprinters from one domain while simultaneously preventing it from others. The second requirement uses a randomization mitigation approach, which takes the form of adding noise to the fingerprint attribute data each time it is collected. As such the fingerprint attribute values between two different collection attempts should never be the same; or at minimum distinct enough to thwart a tracking system. The final requirement uses a blocking approach, which completely prevents the data collection from happening. The formal safety and liveness properties that verify these requirements are defined in Table 4, which will be introduced later.

4.2 Verifying Formal Safety and Liveness Properties

To formally evaluate all three requirements at once, we first directly translate the requirements into a well-defined policy configuration, which is set up to control each **Fingerprinter** in a separate fashion. The policy configuration is comprised of a set of lists, with individual lists configured as an `allowlist` or `blocklist`. We chose this approach to support extensions to our model that aim to evaluate more complex requirements. The resulting configuration, depicted in Table 3, instructs the controller to allow fingerprinting from **FP_0**, randomize the fingerprint of **FP_1**, and completely block the collection of data by **FP_2**. In

Table 3. Policy Configuration. The system's policy configuration adheres to the requirements in Table 2. Policies are implemented as allowlists or blocklists, and are evaluated by the **Controller** during function call interception. Table 1 outlines which policies are evaluated by which function calls.

Policy	Type	FP_0	FP_1	FP_2
p_createElem	blocklist	false	false	false
p_getCtx	blocklist	false	false	false
p_fillText	blocklist	false	false	false
p_toDataURL	blocklist	false	false	*true*
p_poison	allowlist	*true*	false	false

this configuration, all policies are allowed by default except for *p_poison*, which is blocked by default, reflecting the outlined requirements.

Now that the system is setup to enforce our defined requirements, we may begin our formal evaluation. We will perform our verification through the use of safety and liveness properties expressed using Computation Tree Logic (CTL), which are depicted in in Table 4. The first requirement states that component **FP_0** should be allowed to fingerprint the client. We construct safety property A that ensures the fingerprint attribute value of **FP_0** is *never* poisoned and is able to be collected. The second requirement states that component **FP_1** should be allowed to fingerprint the client but the fingerprint attribute value should be poisoned. We construct safety property B that ensures the fingerprint attribute value of **FP_1** is *always* poisoned and is able to be collected. Finally, the third requirement states that component **FP_2** should not be allowed to collect the client's fingerprint data. We construct safety properties C and D that ensure component **FP_2** is never able to collect the fingerprint attribute value; two methods of expressing the same property. By using UPPAAL's verifier, we confirm that our model satisfies all four of the aforementioned safety properties.

We then extend our safety evaluation with a set of reachability and liveness properties. Properties F, G, and H further verify the three requirements respectively by ensuring the components are able to reach the locations their intended to. It follows that property F complements A, G complements B, while property H complements properties C and D. As expected, property H is not satisfied since **FP_2** is blocked from collecting the fingerprint value, i.e. it cannot reach the *Collect* location. Finally, the liveness properties I and J ensure randomization is correctly applied. As expected, property J is not satisfied due to the enforcement of randomization.

Note that as we utilize UPPAAL to verify a network of timed automata, our approach inherits the verification complexity of UPPAAL when checking the system against Computation Tree Logic (CTL) requirements. The time complexity of UPPAAL's verification algorithm is exponential in the number of clocks and variables within the timed automata network, as it relies on symbolic model checking techniques [8,27].

Table 4. Safety properties (*A*-*E*) and liveness properties (*F*-*J*) that reflect the requirements outlined in Table 2. These properties are used to evaluate our system's ability to reliably enforce well-known fingerprinting mitigation methods, namely randomization and API blocking. The **Sat.** column indicates whether or not a property is satisfied. By design, some properties should not be satisfied to validate the expected effects of mitigation methods.

Prop.	Sat.	Format	Value
A	true	CTL	`A[] FP_0.Collect imply (elements[0].value > 0)`
		Meaning	For all reachable states, component **FP_0** being in the location *Collect* implies that its attribute value is not poisoned.
B	true	CTL	`A[] FP_1.Collect imply (elements[1].value < 0)`
		Meaning	For all reachable states, component **FP_1** being in the location *Collect* implies that its attribute value is poisoned.
C	true	CTL	`A[ ] FP_2.Collect imply evalPolicy(p_toDataURL, 2)`
		Meaning	For all reachable states, component **FP_2** being in the location *Collect* implies the policy configuration allows it, i.e. the attribute data is allowed to be collected.
D	true	CTL	`A[ ] !FP_2.Collect`
		Meaning	For all reachable states, component **FP_2** is never in the *Collect* location.
E	true	CTL	`A[ ] Server.db[2].len == 0`
		Meaning	For all reachable states, the server does not store any values for **FP_2**.
F	true	CTL	`E<> FP_0.Collect`
		Meaning	The *Collect* location is reachable in the **FP_0** component.
G	true	CTL	`E<> FP_1.Collect`
		Meaning	The *Collect* location is reachable in the **FP_1** component.
H	false	CTL	`E<> FP_2.Collect`
		Meaning	The *Collect* location is *not* reachable in the **FP_2** component.
I	true	CTL	`A<> ((Sever.db[0].len > 0) && (Server.db[0].entries[0] == Server.db[0].entries[1]) && (Server.db[0].entries[1] == Server.db[0].entries[2]))`
		Meaning	Eventually all database entries for **FP_0** are the same.
J	false	CTL	`A<> ((Server.db[1].len > 0) && (Server.db[1].entries[0] == Server.db[1].entries[1]) && (Server.db[1].entries[1] == Server.db[1].entries[2]))`
		Meaning	Eventually all database entries for **FP_1** are the same.

5 Conclusion and Future Work

In this paper, we modeled a canvas-based browser fingerprinter and an Inlined Reference Monitor (IRM) using timed automata. To evaluate our models, we first defined a set of requirements reflecting well-known fingerprinting mitigation methods. We then used Computation Tree Logic (CTL) to formally express these requirements as well-defined liveness and safety properties. Using the formal verification tool UPPAAL, we assessed our model's behavior against these properties. Our evaluation confirmed that the model effectively enforces several widely recognized mitigation strategies for browser fingerprinting, including randomization, normalization, and API blocking. This result demonstrates that policy enforcement through an IRM is a robust and reliable method for defending against browser fingerprinting attacks. Furthermore, we showed that fine-grained policies can selectively allow fingerprinting from trusted domains while preventing it from malicious ones.

In real-world applications, browser fingerprints are typically constructed using multiple attributes; however, our focus was exclusively on a single canvas-based attribute. Despite the inherent complexity of data-generating fingerprinters, we successfully designed a foundational model that also considers similar, more straightforward fingerprinting techniques. This allowed us to create and verify a flexible framework that is readily extensible to model more comprehensive fingerprinting methods, a task we have reserved for future work. Furthermore, as part of future work, we plan to develop a comprehensive formal model of a real-world browser fingerprinter which includes a variety of fingerprint attributes. Since a comprehensive formal model is beyond the scope of the current study, we also do not provide an attack model at this stage. Such an endeavor should address key questions regarding the minimal mitigation steps necessary to prevent fingerprinting attacks. For instance, it is crucial to determine how many fingerprint attributes need to be randomized to effectively protect the user, as well as to ensure that sensitive information does not leak to untrusted domains through unintended information flows, as explored in [30]. Finally, we see significant potential in automating the translation of a verified system into practical applications. Future research could involve developing code-generation scripts that produce JavaScript for web applications, thereby bridging the gap between anti-fingerprinting research and its real-world implementation.

Acknowledgements. This work received partial support from the Ohio Department of Higher Education (ODHE) through the Strategic Ohio Council for Higher Education (SOCHE) and Ohio Cyber Range Institute (OCRI) sub-awards and from the National Science Foundation (NSF) grant NSF-CRII-2245853. We would like to extend our appreciation to the anonymous reviewers for their valuable feedback.

Disclosure of Interests. The author have no competing interests to declare that are relevant to the content of this article.

References

1. Acar, G., Juarez, M., Nikiforakis, N., Diaz, C., Gürses, S., Piessens, F., Preneel, B.: Fpdetective: dusting the web for fingerprinters. In: Proceedings of the 2013 ACM SIGSAC Conference on Computer and Communications Security,CCS 2013, pp. 1129-1140. Association for Computing Machinery, New York, NY, USA (2013). https://doi.org/10.1145/2508859.2516674
2. Ajay, V.L., Guptha, A.M.: A defense against javascript object-based fingerprinting and passive fingerprinting. In: 2022 International Conference on Computing, Communication, Security and Intelligent Systems (IC3SIS), pp. 1–6. IEEE (2022)
3. Alur, R., Dill, D.L.: A theory of timed automata. Theoret. Comput. Sci. **126**(2), 183–235 (1994)
4. Andriamilanto, N., Allard, T., Le Guelvouit, G., Garel, A.: A large-scale empirical analysis of browser fingerprints properties for web authentication. ACM Trans. Web (TWEB) **16**(1), 1–62 (2021)
5. Behrmann, G., David, A., Larsen, K.G.: A tutorial on uppaal. Formal Methods Des. Real-Time Syst. 200–236 (2004)
6. Commission, E.: Principles of the gdpr. https://commission.europa.eu/law/law-topic/data-protection/reform/rules-business-and-organisations/principles-gdpr (2024), Accessed 29 Sep 2024
7. Datta, A., Lu, J., Tschantz, M.C.: Evaluating anti-fingerprinting privacy enhancing technologies. In: The World Wide Web Conference, pp. 351–362 (2019)
8. David, A., Du, D., Larsen, K.G., Legay, A., Nyman, U., Poulsen, D.B.: Uppaal SMC tutorial. Int. J. Softw. Tools Technol. Transfer **17**(4), 397–415 (2015)
9. Eckersley, P.: How unique is your web browser? In: International Symposium on Privacy Enhancing Technologies Symposium, pp. 1–18. Springer (2010)
10. Erlingsson, U.: The inlined reference monitor approach to security policy enforcement. Ph.D. thesis, Cornell University, USA (2004), aAI3114521
11. Fang, Y., Huang, C., Zeng, M., Zhao, Z., Huang, C.: Jstrong: malicious javascript detection based on code semantic representation and graph neural network. Comput. Secur. **118**, 102715 (2022)
12. Federal trade commission: as nationwide fraud losses top $10 billion in 2023, FTC steps up efforts to protect the public. https://www.ftc.gov/news-events/news/press-releases/2024/02/nationwide-fraud-losses-top-10-billion-2023-ftc-steps-efforts-protect-public, February 2024, Accessed 29 Sep 2024
13. Foster, J.S., Terauchi, T., Aiken, A.: Flow-sensitive type qualifiers. In: Proceedings of the ACM SIGPLAN 2002 Conference on Programming Language Design and Implementation, pp. 1–12. ACM (2006)
14. Fouad, I., Santos, C., Legout, A., Bielova, N.: Did I delete my cookies? cookies respawning with browser fingerprinting. CoRR **abs/2105.04381** (2021), https://arxiv.org/abs/2105.04381
15. Gk: browser fingerprinting: an introduction and the challenges ahead: Tor project, September 2019, https://blog.torproject.org/browser-fingerprinting-introduction-and-challenges-ahead/
16. Hiremath, P.N., Armentrout, J., Vu, S., Nguyen, T.N., Minh, Q.T., Phung, P.H.: Mywebguard: toward a user-oriented tool for security and privacy protection on the web. In: Dang, T.K., Küng, J., Takizawa, M., Bui, S.H. (eds.) Future Data and Security Engineering, pp. 506–525. Springer, Cham (2019)
17. Iqbal, U., Englehardt, S., Shafiq, Z.: Fingerprinting the fingerprinters: learning to detect browser fingerprinting behaviors. In: 2021 IEEE Symposium on Security and Privacy (SP), pp. 1143–1161. IEEE (2021)

18. Iqbal, U., Snyder, P., Zhu, S., Livshits, B., Qian, Z., Shafiq, Z.: Adgraph: a graph-based approach to ad and tracker blocking. In: 2020 IEEE Symposium on Security and Privacy (SP), pp. 763–776. IEEE (2020)
19. Karami, S., Ilia, P., Solomos, K., Polakis, J.: Carnus: exploring the privacy threats of browser extension fingerprinting. In: Proceedings of the 27th Network and Distributed System Security Symposium (NDSS) (2020)
20. Khademi, A.F., Zulkernine, M., Weldemariam, K.: An empirical evaluation of web-based fingerprinting. IEEE Softw. **32**(4), 46–52 (2015)
21. Lanze, F., Panchenko, A., Engel, T.: A formalization of fingerprinting techniques. In: 2015 IEEE Trustcom/BigDataSE/ISPA, vol. 1, pp. 818–825. IEEE (2015)
22. Laperdrix, P.: Morellian analysis for browsers (2019). https://github.com/plaperdr/morellian-canvas
23. Laperdrix, P.: Learn how identifiable you are on the internet (2024). https://amiunique.org/
24. Laperdrix, P., Avoine, G., Baudry, B., Nikiforakis, N.: Morellian analysis for browsers: Making web authentication stronger with canvas fingerprinting. In: International Conference on Detection of Intrusions and Malware, and Vulnerability Assessment, pp. 43–66. Springer (2019)
25. Laperdrix, P., Bielova, N., Baudry, B., Avoine, G.: Browser fingerprinting: a survey. ACM Trans. Web **14**(2) (2020). https://doi.org/10.1145/3386040
26. Laperdrix, P., Rudametkin, W., Baudry, B.: Mitigating browser fingerprint tracking: multi-level reconfiguration and diversification. In: 2015 IEEE/ACM 10th International Symposium on Software Engineering for Adaptive and Self-Managing Systems, pp. 98–108. IEEE (2015)
27. Larsen, K.G., Pettersson, P., Yi, W.: Uppaal in a nutshell. In: International Journal on Software Tools for Technology Transfer, vol. 1, pp. 134–152. Springer (1997)
28. Li, S., Cao, Y.: Who touched my browser fingerprint? a large-scale measurement study and classification of fingerprint dynamics. In: Proceedings of the ACM Internet Measurement Conference, pp. 370–385 (2020)
29. Mowery, K., Shacham, H.: Pixel perfect: fingerprinting canvas in html5. In: Proceedings of W2SP, vol. 2012 (2012)
30. Nguyen, L.V., Mohan, G., Weimer, J., Sokolsky, O., Lee, I., Alur, R.: Detecting security leaks in hybrid systems with information flow analysis. In: Proceedings of the 17th ACM-IEEE International Conference on Formal Methods and Models for System Design, pp. 1–11 (2019)
31. Phung, P.H., Sands, D., Chudnov, A.: Lightweight self-protecting javascript. In: Proceedings of the 4th International Symposium on Information, Computer, and Communications Security, pp. 47–60 (2009)
32. Pugliese, G., Riess, C., Gassmann, F., Benenson, Z.: Long-term observation on browser fingerprinting: users' trackability and perspective. Proc. Priv. Enhancing Technol. **2020**(2), 558–577 (2020)
33. Queiroz, J.S., Feitosa, E.L.: A web browser fingerprinting method based on the web audio API. Comput. J. **62**(8), 1106–1120 (2019)
34. Reynolds, M.: An axiomatization of full computation tree logic. J. Symbol. Logic **66**(3), 1011–1057 (2001)
35. Senol, A., Ukani, A., Cutler, D., Bilogrevic, I.: The double edged sword: identifying authentication pages and their fingerprinting behavior. In: The Web Conference (WWW), vol. 2024 (2024)
36. Team, B.P.: Fingerprint randomization, June 2020. https://brave.com/privacy-updates/3-fingerprint-randomization/

37. Team, F.: Fingerprintjs. https://github.com/fingerprintjs/fingerprintjs (2024). Accessed 29 Sep 2024
38. UNION, E.: Directive 2009/136/ec of the European parliament and of the council. Official J. Eur. Union **337**, 11 (2009)
39. Vastel, A., Laperdrix, P., Rudametkin, W., Rouvoy, R.: Fp-stalker: tracking browser fingerprint evolutions. In: 2018 IEEE Symposium on Security and Privacy (SP), pp. 728–741. IEEE (2018)
40. Zhang, D., Zhang, J., Bu, Y., Chen, B., Sun, C., Wang, T., et al.: A survey of browser fingerprint research and application. Wirel. Commun. Mob. Comput. **2022** (2022)

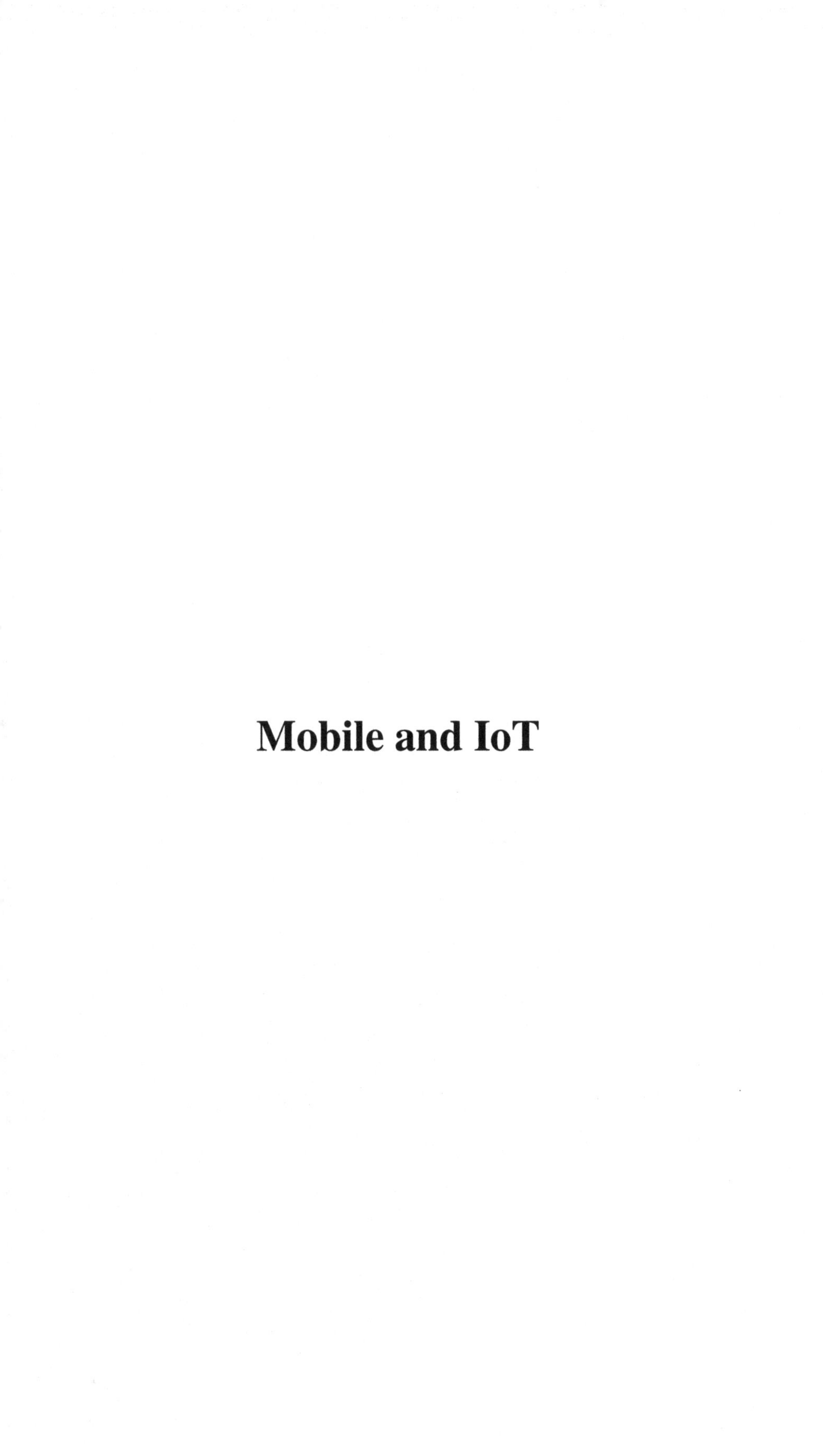

Mobile and IoT

Beware of the Rabbit Hole – A Digital Forensic Case Study of DIY Drones

Samantha Klier(✉) and Harald Baier

Research Institute CODE, University of the Bundeswehr Munich, Neubiberg, Germany
{samantha.klier,harald.baier}@unibw.de
https://unibw.de/digfor

Abstract. In the past years, Unmanned Aerial Vehicles (UAVs), commonly known as drones, have drawn attention for commercial, military and private use and thus emerged as a significant source of digital evidence. As of today both the research community and commercial software manufacturer focus on UAV mainstream brands such as DJI, which holds a market share of roughly 80% of the civil market. On the other side Do-It-Yourself (DIY) drones are well suited for unconventional and illegal activities due to their technical capabilities and the legal limitations of commercial drones. However, the community currently lacks research of the examination of DIY drones. In this paper we address this research gap by conducting a comprehensive case study of a sample DIY drone. Our case study comprises both the assembly *and* the digital forensic perspective of DIY drones. Our systematic digital forensic examination within our case study follows the well-known process steps, i.e. preparation, acquisition, analysis. We provide insights into the peculiarities of each step and reveal that the identification of the hardware components and the corresponding examination is the most critical step.

Keywords: UAV Forensics · UAS Forensics · DIY drone · Drone Forensics

1 Introduction

In the present era, Unmanned Aerial Vehicles (UAVs), colloquially known as drones, have become a ubiquitous form of digital evidence. A plethora of research has been conducted on this subject and a multitude of commercial software solutions are available to facilitate the accessibility of digital drone evidence. However, it is notable that the majority of drone forensics research and practice has been concentrated on the Chinese manufacturer DJI, which has indisputably secured the status of market leader with a market share of roughly 80% in the civil area [21].

While the focus on DJI is comprehensible, the construction of Do-It-Yourself (DIY) drones offers distinctive advantages if the user's intentions extend beyond

L. Horn Iwaya et al. (Eds.): NordSec 2024, LNCS 15396, pp. 325–344, 2025.
https://doi.org/10.1007/978-3-031-79007-2_17

the boundaries of legality or typical use cases. As an illustration, DIY drones are extensively used in the Russian-Ukrainian War [3,26] due to their individual configurable compilation. Despite representing a niche area within the broader market, there is now (i) a vast array of components that are readily available and (ii) an active community[1] that provides detailed construction guides and support for anyone who is interested in the assembly of a DIY drone. Consequently, any individual with a technical inclination can construct his own drone today.

Despite their potential and active military use, research on DIY drones from a forensics perspective is almost entirely absent. To address this research gap, we conduct a case study on a self-crafted DIY drone with the objective to run through the entire digital forensic process and to derive a tested procedure and toolchain.

More precisely the contributions of our case study are as follows: we review the diverse universe of hardware and software of DIY drones and point to legal aspects in this scope. We then present a methodology, which comprises two perspectives, i.e. the assembly *and* the digital forensic perspective of DIY drones with a focus on data generation. In the latter, we propose four representative scenarios including both standard scenarios and unexpected signal loss.

As a key result we present and discuss the examination results with respect to the different modules of our case study DIY UAV. First our comprehensive hardware examination reveals eight USB interfaces, some of which are concealed, as well as two external and five internal data carriers. We present details of the respective acquisition process. Second our analysis of the camera data reveals that videos are recorded both on the sending and the receiving end point. Furthermore, we provide instructions to repair recordings that were truncated due to signal loss and interpret the timestamps and file names. Finally an analysis of the remote control shows that in our case it holds only limited data, namely the SSID of the connected WiFi and some timestamps. However, under different premises, telemetry or flight logs may be found.

The rest of the paper is organised as follows: after this introduction we present the related work (being mostly case studies on DJI drones) and important background information on regulation in Sect. 2. Then we gather key aspects of the world of DIY drones in Sect. 3, with an emphasis on the technical potential of DIY drones when legal limitations are disregarded. We introduce our methodology in Sect. 4 followed by the in-depth examination and discussion of our sample DIY drone including all components in Sects. 5 to 8. Finally, we conclude our paper in Sect. 9 and point to future work.

2 Background and Related Work

To ensure clarity and consistency, this section first outlines the terminology relevant to this work. Subsequently, it examines seminal works on commercial drones and drone forensics, providing a useful context for this study.

[1] For example https://oscarliang.com/.

2.1 UAS or UAV

When we refer to an Unmanned Aircraft System (UAS), we mean the system of Unmanned Aerial Vehicle (UAV) extended by the equipment used alongside, such as a Radio Control (RC) and First Person View (FPV) goggles, in accordance with the definition of Commission of European Union [4]. Furthermore, the term UAV includes, as the name implies, any kind of *Unmanned Aerial Vehicle*, not just the most recognized copter types, but also e.g. wing types.

2.2 Related Work

UAS forensics is a rather new sub-discipline of digital forensics, as one of the first papers in that field was published just in 2016 [9]. The main goals include the extraction of flight paths and media recorded. Right now, the discipline is primarily based on case studies of selected drone models, primarily from the market leader DJI [2,10,19,20,27,28]. Here, the main forensic challenge are proprietary constraints and data formats, as well, as encryption, which are not an issue when handling a basic DIY UAS (see Sect. 5). However, when these challenges are overcome, DJI UAS are known for their accurate and exuberant data recordings, even among other commercial UAS manufacturers [12].

Despite that, to the best of our knowledge, only one paper included a DIY UAV so far [13] whereas the specific implications imposed by DIY UAVs to digital forensics were not the focus of the work. But, they analyzed the flight path data from the DIY UAV in comparison to a DJI UAV and found that the obtained data sets from the DIY drone are "not very informative and elude towards vague patterns in flight path data" whereas the DJI drone is "more informative and enable the investigator to predict the phases of the flight journey". Indeed, the sparsity of the recorded data per default is also a concern of this paper (see Sect. 8).

Despite these numerous case studies efforts to systematize drone forensics date back to 2017 when [11] proposed their *Drone forensic framework* which, however, is more concerned of a general forensic procedure and less of the digital forensics part of it. In 2019 [17] proposed a *comprehensive micro UAV/Drone forensic framework* specifically for the digital forensics community. Their digital forensics subprocess comprises of the acquisition of the *Memory Card*, the extraction of the *System Logs* and the subsequent visualization, however, without further discussion of details.

Recently, [1] reviewed 32 research papers on drones with regard to their forensic procedure and merged the results in their *Comprehensive Collection Analysis and Forensic Model (CCAFM)*, where the "Evidence Acquisition Stage" incorporates three processes, namely "Live Acquisition", "Post-mortem Acquisition" and "Hybrid Acquisition". Although mapping comprehensively, all processes related to the forensic investigation of UAS, the CCAFM offers no guideline on how sub-processes, such as *Post-Mortem Acquisition*, should be executed.

Consequently, investigators must rely on general acquisition procedures if UAS model specific information is not available. While this seems to be straightforward at first glance, as e.g. every digital forensics practitioner is able to acquire an SD card, its way more complex than that, especially for DIY drones, as we discuss in Sect. 5.

2.3 EU Regulations for UAS

We now give an overview on the legal framework which is based on the EU regulations Commission of European Union [4], Commission of European Union [5] and further amendments, as listed in EASA [7]. Furthermore, we assume that offenders refrain from soliciting the endorsement of the regional aviation authority to be able to fly legally in the "specific" or "certified" category, hence, the following remarks are based on the rules of the so-called "open" category.

Remote-ID. Today it is mandatory to officially register a UAVs and the obtained *eID* must be placed on the drone. Consequently, as long as the drone is flying, this information can not be accessed by Law Enforcement Agencies (LEAs), so to remedy this situation, the *Remote-ID* has been introduced, which is consistently sent via radio or network, so that the operator can be identified by LEAs at any time. The idea is similar to the systems used for flight control of airplanes. Therefore, the Remote-ID includes the eID assigned at registration and the serial number, but also its position, the position of the remote control, the take-off point, the flight speed, and the flight direction. Obviously, this is highly disadvantageous for any covert operation of a UAV.

Automatic and Autonomous UAVs. Many UAVs are able to fly automatically which is legal in the EU without strict requirements on the UAS [5]. However, automatic is not autonomous. The first means that a flight mission is planned in advance and the UAS automatically completes the mission while a remote control must be connected to the UAV. Whereas the latter means that the drone is able to react to unforeseen events by itself, hence, is allowed to fly without a connected remote control. Consequently, similar to autonomous cars, autonomous UAS have to be officially certified [5], hence, only few autonomously operating drones for industrial purposes are available on the market right now.

Maximum Range and Altitude. The maximum altitude in the EU is 120 m which must be enforced by the drone manufacturer as of 2024. The range is limited by the decree that it is only allowed to fly within sight. However, DJI states that from a technical viewpoint, e.g. the Mavic 3 Classic [6] has a maximum range of 3km and a maximum altitude of 5km while implementing the EU restrictions on the transmission power of the radio (i.a. 25mW). Consequently, from a technical viewpoint UAVs can fly considerably further and higher than the legal restrictions allow, hence, are clearly limited in their capabilities by the current regulations.

3 The Exciting and Chaotic World of DIY UAS

In this section we introduce the infinite possibilities when building their own UAS. Although, they must also comply with applicable regulations, private manufacturers can simply choose not to. Consequently, the capabilities of DIY UASs are only limited by the available components and skills.

3.1 Evading Regulations

Likely, the attractiveness of DIY UAS for e.g. criminal purposes will increase as the technical possibilities expand while the regulations become stricter(see Sect. 2). Interestingly, no additional skills or special components are required to circumvent most of the regulations when building a UAS. For example, the transmission power of the radio can be configured between 10mW and 2W [23], which is eight times the legal limit in the EU and results in a range of up to 30km. For some regulations, such as the Remote-ID, even an additional component, installation and configuration effort is required to comply.

An autonomous UAV is also easy to build, since the simplest autonomous UAV imaginable is an automatic UAV that can operate without an active connection to a remote controller. Thus, open source UAS software such as Ardupilot can be easily configured to ignore a missing radio link [25] and even provide obstacle avoidance capabilities [24]. Therefore, this offers tempting prospects for covert operations, as an operator does not need to be close to the UAV, and the range of the UAV is limited only by the power supply.

3.2 Hardware of DIY UAS

DIY UAS can be customized for peculiar purposes and to execute a wide range of operations which is only limited by the availability of resources, most notably of qualified technicians.

Basic Example. However, a minimal working UAS can be built cheaply and quickly with just a few components, namely a Radio Control (RC) and the UAV with a Flight Controller (FC), Electronic Speed Controller (ESC) and a Radio Receiver (RX), as well as a frame, motors with propellers and a battery. The RC sends commands from the pilot to the UAV, which are received by the RX and delegated to the FC. The FC, in turn, is the brain of the UAV and translates commands from the RC, based on its sensors such as gyroscopes and accelerometers, into commands for the ESCs (may be included in the FC). The ESCs then regulates the speed of the UAV's motors to achieve the behavior requested by the pilot.

The size of such a minimally equipped UAV can be as small as 90mm and easily up to 800mm, measured diagonally from motor to motor, respectively. These basic UAS can be built based on a plethora of tutorials that are available on the internet, whereas some claim to be as cheap as 150 $ [8]. Furthermore, a UAS can be built very unconcerned and sloppily, for example based on plywood [14]. However, With such a UAS offenders are capable to interfere with air traffic, frighten crowds or execute kamikaze operations. Furthermore, such a UAV can be equipped with any kind of payload, such as explosives, and may also drop the payload over a target area [26].

Endless Possibilities. However, the given minimal example of a UAS can be expanded in numerous ways, most prominently, by adding a GPS and camera system which can be a cheap and lightweight low resolution analogue camera up to a fully fledged camera system with infrared, thermal and 4K resolution. Furthermore, with systems like Pixhawk or BeagleBone which offer i.a. UART, CAN, I2C, USB and WiFi interfaces, by and large any electronically component can be utilized. Furthermore, DIY UAVs can also be built as wing type which are characterized by their very low energy requirements. For instance, it is possible to build a winged UAVs capable of staying in the air for a whole day, since a few mounted solar panels provide enough energy, as demonstrated by several hobby projects [15,16].

3.3 Software of DIY UAS

Additionally, to the hardware a flight control software is necessary whereas at the moment, the following three are most prominent:

- **PX4** which is supported by the Linux Foundation, provides a professional ecosystem and is also used by commercial drone manufacturers, such as Yuneec.
- **ArduPilot** is licensed under the GPLv3, hence, is subject to the copyleft principle which makes it uninteresting to commercial drone manufacturers, but attractive to hobby UAV builders.
- **Betaflight** is also licensed under the GPLv3, but, in contrast the focus is on piloting and agility which results in a limited range of supported sensors and no capabilities for automatic missions.

However, based on a flight control software, such as ArduPilot, technical capable offenders can build extensive functionality on top. For example, there is a project[2] that shows how a ArduPilot UAV can be combined with the machine learning frameworks OpenCV and YOLO[3]. Consequently, fully autonomous UAVs capable of, e.g. identifying targets to attack, are possible. Although these projects exist, the effort to realize a UAV with sophisticated autonomous functions is significant. However, once successfully built and programmed, manufacturing more UAVs is straightforward.

4 Methodology of Case Study

The methodology used in this case study is defined by two major phases: (i) design, build, configuration and test, and (ii) data generation and forensic examination (incl. acquisition and analysis) which are separated by the shift of perspective.

[2] https://github.com/Intelligent-Quads/iq_tutorials.
[3] https://opencv.org/, https://pjreddie.com/darknet/yolo/.

4.1 Design, Build, Configuration and Test

This first phase is characterized by a builders and operator's point of view, which means that the sole focus is on building UAS that meet the requirements of a mission. Hence, the goal was not to record as much data, as possible, as digital forensic scientists may be inclined to do, hence, different team members were assigned to the configuration and the examination of the next phase. Thus, our UAS were manufactured realistically.

Fig. 1. Half assembled small and cheap DIY UAV with digital HD camera.

However, in this paper, we focus on our first DIY UAS which is easy to setup, small and light, and, as such should provide outdoor and indoor "in the middle of the action" camera footage, e.g. for reconnaissance and may also carry a small amount of explosives. Therefore, the UAV needs to be cheap to make a loss in action bearable while providing a good camera footage quality. Based on the input of several DIY drone communities[4], we designed and built a UAV with a HD camera, for under 200 EUR[5] which is shown in Fig. 1 (see Table 6 for the fulls specification).

However, to complete the UAS, a compatible remote control is required and we have also selected FPV goggles as they are advantageous in this scenario. This time, to maximize range, reliability and footage quality we resort to high end components, as in an operation, only the UAV is in danger of damage or

[4] https://oscarliang.com/, https://www.reddit.com/r/diydrones/.

[5] Market prices fluctuate strongly.

loss. However, cheaper compatible components are available on the market. The process of building and configuring the UAV, was straightforward, but to tweak the flight performance of the UAV, several cycles of adapting the configuration and testing it, were required.

As the design, build and test phase was completed, we acquired the data of all UAS components and subsequently wiped the data carriers, before we entered the next phase. For the complete technical specification of the UAS see Sect. A.

4.2 Data Generation and Forensic Examination

We developed four typical scenarios for our experiments with the given UAS, as shown in Table 1. The first scenario, is a standard operation which includes a successful return of the UAV and a recording that was started and stopped with dedicated record button of the FPV goggles. Additionally, we tested loss of connection during recording on the UAV and FPV side, which can occur due to power loss, other technical problems, or during a kamikaze mission. Finally, we have a scenario for the corner case that a recording was started but the UAV was not armed or flying, which can happen when a take off is interrupted or the recording is started accidentally.

Based on these scenarios, we conducted eleven controlled experiments. Finally, the UAS was admitted to our lab and treated as digital forensic evidence.

Table 1. The scenarios tested with the UAS. UAV, FPV Goggles, RC are on and operational in each scenario.

Scenario	Description
STD	Recording of the FPV goggles is started. UAV is armed and started. Flight is executed. UAV is landed and disarmed. Recording is stopped. UAV is turned off.
UAV_LOST	Recording of the FPV goggles is started. UAV is armed and started. Flight is executed. UAV is disconnected from the power source.
FPV_LOST	Recording of the FPV goggles is started. UAV is armed and started. Flight is executed. FPV Goggles are disconnected from the power source.
NO_FLIGHT	Recording of the FPV goggles is started. Recording is stopped.

5 Digital Forensic Examination and Acquisition

In the lab, we conducted a thorough examination of the hardware to identify relevant data carriers and interfaces for the next step, the acquisition. The results are illustrated in Fig. 2 which are now discussed in detail.

5.1 Hardware Examination

UAV. The hardware examination of the UAV revealed two USB interfaces to the FC, the micro USB interface on the top is easily accessible, in contrast to, the

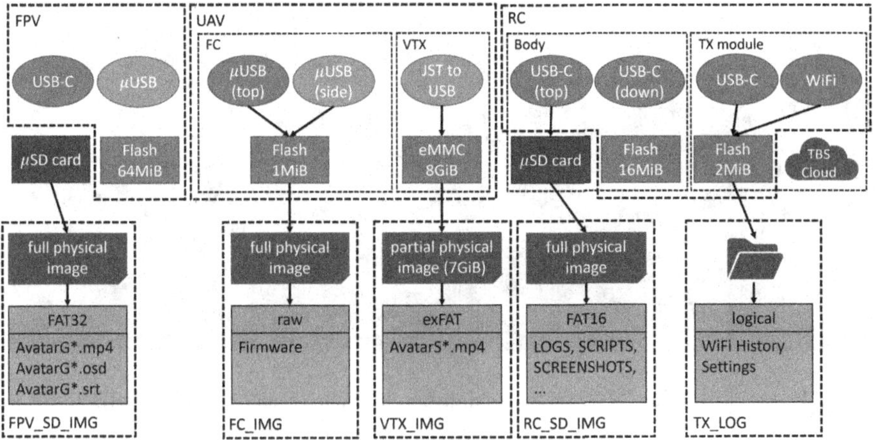

Fig. 2. Overview of (sub-)components, interfaces (light color indicates being hidden), data carriers (external: brown, internal: orange) and the acquired data whereas the arrows indicate the connection between these entities. (Color figure online)

semi hidden micro USB on the side. However, no internal storage was identified besides the memory of the `STM32F405RG` chip.

Another semi-hidden interface on the side, of type JST, belongs to the VTX which core piece is a chip `KMFN60012B-B214` for mobile devices which includes 8GiB of Embedded Multi Media Card (eMMC) storage. Interestingly, the manual of the VTX shows that the JST interface translates to a 4-pole standard USB interface, hence, a compatible cable can be easily manufactured e.g. by cutting a standard 4-pole USB cable and connecting it to the respective pins.

FPV Goggles. Here, the FPV goggles provide a micro SD card slot and a USB-C interface, for "HDMI output" as stated by the user manual. Additionally, dismantling the FPV goggles revealed a concealed mini USB connection to the mainboard, as shown in Fig. 3 which is not accessible externally, and unusually well marked JTAG connector pads. However, only one built-in flash memory of 64MiB was found which strongly indicates that video recordings are not saved internally.

Remote Control. The remote control consists of the body and the inserted TX module. The body has two USB-C ports, one for charging and one to access the micro SD card, which must be inserted for the body to function. For this reason, we decided not to disassemble the body and simply removed the micro SD card. However, the TX module does have its own USB-C interface, which powers the module when it is removed from the body. A WiFi module and a 2MiB flash memory were also found during disassembly.

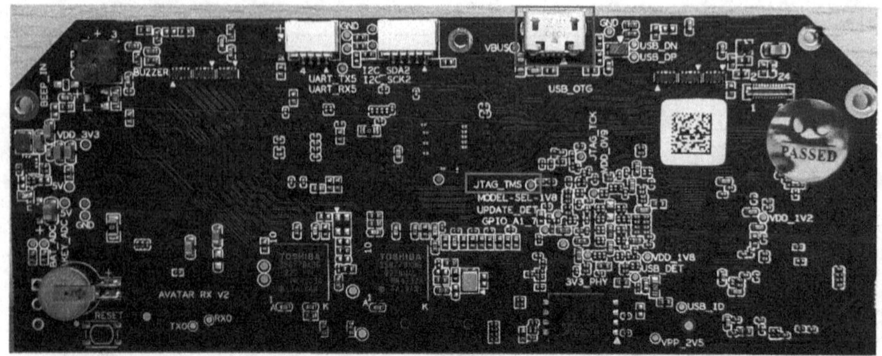

Fig. 3. Backside of the FPV goggles mainboard with concealed mini USB interface (red) and one exemplary JTAG connector (green). (Color figure online)

5.2 Acquisition

UAV. Surprisingly, the internal storage of the VTX can easily be acquired physically via the "JST to USB" interface even with the use of a write blocker, as it is recognized as an ordinary mass storage device. However, following the standard procedure, we only acquired a partial physical image with 7GiB of 8GiB to which we refer as `VTX_IMG` (see Fig. 2). However, it is of utmost importance to ensure sufficient cooling (e.g. with a cool pad or external fan) while acquiring the VTX, as it overheats quickly when not flying, and consequently, shuts down to prevent damage. Additionally, it is worth mentioning, that the VTX can only be acquired if the UAV is connected to its battery, as the power supply from the USB is not sufficient.

In contrast, the FCs internal storage can be acquired physically and completely when booted into its Device Firmware Update (DFU) mode, which is initiated by holding the so-called *boot* button on the board, when plugging the USB cable in. However, the usage of a write blocker, such as *Tableau T8u*[6], is not possible, but, the DFU mode inherently impedes data changes and enables the acquisition of a complete physical image of the internal memory by, e.g. using the firmware development software *STM32CubeProgrammer*[7]. We refer to this image as `FC_IMG`. Oddly, both USB interfaces (see Fig. 2) provide access to the same storage, and yield hash identical images.

FPV Goggles. First off, the micro SD card was extracted from its slot and acquired straightforward, yielding the image `FPV_SD_IMG`. Although, the SD card will be the main source of usage data, there is a 64MiB flash storage built-in which may not just contain the goggles firmware. Therefore, we examined the

[6] "T8u supports USB devices that conform to the USB Mass Storage Bulk-Only specification", as stated by its manual.

[7] https://www.st.com/en/development-tools/stm32cubeprog.html.

USB interfaces to complete the data acquisition, which, was not successful, but we were able to gather some information.

Despite the fact, that the USB-C interfaces supplies the goggles with power which the micro USB interface does not, no major difference was ascertainable and we were not able to acquire the internal storage by any of the two. However, kernel messages of our forensic workstation[8], could be observed when the device is connected (via any USB interface) first, and then powered on, whereas the device is not recognized when its powered on and connected afterwards.

Therefore, as shown in Listing 1.1 we are provided with a serial number, a product name and the dedicated manufacturer (*Artosyn*) which is known for supplying DJI with components [22]. Furthermore, the device registers as a RNDIS host which provides a virtual Ethernet over USB, hence, is registered as network interface (see Listing 1.3 in Sect. B for the bash records). However, an IP address must be manually assigned, but unfortunately, a port scan showed no relevant open ports. Due to the small size of the internal memory, it presumably contains only the firmware of the goggles, as they show a GUI when booted, we decided to let it be. But, as stated, a JTAG acquisition of the internal NOR storage is a possibility if the firmware is of interest in a given case.

Listing 1.1. Kernel messages retrieved for the FPV goggles. Serial number is obscured. Interface name changes on each connection.

```
$ sudo dmesg
[   63.590203] usb 1-2: new high-speed USB device number 4 using xhci_hcd
[   63.759012] usb 1-2: New USB device found, idVendor=1d6b, idProduct=0104, bcdDevice= 3.10
[   63.759094] usb 1-2: New USB device strings: Mfr=1, Product=2, SerialNumber=3
[   63.759111] usb 1-2: Product: Sirius
[   63.759124] usb 1-2: Manufacturer: Artosyn
[   63.759135] usb 1-2: SerialNumber: ZBBM5***MP
[   63.830255] hid-generic 0003:1D6B:0104.0002: hiddev0,hidraw1: USB HID v1.01 Device [
    ↪ Artosyn Sirius] on usb-0000:00:14.0-2/input2
[   63.830346] usbcore: registered new interface driver usbhid
[   63.830349] usbhid: USB HID core driver
[   63.832721] usbcore: registered new interface driver cdc_ether
[   63.836540] rndis_host 1-2:1.0 usb0: register 'rndis_host' at usb-0000:00:14.0-2, RNDIS
    ↪ device, c2:af:08:37:e5:5d
[   63.836583] usbcore: registered new interface driver rndis_host
[   63.846985] rndis_host 1-2:1.0 enxcaddb23e0d15: renamed from usb0
```

Remote Control. Again, the micro SD card of the remote control's body was simply extracted and handled typically. Furthermore, the body inhabits a 16MiB internal flash memory which is not addressable with the given interfaces, hence, an acquisition would require intrusive measures.

However, the data stored in the internal flash memory of the TX module can be viewed, but also not acquired. On the one hand, the TX module provides a WiFi access point and a WebUI to connected devices at `192.168.4.1`. On the other hand, the manufacturers software *TBS Agent*[9] can be used to connect to the device via USB-C.

[8] Kubuntu 24.04 LTS, 6.8.0-31 generic x86_64, auto mount disabled.

[9] https://www.team-blacksheep.com/products/prod:agentx.

5.3 Acquisition Results

Finally, the acquired images were reviewed, as shown in Table 2. To sum up, the SD cards are conventionally partitioned with a DOS partition scheme and can be analyzed with standard tools due to their FAT file systems. Unusually, the SD card, as formatted by the RC, has a FAT16 file system, which is, however, no challenge for standard forensic tools. In contrast, the mass storage of the VTX has no partition scheme which is also unusual but no hindrance for an analysis with standard tools, as there is direct access to an exFAT file system. In contrast, the image of the flight controller, is a firmware image which is not changed during operation, hence, will not be considered any further in this work.

Table 2. The acquired images with initial assessment.

Storage	Size (B)	Partition Scheme	File System	Operational Data
FPV_SD_IMG	31,267,487,744	DOS	FAT32	yes
FC_IMG	1,048,76	none	none	no
VTX*_IMG	7,503,068,672	none	exFAT	yes
RC_SD_IMG	504,365,056	DOS	FAT16	yes

6 Analysis of UAV and FPV Goggles

As there is no GPS module, the most interesting data will be the video files and corresponding data which can be found on FPV side (`FPV_SD_IMG`) and UAV side (`VTX_IMG`), respectively, in the root directory of the dedicated file system.

Generally, the recorded data that can be found on both sides differs. Most importantly, on FPV side there are not only video files (in MP4 format) saved, but also additional information from the On Screen Display (OSD) which are missing on the VTX side[10]. Now, we will discuss the available metadata of the saved files, before addressing the primary data.

6.1 Filenames, Timestamps and Metadata

The metadata will be analyzed on the example of the second controlled flight of which all generated files are shown in Table 3.

Table 3. File system information of the files created for the second controlled flight.

Image	Path	Filename	Modified Time	Access Time	Created Time	Size (B)
VTX_IMG	/	AvatarS0014.mp4	2000-01-01 00:06:24	2000-01-01	2000-01-01 00:06:24	208,586,788
FPV_SD_IMG	/	AvatarG0001.mp4	2000-01-01 00:06:26	2000-01-01	2000-01-01 00:06:26	204,418,187
FPV_SD_IMG	/	AvatarG0001.osd	2000-01-01 00:06:26	2000-01-01	2000-01-01 00:06:26	450,328
FPV_SD_IMG	/	AvatarG0001.srt	2000-01-01 00:06:26	2000-01-01	2000-01-01 00:06:26	26,089

[10] A detailed list of all camera related files can be downloaded from our cloud storage.

Filenames. On the FPV side MP4, SRT and OSD files always appear together and adhere to the naming scheme `^AvatarG[0-9]{4}.(mp4|srt|osd)$`. However, on VTX side only a MP4 file of this flight is saved and instead of a `G` an `S` is present in the filename. On both sides, the four digits act as a counter, which start by 0 and is incremented by one with each recording. Interestingly, the empty SD card on FPV side leads to the counter to be reset, with the first controlled flight. In contrast, the data storage on VTX side was also erased, but, the counter still remembers that 13 videos have been recorded before.

Timestamps and Metadata. In the file system, all files have a created, last modified and last access timestamp which inexplicable points to the `2000-01-01`, also, the flights were not conducted shortly after midnight. The same is the case for the timestamps of the metadata of the MP4 files, as extracted by ExifTool[11]. Although, we have no explanation for the date, the time on both sides, represents the uptime of the FPV goggles. Therefore, from the metadata of the video files the approximate uptime when the recording started (i.e. `5:54`) can be obtained, and, from the file system, when the recording stopped (i.e. `6:24`). This information can be verified with the duration of the video (i.e. 0:32s, see Table 4) (Fig. 4).

Table 4. Timestamps of the files created for the second controlled flight, based on the metadata embedded in the video files.

Filename	CreateDate	ModifyDate	Duration
AvatarG0001.mp4	2000:01:01 00:05:54	2000:01:01 00:05:54	0:00:32
AvatarS0014.mp4	2000:01:01 00:05:53	2000:01:01 00:05:53	0:00:32

6.2 Primary Data

The primary data recorded by the UAS is the camera footage and the corresponding OSD information.

Video Files. When the user starts a recording, a video is usually saved on VTX and FPV side, respectively. However, these recordings are not identical, e.g. the resolution on VTX side (i.a. 1920×1080 px) is higher than on the FPV side (i.a. 1280×720 px). Despite that fact, further difference are shown in Table 5, respectively, in relation to the executed scenario (see Table 1). Due to the counting differences, as discussed in Sect. 6.1, the video files have been joined by executed operation, as identified by the footage, rather than the filenames.

First off, the recordings of the two flights of the standard scenario differ only slightly, in contrast to the flights of the `UAV_LOST` or `FPV_LOST` scenario, as in these case, the MP4 files are truncated on the "lost" side. Fortunately, the video

[11] https://exiftool.org/, version used: 12.65.

files can be repaired, e.g. with `untrunc`[12] which, uses a reference file from the same device to rework the container structure. But, the videos repaired in this way, are approximately 10 s shorter than their untruncated counterparts. Therefore, in the event of an abrupt interruption of a recording, a significant amount of data will be missing and a more sophisticated approach may be required.

However, this suggests, in concordance to the fact that no deleted files can be found on the storage, that the MP4 files are written to the storage without an intermediate temporary file or buffering.

Table 5. Juxtaposition of video files found on FPV side and UAV side.

Cr./Mod. Timestamp	Dur.	Trunc.	File of VTX_IMG	Scenario	File of FPV_SD_IMG	Trunc.	Dur.	Cr./Mod. Timestamp
2000-01-01 00:03:34	02:11	yes	AvatarS0013.mp4	UAV_LOST	AvatarG0000.mp4	no	02:14	2000-01-01 00:06:26
2000-01-01 00:06:24	00:32	no	AvatarS0014.mp4	STD	AvatarG0001.mp4	no	00:31	2000-01-01 00:06:26
2000-01-01 00:09:40	00:08	yes	AvatarS0015.mp4	UAV_LOST	AvatarG0002.mp4	no	00:15	2000-01-01 00:09:46
			–	NO_FLIGHT	AvatarG0003.mp4	no	00:02	2000-01-01 00:10:30
2000-01-01 00:11:26	00:48	no	AvatarS0016.mp4	STD	AvatarG0004.mp4	no	00:48	2000-01-01 00:11:26
2000-01-01 00:11:44	00:11	yes	AvatarS0017.mp4	UAV_LOST	AvatarG0005.mp4	no	00:21	2000-01-01 00:11:56
			–	NO_FLIGHT	AvatarG0006.mp4	no	00:02	2000-01-01 00:16:58
2000-01-01 00:17:58	00:37	yes	AvatarS0018.mp4	UAV_LOST	AvatarG0007.mp4	no	00:46	2000-01-01 00:18:10
			–	NO_FLIGHT	AvatarG0008.mp4	no	00:06	2000-01-01 00:19:38
2000-01-01 00:20:54	01:14	no	AvatarS0019.mp4	FPV_LOST	AvatarG0009.mp4	yes	01:06	2000-01-01 00:20:48
2000-01-01 00:06:06	01:36	yes	AvatarS0020.mp4	UAV_LOST	AvatarG0010.mp4	no	01:43	2000-01-01 00:06:16

Flight Information. Additionally, to every MP4 file on FPV side there is a corresponding SRT and OSD file (see Table 3) which are plain text and binary files, respectively. The SRT files provide subtitles which can be replayed alongside the dedicated MP4 files, e.g. with the VLC player[13], as shown in Fig. 4. Also, the SRT files can be analyzed quantitatively due to their very simple structure, as stated by Rodriguez-Alsina et al. [18]: "Each subtitle entry consists of the subtitle number, the time at which the subtitle should appear on screen, the subtitle itself, and a blank line to indicate the subtitle's end".

For example, in Listing 1.2 an excerpt of `AvatarG0001.srt` and the saved flight information is shown. Therefore, even without GPS we are provided with an accurate approximation of the distance between VTX and FPV goggles, in this case, 11 m, as well, as the duration of the flight independently from the duration of the recording. Furthermore, we can check if e.g. a crash of the UAV was due to low battery. However, the transmitted information depends on the particular UAV and its configuration.

Listing 1.2. Excerpt of AvatarG0001.srt

```
208
00:00:31,049 --> 00:00:31,199
Signal:4 CH:1 FlightTime:22 SBat:5.0V GBat:16.5V Delay:25ms Bitrate:25.0Mbps Distance:11m

209
00:00:31,199 --> 00:00:31,349
Signal:4 CH:1 FlightTime:22 SBat:5.0V GBat:16.5V Delay:25ms Bitrate:25.0Mbps Distance:11m
```

[12] https://github.com/anthwlock/untrunc.

[13] Menu: Subtitle - Add subtitle file..., https://www.videolan.org/.

Fig. 4. AvatarG0000.mp4 with overlaid subtitle, as displayed by VLC.

In contrast, the binary OSD file can be used to replicate the display of this information as it was displayed during flight, e.g. by the Walksnail OSD Tool[14]. However, this re-rendered video may not include all available information, as the OSD is normally configured to show only an excerpt of the transmitted information. Therefore, from a forensics perspective, the re-rendering of the video file with the OSD file is only reasonable when it is important to determine which information the operator of the UAV had while flying.

7 Analysis of Remote Control

The body and the TX module are independent systems from different manufacturers which will be analyzed separately.

7.1 The Body's SD Card

The SD card of the body contains twelve directories, i.a. named `LOGS` and `SCREENSHOTS`[15]. Due to the fact, that we used the remote control in standard configuration and only for controlling the UAV, our tests did not generate files of interest in these directories. However, we had to store our configuration for our UAV in the RC which is saved in the `MODELS` directory as `model16.yml`. Despite the name and a customizable icon, only the sensitivity of the joysticks and such parameters are saved. But, the body has an internal clock, and the

[14] https://github.com/avsaase/walksnail-osd-tool.

[15] A detailed list of all files and directories can be downloaded from our cloud storage.

timestamps of the file and directory are updated, even when the configuration is only activated which can be a hint to the time of the last operation.

7.2 The TX Module

The configuration of the TX Module can be viewed with the "TBS Agent Desktop" software which includes a Telemetry and a Log Viewer and allows to configure the manufacturers cloud service which, however, were empty or disabled here. Therefore, the most interesting data that was saved in the TX Module is the SSID of the WiFi it was connected to, which is accessible in the WiFi category of the WebUI. Furthermore, e.g. the serial number, MAC address an firmware version can be viewed.

8 Discussion and Practical Implications

The aim of our case study was to investigate DIY UAS from a forensics perspective and our results reveal that the challenges are indeed distinct to popular consumer market UAS. One important result is, that DIY UAS can be incredibly sparse in the data they record even if they appear to be data-rich, as seen with the eight USB interfaces in our example. Therefore, if we opted to not record videos, no data of an operation could have been found on the UAV. Therefore, in practice the hardware examination is tremendously important to avoid falling down a rabbit hole.

Consequently, the first step should be the identification of components and sub-components, such as cameras, VTXs and GPS modules, focusing on those that may provide valuable evidence. Moreover, the identification process should guide the forensic strategy toward relevant interfaces for data acquisition. However, simply relying on SD cards or USB sockets may be fatal, as the UAV's VTX demonstrates. This component, although seemingly peripheral, and with an unusual JST socket, might hold key information that other interfaces do not capture. Finally, it must be kept in mind that a DIY UAS could be built completely different, so that any kind of data may be present. These findings underscore the necessity for a structured approach in the forensic examination of DIY UAS.

9 Conclusion and Future Work

In summary, DIY UAS provide unique opportunities for operations beyond the legal scope, while the existing body of research on consumer market UAS is not applicable. Moreover, each DIY UAS is an original, ranging in complexity from bare firmware to full-fledged AI-based IT system. Therefore, to enable a successful forensic examination, we pioneer by building a unique DIY UAS to present a complete case study. As a result, we point out the identified challenges and recommend a general yet rudimentary approach. However, the main characteristic of DIY UAS is their diversity and imponderability.

Therefore, our next step is to build further models with emphasis on market coverage and introduction of more complex software functionalities. Additionally, we will perform JTAG and chip-off procedures for otherwise not addressable data carriers to conclude the data acquisition. Finally, our aim is the proposal of a process model and a tool chain for the forensic examination of DIY UAS, based on empirical research (Fig. 6).

Acknowledgements. We would like to express our sincerest gratitude to Mario Winkler for his invaluable contributions to the construction and operation of the drone, as well as for his unwavering support throughout the course of this research.

This work has been developed in the project FOCUS. FOCUS (reference number: 13N16510) is partly funded by the German ministry of education and research (BMBF) within the research programme "Anwender– Innovativ: Forschung für die zivile Sicherheit II".

A Configuration of the DIY UAS

Table 6. Configuration of the DIY UAS, separated by main component.

UAV	
Flight Controller	F405 AIO 20 A Toothpick V4
ESC	incl. in FC
BEC	incl. in FC
GPS	none
Compass	none
Video Transmitter	Walksnail Avatar HD Mini 1 s Kit
Motors	1404 4500KV Brushless Motors
Propellers	Gemfan D63 3-Blade Propellers 1.5mm
Radio Receiver	TBS Crossfire Nano Receiver RX SE
Battery	Tattu 4 s 450mAh 75C Lipo XT30
Flight Control Software	Betaflight 4.4.3
Remote Control	
Body	RadioMaster TX16S MAX MKII Hall 4.0 4in1
Transmission Module	TBS CrossfireTX V2
FPV	
FPV Goggles	Walksnail Avatar HD

B Details of the FPV's Mainboard Acquistion Procedure

Listing 1.3. Acquisition procedure of the FPV mainboard due to the concealed micro USB interface.

```
$ ifconfig
[...]
enxcaddb23e0d15: flags=4163<UP,BROADCAST,RUNNING,MULTICAST>  mtu 1500
        inet 169.254.122.176  netmask 255.255.0.0  broadcast 169.254.255.255
        ether ca:dd:b2:3e:0d:15  txqueuelen 1000  (Ethernet)
        RX packets 0  bytes 0 (0.0 B)
        RX errors 0  dropped 0  overruns 0  frame 0
        TX packets 292  bytes 58407 (58.4 KB)
        TX errors 0  dropped 0 overruns 0  carrier 0  collisions 0
[...]
$ sudo nmap -A 169.254.122.176
Starting Nmap 7.94SVN ( https://nmap.org ) at 2024-05-02 14:15 CEST
Nmap scan report for * (169.254.122.176)
Host is up (0.00010s latency).
All 1000 scanned ports on * (169.254.122.176) are in ignored states.
Not shown: 1000 closed tcp ports (reset)
Too many fingerprints match this host to give specific OS details
Network Distance: 0 hops
Nmap done: 1 IP address (1 host up) scanned in 1.84 seconds
[...]
$ sudo nmap -sU 169.254.122.176
Starting Nmap 7.94SVN ( https://nmap.org ) at 2024-05-02 14:16 CEST
Nmap scan report for * (169.254.122.176)
Host is up (0.0000040s latency).
Not shown: 998 closed udp ports (port-unreach)
PORT     STATE         SERVICE
631/udp  open|filtered ipp
5353/udp open|filtered zeroconf
Nmap done: 1 IP address (1 host up) scanned in 1.37 seconds
```

C List of Acronyms

CCAFM Comprehensive Collection Analysis and Forensic Model
RC Radio Control
RX Radio Receiver
DFU Device Firmware Update
UAV Unmanned Aerial Vehicle
UAS Unmanned Aircraft System
LEAs Law Enforcement Agencies
eMMC Embedded Multi Media Card
FC Flight Controller
ESC Electronic Speed Controller
FPV First Person View
OSD On Screen Display
DIY Do-It-Yourself

References

1. Alotaibi, F.M., Al-Dhaqm, A., Al-Otaibi, Y.D., Alsewari, A.A.: A comprehensive collection and analysis model for the drone forensics field. Sensors **22**(17), 6486 (2022)
2. Barton, T.E.A., Hannan Bin Azhar, M.: Forensic analysis of popular UAV systems. In: 2017 Seventh International Conference on Emerging Security Technologies (EST), pp. 91–96, IEEE, IEEE Press, Canterbury, UK (2017), https://doi.org/10.1109/EST.2017.8090405
3. Boenke, M., et al.: Sie kreisen, sie jagen, sie töten. Die ZEIT (2024). https://www.zeit.de/politik/ausland/2024-02/ukraine-krieg-drohnen-truppengattung-fpv
4. Commission of European union: regulation (EU) 2019/945 (2019). https://eur-lex.europa.eu/legal-content/EN/TXT/?uri=CELEX:32019R0945
5. Commission of European union: regulation (EU) no 2019/947 (2019). https://eur-lex.europa.eu/legal-content/EN/TXT/PDF/?uri=CELEX:32019R0947
6. DJI: Specs – DJI Mavic 3 Classic (2024). https://www.dji.com/global/mavic-3-classic/specs
7. EASA: easy access rules for unmanned aircraft systems (2022). https://www.easa.europa.eu/document-library/easy-access-rules/online-publications/easy-access-rules-unmanned-aircraft-systems
8. FPV, D.: Build this quality freestyle FPV drone for $150 (2024). https://www.youtube.com/watch?v=Ti9qMJ4LNiI
9. Horsman, G.: Unmanned aerial vehicles: a preliminary analysis of forensic challenges. Digit. Investig. **16**, 1–11 (2016)
10. Husnjak, S., Forenbacher, I., Peraković, D., Cvitić, I.: UAV forensics: DJI Mavic air noninvasive data extraction and analysis. In: Knapčíková, L., Peraković, D., Behúnová, A., Periša, M. (eds.) 5th EAI International Conference on Management of Manufacturing Systems. EICC, pp. 115–127. Springer, Cham (2022). https://doi.org/10.1007/978-3-030-67241-6_10
11. Jain, U., Rogers, M., Matson, E.T.: Drone forensic framework: sensor and data identification and verification. In: 2017 IEEE Sensors Applications Symposium (SAS), pp. 1–6, IEEE, IEEE Press, Glassboro, NJ, USA (2017). https://doi.org/10.1109/SAS.2017.7894059
12. Kumar, R., Agrawal, A.K.: Drone GPS data analysis for flight path reconstruction: a study on DJI, Parrot & Yuneec make drones. Forensic Sci. Int. Digit. Invest. **38**, 301182 (2021)
13. Mekala, S.H., Baig, Z.: Digital forensics for drone data – intelligent clustering using self organising maps. In: Doss, R., Piramuthu, S., Zhou, W. (eds.) FNSS 2019. CCIS, vol. 1113, pp. 172–189. Springer, Cham (2019). https://doi.org/10.1007/978-3-030-34353-8_13
14. Racing, X.C.D.: X Class budget build for under $400 (2024). https://www.youtube.com/watch?v=YyD9GRPMviw
15. rctestflight: RC solar plane flight duration test. https://www.youtube.com/watch?v=1OGrDvInUAY (2021), Accessed 21 June 2024
16. rctestflight: Solar Plane V4 cross-country waypoint mission. https://www.youtube.com/watch?v=vYeYZpBE51I (2021), Accessed 21 June 2024
17. Renduchintala, A., Jahan, F., Khanna, R., Javaid, A.Y.: A comprehensive micro unmanned aerial vehicle (UAV/Drone) forensic framework. Digit. Investig. **30**, 52–72 (2019)

18. Rodriguez-Alsina, A., Talavera, G., Orero, P., Carrabina, J.: Subtitle synchronization across multiple screens and devices. Sensors **12**(7), 8710–8731 (2012)
19. Salamh, F.E., Mirza, M.M., Karabiyik, U.: UAV forensic analysis and software tools assessment: DJI Phantom 4 and Matrice 210 as case studies. Electronics **10**(6), 733 (2021)
20. Stanković, M., Mirza, M.M., Karabiyik, U.: UAV forensics: DJI mini 2 case study. Drones **5**(2), 49 (2021)
21. Statista: Drones – Worldwide (2024). https://www.statista.com/outlook/cmo/consumer-electronics/drones/worldwide#key-players
22. sUASNews: A history of DJI wireless system, is Walksnail using DJI technology? https://www.suasnews.com/2022/06/a-history-of-dji-wireless-system-is-walksnail-using-dji-technology/ (2022), Accessed 16 July 2024
23. TBS: TBS CROSSFIRE R/C System. TBS, August 2022. https://www.team-blacksheep.com/media/files/tbs-crossfire-manual.pdf
24. Team, A.D.: Ardupilot – object avoidance (2024). https://ardupilot.org/copter/docs/common-object-avoidance-landing-page.html
25. Team, A.D.: Ardupilot – Radio Failsafe (2024). https://ardupilot.org/copter/docs/radio-failsafe.html
26. Times, T., Times, T.S.: Inside Ukraine's deadly drone war (2024). https://www.youtube.com/watch?v=Cmv1frnURHA
27. Yousef, M., Iqbal, F.: Drone forensics: A case study on a DJI Mavic Air. In: 2019 IEEE/ACS 16th International Conference on Computer Systems and Applications (AICCSA), pp. 1–3, IEEE, IEEE Press, Abu Dhabi, United Arab Emirates (2019). https://doi.org/10.1109/AICCSA47632.2019.9035365
28. Zhao, Z., Wang, Y., Liao, G.: Digital forensic research for analyzing drone and mobile device: focusing on DJI Mavic 2 Pro. Drones **8**(7), 281 (2024)

GOTCHA: Physical Intrusion Detection with Active Acoustic Sensing Using a Smart Speaker

Hoang Quoc Viet Pham(✉), Hoang D. Nguyen(✉), and Utz Roedig(✉)

University College Cork, Cork T12 K8AF, Ireland
{v.pham,hn,u.roedig}@cs.ucc.ie

Abstract. Voice Assistants (VAs) in the form of smart speakers such as Amazon Alexa, Google Assistant or Apple Siri are now commonplace. Due to their ubiquitous presence they can be useful as home alarm systems. In this work we present the development and evaluation of a novel physical intrusion detection system GOTCHA based on human presence detection with active acoustic sensing. GOTCHA can execute on simple off-the-shelf smart speaker hardware. Periodic audible chirps are employed to gather data which are then processed by a deep autoencoder trained on the acoustic profile of the empty room. As our evaluation shows, GOTCHA achieves promising results of up to 99.2% for the F1-score. Our experiments show that a person can be detected without fail while the system barely generates false alarms. GOTCHA is a viable alternative to passive sensing solutions for physical intrusion detection.

Keywords: Physical Intrusion Detection · Active Acoustic Sensing · Anomaly Detection · Autoencoder · Machine Learning · Deep Learning

1 Introduction

Voice Assistants (VAs) such as Amazon Alexa [6], Google Assistant [14] or Apple Siri [7] are now commonplace. They are used to interact naturally, via voice, with digital infrastructure and services. For example, VAs are used to read out email, to provide weather forecasts or to interact with smart home devices. Often, VAs come in the form of standalone devices referred to as smart speakers. They are sold at affordable prices and they can be found in nearly every home.

As VAs are ubiquitous, users and VAs providers are looking for novel ways of using them to maximise their utility. One application domain considered is home security. Utilising available smart devices such as a smart speaker in a home as a security device can be a very cost-effective solution. The underlying idea here is to analyse anomalous sounds recorded by the smart speaker when a home is supposed to be unoccupied. In a simple setup, any sound above a set threshold will raise the alarm, as an empty house should be quiet. More sophisticated setups analyse the sound and perform classification to only raise

L. Horn Iwaya et al. (Eds.): NordSec 2024, LNCS 15396, pp. 345–363, 2025.
https://doi.org/10.1007/978-3-031-79007-2_18

the alarm when sounds attributed to human presence are detected (e.g. closing a door, footsteps, speech).

Contrary to the aforementioned passive sensing approaches, it is promising to use active acoustic sensing for targetted monitoring, better noise handling and lower false alarms. Here an acoustic signal is sent periodically and the room response is analysed to determine the presence of an intruder. This approach has been explored less and existing work relies on dedicated hardware (e.g. ultrasound transducers, microphone arrays) and makes use of relatively simple methods such as statistic analysis and traditional machine learning.

In this work we detail the novel human presence detection system GOTCHA based on active acoustic sensing. GOTCHA can execute on simple off-the-shelf smart speaker hardware. It uses periodic audible chirps between 6kHz and 8kHZ. The core of GOTCHA is a deep autoencoder trained on the acoustic profile of the empty room. GOTCHA achieves a 99.2%, 99.0% and 91.4% of F1-score testing set with low false alarms rate. Thus, a practical alarm system can be constructed that can identify intruders very quick within miliseconds with minimal false alarms. While our work here focuses on active acoustic sensing it has to be noted that GOTCHA can be combined with existing classical passive acoustic sensing approaches. Passive sensing can execute in silent periods between GOTCHA chirps further improving system effectiveness.

The specific contributions of the paper are:

- *GOTCHA Design*: We provide an end-to-end design of the human presence detection system GOTCHA. It employs an autoencoder based anomaly detection using audio spectrograms from four microphones recording responses to acoustic chirps. The design enables implementation on simple commodity smart speaker hardware.
- *GOTCHA Evaluation*: We evaluate GOTCHA in three environments and show that 99.2%, 99.0% and 91.4% F1-score on the testing set can be achieved respectively with low false alarms rate making GOTCHA a practical system.
- *Public Available Dataset*: We make the datasets (chirp responses in an empty and occupied room) publicly available[1]. Thus, we enable other researchers to validate and reproduce our results and also enable further work such as bench-marking of alternate detection algorithms or improved training.

The remainder of this work is organised as follows. In Sect. 2 we describe related work on active acoustic sensing in monitoring applications and human presence detection studies. The GOTCHA design is presented in Sect. 3. In Sect. 4, we show an experimental evaluation of GOTCHA. In Sect. 5 we discuss limitations and future work. Section 6 concludes the paper.

2 Related Work

Human presence detection is a prominent research topic as it is necessary for a number of applications such as security surveillance, health care and traffic

[1] https://github.com/viet98lx/GOTCHA.git.

management. A vast range of sensing modalities can be used for human presence detection including vision [2,9,10], Infrared (IR) [19,20], Radio Frequency (RF) [12], and audio. In the case of RF, existing communication systems such as WiFi [18] might be used for human presence detection. Vision-based approaches might not work under low illumination conditions and also raise privacy concerns. RF-based detection based on existing communication equipment is often complex to deploy and calibrate. IR and RF based approaches require dedicated hardware and effort to deploy. In this work we consider human presence detection using acoustic signals. We consider a smart speaker to perform this task.

Speakers and microphones are now ubiquitous, integrated into mobiles and many Internet of Things (IoT) devices, facilitating acoustic sensing applications [8]. Acoustic sensing has been employed to observe humans. For example, Xie et al. [24] turn smart speakers into active sonars to determine exercise types using a method based on Doppler shift and short time energy. Xu et al. [25] utilized commercial off-the-shelf equipment to generate acoustic signals to distinguish individuals based on fine-grained gait information. In this work we aim to determine the presence of a person in a room instead of deriving information about a person's behaviour.

2.1 Human Presence Detection - Passive Sensing

Acoustic passive sensing is a method that uses acoustic sensors to hear and analyze ambient sounds. Human presence is either detected by registering noise above a threshold within a specific time window or in more advanced systems by identifying sound linked to human presence (e.g. footsteps).

Al-Khalli et al. [3] built a home security system that can detect burglars by analyzing acoustic signals. An algorithm named *short-time-average through long-time-average* is used to detect noise above a threshold to detect human presence. The decision threshold is computed in an adaptive manner to maintain a constant false alarm rate.

Sharma et al. [21] proposed an end-to-end system for intrusion detection by sensing the sound of footsteps amongst background noise. The algorithm uses energy information (amplitude) and spectral information (size of zero crossing intervals) to identify footsteps; an Machine Learning (ML) approach is not used.

A number of security systems based on ML sound classification have been proposed (e.g. [1,5,15]). Often they aim to identify extreme acoustic events such as a glass break, a gunshot or a fire alarm. Previous studies have used ML approaches in the context of human behaviour classification (e.g. [13,17,23]) but not in the context of human presence detection although they could be used for this purpose.

Our work differs from these existing solutions as we propose an active acoustic sensing approach instead of using passive acoustic sensing.

Table 1. Summary of related works in acoustic active sensing for human presence detection task. Room size is categorized as large (lecture hall - 9(m)x6(m)), medium (common living room - 4(m)x3(m)).

Research	Emitting sound	Omni-directional speaker	No of channels	Approach	Label needed in training	Room size
[4]	Tone (1 kHz)	✓	8	Random Forest	✓	Medium
[11]	Chirp (12.5–15 kHz)	✓	1	Statistical Method	✗	Medium
[22]	Chirp (20–21 kHz)	✓	1	DBSCAN + Regression	✓	Large
[26]	Pulse (6000–7750 Hz)	✓	8	Statistical Method	✗	Medium
GOTCHA	Chirp (6–8 kHz)	✗	4	Autoencoders	✗	Medium

2.2 Human Presence Detection - Active Sensing

For acoustic active sensing a sound signal is emitted and reflections from the surroundings are analysed to characterize the environment. Table 1 provides a summary of the key characteristics of existing works which we discuss in the next paragraphs. The main difference of all existing works to our proposed method is that simple statistical methods are used while we employ an deep autoencoder.

Shih and Rowe [22] use active ultrasonic sensing to count people in a room. DBSCAN combined with a regression model is applied. Good performance is achieved with an average error of 5% relative to the maximum room occupancy. However, the system requires high-end audio equipment to handle the used high-frequcy signal. The system also can distinguish an empty room from an occupied room. However, different to our approach, labelled training data is required for human presence cases. Our approach employs an unsupervised training method.

Alanwar et al. [4] detect human presence after a critical command is issued to a VA to verify that a user is present. Machine learning models SVM, RF, MLP with sound signal characteristics such as mean, standard deviation, skewness, kurtosis and MFCC as input are used. They can achieve 93% in accuracy but their training process required labels for both empty room and human presence cases. The application scenario is also slightly different from our work; there is an acoustic interaction before a pulse is sent.

Cheong et al. [11] employ a two-dimensional spectro-temporal filtering mechanism on a Fourier spectrogram to measure the total energy of the reverberations of the chirp signal to detect the change in the acoustic scene. Their work uses reverberation energy difference between two consecutive chirps to detect a change in the background scene. Their work can achieve 100% accuracy without any false alarms in the case that the human position is 2–5(m) away from the speaker. However, in their work, their system prototype requires an omnidirectional microphone and 4 speakers facing 4 cardinal directions.

Yoneoka et al. [26] analyse signal power correlation between a pulse and received sound to detect a human. They show that there is a different pattern in power attenuation of reflected sound with and without human presence. Their work focuses on detection speed instead of detection accuracy.

3 GOTCHA System Design

The aim is to detect an intruder entering a room using an acoustic signal emitted and analysed by a standard smart speaker device placed in the room.

3.1 Assumptions

We assume standard sized rooms. We do not consider large rooms (halls, open spaces). We assume a quiet environment, no noisy machinery or significant noise from the outside is present. We assume the smart speaker is placed on a table or shelf at a height of around 1 m. We consider a smart speaker that is not obstructed by other items directly in front of it.

3.2 Application Scenario

The user activates GOTCHA, an intrusion detection application on the smart speaker and then leaves the room. After a short time GOTCHA becomes active to detect intruders, similar to a standard burglar alarm. A sound pulse is emitted periodically and microphones of the smart speaker record responses to analyse the acoustic state of the room. Immediately after activation of GOTCHA it is known that the room is empty and the first responses collected by the device can serve as training data to have a clear understanding of the acoustic properties of the empty room. Training of the GOTCHA system can be performed every time the system is activated to accommodate changes in the room layout. This might be for example necessary if furniture has been moved. However, in most cases re-profiling of the empty room may not be necessary. After the system is initialised, GOTCHA sends periodic pulses and uses the recorded responses at multiple microphones to determine if the room state differs significantly from the expected empty room state. If that is the case GOTCHA records a detection but does not raise an alarm yet. Instead, windowing is applied and only if multiple detections are observed within the window an intrusion alarm is raised. Windowing avoids false alarms which is an important design consideration. Windowing increases detection delay, however, a delay of a few seconds is usually not a problem in the context of detecting a human intruder.

3.3 Sensing Signal

A sonar system such as GOTCHA should ideally use ultrasonic sound as commonly used in sensing application [16]. However, low-cost microphones on the market often support only a maximum sampling rate of 16kHz and the highest frequency that can be captured is therefore 8kHz. There are various kinds of sounds that can be used, such as a tone, a chirp, etc. A chirp signal can be robust against background noise as reported by Cheong et al. [11]. Moreover, using a chirp in active acoustic sensing demonstrated good performance in previous work (see [11,22,26]). We did not use the entire frequency range as the higher frequencies provide more information. We decided to use a chirp signal generated by Audacity[2] starting from 6kHz and gradually rising up to 8kHz at the end of the 10ms period.

The sensing signal is audible (but not terribly annoying) and a person entering the space will notice it. That might be useful for the owner as a reminder when returning to disable the system. An intruder may seek out the device and disable it but this would also reveal their presence.

3.4 GOTCHA Autoencoder (AE) Processing Chain

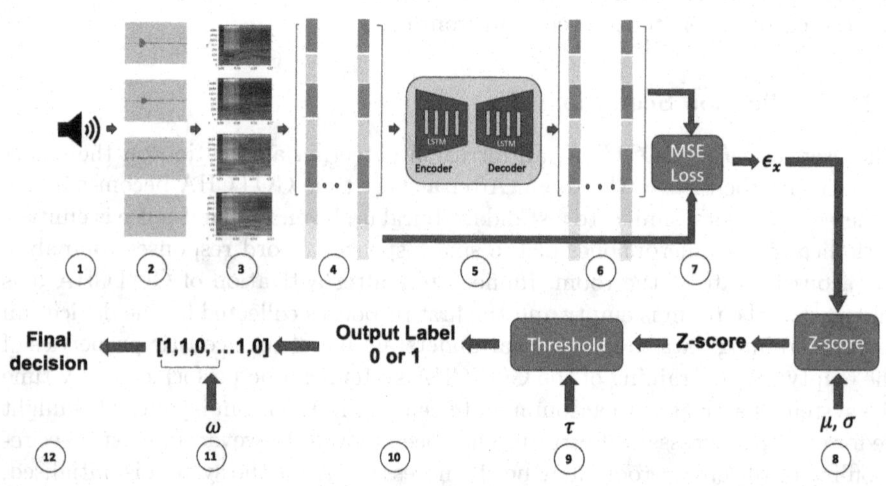

Fig. 1. GOTCHA processing chain. (1) Audio signal (2) Recording on N microphones (3) Signal transformation into Spectogramms (4) Combining inputs into a single input matrix (5) Autoencoder processing (6) Reconstructed output matrix (7) Reconstruction error ϵ_x computation (8) z_score computation (9) Threshold τ comparison (10) Decision output (11) Windowing (12) Final decision output.

The flow of GOTCHA is described in Fig. 1. GOTCHA periodically sends an acoustic signal (Step 1) and then records the response on N microphones (Step 2). Figure 1 depicts GOTCHA for $N = 4$. We apply Short-Time Fourier Transforms (STFTs) to the acoustic signal received on each microphone and transform the input into 2D spectrograms (Step 3). The 2D representations are

[2] https://www.audacityteam.org/.

then fed to the AE to identify whether the current state is anomalous or not. To generate the input for the AE we stack the spectrograms from all N microphones (Step 4). For each time frame t of the spectrogram, we concatenate the frequency values:

$$X_t = [a_{1,t} \oplus a_{2,t} \oplus a_{3,t} \oplus ... \oplus a_{N,t}] \tag{1}$$

$$X = [X_1, X_2, X_3, ..., X_T] \tag{2}$$

where T is the number of time frames in the spectrogram, while N is the number of channels of microphones. Vector $a_{n,t}$ represents t^{th} column of spectrogram from channel n. Now, the raw audio signals from all channels are transformed into temporal representations. The encoder and decoder in our AE are two Long Short-Term Memory (LSTM) networks that are suitable to handle sequential data.

After receiving input, AE in GOTCHA aims to reconstruct the input signal as accurately as possible (Step 5 and Step 6). The encoder is trained to compress an input signal of normal data (data that represents the normal state of operations without an intrusion) into a low-dimensional representation space. The decoder is trained to recover the original signal from the compressed representation. Mean Square Error (MSE) loss is employed to measure differences between input representation and reconstructed output (Step 7). By minimising the MSE loss, our AE can learn the way to reconstruct the profile of an empty room as normal signals accurately. The result of MSE loss also known as the reconstruction error reflects how well our AE did. The AE network can be mathematically described as follows:

$$z = f_e(X) \tag{3}$$

$$\hat{X} = f_d(z) \tag{4}$$

$$\{\theta^*{}_{f_e}, \theta^*{}_{f_d}\} = \underset{\theta_{f_e}, \theta_{f_d}}{\text{argmin}} \sum_{X \in \mathcal{X}} \|X - \hat{X}\|^2 \tag{5}$$

$$\epsilon_X = \|X - \hat{X}\|^2 \tag{6}$$

where f_e and f_d are the encoder and the decoder of the AE with the parameters θ_{f_e} and θ_{f_d}, respectively. ϵ_X is the reconstruction error for input X and recovered output $\hat{X}$.

Because training samples only include normal signals, any anomaly sample fed into our AE will result in a large reconstruction error. Thus, a distribution of reconstruction error from the training set is established to identify anomaly samples. In the inference phase, we feed new data into our trained AE and compare the newly computed reconstruction error to the distribution of training reconstruction errors to identify if the sample is normal or abnormal. Z-score as shown in Eq. 7 is a classical tool to detect outliers from a distribution (Step 8):

$$z\_score = (\epsilon_x - \mu)/\sigma \tag{7}$$

where μ and σ are the mean and standard deviation derived from the AE output on the training set which only includes normal samples. An example input and the reconstructed signal is shown in Fig. 2. An input is considered as an anomaly if the z-score exceeds a pre-defined threshold τ_z (Step 9). Threshold τ is a hyperparameter that will be chosen during the hyperparameter tuning process. We label normal cases as 0(s) and anomalous cases as 1(s) (Step 10).

To eliminate false alarms, windowing is used. A window W is used to evaluate the last w decisions of the AE (Step 11). The majority label of all decisions within the window W are used as label for the entire window (Step 12). Thus, short-term noise does not lead to potential false alarms.

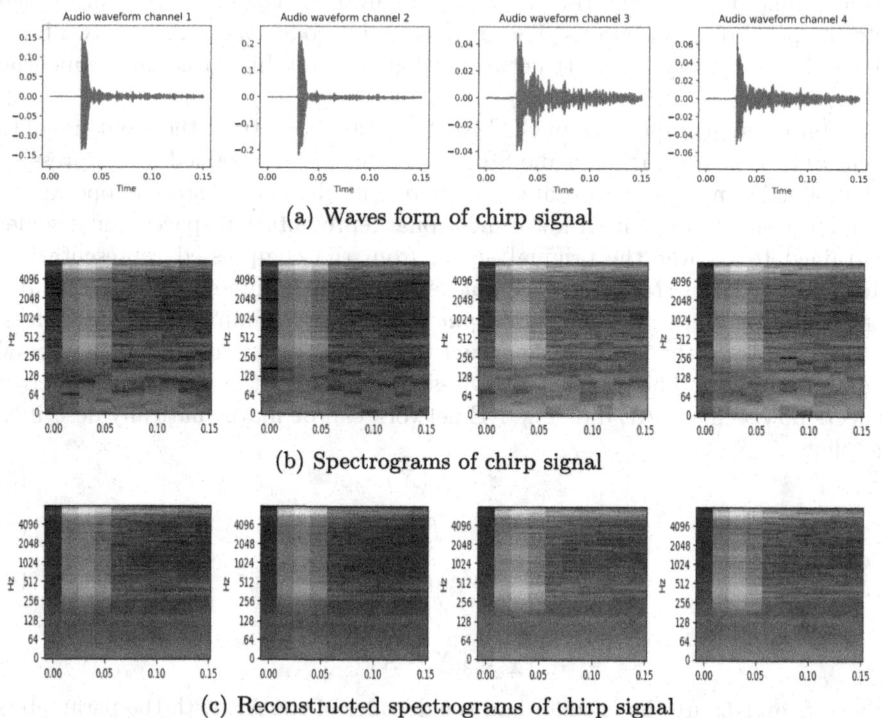

(a) Waves form of chirp signal

(b) Spectrograms of chirp signal

(c) Reconstructed spectrograms of chirp signal

Fig. 2. An example of input signal and reconstructed spectrogram of 4 microphone channels for an example (Output of the processing chain Step (6) as shown in Fig. 1). The reduced noise in the reconstructed output is clearly visible.

3.5 GOTCHA Prototype

We implemented a prototype of GOTCHA to carry out the experimental evaluation described in the next section.

We use an HP S01 speaker as the transmitter of the chirp sensing signal. The speaker is a low-end device. As microphones we use the ReSpeaker Mic Array v2.0 from Seed Studio (see Fig. 3(b)). The ReSpeaker provides four microphones and the ability to record sound on all microphones in a synchronised fashion (i.e. recording starting points are synchronised). The platform is designed as a component to prototype smart speakers. The speaker and microphones are connected to a laptop that executes the GOTCHA algorithms.

Each sensing cycle has a length of 150 ms. At the start of each period, a chirp ranging from 6 kHz to 8 kHz is emitted by the speaker and the microphones are triggered to start recording. The chirp signal duration is 10 ms and the process of emitting sound and recording is synchronised. In our prototype, recordings of cycles are stored for later analysis. However, in a practical system the analysis by the processing chain as shown in Fig. 1 would be executed after each cycle.

GOTCHA is implemented in Python using the API provided by ReSpeaker Mic v2 and to control the speaker via laptop. AE in GOTCHA was trained by Pytorch which is a well known framework for deep learning model and it also supports intergration into embedded system.

We place in the experiments the ReSpeaker microphones on top of the speaker (see Fig. 3(a)). This is not ideal as sound from the speaker is directly transferred to the microphones. However, we chose this configuration as it represents the closest real smart speaker implementation where both components are included in one casing.

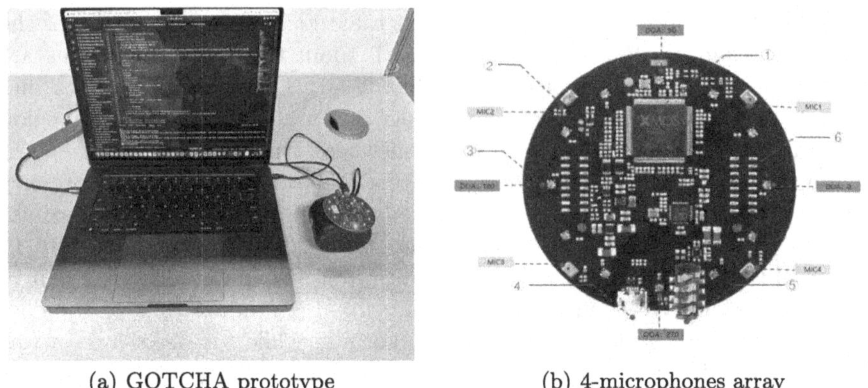

(a) GOTCHA prototype (b) 4-microphones array

Fig. 3. GOTCHA prototype design and microphone array structure.

4 GOTCHA Evaluation

4.1 Experiment Setup

We use the prototype described in Sect. 3.5 for evaluation. The experiments are conducted in a total of 3 rooms, 2 rooms of size 3.5 m x 3.3 m containing a table and cabinets and 1 bed room of size 6 m x 4 m (see Fig. 4).

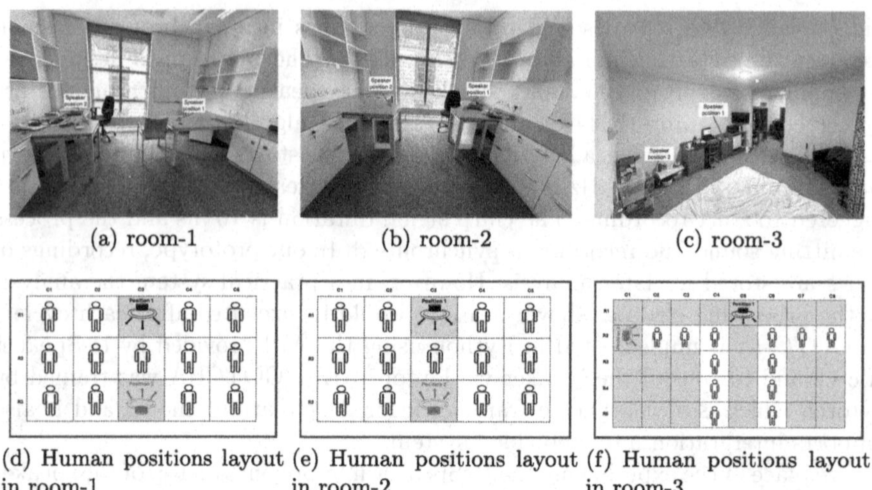

(a) room-1 (b) room-2 (c) room-3

(d) Human positions layout in room-1 (e) Human positions layout in room-2 (f) Human positions layout in room-3

Fig. 4. Room layout and regions with possible human presence. In white regions a human subject can be located, grey cells are obstacles (bed, cabinet, table, ...). (Color figure online)

The GOTCHA prototype is placed on a table located in one corner of the room. The layout is shown in Fig. 4. In each room two experiment runs are conducted with the speaker placed in different locations (shown as black and red speaker symbol). We divide the floor space into multiple regions, each region is a rectangle of size 80cm x 65cm. A region where a person can be are shown in white, grey regions are occupied by furniture and a person cannot be present. We place markers on the floor in the centre of each white square which we use as marker for a test subject to stand. Room-1 and room-2 are divided into 13 regions, while room-3 has 12 regions. Thus, we are able to collect data in a repeatable fashion. We conduct our experiments at a random time of the day; In room-1 and 2 we collected data in the morning while for room-3 data was collected in the afternoon. Some noise from the outside environment was present during experiments but not at significant level (usual background noise).

4.2 Experiments and Dataset

The GOTCHA prototype is started and executes a sensing cycle every 150ms. A chirp ranging from 6 kHz to 8 kHz over 10 ms is emitted and the room response is recorded. The furniture is constant throughout the experiment so that it can be ensured that all changes recorded are due to a human that might be present. Initially, we execute a number of sensing cycles in the empty room for around 50 min to collect training data for the AE. Thereafter we collect validation and testing data. First, sensing cycles in the empty room are collected. Then, a person enters the room for approximately 20 min to record sensing cycles with human presence. The person is moving during this time from one of the regions marked on the floor to the next. We record the positions together with the sensing data such that a ground truth is available. This process is repeated two times, one to collect the validation set and one to gather the testing set.

We collected 9600 recording samples for each speaker position in room-1 and room-2, as well as 9400 for each position in room-3. A summary description of the data is shown in Table 2. For all 3 rooms, the first 5000 samples are fed to the AE in the training phase. For the validation and testing phase, each of human position corresponds to 100 samples and the rest represent the empty room. The dataset and code of GOTCHA are available via our Github repository[3].

Table 2. Datasets summarization (r1, r2 and r3 stand for room-1, room-2 and room-3 while p1 and p2 stand for speaker position-1 and 2, respectively)

Data	Label	Number of samples					
		r1_p1	r1_p2	r2_p1	r2_p2	r3_p1	r3_p2
Training	Empty	5000	5000	5000	5000	5000	5000
Validation	Empty	1000	1000	1000	1000	1000	1000
	Human presence	1300	1300	1300	1300	1200	1200
Testing	Empty	1000	1000	1000	1000	1000	1000
	Human presence	1300	1300	1300	1300	1200	1200

4.3 Comparison and Metrics.

Comparison. Among existing works mentioned in Sect. 2, we found that work by Yoneoka et al. [26] is closest to our work. We reimplemented their method and applied it to our dataset. However, as they showed in their paper, their method was designed to record continuous sound and uses a full 30 s recording for analysis. That is different from our recording process because we only require a chirp signal recording in discrete periods. The result of the reimplemented method by Yoneoka et al. [26] on our dataset is poor (almost a random prediction with an AUC at 50%). GOTCHA improves significantly on existing work as it can work with short pulses and short recordings using off-the-shelf comodity hardware. A comparison against existing work under these conditions is not meaningful and therefore a comparison with other solutions is not provided.

Metrics. We consider an anomaly as label 1 and the empty room as label 0. We use F1-score and False Positive Rate (FPR) as main metrics to evaluate our system, we also use accuracy to show the result of GOTCHA when detecting humans at different positions. It has to be noted that the metrics can be applied to the classification result with or without the last step of applying windowing.

[3] https://github.com/viet98lx/GOTCHA.git.

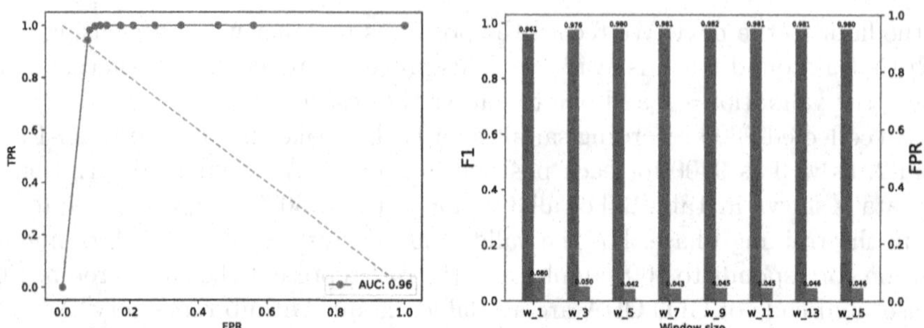

(a) ROC curve for selection of threshold τ by tuning on validation set of room-1 speaker postition-1

(b) F1 (blue) and FPR (red) for different window sizes w on validation set of room-1 speaker position-1

Fig. 5. Hyper-parameter tuning for the selection of μ, σ and τ in step (8) and step (9) in the signal processing chain in room-1 speaker position-1 as depicted in Fig. 1.

4.4 Hyper Parameters Tuning

All hyper parameters tuning process are conducted on validation set. GOTCHA requires parameters μ, σ and τ in step (8) and step (9) in the signal processing chain as depicted in Fig. 1. Furthermore, a window size w should be selected in step (11), used to reduce FPR for the final decision in step (12). Figure 5(a) and Fig. 5(a) describe the process of tuning parameters τ and w for the dataset of speaker at position-1 in room-1. We applied the same approach for the other datasets tuning parameters for these settings.

Threshold τ and z-Score Parameters μ, σ: After training of the AE with the training set we obtain the distribution of the reconstruction error ϵ_x. μ and σ are the mean and standard deviation of this distribution. We use the z-score in Eq. 7 to identify an anomalous sample. For every sample in the validation and testing set, we calculate the reconstruction error and then the z_score. We plot the ROC curve for all possible thresholds τ as shown in Fig. 5(a) for the speaker at position 1 in room-1. W. We chose τ by using the Equal Error Rate (EER) point such that the highest True Positive Rate (TPR) can be achieved while still keeping FPR at a low rate.

Window Size w: An alarm system benefits from preventing false alarms even if the detection accuracy is reduced. An operator will ignore alarms after a while if too many false alarms are issued and the system becomes ineffective. We tested window sizes of odd values 1, 3, 5, ... to 15 to choose the best value. In Fig. 5(b) we can see that for a window size of $w = 5$ the best F1-score of 98.0% on the validation set is achieved while the FPR is kept at 4.2% for speaker position-1 in room-1.

4.5 Data Observations

Figure 2a shows the signal waveform and spectrograms of 4 channels for one sensing sample in dataset of speaker at position-1 in room-1. It can be seen that the chirp starts at around 30 ms and the signal amplitude attenuates after 40ms. In the spectrogram, the signal is as expected strongest at frequencies ranging from 6 kHz to 8 kHz. However, we also see that there are signal artifacts at lower frequencies. The samples in the other datasets have similar visualisation.

We also notice that the signal amplitude of channels 3 and 4 is often smaller than signal amplitude of channel 1 and 2. This is due to the fact that the speaker does not have an omnidirectional characteristic and sound is projected forward and channel 3 and channel 4 receive a stronger signal (see Fig. 3(a) and Fig. 3(b)).

After training, the AE provides the reconstructed spectrogram as output. The comparison between input spectrograms and reconstructed output spectrograms are shown in Fig. 2. It can be seen that reconstructed spectrograms are smoother than the original input and regions at the low frequencies range become darker while the region at high frequencies remains the same. It indicates that the AE can learn to preserve the main signal of our chirp (6 kHz–8 kHz) while noise at lower frequencies is suppressed.

4.6 Detection Performance

Overall Performance. Our system can perform very well on the task of human presence detection. The results on testing set for 6 experiments are shown in Table 3 . Figure 5(b) shows an example for room-1 speaker position-1 that window size 5 has the best F1 score while keeping FPR at a low rate. The window size of $w = 5$ means that 5 sensing cycles are required before a decision can be made. Our cycle is 150 ms long and this means a decision can be made after 750 ms once a person appears in the room. Given the speed with which humans normally move through a room a detection frame of under one second is sufficient. A person may not be detected within one window analysed; however as active sensing is continuous an intruder will eventually be noticed.

Table 3. F1-score and FPR on testing set of 6 experiments (r1, r2 and r3 stand for room-1, room-2 and room-3 while p1 and p2 stand for speaker position-1 and 2, respectively)

Metrics	r1_p1	r1_p2	r2_p1	r2_p2	r3_p1	r3_p2
F1-score	99.2%	98.4%	99.0%	98.8%	91.4%	90.2%
FPR	1.9%	3.5%	2.3%	2.8%	9.4%	5.7%

Effect of Windowing Method. Figure 6 shows that after applying windowing method, for all cases, the F1-score can be improved while the FPR is significantly reduced.

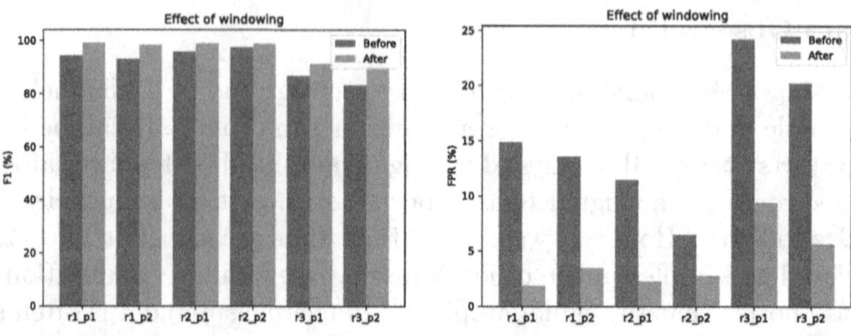

(a) F1 score on testing set of 6 cases before and after windowing

(b) FPR on testing set of 6 cases before and after windowing

Fig. 6. Effects of windowing method on 6 cases (3 rooms with 2 speaker positions of each room. r1, r2 and r3 stand for room-1, room-2 and room-3 while p1 and p2 stand for speaker position-1 and 2, respectively).

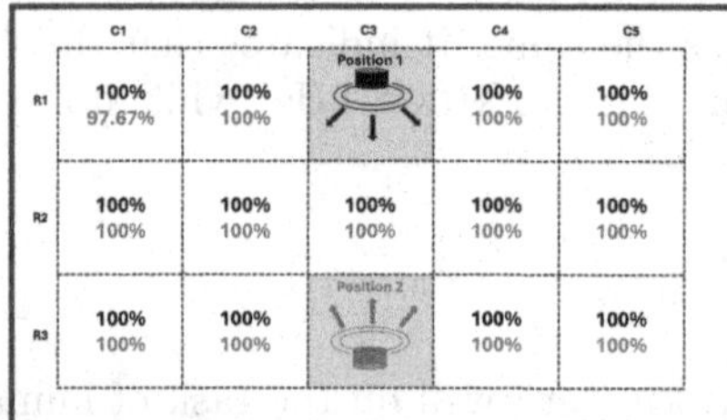

(a) Accuracy on testing set of room-1 after windowing

(b) Accuracy on testing set of room-2 after windowing

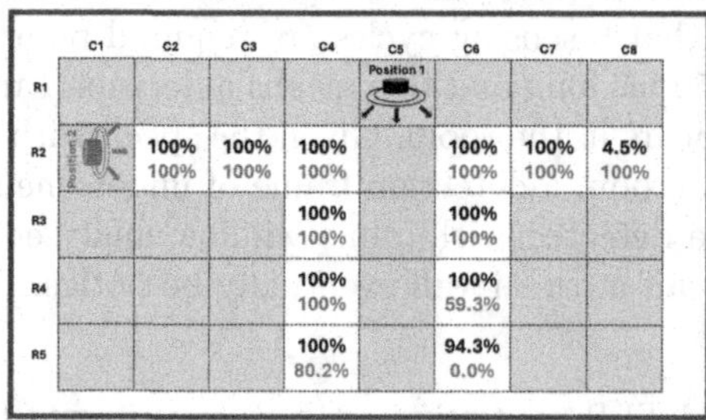

(c) Accuracy on testing set of room-3 after windowing

Fig. 7. Accuracy of detecting a human at different positions in the room after windowing. The black figures show accuracy for speaker at position-1 and the red figures show accuracy for speaker at position-2. (Color figure online)

Accuracy on Positions. An important question is if GOTCHA is able to detect an intruder equally well at all positions within a room. More importantly, are there any blind spots in which the system cannot detect an intruder, given certain hardware? To analyse these aspects we designed our experiment such that data

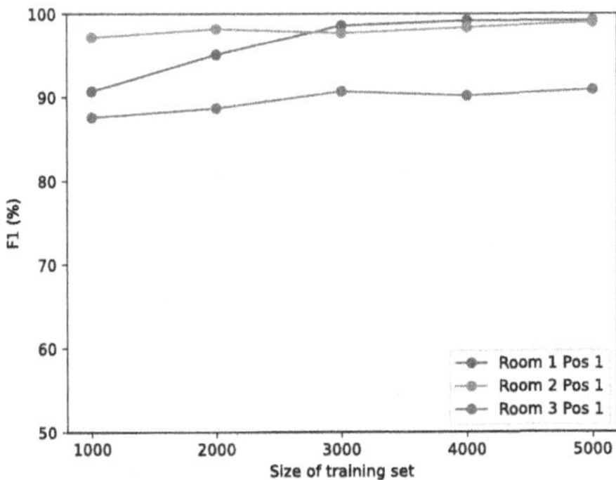

Fig. 8. F1-score on testing set of 3 rooms at speaker position-1 when using different sizes of training set.

is collected with a person present at different marked locations in the room and we conducted two sessions for two different position of speaker as shown in Fig. 4.

Figure 7 shows the achieved accuracy at each position on testing set after applying windowing method for two different positions of speaker. Accuracy is defined as the percentage of correct classification after a sensing cycle; i.e. an 80% accuracy means that 80 out of the 100 cycles were accurately classed as a human is present. The results are shown in Fig. 7(a), Fig. 7(b) and Fig. 7(c) for room-1, room-2 and room-3, respectively.

In room-1 and room-2, we can see that almost all areas achieve 100% of accuracy for both speaker positions while there is no area in the room where the accuracy reaches zero. This means that within the time frame of sample collection at each point at least one alarm was raised; at any position an intruder is detected at least once within the 750ms window. It has to be noted that this result is achieved while keeping very low FPR.

In room-3, there are more obstacles compared to the other two rooms, it showes that there are a few blind-spots that make GOTCHA perform worse than in open areas. For speaker position-1, the position (R2/C8) is partly blocked by a wall so the accuracy drops significantly while at the position (R5/C8), the accuracy drops a bit even though it is in the direct line of sight to the speaker. For speaker position-2, in areas (R5/C4), (R4/C6) and (R5/C6), the accuracy drops significantly, especially at (R5/C6). It can be explained by the fact that these positions are far away and not in direct line of sight (the speaker is not perfectly omnidirectional), as well as that they are close to the wall with a curtain and especially, (R5/C6) is overlapping with a couch and curtain (see Fig. 4c).

In summary, GOTCHA is able to well detect an intruder in reasonable range while the system is not raising many false alarms.

Training Set Size. In previous sections, we used in our evaluation the entire collected dataset of 5000 sensing cycles within an empty room to train the AE. In a practical setting the system will be activated and the user will leave the room. Thereafter active sensing cycles will be executed in the empty room, the AE will be trained and then intrusion detection is activated. Thus, it may be necessary to shorten the time for the collection of empty room data in order to switch to the detection state early. Thus, we investigated how the reduction of training data impacts on the resulting accuracy. We can see in Fig. 8 that all of 3 rooms share a similar trend: the F1 score of testing set tends to increase when the size of training set increases. However, the performance is not significantly improved after the size of training set is over 3000 samples. Clearly, it is possible to reduce the amount of necessary training data significantly.

5 Limitations and Future Work

As shown in our evaluation, GOTCHA is able to detect intruders within short time and barely make false alarms. However, there are a number of system aspects we aim to evaluate in future and improve upon.

We did not investigate the full design spectrum of the sensing chirp pulse we used. It might be possible to improve the system by using different pulses. Also, it could be investigated how to optimise the pulse for user acceptance (reducing nuisance, selecting a pleasant sound) while maintaining system performance.

GOTCHA currently only relies on active sensing. Although its performance is adequate for real-world adoption, it would be interesting to explore the combination of the active sensing approach with a passive sensing approach. In between sensing cycles (in our case of duration 150 ms) it would be feasible to switch to passive sensing and use a sound classification system to identify sound events such as footsteps, door opening/closing or light switching. Using two sensing approaches in combination might enable the system to be more robust.

6 Conclusions

In this paper we proposed GOTCHA, a human presence detection system (i.e. physical intrusion detection system) using active sensing with low-cost devices. To the best of our knowledge our work is the first to employ an AE to detect human presence by active acoustic sensing. This is particularly significant as the AE can be trained with only samples from an empty room; data examples representing an intrusion are not required which are usually hard to obtain. We demonstrated that our system is highly practical with good results in our experimental evaluation. Our system achieved up to 99.2%, 99.0% and 91.4% F1-score on corresponding testing sets of 3 different rooms with low rate of false decisions. In almost all evaluated situations an intruder is always detected except the case that intruder is blocked from the path of signal. Our system can be easily deployed using low-cost devices and can be integrated in ubiquitous deployed smart speakers. We also collected a dataset for human presence detection by an active acoustic signal that can be useful for future research in the field of active acoustic sensing. We noted that it is impossible to compare approaches across the literature as different hardware and application scenarios are used. We hope that our dataset can be used to establish a benchmark for comparison.

Acknowledgements. This publication has emanated from research conducted with the financial support of Science Foundation Ireland under Grant number 19/FFP/6775 and 13/RC/2077_P2. For the purpose of Open Access, the author has applied a CC BY public copyright licence to any Author Accepted Manuscript version arising from this submission.

References

1. Agarwal, S., Khatter, K., Relan, D.: Security threat sounds classification using neural network. In: 2021 8th International Conference on Computing for Sustainable Global Development (INDIACom), pp. 690–694 (2021)
2. Ahire, P., Lokhande, M., Patil, R., Shirsath, T., Zaware, S., Zalki, T.: Intrusion detection using camera and alert management. In: 2023 International Conference on Inventive Computation Technologies (ICICT), pp. 1117–1121 (2023). https://doi.org/10.1109/ICICT57646.2023.10134400
3. Al-Khalli, N.F., Alateeq, S., Almansour, M., Alhassoun, Y., Ibrahim, A.B., Alshebeili, S.A.: Real-time detection of intruders using an acoustic sensor and internet-of-things computing. Sensors (Basel, Switzerland) **23** (2023). https://api.semanticscholar.org/CorpusID:259582958
4. Alanwar, A., Balaji, B., Tian, Y., Yang, S., Srivastava, M.: Echosafe: sonar-based verifiable interaction with intelligent digital agents. In: Proceedings of the 1st ACM Workshop on the Internet of Safe Things, SafeThings 2017, pp. 38–43, New York, NY, USA (2017). https://doi.org/10.1145/3137003.3137014
5. Alsina-Pagès, R.M., Navarro, J., Alías, F., Hervás, M.: homesound: real-time audio event detection based on high performance computing for behaviour and surveillance remote monitoring. Sensors (Basel, Switzerland) **17** (2017). https://api.semanticscholar.org/CorpusID:23015307
6. Amazon: amazon alexa (nd). https://www.apple.com/siri
7. Apple: apple siri (nd). https://www.apple.com/siri
8. Bai, Y., Lu, L., Cheng, J., Liu, J., Chen, Y., Yu, J.: Acoustic-based sensing and applications: a survey. Comput. Networks **181**, 107447 (2020). https://doi.org/10.1016/J.COMNET.2020.107447
9. Bharadwaj K H, A., Deepak, Ghanavanth, V., Bharadwaj R, H., Uma, R., Krishnamurthy, G.: Smart cctv surveillance system for intrusion detection with live streaming. In: 2018 3rd IEEE International Conference on Recent Trends in Electronics, Information & Communication Technology (RTEICT), pp. 1030–1035 (2018). https://doi.org/10.1109/RTEICT42901.2018.9012234
10. Chen, H., Chen, D., Wang, X.: Intrusion detection of specific area based on video. In: 2016 9th International Congress on Image and Signal Processing, BioMedical Engineering and Informatics (CISP-BMEI), pp. 23–29 (2016). https://doi.org/10.1109/CISP-BMEI.2016.7852676
11. Cheong, K.M., Shen, Y.L., Chi, T.: Active acoustic scene monitoring through spectro-temporal modulation filtering for intruder detection. J. Acoust. Soc. Am. **151**(4), 2444 (2022). https://api.semanticscholar.org/CorpusID:248053139

12. Denis, S., Berkvens, R., Weyn, M.: A survey on detection, tracking and identification in radio frequency-based device-free localization. Sensors **19**(23) (2019), ISSN 1424-8220, https://doi.org/10.3390/s19235329, https://www.mdpi.com/1424-8220/19/23/5329
13. Do, H.M., Welch, K.C., Sheng, W.: Soham: a sound-based human activity monitoring framework for home service robots. IEEE Trans. Autom. Sci. Eng. **19**, 2369–2383 (2021). https://api.semanticscholar.org/CorpusID:236408129
14. Google: google assistant (nd). https://assistant.google.com
15. Kim, J., Min, K., Jung, M., Chi, S.: Occupant behavior monitoring and emergency event detection in single-person households using deep learning-based sound recognition. Build. Environ. **181**, 107092 (2020), ISSN 0360-1323, https://doi.org/10.1016/j.buildenv.2020.107092, https://www.sciencedirect.com/science/article/pii/S0360132320304686
16. Lee, Y., et al.: Using sonar for liveness detection to protect smart speakers against remote attackers. Proc. ACM Interact. Mob. Wearable Ubiquitous Technol. **4**(1) (2020). https://doi.org/10.1145/3380991
17. Li, J., Li, X., Liu, B., Liu, Y., Jia, W., Lai, J.: Invisible-guardian: using ensemble learning to classify sound events in healthcare scenes. In: 2019 IEEE 4th Advanced Information Technology, Electronic and Automation Control Conference (IAEAC), vol. 1, pp. 1277–1282 (2019). https://api.semanticscholar.org/CorpusID:211210752
18. Liu, J., Liu, H., Chen, Y., Wang, Y., Wang, C.: Wireless sensing for human activity: a survey. IEEE Commun. Surv. Tutorials **22**(3), 1629–1645 (2020). https://doi.org/10.1109/COMST.2019.2934489
19. Netinant, P., Amatyakul, A., Rukhiran, M.: Alert intruder detection system using passive infrared motion detector based on internet of things. In: Proceedings of the 2022 5th International Conference on Software Engineering and Information Management, ICSIM 2022, pp. 171-175. Association for Computing Machinery, New York, NY, USA (2022). ISBN 9781450395519, https://doi.org/10.1145/3520084.3520112
20. Sahoo, K.C., Pati, U.C.: Iot based intrusion detection system using pir sensor. In: 2017 2nd IEEE International Conference on Recent Trends in Electronics, Information & Communication Technology (RTEICT), pp. 1641–1645 (2017). https://doi.org/10.1109/RTEICT.2017.8256877
21. Sharma, S., Venkata, P.T., Singhal, S., Gopi, G., Kumar, S., Prasad, R.V.: B4w: a smart wireless intruder detection system. In: ICC 2023 - IEEE International Conference on Communications, pp. 191–197 (2023). https://api.semanticscholar.org/CorpusID:264468882
22. Shih, O., Rowe, A.: Occupancy estimation using ultrasonic chirps. In: Proceedings of the ACM/IEEE Sixth International Conference on Cyber-Physical Systems, ICCPS 2015, pp. 149–158. Association for Computing Machinery, New York, NY, USA (2015), ISBN 9781450334556, https://doi.org/10.1145/2735960.2735969
23. Sim, J.M., Lee, Y., Kwon, O.: Acoustic sensor based recognition of human activity in everyday life for smart home services. Int. J. Distrib. Sens. Netw. **11** (2015). https://api.semanticscholar.org/CorpusID:39843971
24. Xie, Y., Li, F., Wu, Y., Wang, Y.: Hearfit: Fitness monitoring on smart speakers via active acoustic sensing. In: 40th IEEE Conference on Computer Communications, INFOCOM 2021, Vancouver, BC, Canada, 10–13 May 2021, pp. 1–10. IEEE (2021). https://doi.org/10.1109/INFOCOM42981.2021.9488811, URL https://doi.org/10.1109/INFOCOM42981.2021.9488811

25. Xu, W., Yu, Z., Wang, Z., Guo, B., Han, Q.: Acousticid: Gait-based human identification using acoustic signal. Proc. ACM Interact. Mob. Wearable Ubiquitous Technol. **3**(3) (2019). https://doi.org/10.1145/3351273
26. Yoneoka, N., Arakawa, Y., Yasumoto, K.: Detecting surrounding users by reverberation analysis with a smart speaker and microphone array. In: 2019 IEEE International Conference on Pervasive Computing and Communications Workshops (PerCom Workshops), pp. 523–528 (2019). https://doi.org/10.1109/PERCOMW.2019.8730674

Security Analysis of Top-Ranked mHealth Fitness Apps: An Empirical Study

Albin Forsberg and Leonardo Horn Iwaya(✉)

Privacy and Security Research Group, Department of Mathematics and Computer Science, Karlstad University, Universitetsgatan 2, 651 88 Karlstad, Sweden
leonardo.iwaya@kau.se

Abstract. Mobile health applications (mHealth apps), particularly in the health and fitness category, have experienced an increase in popularity due to their convenience and availability. However, this widespread adoption raises concerns regarding the security of the user's data. In this study, we investigate the security vulnerabilities of ten top-ranked Android health and fitness apps, a set that accounts for 237 million downloads. We performed several static and dynamic security analyses using tools such as the Mobile Security Framework (MobSF) and Android emulators. We also checked the server's security levels with Qualys SSL, which allowed us to gain insights into the security posture of the servers communicating with the mHealth fitness apps. Our findings revealed many vulnerabilities, such as insecure coding, hardcoded sensitive information, over-privileged permissions, misconfiguration, and excessive communication with third-party domains. For instance, some apps store their database API key directly in the code while also exposing their database URL. We found insecure encryption methods in six apps, such as using AES with ECB mode. Two apps communicated with an alarming number of approximately 230 domains each, and a third app with over 100 domains, exacerbating privacy linkability threats. The study underscores the importance of continuous security assessments of top-ranked mHealth fitness apps to better understand the threat landscape and inform app developers.

Keywords: Security · Penetration Testing · Security Testing · Mobile Health · mHealth · Health and Fitness Apps

1 Introduction

Mobile health applications (mHealth apps) have become increasingly popular due to their availability, convenience, and ability to provide accessible health-related solutions to users across multiple devices [10,16]. While many subcategories of mHealth apps exist, some are more popular and widely used than others. Health and fitness are the most popular categories and have seen a massive increase in usage, especially between January 2019 and January 2020, when

L. Horn Iwaya et al. (Eds.): NordSec 2024, LNCS 15396, pp. 364–381, 2025.
https://doi.org/10.1007/978-3-031-79007-2_19

the downloads of the most popular health and fitness apps worldwide almost doubled from 8.84 million in 2019 to 16.28 million in 2020 [24].

However, previous studies examining the security posture of mHealth apps have found worrying results [11,21], ranging from insecure communication, weak encryption, poor access control, and unfair or unavailable privacy policies. Such findings stress the need for continuous research to assess these threats' extent and impact on mHealth apps' data security. For such reasons, this paper aims to assess the security vulnerabilities of top-ranked mHealth apps for health and fitness. Hence, to guide this study, we developed the following research questions (RQs):

- **RQ1:** *What are the security risks in top-ranked health and fitness apps?* **Objectives:** to identify the security risks specific to health and fitness apps and to conduct penetration tests to evaluate the extent to which these risks exist in current health and fitness apps.
- **RQ2:** *How can these identified risks be mitigated?* **Objective:** to propose recommendations for improving the security of health and fitness apps.

Briefly, the study's methodology involved three key stages: (i) app selection, (ii) static and dynamic security analyses, and (iii) responsible disclosure. The app selection process employed a Google Play Scraper[1] to filter apps available in four English-speaking countries, with a minimum rating of 4 stars and over 1 million downloads, thus focusing only on top-ranked apps. For the security analysis, various tools were used, including the Mobile Security Framework (MobSF[2]) for static and dynamic analysis, Qualys SSL for server-side assessment. A thorough manual analysis of the tools' outputs was conducted in the analysis process. Lastly, the responsible disclosure process involved compiling all findings into comprehensive reports and communicating them to the respective app companies.

This study contributes with valuable insights into the security posture of some of the most popular and top-ranked mHealth fitness apps, empirically assessing them and identifying the prevalence of vulnerabilities within the apps. Furthermore, this study proposes recommendations and mitigation tactics for the identified vulnerabilities, aiming to assist developers and stakeholders in improving the security of their apps. Parts of this work first appeared in the thesis of Forsberg (2024) [7], in which readers can find a more extensive description of the research.

2 Related Work

Many mHealth apps today collect and handle sensitive user data without employing appropriate security measures [11,25,26]. Studies have shown that many

[1] Google Play Scraper (https://github.com/JoMingyu/google-play-scraper).

[2] MobSF is an open-source automated security testing tool for mobile apps (https://github.com/MobSF/Mobile-Security-Framework-MobSF).

mHealth apps rely on vulnerable communication, transmitting data without encryption and sending sensitive user information over insecure channels [25,26]. In addition, a majority of analyzed mHealth apps have been found to transmit sensitive data without encryption over the Internet or use weak encryption and hashing methods such as Electronic Code Book (ECB) cipher mode and Message-Digest 5 (MD5) algorithm [15]. In fact, for many years, studies have highlighted issues such as the misuse of cryptographic Application Programming Interfaces (APIs) and insecure Initialization Vectors (IVs) [5]. Recent research further emphasizes that insecure encryption practices remain prevalent in mHealth apps, with findings revealing the widespread use of vulnerable IVs and ciphers [11].

For instance, an empirical study [11] conducted penetration tests on 27 mHealth apps, revealing numerous security vulnerabilities. These included information disclosure, weak access control, and excessive data permissions, raising severe concerns about user data privacy. Similarly, another study [21] highlighted issues such as excessive permissions and unauthorized data transmission to third parties, with instances of location tracking without user consent. Even earlier studies, such as [12], have highlighted significant shortcomings in mHealth app security, finding that out of 154 mHealth apps studied, health data encryption was rarely provided [12].

Contributions from other researchers evaluating the privacy of mHealth Apps have come to similar conclusions and findings. For instance, [21] found that some applications requested permissions that stretched beyond the intended scope. These permissions included access to Bluetooth and the microphone without any apparent need. The conclusion drawn from the situation was that an ad library used Bluetooth permission to track users' location [21]. Notably, the same study also found that 35% (7/20) [21] of apps transmitted the postal address or geolocation to vendors or third parties, whereas three apps did so insecurely over HTTP.

In addition to examining client-side security measures, studies have conducted comprehensive analyses of Secure Sockets Layer (SSL) web servers using the Qualys SSL Labs tool [11,21]. This tool performs a series of tests on specified web servers, evaluating the validity and trustworthiness of certificates and inspecting server-side SSL configurations. According to the findings of [21], out of 117 HTTPS connections established with third-party servers, 108 servers had a grade of C or higher, while six servers received an F and three received a T grade. Moreover, out of 11 HTTPS connections made to the app vendors, five were rated A[3], three were rated B, one was rated C, and two were rated T [21].

Given that, this study focuses on the top-ranked mHealth apps for health and fitness. Our particular focus on top-ranked apps is currently under-researched since many publications attempt to assess a high number of apps (e.g., [5,25,26]), thereby analyzing apps that are not actually extensively used in the real world. For this reason, we prioritize the security assessment of apps that can indeed

[3] Further details on the Qualys SSL Server Rating Guide can be found at https://github.com/ssllabs/research/wiki/SSL-Server-Rating-Guide.

impact millions of users. We also seek to verify and compare findings with prior work, providing further insights into the security status of mHealth apps.

3 Methods

3.1 App Selection Process

We focus on selecting top-ranked mHealth fitness apps across four English-speaking countries: Australia, Canada, the United States, and the United Kingdom. The Google Play Scraper tool was used to find the top 30 apps from each country under the search terms *"health and fitness"* (searches finalized on February 15, 2024). Only the apps presented in all four countries were retained for consistency. Two main criteria were established to select top-ranked apps: (i) apps with at least 1M downloads and (ii) with a star rating of 4 or higher. These criteria allowed us to narrow it down to 15 apps. However, after attempting to locate these apps' APK files, only 10 top-ranked apps remained to be analyzed. We purposely selected only the top-ranked apps for this study since they have a broad user base that may be affected.

3.2 Security Analysis Process

Our methodology is similar to that of [11], yet focuses more on security than privacy. The analysis begins with a semi-automated **static analysis** based on MobSF, comprising several manual inspection steps summarized in Table 1. This involves evaluating permissions, code, hardcoded secrets, manifest configurations, and domain assessments to verify potential security vulnerabilities.

It is worth noting that MobSF is prone to produce many false positives for certain vulnerabilities [11,21] as it may not always have access to the complete context of an application's behavior or environment. Therefore, the results

Table 1. MobSF Static Analysis Main Tests.

Tests	Descriptions
App's permissions	Evaluate if the requested permissions align with the app's intended functions, detecting potential overprivileged permissions
Abused Permissions	Flag permissions that are commonly abused by known malware
Network Security	Analyze network behavior for vulnerabilities like insecure protocols or unencrypted data transmission
Certificate analysis	Checks digital certificates for issues like expiry or trust, highlighting security weaknesses
Manifest file analysis	Review the app's manifest for misconfigurations or vulnerabilities
Code analysis	Conducts static analysis to identify security vulnerabilities or coding errors
Trackers	Identifies third-party trackers collecting user data without consent
Hardcoded Secrets	Search for sensitive information directly embedded in the code, exposing security risks

obtained from the static analysis output by MobSF were verified manually by the first author and discussed among the team. The following steps were taken:

- *Inspecting Code:* Review flagged code to rule out false positives in MobSF's code analysis for insecure number generators, ciphers, and cipher modes.
- *Evaluating Permissions:* Assess whether permissions labeled as "dangerous" are truly necessary for the app's intended functionality.
- *Assessing Hardcoded Secrets:* Review the hardcoded sensitive information found in the apps' source code, such as API keys, passwords, or cryptographic keys, present potential security risks.
- *Assessing Manifest Misconfigurations:* Evaluate the severity of misconfigurations in the Android manifest, such as allowing an application to be installed on vulnerable unpatched Android versions.

Following that, the **dynamic analysis** in MobSF captures runtime information such as network traffic, system calls, log messages, and API calls. The output of the dynamic analysis includes detailed reports and logs that provide insights into the apps's behavior, enabling us to inspect:

- *Logcat Logs:* Logcat logs are system logs that include runtime information, error messages, warnings, and debugging information generated by the Android operating system and the application itself.
- *HTTP(s) Logs:* HTTP(s) logs capture the network traffic generated by the apps, such as requests and responses exchanged with remote servers.
- *App Data:* Apps store data on the mobile phone, creating folders, files, and databases, which can be inspected to determine if personal data is securely stored.

The apps were thoroughly used for approximately 15 min each, which was more than enough to access, interact, and input data to all the activities and available features. Fake emails and user accounts were created for testing the apps, enabling us to access and input data, upload images, schedule workouts, edit entered information, and explore all features. We stress that the apps were used only for their intended purposes, e.g., creating profiles, adding goals, scheduling workouts, changing user info, etc. We did not perform any interactions that could tamper with the app and its server-side infrastructure, e.g., interfere with or inject malicious inputs or network traffic.

All the data captured in the dynamic analysis was carefully inspected by the first author, and the team reviewed the findings. Logcat logs were also examined to identify whether they reveal any sensitive information about the user's app usage patterns, activities, or web traffic. It is important to note that the Logcat logs generated on the device are accessible to other apps running concurrently, which can lead to the exposure of sensitive information [13]. HTTP(S) logs were examined to determine if the app's traffic was transmitted securely (i.e., check for any personal data sent over unencrypted channels) and to create a list of communicating servers. The app data were analyzed using SQLite Browser, and each stored database query was manually checked for privacy risks and user information.

Based on the captured network traffic, all domains communicating with each app are **assessed with Qualys SSL**, determining their security levels concerning HTTPS protocol configurations. The analysis provides an overall rating of the web server's security (A+, A, B, C, D, E, F, T) and a score and potential weaknesses for its certificate, protocol support, key exchange, and cipher strength. It is important to note that only the root domains were tested, and subdomains were not individually assessed.

3.3 Responsible Disclosure Process

After completing the vulnerability assessment, individual reports outlining the findings for each app were compiled. These reports were emailed to the respective companies and developers on April 9, 2024, utilizing the contact information on the Google Play Store platform or websites. The identified issues were communicated to the companies/developers 60 days before the study was made public [7], allowing time for them to mitigate the vulnerabilities. Notwithstanding, all the results from this research are published de-identified, without disclosing the names of the apps or companies. We argue that this study aims to understand the prevalence of security issues, which can be done without singling out and identifying app companies/developers.

3.4 Ethical Considerations

This project followed internal regulations and received ethical approval from the Ethical Advisor at Karlstad University (registration number HNT 2023/795). Furthermore, we adhere to ethical hacking guidelines for security research to try to find and mitigate security and privacy vulnerabilities in the apps [4]. Before publishing our findings, identified vulnerabilities were reported to the respective app companies or developers, allowing sufficient time for remediation efforts. It is also worth reiterating that during the tests, we never tampered with the application infrastructure (e.g., injecting network traffic or trying to trigger SQL vulnerabilities, etc.), and we did not collect personal data from any other users.

4 Results

Ten top-ranked apps met all the criteria from the initial set of 30 apps across the four English-speaking countries. Cumulatively, these 10 apps have been downloaded over 237 million times, underscoring the relevance of studying them specifically. Even if they constitute a small sample, negative impacts can be far-reaching.

4.1 Hardcoded Secrets

Hardcoding sensitive data such as API keys or cryptographic materials in the app's source code poses significant security risks. Such hardcoded secrets are easily extracted through reverse engineering, and attackers may gain unauthorized access to backend systems or compromise user data, making it an increased security risk [19,20].

We found several instances of hardcoded secrets within the code of the tested mHealth apps in the static analysis. Table 2 summarizes the findings related to hardcoded secrets. While some hardcoded secrets might not pose an immediate security threat [19], such as a database URL, their collective prevalence is worth mentioning. This study found that eight out of ten apps had hardcoded their Firebase URL (8/10 apps) and the corresponding API key (10/10 apps). However, Firebase API keys are not used for authorization and may not directly lead to unauthorized access [6].

Table 2. Summary of Hardcoded Secrets.

Categ.	Findings	Risks
API Keys	– All ten apps in the study had hardcoded API keys	– Hardcoding API keys increase the risk of exposure and unauthorized access to sensitive data or functionalities
Database URLs	– Eight hardcoded database connection URLs were identified within the source code	– Carries no immediate risk by itself
Client Secrets and Tokens	– Six instances of hardcoded client secrets and tokens used for authentication with providers such as Facebook and other third parties were found	– Hardcoding authentication credentials increase the risk of account takeover and unauthorized access to user data

From these findings, the Client Secrets and Tokens shown in Table 2 are the most concerning since Meta has specified that access tokens should never be hardcoded into client-side code, seeing that a decompiled app can give full access to your app secret [14]. Therefore, developers should consider the security of client secrets and tokens exposed in the app's code.

4.2 Code Analysis

Examining mobile application code for vulnerabilities is essential for upholding the security and reliability of mHealth apps. Malicious actors can access and browse application binaries with tools such as MobSF, simplifying the reverse engineering process. Hence, vulnerabilities such as weak pseudorandom number generators (PRNGs) or insecure encryption configurations become easy targets for exploitation [11,19]. The findings from the investigated high-risk flags supplied by MobSF during the static analysis are summarized in Table 3.

The analysis revealed several instances of insecure encryption configurations, posing significant and urgent security risks. Five applications were found to utilize the encryption mode CBC with PKCS5/PKCS7 padding, which is known to be vulnerable to padding oracle attacks under certain conditions. While using CBC with PKCS5/PKCS7 padding indicates a potential problem, it is worth

Table 3. Insecure Code in Apps according to MobSF static analysis.

Apps	High Risk Issues
App1	App uses the encryption mode CBC with PKCS5/PKCS7 padding. This configuration is vulnerable to padding oracle attacks
App2	1. Debug configuration enabled. Production builds must not be debuggable. 2. Remote Web debugging is enabled
App3	App uses the encryption mode CBC with PKCS5/PKCS7 padding. This configuration is vulnerable to padding oracle attacks
App4	Uses ECB mode for encryption
App5	Debug configuration enabled. Production builds must not be debuggable
App7	1. App uses the encryption mode CBC with PKCS5/PKCS7 padding. This configuration is vulnerable to padding oracle attacks. 2. Remote Web debugging is enabled
App8	CBC with PKCS5/PKCS7 padding, ECB mode
App10	App uses the encryption mode CBC with PKCS5/PKCS7 padding. This configuration is vulnerable to padding oracle attacks

noting that this is only an indication and may result in false positives. We recommend further investigation by the app developers. Additional conditions must be met to perform a padding oracle attack, i.e., the application must return distinguishable error messages or responses based on the validity of the padding. If the ciphertext is authenticated with a Message Authentication Code (MAC), the risk of a padding oracle attack can be significantly reduced. Therefore, while MobSF's detection of CBC with PKCS5/PKCS7 padding highlights a potential security issue, developers should interpret it cautiously.

Additionally, one application was found to use ECB mode for encryption (see Fig. 1), further increasing security concerns. Due to its weak encryption, it is not recommended for developers to implement AES/ECB with or without padding [8,17] but instead to use AES/GCM/NoPadding as recommended by Google [8]. Although it is hard to determine the exact data that is insecurely encrypted with AES/ECB, such lousy coding practice is alarming and requires immediate attention. Besides, it is worth mentioning that MobSF's code analysis also flagged several false positives regarding PRNGs, MD5, and SHA1 usage. These issues were discarded as the app used the algorithms in non-cryptographic use cases (e.g., hashes for integrity checks of downloads).

We also found that three apps had debug configurations enabled, allowing for remote web debugging and production build debugging [20]. Enabling debug configurations in production builds could expose sensitive information and functionality to potential attackers. Debuggable production builds simplify the task for malicious actors to scrutinize the application behavior and intercept data, potentially resulting in data leaks.

```
public static byte[] h(byte[] bArr, String str) {
  try {
      SecretKeySpec b10 = b(str);
      System.out.prinln(b10);
      Cipher cipher = Cipher.getInstance("AES/ECB/PKCS5Padding");
      cipher.init(1, b10);
      return cipher.doFinal(bArr);
  } catch (Exception e10){
```

Fig. 1. Use of ECB mode by App4.

4.3 Third-Party Trackers

The examined applications were found to communicate with various trackers, as summarized in Table 4. These trackers serve multiple purposes: analytics, advertisement, crash reporting, and identification. Most apps communicate with well-known analytics trackers, including Google Crashlytics, Google Firebase Analytics, and Facebook Analytics, often employed to collect and analyze app usage data, providing developers with insights into user behavior and app performance. Trackers such as Braze (formerly Appboy), AppsFlyer, and Optimizely were also among the most frequently encountered.

The evaluation of trackers used by the apps revealed several notable findings. Firstly, it was found that at least half of the apps utilize cross-device advertisement networks. Sharing information with trackers can raise privacy and security concerns, particularly those used for user profiling and advertisement. By leveraging user data from browsing states, cookies, and browsing history, cross-device ad networks can deliver targeted ads across various devices [23].

Furthermore, the analysis identified several apps engaging in user profiling activities using specific trackers such as Tealium, Braze, and Amplitude. These trackers are known for their capabilities in analyzing user behavior and preferences to create detailed user profiles, potentially raising concerns about user privacy and data protection. Notably, one tracker, Mixpanel, was found to have a concerning privacy breach clause in its policy. According to an analysis by Exodus Privacy[4], Mixpanel's policy states that end-users tracked by MixPanel's "customers" have no right to delete their personal information[5]. This indicates potential privacy implications for users, such as negating data deletion rights, intervenability, and objection to processing.

[4] Exodus Privacy Trackers List (https://reports.exodus-privacy.eu.org/en/trackers/).
[5] Exodus Report on MixPanel: https://reports.exodus-privacy.eu.org/en/trackers/118/.

Additionally, certain trackers such as Branch[6] and Inmobi[7] are known to collect device-specific information according to Exodus Privacy, including unique identifiers and other device-related data. This raises concerns about the extent of data collection by these trackers and the potential for user privacy infringement.

Table 4. Number of Apps by Tracker.

N. of Apps	Trackers	Used For
7	Google Firebase Analytics	Analytics
7	Google CrashLytics	Crash reporting
7	Facebook Analytics	Analytics
6	Facebook Login	Identification
5	Facebook Share	Sharing
4	Braze (formerly Appboy)	Analytics, Advertisement, Location
3	Branch	Analytics
3	Google AdMob	Advertisement
3	AppsFlyer	Analytics
3	Optimizely	Analytics
3	New Relic	Analytics
2	IAB Open Measurement	Identification, Advertisement
2	Sentry	Crash reporting

4.4 HTTP(S) Traffic Analysis

The HTTP(S) traffic analysis yielded reassuring results as it was found that all apps transmitted sensitive user information over encrypted HTTPS connections. However, two apps were found to use email addresses as identifiers in RESTful URI requests, as depicted in Fig. 2. Additionally, a third app similarly revealed users' usernames through this method. This practice is generally considered insecure, as using email addresses or usernames in RESTful URI requests exposes user information directly in the request path. Although the contents of HTTPS requests, including paths and query parameters, are encrypted and not exposed during transmission, this information may still be logged on the server side. Consequently, server logs could contain sensitive user information, posing privacy risks if unauthorized individuals access the logs.

Moreover, the analysis revealed that four apps transmitted users' passwords in cleartext POST requests. Even in encrypted POST requests, it is not recommended to keep passwords in plaintext. App developers can already use secure hashing functions on the client side, avoiding transmitting passwords in plaintext and hopefully not storing them in plaintext, which would also be considered a bad practice [18].

[6] Exodus Report on Branch: https://reports.exodus-privacy.eu.org/en/trackers/167/.
[7] Exodus Report on Inmobi: https://reports.exodus-privacy.eu.org/trackers/106.

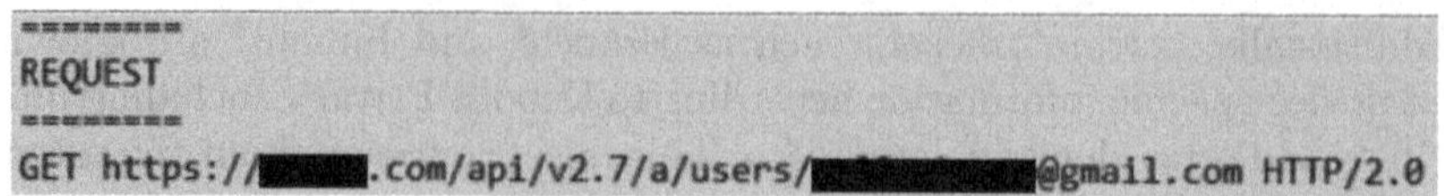

Fig. 2. Email used as an identifier in a RESTful URI.

4.5 Dangerous Permissions Evaluation

Android classifies specific permissions as "dangerous," indicating that their misuse or over-privilege could potentially compromise user privacy or device security [2]. Over-privileged apps pose risks in terms of both user privacy and security. Unnecessary access to sensitive device features (e.g., external storage, photos, media, contacts list) increases the attack surface for potential exploitation by malicious actors, potentially leading to a breach of user privacy [22]. The most common permissions used by the apps are shown in Table 5.

Most of the permissions found to be used by the apps could be justified and aligned with the apps' intended purposes. However, certain permissions such as `BLUETOOTH_SCAN`, `WRITE_CONTACTS`, and `GET_TASKS` indicate over privilege and raise concerns regarding potential misuse.

The `GET_TASKS` permission, although deprecated in API level 21 and no longer enforced, allowed applications to retrieve information about currently and recently running tasks. This permission could potentially enable malicious applications to discover private information about other applications [3].

Similarly, the permission of the `WRITE_CONTACTS` allows an application to modify the contact data stored on a user's phone. Such permission is unnecessary for the apps' intended use and can be promptly removed. Furthermore, the `BLUETOOTH_SCAN` permission is required for an application to discover and pair nearby Bluetooth devices. While this permission might be needed to pair different activity trackers, the app for mobile phones had no such functionality.

Some permissions collectively raised concerns, suggesting over-privilege even if their individual prevalence could be justified. For instance, four of the apps requested for both `READ_EXTERNAL_STORAGE` and `WRITE_EXTERNAL_STORAGE` while also requesting `READ_MEDIA_IMAGES` (4/10 apps), `READ_MEDIA_AUDIO` (4/10 apps), and `READ_MEDIA_VIDEO` (3/10 apps) permissions, which should suffice for the app's media-related functionalities. This redundancy suggests a lack of optimal permission management, potentially exposing user data to unnecessary risks.

Excessive location-related permissions across the examined mHealth apps were also of concern. Five apps were found to request both the permissions of `ACCESS_FINE_LOCATION` (5/10 apps) and `ACCESS_COARSE_LOCATION` (4/10 apps), along with additional permissions such as `ACCESS_MEDIA_LOCATION` (3/10 apps). While it is reasonable for fitness-oriented apps to utilize location tracking in the context of, for example, running, the need for multiple location tracking permissions appears excessive and unnecessary. It is also worth noting that the permission `ACCESS_MEDIA_LOCATION` was only justifiable in one of the three apps.

Table 5. Most common dangerous permissions used by apps.

Dangerous Permissions	# Apps	Dangerous Permissions	# Apps
POST_NOTIFICATIONS	10	READ_MEDIA_VIDEO	3
READ_EXTERNAL_STORAGE	8	ACCESS_MEDIA_LOCATION	3
WRITE_EXTERNAL_STORAGE	8	RECORD_AUDIO	2
ACCESS_FINE_LOCATION	5	BLUETOOTH_CONNECT	2
CAMERA	4	BODY_SENSORS	2
READ_CONTACTS	4	GET_TASKS	1
ACCESS_COARSE_LOCATION	4	GET_ACCOUNTS	1
READ_MEDIA_AUDIO	4	AUTHENTICATE_ACCOUNTS	1
READ_MEDIA_IMAGES	4	READ_MEDIA_VISUAL_USER_SELECTED	1
READ_CALENDAR	4	WRITE_CALENDAR	1
USE_CREDENTIALS	4	BLUETOOTH_SCAN	1
ACTIVITY_RECOGNITION	3	WRITE_CONTACTS	1

4.6 Server-Side Analysis

During the dynamic analysis, we found that some apps communicated with several hundreds of domains over a short testing period (approx. 10–15 min). Table 6 presents the count of domains communicated with by each app during the dynamic analysis. It is apparent from Table 6 that there is considerable variation among the apps in terms of the number of domains they interact with. For instance, App3 and App9 communicated with relatively fewer domains (0 and 15, respectively), while App8 and App10 were found to interact with an astonishing number of domains (236 and 240, respectively). Altogether, the ten apps communicated with 404 unique domains, i.e., excluding same-origin subdomains.

This significant variation in domain communication patterns is concerning, as there seems to be no justifiable reason for an application to communicate with such a large number of domains within a short time frame. This behavior raises privacy and security concerns, as apps interacting extensively with domains exacerbate the risks of data leakage, data linkability, and observability. Further examination of these communications and the related domains is essential to measure the extent of the risks associated with such behavior.

In addition, the security of the domains communicated with by the apps and their TLS/SSL configurations was assessed using Qualys SSL. The summarized results are presented in Table 7. It is important to note that any domain scoring a B or below should evaluate its configurations to enhance security measures, as there is no reason to keep servers configured with lower security levels. Of particular concern is the prevalence of 2.5% (10 domains) receiving a score of T, indicating multiple misconfigurations or vulnerabilities. Given the popularity of the tested apps, communication with such potentially vulnerable domains requires more immediate attention to mitigate potential security risks promptly.

Table 6. Number of domains communicated with the app during dynamic analysis.

Apps	App1	App2	App3	App4	App5	App6	App7	App8	App9	App10
Domains	17	30	0	111	34	18	33	236	15	240

Table 7. Summary of Qualys SSL results from web server analysis ($n = 404$)

Scores	A+	A	B	T	No Res
Domains (%)	86 (21.3%)	148 (36.6%)	107 (26.5%)	10 (2.5%)	53 (13.1%)

5 Discussion

This study sought to investigate security vulnerabilities in top-ranked mHealth fitness apps currently used by millions of users. Ten apps were tested for security, revealing many insecure coding practices, excessive tracking, and permissions. In the following subsections, we discuss our main findings and reflect on prior work in the field. We also provide ten recommendations to app developers, which are summarized in Table 8.

5.1 Insecure Coding in mHealth Apps

Our static analysis revealed hardcoded secrets and weak cryptographic strategies, such as ECB mode and CBC with PKCS5/PKCS7 padding. Other researchers have reached similar findings in a previous study [15], showing that out of 30 apps examined, most employed weak cryptographic methods, ECB mode for data encryption, and decryption [15]. Many other researchers have reported weak cryptography and insecure configurations in Android apps over the years [5,11,21]. It suggests that developers may not be abiding by the basic principles of secure coding and indicates a potential lack of maintenance of the app's security, raising concerns about the overall resilience of these applications against common threats and attacks. These are well-known vulnerabilities that are easy to discover with tools such as MobSF, which makes their prevalence in this study particularly concerning.

We believe such problems are linked to a knowledge gap on the developer's side. For instance, previous studies have found that 80% of mHealth app developers had poor security knowledge and that 85% of developers had an inconsiderable security budget [1]. Given the substantial number of coding vulnerabilities uncovered in this study, including weak cryptographic practices, insecure cipher modes, hardcoded secrets, and app behavior logging, we believe this was also the case for the developers of the apps assessed in this study. Otherwise, it would be hard to explain the existence of these common issues as the mitigation for it is not considered complicated or time-consuming.

5.2 Excessive Communicating Domains and Third-Party Trackers

We found it essential to include an analysis of the domains communicating with the apps and third-party trackers discovered in the static and dynamic analyses. We found that three apps collectively communicated with more than 300 unique domains (i.e., App10 (n = 240), App8 (n = 236), App4 (n = 111)). The sheer volume of communication raises suspicion since we only tested the apps to sufficiently cover all its functionalities and input relevant user data (i.e., approx. 10–15 min). The lack of justification for such extensive interaction with external servers raises additional concerns about the behavior of these apps. In contrast, the remaining apps maintained communication with a more reasonable number of domains, ranging from 0 to 34. The work of [11] reached similar

Table 8. Summary of Recommendations to App Developers.

App's Security Testing & Coding
1. Software companies should allocate sufficient resources and budget for security testing
2. Software companies should enforce secure coding standards and best practices across development teams to ensure consistency and adherence to security guidelines
3. App developers should implement automated security testing as part of the continuous integration and deployment pipeline to detect vulnerabilities early in the development lifecycle and prevent them from reaching production environments
4. App developers should avoid including sensitive user information such as email addresses or usernames in GET requests, RESTful URIs, or parameters. Instead, use non-identifiable attributes, such as an ID number or a hashed value
Domains & Trackers
5. App developers should carefully evaluate the necessity of each domain communicated with by their apps and limit communication to only those essential for the app's functionality
6. Server domain owners should prioritize the security of their TLS/SSL configurations to ensure the confidentiality and integrity of data transmitted between the app and the server
7. App developers should carefully consider the implications of using cross-platform advertisement trackers and minimize their usage wherever possible, as well as thoroughly review the privacy policies of third-party trackers used in their apps to ensure compliance with privacy regulations and user rights
Misconfigurations & Permissions
8. App developers should run a static analysis (e.g., using MobSF) before each new update to identify possible security risks
9. App developers should consider adopting a permissions in-context approach, requesting permissions only when users initiate interactions with corresponding app features
10. App developers should disable non-essential permissions by default, enabling them only when necessary

results, highlighting a small subset of apps making excessive HTTP(S) requests to dozens of servers. In such cases, even if traffic is de-identified (e.g., using a Universally Unique Identifier (UUID) or Android Advertising IDs (AAIDs)), the volume of communication makes it easier to link data and single out users over time, negatively impacting their privacy.

Furthermore, the prevalence of cross-device tracking raises concerns about how user data is shared and utilized for targeted advertising across various devices [23]. This practice not only compromises user privacy by potentially exposing their data and preferences but also makes it harder for users to control their data as it is not fully transparent which trackers gather what information. Moreover, trackers such as Tealium, Braze, and Amplitude, which collect, store, and create comprehensive user profiles, should not be allowed in apps that handle sensitive user data. Their prevalence also raises questions about the transparency and consent mechanisms in place for such data collection activities and the potential for misuse of this data. The identification of Mixpanel's privacy breach clause, which denies users the right to delete their personal information, shines a light on the possible misuse of user data. This clause raises significant concerns about users' ability to control their data and underscores the need for greater transparency and accountability in tracker policies.

We also evaluated each domain TLS/SSL configuration, showing that 29% had some misconfiguration resulting in a lower score (B 26.5%, similar to the findings of [21]. Developers should re-assess such domains to exhibit faulty TLS/SSL configurations, as these misconfigurations not only compromise the security of data transmission but also undermine user trust in the platform's overall security measures.

5.3 Unnecessary Dangerous Permissions

Regarding the dangerous permissions used by the apps, this study shows relatively positive results, with only three apps having one permission each that did not reflect the app's intended use, i.e., an average of 0.33 unnecessary dangerous permissions per app. A previous study [11] discovered that, on average, 4.1 permissions of the examined apps' ($n = 27$) were unnecessary. Developers can adopt several strategies to minimize the number of such unnecessary permissions. Firstly, if permissions are not essential for the app's functionality, developers can simply remove them from its configuration file. Additionally, developers should request permissions "in context," i.e., when the user starts interacting with the feature that requires it [11].

Nonetheless, the prevalence of multiple storage permissions raised some concerns about their relevance to the apps' purposes. For instance, eight apps used the permissions `READ_EXTERNAL_STORAGE` and `WRITE_EXTERNAL_STORAGE` while also requesting for `READ_MEDIA_IMAGES` (4/10 apps), `READ_MEDIA_AUDIO` (4/10 apps), and `READ_MEDIA_VIDEO` (3/10 apps). According to Android's permissions documentation[8], starting in API level 33, the `READ_EXTERNAL_STORAGE`

[8] Additional information about Android permissions: https://developer.android.com/reference/android/Manifest.permission.

permission has no effect and developers are instead advised to use the other `READ_MEDIA` variations mentioned above. Developers can shift their usage of `READ_EXTERNAL_STORAGE` to the `READ_MEDIA` variations to align with best practices and ensure compatibility with future Android versions.

Furthermore, three apps were found to request multiple redundant location permissions, i.e., `ACCESS_COARSE_LOCATION`, `ACCESS_FINE_LOCATION`, and `ACCESS_MEDIA_LOCATION`. These permissions grant apps access to various levels of location information, such as approximate phone location, user's exact coordinates, and location information associated with media files, such as photos or videos, stored on the device. Only one app included a functionality that could utilize the `ACCESS_MEDIA_LOCATION`, but the other two did not. In most cases, `ACCESS_FINE_LOCATION` should suffice for applications that require precise location data for features such as tracking exercise routes or providing location-based reminders. Using `ACCESS_COARSE_LOCATION` may be appropriate for less precise location needs, such as identifying the user's general area for weather updates or nearby points of interest. However, including multiple location tracking permissions without clear justification indicates over privilege and potential privacy concerns.

6 Limitations

Although this study brings valuable insights, readers should consider some limitations. Firstly, we limited our scope to 10 top-ranked apps for Android on the Google Play Store, available in English-speaking countries. This selection criteria may not fully represent the diversity of global health and fitness apps, even though the most successful apps tend to be in English and marketed worldwide. Nonetheless, the focus on top-ranked apps helped us focus on apps with an extensive reach and user base. Secondly, we relied significantly on MobSF for the static and dynamic analysis as it is the most established framework for mobile security testing. However, there are always other tools that could have been considered, such as Privado.ai[9] or more in-depth analysis with Frida[10] for runtime monitoring and manipulation. Thirdly, the server-side analysis relied mainly on Qualys SSL, to assess the TLS/SSL configurations. Although this step was found to be rather time-consuming, researchers can also rely on other tools (e.g., testssl.sh[11]) for even more nuanced results.

7 Conclusion

In this study, we investigated the security of top-ranked mobile health and fitness apps for Android. Our study found a substantial number of vulnerabilities

[9] Privado's Privacy Code Scanning (https://www.privado.ai/open-source).
[10] Frida dynamic instrumentation toolkit (https://frida.re/).
[11] testssl.sh tool for checking TLS/SSL services (https://testssl.sh/).

related to insecure coding practices (10/10 apps), hardcoding sensitive information (10/10 apps), and using known insecure encryption configurations (5/10 apps). Threats also concerned misconfigurations that allowed apps to be installed on older vulnerable Android versions and over-privileged permissions that are unnecessary for the apps' intended use. Some apps also engage with questionable trackers, expose sensitive data in HTTP(s) traffic, log user actions and POST values, and frequent extensive domain communication with inadequate TLS/SSL configurations.

For future research, we encourage expanding the datasets to cover a broader range of health and fitness apps to provide more comprehensive insights into the prevalence of vulnerabilities and potential threats. Additionally, incorporating other tools, such as Privado's privacy code scanning and Frida scripting, could enhance the depth of analysis, allowing for a more nuanced examination of app behaviors and security measures. Future studies might also want to conduct studies over extended periods (e.g., [9,16]) to observe how data sharing and access permissions evolve longitudinally.

Acknowledgments. This work was supported in part by the Knowledge Foundation of Sweden (KKS), Region Värmland (Grant: RUN/230445), and the European Regional Development Fund (ERDF) (Grant: 20365177) in connection to the DHINO 2 project, and Vinnova (Grant: 2018–03025) via the DigitalWell Arena project. We also thank Prof. Dr. Leonardo Martucci for his early feedback on the research, and Dr. Tobias Pulls for reviewing the findings and suggesting improvements to the manuscript.

Disclosure of Interests. The authors declare that they have no known competing financial interests or personal relationships that could have appeared to influence the work reported in this paper.

References

1. Aljedaani, B., Ahmad, A., Zahedi, M., Babar, M.A.: An empirical study on developing secure mobile health apps: the developers' perspective. In: 2020 27th Asia-Pacific Software Engineering Conference (APSEC), pp. 208–217. IEEE (2020)
2. Android: android developer documentation: app permissions overview (2024). https://developer.android.com/guide/topics/permissions/overview
3. Chen, X., Yu, H., Yu, D., Chen, J., Sun, X.: Predicting android malware combining permissions and api call sequences. Software Qual. J. **31**(3), 655–685 (2023)
4. Chow, E.: Ethical hacking & penetration testing: ACC 626: IT research paper (2011). https://citeseerx.ist.psu.edu/document?repid=rep1&type=pdf&doi=cf5080aad2d688f81a3d2666ed90bcecef18964a, accessed: 2024-09-23
5. Egele, M., Brumley, D., Fratantonio, Y., Kruegel, C.: An empirical study of cryptographic misuse in android applications. In: Proceedings of the 2013 ACM SIGSAC Conference on Computer & Communications Security, pp. 73–84 (2013)
6. Firebase: API keys — Firebase documentation (2024). https://firebase.google.com/docs/projects/api-keys, Accessed 12 June 2024
7. Forsberg, A.: Penetration testing and privacy assessment of top-ranked health and fitness apps: an empirical Study. Master's thesis, Karlstad University (2024). https://urn.kb.se/resolve?urn=urn%3Anbn%3Ase%3Akau%3Adiva-100477

8. Google: google support: remediation for unsafe encryption mode usage. https://support.google.com/faqs/answer/10046138?hl=en, Accessed April 2024
9. Hatamian, M., Momen, N., Fritsch, L., Rannenberg, K.: A multilateral privacy impact analysis method for android apps. In: Naldi, M., Italiano, G.F., Rannenberg, K., Medina, M., Bourka, A. (eds.) APF 2019. LNCS, vol. 11498, pp. 87–106. Springer, Cham (2019). https://doi.org/10.1007/978-3-030-21752-5_7
10. Iwaya, L.H., Ahmad, A., Babar, M.A.: Security and privacy for mhealth and uhealth systems: a systematic mapping study. IEEE Access **8**, 150081–150112 (2020)
11. Iwaya, L.H., Babar, M.A., Rashid, A., Wijayarathna, C.: On the privacy of mental health apps: an empirical investigation and its implications for app development. Empir. Softw. Eng. **28**(1), 2 (2023)
12. Knorr, K., Aspinall, D.: Security testing for android mhealth apps. In: 2015 IEEE Eighth International Conference on Software Testing, Verification and Validation Workshops (ICSTW), pp. 1–8. IEEE (2015)
13. Kotipalli, S.R., Imran, M.A.: Hacking Android. Packt Publishing Ltd (2016)
14. Meta: access tokens for meta technologies (2024). https://developers.facebook.com/docs/facebook-login/guides/access-tokens/, Accessed 23 July 2024
15. Mia, M.R., et al.: A comparative study on HIPAA technical safeguards assessment of android mhealth applications. Smart Health **26**, 100349 (2022)
16. Momen, N.: Measuring apps' privacy-friendliness: introducing transparency to apps' data access behavior. Ph.D. thesis, Karlstad University (2020)
17. OWASP: OWASP web security testing guide: testing for weak encryption (2022). https://owasp.org/www-project-web-security-testing-guide/v42/4-Web_Application_Security_Testing/09-Testing_for_Weak_Cryptography/04-Testing_for_Weak_Encryption, Accessed April 2024
18. OWASP: password plaintext storage (2022). https://owasp.org/www-community/vulnerabilities/Password_Plaintext_Storage, Accessed 2 April 2024
19. OWASP: Mobile top 10 - M8: security misconfiguration (2023). https://owasp.org/www-project-mobile-top-10/2023-risks/m8-security-misconfiguration.html, Accessed April 2024
20. OWASP: OWASP mobile top 10: insufficient binary protection (2023). https://owasp.org/www-project-mobile-top-10/2023-risks/m7-insufficient-binary-protection.html, Accessed: April 2024
21. Papageorgiou, A., Strigkos, M., Politou, E., Alepis, E., Solanas, A., Patsakis, C.: Security and privacy analysis of mobile health applications: the alarming state of practice. IEEE Access **6**, 9390–9403 (2018)
22. Raymond, A., Schubauer, J., Madappa, D.: Over-privileged permissions: using technology and design to create legal compliance. J. Bus. Technol. **15**(2020) (2020)
23. Solomos, K., Ilia, P., Ioannidis, S., Kourtellis, N.: Talon: an automated framework for cross-device tracking detection. In: 22nd International Symposium on Research in Attacks, Intrusions and Defenses (RAID 2019), pp. 227–241 (2019)
24. Statista: downloads of leading fitness and workout mobile apps worldwide in the month of january from 2017 to 2024 (2024). https://www.statista.com/statistics/1239806/growth-top-fitness-mobile-apps-downloads/
25. Tangari, G., Ikram, M., Ijaz, K., Kaafar, M.A., Berkovsky, S.: Mobile health and privacy: cross sectional study. bmj 373: n1248. BMJ **373** (2021)
26. Tangari, G., Ikram, M., Sentana, I.W.B., Ijaz, K., Kaafar, M.A., Berkovsky, S.: Analyzing security issues of android mobile health and medical applications. J. Am. Med. Inform. Assoc. **28**(10), 2074–2084 (2021)

Network Security

CCKex: High Bandwidth Covert Channels over Encrypted Network Traffic

Christian Lindenmeier(✉), Sven Gebhard, Jonas Röckl, and Felix Freiling

Friedrich-Alexander-Universität Erlangen-Nürnberg (FAU), Erlangen, Germany
{christian.lindenmeier,sven.gebhard,jonas.roeckl,felix.freiling}@fau.de

Abstract. Covert channels, such as the timing behavior of a process or the lowest order bit in a network protocol nonce, can be used to exchange information in a stealthy manner. Storage covert channels are a class of covert channels that modulate data onto unused or redundant protocol fields of existing network communication. Because of this restriction, but also because of the ubiquity of encrypted communication, such channels usually suffer from severe bandwidth limitations. We propose a novel storage-based covert channel that enables the transmission of data inside encrypted network traffic, thus both drastically increasing bandwidth and stealth. In contrast to prior work, we assume the availability of encryption keys on the sender side, a condition usually met by strong attackers applying key extraction from memory. In this way, we are able to embed information into encrypted network traffic, experimentally increasing covert bandwidth by a factor of 11. We demonstrate the practical feasibility of our approach targeting the Android app Signal on a real-world smartphone.

Keywords: Covert channels · Encrypted communication · Key extraction · Android

1 Introduction

A Covert Channel (CC) is often defined as a communication channel that is neither designed nor intended to transfer information [9]. Common examples are the timing behavior of a process or the system load. CCs are a serious security threat to all types of systems since they occur almost everywhere and are difficult to contain. In particular, classical approaches of access control and perimeter security using reference monitors are not sufficient to prevent information leaking over such channels. This is amplified by the fact that open system architectures are commonly faced with "insider attacks", i.e., attacks that have penetrated the perimeter of the system anyway, including "rooted" computing machines. While they are often considered malicious, CCs can also be used "for the good", e.g., by whistleblowers or dissidents to communicate in autocratic environments [32,33].

The specific class of *storage-based CCs* (as opposed to *timing* channels) modulate information on the content of network packets, e.g., unused header fields or

L. Horn Iwaya et al. (Eds.): NordSec 2024, LNCS 15396, pp. 385–404, 2025.
https://doi.org/10.1007/978-3-031-79007-2_20

different text encodings of content that cannot be distinguished by an unaware observer. Through the multiplicity of ways to encode data, storage CCs generally a little higher bandwidth than timing channels.

Limited bandwidth is a general restriction of CCs, that mainly stems from the requirement of stealthiness, but nowadays also from the increasing fraction of encrypted network traffic. Storage-based CCs need to add, remove or alter values to encode information. This cannot be done on encrypted data because of the built-in integrity protection features of network protocols. Consider for example data transferred using the Transport Layer Security (TLS) protocol which protects the content of the application protocol at the transport layer, so remaining unencrypted parts are either lower network layers or header of for example TCP/IP. This circumstance, together with the fact that these protocols are often highly optimized and leave less space for manipulations, greatly limit the amount of data that can be hidden in a network packet. As a consequence, even the best developed CCs over TLS [6,21] or CCs that restrict themselves to unecrypted parts of communication [7] are limited in bandwidth (we give a more detailed review of the literature in Sect. 7).

1.1 Increasing Bandwidth Using Encryption Keys

Interestingly, all prior works on CC construction assume the unavailability of encryption keys. However, looking at recent malware [20], we notice that sophisticated strains often acquire privileged access to the target system (i.e., the malware has root access). An example is the classical assumption of a Trojan horse on the sender side communicating with the attacker via a command-and-control channel. The existence of privileged malware justifies our assumption that an attacker has access to encryption keys as key material is generally held in the volatile memory of unprivileged processes.

Clearly, these keys can then be used to "open" encrypted parts, covertly add information, and re-encrypt the data, an activity that would be indistinguishable to the unaware receiver. Alternatively, one could even directly inject covert data into network packets while they reside still unencrypted in volatile memory.

Consider the typical scenario of CCs in Fig. 1: A Trojan horse with access to keys wants to send data to an eavesdropper in the network. While the Trojan horse may have access to the keys (through key extraction methods, see Sect. 2), the Covert Receiver (CR) does not have access to keys. The solution that we propose is to send the keys covertly too. This could be done by introducing backdoors into the cryptographic primitives [8,35]. But this involves changes to the underlying cryptosystems which is outside the scope of our scenario. Instead, we directly send the keys as part of the covert data.

The effect of having access to keys is clear: The Trojan horse can use all parts of network packets for covert communication. As we show in the paper, this substantially increases the available bandwidth of the CC. Because of the many options to embed keys in the communication, using the bandwidth effectively is not trivial. For an approach to work, keys have to be embedded securely and allow effective (correct and timely) decryption. Despite the scenario being obvious (key access), we are not aware of this having been investigated before.

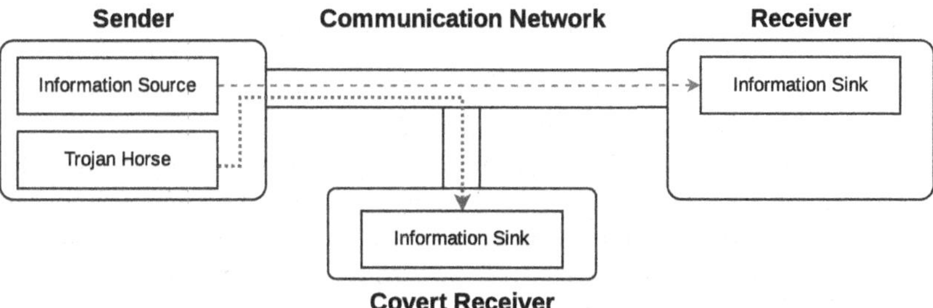

Fig. 1. Our scenario: A Trojan horse with access to encryption keys wishes to send information to a CR in the network. Blue-dashed traffic is legitimate network traffc. Red-dotted traffic is covert communication. (Color figure online)

1.2 Contributions

In the common scenario depicted in Fig. 1, a Trojan horse (covert sender) embeds covert messages in existing network packets, i.e., by using already existent communication between a sender and a receiver as a carrier medium. While previous approaches have excluded encrypted parts of the carrier traffic, in this paper we propose a novel approach that enables the transmission of covert data *inside* encrypted network traffic, drastically increasing bandwidth and stealth.

The basic idea is to transmit cryptographic key material in covert communication, i.e., to intentionally leak necessary keys to the CR such that the CR can decrypt the traffic, albeit in a secure way so that *only* the CR receives the keys. This allows the Covert Sender (CS) to inject covert data inside encrypted traffic, increasing the capacity for covert messages.

In our scenario, the CS operates on a host machine in a way that allows the instrumentation of network packets before they are encrypted, i.e. the sender can manipulate the content of encrypted network data before it is sent. Furthermore, we assume that the CS has access to all the necessary encryption keys, an assumption that can be justified when looking at advanced digital forensic techniques for extracting keys that are used for encrypting network packets [10].

The idea of our approach is to extract associated key material from the volatile memory whenever the host prepares to send an encrypted network packet. The CS embeds the key in unencrypted parts of network packets using traditional CCs. Subsequently, the CS hides covert messages in the encrypted layer of network packets. Conversely, the CR can extract the embedded key from the unencrypted parts of the network packet, use the key to decrypt the encrypted layer of the packet and, thus, access further embedded covert messages. Note that for both the original sender and the original receiver of the (overt) network communication (as well as for any intrusion detection system observing network traffic) the communication looks and feels fully legitimate. Since the usage of cryptographic keys is a central element in our approach, we call this form of CC a *Key extraction-based Covert Channel (KEX-CC).*

To summarize, we provide the following contributions:

1. We propose and formalize CCKex, an approach to construct KEX-CCs that utilize the encrypted parts of network traffic.
2. We showcase CCKex's practical feasibility by covertly transmitting data via the encrypted network traffic of the Android app Signal on a real smartphone. CCKex's source code is openly accessible at https://github.com/cckex/cckex
3. We practically evaluate CCKex and show that we achieve up to 11.1x higher bandwidth compared to state-of-the-art CC proposals.

Overall, our approach shows the practical feasibility to construct high bandwidth and long distance CCs.

1.3 Roadmap

The paper is organized as follows: We first give background knowledge in Sect. 2. In Sect. 3, we introduce and formalize the concept of KEX-CCs. Section 4 demonstrates the practical application of our concepts by presenting CCKex, an end-to-end framework for implementing KEX-CCs. We describe hands-on implementation details for our Proof-of-Concept (PoC) targeting the Signal app on Android in Sect. 5. We practically evaluate CCKex in Sect. 6 to showcase the capabilities of our approach and discuss its limitations. We refer to related work in Sect. 7 and conclude in Sect. 8.

2 Background

2.1 Network-Level Covert Channels

In the context of networking, a CC is a communication established between a CS and a CR with the goal of exchanging data in a stealthy manner, i.e., such that other network participants cannot notice the data transfer. To this end, the CS and the CR exploit legitimate network traffic as a carrier and hide payload data within transmitted data to conceal their communication. CCs use steganographic methods to inject covert information into *overt* channels, like the header or payload of network packets. In general, the CS and CR exploit an underlying carrier protocol by nesting a parasitic channel into already existing network traffic. In practice, CCs can be used both for malicious (e.g., command and control of malware) and legitimate purposes (e.g., circumvent censorship).

2.2 Encryption Protocols

Today, the most dominantly used protocol in the internet for transferring encrypted data is the TLS protocol. When establishing a TLS connection, a client and a server perform a *handshake* resulting in the establishment of a TLS session. With TLS1.3, the client and server negotiate multiple secrets that are used to encrypt payload data in a symmetric fashion.

Due to privacy concerns in the context of instant messaging, TLS is often considered insufficient. For example, Signal [17] and WhatsApp employed an additional layer of encryption to ensure that only the sender and receiver can decrypt communication data, while the forwarding server cannot. Nowadays, the Double Ratchet protocol [18] powering Signal constitues the state-of-the-art in End-to-End Encryption (E2EE). The idea is based on the concept of *ratchets*, that are used to continually generate new one-time key material for encrypting messages. An extended form of the Diffie-Hellman key exchange is employed to continually update key material for chat messages. By moving the session ratchet forward, a new session key is derived that is used as input for messaging ratchets, hence the naming of *double* ratchet protocol. The messaging ratchets are used to derive symmetric keys that are used with the AES cipher to encrypt chat messages.

2.3 Key Extraction from Volatile Memory

Extracting ephemeral artifacts from the volatile memory at runtime is a common challenge in the field of digital forensics [10]. This is even more the case for cryptographic keys, which are typically only present in memory for a very short period of time [3]. While there are multiple approaches for extracting TLS key material [1,4,13,29], none of these directly addresses the extraction of Signal's one-time keys [10]. Only recently, researchers have shown that similar approaches can be used to extract highly-ephemeral one-time key material by continually monitoring a system's control-flow [25].

In summary, the extraction task boils down to mainly two steps: First, the extractor running on the host needs to hit the perfect timing and introspect the memory at exactly the time when key material is present. To this end, state-of-the-art approaches may leverage Dynamic Binary Instrumentation (DBI), that enables hooking the control-flow of the system by injecting custom code at run-time [28]. Second, the extractor routine needs to find the key material in memory in a reasonable time to not hinder the execution of the system. Finding specific key material in memory dumps an be done using heuristic-based approaches based on entropy measurements or including prior knowledge [10]. Our work showcases the extraction of one-time key material of a running Signal app from the volatile memory.

3 Enabling Covert Channels on Encrypted Network Traffic

We derive the central idea of KEX-CCs based on a formal model of communication systems. To this end, we view network communication as a directed stream of packets from a sender to a receiver. Network packets comprise a sequence of *layers*, the number and structure of which depend on the underlying protocol stack (e.g., Signal over TLS over TCP/IP). For simplicity we assume a fixed number of layers which are numbered 0 (lowest *layer*) to n.

We assume that network communication is encrypted. Encrypting layer i protects layer i and all layers above with a specific key. Without the key, the content of encrypted layers cannot be understood. This also holds for multiple encryption layers, e.g., Signal's Double Ratched algorithm *and* TLS. Without loss of generality, we assume that all layers except the lowest layer 0 are encrypted. As shown in Fig. 1, the legitimate traffic is the carrier for covert communication from a CS to a CR.

We provide a schematic overview of our communication model in Fig. 2. We assume an infinite sequence of layered packets from a (covert) sender to a (covert) receiver. An individual layer of a specific packet can be uniquely identified using the pair (p, i) of packet number p and layer number i. If layer (p, i) is encrypted, the notation $key(p, i)$ refers to the keys required to decrypt the content of all layers starting at i in packet p.

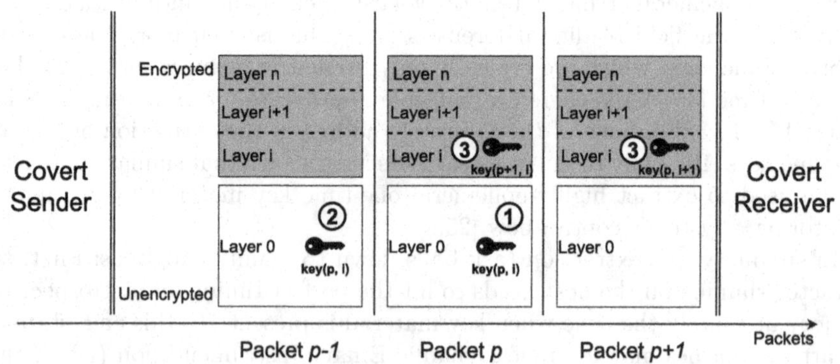

Fig. 2. Communication model of KEX-CC. The CS (left) sends a sequence of network packets to the CR (right). Each network packet consists of layers into which the CS injects keys. Without loss of generality, we assume that all layers $i > 0$ are encrypted. The depicted keys 1–3 are explained in Sect. 3.2 and Sect. 3.4.

3.1 Types of KEX-CC

We formally define three increasingly powerful types of KEX-CCs which depend on the abilities of the CS and CR.

The first distinction depends on the ability of CS and CR to buffer the sequence of packets being transmitted. Storing an arbitrary amount of network traffic may be feasible for the CR. Conversely, it may be cumbersome for the CS who has to operate covertly within the realm of the (overt) sender. The ability to store messages enables the construction of more powerful KEX-CCs. We qualify such channels as *with saving* rather than storing, since this could lead to confusion with the already commonly known storage-based CCs..

The second distinction depends on whether or not the CR can decrypt (and access) the covert message at the exact moment when the associated packet arrives. We call such channels *synchronous.* If CS and CR are with saving, it is also possible to construct *asynchronous* variants of KEX-CCs where key material may arrive *after* the associated packet. As we show below, asynchronous channels offer more flexibility to transmit keys, allowing even higher bandwidth. Since asynchronous KEX-CC necessarily assumes saving capabilities at CS and CR, we end up with three increasingly powerful variants of KEX-CCs.

We define these three variants by stating conditions about the *accessibility of the content of* (p, i), i.e., the fact that CR can understand layer i of packet p. This implicitly describes requirements on how *key*(p, i) must be embedded in the traffic by the CS such that the information in (p, i) can be extracted by the CR, as we now explain.

3.2 Type 1: Synchronous Without Saving

The simplest type of KEX-CC is synchronous and does not assume saving capabilities at CS and CR. Thus, the CR can only inspect the current packet p and does not have access to earlier or later packets. The following two conditions define this type of channel:

C1 The content of layer 0 of packet p is accessible.
C2 The content of some layer i of packet p is accessible iff (if and only if) *key*(p, i) is accessible in layer $j \leq i$ of packet p.

Condition C1 is usually satisfied in modern network protocols since the lowest layer is usually unencrypted. To allow access to encrypted layer i, the key must therefore be transmitted in layers below i. Note that condition C2 can be recursively applied, i.e., *key*$(p, 1)$ is accessible in $(p, 0)$ and *key*$(p, 2)$ is accessible in $(p, 1)$ (① in Fig. 2).

3.3 Type 2: Synchronous with Saving

Channels of type 1 require to embed all necessary key material in one packet. If CS and CR can buffer network packets, it is also possible to embed keys for later packets in earlier ones. This is useful, for example, if the same keys are used to encrypt layers in multiple packets. If we want to maintain synchronous decryption, keys can only be embedded in *previous* packets. This is expressed by the following two conditions:

C3 The content of layer 0 of some packets $p' \leq p$ is accessible.
C4 The content of layer i of packet p is accessible iff all keys for encrypted layers $j \leq i$ are accessible in packets $p' \leq p$.

Note that condition C1 implies C3 and C2 implies C4. Therefore, a synchronous KEX-CC with saving is strictly stronger than a synchronous KEX-CC without saving. The additional network bandwidth stems from the ability to save network packets at each end and retrieve decryption keys "from the past". This is depicted in Fig. 2 at ② where a key for a later packet is embedded in an earlier one.

In our formalization, we assume that CS and CR can save an arbitrary amount of packets, which may appear unrealistic. In practice, this class represents channels where CS and CR can store "enough" network packets.

3.4 Type 3: Asynchronous with Saving

If CS and CR can store network packets, they can not only retrieve decryption keys for (p, i) from the past but also from "the future", i.e., *later* packets. This, however, implies that no synchronous decryption is guaranteed. The asynchronous channel can be formalized using the following two conditions:

C5 The content of layer 0 of some packet p' is accessible.
C6 The content of layer i of packet p is accessible iff all keys for encrypted layers $j \leq i$ in packet p are accessible in some packet p'.

We require that decryption keys can be embedded in arbitrary layers of arbitrary packets. This circumstance is visualized in ③ (Fig. 2). The key for $(p+1, i)$ is embedded in (p, i) and the key for $(p, i+1)$ is embedded in $(p+1, i)$. The CR must therefore wait for packet $p+1$ to be able to access layer $i+1$ in the earlier packet p.

Since C3 implies C5 and C4 implies C6, this type is strictly more powerful in terms of bandwidth at the cost of being asynchronous. In practice, even asynchronous channels allow timely decryption if the network connections which are used as carrier traffic are short-lived. For this reason, we develop and implement a type-3 PoC, which we explain in Sect. 4 and Sect. 5.

4 Kex-Based Covert Communication with CCKex

We now describe CCKex, an end-to-end framework for implementing KEX-CCs on real-world devices. Figure 3 gives an overview of our approach.

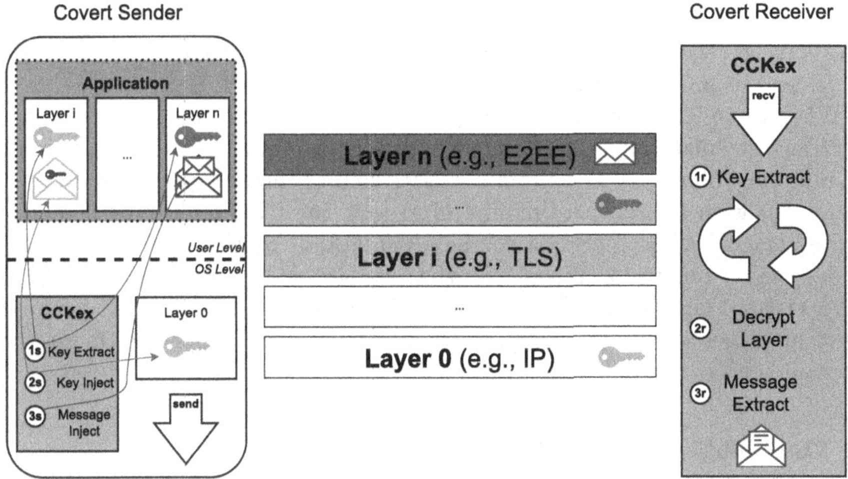

Fig. 3. An overview of CCKex's design. The CS introspects the memory of an application, that employs encryption protocols, extracts key material, and injects covert messages before the encryption process. The CR recursively extracts key material and decrypts network layers while searching for covert messages.

4.1 Requirements

We walk through the process of sending ((1s)-(3s)) and receiving ((1r)-(3r)) a covert message. In total, we identify four requirements:

R1 The CS and CR agree on well-defined functions *embed*(*data*, *layer*) and *extract*(*data*, *layer*) to inject and extract key material into and from network traffic.
R2 The CS can extract ephemeral cryptographic keys from the volatile memory of the host.
R3 The CS can manipulate the content of network packets, especially their encrypted layers, on the host *before* they are sent.
R4 The CR knows decryption functions *dec*(*key*, *layer*) for relevant encryption layers the CS injected data into.

With R1, we ensure that CS and CR know how to embed and extract covertly communicated data over the KEX-CC. This is a common assumption in the field of CCs [30]. In regard to the requirements for the CS (R2 and R3), we propose to operate CCKex's agent at the Operating System (OS) level of the host. To ensure R2 ((1s)), the CS extracts the light gray key from the memory of an application that communicates via layer i. Adressing R3, the CS injects extracted key material in the layers of network traffic using function *embed*(*key*, *layer*) ((2s)). For unencrypted layers this can be directly done on the OS level, while for layers encrypted at the user level, our agent locates the content in volatile memory at runtime *before* it is encrypted using DBI. Similarly, the CS injects covert messages into the later encrypted layers using function *embed*(*message*, *layer*) (3s). We go into technical details of our implementation in Sect. 5.1.

When the CR receives a network packet, it uses the function *extract*(*data*, 0) to retrieve key material hidden in layer 0 ((1r)). For example, the CR extracts TLS key material (light-gray key) from a header field of the IP layer. For decrypting layers ((2r)) with this key, we require (R4) that the CR implements a function *dec*(*key*, *layer*). While TLS is a common encryption protocol, for CCKex's CR we designed a plugin for Wireshark, that enables decrypting the Signal protocol (Sect. 5.2). Our CR repeats this process recursively until all keys and finally covert messages are decrypted (3r). In general, CCKex's CR operates in an *asynchronous with saving* setting (Sect. 3).

4.2 Embedding Keys in Network Layers

Systematic Strategy. For this strategy, we try to embed the key material $key(p,i)$ in the closest layers below in packet p with $embed(key(p,i), i-1)$ and covert messages at the highest layer n. Thus, our strategy strives to fulfill a KEX-CC working *synchronously without saving* (Section 3). However, from a practical perspective, we must consider the available capacity of each layer $capacity(p,i)$ to ensure that there is enough space to inject the necessary key material and message (i.e., $capacity(p,n) > 0$). Thus, $capacity(p,n)$ dictates the overall bandwidth of the CC. We infer that *synchronous without saving* is only possible iff $\forall i \in [0, ..., n] : \sum_{j=0}^{i-1} capacity(p,j) >= \sum_{j=1}^{i} size(key(p,j))$. If the condition does not hold, we split the key over multiple packets and implement *asynchronous with saving*. We implement our PoC for this strategy and explain details in Sect. 5.

Chaining Keys. Each strategy is a trade-off between maximizing bandwidth and stealth. We now describe a strategy promising to maximizes stealth under specific conditions by nearly only operating at the highest encryption layer. We achieve this by *chaining* the injection of key material in encrypted layers such that the next (or previous) packet's layers can be decrypted. If $capacity(p,n) > \sum_{i=0}^{n} size(key(p+1,i))$, we can implement a forward-chaining injection strategy in an *asynchronous with saving* setting as follows: The CS holds a queue with two network packets p and $p+1$. Then, the CS repeatedly injects all required key material for packet $p+1$ into layer n of packet p, i.e., into the next packet. The remaining space can be used to embed covert messages. However, our strategy must start with an initialization phase during which some key material is transmitted in an unencrypted layer, but eventually all covert communication happens in the innermost encrypted layer n. One can also implement a backward-chaining strategy by injecting keys for packet p into packet $p-1$. In this scenario, we require an exiting phase or intermediate phases during which one key has to be communicated in an unencrypted layer.

5 Implementation Details

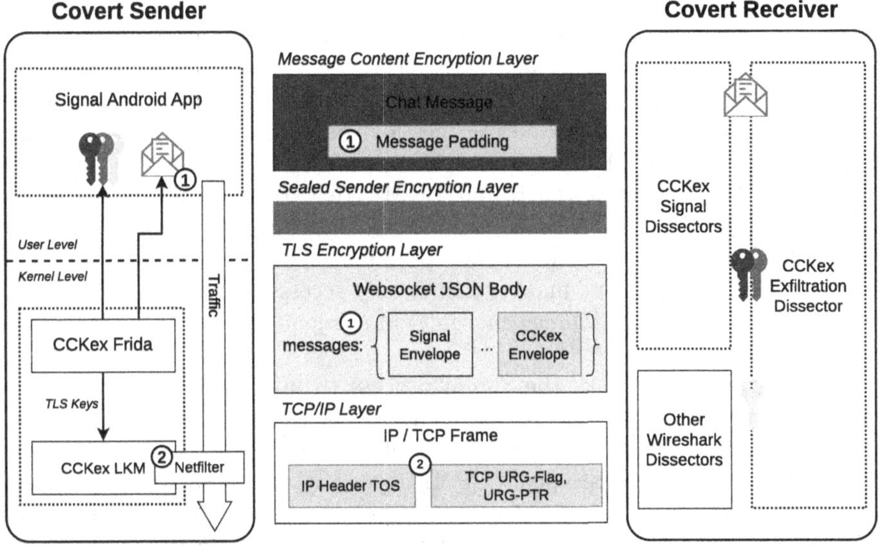

Fig. 4. Overview of the PoC of the CCKex framework. The CS consists of a Frida agent that handles the extraction of key material as well as injection of covert data into memory buffers of Signal chat messages. The Frida agent forwards TLS keys to the CCKex kernel module that leverages the netfilter interface to manipulate outgoing network packets. Our Wireshark plugin implements the CR with three custom dissectors supporting the Signal protocol and a dissector for managing extracted key material and covert messages.

We build our PoC on a Pixel 6 smartphone running Android 14 based on a Linux kernel 5.10.198. We chose a smartphone as a target platform since E2EE communication is ubiquitous on mobile devices. We run Signal (version 7.11.4) on the device and tailor our KEX-CC to Signal's network traffic. Figure 4 depicts an overview of our PoC.

Signal relies on a TCP/IP connection on top of which a TLS 1.3 session is established. Based on the TLS layer, Signal uses the WebSocket protocol to provide a simultaneous two-way communication channel for HTTP requests. The payload of these requests is serialised with JSON and wrapped in a *ProtoBuf*. Signal envelopes are base64-encoded and include the ciphertext for the end-to-end encrypted sealed-sender layer. Each ciphertext holds another *ProtoBuf* wrapping a second layer of E2EE for a serialized chat message. Each raw chat message is padded with zeros for a multiple of 160 bytes. A magic stop byte (`0x80`) marks the end of the serialized message, which also marks the start of the zero padding.

5.1 Covert Sender

CCKex's CS operates at the OS level and comprises two components: A Frida[1] (version 16.4.7) agent and a Loadable Kernel Module (LKM).

The CCKex Frida agent fulfills two main tasks marked with ① in Fig. 4, namely extracting key material and injecting data into memory buffers. First, the agent hooks the execution of the Signal process to extract TLS keys, Signal sealed-sender AES key material, and Signal chat-message AES key material. While we implemented extraction routines for the Signal-specific keys, we integrated friTap[2](version v1.1.0.0) in our framework to handle TLS and directly forward the TLS keys material to our LKM. For extracting the sealed-sender keys we hook the function *aes256_ctr_hmacsha256_encrypt*() in the library *libsignal*. The function receives the unencrypted message buffer as well as the AES key material via parameters, making them easily accessible by CCKex. Similarly, we hook the function *aes_256_cbc_encrypt*() in *libsignal* to retrieve the AES keys for the chat messages.

Second, the agent hooks the Signal process to inject covert data and key material into Signal traffic before its is encrypted. In Fig. 4, we mark the content modified by CCKex in the network traffic in red color. Overall, we inject key material into the unencryped TCP/IP layer (②) and the Websocket JSON body. Our agent hooks the constructor of the class *OutgoingPushMessageList* for injecting a custom Signal envelope at the Websocket layer. For injecting key material, we wrap it in a custom ProtoBuf, serialize it as base64, and write it into the payload of the custom *OutgoingPushMessage*. Covert payload data is injected into the padding bytes at the E2EE chat message layer (①). To this end, we add a custom ProtoBuf record to the serialized chat message with the *LEN* wire type and a custom field number containing the injected payload. We move the padding stop-byte to the end.

To handle the TCP/IP layer, we leverage CCKex's LKM. The module relies on the *netfilter* interface and installs hooks for the TCP/IP protocol, enabling access to the raw data stored in a socket buffer (*struct sk_buff*) of every outgoing packet. The LKM receives TLS secrets via a character device and injects them into the urgent pointer of the TCP header and TOS filed of the IP header.

5.2 Covert Receiver

We use Wireshark (version 4.3.1) to record and parse a *PCAP* file of the recorded network traffic. Our CR works in an *asynchronous with saving* setting, i.e., we recursively search for key material in the entire traffic and try to decrypt any packet repeatedly.

We implement a custom post-dissector that parses the IP and TCP header and retrieves the exfiltrated TLS secrets by reversing the injection process. The CS uses magic values to indicate the start and type of the TLS secrets. Based on the extracted secret, Wireshark can decrypt the TLS traffic.

[1] https://frida.re/.

[2] https://github.com/fkie-cad/friTap.

We also build custom dissectors to identify and parse the WebSocket and HTTP protocols wrapped in the TLS connection. These act as bridges between already existing dissectors since the Signal protocol relies on encodings that are supported by Wireshark (e.g., ProtoBuf and JSON). Our dissector iterates over the base64-encoded messages in the JSON body and identifies the envelope manipulated by CCKex. Subsequently, we parse the envelope that contains the ciphertext of the original Signal chat message. If we recognize a custom ProtoBuf record representing an injected envelope, a further custom dissector extracts the injected Signal key material for both the sealed sender and chat message layer.

In a last step, the dissector takes the ciphertext from the original chat message's envelope and decrypts it with the extracted AES key material. If the special ProtoBuf record that was injected by the CS is found, we extract the injected payload data from the padding of the chat message.

6 Evaluation

We evaluate CCKex and measure the achievable bandwidth of our PoC. Furthermore, we discuss the detectability of KEX-CCs.

6.1 Bandwidth

One of the main benefits of our approach promises to be an increased bandwidth compared to traditional CCs. Thus, we measure the bandwidth of our PoC in experiments on a real-world smartphone. For each experiment, we send a total of 128 Signal messages (one message every five seconds) and measure the payload data, i.e., excluding key data, of covertly transmitted bytes. More specifically, we perform the following two experiments:

- *Random*: In this experiment we send Signal chat messages with random length between one and 128. Since our KEX-CC depends on available capacity in the padding of chat messages, we try to simulate the behavior of a normal human end user with this experiment.
- *Fixed*: As we exploit the zero padding of the Signal message layer for injecting our CC, there exists an optimal chat message length that leads to a maximal padding, i.e., capacity for our CC. In this experiment we fix the length of each Signal message to 111.

We use Appium[3] to automate the evaluation process, repeat each experiment five times, and average the results. In total, we transmitted approximately 1700 TCP packets for every run. Since our results converged and showed a low variability, we argue that five repetitions for every experiment are sufficient. Figure 5 depicts the cumulative covertly transmitted payload data (excluding key material) for our experiments.

The black graph *TCP Urgent Pointer CC* represents a baseline for a traditional storage-based CC that only injects payload data into the urgent pointer

[3] http://appium.io/docs/en/latest/.

field and TOS field of TCP packets. In total, this CC transmitted around 5,100 bytes with a throughput of three bytes per packet. The gray graph *Envelope Injection CC* shows the results of a KEX-CC that injects a fake Signal message envelope at the Websocket layer for transmitting payload data and the *TCP Urgent Pointer CC* for exfiltrating TLS secrets. With this KEX-CC, up to 35,300 bytes were covertly transmitted with a throughput of around 20.7 bytes per packet. The red graph *Random Message ProtoBuf Injection CC* represents the results for our full KEX-CC that leverages both encryption layers (i.e., TLS and Signal's Double Ratchet) in the random chat message setting. We divert key material via both the *TCP Urgent Pointer CC* and *Envelope Injection CC* while injecting payload data exclusively into the zero padding of Signal chat messages. In the random setting, our KEX-CC reached a total of around 45,300 bytes with a throughput of around 26.8 bytes per packet. In an optimal setting represented by the blue graph *Fixed Message ProtoBuf Injection CC*, 57,000 bytes were transmitted with a throughput of 33.3 bytes per packet.

In summary, our results show that KEX-CCs can increase the bandwidth of storage-based CCs compared to traditional variants by up to 11.1 times.

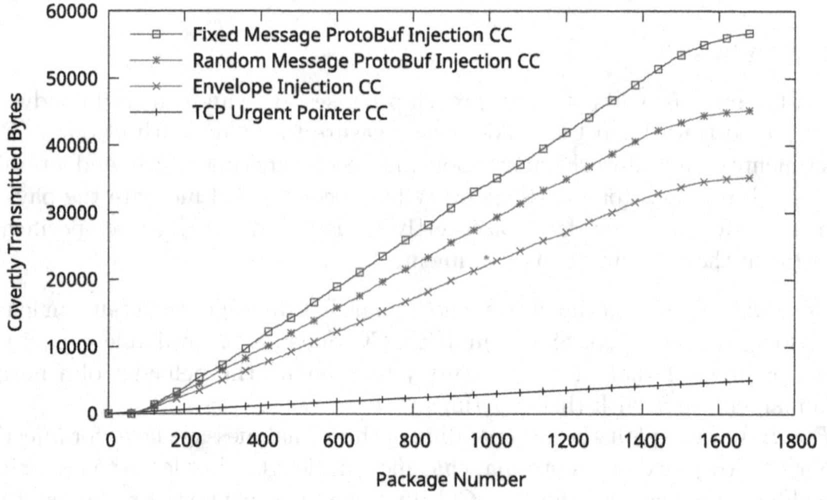

Fig. 5. Cumulatively transmitted covert payload data along sent TCP packets. KEX-CCs greatly outperform traditional CCs in terms of bandwidth. (Color figure online)

6.2 Network Detection

For quantifying the stealth, we measure the ratio of manipulated bytes compared to the overall packet size in percent and present the results in Fig. 6. While TCP/IP header data is accessible by any network participant, our manipulations

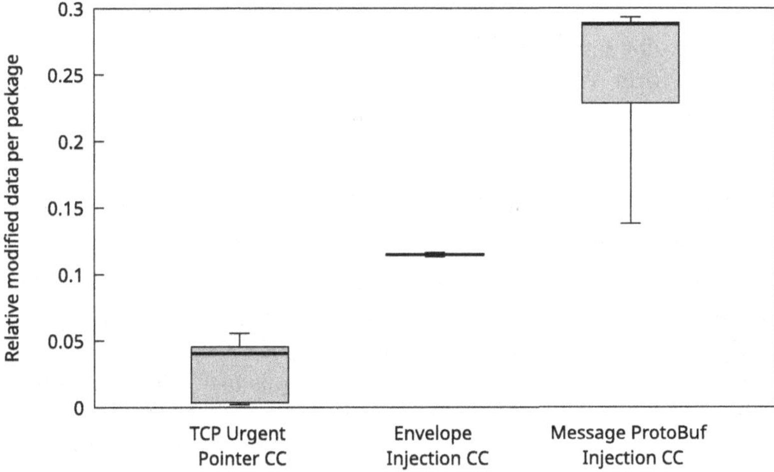

Fig. 6. Ratio of manipulated bytes for each CC compared to the total packet size. While our KEX-CC manipulates more bytes, these manipulations are *inside* encrypted layers, thus less exposed to potential detection techniques.

to encrypted data are only visible to network nodes that can decrypt these layers. Our KEX-CC contributes to the overall changes in a network packet to a varying degree at each of the layers. The lowest manipulation (less than 5%) happens with the *TCP Urgent Pointer CC*. Since we only change three bytes in the TCP/IP header, we argue that these changes are mostly undetected by network detectors. Regarding the *Envelope Injection CC*, we reach constant rates of over 10% manipulation. We note, however, that these parts of the CC are only ever visible to detectors that can access TLS traffic (e.g., the Signal server). The manipulation rate for the *Message ProtoBuf Injection CC* varies between 15% and up to nearly 30%. We point out that these modifications are only visible to participants that can decrypt the E2EE, hence *only* to the end user devices.

6.3 Discussion

Limitations. Because we inject the keys and covert messages in legitimate network traffic, we rely on the user to send messages. However, this limitation is not specific to CCKex but is common to all storage-based covert channels. Further, our reliability can be improved by equipping multiple apps with KEX-CCs. If excessive key sizes are employed, KEX-CCs might be limited in bandwidth in the case that not enough capacity is available for diverting the keys. However, we show that in practice KEX-CCs are feasible even with one-time AES keys.

We assume that CCKex can extract key material from the volatile memory of applications that perform encryption. In practice, most E2EE messengers use symmetric encryption for reasons of performance and hold keys in volatile memory. However, there are techniques that can complicate key extraction by leveraging obfuscation methods [14,26] or isolated execution environments [19].

CCKex comes with some on-device overhead on the host of the CS. However, the overhead is not visible to a network detector, thus does not influence our CC's stealth directly. We consider identifying the CCKex agent on a device with (forensic) measures to be an orthogonal challenge related to malware detection. Furthermore, we note that by modifying parts of the payload of protocols layers (e.g., Signal's padding), a CC could be detected at the original receiver's side. However, for our implementation, we found that the Signal client dropped our modifications silently.

Future Work. With our novel concept of KEX-CCs, we open up various streams of future work. First, one could implement KEX-CCs for other encrypted network traffic or support additional messaging apps like Telegram, WhatsApp, or entirely other application types. Second, we see a potential in coming up with other variants for key injection strategies. While we proposed two strategies, we believe that further variants exist depending on the scenario. Third, CCKex is designed such that the CC on every network layer may be replaced. For example, one could imagine to exchange the TCP/IP layer CC for a timing-based CC.

7 Related Work

To the best of our knowledge, the idea of KEX-CCs is novel. Most closely related to our work are CCs that rely on encrypted network traffic. Schmidbauer et al. [21] exploit the usage of a nonce in TLS to transmit secret data. Heinz et al. [6] investigate methods for CCs targeting TLS traffic. They propose seven different techniques like extending the ClientHello or altering the ciphers and compressions, for using TLS metadata as a CC carrier. Similarly, Merrill et al. [12] implement CCs in SSL negotiation headers. Additionally, there are works that use encrypted and covert DNS queries as CCs for botnets [16] or leverage the Monero blockchain [5] to covertly transmit data in an encrypted fashion. Compared to these works, our KEX-CCs operate *inside* encrypted layers of network packets allowing for a significantly higher bandwidth.

Our work is also partially related to the idea of backdoored cryptosystems. For example, Wuller et al. [34] hide data to calculate a user's key in the RSA modulus and Janovsky et al. [8] propose asymmetric backdoors for all versions of TLS. In contrast to KEX-CCs, these works alter the cryptographic algorithms.

Furthermore, multiple surveys provide taxonomies for network-level CCs that structure the diverse field of CCs. Schmidbauer et al. [23] survey publications addressing indirect CCs over multiple years and identify three common patterns. Wendzel et al. [32] categorize 109 CCs into four different patterns. In a follow-up article, they revise their taxonomy [30] and propose to use steganographic embedding and representing patterns to describe CCs.

There is a wide range of related works addressing storage-based CCs. For example, Marzurczyk et al. [11] propose the idea of *reversible* CCs which allow a CR that sits between the CS and the intended receiver to remove the hidden data from the network packets. Szary et al. [27] implement reversible CCs on multiple protocols. Schmidbauer et al. [22] target detection techniques for reversible CCs via computational measurements. More recently, Wendzel et al. [31] proposed a new class of CCs called *history* CCs. Their idea is that only a small fraction of covert data is transmitted that points to unaltered legitimate traffic, thus enabling higher bandwidth. Zillien et al. [36] design a novel encoding strategy that points to public data in the internet to minimize the amount of traffic that needs to be concealed. Similarly, we see KEX-CCs as a novel type of CCs, that can even be combined with other variants. The literature also discusses numerous other CCs less related to our approach, like for routing protocols [24], inter-protocol steganography [7], and covert data exchange via Dropbox [2].

8 Conclusion

In this paper, we introduce a novel category of network-level CCs that enables including encrypted network data into the equation. We leverage memory introspection techniques to extract key material at runtime from the device's volatile memory while sending legitimate network traffic. By communicating corresponding cryptographic keys to CRs, we drastically expand the available bandwidth for storage-based CCs. By chaining key injections we additionally propose a strategy that enables CCs to operate entirely within encrypted network traffic, leading to new levels of stealth. Our results show that encrypting network traffic does not prevent malware from injecting covert channels, thus urging the development of sophisticated intrusion detection techniques. Especially in the context of so-called "Living-Off-The-Land" attacks, i.e., fileless malware in which attackers leverage native programs of a victim's system to stay undetected [15], KEX-CCs can pose an significant threat. With CCKex, we implement an extendable framework for building KEX-CCs that we openly share to foster future research.

Acknowledgments. We thank our anonymous reviewers for their valuable feedback and comments. This research was partly supported by the German Federal Ministry of Education and Research (BMBF) as part of the CELTIC-NEXT project AI-NET-ANTILLAS ("Automated Network Telecom Infrastructure with inteLLigent Autonomous Systems", grant number 16KIS1314) and by Deutsche Forschungsgemeinschaft (DFG, German Research Foundation) as part of the Research and Training Group 2475 "Cybercrime and Forensic Computing" (grant number 393541319/GRK2475/2-2024).

References

1. Baier, D., Basse, A., Hilgert, J., Lambertz, M.: TLS key material identification and extraction in memory: current state and future challenges. Forensic Sci. Int. Digit. Investig. **49**, 301766 (2024). https://doi.org/10.1016/J.FSIDI.2024.301766
2. Caviglione, L., Podolski, M., Mazurczyk, W., Ianigro, M.: Covert channels in personal cloud storage services: the case of dropbox. IEEE Trans. Ind. Inf. **13**(4), 1921–1931 (2017). https://doi.org/10.1109/TII.2016.2627503

3. Chow, J., Pfaff, B., Garfinkel, T., Rosenblum, M.: Shredding Your Garbage: Reducing Data Lifetime Through Secure Deallocation. In: McDaniel, P.D. (ed.) Proceedings of the 14th USENIX Security Symposium, Baltimore, MD, USA, 31 July–5 August 2005. USENIX Association (2005). https://www.usenix.org/conference/14th-usenix-security-symposium/shredding-your-garbage-reducing-data-lifetime-through
4. Dolan-Gavitt, B., Leek, T., Hodosh, J., Lee, W.: Tappan Zee (North) bridge: mining memory accesses for introspection. In: Sadeghi, A., Gligor, V.D., Yung, M. (eds.) 2013 ACM SIGSAC Conference on Computer and Communications Security, CCS'13, Berlin, Germany, 4–8 November 2013, pp. 839–850. ACM (2013). https://doi.org/10.1145/2508859.2516697
5. Guo, Z., Shi, L., Xu, M., Yin, H.: MRCC: a practical covert channel over monero with provable security. IEEE Access **9**, 31816–31825 (2021). https://doi.org/10.1109/ACCESS.2021.3060285
6. Heinz, C., Zuppelli, M., Caviglione, L.: Covert channels in transport layer security: performance and security assessment. J. Wirel. Mob. Networks Ubiq. Comput. Dependable Appl. **12**(4), 22–36 (2021). https://doi.org/10.22667/JOWUA.2021.12.31.022
7. Jankowski, B., Mazurczyk, W., Szczypiorski, K.: Information hiding using improper frame padding. In: 2010 14th International Telecommunications Network Strategy and Planning Symposium (NETWORKS), pp. 1–6. IEEE (2010)
8. Janovsky, A., Krhovjak, J., Matyas, V.: Bringing kleptography to real-world TLS. In: Blazy, O., Yeun, C.Y. (eds.) WISTP 2018. LNCS, vol. 11469, pp. 15–27. Springer, Cham (2019). https://doi.org/10.1007/978-3-030-20074-9_3
9. Lampson, B.W.: A note on the confinement problem. Commun. ACM **16**(10), 613–615 (1973). https://doi.org/10.1145/362375.362389
10. Lindenmeier, C., Hammer, A., Gruber, J., Röckl, J., Freiling, F.C.: Key extraction-based lawful access to encrypted data: taxonomy and survey. Forensic Sci. Int. Digit. Investig. **50**, 301796 (2024). https://doi.org/10.1016/J.FSIDI.2024.301796
11. Mazurczyk, W., Szary, P., Wendzel, S., Caviglione, L.: Towards reversible storage network covert channels. In: Proceedings of the 14th International Conference on Availability, Reliability and Security, ARES 2019, Canterbury, UK, 26–29 August 2019, pp. 69:1–69:8. ACM (2019).https://doi.org/10.1145/3339252.3341493
12. Merrill, J., Johnson, D.: Covert channels in SSL session negotiation headers. In: Proceedings of the International Conference on Security and Management (SAM), p. 70. The Steering Committee of The World Congress in Computer Science (2015)
13. Moriconi, F., Levillain, O., Francillon, A., Troncy, R.: X-Ray-TLS: transparent decryption of TLS sessions by extracting session keys from memory. In: Zhou, J., Quek, T.Q.S., Gao, D., Cárdenas, A.A. (eds.) Proceedings of the 19th ACM Asia Conference on Computer and Communications Security, ASIA CCS 2024, Singapore, 1–5 July 2024. ACM (2024). https://doi.org/10.1145/3634737.3637654
14. Müller, T., Freiling, F.C., Dewald, A.: TRESOR runs encryption securely outside RAM. In: 20th USENIX Security Symposium, San Francisco, CA, USA, 8–12 August 2011, Proceedings. USENIX Association (2011). http://static.usenix.org/events/sec11/tech/full_papers/Muller.pdf
15. Ongun, T., et al.: Living-off-the-land command detection using active learning. In: Bilge, L., Dumitras, T. (eds.) RAID '21: 24th International Symposium on Research in Attacks, Intrusions and Defenses, San Sebastian, Spain, 6–8 October 2021, pp. 442–455. ACM (2021). https://doi.org/10.1145/3471621.3471858

16. Patsakis, C., Casino, F., Katos, V.: Encrypted and covert DNS queries for botnets: challenges and countermeasures. Comput. Secur. **88** (2020). https://doi.org/10.1016/J.COSE.2019.101614
17. Perrin, T., Marlinspike, M.: The Double Ratchet Algorithm. Technical Report. Revision 1, 2016-11-20, Signal Foundation (2016)
18. Perrin, T., Marlinspike, M.: The Double Ratchet Algorithm. GitHub wiki (2016)
19. Röckl, J., Wagenhäuser, A., Müller, T.: Veto: prohibit outdated edge system software from booting. In: Mori, P., Lenzini, G., Furnell, S. (eds.) Proceedings of the 9th International Conference on Information Systems Security and Privacy, ICISSP 2023, Lisbon, Portugal, 22–24 February 2023, pp. 46–57. SciTePress (2023).https://doi.org/10.5220/0011627700003405, https://doi.org/10.5220/0011627700003405
20. Rudie, J., Katz, Z., Kuhbander, S., Bhunia, S.: Technical analysis of the NSO group's pegasus spyware. In: 2021 International Conference on Computational Science and Computational Intelligence (CSCI) (2021)
21. Schmidbauer, T., Keller, J., Wendzel, S.: Challenging channels: encrypted covert channels within challenge-response authentication. In: ARES 2022: The 17th International Conference on Availability, Reliability and Security, Vienna, Austria, 23–26 August 2022, pp. 50:1–50:10. ACM (2022). https://doi.org/10.1145/3538969.3544455
22. Schmidbauer, T., Wendzel, S.: Hunting Shadows: Towards Packet Runtime-based Detection Of Computational Intensive Reversible Covert Channels. In: Reinhardt, D., Müller, T. (eds.) ARES 2021: The 16th International Conference on Availability, Reliability and Security, Vienna, Austria, 17–20 August 2021, pp. 71:1–71:10. ACM (2021). https://doi.org/10.1145/3465481.3470085, https://doi.org/10.1145/3465481.3470085
23. Schmidbauer, T., Wendzel, S.: SoK: a survey of indirect network-level covert channels. In: Suga, Y., Sakurai, K., Ding, X., Sako, K. (eds.) ASIA CCS '22: ACM Asia Conference on Computer and Communications Security, Nagasaki, Japan, 30 May–3 June 2022, pp. 546–560. ACM (2022). https://doi.org/10.1145/3488932.3517418
24. Schneider, M., Spiekermann, D., Keller, J.: Network covert channels in routing protocols. In: Proceedings of the 18th International Conference on Availability, Reliability and Security, ARES 2023, Benevento, Italy, 29 August–1 September 2023, pp. 42:1–42:8. ACM (2023). https://doi.org/10.1145/3600160.3605021
25. Schulze, M., Lindenmeier, C., Röckl, J., Freiling, F.: IlluminaTEE: effective man-at-the-end attacks from within ARM TrustZone. In: Checkmate@CCS 2024, Proceedings of the Research on offensive and defensive techniques in the Context of Man At The End (MATE) Attacks, Salt Lake City, UT, USA, 14–18 October 2024. ACM (2024). https://doi.org/10.1145/3689934.3690838
26. Simmons, P.: Security through amnesia: a software-based solution to the cold boot attack on disk encryption. In: Zakon, R.H., McDermott, J.P., Locasto, M.E. (eds.) Twenty-Seventh Annual Computer Security Applications Conference, ACSAC 2011, Orlando, FL, USA, 5–9 December 2011, pp. 73–82. ACM (2011).https://doi.org/10.1145/2076732.2076743
27. Szary, P., Mazurczyk, W., Wendzel, S., Caviglione, L.: Analysis of reversible network covert channels. IEEE Access **10**, 41226–41238 (2022). https://doi.org/10.1109/ACCESS.2022.3168018
28. Taubmann, B., Alabduljaleel, O., Reiser, H.P.: DroidKex: fast extraction of ephemeral TLS keys from the memory of android apps. Digit. Investig. **26 Supplement**, S67–S76 (2018). https://doi.org/10.1016/j.diin.2018.04.013

29. Taubmann, B., Frädrich, C., Dusold, D., Reiser, H.P.: TLSkex: harnessing nirtual machine introspection for decrypting TLS communication. Digit. Investig. **16 Supplement**, S114–S123 (2016). https://doi.org/10.1016/j.diin.2016.01.014
30. Wendzel, S., et al.: A revised taxonomy of steganography embedding patterns. In: Reinhardt, D., Müller, T. (eds.) ARES 2021: The 16th International Conference on Availability, Reliability and Security, Vienna, Austria, 17–20 August 2021, pp. 67:1–67:12. ACM (2021). https://doi.org/10.1145/3465481.3470069
31. Wendzel, S., Schmidbauer, T., Zillien, S., Keller, J.: DYST (did you see that?): an amplified covert channel that points to previously seen data. IEEE Trans. Depend. Secure Comput. (2024)
32. Wendzel, S., Zander, S., Fechner, B., Herdin, C.: Pattern-based survey and categorization of network covert channel techniques. ACM Comput. Surv. **47**(3), 50:1–50:26 (2015). https://doi.org/10.1145/2684195
33. Wu, M., et al.: How the great firewall of China detects and blocks fully encrypted traffic. In: Calandrino, J.A., Troncoso, C. (eds.) 32nd USENIX Security Symposium, USENIX Security 2023, Anaheim, CA, USA, 9–11 August 2023, pp. 2653–2670. USENIX Association (2023). https://www.usenix.org/conference/usenixsecurity23/presentation/wu-mingshi
34. Wüller, S., Kühnel, M., Meyer, U.: Information hiding in the RSA modulus. In: Pérez-González, F., Bas, P., Ignatenko, T., Cayre, F. (eds.) Proceedings of the 4th ACM Workshop on Information Hiding and Multimedia Security, IH&MMSec 2016, Vigo, Galicia, Spain, 20–22 June 2016, pp. 159–167. ACM (2016). https://doi.org/10.1145/2909827.2930804
35. Young, A., Yung, M.: Malicious cryptography: kleptographic aspects. In: Menezes, A. (ed.) CT-RSA 2005. LNCS, vol. 3376, pp. 7–18. Springer, Heidelberg (2005). https://doi.org/10.1007/978-3-540-30574-3_2
36. Zillien, S., Schmidbauer, T., Kubek, M., Keller, J., Wendzel, S.: Look what's there! utilizing the internet's existing data for censorship circumvention with OPPRESSION. In: Zhou, J., Quek, T.Q.S., Gao, D., Cárdenas, A.A. (eds.) Proceedings of the 19th ACM Asia Conference on Computer and Communications Security, ASIA CCS 2024, Singapore, 1–5 July 2024. ACM (2024). https://doi.org/10.1145/3634737.3637676

Fingerprinting DNS Resolvers Using Query Patterns from QNAME Minimization

Jonathan Magnusson(✉)

Karlstad University, Karlstad, Sweden
jonathan.magnusson@kau.se

Abstract. The Domain Name System (DNS) plays a pivotal role in the function of the Internet, but if the DNS resolvers are not correctly configured or updated, they could pose security and privacy risks. Fingerprinting resolvers helps the analysis of the DNS ecosystem and can reveal outdated software and misconfigurations. This study aims to evaluate if patterns in queries from DNS resolvers—implementing query name minimization as a privacy enhancing feature—can reveal their characteristics such as their software and versions. We examined the query patterns of minimizing resolvers at the authoritative name server side, and our findings indicate that distinct patterns correlate with specific open-source resolver software versions. Notably, none of the resolvers fully follow the recommended query name minimization algorithm outlined in RFC 9156, suggesting a discrepancy between recommendations and real-world implementations. We also identified high rates of query amplification, possibly caused in part by the combination of minimization and forwarding configurations. Our research contributes to understanding the current state of the DNS ecosystem, highlighting the potential for fingerprinting to enhance Internet security by identifying and addressing resolver-related risks.

Keywords: DNS · QNAME Minimization · Privacy · Fingerprinting · Traffic Analysis

1 Introduction

The Domain Name System (DNS), essential for translating human-readable domain names into IP addresses [17,18], faces significant security and privacy challenges. DNS resolvers, which play a crucial role in the DNS architecture, could be configured in ways that weaken security or harm the privacy of its users [25,28]. The primary motivation behind this study is to evaluate the current state of query name minimization (`QMIN`) [5] implementations in DNS resolvers and to assess whether the patterns observed in these implementations can reveal insights into the resolver software and version. This is crucial because identifying these patterns can help in fingerprinting resolvers, which can expose outdated

L. Horn Iwaya et al. (Eds.): NordSec 2024, LNCS 15396, pp. 405–423, 2025.
https://doi.org/10.1007/978-3-031-79007-2_21

or vulnerable software that may pose security risks. Furthermore, understanding these patterns enhances DNS privacy and security by identifying discrepancies between the recommended standards and real-world implementations.

This study sheds light on the efficacy of current privacy practices in DNS resolution by measuring and analyzing the query patterns from DNS resolvers implementing `QMIN`. The findings provide a snapshot of the DNS ecosystem's current state and highlight areas where further improvements are needed to align implementations with privacy and security standards. Ultimately, the insights gained from this research contribute to the ongoing efforts to secure the Internet's critical infrastructure, ensuring that DNS resolvers function correctly and uphold end-users' privacy and security. A study by De Vries *et al.* [27] in 2018 provided valuable insights into fingerprinting resolvers implementing `QMIN`, but was limited by its dataset (RIPE Atlas probes) and the then-current standards. Since then, the RFC for `QMIN` (RFC 7816 [4]) was obsoleted by new recommendations (RFC 9156 [5]), in part because of the findings of De Vries *et al.*. Our study revisits and applies the established fingerprinting technique in the context of these updated standards, aiming to provide a more comprehensive and current understanding of DNS resolver patterns by also extending the measurements to public resolvers.

RQ1: Have query signatures from minimizing DNS resolvers changed since the study by De Vries *et al.* in the wake of RFC 9156?
RQ2: Is it possible to fingerprint the version in addition to the resolver software using query signatures?
RQ3: What are the effects of `QMIN` implementation approaches in combination with forwarding strategies in the wild?

The key contributions of this study are:

1. We identify distinct patterns of four popular open-source resolvers that implement algorithms for `QMIN` and identify emerging differences in software versions for two of them (Sect. 4.1).
2. We measure public resolvers and RIPE Atlas probe resolvers and find signatures that match those of the open-source resolvers (Sect. 4.4).
3. We discuss various implementations of `QMIN` per the latest RFC (Sect. 5.1), compare our results with De Vries *et al.*, and conclude that we can classify more open-source resolvers by establishing more accurate signatures (Sect. 5.2).
4. We observe significant query amplification, which in part is caused by the combination of `QMIN` and forwarding configurations (Sect. 5.3).

2 Background

2.1 Domain Name System

The DNS is a hierarchical key/value store that translates human-readable names to Resource Records (RRs) on the Internet [11,17,18]. The most common RR, the A record, links a domain name (e.g., `example.com`) to an IPv4 address (e.g., 192.0.2.0). In this example, the type of the query (A) is called Query Type (QTYPE) and the name is referred to as Query Name (QNAME). Another common QTYPE is AAAA, which is used for IPv6 addresses.

DNS servers, known as *name servers*, by default operate on UDP port 53. These servers are either *authoritative*, storing RRs for specific zones, or *resolvers*, which cache or retrieve data from a hierarchy of authoritative servers. The hierarchy includes root servers, Top-Level Domain (TLD) servers (e.g., `.com`, `.net`), and Second-Level Domain (SLD) servers (e.g., `example.com`) with A RR for `www.example.com`. The Name Server (NS) RR is used to refer to other authoritative servers (see Fig. 1).

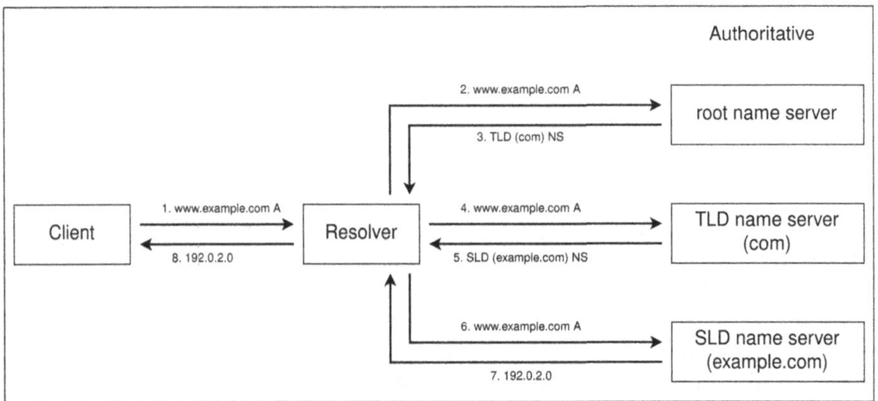

Fig. 1. A lookup for `www.example.com` where the resolver queries the authoritative name servers by sending the full QNAME

Clients use preconfigured resolvers, which may be *recursive* (directly querying authoritative servers) or *forwarding* (relying on another resolver). This forms a *resolver chain*, potentially including several forwarding resolvers and caching at any stage to enhance performance.

Resolvers may also specialize in serving specific client groups. *Local* resolvers, often on private network routers, handle only internal queries. The resolution service of a resolver operated by an Internet Service Provider (ISP) is commonly only offered to clients connected to their networks. *Public* resolvers offer services globally, either intentionally by design or accidentally by misconfiguration. Some popular intentionally public resolvers include Google Public DNS [10], Cloudflare DNS [6], OpenDNS [21], and Quad9 [24]. Local resolvers may forward queries to public resolvers to utilize their caching and filtering capabilities.

2.2 QNAME Minimization

Introduced by RFC 7816 in 2016 to reduce data leakage during DNS queries, `QMIN` limits the information sent to authoritative servers by building the QNAME label by label [4]. For instance, a minimizing recursive resolver looking up `www.example.com` first sends a query containing the TLD label (`.com`) to the root server. This is followed by each subsequent label upon receiving referrals, ensuring that higher-level servers do not see the full QNAME (see Fig. 2).

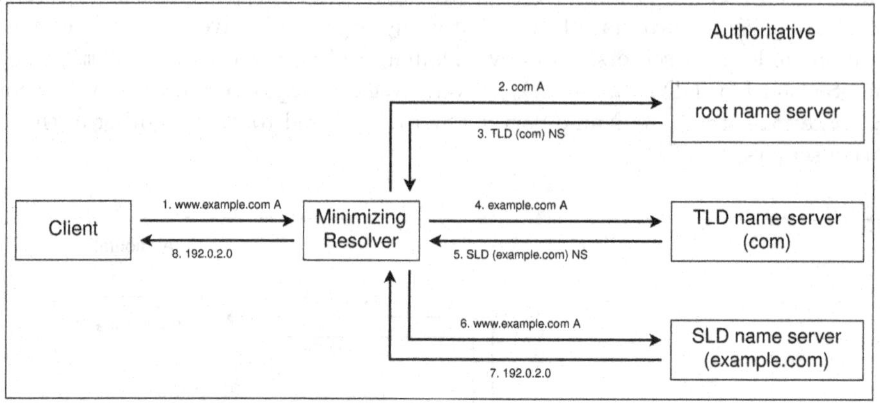

Fig. 2. A lookup for `www.example.com` where the minimizing resolver queries the authoritative name servers by iteratively building the QNAME

This technique, however, presents challenges such as increased potential for traffic amplification in Distributed Denial-of-Service (DDoS) attacks and issues with authoritative name servers that are unable to properly handle the NS queries sent when minimizing. To address these, RFC 9156 replaced RFC 7816, refining `QMIN` to include control over query sequences and adapt to server behaviors more robustly [5]. The reference implementation of `QMIN` now introduced two parameters for prepending labels. MAX_MINIMIZE_COUNT (MAX) is the maximum number of minimized queries to send (recommended: 10) which MUST be selected. The second, MINIMIZE_ONE_LAB (MIN), is the number of initial minimized queries that only prepend a single label (recommended: 4) which MAY be selected. The new RFC recommends using the less error prone A/AAAA QTYPEs to solve the problem with unexpected behaviours from name servers in the wild when queried for an NS record at certain zones.

Additionally, minimizing resolvers operate in either "relaxed" or "strict" modes [3,20]. Relaxed mode allows fallback to full QNAME queries with problematic servers, whereas strict mode does not, prioritizing privacy over query resolution success.

2.3 QNAME Minimization Signatures

De Vries *et al.* [27] enhanced the understanding of `QMIN` by analyzing query patterns from resolvers used by RIPE Atlas probes. These patterns, termed *signatures*, vary across different resolver software and are defined by the sequence of QNAME label count and the requested QTYPE. For instance, a query "`L3.example.com. NS`" is abbreviated as 3NS, while "`L5.L4.L3.example.com. A`" as 5A.

Under the older RFC 7816 standards, a 24-label A record query would be minimized one label at a time using NS queries, resulting in the signature: 1NS-2NS-3NS-...-22NS-23NS-24NS-24A. Under the updated RFC 9156 standards, with parameters MAX = 10 and MIN = 4, the first four labels are appended individually, then the remaining 20 labels are distributed over six queries for a total of 10 queries. The remainder are filled from the end, resulting in the signature 1A-2A-3A-4A-7A-10A-13A-16A-20A-24A. Further, if the SLD is cached (e.g., `example.com`), the signature commences from that cached point, creating the signature 3A-4A-5A-6A-9A-12A-15A-18A-21A-24A under RFC 9156.

Identifying `QMIN` signatures helps in pinpointing the resolver software and version. However, even though the signature 24A at the second-level zone indicates non-minimization, minimization could still happen towards the root and TLD servers (see limitations in Sect. 5.4).

3 Method

We established a virtualized network using Docker containers to create baseline `QMIN` signatures for four prominent open-source resolvers: Bind [12], Knot resolver [7], PowerDNS recursor [23], and Unbound [15]. This testing framework simulates DNS lookups to observe and record the query patterns of these resolvers, facilitating software and version identification during real-world measurements [1]. The chosen four open-source resolvers are widely used and recognized. Their active development communities ensure they are frequently updated and incorporate modern features, making them relevant for current studies. Selecting these four resolvers captures significant and diverse DNS behaviors in real-world traffic while keeping the research manageable. Previous studies such as De Vries *et al.* also focus on a few key resolvers for meaningful insights.

In our experiments, we manage a second-level domain **`fpdns.se`** and utilize a custom logging authoritative name server that starts collecting data from the three-label level. The server is configured to return its own IP address or name whenever a resolver requests an A or NS RR, respectively, for any set of labels under the zone. This enables us to encode identification data into the labels from the client side to map queries between the client and the authoritative name server. The same machine also hosts a web server with measurement and contact information.

When it is necessary to distinguish between a resolver queried by the client or probe and the resolver querying our authoritative name server, we hereinafter call the former *ingress* and the latter *egress*, having IP1 and IP2 respectively. Data collected includes timestamps, recursive resolver IP addresses, requested QNAMEs, and QTYPEs. We employ a 24-label query structure to probe resolvers, incorporating a unique tag to prevent caching effects and trace query-response mapping. To identify public resolvers, we scan the IPv4 space using *zmap*[1], adhering to ethical scanning practices by adjusting the send rate to minimize network impact [8]. We also use the RIPE Atlas probe network [19] to access local and ISP resolvers. This allows for broader insights into resolver configurations commonly used by general Internet users.

4 Measurements

4.1 Establishing Signatures

Our testing framework (see Sect. 3) includes a custom logging authoritative name server capable of using pseudo-top-level domains for dynamic querying of various resolver versions, focusing on those implementing `QMIN`. This setup enables the observation of resolver behaviors across different configurations and software versions.

Table 1. Established signatures of popular open-source resolvers where the SLD is cached.

	Signature
No minimization	24A
RFC 7816	3NS-4NS-5NS-...-22NS-23NS-24NS-24A
RFC 9156	3A-4A-5A-6A-9A-12A-15A-18A-21A-24A
Bind 9.18.14	4A-5A-6A-7A-24A
Bind 9.14.0	3NS-4NS-5NS-6NS-24A
Knot Resolver 5.6.0	3NS-4NS-5NS-...-22NS-23NS-24A
Knot Resolver 3.0.0	3NS-4NS-5NS-...-22NS-23NS-24A
PowerDNS 4.8.4	3A-4A-5A-6A-9A-12A-15A-18A-21A-24A
PowerDNS 4.4.0	3A-4A-5A-6A-7A-10A-13A-16A-19A-22A-24A
Unbound 1.17.1	3A-4A-5A-6A-9A-12A-15A-18A-22A-24A
Unbound 1.8.0	3A-4A-5A-6A-9A-12A-15A-18A-22A-24A

In our test environment, Table 1 illustrates the signatures from the resolvers with two labels (i.e., `SLD.TLD`) cached. Analysis of signature data reveals distinct patterns: the sequence of Bind 9.18.14 starts with 4A, not matching the 3A beginning typical in others, and stops minimizing after 7A. Unbound aligns closely with RFC 9156 standards, albeit with slight deviations at the later stages (e.g., 21A-24A, 22A-24A). PowerDNS closely follows RFC 9156's recommendations, whereas Knot adheres to the older RFC 7816's NS approach. The older version of Bind uses the NS QTYPE until the sixth label, and the older version of PowerDNS uses different MAX and MIN values. Notably, Unbound's responses are the only responses that vary with cache status, displaying unique signatures

[1] https://github.com/zmap/zmap.

Table 2. Unbound signatures at different cache states.

Cache	Unbound Signature
none	3A-4A-7A-10A-13A-16A-20A-24A
TLD	3A-4A-5A-8A-11A-14A-17A-21A-24A
SLD	3A-4A-5A-6A-9A-12A-15A-18A-22A-24A

when either the TLD or SLD is cached, as shown in Table 2. This holds true for both versions of Unbound.

Takeaway: The distinct query patterns of major open-source resolvers utilizing `QMIN` allow for software fingerprinting in practical applications.

4.2 Client Side Queries

Scanning the IPv4 address space for servers on UDP port 53, we identified 5.3 million name servers. Over three days (2024-01-14 to 2024-01-16), we dispatched 26.7 million queries, receiving responses to 24.6 million of the queries from 123,320 unique IP addresses, represented by 3.4 million unique nonces at our authoritative server.

In our study of these public name servers from the client side, 63.8% of responses were `REFUSED`, indicating non-authoritative or unauthorized access, with these scenarios indistinguishable based on the response alone. `TIMEOUT` responses accounted for 13.8%, possibly due to queries being dropped in transit. The `NOERROR` responses made up 9.8%, totaling 2.6 million successful queries, with 689,198 unique resolvers responding with the Recursion Available (RA) flag. `SERVFAIL` responses were observed in 8.2% of queries, suggesting name server misconfiguration.

A "probe" hereinafter refers to a client in the RIPE Atlas network capable of sending DNS queries to its preconfigured resolvers (not using the list from the resulting scan above). Thus, we use probes to investigate resolvers, referring to "client" when we mention "probe" and not the query it sends. Using 991 probes, averaging 1.6 resolvers each, we sent 1,647 queries with unique nonces[2]. This resulted in 12,593 received queries at our authoritative server with 1,599 unique nonces.

For probe resolvers, 93.8% of 1,546 queries returned `NOERROR`, with the majority providing the expected IPv4 address. The incorrect answers in both measurements mainly belonged to networking, DNS filtering, and hosting services predominantly in China, Poland, Italy, and the United States, including some empty responses and addresses like localhost or 0.0.0.0.

Geographical analysis of the Autonomous System (AS) for each unique public resolver showed significant numbers in China, India, and Russia. For RIPE Atlas

[2] https://atlas.ripe.net/measurements/66216489.

probes, the most frequent resolver AS was 0 (49%), which could be local resolvers with private addresses, followed by Google (16.7%) and Cloudflare (10.8%).

Takeaway: The majority of public name servers either operate as restricted resolvers or are authoritative for different zones, predominantly returning `REFUSED`. Only 12.7% of our queries reached our authoritative server. The vast majority of preconfigured resolvers of RIPE Atlas probes worked as intended. A substantial fraction of queries reaching our server did not return to the client, likely due to packet loss (leading to `TIMEOUT`) and missing DNSSEC (resulting in `SERVFAIL`).

4.3 Server Side Queries

At our authoritative server, 3.4M unique nonces allowed us to trace queries from clients to servers using public resolvers. Among these, 689,198 were *responding* resolvers—with `NOERROR` Response Code (RCODE) and RA flag—detected at the client side. Additionally, we identified 231,879 *non-responding* resolvers that initiated queries but resulted in `TIMEOUT`, `SERVFAIL`, `REFUSED`, or other RCODEs, potentially due to the absence of DNSSEC [2] at our server. Combined, these add up to 921,077 public resolvers analyzed.

Table 3. Top 10 amplified nonces observed at our authoritative name server.

Nonce	Count	Nonce	Count
04841028-jan14	16,005	12659023-jan14	9,044
05334945-jan14	15,866	21242404-jan14	8,786
01242404-jan14	15,325	20094944-jan14	7,487
11242404-jan14	11,946	22659023-jan14	6,843
02659023-jan14	11,916	11733696-jan14	4,999

Table 3 illustrates the most frequent nonces observed at our authoritative name server, with the top nonce appearing 16,005 times, despite being sent just once from the client side. This suggests significant query amplification originating from a single ingress resolver.

We examined the top 100 *amplified nonces* to further understand the cause. By analyzing queries by ingress AS, we find that few ASes account for most queries (see Fig. 3 in Appendix). Analysis by egress AS revealed that 42 of the 100 nonces originate from less than five ASes, while the queries for two nonces were distributed across over 600 ASes (Fig. 4, Appendix). Additionally, we investigated `QMIN` patterns (Fig. 5, Appendix), noting that half of the nonces had more than 70% of the queries minimized. For some nonces more than 90% of the queries were minimized.

Takeaway: Significant query amplification towards our authoritative name server is driven by a small number of ingress ASes, with queries for two particular nonces coming from over 600 egress ASes each. High rates of `QMIN` among these queries suggest that minimization practices in combination with forwarding resolver chains contribute to amplification alongside other factors.

4.4 Query Patterns and Signatures

We analyzed the query patterns at the authoritative name server by grouping them according to nonce and using the same notation as `QMIN` signatures. The analysis identified several prevalent patterns. A common yet uninteresting pattern involves non-minimized queries such as repeated instances of 24A. Additionally, we noted patterns of incomplete minimization, where the sequence does not contain the final label, 24A, indicative of attempts that failed to fully minimize. We observed multiple queries executed in either parallel (3A-3A-24A-24A) or sequential (3A-24A-3A-24A) arrangements or combinations thereof, as well as patterns showing retries as sequential duplicates (3A-3A-24A), likely due to responses being lost in transit.

A particularly concerning pattern is 24A-3A-24A, which suggests the simultaneous operations of non-minimizing and minimizing resolvers. This situation undermines the intent of `QMIN` because forwarding queries to multiple resolvers without uniform minimization practices effectively negates the privacy benefits intended by this approach.

Takeaway: Our analysis of ingress resolver query patterns uncovers a range of behaviors from non-minimizing to incomplete minimization. Notably, the simultaneous use of different resolver types complicates the effectiveness of `QMIN`, highlighting the challenges in maintaining DNS query privacy across diverse network environments.

We analyzed *egress* resolver queries grouped by nonce and IP2, identifying patterns and categorizing them based on their minimization behavior. Patterns with repeating 24A sequences were labeled NON-MINIMIZING, and sequences that did not complete minimization were classified as INCOMPLETE. We also simplified patterns by consolidating sequential duplicates due to retries, turning sequences like 4A-5A-6A-**7A-7A**-24A into 4A-5A-6A-**7A**-24A. This allows us to match with the established `QMIN` *signatures* from Sect. 4.1.

The 30 most common signatures observed from public resolvers are shown in Table 6 (Appendix), noting complete and partial matches to established open-source resolver signatures. The most frequent signature, 3A-24A, did not align with any predefined patterns. Approximately 44% of these signatures originated from Cloudflare (AS13335).

Table 4 summarizes signatures that completely match our known resolver patterns and the number of resolver chains observed. We also list the "likely resolver" since some signature overlap and there might be other resolvers outside

Table 4. Egress Resolvers: Instances of matching signatures from public and RIPE Atlas probe resolvers.

Signature	Likely Resolver	Public	Probes
4A-5A-6A-7A-24A	Bind	109,366	83
3A-4A-5A-6A-9A-12A-15A-18A-22A-24A	Unbound (SLD)	43,071	90
3NS-4NS-5NS-6NS-24A	Old Bind	8,661	60
3A-4A-5A-8A-11A-14A-17A-21A-24A	Unbound (TLD)	5,664	139
3A-4A-5A-6A-9A-12A-15A-18A-21A-24A	PowerDNS	1,966	141
3NS-4NS-5NS-...-22NS-23NS-24A	Knot	1,003	114
3A-4A-5A-6A-7A-10A-13A-16A-19A-22A-24A	Old PowerDNS	970	24
3A-4A-7A-10A-13A-16A-20A-24A	Unbound	239	24

the scope of our study that share these signatures. Among public resolvers, the newer version of Bind was the most common (109,366 instances), followed by Unbound (43,071) and an older version of Bind (8,661). We also traced different caching behaviors of Unbound based on the presence of SLD or TLD in the cache. For RIPE Atlas probes, the top signatures included Unbound (253 total across different cache states), followed by PowerDNS (141) and Knot (114), as detailed in Table 7 (Appendix).

Takeaway: Analysis of egress resolver patterns confirms the presence of all established signatures. Bind is the predominant open-source resolver among public queries, with Unbound being the most common egress resolver for RIPE Atlas probes. This analysis also allows for the fingerprinting of different Bind and PowerDNS versions, reflecting changes in their `QMIN` practices over time.

5 Discussion

5.1 Signatures

We observe that most signatures from our measurements follow recommendations from RFC 9156 regarding using A/AAAA QTYPEs instead of NS and limiting how many queries to send when minimizing. The implementation of the algorithm, however, varies a lot.

In Table 5, we can see the open-source resolvers and their version, together with the maximum number of minimized queries (MAX), the minimum number of initial single-label prepending queries (MIN), which QTYPE to use during the minimization and whether the signature changes based on the cache. We do not see Bind 9.18.14 sending a query with three labels, which makes it very difficult to relate to the parameters introduced in RFC 9156. Both versions of Unbound do not evenly distribute the remaining queries towards the end, making it distinct

Table 5. Implementation parameters of resolvers according to RFC 9156.

Resolver	Version	MAX	MIN	QTYPE	Cache
Bind	9.18.14	7	-	A	no
Bind	9.14.0	7	6	NS	no
Knot	5.6.0	-	-	NS	no
Knot	3.0.0	-	-	NS	no
PowerDNS	4.8.4	12	6	A	no
PowerDNS	4.4.0	13	6	A	no
Unbound	1.17.1	10	4	A	yes
Unbound	1.8.0	10	4	A	yes

from PowerDNS 4.8.4, which looks like it is following RFC 9156. However, we did not see the signature of PowerDNS change based on previously cached queries in our testing environment. If a resolver minimizes in relaxed mode, its shortened signature may overlap with other resolvers. The longer the query pattern, the easier it likely is to fingerprint.

The plethora of QMIN implementations indicates that we are in a phase where DNS developers try various parameter values to find a balance between performance and privacy. Most acknowledge RFC 9156 by using the A RR and setting an upper limit to the number of queries to send, but taking the cache into account seems rare. These variations put us in a similar position as De Vries *et al.* [27], where we see deviations from the RFC, and it is precisely these deviations that allow us to fingerprint the resolvers from the authoritative name server.

5.2 Comparison with Previous Study

In 2018, De Vries *et al.* [27] sent unique queries from 9,410 RIPE Atlas probes to establish QMIN signatures with the same method we use in this study, and map them to three open-source resolvers; Bind 9.13.3, Knot 3.0.0, and Unbound 1.8.0. From the authoritative side, 8,894 probes were identified using 8,179 unique resolvers, sending a total of 20,716 queries, which were grouped to create signatures. The most common signature (13,892 occurrences) was 24A, representing a non-minimizing resolver. The second most common, observed 784 times, was 3NS-24A, mapped to the implementation by Knot Resolver 3.0.0. Three other signatures used the A QTYPE instead of NS and added multiple labels. One of these three, occurring 16 times, was consistent with the Unbound 1.8.0 implementation. Looking closer at the two unlabeled signatures from De Vries *et al.*, we note that they are also Unbound but with either the SLD or the TLD in the cache. De Vries *et al.* only attributed Unbound to the signature with an empty cache (3A-4A-7A-10A-13A-16A-20A-24A). Bind 9.13.3 was the least common out of the three, with an occurrence of 11, and none of the signatures matched the implementation reference in RFC 7816.

Our findings indicate significant changes since De Vries *et al.*'s study. Firstly, adding PowerDNS to the set of resolvers has introduced new `QMIN` signatures, reflecting its updated implementation. Moreover, updates in Bind and PowerDNS have resulted in new signature patterns, highlighting advancements in their query minimization techniques. Unlike De Vries *et al.*, we found that Unbound's signatures vary with cache states but remain distinct from other resolvers. Additionally, our study revealed that the proper signature for Knot aligns more closely with the RFC 7816 reference, suggesting potential issues with the custom authoritative name server used by De Vries *et al.*. Notably, while non-minimizing resolvers still dominate, the distribution among open-source resolvers has shifted, with Bind leading public resolver signatures and Unbound topping RIPE Atlas probe measurements, followed by PowerDNS and Knot. This shift suggests a growing preference for alternatives to Bind among probe operators.

5.3 Query Amplification

One of the challenges of `QMIN` is the amplification of queries, one query sent to the resolver could result in multiple queries at the authoritative name server, especially when the QNAME contains many labels. RFC 9156 introduced an upper limit to the number of queries when minimizing. With the recommended implementation, the amplification is less than tenfold. Combined with forwarding configurations, i.e., one resolver forwarding to multiple resolvers, this could contribute to the query amplification that we see in our measurements. A previous study by Yazdani *et al.* [29] investigated "echoing" DNS resolvers and listed IP broadcasting, routing loops, and DNS interception as contributing factors to amplified queries. Leveraging these public (intentionally or not) resolvers could enable the initiation of a DDoS attack targeting authoritative name servers.

5.4 Limitations

We are limited to studying `QMIN` from the second-level zone due to the third label nonce, mitigating caching effects and allowing us to map client and server queries and responses for analysis. The public DNS team at Google had reached out to the authors in light of the results from De Vries *et al.* and explained that they only minimize queries to the root and TLD name servers, which results in a non-minimized query at the SLD. Not being able to identify a minimizing resolver using MAX = 3 and MIN = 2 as values from RFC 9156 is a limitation of this fingerprinting method, which is what Magnusson *et al.* [16], observed in their study of `QMIN` adoption. We also limit our scope to establishing signatures for a few, although popular open-source resolvers. Some of the patterns we observe in our measurements may be from other resolver software.

6 Related Work

Name server fingerprinting typically involves two principal methods. The first is the *fpdns* tool [13] which, although innovative at its inception, has not been updated in recent years and is less effective for profiling contemporary name server implementations. The *fpdns* tool operates from the client side and attempts to determine the software and version of name servers based on their response to various crafted queries. A new variant of the tool called *dnssoft-ver* has since been developed [30]. The second method involves sending a *version.bind* query, a pseudo-top-level domain query originally specific to Bind but adopted by other server implementations under similar or identical labels like *version.server*. This method is designed to elicit information about the server's software and version, though many servers obfuscate this information to mitigate security risks.

Several studies have used these methods to analyze name servers. Sisson [26] combined them to fingerprint a substantial subset of the IPv4 address space. Bind9 was identified as the second most common name server software, but the study noted the potential for false positives and negatives, advising cautious interpretation of the results. Glynn [9] used *fpdns* to identify software on authoritative servers for `.ie` domains, finding Bind9 as the most frequently observed. The study also highlighted the presence of older, less secure versions of Bind. Kührer *et al.* [14] employed *version.bind* and *version.server* queries to classify public resolvers over a year, revealing a landscape dominated by various Bind versions, Unbound, Dnsmasq, PowerDNS, and Microsoft DNS. Park *et al.* [22] scanned the entire IPv4 address space, uncovering over 3 million resolvers. They tracked behavior by running an authoritative server and monitoring query responses. Many of these resolvers were found to deliver incorrect or malicious responses.

In our study we use a fingerprinting method utilizing the query patterns from `QMIN` at the authoritative name server, using a similar mapping method as Park *et al.*. We continue to see a strong preference for Bind among public resolvers, similar to earlier findings, but we also explore newer dynamics and configurations not previously covered in the literature.

7 Conclusion

This study set out to explore the implementation of `QMIN` in DNS resolvers, motivated by the need to enhance privacy and security within the DNS ecosystem. Our findings reveal significant discrepancies between the recommended `QMIN` standards and their real-world implementations, with many resolvers deviating from the prescribed practices. We established `QMIN` signatures for four popular open-source DNS resolvers. We fingerprinted public resolvers and the preconfigured resolvers of RIPE Atlas probes. Most open-source resolvers avoid the ns QTYPE, favoring the less error-prone A QTYPE, and set an upper limit on the number of queries sent when minimizing, adhering to the latest RFC. However, the exact implementation of minimization algorithms varies between software and versions.

We found significant query amplification from certain ingress resolvers forwarding to many egress resolvers across various ASes. While `QMIN` contributes to the increased query volume at authoritative name servers, it is not the only factor. The observed query amplification, a side effect of QMIN combined with forwarding configurations, further underscores the complexities and unintended consequences that can arise from these privacy-enhancing techniques.

We identified public resolver signatures and found the newest version of Bind as the most common, followed by Unbound and an older version of Bind. Within the RIPE Atlas probes, Unbound and PowerDNS are more popular than Bind. Comparing our results with a previous study, we attributed more signatures (Unbound variations) and corrected an old signature (Knot). We also distinguished between older and newer versions of two resolver vendors (Bind and PowerDNS).

This study contributes valuable insights into the DNS ecosystem's current state by identifying distinct signatures associated with different resolver software and versions. These insights are critical for improving DNS security by identifying outdated or misconfigured resolvers that may compromise user privacy. Ultimately, our research underscores the importance of continued vigilance and refinement in implementing privacy standards like QMIN, ensuring that as the Internet evolves, so too do the measures designed to protect its users. The discrepancies and challenges in this study serve as a call to action for the DNS community to bridge the gap between theoretical standards and practical application, reinforcing the privacy and security of one of the Internet's most fundamental infrastructures.

Acknowledgment. This work was founded by the Swedish Internet Foundation. We would like to thank Tobias Pulls, Anna Brunstrom and Johan Stenstam for valuable feedback during the design of the study and drafts of the manuscript.

Appendix

A Ethics

The measurements were following good Internet citizenship by adjusting the rate of queries as not to overwhelm the network and signaling the benign nature of our measurements. We set up a website for informing other parties and listed contact information for discussions. We have also approval from our ethical review board about the data that we collect in this study. We have contacted the operators of ASes hosting top amplifying resolvers from Table 3 and have yet to receive a response about any insights into the exact causes.

B Query Amplification

We explore the top 100 amplified queries from our measurements to understand what is causing them. In Fig. 3 we rank the ingress ASes of our amplified queries by their mean number of queries per nonce. We find that many of the queries comes from a few number of ingress ASes.

In Fig. 4 we rank the top 100 amplified nonces by their number of egress ASes. We see that 42 of the nonces come from less than five ASes. Then we have

56 nonces coming from between 50 and 240 ASes. Most alarmingly, two nonces are sent from over 600 ASes.

In Fig. 5 we rank the nonces by their share of minimized queries. All of the nonces are sent from resolvers which are minimizing. The lowest share of minimized queries for an amplified nonce is 60%, and the highest is 90%.

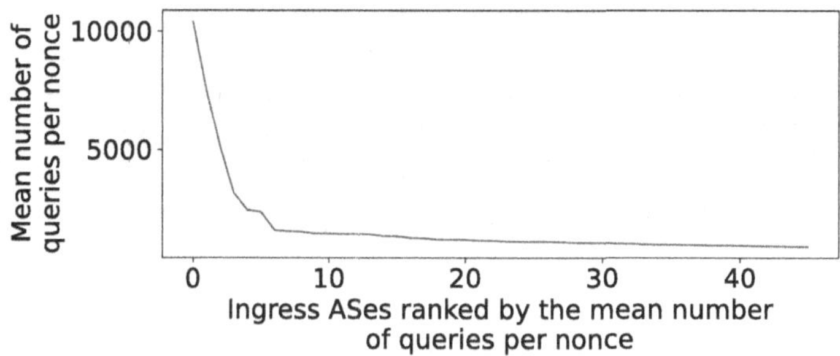

Fig. 3. Amplified Nonces: The mean number of queries per nonce when grouped by the ingress resolver AS.

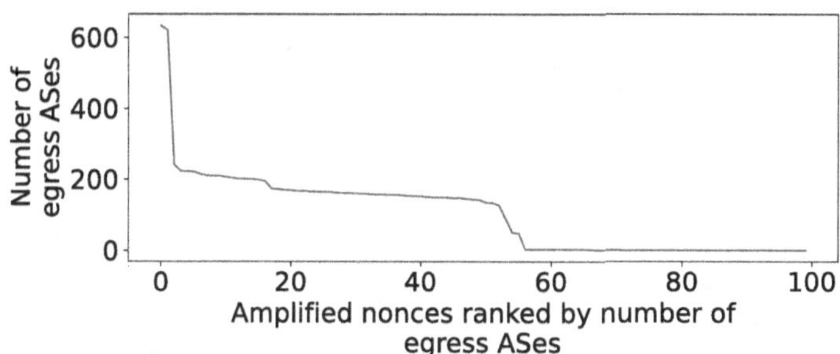

Fig. 4. Amplified Nonces: The number of egress ASes per nonce when grouped by the egress resolver AS.

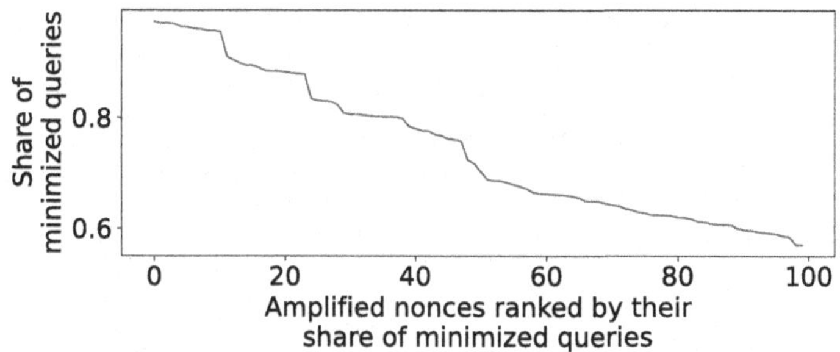

Fig. 5. Amplified Nonces: Share of minimized queries.

C Common Signatures

In Table 6 we show the 30 most common signatures from public resolvers. We see a variety of signatures, some of which we can map to established signarures of open-source resolvers. We count the number of ingress-egress resolver pairs, which means that the amount is *not* representing the number of egress resolvers. At the top of the table we list the open-source resolvers and versions with distinct `QMIN`signatures. If an observed signature is a *complete match*, we mark it with a filled circle (•), and if the signature is a *partial match*, we mark it with an empty circle (○). A signature can be a complete match with one resolver while also being a partial match for another. Using the same method for the RIPE Atlas probes, we extract signatures from query patterns based on nonce and egress resolver IP and show the 15 most common signatures in Table 7.

Table 6. Public Resolvers: Top egress signatures and completely/partly matching resolvers

Signature	Bind	Old Bind	Knot	PowerDNS	Old PowerDNS	Unbound	Count
NON-MINIMIZING							4,492,799
INCOMPLETE							2,204,820
3A-24A				○	○	○	325,287
4A-5A-6A-7A-24A	•				○		109,366
3A-4A-5A-6A-9A-12A-15A-18A-22A-24A						•	43,071
3A-4A-24A				○	○	○	35,592
3A-4A-5A-24A				○	○	○	21,045
5A-6A-7A-24A	○				○		13,684
3A-4A-5A-6A-24A				○	○	○	13,456
4A-6A-7A-24A	○				○		12,339
4A-5A-7A-24A	○				○		11,988
4A-5A-6A-24A	○				○		10,537
3A-4A-5A-6A-9A-24A				○		○	9,738
3NS-4NS-5NS-6NS-24A		•	○				8,661
3A-4A-5A-6A-9A-12A-24A				○		○	7,218
3A-4A-5A-8A-11A-14A-17A-21A-24A						•	5,664
3A-4A-5A-6A-9A-12A-15A-24A				○		○	5,312
4A-24A	○			○	○	○	4,811
3A-4A-5A-6A-9A-12A-15A-18A-24A				○		○	4,314
4A-5A-24A	○			○	○	○	3,309
6A-7A-24A	○				○		2,803
4A-7A-24A	○				○	○	2,646
5A-7A-24A	○				○		2,527

(*continued*)

Table 6. (*continued*)

Signature	Bind	Old Bind	Knot	PowerDNS	Old PowerDNS	Unbound	Count
5A-6A-24A	○			○	○		2,267
4A-6A-24A	○			○	○		2,175
3A-4A-5A-6A-9A-12A-15A-18A-21A-24A				●			1,966
5A-24A	○			○	○	○	1,625
6A-24A	○			○	○	○	1,174
7A-24A	○				○	○	1,080
3NS-4NS-5NS-...-22NS-23NS-24A			●				1003
OTHER							37,081

● (complete match), ○ (partial match)

Table 7. RIPE Atlas Probe Resolvers: Top egress signatures and completely/partly matching resolvers

Signature	Bind	Old Bind	Knot	PowerDNS	Old PowerDNS	Unbound	Count
NON-MINIMIZING							964
3A-24A				○	○	○	407
INCOMPLETE							142
3A-4A-5A-6A-9A-12A-15A-18A-21A-24A				●			141
3A-4A-5A-8A-11A-14A-17A-21A-24A						○	139
3NS-4NS-5NS-...-22NS-23NS-24A			●				114
3A-4A-5A-6A-9A-12A-15A-18A-22A-24A						●	90
4A-5A-6A-7A-24A	●				○		83
3NS-4NS-5NS-6NS-24A		●					60
3A-4A-7A-10A-13A-16A-20A-24A						●	24
3A-4A-5A-6A-7A-10A-13A-16A-19A-22A-24A					●		24
3A-4A-5A-8A-6A-11A-9A-14A- -12A-17A-15A-21A-18A-22A-24A						○	4
3A-4A-5A-6A-8A-9A-11A-12A- -14A-15A-17A-18A-21A-24A						○	3
3A-4A-5A-8A-11A-14A-17A-21A- -6A-9A-12A-15A-18A-22A-24A						○	2
3A-4A-5A-6A-8A-9A-11A-12A- -14A-15A-17A-18A-21A-22A-24A						○	2
OTHER							28

● (complete match), ○ (partial match)

References

1. Arcnilya: Github: resolver-lab. https://github.com/Arcnilya/resolver-lab/. Accessed 23 Sept 2024
2. Arends, R., Austein, R., Larson, M., Massey, D., Rose, S.: DNS security introduction and requirements. RFC 4033, RFC Editor (2005). http://www.rfc-editor.org/rfc/rfc4033.txt
3. Bind: Bind documentation: options (2022). https://bind9.readthedocs.io/en/v9.18.14/reference.html#namedconf-statement-qname-minimization. Accessed 23 Sept 2024
4. Bortzmeyer, S.: DNS query name minimisation to improve privacy. RFC 7816, RFC Editor (2016)
5. Bortzmeyer, S., Dolmans, R., Hoffman, P.: Dns query name minimisation to improve privacy. RFC 9156, RFC Editor (2021)
6. Cloudflare: Cloudflare DNS. https://cloudflare-dns.com/. Accessed 23 Sept 2024
7. CZ-NIC: Knot resolver. https://www.knot-resolver.cz/. Accessed 23 Sept 2024
8. Durumeric, Z., Wustrow, E., Halderman, J.A.: Zmap: fast internet-wide scanning and its security applications. In: USENIX Security Symposium, vol. 8, pp. 47–53 (2013)
9. Glynn, W.J.: Measuring DNS vulnerabilities and DNSSEC challenges from an Irish perspective. In: Proceedings of SATIN (2011)
10. Google: Google public DNS. https://developers.google.com/speed/public-dns. Accessed 23 Sept 2024
11. Hoffman, P., Sullivan, A., Fujiwara, K.: DNS terminology. BCP 219, RFC Editor (2019). https://www.rfc-editor.org/info/rfc8499
12. ISC: Bind 9. https://www.isc.org/bind/. Accessed 23 Sept 2024
13. kirei: Github: fpdns. https://github.com/kirei/fpdns/. Accessed 23 Sept 2024
14. Kührer, M., Hupperich, T., Bushart, J., Rossow, C., Holz, T.: Going wild: large-scale classification of open DNS resolvers. In: Proceedings of the 2015 Internet Measurement Conference, pp. 355–368 (2015)
15. Labs, N.: Unbound. https://nlnetlabs.nl/projects/unbound/about/. Accessed 23 Sept 2024
16. Magnusson, J., Müller, M., Brunstrom, A., Pulls, T.: A second look at DNS QNAME minimization. In: Passive and Active Measurement: 24th International Conference, PAM 2023, Virtual Event, 21–23 March 2023, Proceedings, pp. 496–521. Springer (2023)
17. Mockapetris, P.: Domain names - concepts and facilities. STD 13, RFC Editor (1987). http://www.rfc-editor.org/rfc/rfc1034.txt
18. Mockapetris, P.: Domain names - implementation and specification. STD 13, RFC Editor (1987). http://www.rfc-editor.org/rfc/rfc1035.txt
19. NCC, R.: RIPE Atlas (2017). https://atlas.ripe.net/
20. NLnet Labs: Unbound documentation: Qname minimization (2021). https://unbound.docs.nlnetlabs.nl/en/latest/manpages/unbound.conf.html. Accessed 23 Sept 2024
21. OpenDNS: Opendns. https://www.opendns.com/. Accessed 23 Sept 2024
22. Park, J., Khormali, A., Mohaisen, M., Mohaisen, A.: Where are you taking me? Behavioral analysis of open DNS resolvers. In: 2019 49th Annual IEEE/IFIP International Conference on Dependable Systems and Networks (DSN), pp. 493–504. IEEE (2019)

23. PowerDNS: Powerdns recursor. https://www.powerdns.com/powerdns-recursor. Accessed 23 Sept 2024
24. Quad9: Quad9 DNS. https://www.quad9.net/. Accessed 23 Sept 2024
25. Schomp, K., Allman, M., Rabinovich, M.: DNS resolvers considered harmful. In: Proceedings of the 13th ACM Workshop on Hot Topics in Networks, pp. 1–7 (2014)
26. Sisson, G.: DNS survey: October 2010 (2010)
27. de Vries, W.B., Scheitle, Q., Müller, M., Toorop, W., Dolmans, R., van Rijswijk-Deij, R.: A first look at QNAME minimization in the domain name system. In: Choffnes, D., Barcellos, M. (eds.) PAM 2019. LNCS, vol. 11419, pp. 147–160. Springer, Cham (2019). https://doi.org/10.1007/978-3-030-15986-3_10
28. Yan, Z., Lee, J.H.: The road to DNS privacy. Futur. Gener. Comput. Syst. **112**, 604–611 (2020)
29. Yazdani, R., Nosyk, Y., Holz, R., Korczyński, M., Jonker, M., Sperotto, A.: Hazardous echoes: the DNS resolvers that should be put on mute. In: 2023 7th Network Traffic Measurement and Analysis Conference (TMA), pp. 1–10. IEEE (2023)
30. yevheniya-nosyk: Github: dnssoftver. https://github.com/yevheniya-nosyk/dnssoftver/. Accessed 23 Sept 2024

Formally Discovering and Reproducing Network Protocols Vulnerabilities

Christophe Crochet[(✉)], John Aoga, and Axel Legay

INGI, ICTEAM, Université catholique de Louvain, Place Sainte Barbe 2, L05.02.01, 1348 Louvain-La-Neuve, Belgium
{christophe.crochet,john.aoga,axel.legay}@uclouvain.be

Abstract. The rapid evolution of cyber threats has increased the need for robust methods to discover vulnerabilities in increasingly complex and diverse network protocols. This paper introduces *Network Attack-centric Compositional Testing* (*NACT*) [12], a novel methodology designed to discover new vulnerabilities in network protocols and create scenarios to reproduce these vulnerabilities through attacker models. *NACT* integrates composable attacker specifications, formal specification mutations, and randomized constraint-solving techniques to generate sophisticated attack scenarios and test cases. The methodology enables comprehensive testing of both single-protocol and multi-protocol interactions. Through case studies involving a custom minimalist protocol (`MiniP`) and five widely used `QUIC` implementations, *NACT* is shown to effectively identify, reproduce, and find new real-world vulnerabilities such as version negotiation abuse. Additionally, by comparing the current and older versions of these `QUIC` implementations, *NACT* demonstrates its ability to detect both persistent vulnerabilities and regressions. Finally, by supporting cross-protocol testing within a black-box testing framework, *NACT* provides a versatile approach to improve the security of network protocols.

Keywords: Formal Specifications · Formal Verification · Mutation Testing · Network Attacks · Systems · Internet protocols · `QUIC` · Concrete Implementation · Adverse Stimuli · Framework

1 Introduction

In today's hyperconnected world, network protocols serve as the foundation of global communication infrastructures, yet they remain vulnerable to sophisticated cyber threats. Protocol vulnerabilities provide a fertile ground for attackers to disrupt services, steal sensitive information, and cause widespread damage, as seen in high-profile incidents such as the *Heartbleed* [37] and *Log4Shell* [15] attacks. The unpredictability of cyberattacks lies in their ability to exploit weaknesses in ways not anticipated during the protocol's design. Attackers frequently leverage *zero-day* vulnerabilities and subtle deviations from formal specifications to create unexpected behaviors that lead to breaches [40]. This challenge

L. Horn Iwaya et al. (Eds.): NordSec 2024, LNCS 15396, pp. 424–443, 2025.
https://doi.org/10.1007/978-3-031-79007-2_22

highlights the necessity of anticipating attacks by uncovering potential vulnerabilities before they can be exploited [38]. Testing and simulation approaches play a crucial role in this proactive defense strategy.

Previous studies have delved into various fault-based testing methodologies. Some methods focus on validating protocols according to their defined specifications (conformance testing) [16,32], while others target known vulnerabilities directly [35,36], especially through mutation testing [41], which creates test scenarios by injecting minor controlled errors (mutants) into protocols to gauge their resilience [33]. These strategies typically fall under the umbrella of *black-box* or *fuzz testing* [36]. It is crucial to perform tests directly on implementations to enhance the realism and applicability of these tests for real-world network situations. This is where *Model-Based Testing (MBT)* [28] comes in, using an advanced language to describe protocol specifications and validate them directly against real implementations. This method facilitates the identification of potential code vulnerabilities that an attacker can exploit in practical scenarios, especially given the growing complexity of modern protocol implementations.

Recently, *Network-centric Compositional Testing* (*NCT*) [23] has emerged as a pioneering MBT approach [28] that uses formal protocol specifications, implemented with tools such as *Ivy* [29], to generate test tools automatically. *NCT* has effectively identified bugs and vulnerabilities, particularly in real-world protocols such as `QUIC`.

However, *NCT* focused on individual compliance checks and did not address the dynamic and diverse nature of actual network interactions, which are essential to detect potential vulnerabilities before they can be exploited.

To bridge this gap, we present Network Attack-centric Compositional Testing (*NACT*), a novel *model-based mutation testing* that builds upon *NCT*. *NACT* is tailored to thoroughly evaluate real-world network protocols for security flaws. Using compositional attacker models, mutations in formal specifications, and randomized constraint-solving techniques, *NACT* can uncover previously unknown vulnerabilities by emulating various advanced attack scenarios. Our method facilitates the examination of multi-protocol and cross-protocol interactions in black-box settings, thereby creating realistic, adversarial circumstances reflective of potential exploits in live environments. The capability to conduct multi-protocol testing and multipoint communications is becoming increasingly crucial with the rise of microservice architectures and distributed systems. We validate our method's effectiveness by testing several recent vulnerabilities in the widely used `QUIC` protocol, successfully identifying new significant security weaknesses, including version negotiation issues and buffer overflows.

The remainder of the paper is organized as follows. Section 2 offers an overview of network protocol vulnerabilities, associated attacks, the *NCT* methodology, and its inherent limitations. Section 3 introduces the *NACT* methodology, elaborating on the mutations of formal specification, their implementation, and integration within a compositional testing framework. Section 4 discusses our case studies on five `QUIC` implementations, showcasing the ability of *NACT* to identify complex vulnerabilities. Finally, Sect. 5 concludes and suggests possible directions for future work.

2 Background

This section covers the core concepts of network attacks, how to test network protocols against these threats using network-centric approaches, and the limitations of these approaches, emphasizing the need for more comprehensive testing frameworks.

(1) Network Attack Vectors and Agents. In network security, a **vulnerability** is a defect or weakness present in the design, implementation, or operation of a system that an attacker can exploit to breach the system's security attributes, such as *confidentiality*, *integrity*, *availability*, and *authenticity*. When a malicious entity discovers and exploits a vulnerability, it results in a **network attack**, which is any intentional action to disrupt standard system functioning.

(a) Types of Network Attacks. To understand the different forms of network attacks, we conducted a literature review and identified the most prevalent types of attacks that can occur in network environments. We classify these attacks according to their mode of operation. Table 1 summarizes the general categories of network attacks as referenced in various works [8,10,18,21].

Table 1. Network attacks categories from the literature.

Type of Attack	Description
TLS/SSL Connection Attacks	Exploiting vulnerabilities in the TLS handshake process, such as protocol downgrade or renegotiation attacks, to intercept, decrypt, or alter encrypted communication data
Injection	Injecting malicious data/code into a system or application to manipulate its operations
Eavesdropping	Intercepting communications between two parties without their consent
Service Disruption	Overloading or disrupting services to make them unavailable to legitimate users
Spoofing	Impersonating a legitimate entity to deceive users or systems
Protocol-Based Attacks	Exploiting inherent weaknesses or misconfigurations in communication protocols (e.g., TCP Slowloris) to overwhelm, disrupt services, or gain unauthorized access

These attack types form the basis for our testing framework, allowing us to simulate various attack scenarios and validate the robustness of network protocols under different adversarial conditions.

(b) Attack Vectors. An **attack vector** is the specific method or pathway that an attacker uses to exploit a vulnerability in a system. Understanding attack vectors is essential in constructing effective security models and testing methodologies, as they directly influence how attacks are simulated and mitigated. We identified three main attack vectors relevant to network security testing, presented in Table 2. Although malicious clients and servers might appear similar, the directions of their interactions differ. A malicious client begins communication and strays from protocols to perform attacks. In contrast, a malicious server responds to requests with harmful actions, taking advantage of client trust. The impact of a malicious client is precise and targeted, whereas a malicious server can influence numerous users and disrupt the entire network, magnifying the damage. A special case of this is the Man-in-the-Middle (MitM) attack, where the attacker intercepts and manipulates the communication between a client and server, often impersonating both simultaneously. This dual role allows the attacker to perform activities such as spoofing, eavesdropping, and data injection without the communicating parties' awareness.

Table 2. Identified Attack Vectors in Network Protocols

Attack Vector	Description	Attack Surface	Type of Attack
Man-in-the-Middle (MitM)	Intercepts and potentially alters the communication between two parties without their knowledge, compromising message integrity and authenticity	Network communication between client and server	Eavesdropping Injection TLS/SSL Connection Protocol-Based Attacks Service Disruption Spoofing
Malicious Client	Behaves as a legitimate user but intentionally violates protocol rules to disrupt the system or steal data	Interaction with a legitimate server	
Malicious Server	Controls a seemingly legitimate server that responds to client requests maliciously, violating protocol rules and compromising security	Responses to legitimate client requests	

These attack vectors serve as the foundation for developing our **Network Attack Model Framework**. In this framework, we emulate different attack scenarios to assess network protocols for potential vulnerabilities. Further details will be provided in the next section. Now, let's explain the Network-Centric Testing framework that underpins our methodology.

(2) Network-Centric Testing Approaches. Network-centric compositional testing (NCT) is a specialized approach within model-based testing (MBT) that focuses specifically on network protocols. The principle of compositional testing views formal specifications as a system of interrelated components or processes, each with its own input and output. This method allows for examination of the protocol behaviors in their network interactions, instead of relying exclusively on abstract mathematical models. The emphasis on genuine network behavior is what distinguishes the methodology as "network-centric".

NCT Principle. NCT creates a systematic framework for generating formal specifications of Internet protocols and verifying their implementations for conformity to these specifications [14,23]. After generating the formal model code, a test generator produces concrete and randomized test cases. The testers, which use an *SMT solver* to meet the constraints set by the formal protocol requirements, are then deployed to verify the real-world implementation of the protocol. If any protocol requirements are not met, the resulting traces can be examined to find and identify potential errors or vulnerabilities. Let us consider a minimal network protocol designated as `MiniP` to illustrate how NCT works.

MiniP. The Minimalist Protocol (`MiniP`) is specified as follows. Each packet must contain exactly two frames. There are three types of frames: `PING`, `PONG`, and `TIMESTAMP` frames. The `PING` and `PONG` frames include a *four-byte string* that corresponds to the word 'ping' or 'pong', respectively. A packet must contain one of these two frames. Additionally, the `TIMESTAMP` frame contains an *eight-byte unsigned integer* that represents the time, in milliseconds, when the packet is transmitted. Every packet includes this frame. The client initiates communication by sending a packet with the `PING` frame and the `TIMESTAMP` frame as its payload. The server is required to reply within *three seconds* with a packet that includes the `PONG` frame followed by the `TIMESTAMP` frame. This process repeats until the client disconnects. To end the connection, the client simply stops sending packets for *more than three seconds.*

MiniP Network-Centric Structure. Figure 1 illustrate the design of `MiniP` according to the NCT principle. The "Frame" process generates output that is used as input for the "Packet" process. The assumptions regarding the inputs of a process are treated as guarantees for the outputs of other processes. Each element represents a layer of the `MiniP` stack, including the frame layer ⓐ and the packet layer ⓑ. The *shim* component ⓒ handles the network transmission and packet reception. Once a packet is received, the shim component checks the formal specifications associated with the packet. For example, it ensures that a MiniP packet consistently includes two frames in the appropriate sequence. Should any of the criteria not be satisfied, an error is triggered. Frames are likewise handled according to their own formal specifications.

Formal Specification. NCT employs the Ivy language [22,29] for formal specification purposes. Ivy facilitates describing a program's state through first-order

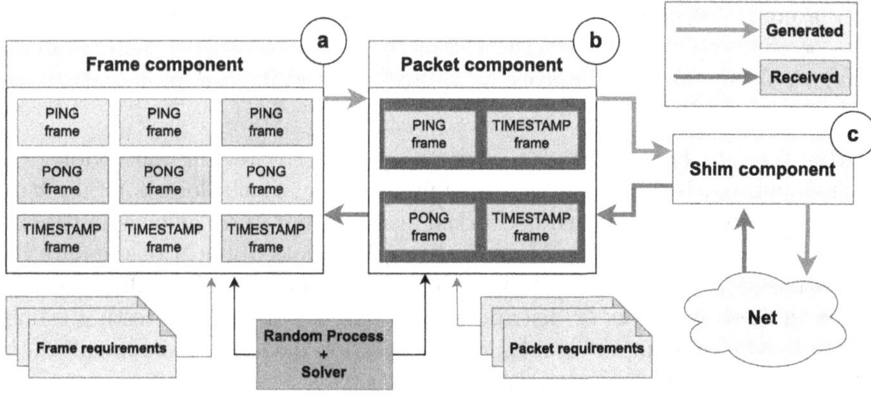

Fig. 1. `MiniP` Network-Centric Testing (*NCT*) structure

logic formulas and incorporates relations (boolean predicates), functions, modules, and type objects as the primary abstractions to model the system's state. For example, the Ivy code snippet 1 defines how the handling of the `PING` frame, which must contain the word 'ping' as a *four-byte string*.

</> 1. Ping frame formal specification code </>

```
before ping_frame.ping.handle {
    require f.data     = ping_data; #data must be 'ping'
    require f.data.end = 4; #length of the data must be 4
}
```

While *NCT* approaches have been effective in identifying protocol compliance issues, it is crucial to extend them to include tests that explore beyond safety properties focus, as outlined in their paper [24].

(3) Network-Centric Testing Limitations. *NCT* and Specification-conforming testing, which focuses on ensuring that implementations strictly adhere to formal specifications, has several inherent limitations:

① *Limited to Specification-Conforming Testing.* Focusing solely on testing that adheres to the specifications restricts the overall extent of coverage. By strictly following the formal specifications, the methodology might overlook potential issues stemming from unexpected or non-specification-conforming inputs and behaviors, which are prevalent in practical scenarios. This aspect is crucial, as real-world networks frequently encounter unforeseen interactions or attacks that are not predicted by a specification. This limitation underscores the necessity to broaden the testing framework to include tests that go beyond the specified boundaries, possibly incorporating formal attack models that mimic adversarial conditions or unusual network behaviors.

② *Single Protocol Testing.* The current approach is designed to test one protocol at a time. This approach limits the framework's applicability to more complex systems where multiple protocols interact, such as in distributed services or multi-layered web applications. These interactions might introduce unforeseen issues or vulnerabilities. Expanding the methodology to support multi-protocol testing would significantly improve its ability to detect interaction-based vulnerabilities.

③ *Restricted to Point-To-Point communications.* The testing methodology is currently limited to point-to-point communications, which does not fully capture the complexity of modern networked systems that often involve multipoint or broadcast communications. Many real-world network applications require the verification of protocols that manage communications among multiple nodes, such as in mesh networks or distributed systems. Extending the testing framework to handle these more complex communication patterns would significantly enhance its usefulness and applicability.

Putting All Together. Addressing these limitations by integrating *formal non-conform (mutation) attack models*, supporting *multi-protocol environments*, and expanding to *multi-node communications* would greatly enhance the robustness and comprehensiveness of protocol testing, ensuring that the protocol performs well not only in controlled environments but also in real-world, dynamic network scenarios.

3 Network Attack Model Framework

Network Attack-centric Compositional Testing (NACT), a method of model-based mutation testing, facilitates the evaluation of network protocols' security and robustness by introducing mutations (minor alterations) to the specifications (*addressing Limitation* ①) and testing these modifications across different use cases (*addressing Limitations* ② & ③). To accomplish this, we suggest a framework for a network attacker model that operates in three phases.

Step1: Defining formal specification mutations. Mutation testing has been successfully applied to network protocols to improve their robustness and security. This approach involves intentionally making small changes (mutations) to the protocol specifications, resulting in mutant versions that might reveal potential weaknesses [9,20,34,39]. Subsequently, the mutants are evaluated against a comprehensive set of test cases to determine the efficacy of existing tests in detecting artificially introduced errors. The main goal is to evaluate the protocol's fault tolerance and to determine potential failure points that may arise in unexpected circumstances.

Table 3 presents various mutation techniques applicable to formal specifications in internet protocol testing. These specific mutations are chosen for their ability to effectively challenge and validate the robustness of protocol implementations.

Furthermore, they specifically target critical protocol behavior aspects that are prone to reveal hidden issues. Other mutations might not be effective in this scenario, either due to insufficiently significant deviations or the generation of invalid mutants that fail to yield meaningful test results.

Table 3. Formal Specification Mutations in Internet Protocol Testing.

Mutation	Description	Problem Investigated	Challenges
Statement Deletion or Addition	Remove or add statements to observe protocol deviations	Functional errors, missing logic, incomplete flows, Protocol deviations, unintended side-effects	Incomplete protocol states, trivial bugs, unreachable or invalid states
Negation Mutation	Negate logical expressions to introduce faults	Logical errors, incorrect conditional handling	Reveal deep logical errors
Value Replacement	Modify variables or constants to test behavior under changes	Edge-cases, faulty variable handling	Maintain meaningful tests
Boundary Value Mutation	Alter values to boundary limits for edge-case testing	Buffer overflows, boundary issues	Select boundaries carefully to avoid meaningless mutations
Control Flow Mutation	Modify control structures to test robustness	Conditional logic failures, Infinite loops, performance bottlenecks	Unreachable states, complex conditions, computational cost
Mutate Data Structures	Change data structure definitions to find vulnerabilities	Memory management, invalid state transitions	Ensure valid structure mutations

At the protocol layer, these mutations are incorporated into both the frame and packet components. Figure 2 illustrates the integration of mutations within `MiniP`'s architecture. Based on the requirements, modifications are made to define the mutations, which are subsequently embedded in the protocol components, thereby exploring how the implementation handles these deviations from the standard specification (*Limitation* ①).

To test these mutations effectively, we must now implement them. This is where *NCT* becomes relevant.

Step2: Implementing composable attacker specifications. Our approach for implementing mutations extends the conventional formal specification mutation testing framework by introducing mutations directly into the formal specification. This is facilitated by *NCT*. Currently, generating mutants is a manual process due to the difficulty of generalizing mutations across all network protocols while maintaining consistent and meaningful system behavior. To ensure a degree of generality, we provide a template for each attack model: the man-in-the-middle, malicious client, and server (Table 2).

At a protocol level, we show below, using our running protocol `MiniP`, how to implement a malicious character injection (a mutation by addition), find possible security vulnerabilities (vs safety vulnerabilities) in this mutant, and implement a test scenario to test the vulnerability.

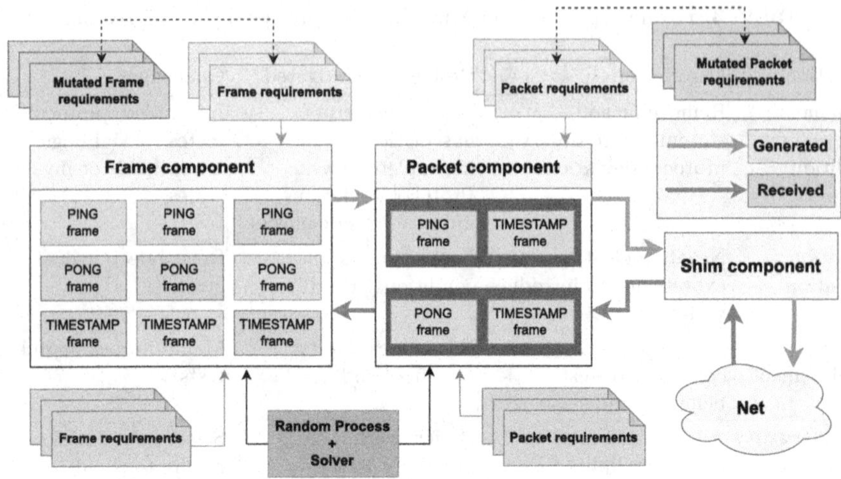

Fig. 2. `MiniP` Formal Specification Mutation

(1) Finding vulnerability with specification mutation. The specific mutation introduced here consists in altering a requirement to allow the inclusion of potentially harmful characters in the packet payload. The following Ivy code snippet 2 represents this mutation showing the modification of the original ping frame handler presented in the code snippet 1 Sect. 2.

</> 2. Format String & Buffer Overflow </>

```
before ping_frame.ping.handle_maliciously {
    require f.data.end < 100000 & exists I. I < f.data.end-8 &
      (f.data.value(I)   = 0x25  & f.data.value(I+1) = 0x78  &
       f.data.value(I+2) = 0x25  & f.data.value(I+3) = 0x6e);
}
```

This mutation is designed to evaluate the `MiniP`'s robustness against format string vulnerabilities, a well-known category of security issues. In addition, we varied the size of the message payload to assess the protocol's handling of unusually large or small messages, a common technique for identifying buffer overflow vulnerabilities. This vulnerability is particularly severe, as it can result in memory corruption, leading to potential system crashes or arbitrary code execution by an attacker. Once a vulnerability is identified using randomized mutation testing, the next step involves creating specific scenario test cases.

(2) Exploiting vulnerability creating a test scenario. A scenario test case is designed to explicitly target the identified vulnerabilities and structured to replicate the exact conditions under which the vulnerability was found. The test scenarios are created using attack vectors (Table 2). For example, we can replicate the protocol's behavior during a *Man-in-the-Middle attack* or its reaction to *malicious clients* sending improperly formatted packets under mutations. By incorporating these vectors into mutation testing, we can validate the system's ability to withstand real-world attacks. These scenario-based tests can be reused in future tests to ensure that the vulnerability remains mitigated in subsequent implementations or protocol versions. One can use *NCT* to craft test scenarios with straightforward assertion directives. The detected vulnerabilities (string format and buffer overflow) can be tested using the following code snippet (3).

</> 3. Malicious Character Injection Specific test </>

```
before ping_frame.ping.handle_maliciously {
    require f.data.end = 50; #Buffer overflow size + format string
    require f.data.value(6) = 0x25 & f.data.value(7) = 0x78;
}
```

Now that we define mutations and test scenarios, we need to test the protocol under test in an appropriate environment.

Step3: Simulating attack scenarios within virtual networks. A crucial stage in developing and validating network protocols involves thorough testing to confirm that protocols operate as expected under various network conditions. Our methodology highlights the significance of testing in settings that closely resemble real-world scenarios. Consequently, we mainly use *virtual networks.*

(1) Using virtual networks. Virtual networks, by leveraging namespaces, enable the creation of isolated network environments that accurately emulate actual deployment settings. This approach facilitates the testing of multipoint communications (*Limitation* ③) and complex topologies, imitating real-world network dynamics. Building upon *NCT*, our framework is compatible with simulators. These simulators provide various benefits, including reproducibility, accurate management of network conditions, and the ability to simulate intricate scenarios such as timing attacks [30]. However, employing simulators necessitates the creation of simulated system calls (syscalls) to emulate the network stack, which can be challenging in proportion to the complexity of the simulation condition. Extending *NCT* to complex network systems, especially in microservices architectures, involves dealing with the added complexity of interacting protocols. Figure 3 illustrates the interaction between our framework and a virtual network. The *NCT* framework integrated with an attack model ⓐ produces model-based testers or attackers ⓑ, which are used within the virtual network consisting of multiple client-tested implementations ⓒ interfaced with a server-tested implementation. Upon completion of the simulation, the network traces are analyzed to investigate vulnerabilities.

(2) Compositional Testing of Networks Services. *NCT* originally focused on testing single protocols through formal specifications and automated testers, ensuring compliance via *SMT solvers* [23]. In a microservice environment, where services may use different protocols (e.g., HTTP over TCP, gRPC over `QUIC`), the challenge is to develop modular formal specifications that capture both individual service behavior and inter-service interactions [7]. To do so, we design the framework with some level of abstraction, illustrated in Fig. 4. The *system component*, a virtual component, serves as a master framework that defines base events common across all protocols, ensuring consistent integration and testing

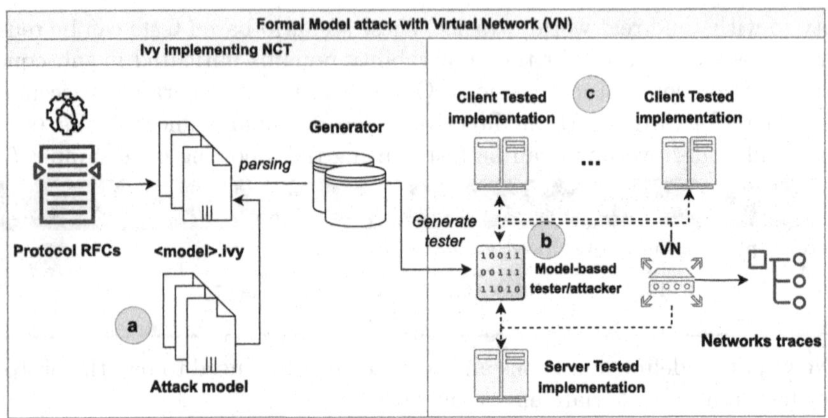

Fig. 3. Virtual networks and *NACT*

(*Limitation* ②). The model can then be expanded with *protocol-specific requirements*, allowing each protocol to be tested both in isolation and as part of the broader system. A *shim* layer manages interactions between different protocols, routing events to the appropriate components and ensuring that protocol-specific requirements are applied while maintaining system integrity.

We implemented a toy example demonstrating a *MitM* attack scenario where `QUIC` packets are reflected towards `MiniP` endpoints ending in buffer overflow. This simple setup provides a valuable scenario into the interaction between different protocols under attack conditions, highlighting potential vulnerabilities in cross-protocol communication environments.

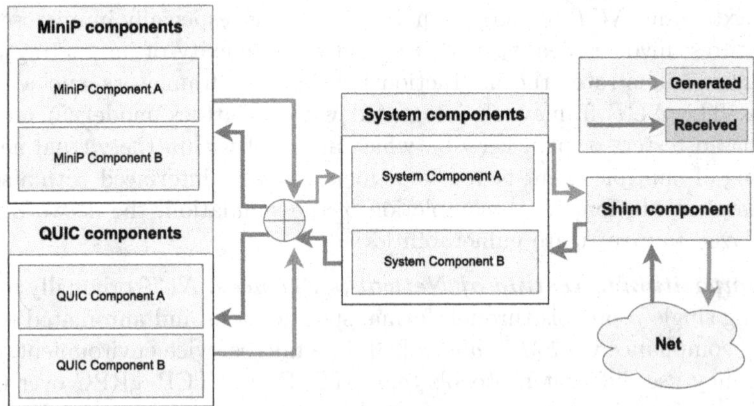

Fig. 4. System Component

Putting All Together. The proposed Network Attack-centric Compositional Testing (*NACT*) framework provides a structured and comprehensive approach to enhancing the security and robustness of network protocols. This framework integrates the mutation of formal specifications, the deployment of attacker specifications that can be composed, and the simulation of attack scenarios in virtual network environments to provide a flexible approach for uncovering hidden vulnerabilities. Our method performs specification-conforming *and* non-conforming testing, managing both individual protocol and multiple protocol interactions in multipoint communication settings.

In the subsequent section, we will demonstrate how this framework is applied to the testing of the real world `QUIC` protocol and its efficacy in uncovering new vulnerabilities.

4 Experiments

This section is organized into two parts. The first part focuses on reproducing known vulnerabilities in various `QUIC` [19] implementations, such as `picoquic`, `quic-go`, `quinn`, `quant`. We apply established attack scenarios to both current and previous versions of these implementations to verify the effectiveness of security patches and identify any regressions. The second part involves the discovery of new vulnerabilities using our Network Attack-centric Compositional Testing (NACT) framework on `lsquic` and `quant` implementation.

(1) Testing recent `QUIC` vulnerabilities. To evaluate vulnerabilities within our framework, it is required to define both the vulnerabilities and the associated attack scenario, given the mutations are defined (Sect. 3). Table 5 shows the chosen `QUIC` vulnerabilities and the respective attack scenario designed to address them (Table 4).

Table 4. Tested implementations informations

Implementation	Language	SLOC	Version
[11] `picoquic` (a)	C	122k	bb6799 (actual)
`picoquic` (b)	C	84k	42c620 (draft 27)
[17] `quic-go` (a)	Go	83k	v0.46.0
`quic-go` (b)	Go	73k	b5ef99a
[31] `quinn` (a)	Rust	33k	0.11.2
`quinn` (b)	Rust	41k	0.10.0 (draft 29)
[25] `quant` (a)	C	18k	dc7721
`quant` (b)	C	18k	bf903d (draft 29)

To thoroughly assess the security of `QUIC` implementations in relation to these vulnerabilities, we performed tests on both the latest and older versions

Table 5. QUIC selected vulnerabilities and our defined attack scenarios

N°	Vulnerability	Description	Known Causes	Occurred Problems	Attack Scenario
(1)	CVE-2022-30591 QUIC Slow Loris [1]	DoS via incomplete QUIC or HTTP/3 requests	Misparsing of the MTU Discovery service by the *quic-go* implementation	CPU consumption and DoS via *Slowloris* attack	Maintain the connection with minimal data transfer, forcing the server to hold resources indefinitely [6]
(2)	CVE-2023-42805 QUIC Frame Parsing Exploitation [2]	Incorrect parsing of unknown QUIC frames causing erroneous responses	Reception of unknown frames within QUIC packets prior to fix	Erroneous server responses	Exploit frame parsing vulnerabilities to manipulate the server response
(3)	CVE-2024-22189 QUIC Memory Exhaustion [3]	Memory exhaustion through excessive transmission of NEW_CONNECTION_ID frames	Exploitation of congestion control by collapsing the window	Denial of service, memory exhaustion	Flood the server with requests to retire connection IDs, overwhelming the server's resources
(4)	GitHub issues *picoquic* Malicious Payload Injection [27]	Malicious QUIC frame triggers an infinite loop, causing a DoS	Crafting maliciously QUIC frames processed during session epoch 3	Infinite loop, server crash, remote exploitation	Inject crafted payloads to trigger an infinite processing loop
(5)	GitHub issues quant Malicious Payload Injection [26]	DoS caused by processing connections with identical connection IDs	Duplicating connection IDs processed by quant	Server crash and denial of service	Inject frames to cause server failure and potentially execute malicious payloads
(6)	Non-conformance bug in QUIC Implementations (NEW_TOKEN frame) [5]	Several QUIC implementations (picoquic 7f2fbdfb & lsquic 3.2.0) fail to handle invalid packets properly	Protocol specification non-conformance	Invalid error codes and server instability	Replay malformed NEW_TOKEN frames to reproduce server errors and non-conformance

of several widely used libraries. Each QUIC implementation was examined for known vulnerabilities using its most recent version as well as a previous version to detect any regressions or persistent issues. By testing multiple versions, we ensure that vulnerabilities identified in earlier versions are indeed present and can be reliably reproduced, while also verifying that these vulnerabilities have been effectively fixed in the most recent versions, preventing their reintroduction.

To guarantee the dependability and consistency of our results, each test was executed three times across the different QUIC implementations. Due to the variability inherent in some tests, this approach allowed us to control for any inconsistencies in the data and better evaluate the robustness of each implementation against the identified vulnerabilities. Table 6 displays the summary of these tests' outcomes. For each test, we allocated a time budget of 150 s per test [13].

Table 6. Reproduction of Vulnerability Testing Results for Various QUIC Implementations. QUIC Implementations versions: (a) *actual* and (b) *old*. Each symbol represents the outcome of the tests, running three times: ✓ indicates that the three trials failed (vulnerable), ✗ indicates that the three trials passed (safe), and ∼ indicates mixed results (some trials passed and some failed). The attacks numbers (i), 1 to 6, are described in Table 5. Grey cells represent the implementation(s) originally detected as vulnerable to the attack scenario. An implementation is considered *safe* if it passes all tests and *unsafe* otherwise.

Implem. / Attacks	picoquic (a)	picoquic (b)	quic-go (a)	quic-go (b)	quinn (a)	quinn (b)	quant (a)	quant (b)
(1)	✗	✗	✗	∼	✗	✗	✗	✗
(2)	✗	✗	✗	✗	✗	∼	✓	✓
(3)	✗	✗	✗	∼	✗	✗	✗	✓
(4)	✗	✓	✗	✗	✗	✓	✗	✓
(5)	✗	✗	✗	✗	✗	✗	✗	✓
(6)	✗	✓	✗	✗	✗	✓	✗	✓
Results	*safe*	*unsafe*	*safe*	*unsafe*	*safe*	*unsafe*	*unsafe*	*unsafe*

The experiments carried out provided valuable information on the behavior and vulnerabilities of various QUIC implementations. As shown in Table 6, our testing revealed that while some implementations demonstrated resilience against specific attack scenarios, others exposed vulnerabilities that could lead to potential security risks. Notably, our findings highlighted the effectiveness of newer versions in addressing previously identified issues, showcasing the ongoing efforts to enhance the security and robustness of QUIC implementations.

The results indicate that while certain implementations, such as quic-go (a), showed no significant issues, others, like quinn (b) and quant (b), revealed persistent vulnerabilities or improper handling of edge cases, as detailed in the various test outcome.

One of the key observations was the effectiveness of newer versions in addressing previously identified vulnerabilities. For example, in the case of `picoquic`, the vulnerabilities observed in version (b), which included issues concerning the frame parsing process and RFC compliance, were successfully mitigated in the newer version (a), demonstrating a clear improvement in security.

However, the experiments also highlighted some persistent challenges. Certain implementations, such as `quinn` (b), showed issues in handling edge cases, such as repeated sending of `CONNECTION_CLOSE` frames (> 10) followed by Stateless Reset packets, indicating a need for further refinement. Similarly, `quant` (b) frequently experienced crashes or improper connection closures when dealing with oversized tokens, illustrating the difficulties in achieving robust `QUIC` implementations across different scenarios.

The experiments faced some difficulties, particularly in consistently triggering specific vulnerabilities like the Slowloris attack on `quic-go` (b). This challenge underscores the complexity of certain attack vectors and the ambiguous nature of some CVE designations, which can make reproducibility and consistent testing outcomes difficult.

In conclusion, these results underscore the significance of comprehensive and rigorous testing frameworks for the assessment of protocol security. The varying degrees of resilience and vulnerability observed across different versions and implementations underscore the necessity for continuous vigilance, rigorous testing, and the refinement of security measures. By addressing these challenges, the security and robustness of `QUIC` and similar network protocols can be significantly enhanced, ensuring their resilience against evolving threats.

(2) Discovering new network protocol vulnerabilities. In the course of our investigation into `QUIC` protocol implementations, we identified a number of vulnerabilities that could potentially be exploited under certain conditions. This section presents our findings, with a particular focus on scenarios involving MitM and client-initiated attacks.

(2.1) Version Negotiation Abuse - Denial of Service. The LiteSpeed `QUIC` (`lsquic`) Library is a fast, flexible, and production-ready open-source implementation of `QUIC` and HTTP/3 for servers and clients. It has been used in LiteSpeed products since 2017 and supports multiple `QUIC` versions. With around 129k SLOC, `lsquic` is significantly larger compared to other implementations. A vulnerability was identified with regard to the version negotiation process. In particular, when `lsquic` initiates a handshake using version 0xff000022 (draft-34) and receives a version negotiation packet responding with 0xff00001d (draft-29), the implementation erroneously applies an incorrect encryption key to subsequent packets. This results in checksum failures, which could potentially lead to a denial of service (*DoS*) condition.

It is noteworthy that this issue does not manifest when transitioning between certain other versions, such as from 0xff00001b (draft-27) to 0xff00001d (draft-29). However, the vulnerability is consistently manifested when moving from version 0xff000022 (draft-34) to 0xff00001b (draft-27). Testing the reverse transition (from 0xff00001d to 0xff000022) is challenging with the current `lsquic` setup, as it defaults to selecting the highest available version.

The root cause of this vulnerability is not related to the key generation process, as each version employs a distinct salt for deriving encryption keys. Rather, the issue arises from the inappropriate application of these keys following version negotiation. This vulnerability presents a potential vector for a MitM attack. While initial packets are encrypted, they do not fully protect against MitM attacks. Furthermore, version negotiation packets, as defined in RFC9000, are entirely unprotected. Consequently, an attacker could intercept and manipulate the version negotiation packet, either by altering the selected version or crafting a fraudulent packet. This could potentially lead to a denial-of-service (DoS) attack.

This vulnerability appears to be specific to the `lsquic` implementation and is not necessarily indicative of a flaw in RFC9000 itself. However, the RFC's relatively vague guidelines on the version negotiation process could contribute to implementation inconsistencies, leading to potential vulnerabilities like the one identified, where an off-path attacker could exploit the protocol's flexibility to deplete server resources.

(2.2) Malformed Frame Encodings - Memory exhaustion attacks Exploits. In the course of our preliminary experiments with a modified specification, we identified a significant error in the implementation of `QUIC`'s `quant` (a) functionality. In particular, when a specific type of frame encoding was employed, the `quant` process entered an infinite loop during the connection close procedure. This issue was particularly evident when the client transmitted a `NEW_TOKEN` frame, which is not permitted by the RFC, in conjunction with a parsing error in the HTTP request contained within the `STREAM` frame. These errors resulted in an infinite loop, as the frame encodings differed slightly from the anticipated format but remained within the acceptable range, prompting the `quant` algorithm to classify them as valid input. Consequently, the connection close state was not correctly exited, leading the server to continue consuming resources and potentially resulting in a system crash.

A subsequent test with a different mutation of the specification yielded comparable results, though through a distinct mechanism. In this scenario, the altered frame encoding modified certain fields within the `NEW_CONNECTION_ID` frame header in a way not anticipated by the original specification. The parsing error in the HTTP request exacerbated the situation, leading to repeated, unsuccessful attempts by the "`quant`" process to close the connection. The unexpected packet structure caused the connection closure process to enter an indefinite loop.

In both cases, the infinite loop was triggered when the server initially sent a `CONNECTION_CLOSE` frame with a `PROTOCOL_VIOLATION` error code twice, followed by an endless sequence of HTTP 505 errors encapsulated within `FLOW_CONTROL_ERROR` frames. In the context of the mutated specification and introduced parsing errors, this combination of frames resulted in the persistent failure of the connection termination process, which ultimately caused the server to become unresponsive.

Notably, this issue does not appear in older versions of `quant` (b), suggesting that it has been introduced in more recent updates. This highlights the importance of continuous testing across different versions to identify and address newly introduced vulnerabilities.

5 Conclusion and Future Works

Robust network protocol testing is crucial in an interconnected digital world due to evolving cyber threats. Our research explores attack vectors and develops a comprehensive, mutation-based testing framework to identify vulnerabilities. We addressed several attacks by constructing the *Network Attack-centric Compositional Testing (NACT)* framework. Mutations generate adversarial conditions by modifying protocol specifications, exposing hidden vulnerabilities that traditional tests might miss, especially within formal specification testing (*NCT*).

While *NCT* has laid the groundwork for testing protocol compliance, it inherits some limitations. One inherited challenge is its focus on specification conformance, which leaves out adversarial behavior and multi-protocol interactions. Another challenge is the point-to-point communication limitation missing the complexity of modern distributed systems. We addressed these limitations by incorporating non-conformant mutation-based attack models, supporting multi-protocol environments, and extending the framework to multi-node communications using virtual networks. These enhancements enable the framework to perform more comprehensive security testing across diverse network environments.

Our experimental results with `QUIC` demonstrate the efficacy of our framework. We developed consistent attack scenarios to validate and discover vulnerabilities, notably in version negotiation and frame encoding errors, leading to *denial of service (DoS)* or *infinite loop conditions.* These findings underscore the need for robust security testing frameworks for both known and emerging vulnerabilities in protocols such as `QUIC`.

Looking ahead, our research aims to enhance the *NACT* framework by incorporating the *Network Simulator-centric Compositional Testing* (*NSCT*) methodology [30]. NSCT has built upon NCT to verify time-dependent network properties, ensuring reproducibility of experiments via simulators. This approach will aid in replicating attacks and allow the modeling of timing attacks.

We also intend to conduct extensive empirical testing on real network systems associated with the AMC3 project. [4].

Acknoledgements. We would like to thank the belgium's "*Defence-related Research Action*" (DEFRA) and the "*Automated Methodology for Common Criteria Certification*" project (AMC3).

References

1. NVD - CVE-2022-30591 (2022). https://nvd.nist.gov/vuln/detail/CVE-2022-30591

2. NVD - CVE-2023-42805 (2023). https://nvd.nist.gov/vuln/detail/CVE-2023-42805
3. NVD - CVE-2024-22189 (2024). https://nvd.nist.gov/vuln/detail/CVE-2024-22189
4. AMC3: What is AMC3 ? (2024). https://www.amc3.be/
5. Asadian, H., Fiterau-Brostean, P., Jonsson, B., Sagonas, K.: Monitor-based testing of network protocol implementations using symbolic execution. In: Proceedings of the 19th International Conference on Availability, Reliability and Security, ARES '24. Association for Computing Machinery, New York (2024). https://doi.org/10.1145/3664476.3664521
6. Balaji, A.S., Anil Kumar, V., Amritha, P.P., Sethumadhavan, M.: QUICLORIS: a slow denial-of-service attack on the quic protocol. In: Dubey, A.K., Sugumaran, V., Chong, P.H.J. (eds.) Advanced IoT Sensors, Networks and Systems, pp. 85–94. Springer, Singapore (2023)
7. Bestavros, A., Kfoury, A., Lapets, A., Ocean, M.: Safe compositional network sketches: tool & use cases, pp. 234–245 (2009)
8. Bhanpurawala, A., El-Fakih, K., Zualkernan, I.: A formal assisted approach for modeling and testing security attacks in IoT edge devices (2022). https://doi.org/10.48550/arXiv.2210.05623
9. Budd, T.A., Gopal, A.S.: Program testing by specification mutation. Comput. Lang. **10**(1), 63–73 (1985). https://doi.org/10.1016/0096-0551(85)90011-6. https://www.sciencedirect.com/science/article/pii/0096055185900116
10. Chatzoglou, E., Kouliaridis, V., Karopoulos, G., Kambourakis, G.: Revisiting QUIC attacks: a comprehensive review on QUIC security and a hands-on study. Int. J. Inf. Secur. **22** (2022). https://doi.org/10.1007/s10207-022-00630-6
11. Huitema, C.: picoquic. https://github.com/private-octopus/picoquic. 4f11445
12. Crochet, C.: PANTHER: protocol formal analysis and formal network threat evaluation resources - nordsec commit (2024). https://github.com/ElNiak/PANTHER/tree/4804a5afba6bc81241c51f6ca71f99e560859fca
13. Crochet, C.: PANTHER: protocol formal analysis and formal network threat evaluation resources - results (2024). https://github.com/ElNiak/PANTHER-Ivy/tree/cf8b80f7bfda33cdd6d285c0110bb3198de28df2/protocol-testing/apt/test/nordsec
14. Crochet, C., Rousseaux, T., Piraux, M., Sambon, J.F., Legay, A.: Verifying QUIC implementations using ivy. In: Proceedings of the 2021 Workshop on Evolution, Performance and Interoperability of QUIC (2021). https://doi.org/10.1145/3488660.3493803
15. Everson, D., Cheng, L., Zhang, Z.: Log4Shell: redefining the web attack surface. In: Proceedings of the Workshop on Measurements, Attacks, and Defenses for the Web (MADWeb), pp. 1–8 (2022)
16. Farooq, F., Nadeem, A.: A fault based approach to test case prioritization. In: 2017 International Conference on Frontiers of Information Technology (FIT), pp. 52–57 (2017). https://doi.org/10.1109/FIT.2017.00017
17. quic go: Github - quic-go/quic-go: a QUIC implementation in pure go (2024). https://github.com/quic-go/quic-go
18. Hoque, N., Bhuyan, M.H., Baishya, R., Bhattacharyya, D., Kalita, J.: Network attacks: taxonomy, tools and systems. J. Netw. Comput. Appl. **40**, 307–324 (2014). https://doi.org/10.1016/j.jnca.2013.08.001. https://www.sciencedirect.com/science/article/pii/S1084804513001756
19. Iyengar, J., Thomson, M.: RFC 9000. https://www.rfc-editor.org/rfc/rfc9000

20. Li, J.H., Dai, G.X., Li, H.H.: Mutation analysis for testing finite state machines. In: 2009 Second International Symposium on Electronic Commerce and Security, vol. 1, pp. 620–624 (2009). https://doi.org/10.1109/ISECS.2009.158
21. Lu, Y., Xu, L.D.: Internet of Things (IoT) cybersecurity research: a review of current research topics. IEEE Internet Things J. **6**(2), 2103–2115 (2019). https://doi.org/10.1109/JIOT.2018.2869847
22. McMillan, K.L., Padon, O.: Ivy: a multi-modal verification tool for distributed algorithms. In: Lahiri, S.K., Wang, C. (eds.) CAV 2020. LNCS, vol. 12225, pp. 190–202. Springer, Cham (2020). https://doi.org/10.1007/978-3-030-53291-8_12
23. McMillan, K.L., Zuck, L.D.: Compositional testing of internet protocols. In: 2019 IEEE Cybersecurity Development (SecDev) (2019). https://doi.org/10.1109/secdev.2019.00031
24. McMillan, K.L., Zuck, L.D.: Formal specification and testing of QUIC. In: Proceedings of the ACM Special Interest Group on Data Communication (2019). https://doi.org/10.1145/3341302.3342087
25. NTAP: Github - NTAP/quant: QUIC implementation for POSIX and IoT platforms (2016). https://github.com/NTAP/quant
26. NTAP: Dos attack: Server crashes when processing new connections ids that have the same cid. Issue 68. NTAP/quant (2020). https://github.com/NTAP/quant/issues/68
27. private octopus: Denial of service vulnerability (infinite loop) while parsing malicious QUIC frame. Issue 969. private-octopus/picoquic (2020), https://github.com/private-octopus/picoquic/issues/969
28. Offutt, J., Abdurazik, A.: Generating tests from UML specifications. In: International Conference on the Unified Modeling Language, pp. 416–429. Springer (1999)
29. Padon, O., McMillan, K.L., Panda, A., Sagiv, M., Shoham, S.: Ivy: safety verification by interactive generalization. ACM SIGPLAN Not. **51**(6), 614–630 (2016). https://doi.org/10.1145/2980983.2908118
30. Rousseaux, T., Crochet, C., Aoga, J., Legay, A.: Network simulator-centric compositional testing. In: Castiglioni, V., Francalanza, A. (eds.) Formal Techniques for Distributed Objects, Components, and Systems, pp. 177–196. Springer, Cham (2024)
31. quinn rs: Github - quinn-rs/quinn: Async-friendly QUIC implementation in rust (2024). https://github.com/quinn-rs/quinn
32. Rutherford, M.J., Carzaniga, A., Wolf, A.L.: Simulation-based test adequacy criteria for distributed systems. In: Proceedings of the 14th ACM SIGSOFT International Symposium on Foundations of Software Engineering, SIGSOFT '06/FSE-14, pp. 231–241. Association for Computing Machinery, New York (2006). https://doi.org/10.1145/1181775.1181804
33. Shahriar, H., Zulkernine, M.: Mutation-based testing of format string bugs. In: 2008 11th IEEE High Assurance Systems Engineering Symposium, pp. 229–238 (2008). https://doi.org/10.1109/HASE.2008.8
34. Sidhu, D., Leung, T.K.: Fault coverage of protocol test methods. In: IEEE INFOCOM '88, Seventh Annual Joint Conference of the IEEE Computer and Communications Societies. Networks: Evolution or Revolution? pp. 80–85 (1988). https://doi.org/10.1109/INFCOM.1988.12901
35. Sui, A.F., Tang, W., Hu, J.J., Li, M.Z.: An effective fuzz input generation method for protocol testing. In: 2011 IEEE 13th International Conference on Communication Technology, pp. 728–731 (2011). https://doi.org/10.1109/ICCT.2011.6157972

36. Tang, W., Sui, A.F., Schmid, W.: A model guided security vulnerability discovery approach for network protocol implementation. In: 2011 IEEE 13th International Conference on Communication Technology, pp. 675–680 (2011).https://doi.org/10.1109/ICCT.2011.6157962
37. Vasiliadis, G., Athanasopoulos, E., Polychronakis, M., Ioannidis, S.: PixelVault: using GPUs for securing cryptographic operations. In: Proceedings of the 2014 ACM SIGSAC Conference on Computer and Communications Security (2014). https://api.semanticscholar.org/CorpusID:1457745
38. Wen, S., Meng, Q., Feng, C., Tang, C.: Protocol vulnerability detection based on network traffic analysis and binary reverse engineering. PLoS ONE **12**, e0186188 (2017). https://doi.org/10.1371/journal.pone.0186188
39. Woodward, M.: OBJTEST: an experimental testing tool for algebraic specifications. In: IEE Colloquium on Automating Formal Methods for Computer Assisted Prototying, p. 2 (1992)
40. Zaib, R.: Zero-day vulnerabilities: unveiling the threat landscape in network security. MJCS 57–64 (2022). https://doi.org/10.58496/mjcs/2022/007
41. Zarrad, A., Alsmadi, I., Yassine, A.: Mutation testing framework for ad-hoc networks protocols. In: 2020 IEEE Wireless Communications and Networking Conference (WCNC), pp. 1–8 (2020). https://doi.org/10.1109/WCNC45663.2020.9120695

Privacy

Enhancing Noise Estimation for Statistical Disclosure Attacks Using the Artificial Bee Colony Algorithm

Alperen Aksoy[1(✉)] and Dogan Kesdogan[2]

[1] Friedrich-Alexander University of Erlangen-Nuremberg, Erlangen, Germany
alperen.aksoy@fau.de
[2] University of Regensburg, Regensburg, Germany
dogan.kesdogan@ur.de

Abstract. The Statistical Disclosure Attack (SDA) is an effective technique for de-anonymizing users in anonymous communication networks. It was presented as a signal detection problem, aiming to distinguish the signal (messaging partners of the targeted user) from the noisy channel (all users). Although the success of signal detection relies on a better understanding of noise properties, the SDA lacks a specific method to analyze the background noise present in the targeted user's signal, i.e., a noise estimation method. Several noise estimation methods have been proposed in previous studies by utilizing communication rounds in which the targeted user does not participate, called *noise rounds*. However, these approaches treat these rounds equally without considering their relation with background noise, limiting their effectiveness. In this paper, we propose a novel noise estimation method that weights the noise rounds based on their relation with the background noise present in the targeted user's signal. We formulate this approach as an optimization problem, where the objective function measures the difference between the current noise estimation and the actual background noise. We minimize this difference by optimizing weights using the Artificial Bee Colony (ABC) algorithm. Our findings indicate that converging noise estimation to the background noise improves the accuracy of the attack.

Keywords: anonymity · traffic analysis · statistical disclosure attack · mix networks · artificial bee colony

1 Introduction

The use of the Internet is expanding to encompass various communication activities in our lives, such as email, instant messaging, and voice calling. This expansion raises concerns about the security and privacy of personal data. Although encryption is a powerful tool for protecting the content of data (e.g., messages) transmitted over the Internet, it does not safeguard critical traffic data, such as the sender and recipient information of data packets. This traffic data contains

L. Horn Iwaya et al. (Eds.): NordSec 2024, LNCS 15396, pp. 447–466, 2025.
https://doi.org/10.1007/978-3-031-79007-2_23

important private information about individuals, such as who is communicating with whom or visiting specific web pages. To protect the confidentiality of this data, Chaum proposed the Mix Networks [7]. He introduced a method for providing anonymity to users by employing specifically designed routers called mixes. Mix nodes hide the link between incoming and outgoing messages by altering their encrypted appearance and processing order. Since then, numerous protocols and anonymous communication systems have been proposed by researchers [10,11,19,25,28]. These systems are crucial to protect the privacy of at-risk individuals, such as whistle-blowers and citizens of totalitarian governments. Other use-case scenarios include protecting sensitive information in military and business corporations. To measure the vulnerability of these systems, several de-anonymization attacks have been revealed by researchers [1,6,8,9,17,21].

Disclosure attacks are an effective method of deanonymising users in anonymous communication networks. They exploit the fact that the messaging behaviour of users is not purely random, but corresponds to their habits, i.e., messages are sent according to the habits of a certain group of users (e.g., friends) [1,8,17]. A well-known example is the Statistical Disclosure Attack (SDA), which was introduced by Danezis to determine the contact list of users based on statistical analyses of traffic data [8]. In the SDA, the adversary observes the network by recording a list of users who receive messages when the targeted user (Alice) sends a message. As other users who send a message at the same time as Alice change over time owing to their different service usage times, the adversary expects Alice's message partners to appear more frequently than other users in the overall recorded recipient lists. Consequently, the SDA is represented as a signal detection problem where Alice's message partners are considered as signals hidden in the list of all recipients (i.e., noise) in the observed recipient lists.

The attack was demonstrated on the Mix Networks [7], an anonymization technique that operates in discrete rounds. In each round, a constant number of messages are collected from distinct users and shuffled[1] before being forwarded to their corresponding recipients. In this context, observations from rounds in which Alice's message is transmitted represent a signal mixed with noise, whereas the other rounds contain only noise. The goal is to estimate Alice's communication profile (e.g. the set of friends) by statistically eliminating noise (e.g. the non-friends of Alice) from the observed recipient lists. As a statistical type of disclosure attack, the SDA can provide results based on any amount of data (observations from the network). If the available data is insufficient, this issue potentially leads to inaccurate results. To increase the accuracy of the attack, several attack variants have been proposed to enhance the SDA by considering more communication assumptions than the original version (e.g. the message-replying behavior of recipients) [9,21,24,29].

One of the most important directions of the SDA approach is the investigation of noise properties. The efficiency of signal detection depends fundamentally on

[1] The shuffling process ensures indistinguishability of messages by changing their processing order and provides bitwise unlinkability through encryption/decryption operations.

a thorough understanding of noise properties. Previous assumptions and models for noise estimation do not adequately reflect reality, i.e., they do not utilize the full potential of all observations. To address this issue, we propose a novel noise estimation method that aims to minimize the disparity between the estimated and actual noise present in Alice's signal by weighting rounds based on their noise characteristics. Our experimental studies demonstrate that the proposed method outperforms previous noise estimation approaches. Also, previous attacks are conducted blindly without knowledge about the potential success of the attack. In contrast, we propose a method to measure the disparity of the current noise estimation, and we show that this information provides insights to the adversary about the potential success of the attack based on the current noise estimation. The main contributions are as follows:

- We provide an overview of the previous noise estimation methods for the SDA and their drawbacks.
- We present a minimization problem that considers the sender information contained in the observations collected by the adversary. The objective function of the problem quantifies how far the current noise estimation is from the actual noise present in the overall signal.
- We demonstrate the process of adapting and solving a problem using meta-heuristic techniques by solving the defined problem using the Artificial Bee Colony (ABC) algorithm.
- Our experimental results demonstrate that minimizing the defined objective function based on sender information of messages improves the accuracy of the SDA by converging the estimated noise to the actual noise present in Alice's signal. Furthermore, we show that the value of the defined objective function provides insights into the potential success of the attack for the adversary.

The remainder of the paper is structured as follows: Sect. 2 covers related works on disclosure attacks and noise estimation methods for the SDA, while the proposed method is presented in Sect. 3. Details and results of the experimental studies are presented in Sect. 4. The results are discussed in Sect. 5 and the conclusions and future works are given in Sect. 6.

2 Related Works

The Disclosure Attack proposed by Agrawal and Kesdogan [1] aims to de-anonymize users in mix networks under the repeated communication scenario. The attack consists of two phases and requires a significant computational effort. To address these issues, a single-phase variant of the attack was proposed in [17], although this remains an NP-complete problem. Danezis proposed a statistical version of the attack, the Statistical Disclosure Attack (SDA), which is efficient and low-complexity [8].

The main drawback of SDA is that, although it is presented as a problem of signal detection in a noisy channel, it does not propose a method for analysing the characteristics of the noise present in the signal in order to achieve better noise filtering. This issue was addressed in [22], where they proposed an approach to estimate the noise that uses the mean of the observations during the rounds in which Alice does not send a message.

Afterward, Emamdoost et al. [12] extended this approach by excluding rounds from noise estimation if any of the senders do not contribute to the background noise present in Alice's signal. However, this approach still treats each included rounds equally without considering the valuable noise contained. Another approach was presented in [26], where they propose assigning weights to users based on their contribution to noise. Instead of directly using noise rounds to estimate noise, they suggest calculating the standalone SDA for each of Alice's cloak senders (see Sect. 3.4) to determine their communication profile and then employing a weighted summation for the calculated profiles as a noise estimation. However, in the profile calculation phase, this approach does not remove the noise from user profiles. The remaining noise causes implicit changes in the assigned weights and reduces the precision of noise estimation. Finally, a lightweight approach was proposed in [3], which introduces a method to detect and exclude noise rounds that corrupt previous attack statistics using cosine similarity analysis. However, this method is limited to providing only a binary decision on whether to include noise rounds in improving the SDA.

In this paper, we introduce a novel noise estimation method by defining a minimization problem aimed at reducing the disparity between the current noise estimation and background noise present in Alice's signal. We achieve this by assigning weights to the noise rounds based on the valuable noise they contain, removing the limitation of previous approaches that treat all noise rounds equally. To optimize these weights, we employ the ABC algorithm, a well-known metaheuristic technique widely utilized across various problem domains [2,4,5,20]. Our experimental findings indicate that converging the estimated noise to the actual noise present in the signal increases the accuracy of the attack results. Furthermore, we address the problem of evaluating the potential success of the SDA from the adversary's perspective. The objective function of the problem quantifies the difference between the current noise estimation and background noise in Alice's signal. The value of this function provides insights to the adversary how effective the SDA can be, depending on the current noise estimation.

For the sake of simplicity we use mix networks to clearly demonstrate our ideas. However, we do not use any technical aspect of the mix network other than the anonymity sets, i.e., anonymity is itself defined by anonymity set as being not identifiable within a set of other items. Thus, our approach can be applied, as demonstrated by other SDA works, to all anonymous communication systems if the attacker can identify anonymity sets and gather information regarding user activity, such as tracking senders and recipients. E.g., Schatz et al. [27] employed the SDA on anonymous voice calling systems and Gaballah et al. [13], employed similar attacks on anonymous microblogging systems, shows this broader applicability.

3 Background

3.1 System Model

Chaum proposed the mix technique to prevent any arriving message from being linked to a departing one through special routers called mixes [7]. In this paper, we consider a system with N users communicating over a mix network that operates in discrete rounds. In each round, the mix waits for a batch of b messages (batch size) from users in set A, before forwarding any message. Once the batch is full, the mix changes the cryptographic appearance and processing order of these messages, then forwards them to the corresponding recipients, completing the round. This process ensures that an incoming message cannot be linked to any departing one. In this context, the subset $A' \subset A$ denotes the senders who have sent messages in the current mixing round (potential sender of each outgoing message, i.e., the sender anonymity set), and the subset $B' \subset B$ shows the recipients who receive any of these messages (potential recipient of each incoming message, i.e., the recipient anonymity set).

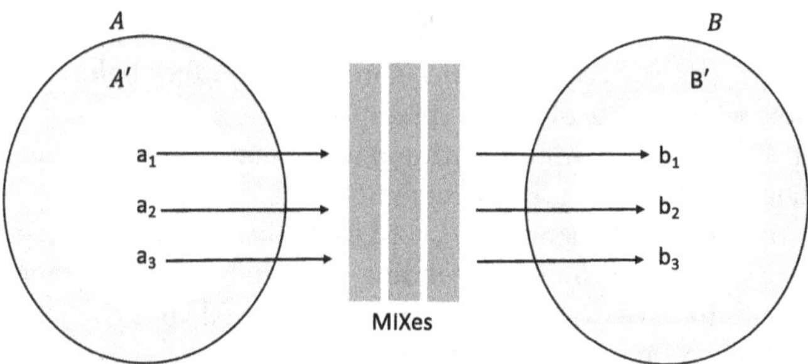

Fig. 1. Overview of communication via mix network

3.2 Attacker Model

The attacker model for disclosure attacks involves the global passive adversary (GPA), who observes the incoming and outgoing traffic of the mix network. The GPA records the interactions (sending and receiving events) for each round, and constructs anonymity sets for messages. As the adversary is passive, she cannot alter, delay, or drop messages and cannot break the cryptographic protocols in use. The adversary's goal is to conduct statistical or combinatorial analyses on anonymity sets to determine the communication partners of the targeted user. Governments and intelligence services are prime examples of the GPA, they capable of gathering sender and recipient data from Internet service providers.

Disclosure attacks can be applied to any anonymity system and mix network design topology since it focuses on anonymity sets. Although using different topologies, such as layered, cascade, or free routing, and increasing the number of mixes may help increase the anonymity set size, these methods cannot protect users from disclosure attacks. This is because disclosure attacks treat anonymous communication systems as a black box, focusing solely on observing the incoming and outgoing traffic. Therefore, we simplify the mix network so that it functions as a single mix, abstract the design and focus on corresponding anonymity sets in our analyses.

In the SDA, the adversary observes rounds in which Alice sends a message by recording the corresponding recipient sets (e.g., the recipient set B' in Fig. 1). Since each round contains a batch of b messages, the recorded recipient set includes one recipient who is the actual recipient of Alice's message, considered as the *signal*, while the other recipients in the set are considered as *background noise*. The main goal of the attack is statistically filter out the background noise to detect Alice's signal (i.e., communication partners) utilizing statistics from observed rounds. In the example provided in Fig. 1, if Alice is designated as sender a_1, one of the recipients between b_1 and b_3 is Alice's signal, while the others are considered noise.

3.3 The (Original) Statistical Disclosure Attack

Let $\vec{v}$ denote a vector representing Alice's message-sending behaviour comprised of N elements, where each element corresponds to a user in the system. It is assumed that Alice has m communication partners and sends messages uniformly to each of them. In this case, m elements of $\vec{v}$ are expected to have a value of $\frac{1}{m}$, while the remaining elements are set to 0. Additionally, $\vec{u}$ is a vector with N elements, representing the message-sending behavior of users other than Alice, and is used to estimate background noise. It is assumed that the noise is uniform across all users; therefore, all elements of $\vec{u}$ are set to $\frac{1}{N}$.

Let $i = 1$ to t, where t denotes the number of communication rounds observed by the adversary. Each observation collected by the adversary contains two elements: the sender and recipient vectors. The sender vector ($\vec{s_i}$) is a vector with N elements corresponding to each user in the system, indicating the number of messages sent by each user in round i. Similarly, the recipient vector ($\vec{r_i}$) consists of N elements denoting the number of messages that each user receives in round i. The recipient vector is normalized ($\hat{r_i} = \frac{\vec{r_i}}{|\vec{r_i}|}$) and used as an observation vector ($\vec{o_i}$). Each element of $\vec{o_i}$ corresponds to a user and denotes the probability that the user is the recipient of a message sent by Alice in round i.

Within a large set of observations, the arithmetic mean of these observations can be calculated based on the law of large numbers as follows [8]:

$$\overline{O} = \frac{1}{t}\sum_{i=1}^{t} \vec{o_i} \approx \frac{\vec{v} + (b-1)\vec{u}}{b} \tag{1}$$

From Eq. 1, Alice's communication behavior ($\vec{v}$) can be derived as:

$$\vec{v} \approx b\frac{\Sigma_{i=1}^{t}\vec{o_i}}{t} - (b-1)\vec{u} \tag{2}$$

Although the SDA is presented as a signal detection problem with a noisy channel (i.e. filtering out the noise would be sufficient to detect the signal), in the original version, the specific characteristics of the noise are not investigated in order to achieve better and faster filtering of noise, i.e., signal detection.

3.4 Investigating Noise

The main idea of this approach is to estimate the background noise by observing rounds. Since noise is independent of rounds with Alice, the idea is to include rounds also without the participation of Alice. In Fig. 2, a simple communication scenario is shown where Alice is designated as sender A. The figure shows the idea of estimating noise by extending four rounds with Alice (i.e., Rounds 1 to 4) with three more rounds without the participation of Alice, called as *noise rounds* (i.e., Rounds 5 to 7). Now the new scenario also changes the task of signal detection with the question of how to use this extra information to better filter the background noise in Rounds 1 to 4.

There are two approaches that have been proposed to utilize noise rounds to investigate the characteristics of the background noise. The first, introduced by Mathewson and Dingledine [22], involves including all noise rounds for statistical estimation of the background noise (e.g., Round 5, 6, and 7). But, including all noise rounds to the noise estimation brings a significant issue: the last noise round (i.e., Round 7) does not provide any noise present in the Rounds 1 to 4 since the sender anonymity set of Round 7 is mutual disjoint to the sender anonymity sets of Rounds 1 to 4. I.e., the senders F, G and H do not contribute to the background noise by joining any round with Alice. Because of this reason, the last noise round could be excluded from the noise estimation. This is the starting point of the approach of Emamdoost et al. named users who contribute to the background noise (participants of Rounds $1-4$ in Fig. 2, i.e., senders B to E for user A) as *cloak senders* [12]. They proposed to include only noise rounds if and only if cloak senders are participating as senders.

Calculation of Noise Observations According [22] and [12]: Obtaining observations from the noise rounds is similar to that of the rounds with Alice. The vector $\vec{u_j}$ represents the observation of the jth noise round, containing N elements calculated as the probability distribution of recipients in that round based on how many messages each recipient received (i.e., probability distribution of $\vec{r_j}$).

For the scenario in Fig. 2, following the mean of the noise observations approach [22], the noise is estimated as $\vec{u} \approx \frac{\vec{u_1}+\vec{u_2}+\vec{u_3}}{3}$ (u_1 points the 1. noise round which is round 5). The cloak sender approach [12] excludes the 3. noise round, and noise is estimated as $\vec{u} \approx \frac{\vec{u_1}+\vec{u_2}}{2}$. Both of these noise estimation approaches treat the included noise rounds equally without considering their relation to the background noise.

The cloak-senders approach utilizes the senders information of noise rounds only to make binary decisions about including a round for calculations. This approach ignores the amount of contribution of each cloak-sender to background

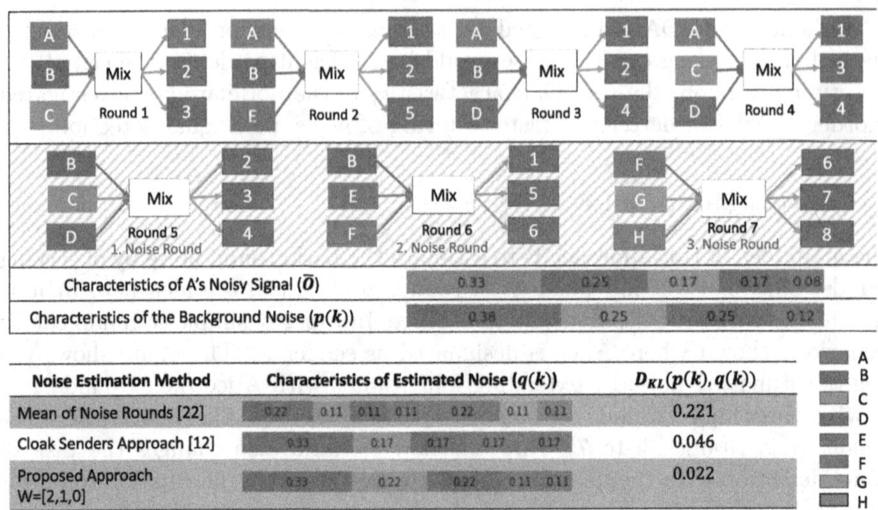

Fig. 2. An example communication scenario and observation characteristics with mix ($b = 3$)

noise in Alice's signal. In the example scenario in Fig. 2, user B has 3 messages in background noise, while user E has only 1 message (in Rounds 1 – 4). If noise rounds are equally considered to estimate the noise, the contribution of each user to the estimated noise may be different from the background noise present in Alice's signal. This issue reduces the precision of noise estimation. The cloak-sender approach does not look at this difference and considers the noise rounds equally if any of the cloak-senders join. We will extend this binary approach with weighting noise rounds based on the senders' contribution to the background noise present in Alice's signal.

3.5 Proposed Noise Estimation Approach

Assuming there are t observations containing Alice's messages and t' observations that do not. Let $\vec{S}$ represents the sum of signals mixed with background noise, and $\vec{S'}$ represents only the noise (sum of sender vectors of noise rounds). If the first element of the sender vectors (a_0) denotes the number of Alice's messages in observations, we obtain:

$$\vec{S} = \sum_{i}^{t} \vec{s_i} = (a_0, a_1 ... a_{N-1}), \quad \vec{S'} = \sum_{j}^{t'} \vec{s'_j} = (0, a'_1 ... a'_{N-1}) \tag{3}$$

We consider the characteristics of observations as the probability distribution of senders corresponding to their amount of messages in the rounds. Let k denotes any user other than Alice. $p(k)$ and $q(k)$ are the probability distributions of noise in the observations corresponding to the users. $p(k)$ is calculated as the probability mass function of $\vec{S}$, excluding the first element, which denotes the number of Alice's messages (not noise). It represents the characteristics of the background noise present in Alice's signal. On the other hand, $q(k)$ represents the characteristics of the noise rounds, calculated as the probability mass function of $\vec{S'}$.

In short, the amount of contribution of each cloak sender in the rounds where Alice is communicating is statistically captured with $p(k)$. This gives us the numbers to consider all these appropriate additional noise rounds and gives us the task to include all cloak users in the same ratio as given by $p(k)$. The statistics of the noise rounds are given by $q(k)$. It would be ideal, when $p(k) = q(k)$ holds, i.e., the characteristics of the background noise and the estimated noise match for all users. In this case, each user's contribution to the noise estimation is considered to be in the same ratio as their contribution to the background noise. This matching helps the adversary to statistically eliminate the noise and extract Alice's signal accurately. But, this expectation is unrealistic and the case is not expected to occur directly in practice. However, it gives us the direction: our objective is now to assign weights to each noise round to approach the ideal scenario. Unfortunately, this is not a linear approximation, since many peers are involved and many possibilities have to be considered to have the minimum difference between $p(k)$ and $q(k)$.

Let $W = [w_1, w_2, \ldots, w_{t'}]$ contains the weights for each noise observation. The probability distribution $q(k) = P(W \cdot \vec{S'} = k)$ represents the estimated noise characteristics after weighting the noise rounds. Our goal is to determine the suitable values of W that converge $q(k) \to p(k)$. After finding suitable weights, the calculation of noise estimation is as follows:

$$\vec{u} \approx \frac{\sum_{i=1}^{t'} w_i * \vec{u_i}}{sum(W)} \tag{4}$$

The final step of the attack involves applying the SDA using Eq. 2, with $\vec{u}$ as specified in Eq. 4.

While converging $q(k)$ to $p(k)$, we have many alternative values for selecting the weights, each of which results in a different value of $q(k)$. To evaluate these choices, we can utilize the Kullback-Leibler (KL) divergence function [18], which measures the difference between two probability distributions. The KL divergence $(D_{KL}(p(k), q(k)))$ quantifies the information loss when $q(k)$ is used to approximate $p(k)$. The output of the function is always non-negative and is zero when the two probability distributions are the same. As the two distributions diverge, the output of the function increases. The difference between $p(k)$ and $q(k)$ using KL-Divergence is calculated as:

$$D_{KL}(p(k), q(k)) = \sum_{k \in Senders - \{Alice\}} p(k) \log \left(\frac{p(k)}{q(k)} \right) \tag{5}$$

Let's revisit the example communication scenario given in Fig. 2. In the third noise round, all participating users (F, G, H) are not cloak-senders of A. Assigning a weight of 0 to exclude this round from the calculations converges the characteristics of the noise estimation to the background noise in A's signal. In our background noise (Rounds $1-4$), we have 3 messages from B, 2 from C and D, and 1 message from E. In included noise rounds, there are 2 messages from B, and 1 message from C, D, E, and F. When these contributions are compared to the characteristics of the background noise in A's signal, we should increase the contribution rate of B or decrease others to converge $q(k)$ to $p(k)$. Assigning a weight of 2 for the first noise round and a weight of 1 for the second noise round means that we consider $2 \times [B, C, D]$ from the first noise round and $1 \times [B, E, F]$ from the second noise round. Overall, we have 3 messages from B, 2 from C and D, and 1 from E and F. As seen in the figure, after weighting the noise rounds, the characteristics of the noise estimation ($q(k)$) converge better to the characteristics of the background noise ($p(k)$) compared to previous approaches by looking at the KL-divergence values.

Defining the Minimization Problem: Some senders who do not contribute to the background noise may join noise rounds with Alice's cloak senders. Because of the messages from cloak-senders are valuable, we cannot exclude these rounds from calculations. For example, in the second noise round of the scenario shown in Fig. 2, user F is not a cloak sender of A, while the other participants are cloak senders. Since there is no contribution from user F to the background noise, this user is not considered in $p(k)$ but is involved in $q(k)$. This issue prevents to met the condition of $p(k) = q(k)$ by weighting noise rounds. Since there is not an exact solution for our problem, we cannot solve using classical equation-solving methods.

In such cases, meta-heuristic techniques are useful where finding an exact solution is difficult or not possible. These methods can efficiently explore solution spaces and find near-optimal solutions. To apply meta-heuristic techniques, the problem must be formulated as an optimization task with the aim of minimizing or maximizing a specific objective function.

Since we know that the output of the KL divergence function decreases as $q(k)$ converges to $p(k)$, this function can be used as an objective function for our problem. We can define an optimization problem with the aim of minimizing the value of objective function as follows:

$$\begin{aligned} &\text{Find } W = [w_1, \ldots, w_{t'}], \text{ which minimizes} \\ &\qquad obj(W) = D_{KL}(p(k), q(k)) \\ &\text{subject to} \quad w_i \geq 0, \quad i = 1, \ldots, t' \end{aligned} \tag{6}$$

The value of the $obj(W)$ function in Eq. 6 quantifies the difference between the characteristics of the current noise estimation and the background noise present in Alice's signal. Also, in the optimization process, the KL divergence function prioritizes the dominant values for convergence, meaning that the noise characteristics of users whose noise contribution is more likely to be considered earlier than the others. For optimizing weights to minimize the objective function, we will use the well-known meta-heuristic technique ABC algorithm, which has demonstrated effectiveness in handling high-dimensional problems [2,4,15].

The ABC algorithm aims to find food sources matched with potential solutions to the problem of interest, using employed, onlooker, and scout bees modeled through different search and utilization characteristics [14]. Each group of bees represents a phase of the algorithm. These phases are iterated in a specific order until the selected termination criteria are met. Completing these consecutive phases is counted as an iteration, and the termination criteria are typically based on a pre-determined iteration count being reached. After completing each iteration, it is expected to obtain a higher-quality solution that minimizes the objective function better. The detailed adoption of the ABC algorithm to the proposed minimization problem is given in Appendix.

4 Experimental Study

We conducted a series of experiments via simulations to evaluate the effectiveness of the proposed noise estimation approach. We developed a simulation program in Python, utilizing the Simpy package [23] to simulate message-sending events and the Hive package [30] for the ABC implementation.

Firstly, we applied the SDA by observing rounds one-by-one from the mix network to track the changes in the estimation error of Alice's communication profile and the KL-divergence value of the noise estimation without weighting the noise rounds to observe their pattern. Then, we investigated the change in the estimation error of Alice's communication profile without additional observations from the network by applying the proposed noise estimation approach. We also observed the effect of the configuration parameters of the ABC algorithm on the convergence performance of the defined minimization problem. Finally, we compared the de-anonymization performance of our method with two previous enhancements, Cloak-Sender SDA [12] and Smart-Noise SDA [26], both of which enhance the noise estimation of the SDA.

During the simulations, we followed the same assumptions as in the original SDA [8], where each user has m communication partners randomly selected from N users. They send messages according to a Poisson process with the same message-sending rate and uniformly select the recipient of each message from their own recipient set. For the ABC Algorithm, while the values for weight matrices (W) are randomly generated, the minimum value set to 0 and the maximum set to the number of rounds containing only noise (t'). The *limit* parameter of the ABC algorithm is set to the default value of 25. The provided simulation results are averaged over 50 repetitions.

4.1 Estimation Error of the SDA and the Divergence of Noise Estimation

In this section, we observe the change in the estimation error of the SDA and the KL divergence value of the noise estimation ($D_{KL}(p(k), q(k))$) which measures the difference between current noise estimation and background noise present in Alice's signal. We do not assign weights to noise rounds in these simulations and estimate the noise by taking the arithmetic mean of cloak-sender observations from noise rounds as proposed in [12]. Here, $\vec{v}$ denotes Alice's actual communication profile, and $\vec{v'}$ is the estimated communication profile by the SDA. We use the mean squared error (MSE) of $\vec{v}$ as a metric to calculate the estimation error of Alice's profile, as shown in Eq. 7.

$$MSE_{\vec{v}} = \frac{1}{N}\sum_{i}^{N}(\vec{v}_i - \vec{v'}_i)^2 \tag{7}$$

We set the network parameters with the batch size (b) as 50, the number of users (N) as 500, and each user has 10 communication partners (m). We observed 200 communication rounds from the mix network for each simulation and recorded the values of the objective function and the MSE of Alice's communication profile after adding each observation. The results are shown in Fig. 3. As shown in the figure, the estimation error of the attack decreases with an increasing number of observations from the network. The decrease in error is rapid for the initial observations, but the rate diminishes for subsequent observations. The value of the KL-divergence between the noise estimation and background noise present in Alice's signal, which we use as an objective function, shows a very similar trend to the estimation error. By observing more rounds from the network, the estimated noise converges to the background noise, resulting in the better and more accurate filtering out the noise from Alice's signal.

4.2 Minimizing the Objective Function Using the ABC Algorithm

In this section, we evaluate the effect of the proposed noise estimation method on the error of the estimated communication profile of Alice. We observe changes in estimation error ($MSE_{\vec{v}}$) without additional observations from the network by applying the proposed noise estimation approach, which minimizes the difference between the characteristics of the estimated noise and the background noise within available observations. Additionally, we analyze the impact of the configuration parameters of the ABC algorithm on the convergence performance of the objective function in the defined minimization problem. We set the network parameters to $b = 50$, $N = 500$, and $m = 10$. For each simulation, we let the adversary has 200 observations of communication rounds.

The configuration parameters of the ABC algorithm are varied as follows: number of food sources (SN) with values [50, 100] and the iterations range from 0 to 200. We record the value of the objective function and $MSE_{\vec{v}}$ in each iteration of the minimization process.

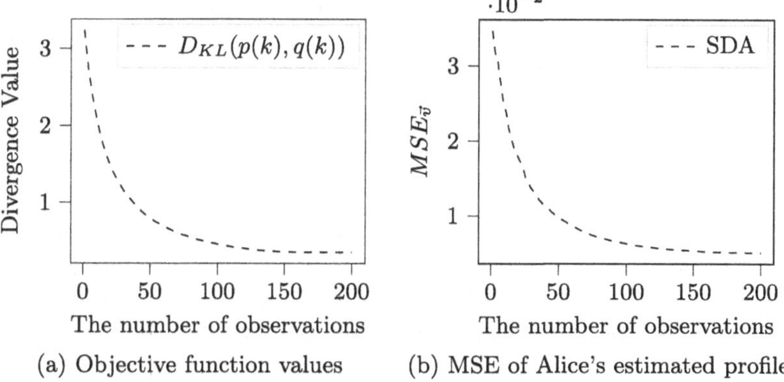

Fig. 3. The value of objective function and error of the estimated Alice's profile by the SDA during observations

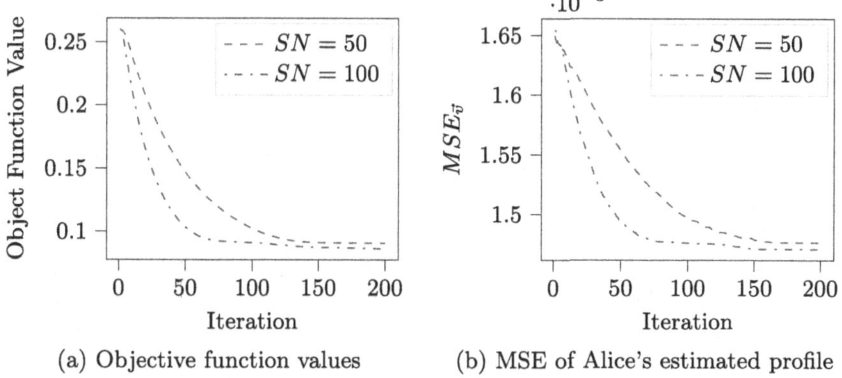

Fig. 4. Minimizing process by the ABC algorithm in defined problem by various food source parameter through 200 iterations

Based on Figs. 4a and 4b, as the value of the objective function decreases throughout the iterations, the error in the estimated communication profile of Alice also decreases. Increasing the number of food sources provides a better minimization performance for the objective function and enhances the accuracy of the estimated communication profile. The convergence rate of the objective function is faster during the initial iterations for both values of the food source parameter. However, as the iterations progress, the convergence rate gradually slows down until it reaches a point where the algorithm appears to become stuck. Beyond this point, the algorithm can only converge to values that are very close to this point. This point can be reached in fewer iterations as the food source parameter increases.

As seen in the results provided in the previous and this section, the estimation error and the value of the objective function show a very similar trend. Briefly, the accuracy of the SDA results increases as the estimated noise converges to the background noise, both by observing more rounds and utilizing the available observations more efficiently following the proposed noise estimation approach.

4.3 Comparison with Previous Methods

One of the useful metric for evaluating the de-anonymization performance of the attack is the number of observations required to de-anonymize a user. Because, observing more rounds requires additional time, results in slower de-anonymization performance. In this section, we compare the de-anonymization performance of our proposed approach (ABC-SDA) under different experimental settings with the Cloak-Sender SDA [12] and Smart-Noise SDA [26], which proposed novel noise estimation approach for the SDA.

Regarding the network parameters, we adopt experimental settings similar to those used in previous studies on disclosure attacks [12, 16]. The batch size (b) is selected as 50, the number of users in the system (N) is set to 20000, and the number of communication partners (m) is 20. In each comparison, we vary one parameter while keeping the other parameters fixed. In the SDA, the m elements with the highest values in the estimated vector $\vec{v'}$ are considered Alice's detected communication partners. The configuration parameters of the ABC algorithm are set as follows: the food source is set to 100 and the termination criteria are defined as iterations reaching 100.

According to Fig. 5a, as the batch size increases, the number of observations required to complete the attack increases for all three SDA variants. When the batch size is set to 25, the ABC-SDA algorithm is completed in 23% fewer rounds than the Cloak-Sender SDA and 20% than the Smart-Noise SDA. Similarly, with a batch size of 150, the number of observations required to complete the attack is 21% less than the Smart-Noise SDA.

The number of required observations increases significantly with m for all given attacks. In Fig. 5b, it can be observed that the difference in the required observations between ABC-SDA and other variants increases with m. This increase indicates that our proposed method is less sensitive to the value of m than previous enhancements. For instance, when m is set to 30, ABC-SDA requires 28% fewer observations than Smart-Noise SDA, even though they are almost the same when m is 5. Furthermore, increasing the value of N reduces the number of observations required to complete the attack for all three SDA variants. Across all the values of N shown in Fig. 5c, ABC-SDA requires approximately 25% fewer observations than Cloak-Sender SDA to complete the attack successfully.

Based on the results, the ABC-SDA demonstrates better de-anonymization performance than the Cloak-Sender SDA and Smart-Noise SDA under the given experimental settings.

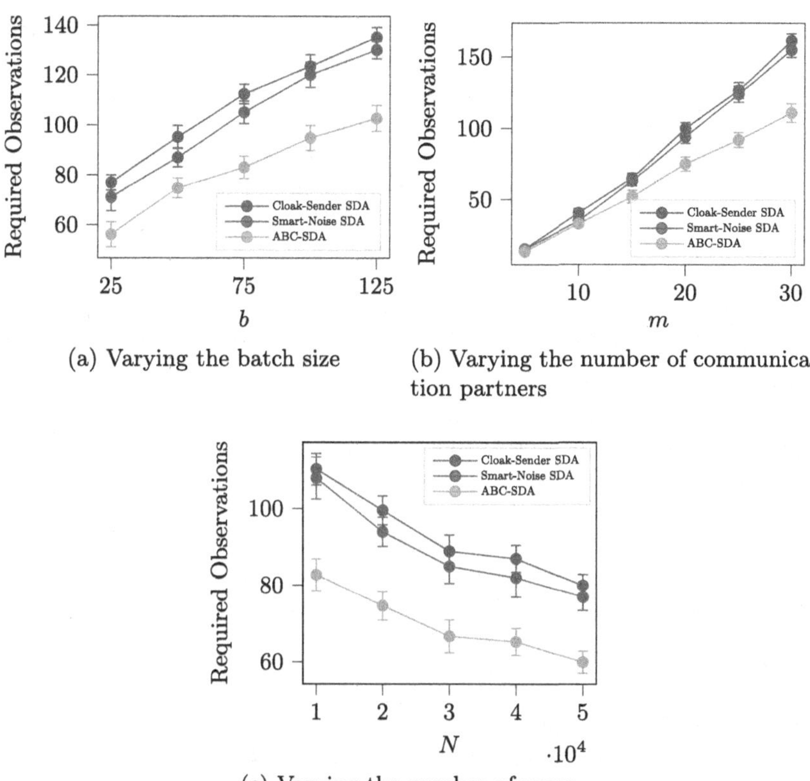

(a) Varying the batch size

(b) Varying the number of communication partners

(c) Varying the number of users

Fig. 5. Comparison of de-anonymization performance of ABC-SDA with the Cloak-Sender SDA and Smart-Noise SDA for varying network parameters (Conf. interval = 0.95)

5 Discussion

The SDA is a statistical attack that does not provide exact results and gives only statistical approximations. Exact type of disclosure attacks such as the Hitting Set Attack [17] guarantee that the provided results are correct but require a certain number of observations to provide any result of the attack. The SDA can provide results based on a given number of observations, even if they are insufficient to produce accurate results. Our experimental results demonstrate that the accuracy of Alice's estimated profile increases as more rounds from the network are observed. With an increase in the number of observed rounds, we observe a reduction in the difference between noise estimation and Alice's background noise, by looking at their divergence values. These results remind us that the SDA is a typical signal detection problem, and the success of the attack relies on accurate noise estimation. Based on this observation, we directed our research towards efficiently utilizing noise rounds to estimate the noise close to the background noise present in Alice's signal within the available observations. We proposed a method to reduce the divergence between noise estimation and background noise by weighting the noise rounds, without needing to observe more rounds. Consequently, we show that the correct contact list of Alice is detected with fewer observations compared to previous methods.

One drawback of the SDA which limits its practical usage is that the adversary has no idea about the potential success of the attack within available observations. In Sect. 4, we show that errors of the estimated Alice's communication profile by the attack decrease with the decreasing value of the defined objective function. The adversary can utilize the value of the objective function to gain insight into the potential success of the SDA with current available observations. In addition, [3] and [26] discuss that some observations may corrupt previous statistics, and adding these observations to the SDA decreases the attack's accuracy. The proposed objective function may help decide whether an observation is useful to be considered by examining the changing values before and after adding it.

Solving the defined minimization problem is limited to the ABC algorithm in this study. We leave the exploration of alternative solution methods to achieve higher-quality solutions as future work.

6 Conclusions

Although the SDA is presented as a signal detection problem, it lacks a specific noise estimation method to investigate the characteristics of the background noise for more accurate signal extraction. Several studies conducted to investigate background noise characteristics in the SDA because the success of signal detection depends on a thorough understanding of the noise characteristics present in the signal. In this study, we provide an overview of previous noise estimation methods and their drawbacks. We then propose a novel approach for noise estimation, which involves weighting noise rounds based on specific noise characteristics. We formulate this as a minimization problem, with the objective function quantifies the difference between the current noise estimation and the background noise present in Alice's signal. We solve the defined problem using the well-known meta-heuristic technique, the Artificial Bee Colony (ABC) algorithm.

We demonstrate that minimizing the defined objective function converges the characteristics of the estimated noise to the noise present in Alice's signal, consequently enhancing the accuracy of the SDA. The results of the experimental studies show that the proposed method outperforms previous approaches in terms of de-anonymization performance. Additionally, the value of the objective function provides insights for the adversary regarding the potential success of the attack within the available observations. In future studies, exploring alternative methods for solving the proposed optimization problem to obtain higher-quality results, defining additional quality criteria to evaluate the current noise estimation, and extending the approach of utilizing noise rounds to combinatorial traffic analysis attacks like the Hitting Set Attack [17] would be worthwhile.

Acknowledgements. The first author would like to express gratitude to the Turkish Ministry of Education for funding his doctoral studies, and we would like to thank Marc Rossberger for the fruitful discussions during the initial phase of this paper.

Appendix

Adapting the ABC Algorithm to the Defined Minimization Problem: In our problem, we seek the optimal values of the weight matrix (W) that minimizes the defined objective function given in Eq. 6. The ABC algorithm starts the optimization process by generating SN (number of food sources) different W matrices randomly using Eq. 8.

$$W_{ij} = min + rand(0,1)(max - min) \quad j = 1, 2, \dots t' \tag{8}$$

In Eq. 8, W_{ij} denotes the generated weight of the $j-th$ noise round for the $i-th$ weight matrix among SN different weight matrices. The dimension of our problem is t', which is the number of noise observations collected by the adversary. The min and max values are the configuration parameters of the algorithm used to restrict the search space.

After the SN different W matrices have been initialized, each generated vector (food source) is assigned to an employed bee. These employed bees are responsible for improving the solution by searching the neighborhood of their assigned food sources. In each iteration, they search for a higher-quality candidate for the weight vectors as follows:

$$C_{ij} = W_{ij} + \phi_{ij}(W_{ij} - W_{kj}) \tag{9}$$

In Eq. 9, C_{ij} represents a new candidate for the j-th weight of the i-th weight matrix. W_{kj} refers to the j-th parameter of a randomly selected weight matrix (W_k) among SN different weight matrices. ϕ_{ij} represents a number drawn randomly from the range $[-1, 1]$.

The next step is checking the quality of the produced candidate weight matrix (C_i). If the fitness value of $\vec{C_i}$, calculated using Eq. 10, is greater than the fitness value of W_i, C_{ij} is replaced with W_{ij}, and the trial counter of W_i is reset[2]. This operation indicates that the source of W_i has been improved in the current iteration. If the fitness value of $\vec{C_i}$ is not greater than $\vec{X_i}$, $\vec{C_{ij}}$ is discarded, and the trial counter is increased by one. This case shows that the source of W_i has not been improved in the current iteration.

$$fit(C_i) = 1 + |obj(C_i)| \tag{10}$$

After the employed bee phase, the quality of food sources is distributed to onlooker bees. In the onlooker bee phase, each bee selects a food source to

[2] The given formula is valid only when $obj() \geq 0$. We do not consider the fitness calculation formula of the ABC algorithm for negative objective function values because the output of our objective function is always non-negative.

improve. This process is carried out based on the selection probabilities for each food source, which are calculated using Eq. 11.

$$p(W_i) = \frac{fit(W_i)}{\sum_j^{SN} fit(W_j)} \tag{11}$$

After the selection procedure, each bee associated with a food source becomes an employed bee and generates candidate solutions using Eq. 9. Upon careful examination of the employed and onlooker bee phases in the ABC algorithm, it is apparent that the utilization or consumption of existing resources is more prominent than the generation or discovery of new resources. However, it is crucial to maintain a balance between these operations for an effective search process. The scout bee phase in the ABC algorithm is responsible for providing this balance. If a food source fails to show improvement over a certain number of iterations, referred to as the *limit*, the associated employed bee abandons the food source. Then, these abandoned food sources are considered to be consumed and replaced with new food sources generated using Eq. 8. These steps are iterated until the termination criteria are met. The highest-quality weight vector among those found is returned as the solution for the problem.

References

1. Agrawal, D., Kesdogan, D.: Measuring anonymity: the disclosure attack. IEEE Secur. Priv. **1**(06), 27–34 (2003). https://doi.org/10.1109/MSECP.2003.1253565
2. Akay, B., Karaboga, D.: A survey on the applications of artificial bee colony in signal, image, and video processing. SIViP **9**(4), 967–990 (2015). https://doi.org/10.1007/s11760-015-0758-4
3. Aksoy, A., Kesdogan, D.: Detecting corruptive noise rounds for statistical disclosure attacks. In: 2024 9th International Conference on Computer Science and Engineering (UBMK) (2024, in press)
4. Aslan, S., Aksoy, A.: Solving wireless sensor deployment problem with parallel artificial bee colony algorithm. In: 2018 26th Signal Processing and Communications Applications Conference (SIU), pp. 1–4 (2018)
5. Badem, H., Basturk, A., Caliskan, A., Yuksel, M.E.: A new efficient training strategy for deep neural networks by hybridization of artificial bee colony and limited-memory BFGS optimization algorithms. Neurocomputing **266**, 506–526 (2017)
6. Cai, X., Zhang, X.C., Joshi, B., Johnson, R.: Touching from a distance: website fingerprinting attacks and defenses. In: Proceedings of the 2012 ACM Conference on Computer and Communications Security, CCS 2012, pp. 605–616. Association for Computing Machinery, New York (2012). https://doi.org/10.1145/2382196.2382260
7. Chaum, D.L.: Untraceable electronic mail, return addresses, and digital pseudonyms. Commun. ACM **24**(2), 84–90 (1981)
8. Danezis, G.: Statistical disclosure attacks. In: Security and Privacy in the Age of Uncertainty, pp. 421–426. Springer, Boston (2003)
9. Danezis, G., Diaz, C., Troncoso, C.: Two-sided statistical disclosure attack. In: Borisov, N., Golle, P. (eds.) Privacy Enhancing Technologies, pp. 30–44. Springer, Heidelberg (2007)

10. Diaz, C., Halpin, H., Kiayias, A.: The nym network | the next generation of privacy infrastructure. https://nymtech.net/nym-whitepaper.pdf. Accessed 12 Apr 2023
11. Dingledine, R., Mathewson, N., Syverson, P.: Tor: the second-generation onion router. In: 13th USENIX Security Symposium (USENIX Security 2004). USENIX Association, San Diego, CA (2004)
12. Emamdoost, N., Dousti, M.S., Jalili, R.: Statistical disclosure: improved, extended, and resisted. arXiv preprint arXiv:1710.00101 (2017)
13. Gaballah, S.A., Abdullah, L., Tran, M.T., Zimmer, E., Mühlhäuser, M.: On the effectiveness of intersection attacks in anonymous microblogging. In: Nordic Conference on Secure IT Systems, pp. 3–19. Springer (2022)
14. Karaboga, D.: Artificial bee colony algorithm. Scholarpedia **5**(3), 6915 (2010)
15. Karaboga, N.: A new design method based on artificial bee colony algorithm for digital IIR filters. J. Franklin Inst. **346**(4), 328–348 (2009)
16. Kesdogan, D., Agrawal, D., Pham, V., Rautenbach, D.: Fundamental limits on the anonymity provided by the mix technique. In: 2006 IEEE Symposium on Security and Privacy (SP 2006), pp. 14 pp.–99 (2006). https://doi.org/10.1109/SP.2006.17
17. Kesdogan, D., Pimenidis, L.: The hitting set attack on anonymity protocols. In: Fridrich, J. (ed.) Information Hiding, pp. 326–339. Springer, Heidelberg (2005)
18. Kullback, S., Leibler, R.A.: On information and sufficiency. Ann. Math. Stat. **22**(1), 79–86 (1951)
19. Kwon, A., Lu, D., Devadas, S.: XRD: scalable messaging system with cryptographic privacy. In: NSDI (2020)
20. Lei, X., Sun, J., Xu, X., Guo, L.: Artificial bee colony algorithm for solving multiple sequence alignment. In: 2010 IEEE Fifth International Conference on Bio-Inspired Computing: Theories and Applications (BIC-TA), pp. 337–342 (2010)
21. Mallesh, N., Wright, M.: The reverse statistical disclosure attack. In: Böhme, R., Fong, P.W.L., Safavi-Naini, R. (eds.) Information Hiding, pp. 221–234. Springer, Heidelberg (2010)
22. Mathewson, N., Dingledine, R.: Practical traffic analysis: extending and resisting statistical disclosure. In: Martin, D., Serjantov, A. (eds.) Privacy Enhancing Technologies, pp. 17–34. Springer, Heidelberg (2005)
23. Matloff, N.: Introduction to discrete-event simulation and the simpy language. Davis, CA. Department of Computer Science. University of California at Davis. Retrieved on August **2**(2009), 1–33 (2008)
24. Pérez-González, F., Troncoso, C.: Understanding statistical disclosure: a least squares approach. In: Fischer-Hübner, S., Wright, M. (eds.) Privacy Enhancing Technologies, pp. 38–57. Springer, Heidelberg (2012)
25. Piotrowska, A.M., Hayes, J., Elahi, T., Meiser, S., Danezis, G.: The loopix anonymity system. In: 26th USENIX Security Symposium (USENIX Security 2017), pp. 1199–1216. USENIX Association, Vancouver, BC (2017)
26. Roßberger, M., Kesdoğan, D.: Smart noise detection for statistical disclosure attacks. In: Secure IT Systems, pp. 87–103. Springer, Cham (2024)
27. Schatz, D., Rossberg, M., Schaefer, G.: Evaluating statistical disclosure attacks and countermeasures for anonymous voice calls. In: Proceedings of the 18th International Conference on Availability, Reliability and Security, ARES 2023. Association for Computing Machinery, New York (2023). https://doi.org/10.1145/3600160.3600186
28. Shen, T., et al.: Daenet: making strong anonymity scale in a fully decentralized network. IEEE Trans. Dependable Secure Comput. **19**(4), 2286–2303 (2022). https://doi.org/10.1109/TDSC.2021.3052831

29. Troncoso, C., Gierlichs, B., Preneel, B., Verbauwhede, I.: Perfect matching disclosure attacks. In: Borisov, N., Goldberg, I. (eds.) Privacy Enhancing Technologies, pp. 2–23. Springer, Heidelberg (2008)
30. Wuilbercq, R.: rwuilbercq/hive: First release of hive (2017). https://doi.org/10.5281/zenodo.1004592

Left Alone Facing a Difficult Choice: An Expert Analysis of Websites Promoting Selected Privacy-Enhancing Technologies

Shirin Shams[1(✉)], Sebastian Reinke[1], and Delphine Reinhardt[2]

[1] Institute of Computer Science, University of Göttingen, Göttingen, Germany
shirin.shams@uni-goettingen.de, reinke@cs.uni-goettingen.de

[2] Institute of Computer Science and Campus Institute Data Science, University of Göttingen, Göttingen, Germany
reinhardt@cs.uni-goettingen.de

Abstract. The privacy community has invested considerable effort in understanding why motivated individuals do not adopt available solutions. As a result, several factors supporting individuals in adopting *Privacy Enhancing Technologies* (PETs) have been revealed. However, the adoption rate remains low. To contribute in changing this current state, we adopt an unexplored approach by analysing 69 online websites promoting four selected PETs: *Virtual Private Network* (VPN), Tor, private browser, and private search engine. In addition to considering the accessibility of these websites, we consider a set of 24 selected criteria grounded in the factors identified in the literature as supporting individuals in adopting PETs. These criteria aim to explore the presentation of PETs to individuals. For example, we consider the presentation of aspects of PET technology, such as coverage, limitations, and speed. Our results show that, on average, only about one-third of our criteria set are fulfilled by the analysed websites. Furthermore, our accessibility audit reveals issues that could create significant obstacles for impaired users. As a result, these websites miss their primary goal of effectively informing individuals about PETs by not utilising the identified supporting factors. These results indicate that individuals are left alone in making privacy choices and do not have sufficient support for adopting PETs. To address this situation, we propose two design templates incorporating supporting factors, offering a foundation for presenting PETs to individuals to assist them in adoption.

Keywords: Usable Privacy · Presentation of PETs · Accessibility Audit

1 Introduction

Numerous PETs are available to the public. For example, over 150 VPNs can be downloaded from the Apple App Store, and more than 30 private browsers with

L. Horn Iwaya et al. (Eds.): NordSec 2024, LNCS 15396, pp. 467–487, 2025.
https://doi.org/10.1007/978-3-031-79007-2_24

various functionalities have been presented to individuals in the Android Google Play. However, the adoption rate of PETs remains notably low, despite individuals expressing privacy concerns [4,23,24,30,38,50]. For example, the most popular VPNs in the App Store show 50 million downloads. As compared to the number of 3.3 billion Android users [13], this represents about 1.5%. Moreover, for instance, only 6% of the 257 participants of the study conducted in [4] had installed privacy-preserving applications on their mobile devices despite more than 80% expressed privacy concerns. The privacy community (i.e., researchers and privacy organisations) has invested considerable effort in understanding why motivated individuals do not adopt available solutions. A prominent outcome of these efforts shows the poor usability of PETs and the manner in which PETs are presented to individuals [1,3,4,12,44]. This indicates that the role of humans has not received adequate attention in the process of developing and presenting PETs. While the poor usability covers various aspects, a more multi-faceted approach is suggested in [1,6,7,12,41] to understand the influential factors contributing to PETs adoption. In this regard, fundamental factors, such as incomplete threat models and limited understanding of the technology, are presented in [29,41,51]. More factors such as individuals' personality traits and privacy concerns and knowledge are highlighted in [5–9,18–20,25,28,32]. Several works presented more fine grain influential factors. For instance, [28] shows that when people perceive an effective response to their actions, it strongly affects their intention to use PETs. This means that when the effectiveness of adopting a PET in addressing privacy concerns is clearly demonstrated, the likelihood of PET adoption significantly increases. Despite knowing these influential factors, the rate of PET adoption remains low. To gain deeper insights, in this paper, we focus on exploring online resources, such as websites, as they, in combination with blogs, are the primary sources where users inform themselves about improving their online privacy [32]. We aim to assess how the identified factors supporting adoption are communicated to visitors of websites promoting PETs. To this end, we have selected four PETs: *Virtual Private Network* (VPN), Tor, *Private Browser* (PB), and *Private Search Engine* (PSE). Our choice is motivated by [10], which highlights that stand-alone solutions are the least utilised compared to non-technology-based and built-in alternatives, emphasising the need for action. We next form our research question as follows: **RQ:** *What are the strengths and weaknesses of websites promoting PETs in supporting individuals in their decision?* Answering this question can shed light on how well (or not) PETs are being presented to individuals. Ultimately, our results can serve as the basis for future investigations of potential correlation with the current low adoption rate. This provides a foundation for better-supporting individuals in privacy preservation, which is the core objective of this paper.

In the following, we summarise the contributions of this paper.

- We, two domain researchers, have analysed 69 websites promoting four targeted PETs using an expert-oriented method. We have categorised these websites into two main categories: (1) *single-product*, which exclusively promotes one product, such as a single VPN application and (2) *comparing- product*, which compares various products, such as seven VPN applications. To analyse these websites, we have compiled a list of 24 criteria primarily based on factors identified by academic research as supporting individuals in adopting PETs. We have classified these criteria into seven categories, including (1) *technology*, which refers to presenting technological aspects to individuals, covering criteria like coverage and limitation, and (2)*information*, which focuses on how information is presented, including criteria such as layout and variety. Furthermore, we have conducted an accessibility audit on the websites mentioned above, guided by the principles outlined in the Web Content Accessibility Guidelines (WCAG) 2 [52].

- Our analysis shows the average coverage across all criteria in *single-product* and *comparing-product* websites is approximately one-third. Additionally, our accessibility audit reveals a consistent pattern of neglecting accessibility guidelines, including easily fixable cases. This reflects that individuals are receiving, at best, one-third of what the privacy community has shown to be supportive in adopting PETs, highlighting a gap between academic knowledge and practical implementation. These results display that individuals are left alone without adequate support to make privacy decisions.
- Based on these results, we have developed two design templates, including factors identified in the literature. These templates intend to present PETs better to support individuals in making a decision to adopt PETs. We further contextualise our research findings within the existing academic resources.

This paper is organised as follows: Sect. 2 explains the related work focusing on supporting individuals in adopting privacy solutions. Section 3 describes our methodology, the selection of websites and criteria, and the analysis process. A detailed explanation of our results is provided in Sect. 4. We propose design templates in Sect. 5. We further discuss our results in Sect. 6. Finally, we conclude our study in Sect. 7.

2 Related Work

In this section, we look into the relatively limited literature focusing on supporting people in adopting security and privacy solutions. These studies, along with our own work, ultimately aim to address the identified gap: low adoption rates of PETs despite users' express of privacy concerns [4,23,24,30,38,50]. In the following, we present these works chronologically.

The first influential study related to our work is ENISA's report from 2015 [26]. ENISA conducted a study to analyse existing websites promoting the use of online privacy tools for the general public based on ten criteria. These criteria include tool selection methodology and frequency of content updates. While ENISA's goal for analysis is on the method used for selecting the proposed privacy tools and the overall quality of offered information, our goal differs. We aim to analyse our website samples in regard to factors supporting individuals in adopting PETs. Therefore, our set of 24 criteria focused on factors such as technology explanation, text readability, and accessibility. While ENISA focused on 12 websites presenting multiple products, we examined 69 websites presenting a single PET or comparing multiple PETs. To the best of our knowledge, our analysis is the first to address the following aspects: (1) providing an overview of websites promoting PETs concerning their support for people in the adoption process and (2) evaluating the extent to which recommendations from academic research and domain experts are delivered to users via websites.

Similar to ours, the study [40] published in 2020 examines the support provided to individuals in adopting privacy and security solutions. The authors initially identified 374 distinct recommended behaviours about online security and privacy. Subsequently, they assessed the quality of these recommendations based on criteria such as comprehensibility and perceived actionability via a user study involving 1,586 participants and 41 professional security experts. While their focus was on analysing individual pieces of advice, our study takes a broader approach, examining the entirety of online websites. This includes various aspects of websites, such as presentation variety, provider information and comparison support. To our understanding, our study is the first to comprehensively analyse the presentation of PETs, encompassing the entirety of websites.

Introduced in 2022, the *Security and Privacy Acceptance Framework* (SPAF) [11] is the most recent related study. SPAF aims to encourage user adoption of security and privacy behaviours and also evaluate the presentation of privacy solutions to people. SPAF proposes a framework comprising three non-independent factors: *Motivation, ability, and awareness.* According to SPAF, these three factors must be present simultaneously for an individual to initiate a behaviour in this context, like adopting a PET. SPAF built this framework based on the fundamental behaviour model called Fogg Behavior Model [16]. Then, SPAF analyses prior academic works providing privacy and security solutions to users through the lens of these three factors. Their evaluation of 100 works revealed that almost all failed to cover these three factors simultaneously. The distinction between our work and SPAF lies in resources and criteria. While SPAF primarily examines academic works, our study focuses on the presentation of PET via websites that are available to the public. Although our criteria conceptually overlap with SPAF's, we have conducted our analysis by using fine-grainer criteria. To the best of our knowledge, our study is the first to analyse the delivery of fine-grained factors for supporting individuals in adopting PETs when they inform themselves online.

3 Methodology

To answer our research question (**RQ:** *What are the strengths and weaknesses of websites promoting PETs in supporting individuals in their decision?*), we first analyse "what" individuals are dealing with when they want to inform themselves about adopting PETs online. "What" means the content and form of websites promoting PETs. By identifying the strengths and weaknesses of the current presentation of PETs, our secondary goal is to propose design templates containing collective strengths and covering the current weaknesses (see Sect. 5).

To this end, we follow an expert-oriented approach similar to the one applied by ENISA [26]. Our decision is also motivated by fundamental human-computer interaction resources [34,45], which recommend an expert-oriented approach as highly valuable in the early stages when design concepts require validation prior to user involvement. As the basis for our analysis, we have first defined the context of the study (Sect. 3.1). Next, we have selected 69 websites (Sect. 3.2) and have developed a set of 24 criteria (Sect. 3.3). We finally detail our analysis process (Sect. 3.4).

3.1 Study Context

We have first made the following decisions that define the context considered in our study due to its importance in the field of privacy [35]. (1) Since the platform defines context [36], we have scoped for computer desktop platform. While mobile devices are comparably used for web browsing [17], we prioritise the desktop due to the larger screen size, allowing for a stable analysing environment. (2) Among the available privacy solutions, we concentrate on stand-alone solutions as shown in [10] to be the least used compared to non-technology-based and built-in solutions, thus calling for action. Consequently, we scoped out four PETs, named: (a) **VPN** as in [10,27,39,46,48], (b) the **Tor** considered in [10,19,20,39, 48], (c) **PB** (e.g., DuckDuckGo as in [39], Ghostery in [10], Brave in [39]), and (d) **PSE** (e.g., Startpage mentioned in [39]).

3.2 Websites Selection

We focus on online searching for the names of four targeted PETs to identify the websites of our study. As shown recently in [32], searching for information online is a common method for individuals motivated to improve privacy. To minimise biases from search history, we utilise Tor [49] and DuckDuckGo [14] as the search browser and search engine, respectively. We gathered 120 websites by scanning the first three pages of search results for the names of each of the four PETs (*Virtual Private Network*, *Tor*, *Private Browser*, and *Private Search Engine*) as search terms. Typically, users do not go until the end of the third page of search results [42], as we did. However, websites that may appear on the third page might appear earlier in search results for queries with alternative terms. Therefore, we decided to include websites up to the end of the third page to ensure we would not miss potentially relevant websites. We excluded websites that were not in English, repetitive, or unrelated. After this filtering, 69 websites were left (see Appendix). We categorised these 69 websites into two main groups based on their content and purpose. The first group, called *single-product*, comprises websites exclusively promoting a single PET, e.g., Surfshark VPN. The second group, which we refer to as *comparing-product*, includes websites that compare multiple PETs of a similar type, for example, comparing ten VPN products.

Table 1. 24 criteria considered in our analysis. Criteria marked with ⋆ are exclusive to *single-product*, while others marked with ⋆⋆ apply solely to *comparing-product* websites.

Category	Criterion	Description
Technology The technology aspects of the PET	**Explanation**	Explanation of the functionality of a PET. Understanding the PET functionality enhances users' perception of its usefulness [6,8,39,41].
	Coverage	Communicating the effects of adopting a PET and how it meets users' needs [15,28].
	Limitations	Communicating the PETs limitation i.e., the threats not addressed [21,29,41,51].
	Easiness	Showing the easiness of PET adoption and usage, increasing the likelihood of adoption [6].
	Speed⋆	Presenting evidence of the low impact of the PET on speed [46].
Trust The role of trust in various aspects in the adoption of PET	**Provider**	Providing information about the PET provider (e.g., the producer company) or the analyser of comparison [19].
	Product	Showing evidence of PET trustworthiness [7]
	User feedback	Delivering other people's opinions about PET. [46] demonstrates that user reviews and ratings influence how people choose a VPN to install.
	Interpersonal	Utilising interpersonal diffusion channels, such as peer recommendations, group and family plans [7,11,12,43].
Information The information and its presentation to individuals	**Layout⋆**	Presenting information in the page layout: appropriately titled, categorised, and easily understandable.
	Presentation variety	Offering information in various formats (e.g., videos, diagrams) to enhance engagement and accommodate different browsing habits.
	Gap coverage	Covering knowledge gaps rooted in jargon and industry-specific language, e.g., text links and teaching in time by information icons.
	Language formality	Avoiding informal and complicated language [47].
Usability The user interaction usability [1,4,12]	**Visual design**	Offering professional-looking, minimal design, and visual aesthetic interface [33].
	Demo	Showing PET environment, e.g., via screenshots or screen recording.
	Interaction	Considering individuals' needs and concerns, avoid statistic presentation of information [33].
Comparison⋆⋆ The styles and elements of comparing PETs	**Review per product⋆⋆**	Providing a detailed review for each PET.
	Key benchmarks⋆⋆	Educating individuals on the parameters to consider in choosing PET.
	Snapshot⋆⋆	Offering a comparison of various PET products at a glance, e.g., via a table to improve comprehension, easier assessment of the pros and cons.
	Ratting per product⋆⋆	Accompanying each PET by the reviewer rating.
Readability The readability of the text	**Reading ease**	Estimating the ease of understanding the text by Flesch-Kincaid tests [22].
	Grade level	Estimating the required educational level to comprehend the text by Flesch-Kincaid tests [22].
Price The price range [46]	**Start⋆**	Providing easy start via free version or trial period.
	Availability⋆⋆	Displacing the price range for each discussed PET.

3.3 Criteria Selection

To establish our criteria, we first analysed existing academic resources in the domain. The objective was to identify factors that have been recognised as influential in supporting individuals in adopting security and privacy solutions, such as providing easy-to-understand technology explanation [6,8,39,41] referred to as the explanation criterion in what follows. Then, we have considered usability factors [31,37,51] like the interaction criterion in what follows. Last, we have also incorporated criteria based on our own experiences, such as the demo criterion, which looks into the availability of the demonstration of the PET environment. In total, we have collected a set of 24 criteria grouped into seven categories detailed in Table 1. Among these, speed, layout, and start criteria apply to *single-product* only, and review per product, key benchmarks, snapshot, ratting per product, and availability criteria apply to *comparing-product* only. This discrepancy stems from the difference in the characteristics of websites. For example, the criteria review and rating per product only apply to *comparing-product* websites.

3.4 Analysis Process

After compiling our website list and defining the criteria set, we conducted a pre-analysis. This pre-analysis focused on evaluating the criteria on a small sample of websites to ensure the analysis was applicable and measurable. After several iterations, we finalised our analysis material. Subsequently, two of the authors, as independent domain researchers, evaluated the selected websites and rated them against the criteria. Next, we implemented a structured discussion process that involved comparing ratings to identify specific areas of disagreement. We then conducted collaborative reviews of the websites, focusing on the criteria where differences arose. Through these reviews, we discussed the evidence and reasoning for the ratings until an agreement on the rating was reached. This process finished at the end of March 2024.

Rating Measuring Scale. We have introduced a measuring scale for each criterion to ensure the accuracy of our analysis. Our primary aim was not to assign fine-grain points to each criterion but to ensure that the criterion was met fully, partially, or not at all. Therefore, we maintained a three-level measuring scale: full (assigned score: 1), half (assigned score: 0.5), and none (assigned score: 0). In the following Table 2 and Table 4, we have aggregated the rating results obtained for each of the four PET types, thus averaging and rounding them. To increase the readability of the tables, we omitted the repeated presentation of the number 0 before the decimal, meaning that, e.g., .5 is equivalent to 0.5.

Automatic Evaluation. In addition to the above-mentioned manual analysis conducted by two of the authors, we have used automatic tools to analyse the *readability* and *accessibility*. For *readability*, we have used Webfx [55], which supplied us with scores for reading ease and grade level criteria based on Flesch-Kincaid tests [22]. The reading ease criterion ranges from 0 to 100, with higher scores indicating easier readability. In contrast, the grade level criterion ranges from 0 to 12 with lower scores indicating easier readability as they correspond to lower school grades. For the *accessibility* audit, we have applied Accessi [2], which provided us with the violations of Web Content Accessibility Guidelines (WCAG) 2 [52] by our website samples.

4 Results

We present the results of analysing 69 websites against a set of 24 criteria and the result of the accessibility audit in three subsections. The analysis of the *single-product* websites is presented in Sect. 4.1, while the analysis of the *comparing-product* websites is detailed in Sect. 4.2. We then focus on our accessibility audit result in Sect. 4.3, before summarising our results in Sect. 4.4.

Table 2. Mean score of 45 *single-product* websites. The higher the score (the darker the blue), the better the criterion fulfilled. $\bar{x}$: weighted mean, -: not applicable.

		Categories																	
		Technology					Trust				Information				Usability				
Number of websites	PETs	Explanation	Coverage	Limitation	Easiness	Speed	Provider	Product	User feedback	Interpersonal	Layout	Presentation variety	Gap coverage	Language formality	Visual design	Demo	Interaction	$\bar{x}$
20	VPN	.4	.2	.1	.3	.6	.5	.5	.9	.3	.6	.3	.4	.5	.8	.6	.0	.4
11	Tor	.5	.2	.2	.2	.3	.5	.3	.2	.0	.4	.3	.2	.5	.5	.5	.0	.3
4	PB	.0	.6	.0	.4	.4	.8	.6	.6	.0	.8	.6	.1	.4	.8	.5	.0	.4
10	PSE	.2	.4	.0	-	.1	.3	.4	.2	.0	.5	.4	.1	-	.5	-	.0	.4
	$\bar{x}$	.4	.3	.1	.3	.4	.5	.4	.5	.1	.5	.3	.3	.5	.7	.6	.0	$\approx \frac{1}{3}$

4.1 Single-Product Websites

Based on the search strategy outlined in Sect. 3.2, we have identified 45 websites exclusively presenting a single PET. They comprise 20 websites presenting a VPN, eleven Tor, four PB, and ten PSE. The variation in the number of identified websites per PET mainly stems from differences in product availability. Next, we analysed these websites based on the 19 criteria that apply to this category of websites (see Table 1). Note that three out of the 19 criteria did not apply to PSE websites due to their specific characteristics. For instance, we could not assess the language formality criterion for PSE, as these websites commonly offered minimal text, making it impossible to evaluate this aspect. Table 2 shows the average scores for each criterion for *single-product* websites except for the *readability* and *price* category, shown in Table 3. In the following, we elaborate on the notable findings.

Criteria-Based Insights. We first consider various aspects of PET *technology* being presented to individuals. On average, 4 out of 10 websites explained the technology behind the PET they presented and clarified its effect on the connection speed. This number is slightly lower when objectively communicating what a PET can cover for one's privacy upon adoption. On the other hand, showing what a PET can not cover is down to 0.1. This means that our sample of websites does not transparently familiarise individuals with the functionality and limitations of PETs. Such a situation can develop unrealistic expectations about the effectiveness of a PET. In some cases, even misleading information about the coverage of a PET is presented, such as *"The One-Click Solution for All Your Privacy Needs"*. This misleading information further complicates the adoption process as it creates the unrealistic belief that only one tool, like a VPN, can bring full privacy protection to the adopter. This result sheds light on the findings of [4], highlighting a clear gap between users' perceived privacy risks and the defences they employ. In addition, only one-third of our sample addressed the ease of adopting or using a PET. Failing to communicate the time or technical skill required creates uncertainty and can reduce users' perceived ability.

Looking into the *trust* category, half of our sample does not present any information about the PET provider, such as the producer company. In addition, less than half of them present some information about the trustworthiness of the PET. Some websites provide quotes like *"No log policy"*, which may not be convincing for users concerned about PET itself privacy threats. In other examples, we have found statements like *"VerSprite has also tested the security of our IOS app and proved it to be completely safe."* However, the question arises: how qualified is VerSprite to make such a statement? The potential of interpersonal connections to increase the adoption rate, such as peer promotions and friends and family plans, is also neglected. Therefore, the potential of trusting through human-to-human connections is not supported.

Within the *information* category, one of the most neglected criteria is the presentation variety. This indicates that diverse formats, such as video, demo, voice, and diagram, are not widely utilised. Instead, a significant portion of the websites heavily rely on text to present information, making it less engaging and more challenging for individuals to learn about and ultimately adopt PETs. In some poorly designed cases, large blocks of text lacking detailed sectioning were presented. However, bullet points, bold font, underlining and highlighting were leveraged in better cases. Another criterion with the same low score is gap coverage. This score indicates that our sample does not effectively explain the meaning of jargon and technical terminologies. These technical terminologies can be, e.g., *"IP address"*. Without an adequate explanation, users may encounter confusion and uncertainty, resulting in abandoning the adoption process.

In the *usability* category, the visual design criterion received the highest average, while the interaction criterion received the lowest. For the former, this means that the design of the interfaces was evaluated as minimal and professional-looking in most cases. For the latter, we did not find evidence of interaction or personalisation in presenting information to individuals. This indicates that the websites are not engaging in dialogue with users and mainly offer information in monologue. A practical interaction could start with gathering users' needs to deliver tailored information.

Table 3 shows a reading easy score of 62, which indicates moderately easy readability. PB falls behind the other three PET types as it uses more complex explanations and terminologies. The grade level score was 6, suggesting that the content was accessible to individuals with a sixth-grade reading level. For all PETs of this study, either a free version or a free trial was available.

Comparison Between Considered PETs. The average coverage scores per PET in Table 2 are similar among all four PETs, Tor being slightly lower. Indicating that only about one-third of the identified criteria supporting the adoption of PETs are effectively conveyed to individuals by each of the PET types.

Table 3. Mean score of readability and price of 45 *single-product* websites

		Readability		Price
Number of websites	PETs	Reading ease	Grade level	Starting
20	VPN	65	6	free
11	Tor	63	6	free
4	PB	49	4	free
10	PSE	61	5	free
$\bar{x}$		**62**	**6**	**free**

Table 4. Mean score of 24 *comparing-product* websites. The higher the score (the darker the blue), the better the criterion fulfilled. $\bar{x}$: weighted mean.

		Categories																		
		Technology				Trust				Information			Usability			Comparison				
Number of websites	PETs	Explanation	Coverage	Limitation	Easiness	Provider	Product	User feedback	Interpersonal	Presentation variety	Gap coverage	Language formality	Visual design	Demo	Interaction	Review per product	Key benchmarks	Snapshot	Ratting per product	$\bar{x}$
6	VPN	.7	.5	.6	.1	.8	.3	.0	.0	.8	.3	.2	.7	.4	.0	.8	.9	.6	.7	.5
8	PB	.0	.1	.3	.1	.9	.1	.0	.0	.3	.4	.5	.5	.6	.0	.6	.3	.2	.1	.3
10	PSE	.1	.2	.2	.1	.8	.4	.0	.1	.3	.4	.5	.7	.5	.0	.7	.5	.4	.1	.3
	$\bar{x}$	.2	.2	.3	.1	.8	.3	.0	.0	.4	.4	.4	.6	.5	.0	.7	.5	.4	.3	$\approx \frac{1}{3}$

4.2 Comparing-Product Websites

In this section, we focus on a total of 24 websites, comprising six for VPN, eight for PB, and ten for PSE identified and analysed as described in Sect. 3.2. Unlike in Sect. 4.1, these websites do not concentrate on a *single-product* but present a comparison of multiple products of one PET type (e.g., comparing seven VPNs). It is worth noticing that Tor is a singular product and is therefore omitted in this analysis. We hence analyse these websites based on the 21 dedicated criteria shown in Table 1. The average scores for each criterion for *comparing-product* websites shown in Table 4, and Table 5 shows their *readability* and *price* categories.

Criteria-Based Insights. In the *technology* category, the highest score is 0.3 for the limitation criterion, while the lowest is 0.1 for easiness. In one case, a limitation was explained using an example: *"while using a VPN and providing credentials to an online web page, your privacy will be at risk, and a VPN cannot protect you."* Such examples enhance users' understanding of risks. The explanation and coverage criteria scored slightly higher but remained low, indicating insufficient efforts to educate users about PET and its privacy benefits objectively.

Considering the *trust* category, we observed that the provider criterion has the best score across all criteria. This means the users have been informed of the person or organisation that provided the comparison analysis. However, the websites do not rely on user feedback or interpersonal connections, meaning they do not count on the community, also observed by [11], which neglects excellent potential [43]. For instance, when websites compare multiple PBs, no comment or rating of other users about the comparing analysis of PET products was observed.

Within the *information* category, we observe that our sample mainly relies on text, with other communication formats not included. In addition, we found repetitive examples of technical words that did not accompany an explanation. For instance, in the case of PSE, *"Features: SSL encryptions"*.

In the *usability* category, approximately half of our sample provides a demo of the PET environment, such as a screenshot, video, or animation. However, we could not find any evidence of websites interacting with individuals. This further shows that interaction and receiving users' needs for presenting relevant information about PETs to them are missing.

Looking into the *comparison* category, which is exclusive to *comparing-product* websites, review per product scores the best. In about two-thirds of the cases, we found detailed analyses for each PET, rather than just mentioning the name with brief pros and cons. Half of our samples provided key benchmarks of what elements to consider when adopting a specific PET to empower individuals in decision-making and increase awareness. We only found evidence for the snapshot criterion, e.g., in the form of a table, which is usually a more efficient way to compare different PET products in less than half of the cases. For example, a common format we observed presents PETs sequentially: Name, explanation, and pros and cons for each. This layout requires extensive scrolling and makes comparing parameters between PETs time-consuming and mentally demanding.

Table 5. Mean score of readability and price of 24 *comparing-product* websites

		Readability		Price
Number of websites	PETs	Reading ease	Grade level	Availability
6	VPN	65	7	0.6
8	PB	53	6	0.2
10	PSE	65	6	0.3
$\bar{x}$		**61**	**6**	**0.3**

As shown in Table 5, the average reading easy score is 61, indicating moderately easy readability. Again, we observe that the reading ease is lower for the websites comparing PB as compared to the other PETs. Additionally, the overall average grade level score was 6, suggesting that the content was accessible to individuals with a sixth-grade reading level same score as in *single-product*. Regarding the price availability criterion, only about 3 out of 10 websites provided pricing information when comparing PET products. Notably, most PETs offer a free version or trial in the *single-product* section, yet this information is often not communicated to the users in comparison websites.

PETs-Based Insights. When comparing the average scores across all criteria per PET, we observed minimal variation among the three PETs. On average, only one-third of the factors that support adoption are applied to the 24 *comparing-product* websites. Recall that it is the same ratio as for *single-product* websites (see Sect. 4.1).

4.3 Accessibility

Table 6 shows the average number of accessibility issues found using Accessi [2], categorised as high, medium, and low impact per type of PET. Based on the WCAG 2 guideline [52], high-impact errors severely obstruct or block access to content for users with disabilities. Medium-impact errors create significant difficulties but do not make access impossible. Low-impact errors cause minor inconveniences or slow down interaction but do not prevent access.

As shown in Table 6, there is an average of 18 high-impact issues per website. In addition, the average sum of all issues per website is 147. Interestingly, VPNs have the highest number of issues, while PSE websites have the lowest. This difference can be due to PSE websites having considerably less content and web pages than other types. In the following, we present the two most frequent issues observed across all the reviewed websites.

Table 6. Mean score of observed **accessibility issues**

Number of websites	**Issues** / **PETs**	Impact			Sum
		High	**Medium**	**Low**	
26	VPN	22	33	143	198
11	Tor	16	17	82	115
12	PB	20	27	97	144
20	PSE	12	25	62	99
69	$\bar{x}$	**18**	**27**	**73**	**147**

Violation of 1.3.1 Guideline: "Structure your website so that content is read by a screen reader in the same way it is presented visually" [53]. An example is headings. When a large, bold font precedes an article, it visually suggests it is a heading for the following text. However, without proper coding to designate a heading level, this visual cue is not conveyed to individuals using screen readers. This means that individuals relying on screen readers do not hear the headlines as headings, making navigating the websites difficult.

Violation of 4.1.2 Guideline: "For all user interface components (e.g., forms, links, scripts, controls), the name and role of those components should be coded in" [54]. For example, while forms may visually indicate their function, this is not conveyed to screen reader users unless properly coded. This issue also affects elements like drop-down lists and progress bars. In our study, some websites used progressive disclosure to enhance readability, but if this feature is not coded correctly, users relying on auditory cues may miss important content.

Solving the above issues can be low-cost in time and resources for providers. For example, easy fixes are assigning a heading level in code to meet the 1.3.1 guideline or providing roles for interface components to meet the 4.1.2 guideline.

4.4 Summary

When considering the average criteria coverage of both *single-product* and *comparing-product* websites, we observe that approximately one-third of the influential supporting factors recommended by academic findings have been effectively provided to individuals. Additionally, our accessibility audit revealed that even easily fixable issues were overlooked, potentially posing significant obstacles for impaired users. These results highlight a lack of optimal support and even difficulties that users interested in protecting their privacy may encounter when informing themselves to choose a PET to install. This shows great potential for improvement in presenting PETs to motivated individuals and supporting the adoption process.

5 Design Templates

Based on our observations and results presented in Sect. 4, we propose two design templates, illustrated in Fig. 1 for a single product and Fig. 2 for comparing multiple products, for effectively presenting PETs to individuals. These templates are grounded in (1) our analysis of the strengths of the best-rated websites per criteria and per PET and (2) the integration of relevant design elements to ensure current practices to address neglected criteria. The yellow boxes provided on the two design templates refer to the related criteria.

Supplementary Considerations for Effective Implementation. While the two design templates serve as a foundational framework, additional considerations to ensure a more effective design implementation are: (1) Use diverse formats like videos, diagrams, and animations to present information effectively. (2) Organise the page layout with clear titles and proper categorisation subsequently coded. (3) Avoid informal language; keep content jargon-free and easy to read. (4) Opt for a minimalist, professional, and visually appealing user interface design. (5) Provide an explanation on the spot of the potential unknown terminologies. (6) Conduct accessibility audits regularly.

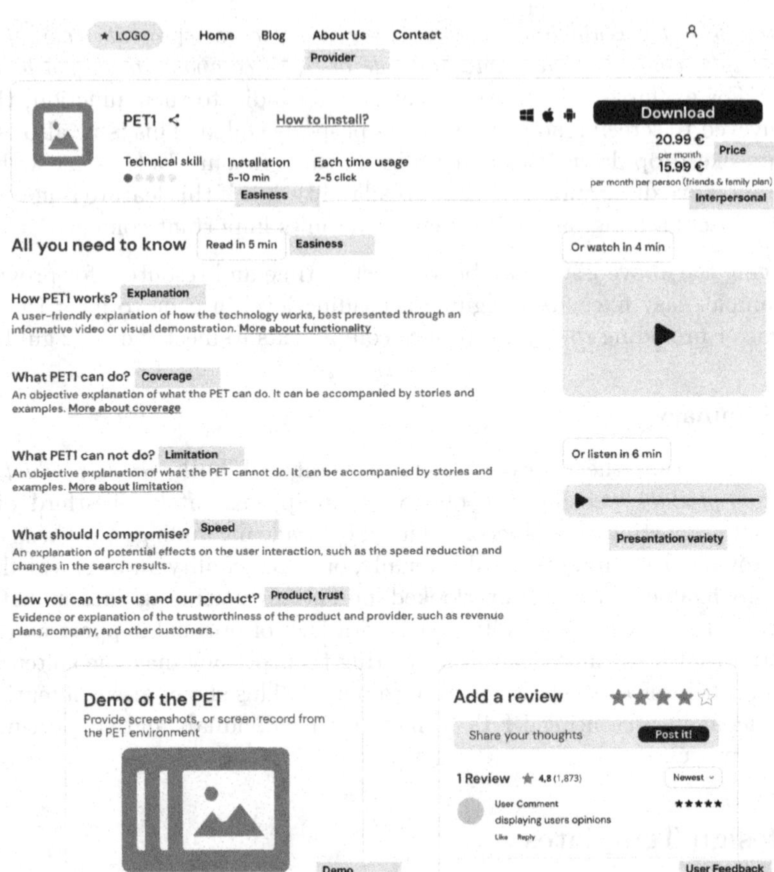

Fig. 1. Design template for a single product.

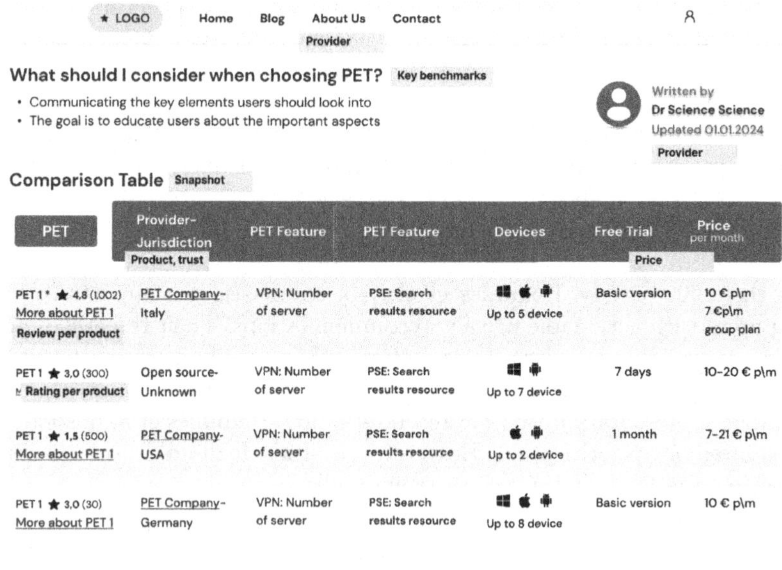

Fig. 2. Design template for comparing multiple products.

6 Discussion

Our results indicate a widespread disregard for following the supporting factors and accessibility guidelines in our sample. This section further compares our results with existing works in Sect. 6.1, the scope and limitations of our work in Sect. 6.2, and the future works in Sect. 6.3.

6.1 Comparative Analysis of Our Findings with Existing Works

As mentioned in (Sect. 2), a recent fundamental work related to our study is SPAF [11], which outlines awareness, motivation and ability as crucial factors for users to accept security and privacy behaviour, such as adopting a PET. Awareness refers to users' understanding of privacy risks and mitigation strategies. SPAF identifies training, digital literacy, and social engagement as influencing awareness. Our analysis indicates shortcomings in addressing these factors with criteria such as explanation, limitation, user feedback, and interpersonal. Motivation encompasses the willingness of individuals to enhance privacy. SPAF identifies perceived advantages, trial ability, and compatibility as motivation factors. Our analysis shows weaknesses in addressing these factors with criteria such as coverage. However, we could find evidence of a free version or trial for all PET types considered in this study, supporting the recommended trial ability. Ability highlights the challenge of translating intentions into protective actions, influenced by usability and accessibility [11]. Although the visual design and demo are partly applied in our study, the interaction criterion is not respected. Furthermore, our analysis reveals widespread accessibility issues. Our results confirm, with SPAF, that users are left without adequate support for adopting a PET.

In their 2020 study, Redmiles et al. [40] emphasise the importance of providing users with actionable privacy recommendations. Their research highlights that many available websites lack practicality. Our findings support this, as we observed a lack of comprehensive coverage in criteria such as easiness, gap coverage, demo, presentation variety, and interaction. Redmiles et al. also identified a crisis in advice prioritisation. However, our study focused on the specific goal of choosing one PET and not prioritising multiple PETs.

As a result, our exploration confirms the differing outcomes of SPAF [11] and Redmiles et al. [40] in practice while extending their work by analysing additional factors such as trust in providers and products, presentation of information to end users, and accessibility. Furthermore, we introduce design templates to help bridge the gap between academic recommendations and practical implementation, ultimately supporting users in making privacy decisions.

6.2 Scope and Limitations

The scope of this study is limited in several ways. Firstly, we have only analysed the websites on a desktop display. Accessing them on mobile devices may lead to different results. Future analyses on various screen sizes may reveal other challenges that need to be addressed, given the increasing prevalence of mobile browsing. Secondly, while this study focused on analysing four specific PETs, it is important to note that there are other PETs available that users may seek information about through online resources, such as encrypted messaging services or ad-blockers, which require attention to provide a more comprehensive understanding of the landscape. Lastly, our approach involved using the names of PETs as search terms in an online search engine to access websites. However, we recognise that users may discover websites through various means, such as advertisements or recommendations from friends. These alternative pathways to access websites can impact users' adoption experiences.

6.3 Future Work

While our current study focuses on expert perspectives, gathering insights directly from users can help us understand the obstacles they encounter. Combining both methods will provide a more thorough understanding of the gaps between users' desire to protect their privacy and their actual behaviours. Future research could involve conducting in-depth interviews and user studies with diverse groups to uncover their specific challenges. Combining these user-centred findings with our expert-driven results provides a strong foundation for developing strategies or design recommendations to support the adoption of PETs. Moreover, as privacy concerns are global, and websites in other languages could vary in how they present information, analysing websites in different languages can be followed as future work.

7 Conclusion

Despite individuals expressing privacy concerns, only a fraction of them actively adopt PETs, which raises questions about the effectiveness of the presentation of the PETs. To understand the reasons behind this situation, we conducted a comprehensive analysis of 69 websites that promote four specific PETs. Our expert-driven analysis, guided by a set of 24 criteria, showed that websites, on average, cover only about one-third of the identified supporting factors. This likely contributes to PETs' persistently low adoption rates. Additionally, our accessibility audit showed the repeated presence of issues that create obstacles for impaired users. To address these issues, we have proposed two design templates that comprise supporting factors to help individuals adopt PETs. These measures can help in steps fostering greater adoption of PETs among individuals who are informing themselves about PETs online.

Acknowledgements. This work is partly funded by the Deutsche Forschungsgemeinschaft (DFG, German Research Foundation), referenced with the number 505982147.

Appendix

Table 7 shows the websites included in our study.

Table 7. The 69 websites included in our study

Single-product Websites	VPN	**Surfshark:**https://surfshark.com/ **Atlas:** https://atlasvpn.com/ **Express:** https://www.expressvpn.com/ **Cyberghost:** https://www.cyberghostvpn.com/ **Ip Vanish:** https://www.ipvanish.com/ **Pure:** https://www.purevpn.com/ **Ivacy:** https://www.ivacy.com/ **Norton:** https://de.norton.com/ **Private:** https://privatevpn.com/cybernews/ **Nord:** https://nordvpn.com/download/ **Proton:** https://protonvpn.com/ **Hostspot Shield:** https://www.hotspotshield.com/ **Avira:** https://www.avira.com/ **Veepen:** https://veepn.com/ **Hide Me:** https://hide.me/ **Avast:** https://www.avast.com/c-vpn-for-pc **Turbo:** https://turbovpn.com/download/windows **Touch:** https://touchvpn.net/ **Unlimited:** https://www.vpnunlimited.com/downloads/macos **Privado:** https://privadovpn.com/
	Tor	**Tor Project:** https://www.torproject.org/ **Softonic:** https://tor-browser.en.softonic.com/**Techradar:** https://www.techradar.com/how-to/how-to-get-started-with-tor-browser**Techspot:** https://www.techspot.com/downloads/5183-tor-browser.html**PCMag:** https://www.pcmag.com/reviews/tor-browser**Wikipedia:** https://www.en.wikipedia.org/wiki/Tor_(network)**CSO:** https://www.csoonline.com/article/565798/what-is-the-tor-browser-how-it-works-and-how-it-can-help-you-protect-your-identity-online.html**Microsoft:** https://www.microsoft.com/en-us/microsoft-365-life-hacks/privacy-and-safety/what-is-tor**VPN Overview:** https://vpnoverview.com/privacy/anonymous-browsing/tor/**Free Download Manager:** https://en.freedownloadmanager.org/Windows-PC/Tor-Browser-FREE.html**Source for Age:** https://sourceforge.net/projects/tor-browser.mirror/
	Private browser	**Duckduckgo:** https://duckduckgo.com/ - **Brave:** https://brave.com/ - **Epic:** https://www.epicbrowser.com/ - **Aloha:** https://alohabrowser.com/
	Private search engine	**Start Page:** https://www.startpage.com/ - **Brave:** https://search.brave.com/ - **Privacia:** https://privacia.org/ - **Ghostery:** https://www.ghostery.com/private-search - **GoGo Private:** https://www.gogoprivate.com/ - **One Search:** https://www.onesearch.com/ - **Privacy Wall:** https://www.privacywall.org/ - **Metager:** https://metager.org/ - **Lukol:** https://www.lukol.com/ - **Seekly:** https://www.seekly.net/
Comparing-product Websites	VPN	**PCMag:** https://www.pcmag.com/picks/the-best-vpn-services **Techradar:** https://www.techradar.com/vpn/best-free-vpn - **Tomsguide:** https://www.tomsguide.com/best-picks/best-vpn - **Forbes:** https://www.forbes.com/advisor/business/software/best-vpn/ - **Cnet:** https://www.cnet.com/tech/services-and-software/best-free-vpn/ - **Privacy Tool:** https://www.privacytools.io/
	Private browser	**PCMag:** https://uk.pcmag.com/browsers/134703/stop-trackers-dead-the-best-private-browsers-for-2021 - **Brave:** https://brave.com/learn/best-private-browser/ - **Vpninsights:**https://vpninsights.com/privacy/browsing/best-private-browsers/ - **Hongkiat:** https://www.hongkiat.com/blog/private-browsers-windows-11/ - **Restor Privacy:** https://restoreprivacy.com/browser/secure/ - **Pro Privacy:** https://proprivacy.com/privacy-service/comparison/most-secure-browsers - **Blokt:** https://blokt.com/guides/best-secure-browsers-for-private-browsing - **IP Vanish:** https://www.ipvanish.com/blog/best-private-browsers-2022/
	Private search engine	**Restore Privacy:** https://restoreprivacy.com/private-search-engine/ - **Privacy Savvy:** https://privacysavvy.com/security/safe-browsing/private-search-engines/ - **Panda Security:** https://www.pandasecurity.com/en/mediacenter/security/best-private-search-enginges/ - **Comparitech:** https://www.comparitech.com/blog/vpn-privacy/best-private-search-engine/ - **VPN Overview:** https://vpnoverview.com/privacy/anonymous-browsing/best-private-search-engines/ - **Surfshark:** https://surfshark.com/blog/private-search-engines - **GUR99** https://www.guru99.com/private-search-engines-anonymous-no-tracking.html - **USA Today** https://eu.usatoday.com/story/tech/columnist/komando/2020/11/21/6-internet-search-engines-respect-your-privacy/6306467002/ - **Pro Privacy** https://proprivacy.com/privacy-service/comparison/private-search-engines - **VPN Mentor** https://www.vpnmentor.com/blog/best-private-search-engines-true-no-log-services/

References

1. Abu-Salma, R., Sasse, M.A., Bonneau, J., Danilova, A., Naiakshina, A., Smith, M.: Obstacles to the adoption of secure communication tools. In: Proceedings of the IEEE Symposium on Security and Privacy (2017)
2. Accessi.org: Accessi: Accessibility Test (2024). https://www.accessi.org/
3. Adams, A., Sasse, M.A.: Users are not the enemy. Commun. ACM (1999)
4. Assal, H., Hurtado, S., Imran, A., Chiasson, S.: What's the deal with privacy apps? A comprehensive exploration of user perception and usability. In: Proceedings of the 14th International Conference on Mobile and Ubiquitous Multimedia (2015)
5. Benenson, Z., Girard, A., Krontiris, I.: User acceptance factors for anonymous credentials: an empirical investigation. In: Proceedings of the Workshop on the Economics of Information Security (WEIS) (2015)
6. Benenson, Z., Girard, A., Krontiris, I., Liagkou, V., Rannenberg, K., Stamatiou, Y.: User acceptance of privacy-abcs: an exploratory study. In: Proceedings of the 2nd Human Aspects of Information Security, Privacy, and Trust (2014)
7. Bracamonte, V., Pape, S., Kiyomoto, S.: Investigating user intention to use a privacy sensitive information detection tool. In: Symposium on Cryptography and Information Security (SCIS) (2021)
8. Brecht, F., Fabian, B., Kunz, S., Mueller, S.: Are you willing to wait longer for Internet privacy? In: Proceedings of the European Conference on Information Systems (ECIS) (2011)
9. Cabinakova, J., Zimmermann, C., Mueller, G.: An empirical analysis of privacy dashboard acceptance: the Google case. In: Proceedings of the European Conference on Information Systems (ECIS) (2016)
10. Coopamootoo, K.P.: Usage patterns of privacy-enhancing technologies. In: Proceedings of the ACM SIGSAC Conference on Computer and Communications Security (2020)
11. Das, S., Faklaris, C., Hong, J.I., Dabbish, L.A., et al.: The security & privacy acceptance framework (SPAF). Found. Trends Priv. Secur. (2022)
12. De Luca, A., Das, S., Ortlieb, M., Ion, I., Laurie, B.: Expert and non-expert attitudes towards (secure) instant messaging. In: Proceedings of the 12th Usable Privacy and Security (SOUPS) (2016)
13. Demandsage.com: Android Statistics 2024 (2023). https://www.demandsage.com/android-statistics/
14. Duckduckgo.com: DuckDuckGO (2024). https://duckduckgo.com/
15. Fishbein, M.: A Theory of Reasoned Action: Some Applications and Implications (1979)
16. Fogg, B.J.: A behavior model for persuasive design. In: Proceedings of the 4th International Conference on Persuasive Technology (2009)
17. Gs.statcounter.com: Desktop vs Mobile vs Tablet Market Share Worldwide (2021). https://gs.statcounter.com/platform-market-share/desktop-mobile-tablet/
18. Harborth, D., Pape, S.: Examining technology use factors of privacy-enhancing technologies: the role of perceived anonymity and trust. In: 24th Americas Conference on Information Systems (2018)
19. Harborth, D., Pape, S.: How privacy concerns and trust and risk beliefs influence users' intentions to use privacy-enhancing technologies-the case of tor. In: 52nd Hawaii International Conference on System Sciences (2019)
20. Harborth, D., Pape, S., Rannenberg, K.: Explaining the technology use behavior of privacy-enhancing technologies: the case of tor and jondonym. Priv. Enhancing Technol. (2020)

21. Herbert, F., et al.: A world full of privacy and security (MIS) conceptions? Findings of a representative survey in 12 countries. In: Proceedings of the ACM Conference on Human Factors in Computing Systems (CHI) (2023)
22. Kincaid, J.P., Fishburne, R.P., Jr., Rogers, R.L., Chissom, B.S.: Derivation of New Readability Formulas. Automated Readability Index, Fog Count and Flesch Reading Ease Formula) for Navy Enlisted Personnel (1975)
23. Klasnja, P., Consolvo, S., Choudhury, T., Beckwith, R., Hightower, J.: Exploring privacy concerns about personal sensing. In: Proceedings of the 7th Pervasive Computing (2009)
24. Kokolakis, S.: Privacy attitudes and privacy behaviour: a review of current research on the privacy paradox phenomenon. Comput. Secur. (2017)
25. Krontiris, I., Benenson, Z., Girard, A., Sabouri, A., Rannenberg, K., Schoo, P.: Privacy-abcs as a case for studying the adoption of pets by users and service providers. In: Proceedings of the 3rd Privacy Technologies and Policy (2016)
26. Encinas, L.H., et al.: Online Privacy Tools for the General Public (2015). https://www.enisa.europa.eu/publications/privacy-tools-for-the-general-public
27. Mangiò, F., Andreini, D., Pedeliento, G.: Hands off my data: users' security concerns and intention to adopt privacy enhancing technologies. Italian J. Mark. (2020)
28. Matt, C., Peckelsen, P.: Sweet idleness, but why? How cognitive factors and personality traits affect privacy-protective behavior. In: 2016 49th Hawaii International Conference on System Sciences (HICSS). IEEE (2016)
29. Mehrnezhad, M., Coopamootoo, K., Toreini, E.: How can and would people protect from online tracking? In: Proceedings of the Privacy Enhancing Technologies (2021)
30. Miltgen, C.L., Peyrat-Guillard, D.: Cultural and generational influences on privacy concerns: a qualitative study in seven European countries. Eur. J. Inf. Syst. (2014)
31. Molich, R., Nielsen, J.: Improving a human-computer dialogue. Commun. ACM (1990)
32. Namara, M., Wilkinson, D., Caine, K., Knijnenburg, B.P.: Emotional and Practical Considerations Towards the Adoption and Abandonment of VPNs as a Privacy-Enhancing Technology (2020)
33. Nielsen, J.: Enhancing the explanatory power of usability heuristics. In: Proceedings of the Human Factors in Computing Systems (SIGCHI) (1994)
34. Nielsen, J.: Usability Engineering (1994)
35. Nissenbaum, H.: Privacy as contextual integrity. Wash. L. Rev. (2004)
36. Nissenbaum, H.: Respecting context to protect privacy: why meaning matters. Sci. Eng. Ethics (2018)
37. Nngroup.com: 10 Usability Heuristics for User Interface Design (2024). https://www.nngroup.com/articles/ten-usability-heuristics/
38. Phelps, J., Nowak, G., Ferrell, E.: Privacy concerns and consumer willingness to provide personal information. J. Public Policy Mark. (2000)
39. Racine, E., Skeba, P., Baumer, E.P., Forte, A.: What are PETs for privacy experts and non-experts. In: Proceedings of the Symposium on Usable Privacy and Security (2020)
40. Redmiles, E.M., et al.: A comprehensive quality evaluation of security and privacy advice on the web. In: Proceedings of the 29th USENIX Security Symposium (2020)
41. Renaud, K., Volkamer, M., Renkema-Padmos, A.: Why doesn't jane protect her privacy? In: Proceedings of the 14th International Symposium om Privacy Enhancing Technologies (2014)
42. Research.chitika.com: The Value of Google Result Positioning (2013). https://research.chitika.com/wp-content/uploads/2022/02/chitikainsights-valueofgoogleresultspositioning.pdf

43. Rogers, E.M.: Diffusion of Innovations the Free Press of Glencoe. NY (1962)
44. Shams, S., Reinhardt, D.: Vision: supporting citizens in adopting privacy enhancing technologies. In: Proceedings of the European Symposium on Usable Security (2023)
45. Shneiderman, B., Plaisant, C.: Designing the user interface: strategies for effective human-computer interaction (2010)
46. Sombatruang, N., Omiya, T., Miyamoto, D., Sasse, M.A., Kadobayashi, Y., Baddeley, M.: Attributes affecting user decision to adopt a virtual private network (VPN) app. In: Meng, W., Gollmann, D., Jensen, C.D., Zhou, J. (eds.) ICICS 2020. LNCS, vol. 12282, pp. 223–242. Springer, Cham (2020). https://doi.org/10.1007/978-3-030-61078-4_13
47. Stokes, J., et al.: How language formality in security and privacy interfaces impacts intended compliance. In: Proceedings of the Human Factors in Computing Systems (CHI) (2023)
48. Story, P., et al.: Awareness, adoption, and misconceptions of web privacy tools. In: Proceedings of the Privacy Enhancing Technologies (2021)
49. Torproject.org: Tor Project (2024). https://torproject.org/
50. Udo, G.J.: Privacy and security concerns as major barriers for e-commerce: a survey study. Inf. Manag. Comput. Secur. (2001)
51. Ur, B., Leon, P.G., Cranor, L.F., Shay, R., Wang, Y.: Smart, useful, scary, creepy: perceptions of online behavioral advertising. In: Proceedings of the 8th Symposium on Usable Privacy and Security (SOUPS) (2012)
52. W3.org: WCAG 2 at a Glance (2024). https://www.w3.org/WAI/standards-guidelines/wcag/glance/
53. WCAG.com: Designers Guid (2021). https://wcag.com/developers/1-3-1-info-and-relationships/
54. WCAG.com: Designers Guid (2021). https://wcag.com/developers/4-1-2-name-role-value/
55. Webfx.com: Webfx.com: Readability Test (2024). https://www.webfx.com/tools/read-able/

Optimizing Onionbalance: Improving Scalability and Security for Tor Onion Services

Laura Donah and Pascal Tippe(✉)

FernUniversität in Hagen, Hagen, Germany
pascal.tippe@fernuni-hagen.de

Abstract. This paper addresses the critical issue of denial-of-service (DoS) attacks on Tor Onion Services by focusing on load balancing mechanism. We analyze the current available mechanisms and discuss potential options for enhancing scalability and security of Onion Services. We leverage and modify the existing tool Onionbalance to be fully backward compatible and increase the acceptance of our modifications. Our approach includes optimizing the creation and distribution of service descriptors introducing a more efficient load-balancing mechanism. We also analyze and discuss the security implications of these enhancements and provide a practical implementation with comprehensive tests in a test bed and the real Tor network. Our results demonstrate that the proposed improvements significantly increase the resilience of Onion Services against DoS attacks, ensuring better service availability and security for users.

Keywords: Onion Service · Tor load balancing · Onionbalance

1 Introduction

Anonymity is increasingly threatened as tracking technologies advance and society becomes more digitalized. The extensive collection of private data by various entities can influence individuals' behavior and decisions, potentially undermining freedom even in democratic countries. Cases like the prosecution of prominent whistleblowers and actions by authoritarian regimes to restrict access to information highlight the need for a decentralized, privacy-preserving internet [3,12]. Tor [13] is the most influential anonymization network with more than 2 million daily users [22]. A key feature of Tor are Onion Services, which allow users to host internet services within the Tor network while concealing their locations. This capability enables activists and journalists to share sensitive information and opinions while making it difficult for third parties to identify or censor them. Additionally, Onion Services enhance internet security by using self-authenticated addresses, distributed to clients as .onion links, instead of relying on centralized Certification Authorities.

L. Horn Iwaya et al. (Eds.): NordSec 2024, LNCS 15396, pp. 488–499, 2025.
https://doi.org/10.1007/978-3-031-79007-2_25

However, Onion Services are particularly vulnerable to denial-of-service (DoS) attacks and have been frequently targeted in the past [1]. The computational effort required to establish new connections can overwhelm these services, allowing attackers to effectively censor content by making it unavailable. Traditional methods from the internet like detecting bot requests, blocking IP ranges, or using centralized providers are inadequate for Onion Services. They cannot distinguish between benign and malicious requests due to the unified attributes like IPs or user agents. This has led to the development of a proof-of-work mechanism to increase the cost of DoS attacks [6]. To further mitigate DoS attacks and potential security issues, we discuss the existing availability mechanisms for Tor Onion Services and propose improvements for better scalability. We integrate our suggestions into an existing load balancing tool and test it in multiple settings. We also discuss the potential security impacts of these enhancements.

The remainder of this paper is structured as follows: Sect. 2 explains the basics of Tor and Onion Services to later understand the basic load balancing approaches discussed in Sect. 3 with a security analysis for our approach. The implementation, its limitation and extensive tests are presented in Sect. 4 followed by the discussion of our results and future work in Sect. 5. Section 6 concludes.

2 Tor Onion Services

The Tor network consists of volunteer-run Tor relays that route data on behalf of other participants based on the current Tor protocol specifications [21]. Tor enables participants to tunnel low-latency TCP connections over the Tor network, making it difficult to link communication parties. Directory authorities, which are a select few trustworthy Tor relays, synchronize and vote each hour to create a status document called the consensus. This document describes the current Tor network. Information about all Tor relays participating in the network is included to allow clients to individually select Tor relays based on their flags, bandwidth, or other properties, along with cryptographic keys to establish secure communication channels.

Circuits enable clients to incrementally establish TCP connections over multiple Tor relays. First, the initial relay is contacted and a secure communication channel is set up. Subsequently, the client extends the current circuit by instructing the last relay in the circuit to establish an additional connection to a new Tor relay. With each relay, a new symmetric key is negotiated through cryptographic handshakes to prevent other relays in the circuit from modifying or eavesdropping on packets. This process continues until the circuit is fully built. Clients are effectively anonymized because only the first relay knows the client's IP address, while only the last relay can see the target IP address. The last relay in the circuit appears as the communication partner for the target. Clients encrypt all traffic in layers with the respective negotiated symmetric keys so that each relay peels off one layer until the packet is sent to the target. Packets originating from the target are encrypted by each relay so that the client can decrypt them again.

Besides providing sender anonymity, Tor also enables receiver anonymity through Onion Services [20]. These are web services exclusively accessible within the Tor network, shielded by Tor circuits to obfuscate their IP addresses. Administrators can host all internet services over TCP, protecting both their identity and that of the servers. Onion Services regularly publish a service descriptor, which contains introduction points and cryptographic keys, enabling clients to contact them. These introduction points are selected by the Onion Services from the pool of all active Tor relays. A long-lived circuit established by Onion Services allows them to forward connection requests. Incoming client requests are relayed over the circuit by the introduction point to inform Onion Services. With the contained information, Onion Services can establish a separate circuit to a rendezvous point chosen by the client, connecting the client and Onion Service circuits to enable communication. Each Onion Service has an .onion address derived from a secret key that clients must know to fetch service descriptors and initiate connection requests. The service descriptors are stored by Tor relays with a special flag (HSDir) and are ordered in a distributed hash ring based on their fingerprint and a shared random value in the consensus document. Onion Services regularly publish their descriptors on the HSDirs currently responsible, based on a separate signing key. The descriptors are encrypted and blinded so that HSDirs cannot read their contents, while clients can use the knowledge of the 56-character .onion key to unblind and decrypt them. Every 60 to 120 min, Onion Services publish descriptors for the current and previous consensus time periods to ensure periodic updates.

Similarly, clients fetch descriptors for Onion Services and select a Tor relay to act as a rendezvous point [19]. These requests are cached to reduce the need for costly refetches. By initiating a circuit to one of the specific introduction points in the descriptor, clients send their selected Tor relay, the first half of a handshake to the Onion Service, and a cookie to allow the rendezvous point to identify and connect the two circuits. Both parties then have a bidirectional connection without revealing their locations. However, the traffic content is not protected by Tor and might reveal sensitive information. Regular attack vectors for web services can be even more devastating because their identity is also at risk. Additionally, there are attacks on the Tor protocol level for Onion Services. For example, Øverlier and Syverson [5] describe a correlation attack involving the entry guard, the first Tor relay in the circuit, and the exit relay, both of which must be controlled by an adversary. This can link communication parties and decloak IP addresses. The computational asymmetry mentioned by Döpmann et al. [2] between Onion Services and clients exacerbates problems, as adversaries could use fake data to directly send connection requests over introduction points, skipping computationally expensive parts of the circuit building. This incurs significantly more cost for the Onion Service to build a full default circuit. Since Tor is an established protocol that relies on volunteers to manage their infrastructure decentrally, protocol changes advance slowly, and new changes suffer from slow adoption rates.

3 Scaling Tor Onion Services

3.1 Current Protocol and Onionbalance

Figure 1 illustrates how Onion Services control the upload of descriptors using the parameters *Replica* and *HSDir-Spread-Store*. The *Replica* parameter determines the number of unique positions in the hash ring for starting the descriptor upload, while *HSDir-Spread-Store* controls how many subsequent Tor relays the descriptors will be uploaded to. Although this theoretically allows uploading the descriptor many times, clients use similar parameters for fetching descriptors. The *Replica* parameter is set to two, and *HSDir-Spread-Fetch* is set to three, resulting in clients fetching descriptors from six different Tor relays. The descriptors can contain up to 20 Introduction Points, with an overall maximum file size of 50,000 bytes [15].

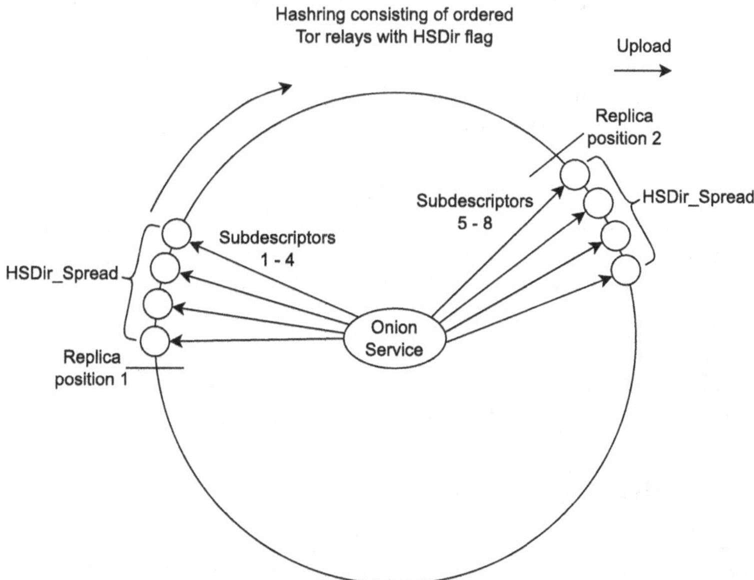

Fig. 1. Upload of several service descriptors to their responsible Tor relays.

By default, Onion Services select three Introduction Points linking to the same server, assemble a descriptor, and then upload the same descriptor to the responsible Tor relays. Balancing the load across multiple servers in this setup would require different .onion addresses for each instance. This is cumbersome for administrators and users who need to manage numerous addresses. It also potentially makes it easier for malicious third parties to impersonate websites, as users might not save all links and may search for new ones each time they use the service. Worse, attackers only need to compromise one of the servers to exfiltrate the private master key, allowing them to snoop on all traffic for a .onion address or impersonate it. For the same reason, having multiple servers share the same .onion address is dangerous. Additionally, each server uploading its service descriptor will override the existing ones, making them effectively inaccessible.

3.2 Improving the Availability of Onion Services

Ceysun Sucu [11] developed a tool that eventually led to Onionbalance [16], based on the idea that one server is solely responsible for publishing service descriptors linking to several backend instances. In this setup, the backend instances each host an individual Onion Service, and the Onionbalance instance collects their descriptors to assemble a master descriptor, which is then published. Users fetch the master descriptor, randomly select one of the included Introduction Points, and transparently connect to one of the backend instances, effectively providing load balancing. Currently, Onionbalance supports only up to eight backend instances and uploads one descriptor to all backend instances. The first improvement we implement is creating multiple descriptors containing different Introduction Points. The default values direct Tor clients to fetch them from six different Tor relays, and there is no check to ensure all of them are identical. Therefore, capacity can be increased sixfold by uploading different descriptors. Additionally, the size of an individual service descriptor is not fully utilized in the current Onionbalance version. We adhere to the protocol's maximums, which state that service descriptors can include up to 20 Introduction Points and have an overall size of 50,000 bytes. Consequently, the second improvement will involve including more Introduction Points while respecting the size limit. This approach allows for up to 120 backend instances, each contributing one Introduction Point. To fully utilize the default three Introduction Points that each Onion Service uses, 40 backend instances can be employed, significantly improving the existing load balancing mechanism.

3.3 Alternative Approaches

Replacing current service descriptors with frequent reuploads can also offer load balancing, as clients fetch the new descriptors with updated introduction points. Depending on the fetch time, clients receive different descriptors. However, this approach is hindered in practice by clients caching descriptors, meaning that new descriptors only affect clients who haven't recently established a connection to the .onion address. Integrating new backend instances has limited benefits, as they can push out existing backend instances, preventing them from receiving new visitors. This reduces efficiency, as these backend instances only serve existing user connections until a future rotation of service descriptors includes them again and makes them visible for new clients fetching the updated descriptors. To efficiently rotate workload among a fixed set of backend instances by including more introduction points from idling backends and fewer from heavily used backends, the master server would need additional information about their workload instead of simply fetching their descriptors. This depends on the use case of individual Onion Services and is therefore out of scope for a simple load balancing tool for users with limited technical backgrounds. Other approaches require changes to the Tor protocol and are unlikely to be backward compatible, which poses an issue for decentrally run networks like Tor. For example, Tor protocol proposal 255 [23] from 2015 presents a solution but is currently neither discussed nor implemented.

3.4 Security Analysis

Our proposed enhancements to Onionbalance introduce several security considerations that require careful examination. This analysis focuses on the potential implications of our modifications, particularly regarding descriptor uploads and multi-backend functionality. Descriptor fingerprinting remains a primary concern. As noted in previous research [7], service descriptors can reveal the use of Onionbalance through structural differences in size and number of introduction points. Adversaries may infer Onionbalance usage, detect custom modifications, or identify relationships between .onion addresses based on unique descriptor characteristics. To mitigate these risks, we recommend integrating our improvements directly into the Onionbalance codebase, limiting adversaries to learning only that a standard load balancing tool was used. Our manual analysis of Onionbalance descriptors with and without our modifications revealed no significant structural differences beyond the number of introduction points.

Onionbalance enhances security by isolating master keys for the .onion address on a single instance that doesn't interact directly with clients [9]. This setup preserves .onion address integrity even if backend instances are compromised, allowing administrators to easily replace compromised backends by updating the Onionbalance configuration. However, if adversaries compromise the Onionbalance instance or extract the .onion address private keys, they can impersonate the service or perform man-in-the-middle attacks. The Onionbalance instance is primarily vulnerable during the descriptor upload process. Adversaries may attempt to run or compromise HSDirs to target Onion Services during this phase, but without knowing the .onion address, they cannot identify the specific service even if deanonymization occurs. The upload process, initiated by Onionbalance, is comparatively short, presenting a smaller attack surface than traditional Onion Services. Onionbalance mitigates traditional web vulnerabilities and reduces the number of circuits compared to standard Onion Services as clients don't directly interact with the Onionbalance instance. This lowers the risk of selecting malicious Tor relays and minimizes traffic information available for correlation attacks.

Additionally, simple availability correlations by monitoring and comparing the downtime of an Onion Service and other network infrastructure leak less information, depending on the configuration. While adversaries can monitor all introduction points, distributing backend instances across multiple locations and providers ensures that only the introduction points for affected servers fail. With more backend instances, it becomes more challenging for adversaries to attribute outages to specific server backends, as circuit failures can also result from affected

Tor relays. For instance, using three backend instances, each with three introduction points, results in a master descriptor with nine introduction points. If one server fails, three introduction points lose connectivity simultaneously, presenting a stronger correlation than if only one or two out of twenty introduction points fail. Distributing backend instances across multiple locations further complicates availability correlation attacks, making it harder for adversaries to attribute outages to specific servers. While the Onionbalance server remains a single point of failure, its infrequent connections make short downtimes less noticeable and it can recover quickly by fetching the descriptors from backend instances and uploading the master descriptor. To address prolonged failures, administrators could implement a secondary Onionbalance instance, though this introduces key management challenges that could be mitigated by using multiple .onion addresses with dedicated Onionbalance instances.

While Onionbalance offers security benefits, scaling Onion Services increases complexity for administrators. Managing multiple backend instances requires regular updates, maintenance, and proper configuration. As securing a single service is already prone to errors, misconfiguration risks likely increase with more backend instances. Administrators must also configure their services to run on distributed systems, necessitating mechanisms to synchronize data and actions between instances. Tor configurations should be synchronized across backend instances to mitigate risks from malicious Tor relays attempting to identify Onion Services. Without synchronization, the number of chosen Tor relays for all backend instances increases, raising the likelihood of malicious relay involvement in circuits resulting in the deanonymization of some backend instances. This consideration extends to potential multiple Onionbalance instances as well.

The Vanguards security addon [7] introduces additional considerations for Onionbalance implementations. Its default 30,000 kilobyte limit on service descriptor size may conflict with larger Onionbalance master descriptors, necessitating careful configuration to accommodate the 50,000 kilobyte protocol limitation. While disabling or modifying this parameter allows for larger descriptors, it may impact a small fraction of clients using Vanguards. Additionally, Vanguards offers a non-default feature that tears down introduction point circuits based on traffic volume, potentially causing introduction point rotations. Adversaries exploiting this or failures occurring could lead to backend instances choosing new introduction points and creating new service descriptors. To mitigate this issue, Onionbalance would need to frequently check for changes and reupload updated descriptors.

In conclusion, our enhancements to Onionbalance offer significant improvements in scalability and performance for Onion Services, but they also introduce new security considerations that require careful management. The proposed modifications maintain many of Onionbalance's inherent security benefits, such as isolated key management and reduced attack surfaces. However, they also present challenges related to increased system complexity, potential fingerprinting risks, and interactions with security addons like Vanguards. By integrating our improvements directly into the Onionbalance codebase and following best practices in distributed system management, Onion Service operators can leverage the benefits of our modifications while reducing potential negative effects.

4 Implementation

4.1 Modifying Onionbalance

To promote practical usage, we decided to integrate our improvements into Onionbalance with minimal modifications to the existing Python code. Our enhancements are available as a merge request in the official Onionbalance repository and are currently under review [4]. Onionbalance currently saves the latest generated descriptor and offers multiple classes for generating and validating them. We focused solely on the current V3 Onion Service protocol version, ignoring legacy code for the previous V2 protocol version. First, we modified the configuration settings to allow up to 120 backend instances, which is the maximum according to the current protocol specifications. The parts responsible for downloading the specified service descriptors from the given .onion addresses representing the backend instances, processing the collected introduction points, and calculating blinding parameters were left untouched. We then added code to calculate the necessary number of descriptors based on the number of introduction points. To ensure the new descriptors comply with the size limitations, we create a new empty descriptor and measure its size. The list of introduction points is serialized in Python to calculate the estimated required additional descriptor size. Introduction points are added to the first descriptor until the size limit of 50,000 bytes is approached or the maximum number of 20 is reached. This process repeats with the next descriptor using the remaining list items until the number of needed descriptors is calculated. With this number, the introduction points are fairly distributed among the descriptors so that all include roughly the same number, enabling more efficient load balancing. New program code creates the different descriptors, adapts the logging messages, and calculates the position in the hash ring for each. The default values for the *HS_SPREAD_STORE* parameter are overwritten to match client fetching behavior. The number of usable HSDirs is calculated based on the provided configuration and helps to evenly distribute the descriptors. For example, if five descriptors are generated, the first one will be duplicated and uploaded to the sixth position. The remaining parts of Onionbalance are not modified.

4.2 Limitation of the Implementation

Due to the potential mismatch between available HSDirs and required descriptors, the implementation will start copying existing descriptors to fill the number of available HSDirs. This generally provides decent load balancing, but in some cases, it doesn't provide an optimal distribution. For example, if five descriptors are required because each backend instance will have one introduction point and there are 100 backend instances, then the first descriptor will be included twice for the default six available HSDirs. This scenario doubles the expected workload on the affected 20 backend instances compared to the remaining ones. The descriptor size limitation is also just approximated in the current version, as measuring the size before encryption does not yield accurate results. Additionally, certain security add-ons like Vanguards [8], available to Tor users, set further restrictions on the descriptor size with a default maximum value of 30,000 bytes. As a solution, a simple buffer value, such as 25,000 bytes, could be used in the configuration to comply with additional security add-ons and account for the size overhead introduced by encryption. Reuploads for failed descriptor upload attempts are not undertaken, as the original Onionbalance doesn't perform these either. Administrators would need to manually restart the entire upload process in such cases. Also, as in the original Onionbalance implementation, our modifications don't support the modifications of descriptors to support the new proof-of-work protocol or to enable client authorization, which would require clients to use a pre-shared key to decrypt the descriptor as access control mechanism.

4.3 Tests

During the development, we used a static code analyzer to check for potential vulnerabilities and fix any issues. Additionally, we created six tests for classes and functions to evaluate basic functionality, such as the correct distribution of introduction points to descriptors and the assignment of correct HSDirs to them. After verifying these tests, we deployed our tool to the Tor network simulator Chutney [14] to prevent potential unwanted side effects on the real Tor network. We confirmed correct usage by configuring Onionbalance and setting up the test network with 25 Onion Service backends.

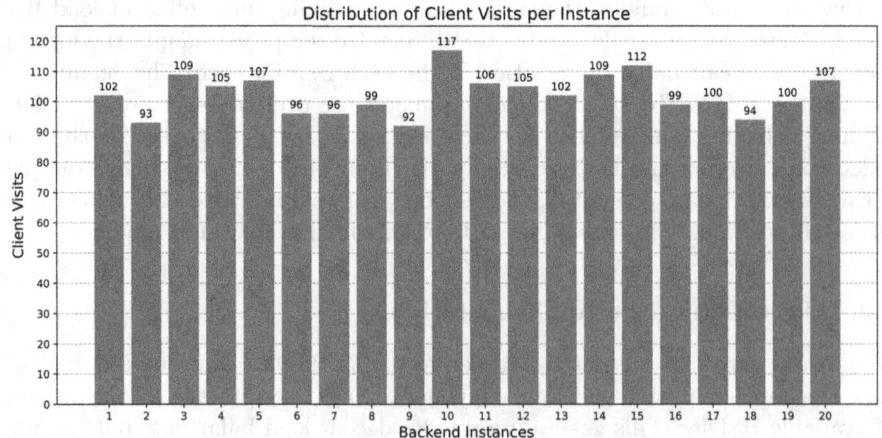

Fig. 2. Distribution of client requests to backend instances.

Following the Tor research guidelines [18], we designed a test setup for the real Tor network without introducing unreasonable workloads or endangering other users. We created different backend instances running simple web servers that displayed their number, and a server with Onionbalance assembling the master descriptor. Several Tor clients fetched it, and depending on the displayed number from the site, we could infer which backend instance was visited. We used Docker containers to simulate a total of 20 backend instances and 50 clients fetching the master descriptor 2,050 times over 2.5 h. Between each request, we rebuilt the Docker instance to ensure that Tor established new circuits and conducted clean fetches. The log files additionally confirmed the correct creation and upload of the descriptors. Figure 2 shows the distribution of client visits from our experiments to the backend instances. As expected, not all backend instances received the same number of visits because clients randomly selected the responsible HSDir and the included Introduction Point from the descriptor. The median number of visits per instance was 102, showing equal load balancing across the backend instances. For the tests, we configured the clients to retry establishing a connection three times, which explains the absence of unsuccessful connection attempts. Lastly, we manually tested a scenario with 60 backend instances, each with two introduction points to entirely fill the descriptors, and verified that the site was reachable and no errors occurred. During our test attempts, we noticed that Onionbalance requires an initial waiting time after starting the backend instances until it successfully includes all in the master descriptors, as they need time to individually upload their descriptors first.

5 Discussion

In Sect. 3, we presented the current state of load balancing for Onion Services and possible alternatives. Our approach does not introduce protocol-breaking changes and is completely backward compatible. Individual administrators can choose to use our solution independently. The tests demonstrate the functionality and can build trust for third parties to adopt our modifications. The Tor project provides a simple tutorial [17] for Onion Service administrators to set up Onionbalance, and no changes are required as our modifications integrate seamlessly. However, Onionbalance offers limited guidance on selecting an appropriate number of backends or determining for whom this program can be useful. We believe this likely causes administrators to instead deploy more Onion Services and distribute numerous .onion addresses, which has the drawbacks discussed in Subsect. 3.1. The security benefits might convince administrators to use Onionbalance instead. We suggest recommending administrators with some experience to consider the security benefits of an additional Onionbalance instance, especially for Onion Services that suffer from DoS attacks or high volumes of legitimate client visits.

For further improvements, Onionbalance should implement the reuploading load balancing approach discussed in Subsect. 3.1. While this should be targeted towards large and very popular Onion Services, administrators might have more technical expertise to customize certain configurations. For example, individual backends could provide load information to Onionbalance by exposing a number over their Onion Service. Instead of solely fetching descriptors, Onionbalance could also query this number to balance the number of Introduction Points according to the load information. This approach would not affect the anonymity of the backends because these requests run over Tor. Administrators would be responsible for calculating numbers for their individual use cases, for example, depending on CPU loads or the number of open circuits. Integrating the proof-of-work system into Onionbalance can further increase resistance against DoS attacks and is currently under discussion [10].

6 Conclusion

In conclusion, the proposed improvements to Tor Onion Services address significant challenges related to denial-of-service attacks and scalability. The modifications affecting the service descriptor composition and distribution demonstrated a substantial increase in the resilience and availability of Onion Services. The integration of these improvements into the Onionbalance tool provides a practical solution that can be readily adopted by the Tor community. Existing tutorials and setup procedures can continue to be used, as the changes are adapted to the current codebase. Future work should focus on further refining these mechanisms and exploring additional security measures to ensure the continued robustness of Tor Onion Services.

Disclosure of Interests. The authors have no competing interests to declare that are relevant to the content of this article.

References

1. Bagueros, I.: Responding to Tor censorship in Russia (2023). https://blog.torproject.org/tor-network-ddos-attack/. Accessed 9 Aug 2024
2. Döpmann, C., Franck, V., Tschorsch, F.: Onion pass: token-based denial-of-service protection for tor onion services. In: 2021 IFIP Networking Conference (IFIP Networking), pp. 1–9 (2021). https://doi.org/10.23919/IFIPNetworking52078.2021.9472207
3. ggus.: Responding to Tor censorship in Russia (2021). https://blog.torproject.org/tor-censorship-in-russia/. Accessed 9 Aug 2024
4. nr24119: Implement Distinct Descriptor Mode (2024). https://gitlab.torproject.org/tpo/onion-services/onionbalance/-/merge_requests/18. Accessed 9 Aug 2024
5. Overlier, L., Syverson, P.: Locating hidden servers. In: Proceedings of the 2006 IEEE Symposium on Security and Privacy, SP 2006, pp. 100–114. IEEE Computer Society, USA (2006). https://doi.org/10.1109/SP.2006.24
6. isabela: Introducing Proof-of-Work Defense for Onion Services (2023). https://blog.torproject.org/tor-network-ddos-attack/. Accessed 9 Aug 2024
7. Perry, M.: README_SECURITY.md (2021). https://github.com/mikeperry-tor/vanguards/blob/master/README_SECURITY.md. Accessed 9 Aug 2024

8. Perry, M.: Vanguards (2023). https://github.com/mikeperry-tor/vanguards. Accessed 9 Aug 2024
9. Rhatto, S.: Onionbalance Security Analysis. https://gitlab.torproject.org/tpo/onion-services/onionbalance/-/issues/25. Accessed 9 Aug 2024
10. Rhatto, S.: Proof of Work (PoW) Support in Onionbalance. https://gitlab.torproject.org/tpo/onion-services/onionbalance/-/issues/13. Accessed 9 Aug 2024
11. Sucu, C.: Tor: Hidden service scaling. Master's thesis, University College London (2015)
12. Thrush, G., Specia, M.: Assange Agrees to Plead Guilty in Exchange for Release, Ending Standoff With U.S. (2024). https://www.nytimes.com/2024/06/24/us/politics/julian-assange-plea-deal.html. Accessed 9 Aug 2024
13. Tor Project: Browse Privately. Explore Freely. https://www.torproject.org/. Accessed 9 Aug 2024
14. Tor Project: Chutney. https://gitlab.torproject.org/tpo/core/chutney/. Accessed 9 Aug 2024
15. Tor Project: Hidden service descriptors: encryption format. https://spec.torproject.org/rend-spec/hsdesc-encrypt.html. Accessed 9 Aug 2024
16. Tor Project: Onionbalance. https://gitlab.torproject.org/tpo/onion-services/onionbalance/. Accessed 9 Aug 2024
17. Tor Project: Onionbalance v3 Installation Guide. https://onionservices.torproject.org/apps/base/onionbalance/v3/tutorial/. Accessed 9 Aug 2024
18. Tor Project: Research Safety Board. https://research.torproject.org/safetyboard/. Accessed 9 Aug 2024
19. Tor Project: The rendezvous protocol. https://spec.torproject.org/rend-spec/rendezvous-protocol.html. Accessed 9 Aug 2024
20. Tor Project: Tor Rendezvous Specification - Version 3. https://spec.torproject.org/rend-spec/index.html. Accessed 9 Aug 2024
21. Tor Project: Tor specifications. https://spec.torproject.org/. Accessed 9 Aug 2024
22. Tor Project: Tor Metrics (2024). https://metrics.torproject.org/userstats-relay-country.html. Accessed 9 Aug 2024
23. van der Woerdt, T.: 255-hs-load-balancing.txt (2015). https://spec.torproject.org/proposals/255-hs-load-balancing.html. Accessed 9 Aug 2024

Author Index

L. Horn Iwaya et al. (Eds.): NordSec 2024, LNCS 15396, pp. 501–502, 2025.
https://doi.org/10.1007/978-3-031-79007-2

Printed in the United States
by Baker & Taylor Publisher Services